2017
北京统计年鉴
Beijing Statistical Yearbook

图书在版编目(CIP)数据

北京统计年鉴. 2017 ：汉英对照 / 北京市统计局，国家统计局北京调查总队编. -- 北京：中国统计出版社，2017.10
ISBN 978-7-5037-8299-2

Ⅰ. ①北 Ⅱ. ①北 ②国 Ⅲ. ①统计资料－北京－2017－年鉴－汉、英 Ⅳ. ①C832.1-54

中国版本图书馆CIP数据核字(2017)第209507号

北京统计年鉴-2017

作　　者/北京市统计局　国家统计局北京调查总队
责任编辑/李　冲
封面设计/高　立
出版发行/中国统计出版社
通信地址/北京市丰台区西三环南路甲6号　邮政编码/100073
电　　话/邮购（010）63376909　书店（010）68783171
网　　址/http://www.zgtjcbs.com
印　　刷/北京联兴盛业印刷有限公司
经　　销/新华书店
开　　本/880mm × 1230mm　1/16
字　　数/1200千字
印　　张/38.5印张　彩插/1.5印张
版　　别/2017年10月第1版
版　　次/2017年10月第1次印刷
定　　价/350.00元

本书附同版本CD-ROM一张，光盘内容以书面文字为准。
如有印装差错，由本社发行部调换。

2016年的北京
Beijing in 2016

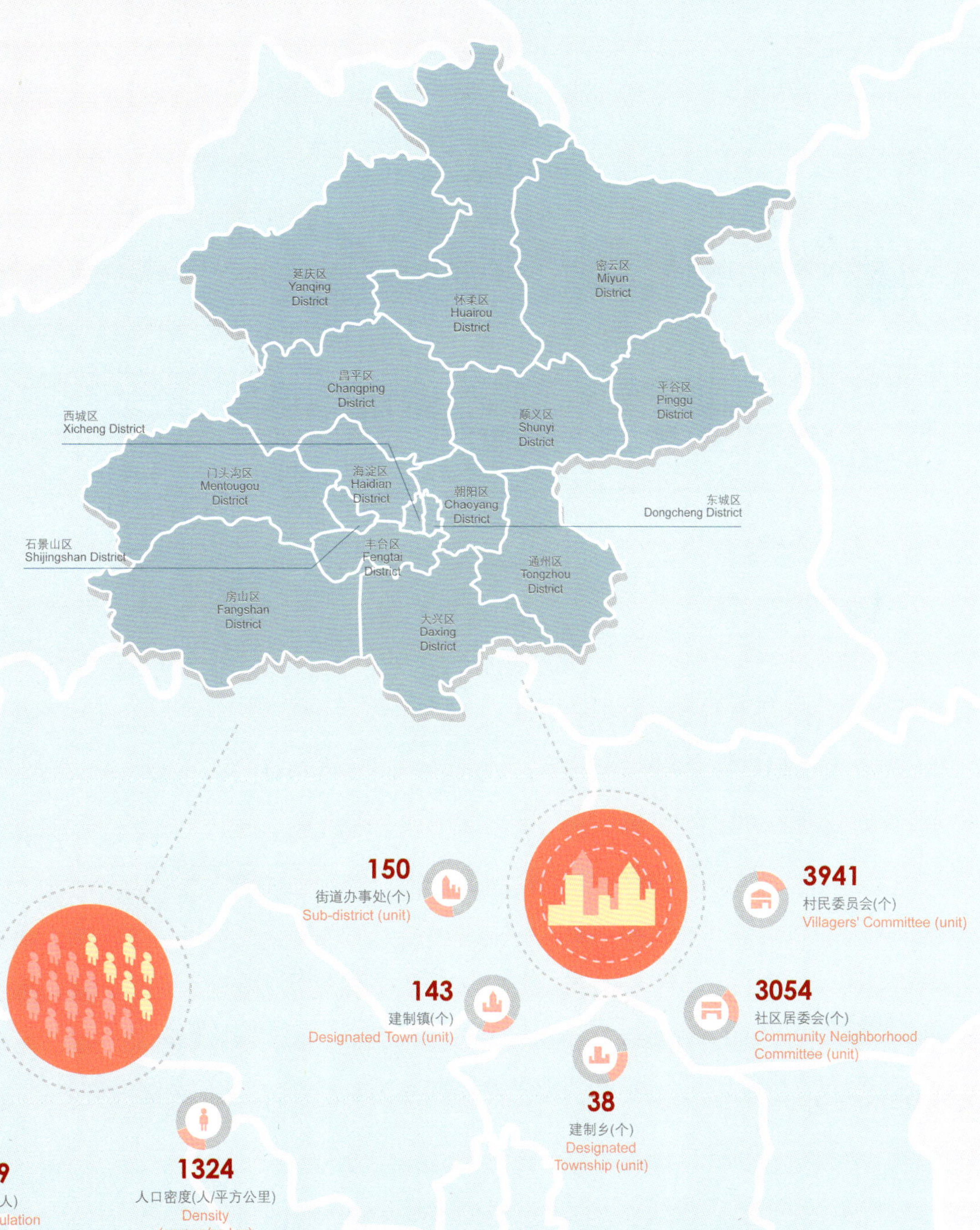

2016年的北京
Beijing in 2016

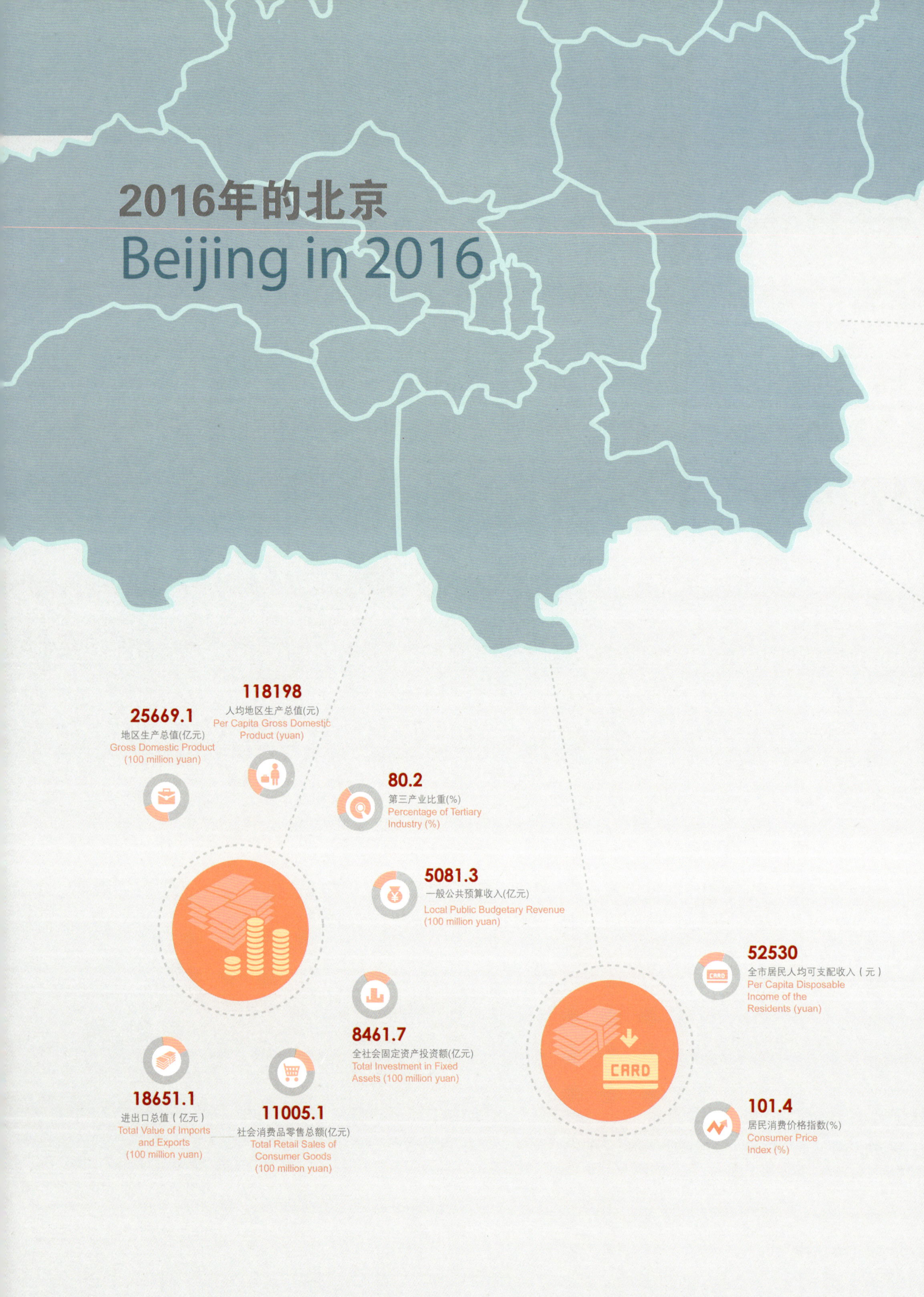

5.78
研究与试验发展(R&D)经费内部支出相当于地区生产总值比例(%)
Internal R&D Expenditure as Percentage of GDP (%)

48.2
万人发明专利申请数(件)
Number of Invention Patent Applications per 10,000 Persons (piece)

3940.8
技术合同成交总额(亿元)
Total Amount of Technological Contracts Signed (100 million yuan)

5.42
每千常住人口注册护士(人)
Number of Certified Nurses per 1000 Permanent Population (person)

4.64
每千常住人口执业医师(人)
Number of Licensed Doctors per 1000 Permanent Population (person)

5.06
每千常住人口医院床位(张)
Number of Hospital Bed per 1000 permanent population (person)

0.8
每十万常住人口博物馆数(个)
Number of Museums per 100000 Permanent Population (unit)

7.2
每十万常住人口幼儿园数(个)
Number of Kindergartens per 100000 Permanent Population (unit)

48.4
城市绿化覆盖率(%)
Urban Green Area Coverage (%)

14.0
平均每一专任教师负担小学生数(人)
Average Number of Students in Primary School Instructed by a Full-time Teacher (person)

16.1
人均公园绿地面积(平方米)
Per Capital Park Green Areas (square meter)

574
轨道交通运营线路长度(公里)
Length of Rail Transportation Lines in Operation (kilometer)

161.4
人均水资源(立方米/人)
Per-capita Water Resource(cu.m)

北京一日
A Day in Beijing

每日创造
Daily Production

138832.2
一般公共预算收入(万元/日)
Local Public Budgetary Revenue (10000 yuan/day)

175048.3
一般公共预算支出(万元/日)
Local Public Budgetary Expenditure (10000 yuan/day)

11848.9
发电量(万千瓦时/日)
Generating Capacity (10000 kWh/day)

7115
汽车生产量(辆/日)
Output of Motor Vehicles (unit/day)

189178
移动电话机生产量(台/日)
Output of Mobile Telephone (unit/day)

415870.4
海关进口总值(万元/日)
Total Value of Import at Customs (10000 yuan/day)

13756
显示器(台/日)
Display (unit/day)

3546.4
第一产业(万元/日)
Primary Industry (10000 yuan/day)

135092.9
第二产业(万元/日)
Secondary Industry (10000 yuan/day)

562702.2
第三产业(万元/日)
Tertiary Industry (10000 yuan/day)

701341.5
地区生产总值 (万元/日)
Gross Domestic Product (10000 yuan/day)

93722.5
海关出口总值(万元/日)
Total Value of Export at Customs (10000 yuan/day)

1008.2
公共电汽车客运量(万人次/日)
Passengers Carried by Buses and Trolley Buses (10000 person-times/day)

127950.8
国内旅游收入(万元/日)
Domestic Tourism Income (10000/day yuan/day)

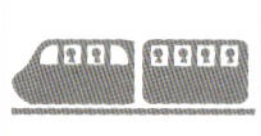
1000
轨道交通客运量(万人次/日)
Passengers Carried by Rail Transit (10000 person-times/day)

1385.0
旅游外汇收入(万美元/日)
Foreign Exchange Earnings from Tourism (USD 10000/day)

1.14
接待入境旅游人数(万人次/日)
Inbound Tourists (10000 persons /day)

21.5
民航客运量(万人次/日)
Civil Aviation Passenger Traffic (10000 person-times/day)

131.3
公路客运量(万人次/日)
Highway Passenger Traffic (10000 person-times/day)

36.6
铁路客运量(万人次/日)
Railway Passenger Traffic (10000 person-times/day)

2016
年 Year

每日生活
Daily Life

553
常住出生人口（人/日）
Birth Population (Permanent Population) (person/day)

309
常住死亡人口（人/日）
Death Population (Permanent Population) (person/day)

454
登记结婚对数（对/日）
Marriage Registered (couple/day)

289
离婚对数（对/日）
Registered Divorces (couple/day)

143.5
全市居民人均可支配收入(元/日)
Per Capita Disposable Income of the Residents (yuan/day)

535.6
特快专递业务量（万件/日）
Business Volume of EMS (10000/day)

96.8
全市居民人均消费支出(元/日)
Per Capita Consumption Expenditure of the Residents (yuan/day)

62751.4
吃类商品(万元/日)
Food (10000 yuan/day)

21352.5
穿类商品(万元/日)
Clothing(10000 yuan/day)

202844.3
用类商品(万元/日)
Daily Supplies(10000 yuan/day)

13737.7
烧类商品(万元/日)
Fuel(10000 yuan/day)

300685.8
社会消费品零售总额（万元/日）
Retail Sales of Consumer Goods (10000 yuan/day)

612
污水处理能力（万立方米/日）
Sewage Treatment Capacity (10000cu.m/day)

287.3
法人单位从业人员平均工资（元/日）
Average Wage of Employed Person in Legal Entities(yuan/day)

2.38
生活垃圾清运量（万吨/日）
Domestic Waste Removed and Transported (10000 tons/day)

5339.7
城乡居民生活用电量（万千瓦时/日）
Urban and Rural Residential Electricity Consumption (10000 kWh/day)

349.0
居民家庭用天然气（万立方米/日）
Natural Gas for Living Use (10000 cu.m/day)

296.1
自来水销售总量（万立方米/日）
Total Sales Volume of Tap Water (10000 cu.m/day)

6243
电影放映场次（场次/日）
Film Show Times (Times/day)

总体经济
Overall Economy

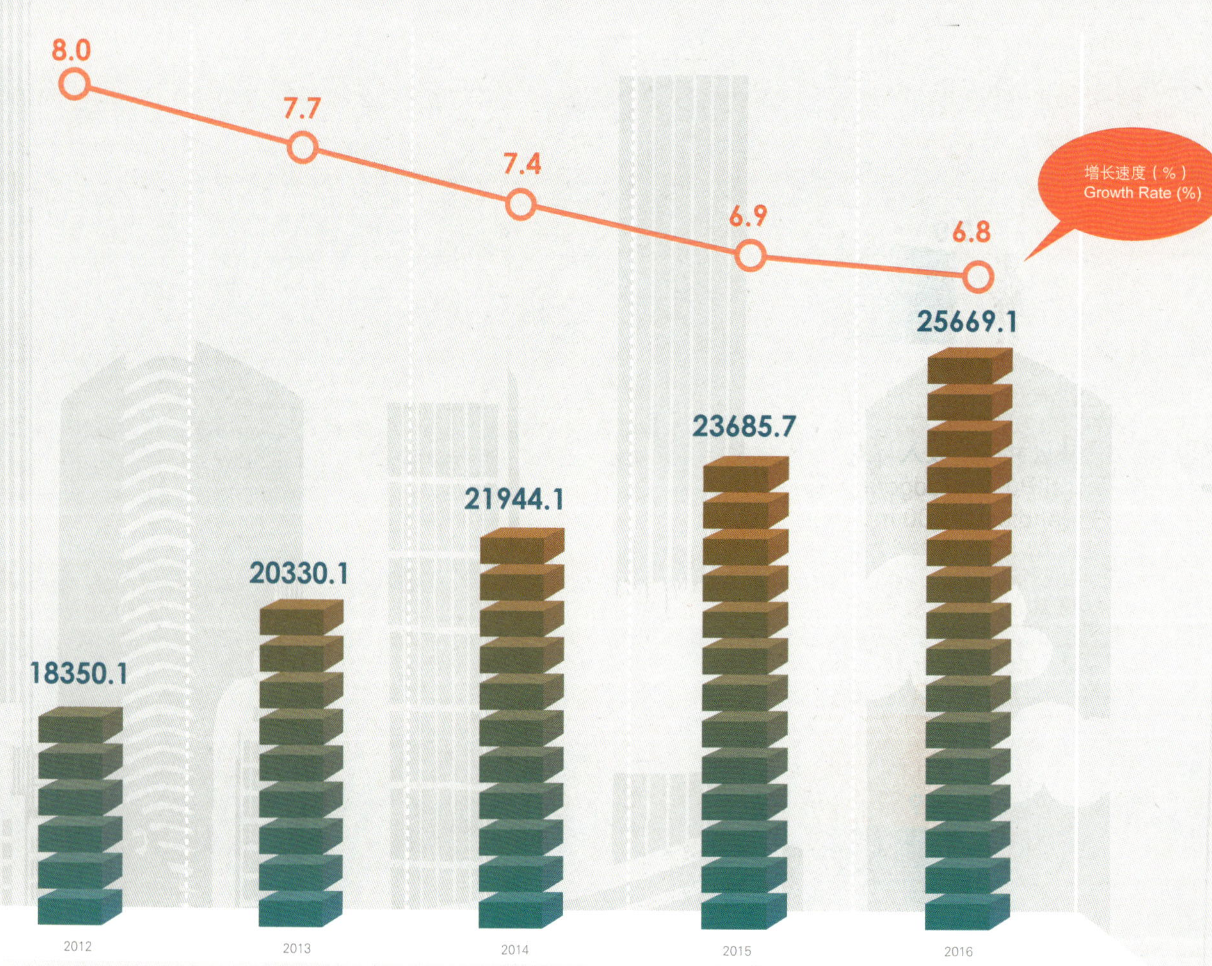

人均地区生产总值（万元/人）
Per Capita Gross Domestic Product (10000 yuan/person)

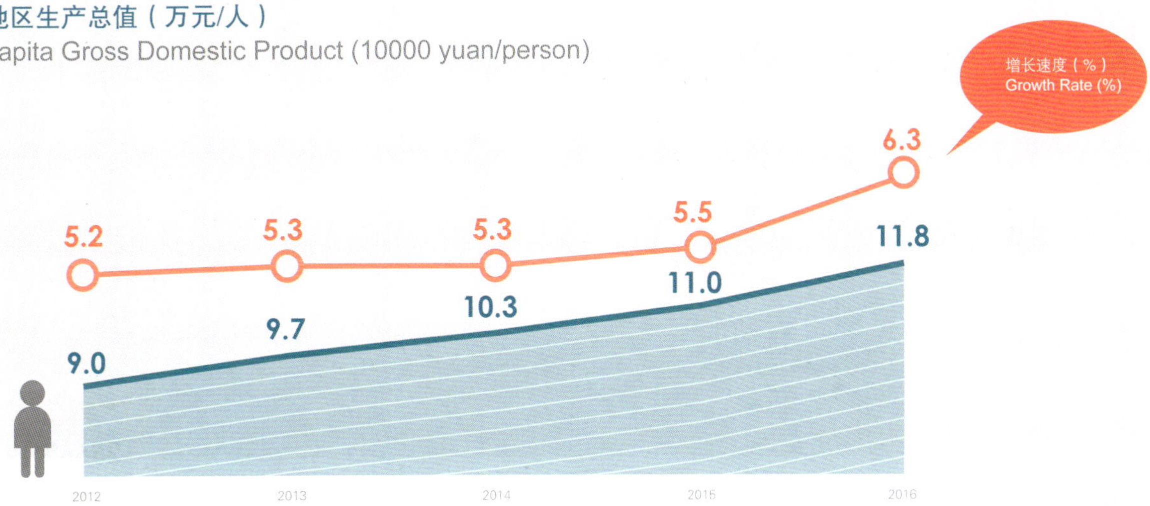

增长速度（%）
Growth Rate (%)

	2012	2013	2014	2015	2016
人均地区生产总值	9.0	9.7	10.3	11.0	11.8
增长速度（%）	5.2	5.3	5.3	5.5	6.3

一般公共预算收入与支出（亿元）
Local Public Budgetary Revenue and Expenditures(100 million yuan)

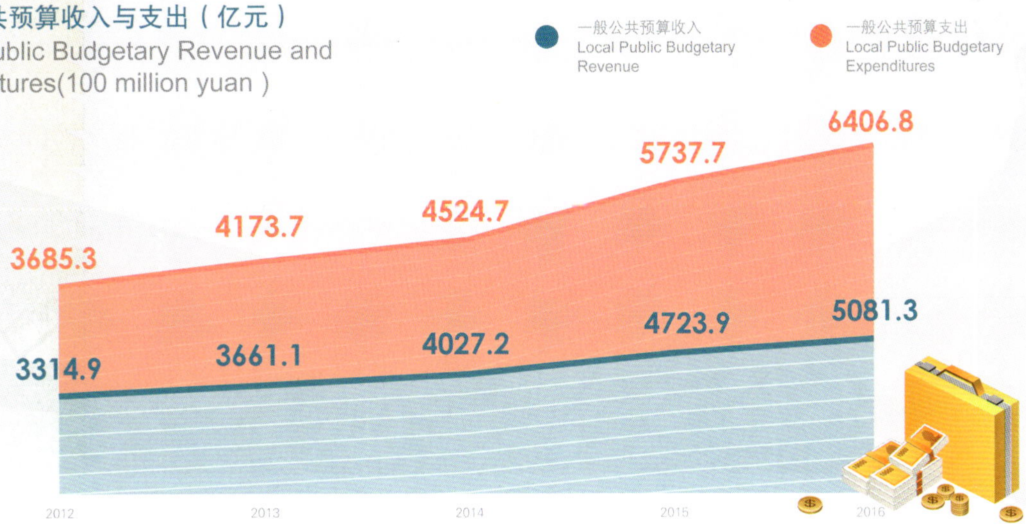

	2012	2013	2014	2015	2016
一般公共预算收入 Local Public Budgetary Revenue	3314.9	3661.1	4027.2	4723.9	5081.3
一般公共预算支出 Local Public Budgetary Expenditures	3685.3	4173.7	4524.7	5737.7	6406.8

人口与就业
Population and Employment

常住人口（万人）
Permanant Population (10000 persons)

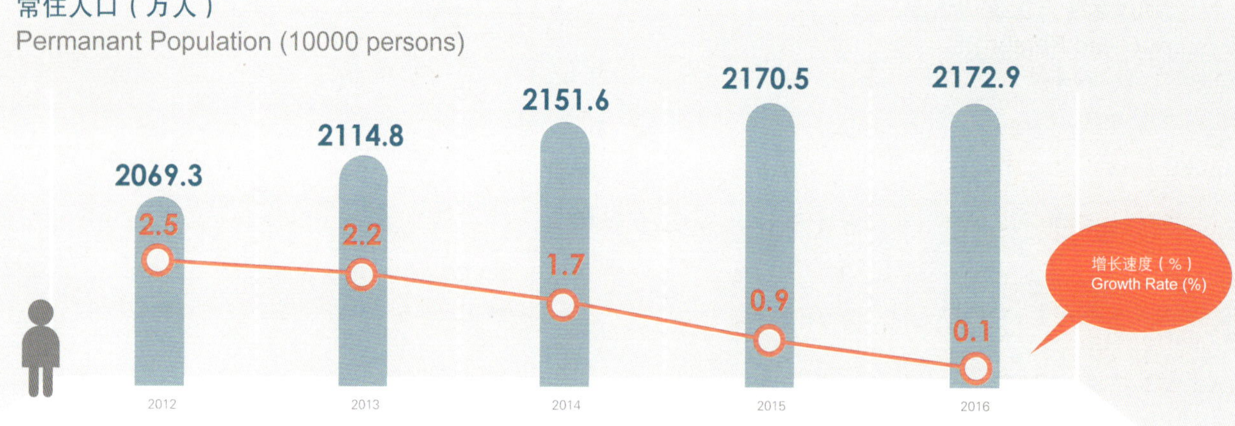

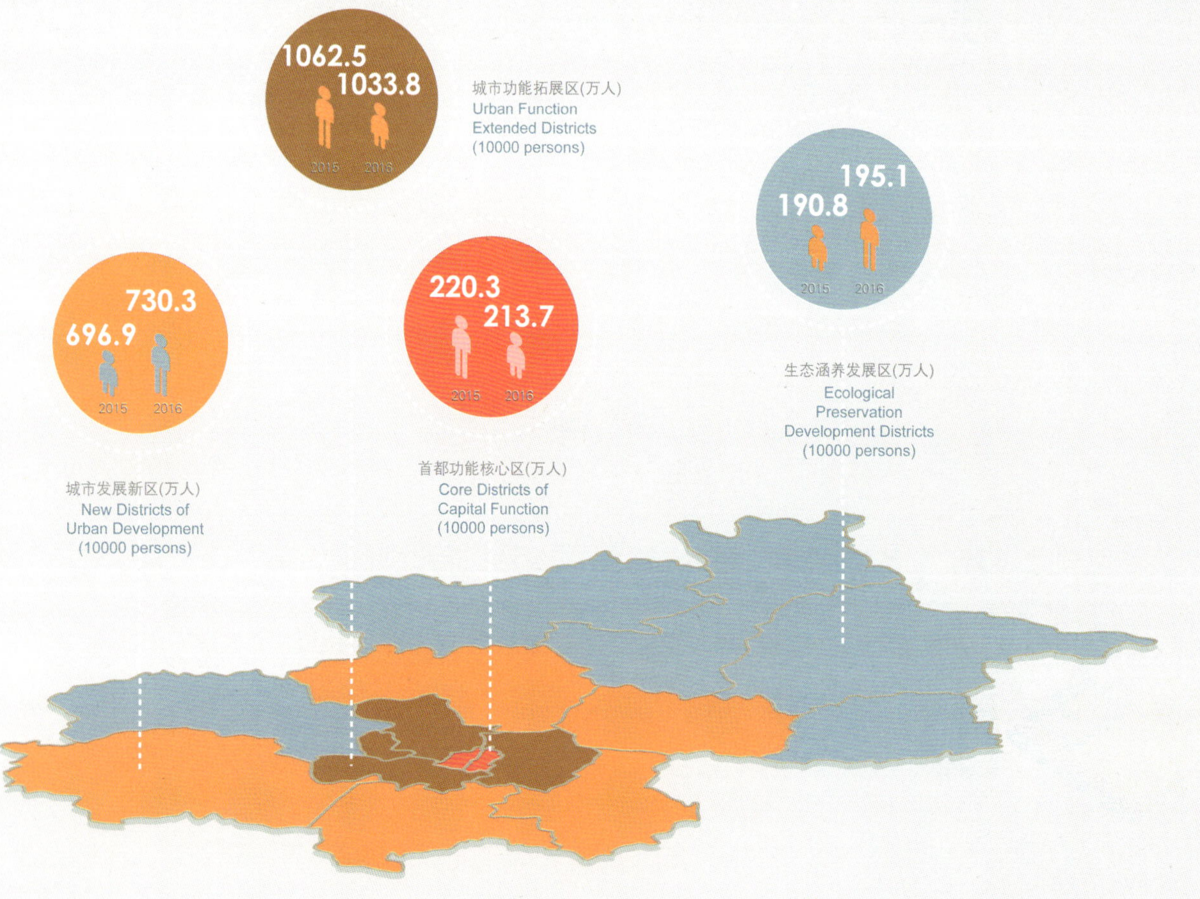

从业人员（万人）
Employed Persons (10000 persons)

增长速度（%）
Growth Rate (%)

	2012	2013	2014	2015	2016
Growth Rate (%)	3.5	3.0	1.4	2.5	2.9
Employed Persons	1107.3	1141.0	1156.7	1186.1	1220.1

法人单位从业人员平均工资（元）
Average Wage of Employed Persons in Legal Entities(yuan)

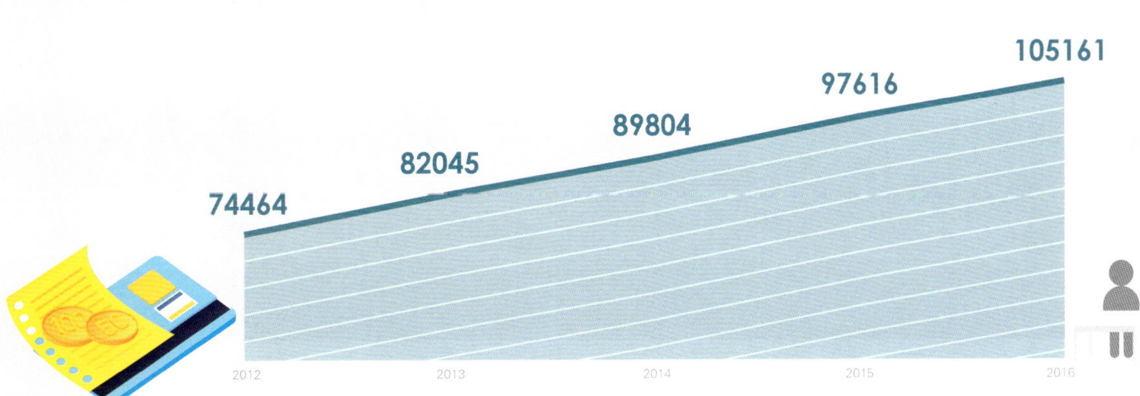

价格指数
Price Index

价格指数（上年=100）（%）
Price Index (preceding year=100) (%)

居民消费价格指数
Consumer Price Index

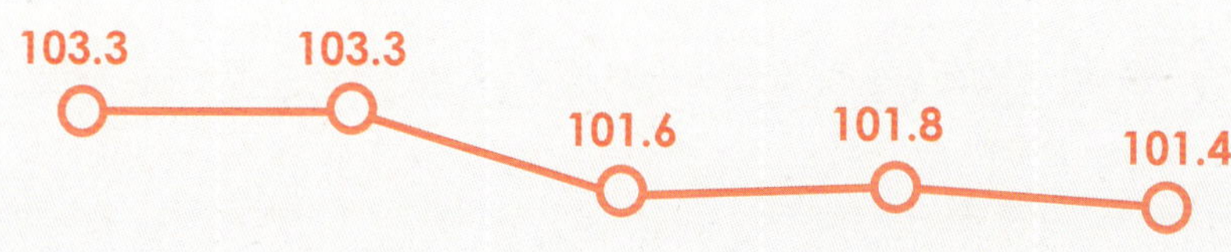

商品零售价格指数
Retail Price Index

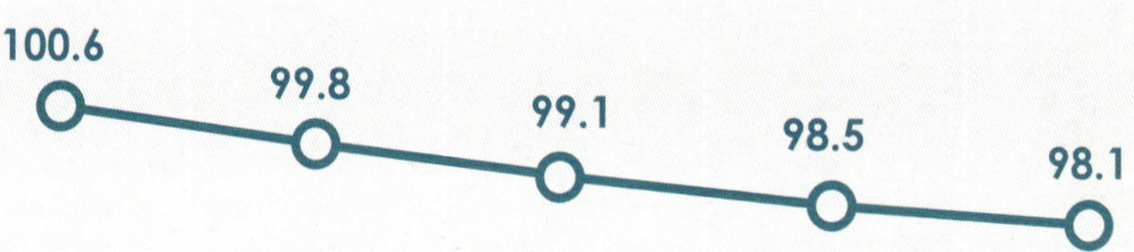

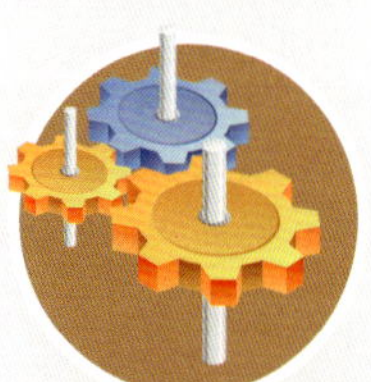

工业生产者出厂价格指数
Producer Price Index for Industrial Products

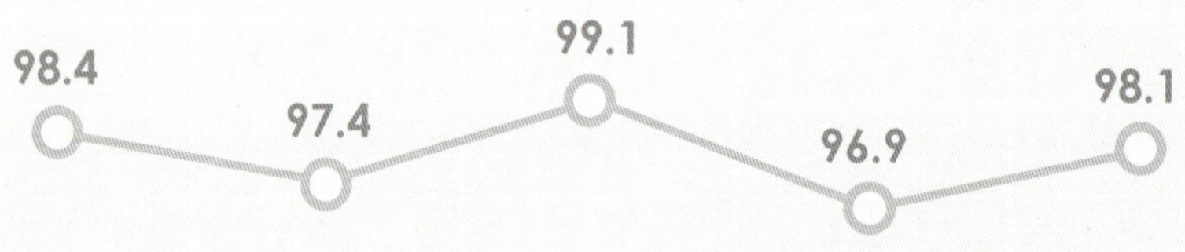

工业生产者购进价格指数
Purchasing Price Index for Industrial Products

2012 2013 2014 2015 2016

人民生活
People's Life

居民人均可支配收入（元）
Per Capita Disposable Income of the Residents (yuan)

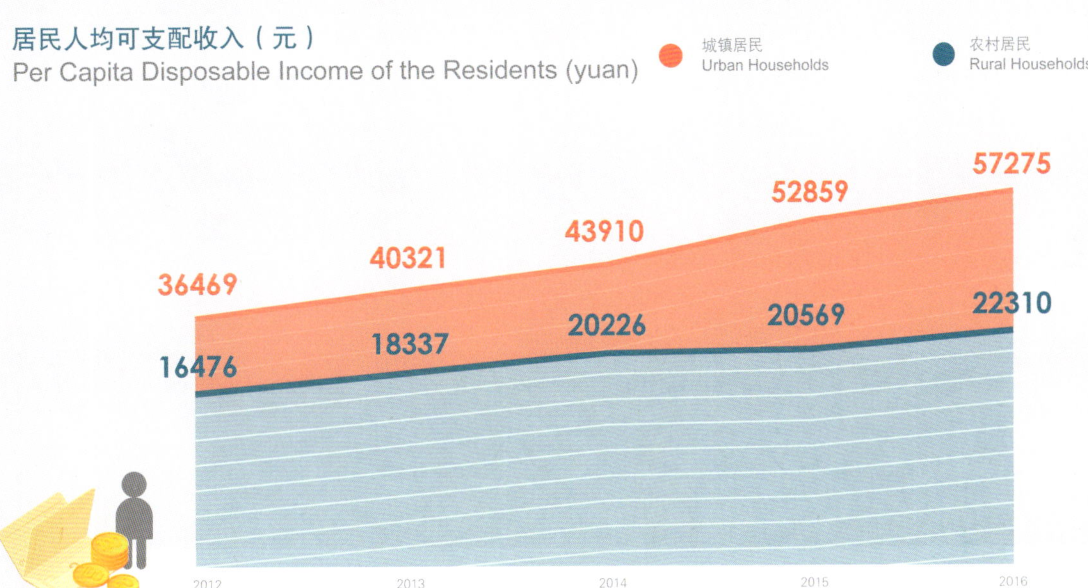

居民人均消费支出（元）
Per Capita Consumption Expenditure of the Residents (yuan)

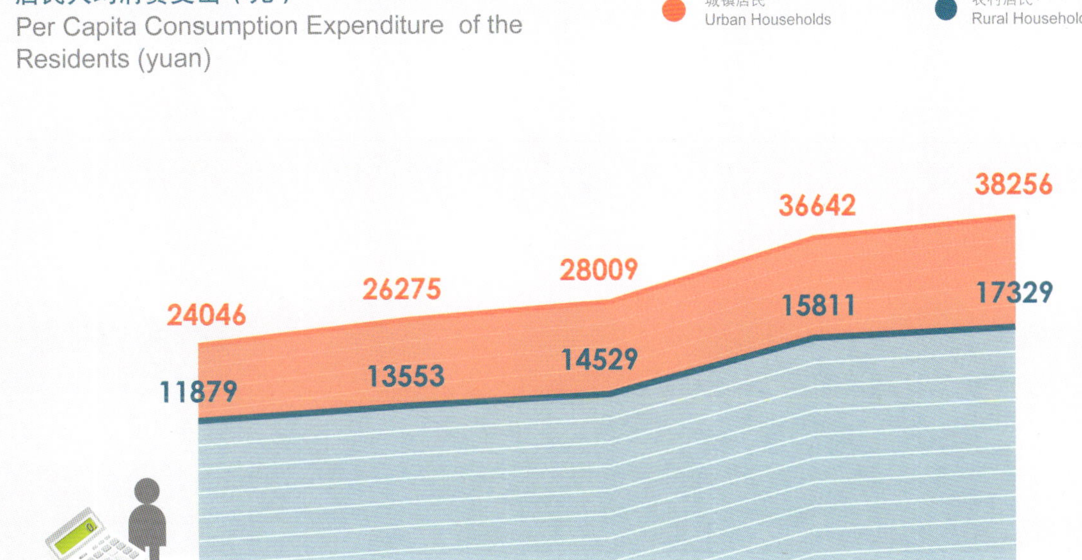

产业发展
Industry Development

地区生产总值构成（%）
Composition of Gross Domestic Product By Three Industies(%)

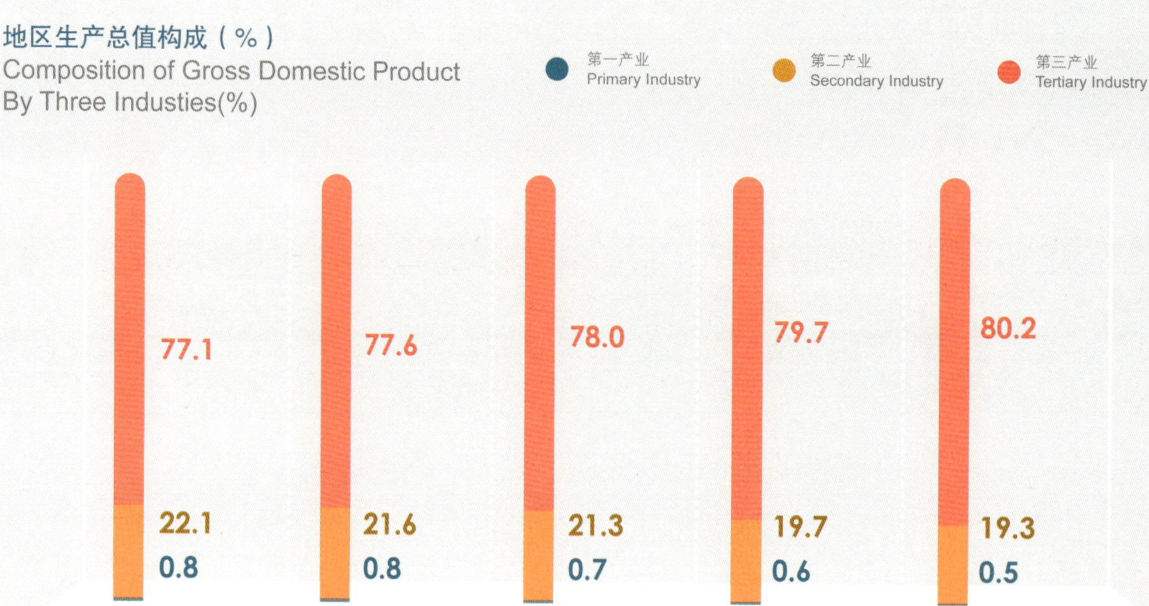

部分新兴产业增加值（亿元）
Added Value of Some Emerging Industries(100 million yuan)

投资与消费
Investment and Consumption

全社会固定资产投资（亿元）
Total Investment in Fixed Assets (100 million yuan)

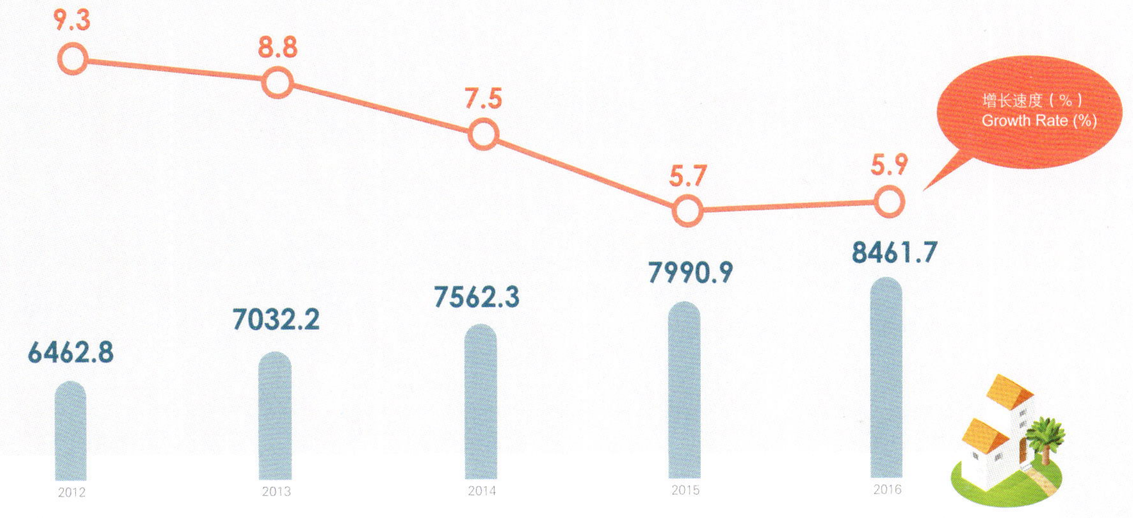

社会消费品零售总额（亿元）
Total Retail Sales of Consumer Goods (100 million yuan)

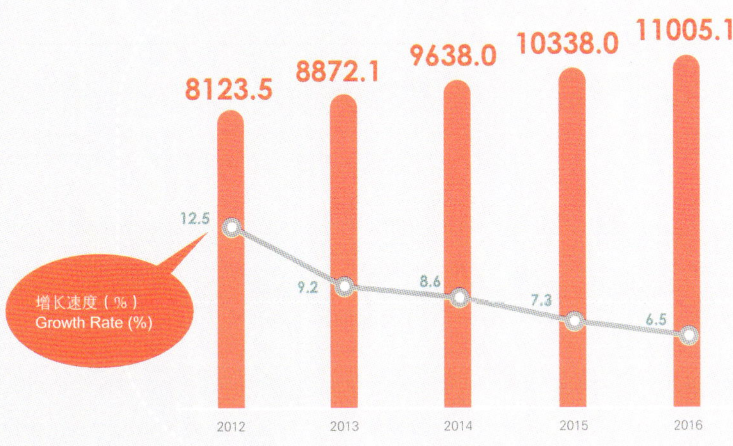

对外开放
Opening to the Outside World

进出口总值
Total Value of Imports and Exports

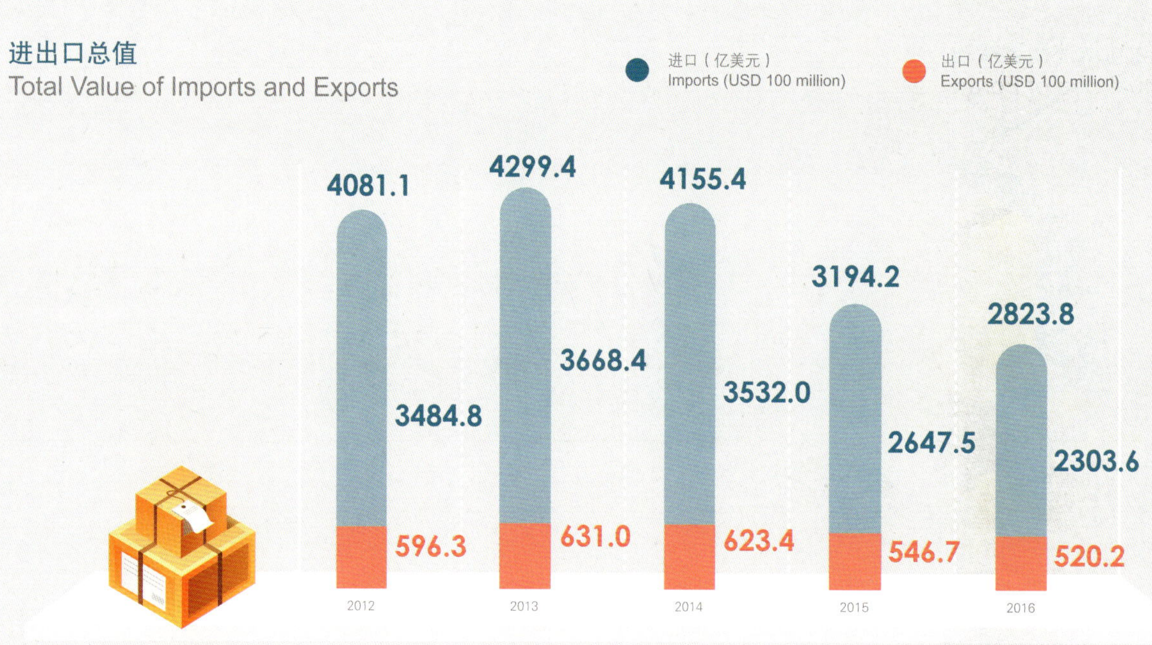

服务贸易总额
Total Service Trade

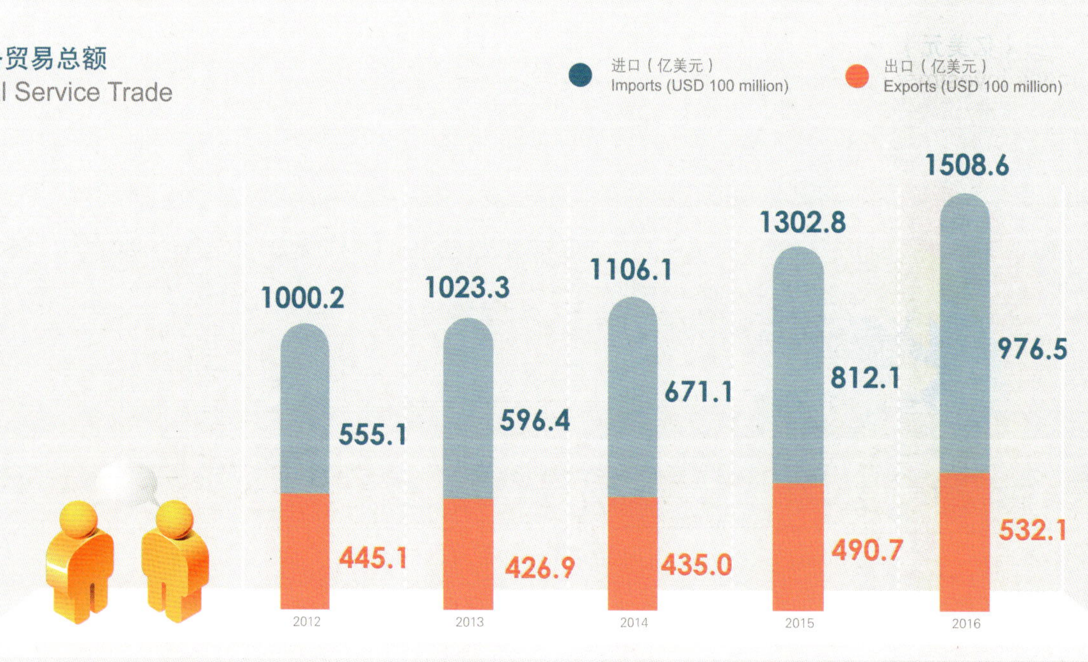

实际利用外商直接投资额（亿美元）
Actual Use of Foreign Direct Investment (USD 100 million)

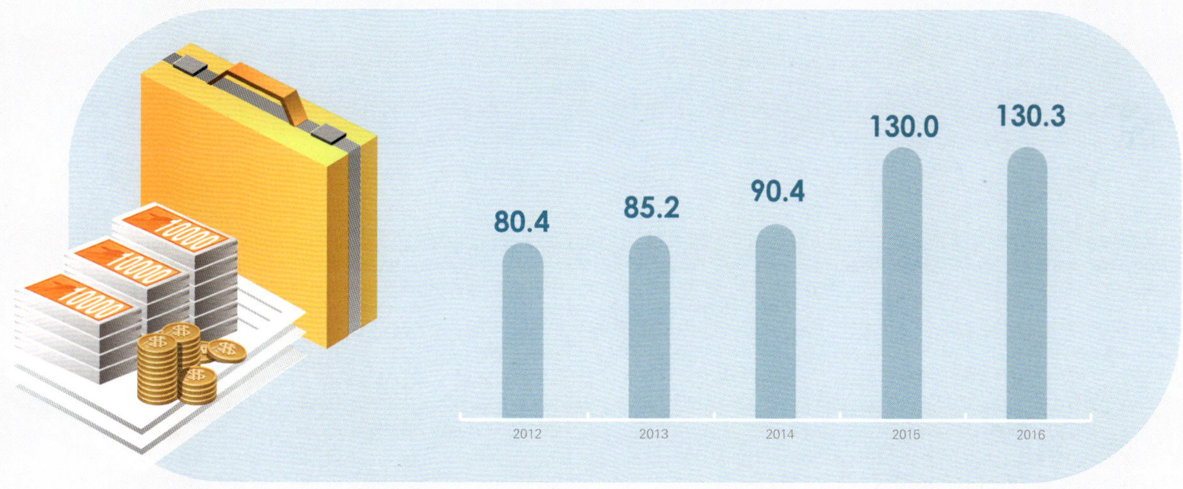

境外投资（亿美元）
Overseas Investment (USD 100 million)

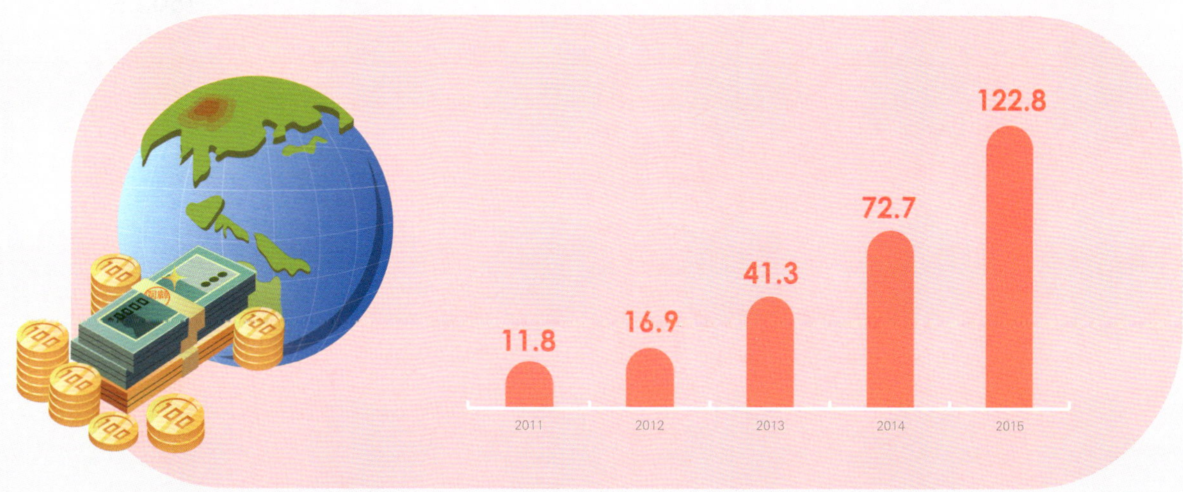

资源与环境
Resource and Environment

万元地区生产总值能耗（吨标准煤）
Energy Consumption per 10000 yuan of GDP (ton of SCE)

万元地区生产总值水耗（立方米）
Water Consumption per 10000 yuan of GDP (cu.m)

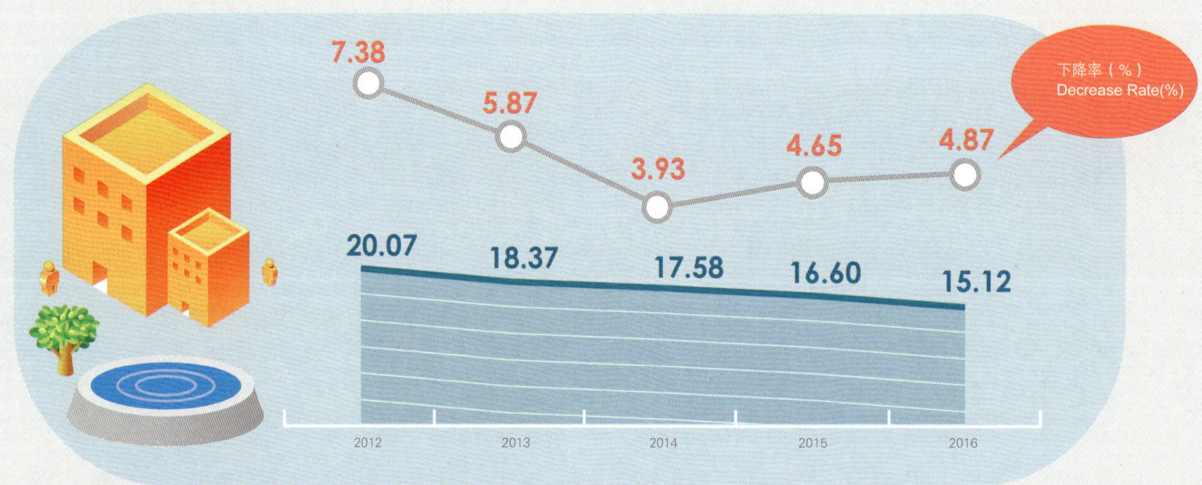

生活垃圾无害化处理率（%）
Rate of Harmless Disposal of Domestic Waste(%)
污水处理率（%）
Sewage Treatment Rate(%)
城市绿化覆盖率（%）
Green Land Coverage(%)
细颗粒物（PM2.5）年均浓度(微克/立方米)
Annual Concentration of PM2.5 (μg/m3)
99.1
99.3
99.6
99.8
99.8
83.0
84.6
86.1
87.9
90.0
46.2
46.8
47.4
48.4
48.4
89.5
85.9
80.6
73.0
2012
2013
2014
2015
2016

科技创新
Technology Innovation

研究与试验发展(R&D)经费内部支出（亿元）
Internal R&D Expenditures (100 million yuan)

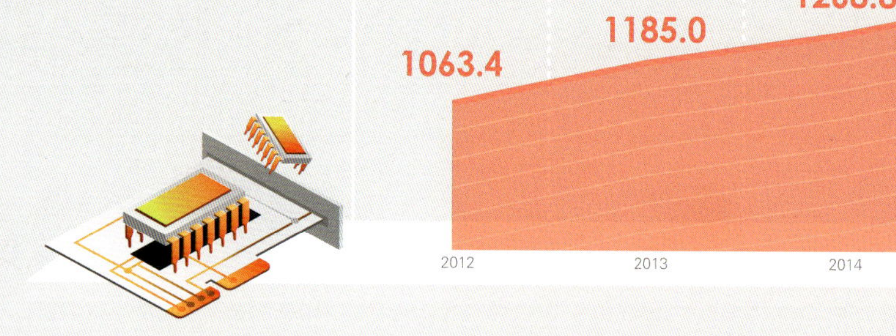

技术合同成交（亿元）
Technological Contracts (100 million yuan)

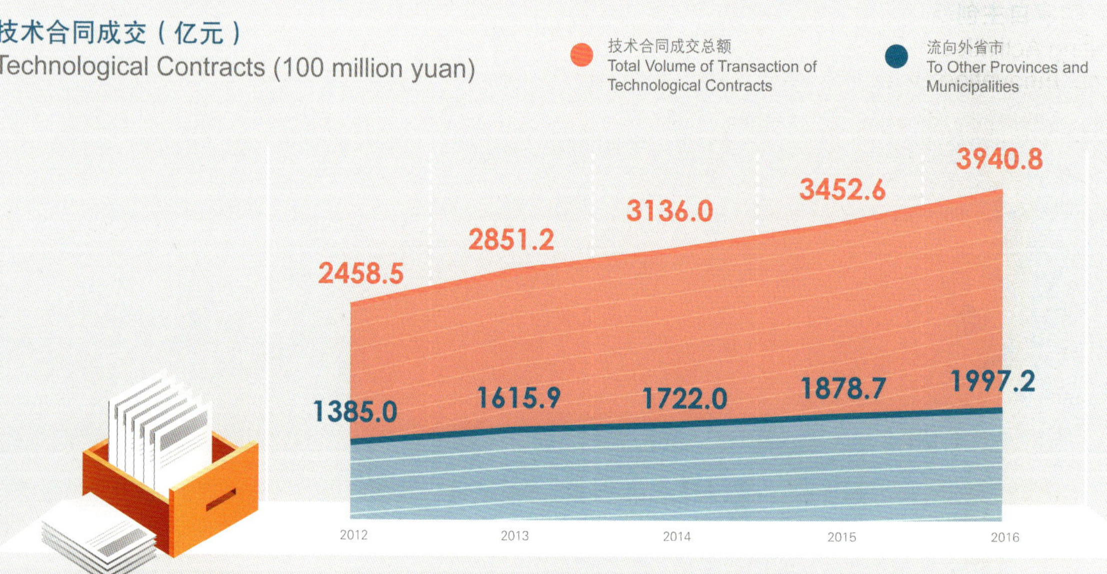

专利情况（件）
Patent (unit)

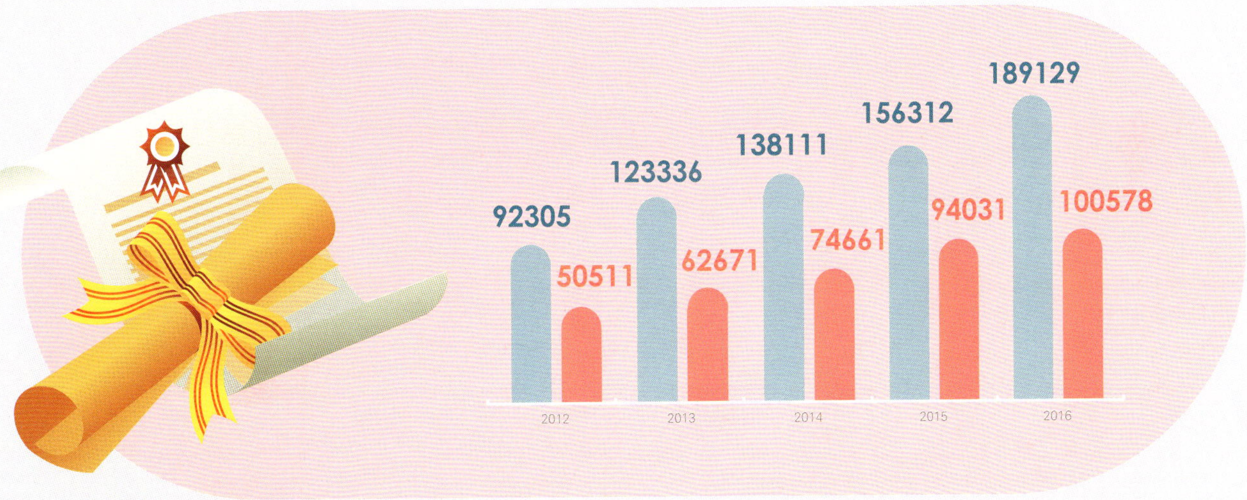

中关村国家自主创新示范区企业经营情况（亿元）
Operating Activities of Enterprises in Zhongguancun National Innovation Demonstration Zone (100 million yuan)

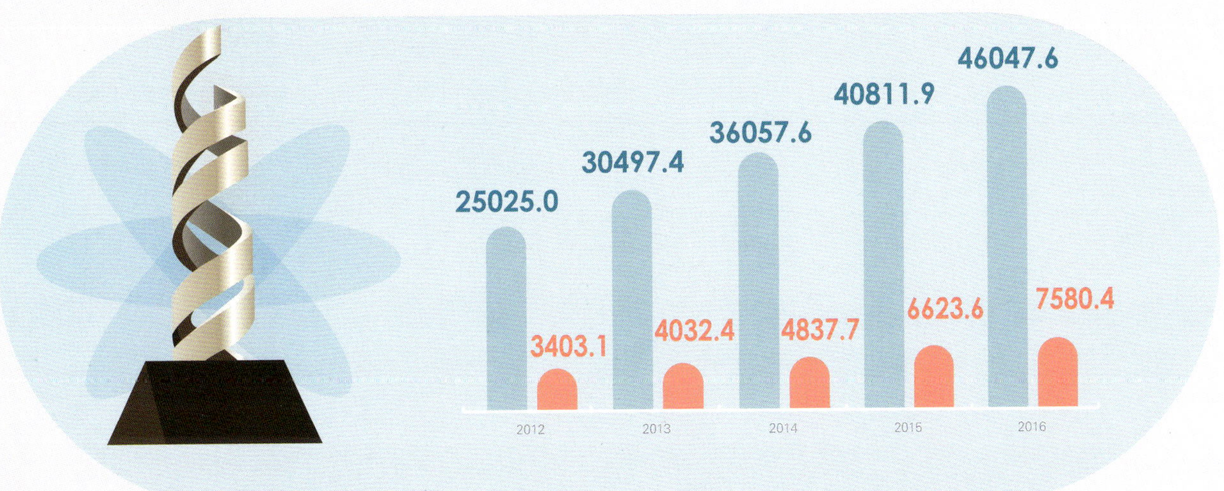

公共服务
Public Service

教育
Education

学校数（个）
Number of Schools (unit)

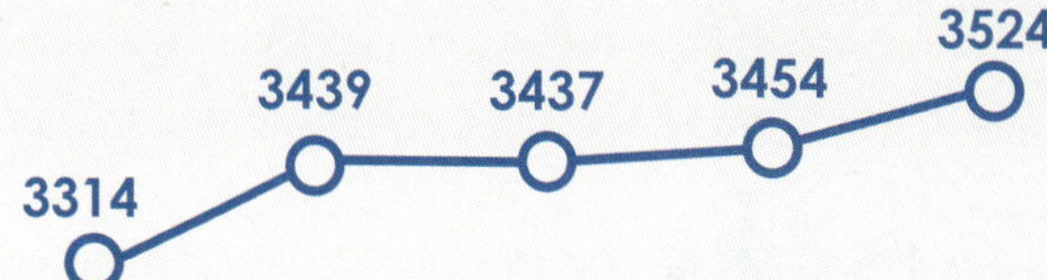

在校学生数（万人）
Enrolled Students in Schools
(10000 person)

专任教师数（万人）
Full-time Teachers
(10000 person)

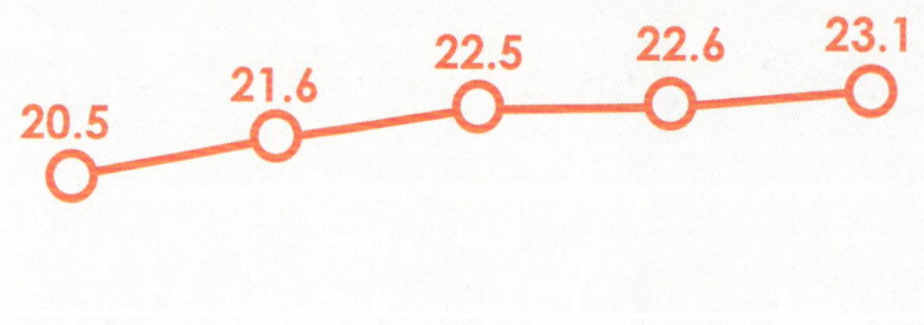

2012 2013 2014 2015 2016

卫生
Healthcare

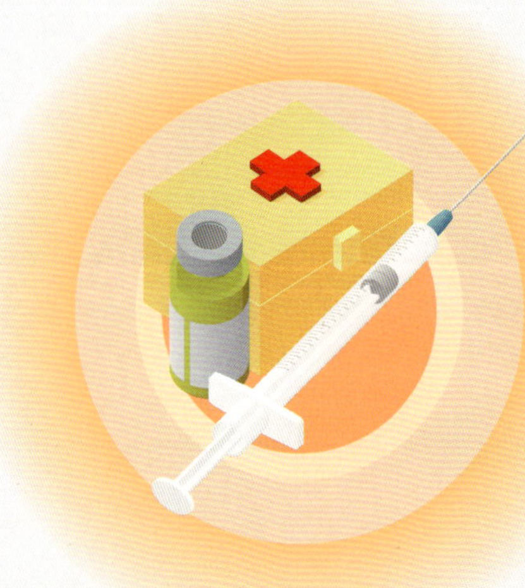

每千常住人口执业医师数（人）
Certified Physicians per 1,000 Permanent Residents (person)

每千常住人口床位数（人）
Number of Hospital Beds per 1,000 Permanent Residents (unit)

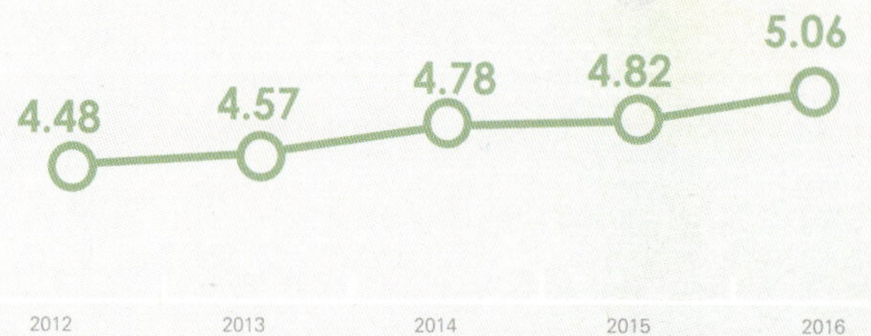

文化
Culture

公共图书馆总藏书（万册、万件）
Total Collections of Public Libraries (10000 volumes)

博物馆数（个）
Number of Museums (unit)

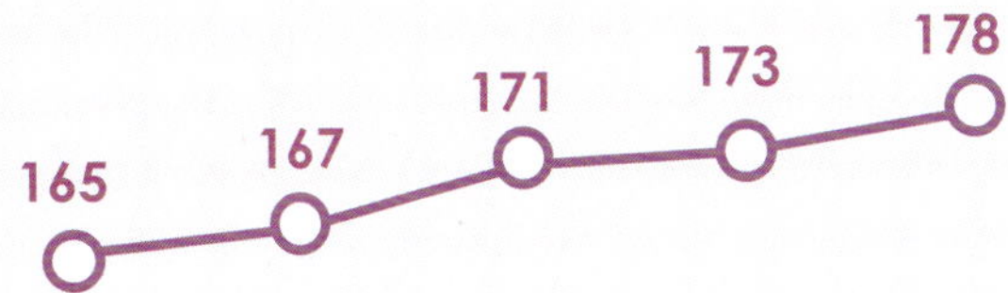

电影放映场次（万场次）
Show Times of Films (10000 Times)

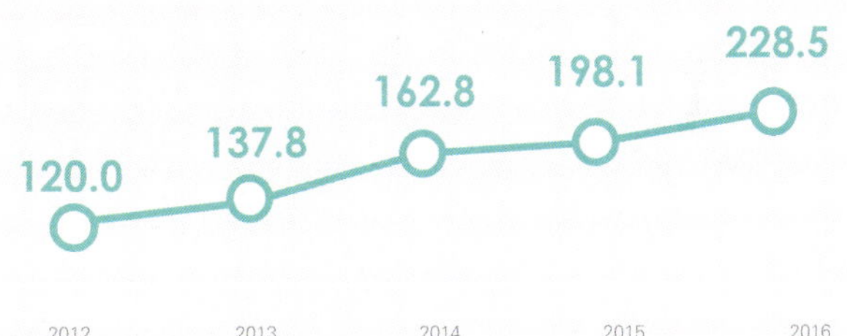

公共交通客运量
Passenger Carried by Public Transport

公共电汽车（万人次）
Buses and Trolley Buses (10000 person-times)

轨道交通（万人次）
Rail Transit (10000 person-times)

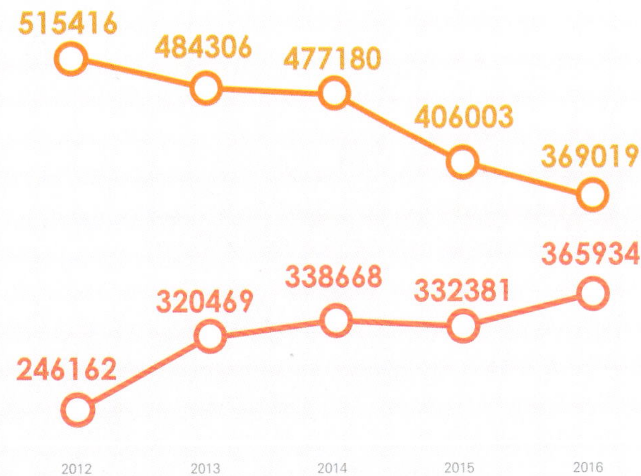

社会保障
Social Security

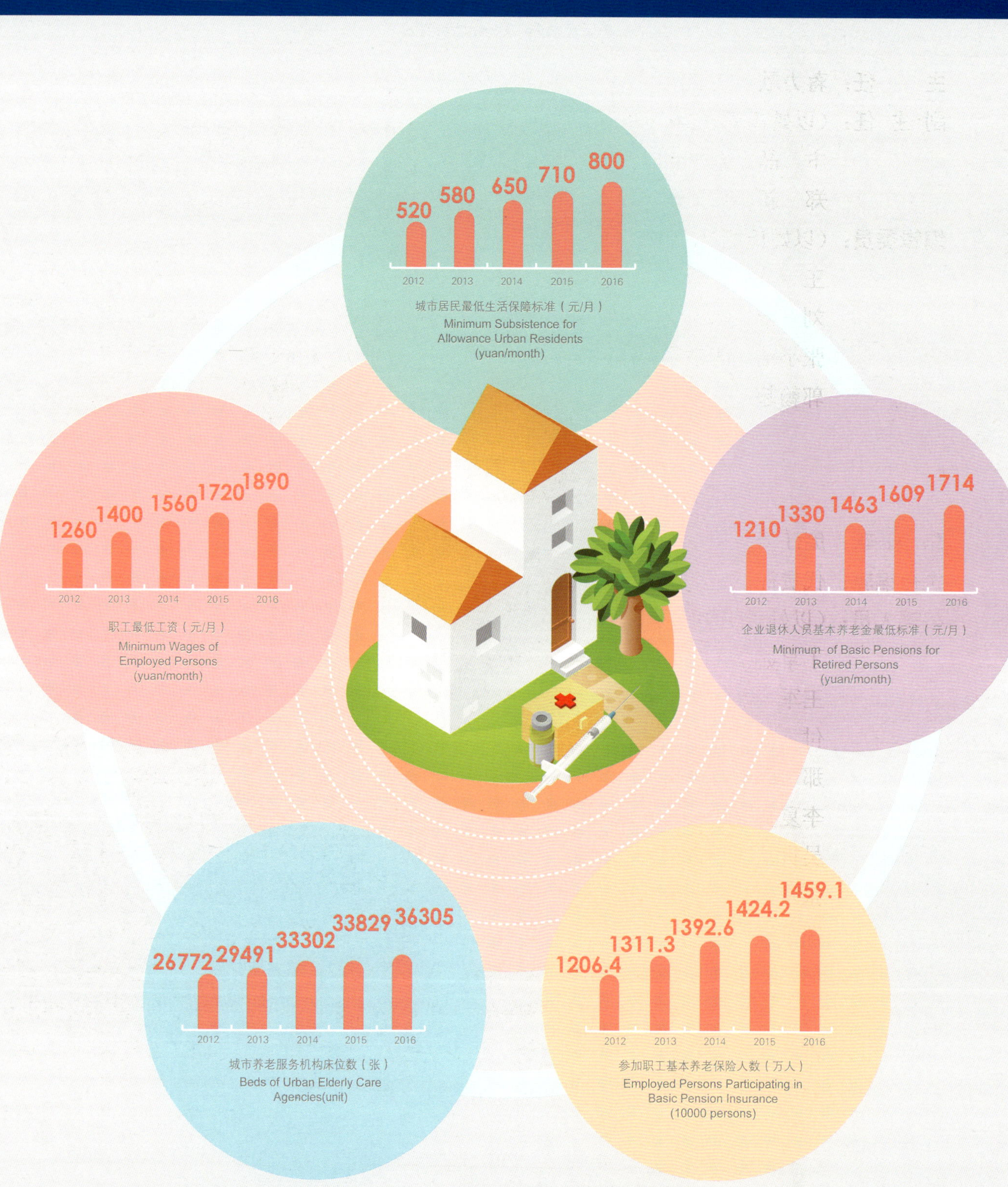

《北京统计年鉴—2017》
编辑委员会及编辑工作人员

编委会

编辑工作人员

使用指南

《北京统计年鉴》是一部按年连续出版的大型统计资料。本年鉴通过大量的统计数据，真实地记录了北京市一年来经济社会发展变化情况，是国内外各界人士了解北京、认识北京的重要资料工具书。

一、关于框架结构

（一）总体结构

《北京统计年鉴》整体框架基本保持稳定，彩页内容以图文并茂的形式反映了本地区经济社会发展主要趋势和变化；统计表是年鉴的主体内容，主要包括综合，国民经济核算，人口与就业，财政与税收，能源、资源和环境，全社会固定资产投资和房地产开发，对外经济贸易，价格指数，人民生活，城市公用事业，农业及农村经济，工业，建筑业，第三产业，交通运输邮电，批发和零售业、住宿和餐饮业，旅游业，金融和保险，教育、文化，科技，卫生、体育，社会福利、社区、政法及其他，开发区等 23 个章节，从多行业、多领域客观反映全市经济和社会发展情况。

（二）章节结构

章节内结构：每一章节由简要说明、统计表和主要统计指标解释三部分组成。简要说明在每一章节首页，主要介绍该章节的主要内容、资料来源、统计范围、指标口径和历史数据调整方法；主要统计指标解释在每章节页尾，主要对本章节内所涉及的主要指标、计算方法等做简要解释；统计表是各章节的核心内容。

统计表排列：每一章节注重从反映该领域主要情况出发，编排统计表内容。统计表的排列顺序一般先是主要指标历史数据表，后为当年数据表。

二、关于使用要领

（一）年份

按照惯例，书名中标注的年份为出版年份，年鉴中统计表内最新数据为上一年数据。例如，书名为《北京统计年鉴 2017》表示此本年鉴为 2017 年出版，年鉴中最新数据年份截至 2016 年。

统计表名中的“年份”大致会有三种标识方法，分别代表三种含义：一是“表格名称（****年-****年）”表示表内所列数据是包含了这两个年份之间的各年资料；二是统计表名中未显示年份，表示表内所列数据为当年和上年两年数据；三是“表格名称（****年）”表示表内所列数据仅为某一年资料。

（二）符号

统计表中常见符号如下：

：表示总计中的其中项；有“#”号的分组指标表示总计的部分项目，无“#”号的分组指标则表示其中项之和等于总计。

‖ ：宾栏中的“‖”为分组符号，代表某个指标存在几种分组数据。

… ：表示该数据不足该表最小计量单位数。

空格：表示该项指标数据不详或没有数据。

*** ：表示为使个体数据得以保密，该数据不予公布。

（三）文字说明

文字说明包括使用指南、目录、简要说明、指标解释和表下注解。使用指南在目录之前，是对年鉴整体框架进行介绍，对主要调整内容进行说明；简要说明在每一章节首页，主要介绍该章节的主要内容、资料来源、统计范围、指标口径和历史数据调整方法等；统计表下的注释则是对部分统计指标口径、方法、范围等内容的说明。

（四）数据

一般情况下，每一章节的前几张表均为该专业或该领域核心指标的历史数据。历史数据如果按年份连续反映在一张表内的，一般可以连续使用，但也需要留意表下的注释，以便对指标内涵有更详尽的了解；如果历史数据分成若干张表显示，则表示相关指标统计有过重大调整，需要分段反映。

此外，最新出版的年鉴上发布的部分历史数据会与以往年鉴上的数据有调整，存在差异，因此在查询和使用历史数据时应以最新出版的年鉴为准。

（五）电子光盘

《北京统计年鉴》配有电子光盘，包括中文和英文两种语言的版本，辅助用户对数据进行加工处理。

（六）本年鉴中部分数据合计数或相对数由于计量单位取舍不同而产生的计算误差，均未作机械调整。

三、关于 2017 年版《北京统计年鉴》说明

与 2016 年版《北京统计年鉴》相比较，本年鉴在内容上主要做了如下调整：

1. 本书对部分章节顺序进行调整。

2. 按照国家统计局统一要求，自 2016 年 1 月起，北京流通消费价格统计执行新的《流通和消费价格统计报表制度》，其中居民消费价格和商品零售价格调查项目目录均重新进行了修订调整。根据国家统计制度要求，工业生产者价格统计调查每五年进行一次基期轮换，2016 年开始使用 2015 年作为新一轮的对比基期。

3. 按照国家统计局部署，2016 年开始实施地区研发支出核算方法改革，将研发支出未计入地区生产总值部分进行补充核算，对 1996—2015 年地区生产总值进行了调整，同时调整了研发与试验发展（R&D）经费内部支出相当于地区生产总值比例数据，以及 2016 年万元地区生产总值能耗及下降率、平均每万元地区生产总值能源消费量。

4. 继续加强文字内容修订，方便读者了解数据变化情况。一是修订各章节简要说明内容，将各章节反映的数据内容、数据来源、统计标准以及数据历史变化等情况全面呈现；二是及时增减章节后的主要指标解释内容，根据当年指标变化等情况对各章节指标解释进行统一的修订、调整；三是更新表下注释内容，准确反映当年数据口径内容调整变化情况；四是根据北京市行政机构调整情况，对相关单位名称进行统一修订。

USER GUIDE

Beijing Statistical Yearbook is a large statistical book published continuously on a chronological basis. With a great deal of statistical data, this Yearbook gives a true reflection of the social and economic development and changes in Beijing over the past year. It serves as an important reference book for domestic and foreign personnel in all circles to understand and know Beijing.

I. Framework Structure

(I) Overall Structure

The overall structure of *Beijing Statistical Yearbook* remains basically stable. In color pages, main tendency and changes about economic and social development of Beijing have been presented with both illustration and pictures; statistical tables are the main part of this Yearbook, mainly including 23 chapters, i.e. General Survey; National Accounts; Population and Employment; Government Finance and Tax Revenues; Energy, Resources and Environmental Protection; Total Investment in Fixed Assets and Real Estate Development; Foreign Trade; Price Index; People's Livelihood; Public Utilities; Agriculture and Rural Economy; Industry; Construction; Tertiary Industry; Transport, Post and Telecommunication Service; Wholesale and Retail Trade, Accomodation and Restaurants; Tourism; Finance and Insurance; Education and Culture; Science and Technology; Health Care and Sports; Social Welfare, Community, Plicies & Laws and Others; and Development Zones 23 chapters in total, reflecting the economic and social development situation across the city through multiple industries and fields.

(II) Structure of Chapters

Internal structure of chapters: Each chapter is composed of the Brief Introduction, Statistical Tables and Explanatory Notes to Main Statistical Indicators. Brief Introduction appears on the first page of each chapter, mainly introducing the main content, source of data, statistical scope, indicator standards, method of adjustment to historical data in each chapter; Explanatory Notes to Main Statistical Indicators come on the last page of each chapter, mainly giving a brief explanation to the main indicators and calculation method, etc. involved in the chapter; Statistical Tables are the core content of each chapter.

Arrangement of statistical tables: In each chapter, statistical tables are arranged for the purpose of reflecting the main conditions in the field. Generally speaking, historical statistical tables come before current year statistical tables.

II. How to Use

(I) Years

Conventionally, the year indicated in the book is the year of publication. The latest data indicated in the statistical tables in this Yearbook are data in the previous years. For example, this book is titled *2017 Bejing Statistical Yearbook*, which means it will be published in 2017 while the lastest data in the book is by the end of 2016.

"Years" in the statistical tables are marked in three ways, each indicating a different meaning. Firstly, the statistical table is named "****** (AAAA- BBBB)", which refers to that the data listed in the table are those from the year of AAAA to BBBB; Secondly, the statistical table contains no years, indicating that the data listed in the table are those of current year and last year; Thirdly, the statistical table is named "****** (AAAA)", indicating that the data listed in the table are those of the year of AAAA.

(II) Symbols

Symbols in statistical tables include:

#: means that the item is included in the total. Grouped indicators marked with "#" are part of the total, while those without "#" mean that sum of inclded items equals to the total.

||: means that there are multiple ways of grouping the indicators.

…: means that the figure is less than the minimum measurement unit of the table.

Blank: mean that the figure is unknown or unavailable.

***: means that the figure is not disclosed for secrecy reasons.

(III) Explanations

Explanations include User Guide, Table of Contents, Brief Introduction, Explanatory Notes to Main Statistical Indicators and notes under the tables. User Guide appears before the Table of Contents, giving an introduction to the overall framework of this Yearbook, and explaining the main adjustments; Brief Introduction appears on the first page of each chapter, giving an introduction to the chapter's main content, source of data, statistical scope, standards of indicators, adjustment method of historical data, etc; Notes under the statistical tables make an explanation on standard of some indicators, method and scope, etc.

(IV) Data

In general cases, the first tables in each chapter contain historical data of core indicators in the area or field. Generally speaking, historical data that are shown in one table continuously by year can be used continuously. But it is also necessary to refer to the notes under the table in order to have a full understanding of the connation of indicators; historical data that are shown in several tables indicate that there were major adjustments to relevant indicators, and they need to be reflected by sections.

In addition, some of the historical data in the latest yearbook may have been adjusted over data in previous yearbooks. Therefore please refer to the latest yearbook when enquiring or using historical data.

(V) Electronic CD-ROM

Beijing Statistical Yearbook is provided with a CD-ROM, which containes Chinese and English versions of this Yearbook. The CD-ROM helps users in working with and processing the data.

(VI) The sum of some statistics or some relative numbers in this Yearbook might have certain calculation errors because of the choice of different units of measurement. All the statistics have not undergone mechanical adjustment.

III. About 2017 *Beijing Statistical Yearbook*

Compared with 2016 *Beijing Statistical Yearbook*, the following adjustments have been mainly made:

1. The order of certain chapters has been adjusted in this Yearbook.

2. In accordance with the unified requirements of the National Bureau of Statistics of the People's Republic of China (NBS), since January 2016, a new Circulation and Consumer Price Statistical Form System has been implemented by the circulation and consumer price statistics in Beijing, of which the survey item directories for consumer price and retail price were revised. According to the requirements of national statistical system, the statistical year of 2015 began to be used as a new round of base period for comparison in 2016.

3. In accordance with the deployment of the National Bureau of Statistics of the People's Republic of China (NBS), the reform of calculation method of regional R&D expenditure has been implemented since 2016, according to which the part of R&D expenditure not included in GDP figures were calculated additionally and GDP figures of 1996-2015 were adjusted. Moreover, the proportional data of internal spending of R&D expenditure in GDP, the energy consumption per RMB 10,000 GDP and decrease rate in 2016 and the energy consumption per RMB 10,000 GDP have also been adjusted.

4. Continue to strengthen the text revision work to make it easier for readers to understand the data changes. 1) To revise the content of the overview part of each chapter, comprehensively reflecting the data content, data sources, statistical standards and the historical changes of data and so on; 2) To timely revise or adjust the explanation part of the major indicators attached after the body text in each chapter according to the changes of indicators and the content of indicators of that very year and so on; 3) To update the content of notes under the tables, accurately reflecting the changes and adjustments of the data approach of that very year to make readers understand the data changes and accurately use the annual statistical data in different periods and different sectors; 4) The names of certain units have been revised uniformly according to the adjustments to the administrative bodies in Beijing.

目 录

Contents

一、综合

GENERAL SURVEY

二、国民经济核算
NATIONAL ACCOUNTS

三、人口与就业
POPULATION AND EMPLOYMENT

四、财政与税收

GOVERNMENT FINANCE AND TAX REVENUES

五、能源、资源和环境

ENERGY, RESOURCES AND ENVIRONMENT

六、全社会固定资产投资和房地产开发

TOTAL INVESTMENT IN FIXED ASSETS AND REAL ESTATE DEVELOPMENT

七、对外经济贸易

FOREIGN ECONOMY AND TRADE

八、价格指数
PRICE INDEX

九、人民生活
PEOPLE'S LIFE

十、城市公用事业

PUBLIC UTILITIES

十一、农业及农村经济

AGRICULTURE AND RURAL ECONOMY

十二、工业
INDUSTRY

十三、建筑业
CONSTRUCTION

十四、第三产业
TERTIARY INDUSTRY

十五、交通运输邮电
TRANSPORT，POST AND TELECOMMUNICATON SERVICES

十六、批发和零售业、住宿和餐饮业
WHOLESALE AND RETAIL TRADE，ACCOMMODATION AND RESTAURANTS

十七、旅游业
TOURISM

十八、金融和保险
FINANCE AND INSURANCE

十九、教育、文化
EDUCATION AND CULTURE

二十、科技
SCIENCE AND TECHNOLOGY

二十一、卫生、体育
HEALTH CARE AND SPORTS

二十二、社会福利、社区、政法及其他
SOCIAL WELFARE，COMMUNITY，LAW AND OTHERS

二十三、开发区
DEVELOPMENT ZONES

北京统计年鉴2017　BEIJING STATISTICAL YEARBOOK

综　合
GENERAL SURVEY

简要说明

一、本章资料的主要内容

本章主要包括北京市行政区划、法人及产业活动单位数、私营个体、非公经济、中小微型企业基本情况、全市社会经济发展的主要指标以及“十三五”时期监测指标等。

二、本章资料的数据来源

北京市行政区划情况来自北京市民政局；全市法人及产业活动单位情况来自北京市统计局；全市私营个体经济基本情况来自北京市工商行政管理局、北京市地方税务局、北京市国家税务局；非公经济数据和中小微型企业数据来自北京市统计局；全市社会经济主要指标及“十三五”时期主要监测指标资料由北京市统计局及国家统计局北京调查总队根据相关资料整理取得。

三、有关统计标准的变化说明

（一）《国民经济行业分类与代码》（GB/T 4754—2002版）与原（GB/T 4754—1994版）的主要框架结构变化：

增加的门类：a).信息传输、计算机服务和软件业 b).租赁和商务服务业 c).住宿和餐饮业 d).水利、环境和公共设施管理业 e).教育 f).国际组织。

名称或范围进行调整的门类：a).农、林、牧、渔业 b).采矿业 c).制造业 d).交通运输、仓储和邮政业 e).批发和零售业 f).金融业 g).科学研究、技术服务和地质勘查业 h).居民服务和其他服务业 i).卫生、社会保障和社会福利业 j).文化、体育和娱乐业 k).公共管理和社会组织。

取消的门类：a).地质勘查、水利管理 b).其它行业

（二）《国民经济行业分类》（GB/T 4754—2011版）与原（GB/T 4754—2002版）的主要框架结构变化：

门类名称调整：(1)“电力、燃气及水的生产和供应业”更名为“电力、热力、燃气及水生产和供应业”；(2)“信息传输、计算机服务和软件业”更名为“信息传输、软件和信息技术服务业”；(3)“科学研究、技术服务和地质勘查业”更名为“科学研究和技术服务业”；(4)“居民服务和其他服务业”更名为“居民服务、修理和其他服务业”；(5)“卫生、社会保障和社会福利业”更名为“卫生和社会工作”；(6)“公共管理和社会组织”更名为“公共管理、社会保障和社会组织”。

门类位次调整：(1)“批发和零售业”调至“建筑业”后面；(2)“住宿和餐饮业”调至“交通运输、仓储和邮政业”后面。

门类范围调整：A 农、林、牧、渔业；C 制造业；G 交通运输、仓储和邮政业；I 信息传输、软件和信息技术服务业；J 金融业；L 租赁和商务服务业；M 科学研究和技术服务业；O 居民服务、修理和其他服务业；P 教育；Q 卫生和社会工作；R 文化、体育和娱乐业；S 公共管理、社会保障和社会组织。

Brief Introduction

I. Main Content

Statistics in this chapter mainly show the basic information of administrative divisions of Beijing, number of corporate and industrial entities, non-public economy, small-, medium- and micro-sized enterprises, main indicators for social and economic development of the city, and monitoring indicators for the 13th Five-Year Plan, etc.

II. Source of Statistics

Statistics on administrative divisions of Beijing are from Beijing Municipal Bureau of Statistics. Statistics on municipal corporate and industrial entities are from Beijing Municipal Bureau of Statistics. Statistics on private and self-employment economy in the city are from Beijing Administration for Industry and Commerce, Beijing Municipal Bureau of Local Tax and Beijing Municipal Bureau of State Tax. Statistics on non-public economy, small-, medium- and micro-sized enterprises are from Beijing Municipal Bureau of Statistics. Statistics on social and economic indicators and main monitoring indicators for the 13th Five-Year Plan of the city are sorted out by Beijing Municipal Bureau of Statistics and National Bureau of Statistics Survey Office in Beijing on the basis of relevant statistics.

III. Adjustment to Historical Statistics According to New Industrial Standards

(I) Changes to the main framework of the *Classification and Codes of Sectors in National Economy* (GB/T 4754-2002) as compared with the previous version (GB/T 4754-1994):

Sectors added: a). information transmission, computer service and software, b). renting and leasing activities and business services, c). accommodation and restaurants, d). management of water conservancy, environment and public facilities, e). education, f). international organizations.

Sectors with name or range changed: a). agriculture, forestry, animal production and hunting, fishing, b). mining and quarrying, c). manufacturing, d). transport, storage and post, e). wholesale and retail trade, f). finance, g). scientific research, technical service, geological prospecting, h). resident service and other service, i). health care, social security, and social welfare, j). culture, sports and recreation, k). public administration and social organizations.

Sectors cancelled: a). geological prospecting, water conservancy management, b). other sectors.

(II) Compared with the previous (GB/T 4754-2002) version, the *Industrial Classification for National Economic Activities* (GB/T 4754-2011) mainly involves the following framework changes:

Changes to the name of category: (1) The "electric power, gas and water production and supply" is renamed "production and distribution of electricity, heating power, gas and water"; (2) the "information transmission, computer service and software" is renamed "information transmission, software and information technology services"; (3) the "scientific research, technical service and geological prospecting" is renamed "scientific research and development, technical services"; (4) the "resident service and other service" is renamed "resident services, repair and other services"; (5) the "health, social security and social welfare" is renamed "health care and social works"; (6) "public administration and social organization" is renamed "public administration, social security and social organizations".

Changes to the order of categories: (1) the "wholesale and retail trade" is put after the "construction"; (2) the "accommodation and restaurants" is put after the "transport, storage and post".

Changes to the scope of category: A. Agriculture, Forestry, Animal production and Hunting, Fishing; C. Manufacturing; G. Transport, Storage and Post; I. Information Transmission, Software and Information Technology Services; J. Finance; L. Renting and Leasing Activities and Business Services; M. Scientific Research and Development, Technical Service; O. Resident Services, Repair and Other Services; P. Education; Q. Health care and Social Works; R. Culture, Sports and Entertainment; S. Public Administration, Social Security and Social Organizations.

1-1 行政区划(2016年)
ADMINISTRATIVE DIVISIONS (2016)

单位：个 (unit)

地 区	District	街道办事处 Sub-district	建制镇 Designated Town	建制乡 Designated Township	社区居委会 Community Neighborhood Committee	村民委员会 Villagers' Committee
全 市	**Total**	**150**	**143**	**38**	**3054**	**3941**
首都功能核心区	**Core Functional Area of the Capital**	**32**			**443**	
东 城 区	Dongcheng District	17			182	
西 城 区	Xicheng District	15			261	
城市功能拓展区	**Urban Function Extension Area**	**71**	**9**	**22**	**1469**	**303**
朝 阳 区	Chaoyang District	24		19	431	154
丰 台 区	Fengtai District	16	2	3	309	65
石景山区	Shijingshan District	9			153	
海 淀 区	Haidian District	22	7		576	84
城市发展新区	**New Area of Urban Development**	**34**	**71**	**7**	**811**	**2193**
房 山 区	Fangshan District	8	14	6	145	459
通 州 区	Tongzhou District	4	10	1	115	480
顺 义 区	Shunyi District	6	19		125	426
昌 平 区	Changping District	8	14		229	301
大 兴 区	Daxing District	8	14		197	527
生态涵养发展区	**Ecological Conservation Area**	**13**	**63**	**9**	**331**	**1445**
门头沟区	Mentougou District	4	9		119	178
怀 柔 区	Huairou District	2	12	2	34	284
平 谷 区	Pinggu District	2	14	2	36	273
密 云 区	Miyun District	2	17	1	96	334
延 庆 区	Yanqing District	3	11	4	46	376

资料来源：北京市民政局。
Source: Beijing Municipal Bureau of Civil Affairs.

1—2 规模(限额)以上法人单位基本情况(2016年)
NUMBER OF LEGAL ENTITIES ABOVE DESIGNATED SIZE (2016)

单位：个 (unit)

项目	Item	法人单位数合计 Total Number of Legal Entities	单产业法人 Single-industry Legal Entities	多产业法人 Multi-industry Legal Entities
合计	**Total**	**40207**	**33815**	**6392**
按登记注册类型分组	**By Registration Type**			
内资	Domestically-invested Enterprises	36443	31131	5312
国有	State-owned Enterprises	6001	5186	815
集体	Collectively-owned Enterprises	563	490	73
股份合作	Joint-equity Cooperative Enterprises	355	307	48
联营	Associated Enterprises	26	22	4
有限责任公司	Limited Liability Companies	14151	11776	2375
股份有限公司	Companies Limited by Shares	1417	1013	404
私营	Private Enterprises	13499	11931	1568
其他	Others	431	406	25
港澳台商投资	Hong Kong, Macao and Taiwan-invested Enterprises	1487	1069	418
与港澳台商合资经营	Joint Ventures	461	353	108
与港澳台商合作经营	Cooperative Enterprises	99	86	13
港澳台商独资	Solely-funded Enterprises	895	615	280
港澳台商投资股份有限公司	Companies Limited by Shares	30	15	15
其他港澳台商投资	Others	2		2
外商投资	Foreign-invested Enterprises	2277	1615	662
中外合资经营	Joint Ventures	660	505	155
中外合作经营	Cooperative Enterprises	85	66	19
外资企业	Solely-funded Enterprises	1479	1012	467
外商投资股份有限公司	Companies Limited by Shares	39	22	17
其他外商投资	Others	14	10	4
按隶属关系分组	**By Affiliation**			
中央	Central	4364	3630	734
地方	Local	35843	30185	5658
按机构类型分组	**By Organization Type**			
企业	Enterprises	34944	29144	5800
事业单位	Institutions	3384	3126	258
机关	Government Agencies and Organizations	1140	873	267
社会团体	Social Organizations	248	190	58
其他机构	Others	491	482	9

注：本表为2016年年报规模(限额)以上法人单位数据。
Note: This table covers legal entities above designated size in the 2016 annual report.

1-3 国民经济各行业规模(限额)以上法人单位情况(2016年)
NUMBER OF LEGAL ENTITIES IN DIFFERENT SECTORS OF THE NATIONAL ECONOMY ABOVE DESIGNATED SIZE (2016)

单位：个 (unit)

行业	Sector	法人单位数合计 Total Number of Legal Entities	单产业法人 Single-industry Legal Entities	多产业法人 Multi-industry Legal Entities
合 计	**Total**	**40207**	**33815**	**6392**
农、林、牧、渔业	**Agriculture, Forestry, Animal Production and Hunting, Fishing**			
采矿业	**Mining and Quarrying**	**19**	**13**	**6**
煤炭开采和洗选业	Mining and Washing of Coal	1		1
石油和天然气开采业	Extraction of Petroleum and Natural Gas	2		2
黑色金属矿采选业	Mining of Ferrous Metal Ores	7	6	1
有色金属矿采选业	Mining of Non-Ferrous Metal Ores			
非金属矿采选业	Mining and Processing of Nonmetal Ores	3	3	
开采辅助活动	Mining Support Service Activities	6	4	2
其他采矿业	Mining of Other Ores			
制造业	**Manufacturing**	**3204**	**2707**	**497**
农副食品加工业	Processing of Food from Agricultural Products	133	110	23
食品制造业	Manufacture of Foods	124	102	22
酒、饮料和精制茶制造业	Manufacture of Wine, Beverage and Refined Tea	42	29	13
烟草制品业	Manufacture of Cigarettes and Tobacco	1		1
纺织业	Manufacture of Textile	19	17	2
纺织服装、服饰业	Manufacture of Textile, Wearing Apparel and Ornament	117	83	34
皮革、毛皮、羽毛及其制品和制鞋业	Manufacture of Leather, Fur, Feather and Its Products, and Footwear	8	6	2
木材加工和木、竹、藤、棕、草制品业	Processing of Timbers, Manufacture of Wood, Bamboo, Rattan, Palm and Straw Products	12	10	2
家具制造业	Manufacture of Furniture	60	49	11
造纸和纸制品业	Manufacture of Paper and Paper Products	41	39	2
印刷和记录媒介复制业	Printing, Reproduction of Recording Media	99	92	7
文教、工美、体育和娱乐用品制造业	Manufacture of Articles for Culture, Education, Artwork, Sport and Entertainment Activities	30	24	6
石油加工、炼焦和核燃料加工业	Processing of Petroleum, Coking, Processing of Nucleus Fuels	16	14	2
化学原料和化学制品制造业	Manufacture of Chemical Raw Materials and Chemical Products	184	164	20
医药制造业	Manufacture of Medicines	209	177	32
化学纤维制造业	Manufacture of Chemical Fibres	3	2	1
橡胶和塑料制品业	Manufacture of Rubber and Plastics Products	108	95	13
非金属矿物制品业	Manufacture of Non-metallic Mineral Products	219	189	30
黑色金属冶炼和压延加工业	Manufacture and Pressing of Ferrous Metals	20	18	2

注：1. 本表为2016年年报规模(限额)以上法人单位数据。
2. 本表行业划分执行2011年国民经济行业分类标准(GB/T 4754—2011)。

Note: a) This table covers legal entities above designated size in the 2016 annual report.
b) Sectors in this table are classified in accordance with the Standard for Classification of National Economic Sectors 2011 (GB/T 4754-2011).

1-3 续表 1 Continued 1

单位：个 (unit)

行业	Sector	法人单位数合计 Total Number of Legal Entities	单产业法人 Single-industry Legal Entities	多产业法人 Multi-industry Legal Entities
有色金属冶炼和压延加工业	Manufacture and Processing of Non-ferrous Metals	35	31	4
金属制品业	Manufacture of Fabricated Metal Products	182	157	25
通用设备制造业	Manufacture of General-Purpose Machinery	213	165	48
专用设备制造业	Manufacture of Special-Purpose Machinery	287	234	53
汽车制造业	Manufacture of Motor Vehicles	240	219	21
铁路、船舶、航空航天和其他运输设备制造业	Manufacture of Railway Locomotives, Building of Ships and Boats, Manufacture of Air and Spacecrafts and Other Transportation Equipments	78	71	7
电气机械和器材制造业	Manufacture of Electrical Machinery and Equipment	233	207	26
计算机、通信和其他电子设备制造业	Manufacture of Computers, Communication Equipment and Other Electronic Equipment	284	239	45
仪器仪表制造业	Manufacture of Measuring Instrument and Meter	158	124	34
其他制造业	Other Manufacturing	24	20	4
废弃资源综合利用业	Waste Rrecycling and Recovery	9	9	
金属制品、机械和设备修理业	Repair of Fabricated Metal Products, Machinery and Equipment	16	11	5
电力、热力、燃气及水生产和供应业	**Production and Distribution of Electricity, Heating Power, Gas and Water**	**117**	**95**	**22**
电力、热力生产和供应业	Production and Supply of Electric Power and Heat Power	74	62	12
燃气生产和供应业	Production and Distribution of Gas	20	15	5
水的生产和供应业	Production and Distribution of Water	23	18	5
建筑业	**Construction**	**3443**	**2758**	**685**
房屋建筑业	Construction of Building	668	423	245
土木工程建筑业	Civil Engineering Construction	586	453	133
建筑安装业	Construction Installation	846	718	128
建筑装饰和其他建筑业	Building Completion, Finishing and Other Construction	1343	1164	179
批发和零售业	**Wholesale and Retail Trade**	**6029**	**4958**	**1071**
批发业	Wholesale	4106	3552	554
零售业	Retail Trade	1923	1406	517
交通运输、仓储和邮政业	**Transport, Storage and Post**	**992**	**795**	**197**
铁路运输业	Transport via Railway	17	11	6
道路运输业	Transport via Road	482	415	67
水上运输业	Water Transport	5	3	2
航空运输业	Air Transport	28	21	7
管道运输业	Transport via Pipeline	2	2	
装卸搬运和运输代理业	Loading, Unloading, Portage and Other Transport Services	319	225	94
仓储业	Storage	108	98	10
邮政业	Post	31	20	11
住宿和餐饮业	**Accommodation and Restaurants**	**2288**	**1778**	**510**
住宿业	Accommodation	964	818	146
餐饮业	Restaurants	1324	960	364
信息传输、软件和信息技术服务业	**Information Transmission, Software and Information Technology Services**	**3012**	**2470**	**542**
电信、广播电视和卫星传输服务	Telecommunications, Broadcasting, Television and Satellite Transmission Services	222	173	49
互联网和相关服务	Internet and Related Services	333	281	52
软件和信息技术服务业	Software and Information Technology Services	2457	2016	441

1-3 续表 2 Continued 2

单位：个 (unit)

行 业	Sector	法人单位数合计 Total Number of Legal Entities	单产业法人 Single-industry Legal Entities	多产业法人 Multi-industry Legal Entities
金融业	**Finance**	**1915**	**1637**	**278**
货币金融服务	Monetary Financial Services	520	437	83
资本市场服务	Capital Market Services	563	510	53
保险业	Insurance	402	301	101
其他金融业	Other Financial Services	430	389	41
房地产业	**Real Estate**	**4255**	**3650**	**605**
租赁和商务服务业	**Renting and Leasing Activities and Business Services**	**5398**	**4677**	**721**
租赁业	Renting and Leasing Activities	107	83	24
商务服务业	Business Services	5291	4594	697
科学研究和技术服务业	**Scientific Research and Development, Technical Services**	**3382**	**2924**	**458**
研究和试验发展	Research and Experimental Development	562	520	42
专业技术服务业	Professional Technique Services	1501	1218	283
科技推广和应用服务业	Technique Generalization and Application Services	1319	1186	133
水利、环境和公共设施管理业	**Management of Water Conservancy, Environment and Public Facilities**	**554**	**502**	**52**
水利管理业	Management of Water Conservancy	36	32	4
生态保护和环境治理业	Ecological Protection and Environmental Control	65	54	11
公共设施管理业	Management of Public Facilities	453	416	37
居民服务、修理和其他服务业	**Resident Services, Repair and Other Services**	**432**	**372**	**60**
居民服务业	Resident Services	142	111	31
机动车、电子产品和日用产品修理业	Repair of Motor Vehicles, Electronics and Household Appliances	137	117	20
其他服务业	Other Services	153	144	9
教育	**Education**	**1500**	**1383**	**117**
卫生和社会工作	**Health Care and Social Works**	**726**	**593**	**133**
卫生	Health Care	673	542	131
社会工作	Social Work Activities	53	51	2
文化、体育和娱乐业	**Culture, Sports and Entertainment**	**1263**	**1156**	**107**
新闻和出版业	Journalism and Publishing	468	423	45
广播、电视、电影和影视录音制作业	Radio Broadcasting, Television, Movies, Videos and Sound Recording	268	246	22
文化艺术业	Cultures and Arts	281	267	14
体育	Sports Activities	186	167	19
娱乐业	Entertainments	60	53	7
公共管理、社会保障和社会组织	**Public Administration, Social Security and Social Organizations**	**1678**	**1347**	**331**
中国共产党机关	Organs of Communist Party of China	48	41	7
国家机构	Organs of State	1260	998	262
人民政协、民主党派	Peole's Political Consultative Conference and Democratic Parties	25	24	1
社会保障	Social Security	10	10	
群众团体、社会团体和其他成员组织	Mass Communities, Social Organizations and Other Membership Organizations	295	235	60
基层群众自治组织	Grass Roots Self-Government Organization	40	39	1
国际组织	**International Organizations**			

1-4 规模(限额)以上企业法人单位情况(2016年)
NUMBER OF CORPORATE ENTERPRISES ABOVE DESIGNATED SIZE (2016)

单位：个 (unit)

项目	Item	法人单位合计 Total Number of Legal Entities	项目	Item	法人单位合计 Total Number of Legal Entities
合计	Total	34944	与港澳台商合资经营	Joint Ventures	461
按开业时间分	By Openning Time		与港澳台商合作经营	Cooperative Enterprises	99
1949年以前	Before 1949	32	港澳台商独资	Solely-funded Enterprises	894
1950-1965	From 1950 to 1965	245	港澳台商投资股份有限公司	Companies Limited by Shares	30
1966-1979	From 1966 to 1979	145	其他港澳台商投资	Others	2
1980-1989	From 1980 to 1989	1313	外商投资企业	Foreign-invested Enterprises	2274
1990年以后	After 1990	33209	中外合资经营	Joint Ventures	660
按登记注册类型分	By Registration Type		中外合作经营	Cooperative Enterprises	83
内资企业	Domestically-invested Enterprises	31184	外资企业	Solely-funded Enterprises	1478
国有企业	State-owned Enterprises	1437	外商投资股份有限公司	Companies Limited by Shares	39
集体企业	Collectively-owned Enterprises	479	其他外商投资	Other	14
股份合作企业	Joint-equity Cooperative Enterprises	349	按控股情况分	By Share Holding Status	
联营企业	Associated Enterprises	21	国有控股	State-owned Enterprises	7318
有限责任公司	Limited Liability Companies	14146	集体控股	Collectively-controlled Enterprises	1569
股份有限公司	Companies Limited by Shares	1417	私人控股	Privately-controlled Enterprises	22083
私营企业	Private Enterprises	13328	港澳台商控股	Hong Kong, Macao and Taiwan-controlled Enterprises	1348
其他内资企业	Other Domestically-invested Enterprises	7	外商控股	Foreign-controlled Enterprises	2052
港澳台商投资企业	Hong Kong, Macao and Taiwan-invested Enterprises	1486	其他	Others	574

注：本表为2016年年报规模(限额)以上企业法人单位数据。
Note: This table covers legal entities above designated size in the 2016 annual report.

1–5 全市私营个体经济基本情况
STATISTICS FOR PRIVATE AND INDIVIDUAL ECONOMY

单位：万元 (10000 yuan)

项 目	Item	私 营 Private			个 体 Individual		
		2016	2015	2016为2015年% 2016 as % of 2015	2016	2015	2016年为2015年% 2016 as % of 2015
工商登记注册*	**Registered at Administration for Industry and Commerce**						
户 数 (户)	Number of Business Entities (unit)	1209704	1037789	116.6	608142	659357	92.2
从业人员 (人)	Number of Employed Persons (person)	9513227	8485995	112.1	954138	1031314	92.5
注册资本	Registered Capital	1249896616	839869344	148.8	2202464	2266780	97.2
国税、地税入库税收合计	Taxes Put into Local and National Treasury	8086229	6653286	121.5	3835631	2447182	156.7

注：*为期末时点数。
资料来源：北京市工商行政管理局、北京市地方税务局、北京市国家税务局。
Note: Figures with * indicate the accumulative figures at end of the year.
Source: Beijing Administration for Industry and Commerce, Beijing Municipal Bureau of Local Taxation, Beijing Municipal Bureau of State Taxation.

1-6 规模以上非公经济主要指标(2016年)
MAIN INDICATORS OF NON-PUBLIC SECTORS OF THE ECONOMY ABOVE DESIGNATED SIZE (2016)

项目	Item	单位数 (个) Number of Enterprises (unit)	收入合计 (亿元) Total Income (100 million yuan)	利润总额 (亿元) Total Profits (100 million yuan)	应交税金合计 (亿元) Taxes Payable (100 million yuan)	从业人员平均人数 (万人) Average Number of Persons Employed (10000 persons)
合计	**Total**	**26452**	**55643.9**	**4436.8**	**2407.6**	**404.9**
按登记注册类型分组	**Grouped by Registration Type**					
内资	Domestic-funded	22954	31944.9	2157.1	1404.5	291.7
港澳台商投资	Hong Kong, Macao and Taiwan-funded	1390	9689.3	541.2	345.4	50.5
外商投资	Foreign-funded	2108	14009.6	1738.4	657.6	62.7
按规模分	**Grouped by Size**					
#大型企业	Large-sized Enterprises	1034	23259.7	2078.8	909.2	147.6
中小微型企业	Mini-, Small-, Mediume-sized Enterprises	23384	28018.1	1090.7	1097.6	228.3
中型	Medium Size	5748	17096.7	736.5	723.1	131.0
小型	Small Size	12983	9438.3	416.2	332.2	91.0
微型	Mini Size	4653	1483.2	-62.0	42.2	6.4
按行业分组	**Grouped by Sector**					
#制造业	Manufacturing	2510	8113.3	528.2	377.7	54.3
建筑业	Construction	2804	2464.9	47.8	87.7	30.9
批发和零售业	Wholesale and Retail Trade	4710	22326.6	512.8	453.6	51.9
交通运输、仓储和邮政业	Transport, Storage and Post	712	1032.7	37.0	25.0	17.3
住宿和餐饮业	Accommodation and Restaurants	1696	653.8	16.8	34.9	25.5
信息传输、软件和信息技术服务业	Information Transmission,Software and Information Technology Services	2511	6014.9	1125.0	329.1	61.3
金融业	Finance	1244	3493.1	1203.1	359.5	16.4
房地产业	Real estate	2672	2825.5	251.6	397.7	29.5
租赁和商务服务业	Renting and Leasing Activities and Business Services	4050	5344.8	536.0	210.0	68.4
科学研究和技术服务业	Scientific Research and Development, Technical Services	1968	1641.9	102.0	77.4	22.8
水利、环境和公共设施管理业	Management of Water Conservancy, Environment and Public Facilities	181	218.8	20.2	9.0	2.4
居民服务、修理和其他服务业	Resident Services, Repair and Other Services	320	126.8	-0.7	6.8	7.9
教育	Education	264	238.6	17.3	10.4	7.5
卫生和社会工作	Health Care and Social Works	222	139.7	-2.5	2.0	3.6
文化、体育和娱乐业	Culture, Sports and Entertainment	447	313.2	7.9	15.7	3.3
公共管理和社会组织	Pulic Administration, Social Security and Social Organizations	105	329.7	…	0.6	0.4

注：1. 非公经济是指资产由我国私人、港澳台商、外商控股的“非公有控股”的企业法人单位，以及主要经费来源于私人、港澳台资和外资的非企业法人单位和个体工商户。私人、港澳台及外商控股是指由其绝对控股和相对控股的经济成分。本表不包含个体经营户数据。

2. 按规模分组中，各类型非公经济是指执行企业会计制度的非公企业数据，不包含执行事业会计制度的非公单位数据，因此，规模分组合计数不等于其他分组合计数。

3. 2016年，全市非公经济实现增加值9263.5亿元，其中第二产业增加值1559.4亿元，第三产业增加值7704.1亿元(增加值为实施地区研发支出核算改革后数据)。

Note: a) Non-public economies mean enterprises as legal persons whose assets equity are held by non-public entities such as private, Hong Kong, Macao and Taiwan, and foreign businesses, as well as non-legal-person enterprises and self-employed entities whose main outlays come from private, Hong Kong, Macao and Taiwan, and foreign businesses. Economies with share held by private, Hong Kong, Macao and Taiwan, and foreign businesses mean economic elements with shares absolutely held by such businesses. This table excludes figures for self-employed entities.

b) In the group by size, figures of various types of non-public sectors in the economy are those of non-public enterprises implementing enterprise accounting system, excluding those of non-public entities implementing public institution accounting system. Therefore, total amounts in the group by size are not equal to total amounts of other groups.

c) In 2016, non-public sectors of the economy in Beijing achieved added value of RMB 926.4 billion, of which the added value in the secondary industry reached RMB 156 billion and that in the tertiary industry hit RMB 770.4 billion (the added value is based on the data after implementation of the reform of R&D expenditure).

1−7 规模以上中小微型企业主要指标(2016年)
MAIN INDICATORS OF MICRO- SMALL- AND MEDIUM-SIZED ENTERPRISES ABOVE DESIGNATED SIZE (2016)

项 目	Item	单位数 (个) Number of Enterprises (unit)	收入合计 (亿元) Total Income (100 million yuan)	利润总额 (亿元) Total Profits (100 million yuan)	应交税金合计 (亿元) Taxes Payable (100 million yuan)	从业人员平均人数 (万人) Average Number of Persons Employed (10000 persons)
合 计	**Total**	**30659**	**50872.1**	**4077.9**	**1990.5**	**320.1**
按规模分	**Grouped by Size**					
中 型	Medium Size	8459	34447.1	2191.2	1367.5	193.3
小 型	Small Size	16429	13790.0	1193.7	528.6	117.6
微 型	Mini Size	5771	2635.0	693.0	94.3	9.1
按登记注册类型分	**Grouped by Registration Type**					
内 资	Domestic-funded	27674	43700.1	3663.0	1635.2	277.2
港澳台商投资	Hong Kong, Macao and Taiwan-funded	1166	2475.5	49.5	120.9	18.4
外商投资	Foreign-funded	1819	4696.5	365.4	234.4	24.4
按行业分	**Grouped by Sector**					
#制造业	Manufacturing	3083	7063.5	497.5	387.5	56.4
建筑业	Construction	3253	2543.7	121.0	96.3	34.7
批发和零售业	Wholesale and Retail Trade	5679	23938.8	351.2	343.5	32.0
交通运输、仓储和邮政业	Transport, Storage and Post	933	1335.7	31.6	2.5	15.7
住宿和餐饮业	Accommodation and Restaurants	2147	433.6	-10.1	20.5	18.4
信息传输、软件和信息技术服务业	Information Transmission,Software and Information Technology Services	2624	2908.0	585.7	118.4	32.5
房地产业	Real estate	3713	3087.2	456.7	494.1	25.6
租赁和商务服务业	Renting and Leasing Activities and Business Services	5031	5641.8	1611.9	323.4	68.7
科学研究和技术服务业	Scientific Research and Development, Technical Services	2505	2389.0	251.5	109.4	20.4
水利、环境和公共设施管理业	Management of Water Conservancy, Environment and Public Facilities	309	228.5	15.7	10.8	2.5
居民服务、修理和其他服务业	Resident Services, Repair and Other Services	322	93.5	1.8	5.4	3.3
卫生和社会工作	Health Care and Social Works	7	1.6	-1.0	0.0	0.1
文化、体育和娱乐业	Culture, Sports and Entertainment	932	749.5	86.9	42.9	6.9

注：1. 本表中的企业规模划型标准执行国家统计局《关于统计上大中小微型企业划分办法》(国统字〔2011〕75号)。按照国家统计局要求，铁路运输业、教育、卫生、自有房地产经营活动、金融业不划分规模，因此中小微数据不含这五个行业数据。

2. 行业划分执行2011年国民经济行业分类标准(GB/T 4754−2011)。

3. 2016年，全市中小微型企业实现增加值7524.7亿元，其中第二产业增加值1609.4亿元，第三产业增加值5915.3亿元(增加值为实施地区研发支出核算改革后数据)。

Note: a) In this table, enterprise size is identified in accordance with the provisions stated in the Statistical Division Standards of Micro-, Small-, Medium- and Large-sized Enterprises released by the National Bureau of Statistics (G.T.Z. (2011) No. 75). According to requirements of National Bureau of Statistics, size division is unnecessary in sectors of railway transportation, education, health care, self-owned real estate operation and finance, so no data related to the five sectors is included in the table.

b)Sectors in this table are classified in accordance with the Standard for Classification of National Economic Sectors in 2011(GB/T4754-2011).

c) In 2016, micro-, small- and medium-sized enterprises in Beijing achieved added value of RMB 752.4 billion, of which added value in the secondary industry reached RMB 160.9 billion and that in the tertiary industry reached RMB 591.5 billion (the added value is based on the data after implementation of the reform of R&D expenditure).

1-8 主要经济指标增长速度(1979-2016年)

单位：%

年份 Year	地区生产总值比上年增长 YoY Growth Rate of Gross Domestic Product	全社会固定资产投资比上年增长 YoY Growth Rate of Fixed Asset Investment	房地产开发投资比上年增长 YoY Growth Rate of Real Estate Development Investment	社会消费品零售总额比上年增长 YoY Growth Rate of Retail Sales of Consumer Goods	进出口总值比上年增长 YoY Growth Rate of Gross Value of Imports & Exports
1979	9.7	17.3		20.6	
1980	11.8	25.3		17.8	
1981	-0.5	10.2		12.6	
1982	7.4	5.5		6.6	
1983	16.4	32.9		14.6	
1984	17.4	29.2		22.5	16.3
1985	8.7	41.8		27.0	-8.6
1986	8.0	13.0		15.3	-6.0
1987	9.6	28.2		21.9	-12.7
1988	12.8	19.7		35.5	11.9
1989	4.4	-14.4		15.2	-4.3
1990	5.2	28.5		17.1	-17.4
1991	9.9	7.1	6.7	18.3	2.5
1992	11.3	38.5	40.4	23.2	3.1
1993	12.3	54.3	73.3	21.5	11.7
1994	13.7	58.1	70.4	25.4	3.5
1995	12.0	29.7	254.6	24.0	28.2
1996	9.8	4.2	-7.0	11.7	-20.8
1997	10.2	9.6	0.6	13.8	3.7
1998	9.6	20.2	14.3	13.7	0.4
1999	11.0	1.3	11.7	9.9	12.6
2000	12.0	10.8	23.9	9.9	43.8
2001	11.8	18.0	50.1	10.4	4.2
2002	11.8	18.5	26.2	9.5	2.0
2003	11.1	18.9	21.5	14.5	30.5
2004	14.3	17.2	22.5	14.4	38.1
2005	12.3	11.8	3.5	10.9	32.7
2006	12.8	19.3	12.8	13.2	25.9
2007	14.4	17.6	16.0	16.4	22.1
2008	9.0	-3.0	-4.4	21.1	40.8
2009	10.0	26.2	22.5	16.0	-20.9
2010	10.4	13.1	24.1	17.7	40.4
2011	8.1	13.3	10.1	13.9	29.1
2012	8.0	9.3	3.9	12.5	4.8
2013	7.7	8.8	10.5	9.2	5.4
2014	7.4	7.5	12.3	8.6	-3.4
2015	6.9	5.7	8.1	7.3	-23.1
2016	6.8	5.9	-4.3	6.5	-11.6

注：1．地区生产总值增长速度按可比口径计算。
2．农林牧渔业总产值增长速度按现价计算。
3．进出口总值比上年增长速度为按美元计进出口总值数据计算。

YOY GROWTH RATE OF MAIN INDICATORS (1979-2016)

(%)

农林牧渔业总产值比上年增长 YoY Growth Rate of Gross Output Value of Agriculture, Forestry, Animal Production and Hunting, Fishing	规模以上工业总产值比上年增长 YoY Growth Rate of Gross Output Value of Industrial Enterprises Above Designated Size	居民消费价格指数(上年=100) Consumer Price Index (Previous year=100)	城镇居民人均可支配收入 Per-capita Disposable Income of Urban Households		农村居民人均可支配收入 Per-capita Net Income of Rural Households	
			比上年名义增长 Nominal Growth Rate as Compared with That in the Last year	比上年实际增长 Real Growth Rate as Compared with That in the Last year	比上年名义增长 Normal Growth Rate as Compared with That in the Last year	比上年实际增长 Real Growth Rate as Compared with That in the Last year
7.0		101.8	13.6	11.6	11.1	10.9
16.3		106.0	20.8	14.0	23.2	22.1
4.2		101.3	2.5	1.2	17.2	17.1
12.8		101.8	9.1	7.2	19.1	17.3
16.7		100.5	5.2	4.7	20.7	20.9
13.3		102.2	17.5	15.0	27.9	25.7
16.7	17.4	117.6	30.8	11.3	16.7	14.5
8.5	3.8	106.8	17.6	10.1	6.2	3.7
22.4	15.2	108.6	10.7	1.9	11.3	6.5
52.9	27.9	120.4	21.6	1.0	16.0	3.1
14.8	21.6	117.2	11.1	-5.2	15.8	2.2
16.2	3.8	105.4	11.9	6.2	5.4	2.1
9.0	16.7	111.9	14.2	2.1	9.6	1.7
10.5	17.8	109.9	15.8	5.4	10.3	2.0
18.8	35.7	119.0	39.4	17.1	18.2	5.1
43.7	35.1	124.9	43.5	14.9	30.6	9.1
13.9	-5.3	117.3	24.0	5.7	32.5	6.3
2.7	6.5	111.6	17.3	5.1	11.1	4.8
0.9	14.4	105.3	13.5	7.8	5.6	5.1
2.5	7.0	102.4	8.4	5.9	7.1	6.7
3.3	12.1	100.6	8.4	7.8	7.1	7.2
4.4	30.2	103.5	12.7	8.9	8.6	7.3
7.2	15.1	103.1	11.9	8.5	12.5	8.7
5.6	10.7	98.2	13.5	15.6	11.5	12.3
5.2	21.8	100.2	11.4	11.2	10.5	11.5
4.5	30.0	101.0	12.6	11.5	10.4	9.2
1.9	21.2	101.5	12.9	11.2	9.6	8.1
0.4	18.2	100.9	13.2	12.2	9.7	8.7
13.4	17.5	102.4	13.9	11.2	10.9	8.2
11.6	7.9	105.1	12.4	7.0	12.4	6.5
3.6	6.0	98.5	8.1	9.7	11.5	13.4
4.1	24.1	102.4	8.7	6.2	10.6	8.1
10.7	5.9	105.6	13.2	7.2	13.6	7.6
9.0	7.5	103.3	10.8	7.3	11.8	8.2
6.6	11.4	103.3	10.6	7.1	11.3	7.7
-0.4	6.2	101.6	8.9	7.2	10.3	8.6
-12.3	-5.4	101.8	8.9	7.0	9.0	7.1
-8.2	3.7	101.4	8.4	6.9	8.5	7.0

Note: a)The Growth Rate of Gross Domestic Product shall be calculated based on a comparable caliber.
Development Investment in 2011 are calculated at comparable basis.
b)The Growth Rate of Gross Output Value ofAgriculture, Forestry, Animal Husbandry and Fishery shall be calculated based on the current price.
c)Data of YoY Growth Rate of Gross Value of Imports & Exports shall be calculated based on gross value of imports and exports in USD.

1-9 主要年份国民经济和社会发展总量与速度指标

项目		Item		1990	1995
人口与就业		**Population and Employment**			
人口		**Population**			
年末全市常住人口	(万人)	Year-end Permanent Population	(10000 persons)	1086.0	1251.1
按性别分		By Sex			
男性人口		Male		545.0	627.0
女性人口		Female		541.0	624.1
按城乡分		By Urban Area and Rural Area			
城镇人口		Urban Population		798.0	946.2
乡村人口		Rural Population		288.0	304.9
年末户籍人口	(万人)	Year-end Registed Population	(10000 persons)	1032.2	1070.3
就业		**Employment**			
从业人员年末人数	(万人)	Year-end Employed Persons	(10000 persons)	627.1	665.3
#城镇单位在岗职工人数		On-the-job Staff and Workers		454.9	470.9
年末实有城镇登记失业人员	(万人)	Registered Unemployed Persons in Urban Areas at Year End	(10000 persons)	1.7	2.2
宏观经济		**Macro Economy**			
国民经济核算		**National Accounts**			
地区生产总值	(亿元)	Gross Domestic Product	(100 million yuan)	500.8	1507.7
第一产业		Primary Industry		43.7	72.2
第二产业		Secondary Industry		262.0	643.6
第三产业		Tertiary Industry		195.1	791.9
人均地区生产总值	(元/人)	Per Capita Gross Domestic Product	(yuan/person)	4635	12690
固定资产投资		**Fixed Asset Investment**			
全社会固定资产投资	(亿元)	Total Fixed Asset Investment	(100 million yuan)	179.2	841.5
#房地产开发投资		Real Estate Development		22.5	352.8
全社会房屋施工面积	(万平方米)	Floor Space of Houses under Construction	(10000 sq.m)	2864.9	5524.3
全社会房屋竣工面积	(万平方米)	Floor Space of Houses Completed	(10000 sq.m)	1081.2	1530.2
财政		**Government Finance**			
一般公共预算收入	(亿元)	Local Public Budgetary Revenue	(100 million yuan)		
一般公共预算支出	(亿元)	Local Public Budgetary Expenditures	(100 million yuan)		
价格指数(上年=100)		**Price Indices (Preceding Year=100)**			
居民消费价格指数	(%)	Consumer Price Index	(%)	105.4	117.3
商品零售价格指数	(%)	Retail Price Index	(%)	104.1	112.6
农产品生产价格指数	(%)	Farm Product Price Index	(%)	101.9	130.6
工业生产者出厂价格指数	(%)	Producer Price Index for Industrial Products	(%)	107.9	107.3
工业生产者购进价格指数	(%)	Purchase Price Index for Industrial Products	(%)	114.8	106.7
固定资产投资价格指数	(%)	Price Index of Investment in Fixed Asset	(%)		113.9
能源消费总量	**(万吨标准煤)**	**Total Energy Consumption**	**(10000 tons of SCE)**	**2709.7**	**3533.3**
产业		**Industry**			
农村经济		**Rural Economy**			
耕地面积	(万公顷)	Cultivated Areas	(10000 hectare)	41.3	39.4
农林牧渔业总产值(现价)	(亿元)	Gross Output Value of Agriculture, Forestry Animal Production and Hunting, Fishing (at current prices)	(100 million yuan)	70.2	164.4

注：1. 地区生产总值绝对值按现价计算，发展速度按可比价格计算；2006—2010年人均地区生产总值根据第六次人口普查数据进行修正
自2013年开始，地区生产总值三次产业分组口径根据国家统计局规定调整，并对2012年以前三次产业数据进行相应调整。
2. 从2011年起，根据国家统计局相关规定，固定资产投资起点由50万元调整至500万元。

AGGREGATE INDICATORS AND SPEED INDICATORS ON NATIONAL ECONOMIC AND SOCIAL DEVELOPMENT IN KEY YEARS

总量指标 Aggregate Indicator					速度指标(%) Speed Indicator (%)					
2000	2005	2010	2015	2016	指 数(2016年为以下各年) Index (2016 as Percentage of the Following Year)					
					1990	1995	2000	2005	2010	2015
1363.6	1538.0	1961.9	2170.5	2172.9	200.1	173.7	159.4	141.3	110.8	100.1
710.9	778.7	1013.0	1113.4	1112.7	204.2	177.5	156.5	142.9	109.8	99.9
652.7	759.3	948.9	1057.1	1060.2	196.0	169.9	162.4	139.6	111.7	100.3
1057.4	1286.1	1686.4	1877.7	1879.6	235.5	198.6	177.8	146.1	111.5	100.1
306.2	251.9	275.5	292.8	293.3	101.8	96.2	95.8	116.4	106.5	100.2
1107.5	1180.7	1257.8	1345.2	1362.9	132.0	127.3	123.1	115.4	108.4	101.3
619.3	878.0	1031.6	1186.1	1220.1	194.6	183.4	197.0	139.0	118.3	102.9
434.2	448.4	587.7	724.8	733.5	161.2	155.8	168.9	163.6	124.8	101.2
3.3	10.6	7.7	9.2	9.1	537.6	415.5	275.3	86.5	118.2	99.8
3212.8	7141.4	14441.6	23685.7	25669.1	1353.2	773.6	469.4	263.4	154.2	106.8
79.3	86.9	122.8	140.4	129.8	107.8	103.3	96.8	93.9	87.3	91.3
1040.6	2045.6	3387.9	4660.6	4944.4	1018.0	607.8	385.1	224.7	144.5	106.3
2092.9	5008.9	10930.9	18884.7	20594.9	1872.4	932.5	519.4	281.5	158.0	107.0
24518	47127	75573	109603	118198	674.9	424.6	283.8	184.1	135.8	106.3
1297.4	2827.2	5493.5	7990.9	8461.7						
522.1	1525.0	2901.1	4226.3	4045.4						
6995.9	14096.2	15572.1	20009.1	22721.4	793.1	411.3	324.8	161.2	145.9	113.6
2358.2	4679.2	3908.4	4170.2	3594.0	332.4	234.9	152.4	76.8	92.0	86.2
345.0	919.2	2353.9	4723.9	5081.3						
443.0	1058.3	2717.3	5737.7	6406.8						
103.5	101.5	102.4	101.8	101.4						
98.9	99.7	100.4	98.5	98.1						
95.0	102.9	106.5	99.8	99.7						
102.5	101.3	102.2	96.9	98.1						
100.0	111.4	110.5	93.7	98.5						
101.0	100.7	102.5	97.6	99.7						
4144.0	**5049.8**	**6359.5**	**6852.6**	**6961.7**	**256.9**	**197.0**	**168.0**	**137.9**	**109.5**	**101.6**
32.9	23.3	22.4	21.9							
188.6	239.3	328.0	368.2	338.1	481.6	205.7	179.3	141.3	103.1	91.8

Note: a) Absolute values on GDP are calculated at current prices, whereas growth rates are calculated at comparable prices.Per Capita Gross Domestic Product from 2006 to 2010 were adjusted according to the 6th population census.From 2013, The Gross Domestic Product of three industries were changed according to provisions of the National Bureau of Statistics, and the data on the three industries before 2012 was adjusted .
Bureau of Statistics, and the data on the three industries before 2012 was adjusted .

b) From 2011, the starting point of fixed asset investment is changed from RMB 500,000 to RMB 5 million according to relevant regulations of National Bureau of Statistics.

1-9 续表 1

项目		Item		1990	1995
工业		**Industry**			
工业增加值(规模以上)	(亿元)	Added Value of Industry (Above Designated Size)	(100 million yuan)		473.1
工业企业主要经济指标(规模以上)		Main Indicators of Industrial Enterprises (Above Designated Size)			
资产总计	(亿元)	Total Asset	(100 million yuan)	498.3	2582.6
负债总额	(亿元)	Total Liability	(100 million yuan)		1528.8
主营业务收入	(亿元)	Revenue from Main Businesses	(100 million yuan)	610.5	1590.4
利润总额	(亿元)	Total Profit	(100 million yuan)	48.9	85.3
建筑		**Construction**			
建筑业总产值	(亿元)	Gross Output Value	(100 million yuan)	94.7	426.6
建筑业企业年末从业人员	(万人)	Year-end Employed Persons	(10000 persons)	60.2	82.6
运输		**Transport**			
货物周转量	(亿吨公里)	Total Freight Turnover	(100 million ton-km)	268.8	323.1
铁路		Railway		206.7	239.3
公路		Road		57.5	76.2
民航		Civil Aviation		4.5	7.5
管道		Pipeline		0.2	0.1
旅客周转量	(亿人公里)	Total Passenger Turnover	(100 million passenger-km)	119.8	207.7
邮电		**Post and Telecommunication Services**			
邮电业务总量	(亿元)	Business Volume of Post and Telecommunications	(100 million yuan)	11.9	56.1
固定电话用户	(万户)	Fixed Telephone Subscribers	(10000 subscribers)	33.3	150.5
固定电话主线普及率	(线/百人)	Penetration Rate of Main Line	(lines/100 persons)	3.1	12.0
移动电话用户	(万户)	Mobile Telephone Subscribers	(10000 subscribers)	0.3	16.9
移动电话普及率	(户/百人)	Penetration Rate of Mobile Telephone	(sets/100 persons)	0.03	1.4
商业		**Commerce**			
社会消费品零售总额	(亿元)	Retail Sales of Consumer Goods	(100 million yuan)	345.1	950.4
对外经济贸易和旅游		**Foreign Trade and Tourism**			
北京地区进出口总值	(亿美元)	Total Value of Imports and Exports	(USD 100 million)	236.4	370.4
进口值		Imports		192.3	267.9
出口值		Exports		44.1	102.5
实际利用外商直接投资额	(亿美元)	Paid-in Foreign Investment	(USD 100 million)	2.8	14.0
接待入境旅游者人数	(万人次)	Inbound Tourists	(10000 persons)	100.0	207.0
旅游外汇收入	(亿美元)	Foreign Exchange Earning from Tourism	(USD 100 million)	6.6	21.8
金融保险		**Finance and Insurance**			
金融机构(含外资)本外币存款余额	(亿元)	Deposits of Financial Institutions (Including Foreign Institutions)	(100 million yuan)		
金融机构(含外资)本外币贷款余额	(亿元)	Loans of Financial Institutions (Including Foreign Institutions)	(100 million yuan)		
原保险保费收入	(亿元)	Premiums Revenue	(100 million yuan)		

注：1．工业增加值按生产法计算。
2．邮电业务总量2000年及以前按1990年不变价格计算，2010年及以前按2000年不变价格计算，从2011年开始按2010年不变价格计算。
3．社会消费品零售总额2010年数据根据第三次全国经济普查数据进行了修订。

1-9 Continued 1

总量指标 Aggregate Indicator					速度指标(%) Speed Indicator (%)					
					指 数(2016年为以下各年) Index (2016 as Percentage of the Following Year)					
2000	2005	2010	2015	2016	1990	1995	2000	2005	2010	2015
776.0	1627.0	2751.7	3676.6	3748.7						
4612.7	12829.8	22750.6	38609.8	43093.7	8648.1	1668.6	934.2	335.9	189.4	111.6
2676.4	4706.7	11548.1	18102.4	19798.1		1295.0	739.7	420.6	171.4	109.4
2821.4	7279.1	14807.1	18864.9	19747.0	3234.8	1241.7	699.9	271.3	133.4	104.7
127.1	413.5	1028.3	1597.7	1608.3	3286.4	1885.6	1265.5	388.9	156.4	100.7
812.5	1894.0	5196.0	8436.7	8841.2	9336.0	2072.5	1088.1	466.8	170.2	104.8
56.6	67.2	59.9	59.0	59.2	98.3	71.7	104.6	88.1	98.8	100.3
299.6	457.7	513.7	623.7	671.3	249.7	207.8	224.0	146.7	130.7	107.6
200.2	310.8	257.5	224.8	229.0	110.8	95.7	114.4	73.7	89.0	101.9
82.6	85.5	101.6	156.4	161.3	280.7	211.7	195.2	188.7	158.8	103.2
16.8	28.2	48.2	63.7	67.1	1503.3	895.9	400.4	238.4	139.2	105.4
0.04	33.3	106.4	178.9	213.8				642.9	201.0	119.5
314.0	838.1	1399.5	1747.7	1889.3	1577.1	909.6	601.7	225.4	135.0	108.1
214.7	413.0	1108.9	991.2	1468.6						148.2
451.2	943.5	885.6	784.7	694.4	2085.6	461.3	153.9	73.6	78.4	88.5
33.1	61.3	45.1	36.2	32.0						
347.2	1459.8	2129.8	4051.6	3868.7			1114.3	265.0	181.6	95.5
25.5	94.9	108.6	186.7	178.0						
1658.7	2911.7	6340.3	10338.0	11005.1	3189.0	1157.9	663.5	378.0	173.6	106.5
494.0	1255.1	3016.6	3194.2	2823.8	1194.3	762.5	571.6	225.0	93.6	88.4
374.3	946.4	2462.2	2647.5	2303.6	1197.8	860.0	615.4	243.4	93.6	87.0
119.7	308.7	554.4	546.7	520.2	1178.7	507.5	434.6	168.5	93.8	95.2
24.6	35.3	63.6	130.0	130.3	4704.2	928.8	530.1	369.5	204.7	100.2
282.1	362.9	490.1	420.0	416.5	416.5	201.2	147.6	114.8	85.0	99.2
27.7	36.2	50.4	46.1	50.7	771.5	232.3	183.1	140.0	100.5	110.1
11526.0	28969.9	66584.6	128573.0	138408.9			1200.8	477.8	207.9	107.7
6407.9	15335.5	36479.6	58559.4	63739.4			994.7	415.6	174.7	108.8
93.4	498.2	966.5	1403.9	1839.0			1968.0	369.1	190.3	131.0

Note: a) Added value of industry is calculated with the production approach.

b) Business volumes of post and telecommunications before and in 2000 were calculated at 1990's constant price, those before and in 2000 were calculated at 2000's constant price, and those since 2011 were calculated at 2010's constant price.

c) Data of Retail Sales of Consumer Goods were revised according to the third national economic census in 2010.

1-9 续表 2

项 目		Item		1990	1995
教育、文化、科技、卫生		**Education, Culture, Science and Technology and Health Care**			
教 育		**Education**			
在校学生数	(万人)	Students Enrollment	(10000 persons)		238.0
专任教师数	(万人)	Full-time Teachers	(10000 persons)		17.7
文 化		**Culture**			
公共图书馆总藏数	(万册、万件)	Collection of Public Libraries	(10000 volumes)	2205	2629
科 技		**Science and Technology**			
研究与试验发展经费内部支出	(亿元)	Internal R&D Expenditures	(100 million yuan)		
技术合同成交总额	(亿元)	Total Volume of Transaction of Technological Contracts Concluded	(100 million yuan)	20.3	41.2
专利授权量	(件)	Number of Patent Granted	(case)	2268	4025
卫 生		**Health Care**			
卫生机构个数	(个)	Health Care Institutions	(unit)	4953	4955
卫生机构病床数	(万张)	Beds at Health Care Institutions	(10000 beds)	5.9	6.7
卫生技术人员数	(万人)	Medical Technical Personnel	(10000 persons)	11.2	11.6
#执业(助理)医师		Certified Doctors		5.1	5.4
注册护师(士)		Registered Nurses		3.5	3.7
生活与环境		**People's Living and Environment**			
婚 姻		**Marriage and Divorce**			
登记结婚对数	(万对)	Number of Registered Marriages	(10000 couples)	9.30	8.55
离婚对数	(万对)	Number of Registered Divorces	(10000 couples)	1.47	2.02
居民收入		**Resident Income**			
城镇居民人均可支配收入	(元)	Per Capita Annual Disposable Income of Urban Residents	(yuan)	1787	5868
农村居民人均可支配收入	(元)	Per Capita Net Income of Rural Residents	(yuan)	1297	3209
工 资		**Wages**			
城镇单位在岗职工工资总额	(亿元)	Total Wages of Fully Employed Staff and Workers in Urban Entities	(100 million yuan)	118.9	382.0
城镇单位在岗职工平均工资	(元)	Average Wages of Fully Employed Staff and Workers in Urban Entities	(yuan)	2653	8144
市政建设		**Municipal Facilities**			
全社会用电量	(亿千瓦时)	Electricity Consumption	(100 million kwh)	150.5	222.6
自来水销售总量	(亿立方米)	Total Sales Volume of Tap Water	(100 million cu.m)	5.3	6.8
居民燃气用户	(万户)	Households Gas Users	(10000 households)	176.1	219.8
城市公共交通客运量	(亿人次)	Passengers Carried by Urban Public Transport	(100 million person-times)	33.5	37.2
环 境		**Environment**			
城市绿化覆盖率	(%)	Green Area Coverage	(%)	28.0	32.7
污水处理率	(%)	Sewage Treatment Rate	(%)	7.3	19.4

注：1．北京地区用电量来源于北京市电力公司，2000年以前工业用电量不包含输配损失和发电企业自产自用电量。

2．从2001年开始，有关职工的指标调整为在岗职工的指标。2007年及以前城镇单位在岗职工工资包括乡及乡以上独立核算法人单位不包括乡镇企业、私营单位和个体工商户；2008年及以后包括乡镇企业。

3．离婚对数包括在民政部门登记的对数和经法院调离和判离的对数。

4．2010年及以前，本表中卫生机构数据都不包含村卫生室及驻京部队医院情况。2011年开始，包含村卫生室情况。2012年开始，卫生机构数、卫生技术人员数据中包含驻京部队医院，床位数不包含。

1-9 Continued 2

总量指标 Aggregate Indicator					速度指标(%) Speed Indicator (%)					
					指 数(2016年为以下各年) Index (2016 as Percentage of the Following Year)					
2000	2005	2010	2015	2016	1990	1995	2000	2005	2010	2015
229.9	226.4	330.0	373.4	373.4		156.9	162.4	164.9	113.2	100.0
16.7	17.5	20.7	22.6	23.1		131.0	138.4	132.5	111.9	102.3
3020	3626	4613	5943	6229	282.4	236.9	206.3	171.8	135.0	104.8
155.7	379.5	821.8	1384.0	1484.6			953.5	391.1	180.6	107.3
140.3	434.4	1579.5	3452.6	3940.8	19441.5	9572.0	2809.0	907.2	249.5	114.1
5905	10100	33511	94031	100578	4434.7	2498.8	1703.3	995.8	300.1	107.0
6176	4818	6539	10425	10637	214.8	214.7	172.2	220.8	162.7	102.0
7.1	7.9	9.3	11.2	11.7	198.1	174.8	164.2	147.9	125.9	104.8
11.6	12.0	17.1	25.7	26.5	237.3	228.4	229.3	220.9	154.8	103.2
5.2	5.1	6.6	9.6	10.1	198.1	186.4	195.6	199.3	153.0	104.6
4.0	4.3	6.7	11.4	11.8	340.7	320.7	295.1	274.5	175.0	103.0
8.02	9.70	13.81	16.60	16.62	178.7	194.4	207.2	171.4	120.3	100.1
2.66	3.42	4.40	8.22	10.58	717.4	524.8	397.5	309.0	240.6	128.7
10350	17653	29073	52859	57275						108.4
4687	7860	13262	20569	22310						108.5
695.5	1520.1	3789.1	8225.2	9005.0	7573.6	2357.3	1294.8	592.4	237.7	109.5
15726	34191	65683	113073	122749	4626.8	1507.2	780.5	359.0	186.9	108.6
384.4	570.5	809.9	952.7	1020.3	678.0	458.4	265.4	178.8	126.0	107.1
7.5	7.2	8.9	10.4	10.8	205.6	159.7	143.8	151.4	121.5	104.3
291.9	462.6	634.2	885.7	900.7	511.5	409.8	308.6	194.7	142.0	101.7
40.7	51.8	69.0	73.8	73.5	219.6	197.8	180.7	141.9	106.5	99.5
36.5	42.0	45.0	48.4	48.4						
39.4	62.4	81.0	87.9	90.0						

Note: a) Figures on electricity consumption are provided by State Grid Beijing Electric Power Company. Before 2000, electricity consumption by industry excluded transmission and distribution losses and electricity generated and consumed by power generating enterprises.

b) From 2001, indicators related to the "staff and workers" have been changed to those of "fully employed staff and workers". In and before 2007, figures on wages of urban fully employed staff and workers in urban entities had been kept separate accounts at and above the township level, excluding township enterprises, private entities and self-employed operators; in and after 2008, such figures have included township enterprises.

c) Number of registered divorces includes those registered with civil affair authorities and those mediated and ruled in courts.

d) In and before 2010, figures on health centers were emerged with other health institutions such as community health service centers (stations). From 2011, health care institutions included village health centers. From 2012, figures of health care institutions and health care technical personnel have included military hospitals in Beijing, but beds are exclusive.

1-10 主要年份国民经济和社会发展结构指标
STRUCTURAL INDICATORS ON NATIONAL ECONOMIC AND SOCIAL DEVELOPMENT IN KEY YEARS

单位：%　　(%)

项目	Item	1990	1995	2000	2005	2010	2015	2016
人口与就业	**Population and Employment**							
常住人口	**Permanent Population**							
按性别分	By Sex							
男	Male	50.2	50.1	52.1	50.6	51.6	51.3	51.2
女	Female	49.8	49.9	47.9	49.4	48.4	48.7	48.8
按城乡分	By Urban Area and Rural Area							
城镇	Urban	73.5	75.6	77.5	83.6	86.0	86.5	86.5
乡村	Rural	26.5	24.4	22.5	16.4	14.0	13.5	13.5
就业	**Employment**							
从业人员年末人数	Year-end Employed Persons							
第一产业	Primary Industry	14.5	10.6	11.8	7.1	6.0	4.2	4.1
第二产业	Secondary Industry	44.9	40.7	33.6	26.3	19.6	17.0	15.8
第三产业	Tertiary Industry	40.6	48.7	54.6	66.6	74.4	78.8	80.1
宏观经济	**Macro Economy**							
国民经济核算	**National Accounts**							
地区生产总值	Gross Domestic Product							
第一产业	Primary Industry	8.7	4.8	2.5	1.2	0.9	0.6	0.5
第二产业	Secondary Industry	52.3	42.7	32.4	28.6	23.5	19.7	19.3
第三产业	Tertiary Industry	39.0	52.5	65.1	70.1	75.7	79.7	80.2
投资	**Investment**							
全社会固定资产投资	Fixed Asset Investment							
城镇	Urban	88.2	94.4	91.9	91.8	91.1	90.9	91.3
农村	Rural	9.7	4.8	6.5	8.2	8.9	9.1	8.7
资金来源结构	Source of Capital							
国家预算内资金	State Budgetary Appropriation	25.3	7.7	7.4	2.8	1.2	1.7	0.9
国内贷款	Domestic Loans	16.7	13.4	26.0	23.2	26.6	22.2	22.2
利用外资	Foreign Investment	11.2	20.5	3.6	1.6	0.5	0.1	0.1
债券、自筹和其他资金	Securities, Fundraising and Other Investment	46.8	58.4	63.0	72.4	71.6	76.0	76.8
财政	**Government Finance**							
一般公共预算收入主要税种	Main Taxes of Public Finance Budget Revenue							
增值税	Value Added Tax			13.3	10.6	8.9	15.2	23.9
房产税	Housing Property Tax				3.8	3.6	3.2	3.9
土地增值税	Increment Tax On Land Value				0.3	3.6	3.7	3.5
契税	Deed Tax				6.6	5.7	4.5	5.0
营业税	Business Tax			43.2	41.7	36.3	25.1	11.5
个人所得税	Private Income Tax			16.3	9.2	9.1	10.1	11.2
企业所得税	Corporate Income Tax			16.8	17.9	21.8	21.7	21.6
能源消费总量	**Energy Consumotion**							
第一产业	Primary Industry	3.9	3.4	2.5	1.7	1.5	1.2	1.2
第二产业	Secondary Industry	63.5	65.9	58.5	46.8	37.2	27.8	26.9
第三产业	Tertiary Industry	19.0	17.9	26.1	35.1	41.7	48.3	49.0
生活消费	Living Consumption	13.6	12.8	12.9	16.4	19.5	22.7	22.9

注：1．自2012年开始，从业人员年末人数和能源消费总量三次产业分组口径根据国家统计局规定进行了调整。
2．自2013年开始，地区生产总值三次产业分组口径根据国家统计局规定调整，并对2012年以前三次产业数据进行相应调整。

Note: a) From 2012, The grouping standards for Year-end Employed Persons and Energy Consumption of three industries were changed according to provisions of the National Bureau of Statistics.

b) From 2013, The Gross Domestic Product of three industries were changed according to provisions of the National Bureau of Statistics, and the data on the three industries before 2012 was adjusted .

1-10 续表 1 Continued 1

单位：% (%)

项 目	Item	1990	1995	2000	2005	2010	2015	2016
产 业	**Industry**							
农 业	**Agriculture**							
农林牧渔业产值结构	Structure of Gross Output Value of Agriculture							
农 业	Agriculture	55.6	52.8	46.7	38.0	47.0	42.0	42.9
林 业	Forestry	1.3	1.7	2.8	5.2	5.1	15.6	15.4
牧 业	Animal Production and Hunting	39.8	41.8	46.4	50.5	42.6	36.9	36.3
渔 业	Fishing	3.3	3.7	4.1	3.6	3.5	3.2	2.7
农林牧渔服务业	Service Activities for Agriculture, Forestry, Animal Production and Hunting, Fishing				2.7	1.8	2.3	2.6
工 业	**Industry**							
规模以上工业主要行业增加值结构	Structure of Added Value of Industry by Sector (Above Designated Size)							
#医药制造业	Manufacture of Medicines		1.6	3.6	3.0	5.6	8.2	9.0
汽车制造业	Manufacture of Motor Vehicles		9.4	3.7	8.7	16.6	21.8	25.3
计算机、通信和其他电子设备制造业	Manufacture of Computer, Communication Equipment and Other Electronic Equipment		9.9	24.7	16.7	8.7	7.7	4.9
电力、热力的生产和供应业	Production and Distribution of Electricity and Heating Power		7.0	6.4	11.8	14.9	18.0	19.4
建筑业	**Construction**							
建筑业总产值结构	Stucture of Gross Output Value of Construction							
#国有企业	State-owned Enterprises	68.7	69.1	44.8	27.4	6.3	3.0	2.6
集体企业	Collectively-owned Enterprises	31.3	26.4	21.7	4.7	2.0	1.2	1.1
港澳台商投资企业	Hong Kong, Macao and Taiwan-invested Enterprises		1.4	1.4	1.2	1.8	0.7	0.8
外商投资企业	Foreign-invested Enterprises		1.2	2.0	1.7	1.0	0.5	0.4
交通运输业	**Transport**							
货运量结构(按运输方式分)	Structure of Freignt (By Means of Transportation)							
铁 路	Railway	11.4	9.2	8.5	6.1	6.6	4.3	3.0
公 路	Road	87.5	90.4	91.2	92.4	85.1	82.0	82.9
民 航	Civil Aviation	0.04	0.05	0.1	0.2	0.5	0.7	0.7
管 道	Pipeline	1.0	0.3	0.2	1.2	7.7	13.0	13.4
客运量结构(按运输方式分)	Structure of Passenger (By Means of Transportation)							
铁 路	Railway	50.4	45.1	24.2	9.5	6.3	18.3	19.3
公 路	Road	46.7	47.7	70.7	85.3	89.7	71.4	69.3
民 航	Civil Aviation	2.9	7.2	5.1	5.2	4.0	10.3	11.4
国内贸易	**Domestic Trade**							
社会消费品零售总额结构	Structure Retail Sales of Consumer Goods							
吃类商品	Food	39.6	42.7	28.4	25.8	21.4	19.0	20.9
穿类商品	Clothing	13.2	14.6	12.0	9.7	8.8	7.2	7.1
用类商品	Daily Use Articles	44.8	40.8	56.2	56.5	62.4	69.2	67.5
烧类商品	Fuels	2.4	1.9	3.4	8.1	7.5	4.6	4.6
对外贸易	**Foreign Trade**							
海关出口商品结构	Structure of Export Commodities							
#一般贸易	General Trade		70.6	65.9	54.5	45.0	54.8	51.5
加工贸易	Processing Trade		21.3	29.6	39.6	42.1	28.0	29.5
海关进口商品结构	Structure of Import Commodities							
#一般贸易	General Trade		84.4	87.3	85.2	88.7	85.7	85.5
加工贸易	Processing Trade		5.2	3.5	8.2	5.9	7.7	8.4
入境旅游	**Inbound Tourism**							
接待海外旅游人数结构	Structure of Inbound Tourist							
外国人	Foreigners	63.7	80.5	84.4	85.9	86.0	85.1	85.2
港澳台同胞	Compatriots from Hong Kong, Macao and Taiwan	34.6	17.6	15.6	14.1	14.0	14.9	14.8

1-10 续表 2 Continued 2

单位：% (%)

项目	Item	1990	1995	2000	2005	2010	2015	2016
教育、科技、文化、卫生	**Education, Science and Technology, Culture, Health Care**							
教育	**Education**							
在校学生结构	Structure of Students Enrollment							
#普通本专科	Regular Undergraduates and College Students		7.7	12.3	23.7	17.5	15.9	15.8
中等教育	Secondary Education		35.1	42.3	37.9	22.1	15.7	14.8
小学教育	Primary Education		42.3	32.3	21.8	19.8	22.8	23.3
专任教师结构	Structure of Full-time Teachers							
#高等教育	Higher Education	24.6	22.7	22.2	32.7	35.9	30.3	30.0
中等教育	Secondary Education	38.3	38.6	40.5	33.6	29.1	32.0	31.5
小学教育	Primary Education	36.7	37.9	36.8	25.3	23.9	22.1	22.4
科技	**Science and Technology**							
研究与试验发展(R&D)人员折合全时当量结构	Structure of R&D Personnel							
基础研究	Basic Research				12.9	15.2	16.8	18.3
应用研究	Applied Research				29.8	27.1	25.1	25.1
试验发展	Experimental Development				57.3	57.7	58.1	56.6
研究与试验发展(R&D)经费内部支出结构	Structure of Full-time and Non-full Time R&D Personnel							
基础研究	Basic Research				10.1	11.6	13.8	14.2
应用研究	Applied Research				27.8	26.4	23.0	23.4
试验发展	Experimental Development				53.1	62.0	63.2	62.3
卫生	**Health Care**							
卫生技术人员结构	Structure of Medical Personnel							
#执业(助理)医师	Certified Doctors	45.6	46.7	44.6	42.2	38.5	37.6	38.1
注册护士	Registered Nurses	31.0	31.7	34.5	35.8	39.3	44.6	44.5
生活与环境	**People's Livelihood and Environment**							
生活	**People's Livelihood**							
城镇居民消费结构	Consumption Structure of Urban Residents							
#食品烟酒(恩格尔系数)	Food (Engel Coefficient)	54.2	48.5	36.3	31.8	32.1	22.1	21.1
衣着	Clothing	14.8	15.1	8.9	8.9	10.4	7.2	6.9
医疗保健	Health Care and Medical Services	1.4	2.9	6.9	9.8	6.7	6.5	6.9
交通和通信	Transport and Communications	1.5	4.7	7.1	14.7	17.2	13.3	13.3
教育文化娱乐服务	Education, Cultural and Entertainment Services	11.5	10.2	15.1	16.5	14.6	11.0	10.6
农村居民消费结构	Consumption Structure of Rural Residents							
#食品烟酒(恩格尔系数)	Food (Engel Coefficient)	50.7	49.6	36.7	32.8	30.9	27.7	26.9
衣着	Clothing	9.5	10.9	7.6	7.8	7.7	6.3	6.3
医疗保健	Health Care and Medical Services	3.8	4.8	8.0	9.0	8.9	8.5	7.8
交通和通信	Transport and Communications	1.7	4.1	6.3	11.0	13.1	13.5	13.3
教育文化娱乐服务	Education, Cultural and Entertainment Services	6.6	10.6	14.4	15.1	9.7	7.2	7.7
环境	**Environment**							
林木绿化率	Green Area Coverage	28.3	36.3	42.0	50.5	53.0	59.0	59.3

1-11 国民经济和社会发展比例和效益指标
INDICATORS ON PROPORTIONS AND EFFICIENCY IN NATIONAL ECONOMIC AND SOCIAL DEVELOPMENT

项目		Item		2016	2015
人口与就业		**Population and Employment**			
人 口		**Population**			
常住人口出生率	(‰)	Birth Rate of Permanent Population	(‰)	9.32	7.96
常住人口死亡率	(‰)	Death Rate of Permanent Population	(‰)	5.20	4.95
常住人口自然增长率	(‰)	Natural Growth Rate of Permanent Population	(‰)	4.12	3.01
就 业		**Employment**			
城镇登记失业率	(%)	Registered Unemployment Rate in Urban Areas	(%)	1.41	1.39
宏观经济		**Macro Economy**			
国民经济核算		**National Accounts**			
人均地区生产总值	(元/人)	Per Capita Gross Domestic Product	(yuan/person)	118198	109603
社会劳动生产率	(元/人)	Overall Labor Productivity	(yuan/person)	213356	202200
第一产业		Primary Industry		25984	27339
第二产业		Secondary Industry		251114	226963
第三产业		Tertiary Industry		215372	206459
固定资产投资		**Fixed Asset Investment**			
全社会固定资产投资相当于地区生产总值比例	(%)	Proportion of Fixed Asset Investment to Gross Domestic Product	(%)	32.96	33.74
能源消费		**Energy Consumption**			
能源消费弹性系数		Energy Consumption Elasticity Coefficient		0.23	0.05
电力消费弹性系数		Electricity Consumption Elasticity Coefficient		1.07	0.28
万元地区生产总值能耗(可比价)	(吨标准煤)	Energy Consumption per 10000 yuan of GDP (Comparable Price)	(ton of SCE)	0.28	0.34
万元地区生产总值水耗(现价)	(立方米)	Water Consumption per 10000 yuan of GDP (Current Price)	(cu.m)	15.12	16.60
产 业		**Industry**			
规模以上工业企业效益		**Efficiency of Industrial Enterprises Above Designated Size**			
综合效益指数	(%)	General Efficiency Index	(%)	313.42	302.38
总资产贡献率	(%)	Total Asset Contribution Rate	(%)	6.19	6.79
资产保值增值率	(%)	Capital Maintenance and Appreciation Rate	(%)	113.63	124.95

1-11 续表 Continued

项目	Item	2016	2015
资产负债率 (%)	Asset-liability Ratio (%)	45.94	46.89
流动资产周转率 (次)	Turnover Rate of Working Capital (time)	1.21	1.27
成本费用利润率 (%)	Ratio of Profits to Total Industrial Cost (%)	8.45	8.83
全员劳动生产率 (元/人)	Overall Labor Productivity (yuan/person)	358907	332913
产品销售率 (%)	Ratio of Sales to Gross Output Value (%)	98.62	99.02
建筑业	**Construction**		
产值竣工率 (%)	Rate of Buildings Completed (by Output Value) (%)	48.9	50.8
面积竣工率 (%)	Rate of Buildings Completed (by Floor Space) (%)	17.5	16.5
邮电通信业	**Post and Communications**		
移动电话普及率 (户/百人)	Penetration Rate of Mobile Phone (sets/100 persons)	178.0	186.7
固定电话主线普及率 (线/百人)	Penetration Rate of Main Line of Fixed Telephone (line/100 persons)	32.0	36.2
国内贸易	**Domestic Trade**		
人均社会消费品零售总额 (元)	Per Capita Retail Sales of Consumer Goods (yuan)	50675	47838
教育、科技、文化、卫生	**Education, Science and Technology, Culture and Health Care**		
教育	**Education**		
平均每一专任教师负担学生数	Average Number of Students Instructed by a Full-time Teacher		
#普通中学 (人)	Ordinary Secondary Education (person)	7.9	8.4
小学学校 (人)	Primary Education (person)	14.0	14.3
科技	**Science and Technology**		
研究与试验发展经费内部支出相当于地区生产总值比例 (%)	Internal R&D Expenditures as % of GDP (%)	5.78	5.84
文化	**Culture**		
每万人拥有公共图书馆 (个)	Public Libraries per 10,000 persons (library)	0.01	0.01
每万人拥有博物馆 (个)	Museums per 10,000 persons (museum)	0.08	0.08
卫生	**Health Care**		
婴儿死亡率 (‰)	Infant Mortality Rate (‰)	2.21	2.42
孕产妇死亡率 (1/10万)	Maternal Mortality Rate (1/100,000)	10.83	8.69
平均每千人口拥有执业医师数(常住人口) (人)	Certified Doctors per 1,000 Persons (Permanent Resident) (person)	4.64	4.44
家庭、生活、环境、灾害	**Household, Livelihood, Environment and Accidents**		
家庭	**Household**		
少儿抚养比(常住人口) (%)	Child-age Dependency Rate (Permanent Population) (%)	13.02	12.67
老年抚养比(常住人口) (%)	Old-age Dependency Rate (Permanent Population) (%)	13.41	12.89
居民收入	**Resident Income**		
城镇与农村居民收入比例(以农村居民收入为1)	Ratio of Urban Residents' Income to Rural Residents' Income (Rural Residents' Income = 1)	2.57	2.57
环境、灾害	**Environment and Accidents**		
人均公园绿地面积 (平方米)	Per Capita Park and Green Area (sq.m)	16.1	16.0
平均每起火灾直接经济损失 (元)	Average Direct Losses per Fire Accident (yuan)	13867	16195
平均每起交通事故直接经济损失 (元)	Average Direct Losses per Traffic Accident (yuan)	8916	7918
重点食品安全监测抽检合格率 (%)	Up-to-standard Rate of Key Foods Security Monitor Spot Checks (%)	98.50	98.42
药品抽验合格率 (%)	Up-to-standard Rate of Druy Spot Checks (%)	99.85	99.71

1-12 北京一日
A DAY IN BEIJING

项 目		Item		2016	2015
每天创造的财富		**Daily Production**			
地区生产总值	(万元)	Gross Domestic Product	(10000 yuan)	701341.5	648923.3
第一产业		Primary Industry		3546.4	3846.6
第二产业		Secondary Industry		135092.9	127687.7
第三产业		Tertiary Industry		562702.2	517389.0
#批发和零售业		Wholesale and retail trade		64833.3	64446.6
信息传输、软件和信息技术服务业		Information transmission,software and information technology services		76661.2	66901.4
金融业		Finance		116688.5	107572.6
科学研究和技术服务业		Scientific research and development, technical services		68633.9	60991.8
一般公共预算收入	(万元)	Local Public Budgetary Revenue	(10000 yuan)	138832.2	129420.8
一般公共预算支出	(万元)	Local Public Budgetary Expenditures	(10000 yuan)	175048.3	157197.3
发电量	(万千瓦时)	Electricity Generated	(10000 kWh)	11848.9	11435.2
汽车生产量	(辆)	Output of Motor Vehicles	(vehicle)	7115	6080
移动电话机生产量	(台)	Output of Mobile Telephones	(set)	189178	261392
每天收入与消费量		**Daily Income and Consumption**			
城镇居民人均可支配收入	(元)	Per Capita Disposable Income of Urban Residents	(yuan)	156.5	144.8
城镇居民人均消费性支出	(元)	Per Capita Living Expenditures of Urban Residents	(yuan)	104.5	100.4
农村居民人均可支配收入	(元)	Per Capita Disposable Income of Rural Residents	(yuan)	61.0	56.4
农村居民人均生活消费支出	(元)	Per Capita Living Expenditures of Rural Residents	(yuan)	47.3	43.3
城镇单位在岗职工平均工资	(元)	Average Wage of On-the-job Staff and Workers	(yuan)	335.4	309.8
社会消费品零售总额	(万元)	Retail Sales of Consumer Goods	(10000 yuan)	300685.8	283232.9
居民生活用电量	(万千瓦时)	Resident Electricity Use	(10000 kWh)	5339.7	4787.9
每天其他活动		**Other Daily Activities**			
地区出口值	(万元)	Exports of Local Enterprises	(10000 yuan)	93722.5	93013.3
旅游外汇收入	(万美元)	Foreign Exchange Earning from Tourism	(USD 10000)	1385.0	1261.6
国内旅游收入	(万元)	Domestic Tourism Earnings	(10000 yuan)	127950.8	118356.2
接待入境旅游人数	(人次)	Inbound Tourists	(person-time)	11380	11506
接待国内旅游者人数	(人次)	Domestic Tourists	(person-time)	768169	735863
市内公共交通客运量	(万人次)	Urban Public Transport Turnover	(10000 person-times)	2008.1	2023.0
每天人口和婚姻变动		**Daily Population and Marriage Changes**			
出生人口(常住人口)	(人)	Births (Permanent Residence)	(person)	553	471
死亡人口(常住人口)	(人)	Deaths (Permanent Residence)	(person)	309	293
登记结婚对数	(对)	Registered Marriages	(couple)	454	455
离婚对数	(对)	Divorces	(couple)	289	225

注：离婚对数包括在民政部门登记的对数和经法院调离和判离的对数。

Note: Divorces include those registered with civil affair authorities and those mediated and ruled in courts.

1-13 “十三五”时期经济社会发展主要监测指标
MAIN MONITORING INDICATORS OF SOCIAL AND ECONOMIC DEVELOPMENT IN THE THIRTEENTH FIVE-YEAR PLAN PERIOD

项目	Item	十三五”时期监测发展目标 Target in the 13th Five-year Plan	2016
常住人口规模 (万人)	Permanant Population (10000 Persons)	<2300	2172.9
用水总量 (亿立方米)	Total Volume of Water Consumed (100 Million Cu.m)	<43	38.8
森林覆盖率 (%)	Forest Coverage Rate (%)	44.0	42.3
生活垃圾无害化处理率 (%)	Rate of Harmless Disposal of Domestic Waste (%)	>99.8%	99.8
全市污水处理率 (%)	Sewage Treatment Rate (%)	<95%	90
全市居民人均可支配收入实际增长 (%)	Actual Growth Rate of Per-capita Disposable Income of Residents (%)	与经济增长同步	6.9
城镇登记失业率 (%)	Urban Registered Unemployment Rate (%)	控制在4%以内	1.41
重点食品安全监测抽检合格率 (%)	Up-to-standard Rate of Key Foods Security (%)	达到98%以上	98.50
药品抽验合格率 (%)	Up-to-standard Rate of Drug Spot Checks (%)	达到99%以上	99.85
亿元地区生产总值生产安全事故死亡率 (人/亿元)	Death Rate of Work Accidents Per 100 million yuan GDP (person/100 million yuan)	累计降低20%	0.024
地区生产总值年均增速 (%)	Growth Rate of GDP (%)	年均增长6.5%	6.8
社会劳动生产率 (万元/人)	Overall Labor Productivity (10000 yuan/person)	达到23	21.3
第三产业占地区生产总值比重 (%)	Tertiary Industry as % of GDP (%)	>80%	80.2
全社会研究与试验发展经费支出占地区生产总值的比例 (%)	R&D Expenditure as % of GDP (%)	6%左右	5.78
服务贸易总额 (亿美元)	Total Service Trade (USD 100000000)	达到2000亿美元	1508.6
万元地区生产总值能耗降低 (%)	Decrease of Energy Consumption per 10000 yuan of GDP (%)	达到国家要求	4.87
万元地区生产总值水耗降低 (%)	Decrease of Water Consumption per 10000 yuan of GDP (%)	累计降低15%	4.87

主要统计指标解释

法人单位 指有权拥有资产、承担负债，并独立从事社会经济活动（或与其他单位进行交易）的组织。法人单位应同时具备以下条件：(1) 依法成立，有自己的名称、组织机构和场所，能够独立承担民事责任；(2) 独立拥有（或授权使用）资产或者经费，承担负债，有权与其他单位签订合同；(3) 具有包括资产负债表在内的账户，或者能够根据需要编制账户。

单产业法人 指仅包含一个产业活动单位的法人单位，该法人单位同时也是一个产业活动单位。

多产业法人 指由两个及以上产业活动单位组成的法人单位，这些产业活动单位接受法人单位的管理和控制。

登记注册类型 企业法人或企业产业活动单位的登记注册类型，按其在工商行政管理机关登记注册的类型填写。如企业登记注册类型发生变化，但未及时到工商部门变更登记，企业应根据变化后的实际情况填写。其他法人和产业活动单位的登记注册类型，按其主要经费来源和管理方式，根据实际情况，比照《企业登记注册类型与代码》填写。

国有企业 指企业全部资产归国家所有，并按《中华人民共和国企业法人登记管理条例》规定登记注册的非公司制的经济组织。不包括有限责任公司中的国有独资公司。

集体企业 指企业资产归集体所有，并按《中华人民共和国企业法人登记管理条例》规定登记注册的经济组织。

股份合作企业 指以合作制为基础，由企业职工共同出资入股，吸收一定比例的社会资产投资组建，实行自主经营，自负盈亏，共同劳动，民主管理，按劳分配与按股分红相结合的一种集体经济组织。

联营企业 指两个及两个以上相同或不同所有制性质的企业法人或事业单位法人，按自愿、平等、互利的原则，共同投资组成的经济组织称为联营企业。联营企业包括国有联营企业、集体联营企业、国有与集体联营企业和其他联营企业。

有限责任公司 指根据《中华人民共和国公司登记管理条例》规定登记注册，由两个以上，五十个以下的股东共同出资，每个股东以其所认缴的出资额对公司承担有限责任，公司以其全部资产对其债务承担责任的经济组织。有限责任公司包括国有独资公司、其他有限责任公司。

私营企业 指由自然人投资设立或由自然人控股，以雇佣劳动为基础的营利性经济组织。包括按照《公司法》、《合伙企业法》、《私营企业暂行条例》、《个人独资企业法》规定登记注册的私营独资企业、私营合伙企业、私营有限责任公司、私营股份有限公司和个人独资企业。

其他企业 指上述类型之外的其他内资经济组织。

港澳台商投资企业 指港澳台地区投资者依照中华人民共和国有关涉外经济的法律、法规成立的企业，包括与港澳台商合资经营企业、与港澳台商合作经营企业、港澳台商独资经营企业、港澳台商投资股份有限公司、其他港澳台商投资企业。

外商投资企业 指外国企业或外国人依照中华人民共和国有关涉外经济的法律、法规成立的企业，包括中外合资经营企业、中外合作经营企业、外资企业、外商投资股份有限公司、其他外商投资企业。

非公经济 指资产由我国私人控股、港澳台商控股、外商控股的“非公有控股”的企业法人单位，以及主要经费来源于私人、港澳台资和外资的非企业法人单位和个体工商户。其中，私人、港澳台及外商控股是指由其绝对控股和相对控股的经济成分。

Explanatory Notes on Main Statistical Indicators

Legal Entity refers to any organization that has the right to own assets and bear liabilities, and conducts social and economic activities independently (or conducts transactions with other entities). A business entity shall meet all of such conditions as: (1) established in accordance with law, having its own name, organization and site, capable of assuming civil responsibilities independently; (2) independently owning and using (or using under authorization) assets or outlays, assuming liabilities, having the right to sign contracts with other entities; (3) maintaining accounts including balance sheet, or capable of preparing accounts as needed.

Single-industry Legal Entity refers any business entity conducting only one industrial activity. Such business entity is also an industrial activity entity.

Multi-industry Legal Entity refers to any business entity composed of two or more industrial activity entities which are managed and controlled by the business entity.

Registration type of an enterprise as legal person or as industrial activity entity shall be completed according to the type registered at the administration for industry and commerce. In the event of any change in registration type, and no registration alteration is made with administration for industry and commerce in good time, the registration type shall be completed according to the actual situation. Registration type for other legal persons and industrial activity entities shall be completed according to the main source of outlays and management manner, pursuant to the actual conditions, and by referring to the *Type of Enterprise Registration and Code*.

State-owned Enterprise refers to non-corporation economic organizations where the entire assets are owned by the state and which have registered in accordance with the *Regulation of the People's Republic of China on the Management of Registration of Corporate Enterprises*, excluding solely state-funded corporations in limited liability companies.

Collectively-owned Enterprise refer to economic organizations where the assets are owned collectively and which have registered in accordance with the *Regulation of the People's Republic of China on the Management of Registration of Corporate Enterprises*.

Joint-equity Cooperative Enterprise refers to a form of collective economic organizations based on cooperative system, where capitals come mainly from employees as their shares, with certain proportion of capital from the public, where production is organized on the basis of independent operation, independent accounting for profits and losses, joint work, democratic management, and where the distribution system integrates distribution according to work with distribution according to capital share.

Associated Enterprise refers to organizations established by two or more corporate legal persons or institutional legal persons of the same or different ownership, through joint investment on the basis of equality, voluntary participation and mutual benefits. They include state-owned associated enterprises, collectively-owned associated enterprises, state-collective associated enterprises and other associated enterprises.

Limited Liability Company refers to organizations established with investment from 2-50 shareholders and registered in accordance with the *Regulation of the People's Republic of China on the Management of Registration of Corporations*, each shareholder bearing limited liability to the corporation depending on its share of investment, and the corporation bearing liability to its debt to the maximum of its total assets. Limited liability companies include solely state-funded limited liability companies and other limited liability companies.

Private Enterprise refers to profit-making organizations established by natural persons or controlled by natural persons using employed labor. Private enterprises include solely private-funded enterprises, private partnership enterprises, private limited liability companies, private companies limited by shares, and private-funded enterprises registered in accordance with provisions in the *Corporation Law*, *Partnership Enterprises Law*, *Interim Regulations on Private Enterprises* and *Sole Proprietorship Enterprise Law*.

Other Enterprise refers to domestically funded organizations other than those mentioned above.

Hong Kong, Macao and Taiwan-invested Enterprise refers to enterprises established by investors from Hong Kong, Macao and Taiwan in accordance with laws and rules of the People's Republic of China on foreign-related businesses. They include joint ventures with investors from Hong Kong, Macao and Taiwan, cooperative enterprises with investors from Hong Kong, Macao and Taiwan, enterprises wholly funded by investors from Hong Kong, Macao and Taiwan, companies limited by shares and funded by investors from Hong Kong, Macao and Taiwan, and other enterprises funded by investors from Hong Kong, Macao and Taiwan.

Foreign-invested Enterprise refers to enterprises

established by foreign enterprises or foreigners in accordance with laws and regulations of the People's Republic of China on foreign-related businesses. They include Sino-foreign joint ventures, Sino-foreign cooperative enterprises, foreign wholly-funded enterprises, foreign-funded companies limited by shares, and other foreign-funded enterprises.

Non-public Economy means enterprises as business entities whose shares are controlled by "non-public entities" and whose assets are controlled by individuals, investors from Hong Kong, Macao and Taiwan, and foreign investors, along with enterprises not as business entities and self-employed operators whose main funds are from individuals, investors from Hong Kong, Macao and Taiwan, and foreign investors. Here, enterprises controlled by individuals, investors from Hong Kong, Macao and Taiwan, and foreign investors mean economic sectors with absolute or relative control by such companies.

北京统计年鉴2017 BEIJING STATISTICAL YEARBOOK

国民经济核算
NATIONAL ACCOUNTS

简要说明

一、本章资料的主要内容

本章主要包括历年北京市地区生产总值、部分新兴产业增加值、各行业增加值、居民消费水平、全社会劳动生产率、三次产业的贡献率等资料。其中，地区生产总值是由北京市统计局根据统计资料、会计资料和部门财务资料采用不同方法核算的数据。

二、本章中关于历史数据调整的问题

本章中 1997–2008 年地区生产总值的数据及其分组资料，按照国家统一规定，根据“北京市第二次全国经济普查”和“北京市第二次全国农业普查”的数据结果进行了修正。

2006–2010 年人均地区生产总值数据根据全国第六次人口普查数据进行了修正。

2013 年数据为第三次全国经济普查数据。

按照国家统计局部署，2016 年开始实施地区研发支出核算方法改革，将研发支出未计入地区生产总值部分进行补充核算，对 1996–2015 年地区生产总值进行了调整。

三、有关统计标准的变化说明

（一）关于行业划分。2013 年开始，地区生产总值行业划分执行《国民经济行业分类》GB/T 4754–2011 标准。

（二）关于三次产业划分。根据国家统计局《三次产业划分规定》（国统字[2012]108 号），对三次产业的范围进行了调整。第一产业是指农、林、牧、渔业（不含农、林、牧、渔服务业）；第二产业是指采矿业（不含开采辅助活动），制造业（不含金属制品、机械和设备修理业），电力、热力、燃气及水生产和供应业，建筑业；第三产业是指除第一产业、第二产业以外的其他行业。

Brief Introduction

I. Main Content

Statistics in this chapter include the GDP of Beijing, added value of some emerging sectors, added value of different sectors, residents' consumption level, total productivity, contribution rate of three industries in previous years. Among them, the GDP of Beijing is calculated by Beijing Municipal Bureau of Statistics using different measures according to statistical data, accounting data and financial data of different sectors.

II. Adjustment to Historical Statistics

Figures of GDP 1997-2008 and grouping data have been corrected in accordance with the national uniform regulation and the results of “the 2nd National Economic Census in Beijing” and “the 2nd National Agricultural Census in Beijing”.

2006-2010 per-capita GDP figures were adjusted according to figures from the 6th national census.

The data of 2013 was adjusted to be the statistics for the 3rd National Economic Census.

In accordance with the deployment of the National Bureau of Statistics of the People's Republic of China (NBS), the reform of calculation method of regional R&D expenditure has been implemented since 2016, according to which the part of R&D expenditure not included in GDP figures were calculated additionally and GDP figures of 1996-2015 were adjusted.

Ⅲ. Explanation on Changes of Statistical Standards

(I) Industrial Classification. As regulated by National Bureau of Statistics, *Classification of National Economic Sectors* Standard GB/T 4754-2011 shall be adopted and accounting shall follow the standards.

(II) Classification of Three Industries. According to *Regulations on Three Industries Classification* (G.T.Z. [2012] No. 108) of National Bureau of Statistics, the scope of three industries has been adjusted. The primary industry refers to agriculture, forestry, animal production and hunting, fishing (excluding service activities for agriculture, forestry, animal production and hunting, fishing); secondary industry refers to mining and quarrying (excluding mining support service activities), manufacturing (excluding repair of fabricated metal products, machinery and equipment), production and distribution of electricity, heating power, gas and water and construction; the tertiary industry refers to others excluding the primary and secondary industries.

2-1 地区生产总值(1978—2016年)
GROSS DOMESTIC PRODUCT (1978-2016)

单位：亿元 (100 million yuan)

年份 Year	地区生产总值 Gross Domestic Product	按产业分组 By Three Industies 第一产业 Primary Industry	第二产业 Secondary Industry	第三产业 Tertiary Industry	按行业分组 By Sector #工业 Industry	#建筑业 Construction	人均地区生产总值(元/人) Per Capita Gross Domestic Product (yuan/person)	人均地区生产总值(美元/人) Per Capita Gross Domestic Product (USD/person)
1978	108.8	5.6	77.2	26.0	70.2	7.2	1257	797
1979	120.1	5.2	85.0	29.9	77.4	7.8	1358	908
1980	139.1	6.1	95.6	37.4	86.9	8.9	1544	1009
1981—1985	**950.9**	**61.9**	**588.4**	**300.6**	**515.5**	**73.9**		
1981	139.2	6.6	92.3	40.3	82.7	9.8	1526	895
1982	154.9	10.2	99.6	45.1	89.3	10.5	1671	883
1983	183.1	12.7	112.5	57.9	98.8	13.9	1943	983
1984	216.6	14.7	130.5	71.4	114.0	16.7	2262	972
1985	257.1	17.7	153.5	85.9	130.7	23.0	2643	900
1986—1990	**1978.7**	**162.1**	**1082.5**	**734.1**	**917.3**	**167.0**		
1986	284.9	19.0	165.6	100.3	141.2	24.6	2836	821
1987	326.8	24.2	182.2	120.4	154.5	28.1	3150	846
1988	410.2	36.9	220.9	152.4	189.5	31.8	3892	1046
1989	456.0	38.3	251.8	165.9	212.8	39.4	4269	1134
1990	500.8	43.7	262.0	195.1	219.3	43.1	4635	969
1991—1995	**4847.2**	**286.4**	**2213.0**	**2347.8**	**1833.5**	**386.9**		
1991	598.9	45.5	290.5	262.9	255.6	35.9	5494	1032
1992	709.1	48.7	344.7	315.7	293.0	52.9	6458	1171
1993	886.2	53.2	418.2	414.8	339.2	80.4	8006	1389
1994	1145.3	66.8	516.0	562.5	417.9	99.7	10240	1188
1995	1507.7	72.2	643.6	791.9	527.8	118.0	12690	1520
1996—2000	**12234.3**	**387.6**	**4296.6**	**7550.0**	**3479.6**	**831.5**		
1996	1805.0	75.0	715.8	1014.3	579.2	139.0	14380	1729
1997	2096.8	77.2	783.6	1236.0	639.7	146.5	16778	2024
1998	2406.2	77.9	844.4	1483.9	676.0	171.0	19361	2339
1999	2713.5	78.4	912.2	1722.9	730.7	184.3	21684	2619
2000	3212.8	79.3	1040.6	2092.9	853.9	190.7	24518	2962
2001—2005	**26576.3**	**419.6**	**7818.1**	**18338.6**	**6521.6**	**1328.4**		
2001	3769.9	80.8	1147.6	2541.6	947.6	205.3	27430	3314
2002	4396.0	82.4	1259.4	3054.2	1032.6	231.1	31307	3782
2003	5104.1	84.1	1497.9	3522.1	1237.3	265.4	35450	4283
2004	6164.9	85.4	1867.7	4211.9	1573.4	302.5	41809	5051
2005	7141.4	86.9	2045.6	5008.9	1730.7	324.2	47127	5753
2006—2010	**56637.2**	**537.5**	**13638.4**	**42461.2**	**11311.4**	**2503.5**		
2006	8312.6	87.2	2217.8	6007.7	1856.3	375.0	52964	6644
2007	10071.9	99.4	2534.1	7438.4	2116.7	432.9	61470	8084
2008	11392.0	111.4	2641.8	8638.8	2173.0	502.3	66098	9517
2009	12419.0	116.8	2856.9	9445.4	2348.3	559.8	68406	10014
2010	14441.6	122.8	3387.9	10930.9	2817.1	633.5	75573	11164
2011—2015	**100937.9**	**742.3**	**21530.0**	**78665.6**	**17848.6**	**4199.9**		
2011	16627.9	134.5	3753.2	12740.2	3115.0	712.8	83547	12935
2012	18350.1	148.4	4060.0	14141.7	3381.7	775.0	89778	14222
2013	20330.1	159.8	4392.8	15777.4	3661.6	839.2	97178	15692
2014	21944.1	159.2	4663.4	17121.5	3859.6	910.9	102869	16746
2015	23685.7	140.4	4660.6	18884.7	3830.7	961.9	109603	17597
2016	25669.1	129.8	4944.4	20594.9	4026.7	1025.5	118198	17795

注：1.本表数据按当年价格计算。
2.人均地区生产总值按年平均常住人口计算。

Note: a) Figures in this table are calculated at current year's prices.
b) Per capita GDP is calculated at average permamnent population.

2-2 地区生产总值指数(上年=100)(1978-2016年)
INDICES OF GROSS DOMESTIC PRODUCT (PRECEDING YEAR=100) (1978-2016)

单位：% (%)

年 份 Year	地区生产总值 Gross Domestic Product	按产业分组 By Three Industies 第一产业 Primary Industry	 第二产业 Secondary Industry	 第三产业 Tertiary Industry	按行业分组 By Sector #工业 Industry	 #建筑业 Construction	人均地区生产总值 Per Capita Gross Domestic Product
1978	110.5	109.0	115.1	97.7	112.4	153.0	109.1
1979	109.7	105.0	109.2	113.2	110.1	108.4	107.4
1980	111.8	109.3	110.1	118.5	110.1	110.3	109.8
1981	99.5	109.1	96.3	106.0	95.3	106.4	98.3
1982	107.4	113.4	105.8	109.9	105.8	106.1	105.6
1983	116.4	107.5	113.6	124.2	111.5	132.3	114.5
1984	117.4	106.8	116.1	121.8	115.7	118.8	115.6
1985	108.7	106.3	111.0	104.4	109.1	124.7	106.9
1986	108.0	100.1	104.8	115.7	105.0	103.7	104.6
1987	109.6	113.4	105.6	116.7	105.5	106.3	106.1
1988	112.8	111.2	112.1	114.1	113.0	106.5	111.0
1989	104.4	101.1	108.9	97.3	108.4	112.2	103.1
1990	105.2	103.3	101.1	113.3	101.9	95.6	104.0
1991	109.9	103.7	107.5	114.5	112.6	81.6	108.9
1992	111.3	103.1	112.2	111.9	110.3	125.7	110.5
1993	112.3	103.2	113.0	113.1	110.5	128.5	111.4
1994	113.7	102.8	114.1	115.0	113.5	117.0	112.5
1995	112.0	92.0	107.7	120.5	107.7	107.6	105.4
1996	109.8	96.8	106.6	114.7	106.5	107.3	103.9
1997	110.2	103.0	108.1	113.1	108.7	105.1	110.7
1998	109.6	101.1	109.7	110.3	108.8	114.3	110.2
1999	111.0	102.5	112.0	110.7	112.8	108.0	110.3
2000	112.0	103.2	111.4	113.2	113.3	102.2	107.0
2001	111.8	103.6	109.2	113.3	109.9	106.7	106.6
2002	111.8	103.0	108.7	113.6	108.1	111.1	109.4
2003	111.1	98.5	111.9	111.2	112.1	110.7	108.4
2004	114.3	99.6	117.0	113.5	119.5	106.4	111.6
2005	112.3	98.4	110.2	113.6	110.9	106.5	109.3
2006	112.8	100.8	110.6	113.9	109.8	115.9	108.9
2007	114.4	102.0	112.4	115.4	112.8	110.9	109.6
2008	109.0	101.6	100.1	112.5	100.2	103.7	103.6
2009	110.0	104.6	109.9	110.1	108.9	118.2	104.5
2010	110.4	98.4	113.6	109.4	114.8	108.4	104.9
2011	108.1	100.9	106.6	108.6	107.7	102.8	103.8
2012	108.0	103.2	107.4	108.3	107.4	109.7	105.2
2013	107.7	103.0	107.6	107.8	107.7	109.2	105.3
2014	107.4	100.0	107.0	107.6	106.2	110.2	105.3
2015	106.9	89.2	103.2	108.2	101.1	112.3	105.5
2016	106.8	91.3	106.3	107.0	105.1	107.9	106.3

注：本表数据按可比价格计算。
Note: Statistics in this table are calculated at comparable prices.

2-3 地区生产总值指数(1978年=100)(1978-2016年)
INDICES OF GROSS DOMESTIC PRODUCT (YEAR OF 1978=100) (1978-2016)

单位：% (%)

年份 Year	地区生产总值 Gross Domestic Product	按产业分组 By Three Industies 第一产业 Primary Industry	第二产业 Secondary Industry	第三产业 Tertiary Industry	按行业分组 By Sector #工业 Industry	#建筑业 Construction	人均地区生产总值 Per Capita Gross Domestic Product
1978	100.0	100.0	100.0	100.0	100.0	100.0	100.0
1979	109.7	105.0	109.2	113.2	110.1	108.4	107.4
1980	122.6	114.8	120.2	134.1	121.2	119.6	117.9
1981	122.0	125.2	115.8	142.2	115.5	127.2	115.9
1982	131.1	142.0	122.5	156.3	122.2	135.0	122.4
1983	152.6	152.6	139.2	194.1	136.3	178.6	140.2
1984	179.1	163.0	161.6	236.4	157.7	212.1	162.0
1985	194.7	173.3	179.3	246.8	172.0	264.5	173.2
1986	210.3	173.5	187.9	285.5	180.6	274.3	181.2
1987	230.4	196.7	198.5	333.2	190.6	291.6	192.2
1988	259.9	218.7	222.5	380.2	215.3	310.6	213.4
1989	271.4	221.1	242.3	369.9	233.4	348.5	220.0
1990	285.5	228.4	244.9	419.2	237.9	333.1	228.8
1991	313.8	236.9	263.3	479.9	267.8	271.8	249.1
1992	349.2	244.2	295.4	537.0	295.4	341.7	275.3
1993	392.2	252.0	333.8	607.4	326.4	439.1	306.7
1994	445.9	259.1	380.9	698.5	370.5	513.7	345.0
1995	499.4	238.4	410.2	841.7	399.0	552.8	363.7
1996	548.1	230.8	437.3	965.8	424.9	593.2	377.9
1997	604.0	237.8	472.8	1092.7	461.9	623.4	418.3
1998	662.0	240.4	518.6	1205.2	502.6	712.6	461.0
1999	734.8	246.5	581.0	1334.5	566.9	769.6	508.5
2000	823.0	254.5	647.4	1511.2	642.3	786.5	544.1
2001	920.1	263.8	707.2	1712.8	705.9	839.2	580.0
2002	1028.7	271.8	768.9	1945.5	763.0	932.3	634.5
2003	1142.8	267.7	860.4	2162.6	855.4	1032.1	687.8
2004	1306.3	266.7	1006.7	2454.0	1022.2	1098.1	767.6
2005	1466.9	262.3	1109.3	2788.1	1133.6	1169.5	838.9
2006	1654.7	264.4	1227.0	3175.8	1244.7	1355.5	913.6
2007	1893.0	269.6	1379.7	3664.0	1404.0	1503.2	1001.3
2008	2063.4	274.0	1381.4	4122.1	1406.8	1558.8	1037.4
2009	2269.7	286.6	1518.4	4540.0	1532.0	1842.6	1084.1
2010	2505.8	282.0	1724.7	4967.9	1758.7	1997.3	1137.2
2011	2708.7	284.5	1838.4	5396.7	1894.1	2053.3	1180.4
2012	2925.4	293.5	1974.4	5842.4	2034.3	2252.4	1241.8
2013	3150.7	302.2	2123.8	6300.4	2191.0	2459.6	1307.6
2014	3383.8	302.2	2272.7	6778.4	2326.8	2710.5	1376.9
2015	3617.3	269.7	2344.7	7333.9	2352.4	3043.9	1452.6
2016	3863.3	246.3	2493.0	7849.1	2472.4	3284.4	1544.1

注：本表数据按可比价格计算。
Note:Statistics in this table are calculated at comparable prices.

2-4 地区生产总值指数(2000年=100)(2000-2016年)
INDICES OF GROSS DOMESTIC PRODUCT (YEAR OF 2000=100) (2000-2016)

单位：% (%)

年份 Year	地区生产总值 Gross Domestic Product	按产业分组 By Three Industies			按行业分组 By Sector		人均地区生产总值 Per Capita Gross Domestic Product
		第一产业 Primary Industry	第二产业 Secondary Industry	第三产业 Tertiary Industry	#工业 Industry	#建筑业 Construction	
2000	100.0	100.0	100.0	100.0	100.0	100.0	100.0
2001	111.8	103.6	109.2	113.3	109.9	106.7	106.6
2002	125.0	106.8	118.8	128.7	118.8	118.5	116.6
2003	138.9	105.2	132.9	143.1	133.2	131.2	126.4
2004	158.7	104.8	155.5	162.4	159.1	139.6	141.1
2005	178.2	103.1	171.3	184.5	176.5	148.7	154.2
2006	201.1	103.9	189.5	210.1	193.8	172.3	167.9
2007	230.0	105.9	213.1	242.4	218.6	191.1	184.0
2008	250.7	107.7	213.4	272.8	219.0	198.2	190.7
2009	275.8	112.6	234.5	300.4	238.5	234.3	199.3
2010	304.5	110.8	266.4	328.7	273.8	254.0	209.0
2011	329.1	111.8	284.0	357.1	294.9	261.1	217.0
2012	355.5	115.3	305.0	386.6	316.7	286.4	228.2
2013	382.8	118.7	328.0	416.9	341.1	312.7	240.3
2014	411.2	118.7	351.0	448.5	362.3	344.6	253.1
2015	439.5	105.9	362.2	485.3	366.3	387.0	267.0
2016	469.4	96.8	385.1	519.4	384.9	417.6	283.8

注：本表数据按可比价格计算。

Note:Statistics in this table are calculated at comparable prices.

2-5 地区生产总值构成(1978−2016年)
COMPOSITION OF GROSS DOMESTIC PRODUCT (1978-2016)

单位：% (%)

年份 Year	地区生产总值 Gross Domestic Product	按产业分组 By Three Industies			按行业分组 By Sector	
		第一产业 Primary Industry	第二产业 Secondary Industry	第三产业 Tertiary Industry	#工业 Industry	#建筑业 Construction
1978	100.0	5.1	71.0	23.9	64.5	6.6
1979	100.0	4.3	70.8	24.9	64.4	6.5
1980	100.0	4.4	68.7	26.9	62.5	6.4
1981	100.0	4.7	66.3	29.0	59.4	7.1
1982	100.0	6.6	64.3	29.1	57.6	6.8
1983	100.0	6.9	61.4	31.7	53.9	7.6
1984	100.0	6.8	60.2	33.0	52.6	7.7
1985	100.0	6.9	59.7	33.4	50.8	9.0
1986	100.0	6.7	58.1	35.2	49.6	8.6
1987	100.0	7.4	55.8	36.8	47.3	8.6
1988	100.0	9.0	53.9	37.1	46.2	7.8
1989	100.0	8.4	55.2	36.4	46.7	8.6
1990	100.0	8.7	52.3	39.0	43.8	8.6
1991	100.0	7.6	48.5	43.9	42.7	6.0
1992	100.0	6.9	48.6	44.5	41.3	7.5
1993	100.0	6.0	47.2	46.8	38.3	9.0
1994	100.0	5.8	45.1	49.1	36.5	8.7
1995	100.0	4.8	42.7	52.5	35.0	7.8
1996	100.0	4.2	39.7	56.2	32.1	7.7
1997	100.0	3.7	37.4	58.9	30.5	7.0
1998	100.0	3.2	35.1	61.7	28.1	7.1
1999	100.0	2.9	33.6	63.5	26.9	6.8
2000	100.0	2.5	32.4	65.1	26.6	5.9
2001	100.0	2.1	30.4	67.4	25.1	5.4
2002	100.0	1.9	28.6	69.5	23.5	5.3
2003	100.0	1.6	29.3	69.0	24.2	5.2
2004	100.0	1.4	30.3	68.3	25.5	4.9
2005	100.0	1.2	28.6	70.1	24.2	4.5
2006	100.0	1.0	26.7	72.3	22.3	4.5
2007	100.0	1.0	25.2	73.9	21.0	4.3
2008	100.0	1.0	23.2	75.8	19.1	4.4
2009	100.0	0.9	23.0	76.1	18.9	4.5
2010	100.0	0.9	23.5	75.7	19.5	4.4
2011	100.0	0.8	22.6	76.6	18.7	4.3
2012	100.0	0.8	22.1	77.1	18.4	4.2
2013	100.0	0.8	21.6	77.6	18.0	4.1
2014	100.0	0.7	21.3	78.0	17.6	4.2
2015	100.0	0.6	19.7	79.7	16.2	4.1
2016	100.0	0.5	19.3	80.2	15.7	4.0

注：本表数据按当年价格计算。

Note: Figures in this table are calculated at current year's prices.

2-6 按行业分地区生产总值(2013-2016年)
GROSS DOMESTIC PRODUCT BY SECTOR(2013-2016)

单位：亿元 (100 million yuan)

项 目	Item	2013	2014	2015	2016
地区生产总值	**Gross Domestic Product**	**20330.1**	**21944.1**	**23685.7**	**25669.1**
按产业分组	**By Three Industies**				
第一产业	Primary Industry	159.8	159.2	140.4	129.8
第二产业	Secondary Industry	4392.8	4663.4	4660.6	4944.4
第三产业	Tertiary Industry	15777.4	17121.5	18884.7	20594.9
按行业分组	**By Sector**				
农、林、牧、渔业	Agriculture, Forestry, Animal Production and Hunting, Fishing	162.0	161.5	142.8	132.2
采矿业	Mining and Quarrying	174.6	179.7	152.3	74.4
制造业	Manufacturing	2836.1	2931.8	2927.3	3141.0
电力、热力、燃气及水生产和供应业	Production and Distribution of Electricity, Heating Power, Gas and Water	650.8	748.1	751.1	811.3
建筑业	Construction	839.2	910.9	961.9	1025.5
批发和零售业	Wholesale and Retail Trade	2340.7	2411.1	2352.3	2372.9
交通运输、仓储和邮政业	Transport, Storage and Post	871.9	948.4	984.4	1061.0
住宿和餐饮业	Accommodation and Restaurants	374.8	363.8	397.6	399.4
信息传输、软件和信息技术服务业	Information Transmission,Software and Information Technology Services	1901.5	2136.1	2441.9	2805.8
金融业	Finance	2943.2	3357.8	3926.4	4270.8
房地产业	Real Estate	1339.5	1329.2	1438.4	1672.7
租赁和商务服务业	Renting and Leasing Activities and Business Services	1569.8	1705.0	1770.9	1838.3
科学研究和技术服务业	Scientific Research and Development, Technical Services	1783.2	2021.9	2226.2	2512.0
水利、环境和公共设施管理业	Management of Water Conservancy, Environment and Public Facilities	121.0	137.8	182.2	204.4
居民服务、修理和其他服务业	Resident Services, Repair and Other Services	139.9	155.0	142.8	159.7
教 育	Education	831.6	929.4	1045.4	1173.2
卫生和社会工作	Health Care and Social Works	416.9	469.0	578.5	636.6
文化、体育和娱乐业	Culture, Sports and Entertainment	450.6	470.7	528.1	565.3
公共管理、社会保障和社会组织	Pulic Administration,Social Security and Social Organizations	582.7	576.9	735.3	812.7
国际组织	International Organizations				

注：本表数据按当年价格计算。
Note: Figures in this table are calculated at current year's prices.

2-7 按行业分地区生产总值指数(上年=100)(2013–2016年)
INDICES OF GROSE DOMESFIC PRODUCT BY SECTOR (PRECEDING YEAR=100) (2013-2016)

单位：% (%)

项目	Item	2013	2014	2015	2016
地区生产总值	**Gross Domestic Product**	**107.7**	**107.4**	**106.9**	**106.8**
按产业分组	**By Three Industies**				
第一产业	Primary Industry	103.0	100.0	89.2	91.3
第二产业	Secondary Industry	108.0	107.0	103.2	106.3
第三产业	Tertiary Industry	107.7	107.6	108.2	107.0
按行业分组	**By Sector**				
农、林、牧、渔业	Agriculture, Forestry, Animal Production and Hunting, Fishing	103.0	100.1	89.4	91.5
采矿业	Mining and Quarrying	102.9	98.2	92.9	74.0
制造业	Manufacturing	108.5	107.8	101.5	107.6
电力、热力、燃气及水生产和供应业	Production and Distribution of Electricity, Heating Power, Gas and Water	106.3	101.8	102.7	101.4
建筑业	Construction	109.2	110.2	112.3	107.9
批发和零售业	Wholesale and Retail Trade	106.5	105.0	98.6	102.7
交通运输、仓储和邮政业	Transport, Storage and Post	106.9	106.8	104.1	106.6
住宿和餐饮业	Accommodation and Restaurants	96.8	99.1	100.2	100.1
信息传输、软件和信息技术服务业	Information Transmission,Software and Information Technology Services	107.0	111.8	111.9	112.3
金融业	Finance	111.1	112.7	118.1	109.1
房地产业	Real Estate	103.4	97.8	104.2	105.5
租赁和商务服务业	Renting and Leasing Activities and Business Services	109.4	105.9	98.3	101.5
科学研究和技术服务业	Scientific Research and Development, Technical Services	112.5	111.3	113.8	109.6
水利、环境和公共设施管理业	Management of Water Conservancy, Environment and Public Facilities	106.1	112.1	113.1	108.6
居民服务、修理和其他服务业	Resident Services, Repair and Other Services	103.1	112.8	102.1	109.1
教　育	Education	106.1	109.9	111.9	108.5
卫生和社会工作	Health Care and Social Works	111.4	110.7	113.7	107.1
文化、体育和娱乐业	Culture, Sports and Entertainment	106.0	101.9	103.5	106.5
公共管理、社会保障和社会组织	Pulic Administration,Social Security and Social Organizations	102.2	97.4	108.6	107.2
国际组织	International Organizations				

注：本表数据按可比价格计算。
Note: Figures in this table are calculated at current year's prices.

2-8 部分新兴产业增加值
ADDED VALUE OF SOME EMERGING INDUSTRIES

单位：亿元 (100 million yuan)

项目	Item	2016	2015
地区生产总值	**Gross Domestic Product**	**25669.1**	**23685.7**
文化创意产业	**Cultural and Creative Industry**	**3581.1**	**3253.8**
文化艺术	Culture and Arts	161.2	138.9
新闻出版	Journalism and Publishing	322.8	281.9
广播、电视、电影	Radio Broadcasting, Television and Movies	231.5	225.0
软件、网络及计算机服务	Software, Internet and Computer Services	2109.4	1900.0
广告会展	Advertising and Exhibitions	221.8	217.4
艺术品交易	Artwork Trading	65.6	64.3
设计服务	Design Service	163.5	134.9
旅游、休闲娱乐	Tourism, Leisure and Entertainment	119.1	107.7
其他辅助服务	Other Auxiliary Service	186.2	183.5
信息产业	**Information Industry**	**3794.8**	**3562.1**
电子信息设备制造	Manufacture of Electronic Information Equipment	309.3	389.0
电子信息设备销售和租赁	Sales and Renting of Electronic Information Equipment	262.7	312.3
电子信息传输服务	Electronic Information Transmission Service	1130.2	992.6
计算机服务和软件业	Computer Service and Software	1675.6	1471.7
其他信息相关服务	Other Information-related Service	417.1	396.5
高技术产业	**High-tech Industry**	**5833.7**	**5214.0**
医药制造业	Manufacture of Medicines	347.7	282.5
航空、航天器及设备制造业	Manufacture of Aircrafts and Spacecrafts	94.3	58.0
电子及通信设备制造业	Manufacture of Electronic and Communication Equipment	205.9	281.1
计算机及办公设备制造业	Manufacture of Computers and Office Equipments	41.2	49.2
医疗仪器设备及仪器仪表制造业	Manufacture of Medical Equipments and Meters	150.9	137.7
信息化学品制造业	Information Chemical Manufacturing	2.7	0.9
信息服务	Inforamtion Service	2696.7	2361.1
电子商务服务	E-commerce Services	54.9	46.7
检验检测服务	Examination and Inspection Service	115.4	99.9
专业技术服务业的高技术服务	High-tech Service in Professional Technology Service Sector	774.5	656.2
研发与设计服务	Research and Design Service	923.4	834.7
科技成果转化服务	Transformation Service on Technological Achievements	328.8	279.0
知识产权及相关法律服务	Intellectual Property and Relevant Legal Services	48.4	93.2
环境监测及治理服务	Environmental Monitoring and Governance Service	48.9	33.8
现代制造业	**Modern Manufacturing Industry**	**2007.2**	**1762.0**
电子类	Electronics	220.1	304.9
机电类	Electromechanical	359.2	347.1
交通类	Transport	1013.9	827.5
医药类	Pharmaceutical	375.2	309.1
其他类	Other	38.7	-26.6
现代服务业	**Modern Service Industry**	**15365.3**	**13861.9**
信息传输、软件和信息技术服务业	Information Transmission,Software and Information Technology Services	2805.8	2464.3
金融业	Finance	4270.8	3926.4
房地产业	Real Estate	1672.7	1438.4
商务服务业	Business Services	1727.8	1676.1
科学研究和技术服务业	Scientific Research and Development, Technical Services	2512.0	2219.4
环境管理业	Management of Environment	48.0	34.4
教育	Education	1173.2	1040.2
卫生	Health Care	589.7	534.6
文化、体育和娱乐业	Culture, Sports and Entertainment	565.3	528.1
信息服务业	**Inforamtion Service**	**3222.9**	**2861.8**
信息传输服务	Inforamtion Transmission Service	503.5	448.7
信息技术服务	Information Technology Service	1719.1	1508.9
信息内容服务	Information Content Service	1000.3	904.2

注：1. 本表数据按当年价格计算。
2. 新兴产业执行《国民经济行业分类》(GB/T4754—2011)标准。
3. 北京市从2013年开始执行国家高技术产业标准，包括高技术制造业和高技术服务业。

Note: a) Data in the table is calculated based on price in current year.
b) New emerging industries are subject to Classification of National Economic Sectors (GB/T4754-2011).
c) Beijing has implemented standards for national high-tech industries since 2013, industries on high-tech manufacturing and high-tech service are included.

2-9 收入法地区生产总值(1978–2016年)
GROSS DOMESTIC PRODUCT BY INCOME APPROACH (1978-2016)

单位：亿元 (100 million yuan)

年份 Year	地区生产总值 Gross Domestic Product	劳动者报酬 Compensation for Labors	生产税净额 Net Taxes on Production	固定资产折旧 Depreciation of Fixed Assets	营业盈余 Operating Surplus
1978	108.8	37.1	16.5	11.5	43.7
1979	120.1	42.0	18.3	13.4	46.4
1980	139.1	48.9	21.0	15.4	53.8
1981–1985	**950.9**	**350.9**	**142.8**	**111.0**	**346.2**
1981	139.2	52.9	22.0	16.9	47.4
1982	154.9	57.4	23.2	17.7	56.6
1983	183.1	66.0	26.8	20.7	69.6
1984	216.6	79.1	31.8	25.4	80.3
1985	257.1	95.5	39.0	30.3	92.3
1986–1990	**1978.7**	**773.7**	**290.5**	**244.9**	**669.6**
1986	284.9	107.8	43.4	34.9	98.8
1987	326.8	125.4	48.0	40.9	112.5
1988	410.2	153.9	59.7	49.9	146.7
1989	456.0	179.3	66.5	57.1	153.1
1990	500.8	207.3	72.9	62.1	158.5
1991–1995	**4847.2**	**2102.6**	**717.3**	**608.1**	**1419.2**
1991	598.9	254.2	86.4	75.7	182.6
1992	709.1	304.7	103.3	89.5	211.6
1993	886.2	387.7	131.4	109.0	258.1
1994	1145.3	508.1	168.9	140.2	328.1
1995	1507.7	647.9	227.3	193.7	438.8
1996–2000	**12234.3**	**5112.5**	**1761.0**	**1760.4**	**3600.4**
1996	1805.0	760.9	264.9	248.6	530.7
1997	2096.8	880.1	302.6	288.9	625.1
1998	2406.2	1008.5	341.3	336.9	719.5
1999	2713.5	1135.3	388.1	399.5	790.6
2000	3212.8	1327.7	464.1	486.5	934.5
2001–2005	**26576.3**	**11244.4**	**3999.6**	**4428.4**	**6903.8**
2001	3769.9	1538.7	549.8	600.6	1080.8
2002	4396.0	1810.6	643.0	731.1	1211.3
2003	5104.1	2119.7	753.1	854.7	1376.6
2004	6164.9	2595.5	960.4	1041.2	1567.9
2005	7141.4	3179.9	1093.4	1200.8	1667.3
2006–2010	**56637.2**	**26740.5**	**8959.8**	**8828.3**	**12108.5**
2006	8312.6	3657.3	1286.7	1395.1	1973.6
2007	10071.9	4405.8	1625.8	1535.8	2504.5
2008	11392.0	5615.8	1896.6	1790.3	2089.3
2009	12419.0	6141.6	1953.5	1943.6	2380.3
2010	14441.6	6920.0	2197.2	2163.6	3160.8
2011–2015	**100937.9**	**51149.3**	**15166.8**	**14482.3**	**20139.5**
2011	16627.9	7992.4	2566.2	2534.5	3534.9
2012	18350.1	9102.6	2894.6	2725.6	3627.3
2013	20330.1	10238.6	3179.8	2903.5	4008.2
2014	21944.1	11118.4	3227.5	3001.9	4596.3
2015	23685.7	12697.3	3298.7	3316.8	4372.9
2016	25669.1	13483.7	3480.9	3400.6	5303.9

注：本表数据按当年价格计算。

Note: Figures in this table are calculated at current year's prices.

2-10 收入法地区生产总值(2016年)
GROSS DOMESTIC PRODUCT BY INCOME APPROACH (2016)

单位：亿元 (100 million yuan)

项 目	Item	地区生产总值 Gross Regional Product	劳动者报酬 Renumeration of Labor	生产税净额 Net Production Tax	固定资产折旧 Depreciation of Fixed Asset	营业盈余 Operating Surplus
地区生产总值	**Gross Domestic Product**	**25669.1**	**13483.7**	**3480.9**	**3400.6**	**5303.9**
按产业分组	**By Three Industies**					
第一产业	Primary Industry	129.8	113.2	1.1	15.5	…
第二产业	Secondary Industry	4944.4	1901.9	1041.3	819.5	1181.8
第三产业	Tertiary Industry	20594.9	11468.6	2438.5	2565.7	4122.2
按行业分组	**By Sector**					
农、林、牧、渔业	Agriculture, Forestry, Animal Production and Hunting, Fishing	132.2	114.7	1.4	16.1	…
采矿业	Mining and Quarrying	74.4	70.1	32.8	18.7	-47.3
制造业	Manufacturing	3141.0	1239.5	715.6	414.0	771.9
电力、热力、燃气及水生产和供应业	Production and Distribution of Electricity, Heating Power, Gas and Water	811.3	174.5	56.9	330.4	249.4
建筑业	Construction	1025.5	488.0	264.2	65.6	207.7
批发和零售业	Wholesale and Retail Trade	2372.9	1184.9	854.7	118.7	214.7
交通运输、仓储和邮政业	Transport, Storage and Post	1061.0	615.7	-157.5	274.8	327.9
住宿和餐饮业	Accommodation and Restaurants	399.4	299.1	38.2	43.9	18.2
信息传输、软件和信息技术服务业	Information Transmission,Software and Information Technology Services	2805.8	1581.9	190.4	378.1	655.4
金融业	Finance	4270.8	1429.5	690.6	149.4	2001.3
房地产业	Real Estate	1672.7	489.7	436.0	396.7	350.3
租赁和商务服务业	Renting and Leasing Activities and Business Services	1838.3	1464.4	124.4	170.9	78.5
科学研究和技术服务业	Scientific Research and Development, Technical Services	2512.0	1432.3	165.1	604.4	310.2
水利、环境和公共设施管理业	Management of Water Conservancy, Environment and Public Facilities	204.4	126.0	14.6	24.9	39.0
居民服务、修理和其他服务业	Resident Services, Repair and Other Services	159.7	121.5	15.4	7.0	15.9
教 育	Education	1173.2	927.5	19.9	188.9	37.0
卫生和社会工作	Health Care and Social Works	636.6	597.1	1.1	49.9	-11.5
文化、体育和娱乐业	Culture, Sports and Entertainment	565.3	404.6	12.0	63.2	85.5
公共管理、社会保障和社会组织	Pulic Administration,Social Security and Social Organizations	812.7	722.7	5.0	85.0	
国际组织	International Organizations					

注：本表数据按当年价格计算。
Note: Figures in this table are calculated at current year's prices.

2-11 支出法地区生产总值(1978–2016年)

GROSS DOMESTIC PRODUCT BY EXPENDITURE APPROACH (1978-2016)

单位：亿元 (100 million yuan)

年份 Year	地区生产总值 Gross Domestic Product	最终消费支出 Final Consumption Expenditure	居民消费 Households Consumption	政府消费 Government Consumption	资本形成总额 Gross Capital Formation	固定资本形成总额 Completed Fixed Assets	存货增加 Changes in Inventories	货物和服务净流出 Net Outflow of Goods and Services	最终消费率(消费率)(%) Final Consumption Rate (%)	资本形成率(投资率)(%) Capital Formation Rate (%)
1978	108.8	53.0	28.6	24.4	31.7	24.9	6.8	24.1	48.7	29.1
1979	120.1	55.4	31.5	23.9	37.0	29.1	7.9	27.7	46.1	30.8
1980	139.1	57.3	39.6	17.7	45.1	36.5	8.6	36.7	41.2	32.4
1981	139.2	61.8	44.2	17.6	50.5	40.2	10.3	26.9	44.4	36.3
1982	154.9	68.6	48.8	19.8	51.8	42.3	9.5	34.5	44.3	33.4
1983	183.1	77.6	54.6	23.0	62.9	56.1	6.8	42.6	42.4	34.4
1984	216.6	96.5	64.8	31.7	84.7	72.5	12.2	35.4	44.6	39.1
1985	257.1	127.1	88.7	38.4	150.6	102.7	47.9	-20.6	49.4	58.6
1986	284.9	161.1	109.9	51.2	178.8	116.0	62.8	-55.0	56.5	62.8
1987	326.8	181.5	124.3	57.2	201.2	148.6	52.6	-55.9	55.5	61.6
1988	410.2	222.6	161.9	60.7	251.1	177.7	73.4	-63.5	54.3	61.2
1989	456.0	244.0	176.1	67.9	271.5	151.9	119.6	-59.5	53.5	59.5
1990	500.8	269.7	194.1	75.6	296.5	195.0	101.5	-65.4	53.9	59.2
1991	598.9	302.6	225.7	76.9	327.3	208.8	118.5	-31.0	50.5	54.7
1992	709.1	341.5	260.7	80.8	414.6	289.0	125.6	-47.0	48.2	58.5
1993	886.2	445.6	354.9	90.7	535.0	445.5	89.5	-94.4	50.3	60.4
1994	1145.3	614.1	504.2	109.9	787.5	703.8	83.7	-256.3	53.6	68.8
1995	1507.7	844.2	672.8	171.4	1036.0	912.0	124.0	-372.5	56.0	68.7
1996	1805.0	1010.0	815.5	194.5	1063.3	978.1	85.2	-268.3	56.0	58.9
1997	2096.8	1199.1	993.7	205.4	1271.1	1076.1	195.1	-373.5	57.2	60.6
1998	2406.2	1307.1	1068.8	238.4	1417.7	1306.7	110.9	-318.6	54.3	58.9
1999	2713.5	1482.1	1176.4	305.7	1596.9	1327.5	269.3	-365.5	54.6	58.8
2000	3212.8	1636.0	1278.8	357.1	1800.6	1503.5	297.0	-223.7	50.9	56.0
2001	3769.9	1859.1	1398.9	460.2	2050.9	1716.5	334.4	-140.2	49.3	54.4
2002	4396.0	2232.0	1706.5	525.5	2482.0	2101.1	380.9	-318.0	50.8	56.5
2003	5104.1	2558.0	1939.4	618.6	2913.2	2613.3	299.9	-367.1	50.1	57.1
2004	6164.9	3002.7	2235.2	767.5	3381.8	3058.6	323.2	-219.6	48.7	54.9
2005	7141.4	3401.8	2514.2	887.6	3837.5	3461.3	376.2	-97.9	47.6	53.7
2006	8312.6	4043.6	2946.2	1097.5	4226.5	3840.9	385.6	42.5	48.6	50.8
2007	10071.9	4976.2	3518.2	1458.0	4826.8	4380.2	446.7	268.9	49.4	47.9
2008	11392.0	5883.3	4058.3	1824.9	5143.0	4409.6	733.4	365.7	51.6	45.1
2009	12419.0	6781.8	4676.1	2105.7	5464.6	4849.6	614.9	172.7	54.6	44.0
2010	14441.6	7824.3	5527.4	2296.9	6596.3	5879.0	717.3	21.1	54.2	45.7
2011	16627.9	9239.2	6441.2	2797.9	7308.6	6578.9	729.8	80.1	55.6	44.0
2012	18350.1	10405.0	7232.5	3172.6	8130.3	7753.5	376.8	-185.3	56.7	44.3
2013	20330.1	11877.5	8267.0	3610.5	8789.5	8512.3	277.2	-337.0	58.4	43.2
2014	21944.1	13086.2	8994.9	4091.2	9165.7	8813.5	352.2	-307.8	59.6	41.8
2015	23685.7	14255.5	9865.9	4389.5	9409.2	9074.6	334.6	21.0	60.2	39.7
2016	25669.1	15406.5	10621.7	4784.8	10074.1	9716.1	358.0	188.5	60.0	39.2

2-12 支出法地区生产总值
GROSS DOMESTIC PRODUCT BY EXPENDITURE APPROACH

单位：亿元 (100 million yuan)

项　目	Item	2016	2015	2016年为2015年% 2016 as % of 2015
地区生产总值	**Gross Domestic Product**	**25669.1**	**23685.7**	**106.8**
最终消费支出	**Final Consumption Expenditure**	**15406.5**	**14255.5**	**107.0**
居民消费	Households Consumption	10621.7	9865.9	106.8
城镇居民	Urban Resident	9909.5	9212.8	106.7
农村居民	Rural Resident	712.3	653.2	107.6
政府消费	Government Consumption	4784.8	4389.5	107.6
资本形成总额	**Gross Capital Formation**	**10074.1**	**9409.2**	**105.4**
固定资本形成总额	Completed Fixed Asset	9716.1	9074.6	105.3
存货增加	Changes in Inventories	358.0	334.6	107.0
货物和服务净流出	**Net Outflow of Goods and Services**	**188.5**	**21.0**	

2-13 三大需求对地区生产总值增长的拉动(2001-2016年)
CONTRIBUTION OF THREE DEMANDS TO GROWTH OF GDP (2001-2016)

年　份 Year	最终消费支出 Final Consumption Expenditure		资本形成总额 Gross Capital Formation		货物和服务净流出 Net Outflow of Goods and Services	
	贡献率(%) Contribution Rate(%)	拉动(百分点) Impetus (Percentage Points)	贡献率(%) Contribution Rate(%)	拉动(百分点) Impetus (Percentage Points)	贡献率(%) Contribution Rate(%)	拉动(百分点) Impetus (Percentage Points)
2001	32.0	3.8	44.2	5.2	23.8	2.8
2002	70.1	8.3	66.8	7.9	-36.9	-4.4
2003	39.2	4.3	67.7	7.5	-6.9	-0.7
2004	39.0	5.6	39.2	5.6	21.8	3.1
2005	36.6	4.5	46.9	5.8	16.4	2.0
2006	59.1	7.6	25.6	3.3	15.3	1.9
2007	57.5	8.3	24.8	3.6	17.6	2.5
2008	82.3	7.4	8.3	0.7	9.3	0.9
2009	74.9	7.5	40.4	4.0	-15.4	-1.5
2010	61.3	6.4	51.9	5.4	-13.1	-1.4
2011	80.4	6.5	15.7	1.3	3.8	0.3
2012	69.4	5.6	46.4	3.7	-15.8	-1.3
2013	65.4	5.0	40.1	3.1	-5.6	-0.4
2014	72.0	5.3	23.0	1.7	5.0	0.4
2015	64.5	4.4	23.6	1.6	11.9	0.9
2016	62.4	4.2	31.3	2.1	6.3	0.5

注：1. 三大需求指支出法地区生产总值的三大构成项目，即最终消费支出、资本形成总额、货物和服务净流出。
2. 贡献率指三大需求增量与支出法地区生产总值增量之比。
3. 拉动百分点为地区生产总值增长速度与三大需求贡献率的乘积。
4. 本表数据按可比价格计算。

Note: a) Three demands of GDP by expenditure method are final consumption expenditure,gross capital formation and net outflow of goods and services.
b) Contribution rate of the three demands to GDP growth refers to the proportion of the increment of the each component of GDP by expenditure method to the increment of GDP.
c) Impetus of the three demands to GDP growth refers to the growth rate of GDP multiplied by the contribution share of the three demands.
d) Figures in this table are calculated at comparable prices.

2–14 居民消费水平(1978–2016年)
HOUSEHOLDS CONSUMPTION LEVEL (1978-2016)

年份 Year	居民消费水平(元) Level(yuan)			城乡消费水平对比(农村居民=1) Uban/Rural Consumption Ratio(Rural Households=1)	指数(1978年=100) Index(1978=100)			指数(上年=100) Index(Preceding=100)		
	全市 All Households	城镇居民 Urban Households	农村居民 Rural Households		全市 All Households	城镇居民 Urban Households	农村居民 Rural Households	全市 All Households	城镇居民 Urban Households	农村居民 Rural Households
1978	330	451	185	2.4	100.0	100.0	100.0	112.3	110.1	122.6
1979	356	464	221	2.1	117.5	114.5	120.8	117.5	114.5	120.8
1980	440	562	280	2.0	147.6	140.0	159.0	125.6	122.1	131.5
1981	485	590	338	1.7	160.3	144.8	189.4	108.6	103.6	119.2
1982	526	622	384	1.6	170.6	149.7	211.2	106.4	103.4	111.5
1983	579	674	432	1.6	175.4	151.2	222.6	102.8	101.0	105.4
1984	677	789	494	1.6	201.4	173.9	250.4	114.8	115.0	112.5
1985	912	1101	585	1.9	263.2	235.3	289.2	130.7	135.3	115.5
1986	1094	1284	749	1.7	312.9	272.0	365.8	118.9	115.6	126.5
1987	1198	1391	827	1.7	316.7	272.0	375.3	101.2	100.0	102.6
1988	1536	1779	1046	1.7	367.7	313.3	435.7	116.1	115.2	116.1
1989	1648	1874	1169	1.6	398.2	337.1	472.7	108.3	107.6	108.5
1990	1797	2045	1186	1.7	466.7	393.4	527.5	117.2	116.7	111.6
1991	2071	2330	1345	1.7	528.3	440.2	587.1	113.2	111.9	111.3
1992	2375	2696	1456	1.9	553.7	465.3	583.0	104.8	105.7	99.3
1993	3206	3743	1634	2.3	619.6	529.0	588.8	111.9	113.7	101.0
1994	4508	5307	2114	2.5	717.5	618.4	630.6	115.8	116.9	107.1
1995	5663	6497	3101	2.1	774.2	656.7	737.2	107.9	106.2	116.9
1996	6497	7477	3420	2.2	814.5	694.1	742.4	105.2	105.7	100.7
1997	7951	9294	3638	2.6	996.9	862.8	792.1	122.4	124.3	106.7
1998	8600	10037	3874	2.6	1025.8	887.8	798.4	102.9	102.9	100.8
1999	9401	10957	4163	2.6	1116.1	964.2	856.7	108.8	108.6	107.3
2000	9759	11358	4277	2.7	1129.5	973.8	861.8	101.2	101.0	100.6
2001	10179	11743	4695	2.5	1134.0	968.0	917.0	100.4	99.4	106.4
2002	12153	14129	5020	2.8	1322.2	1137.4	954.6	116.6	117.5	104.1
2003	13470	15674	5275	3.0	1393.6	1200.0	956.5	105.4	105.5	100.2
2004	15158	17624	5713	3.1	1507.9	1296.0	1002.4	108.2	108.0	104.8
2005	16591	18843	6602	2.9	1589.3	1334.9	1107.7	105.4	103.0	110.5
2006	18771	20905	7580	2.8	1751.4	1443.0	1238.4	110.2	108.1	111.8
2007	21472	23777	8984	2.6	1905.5	1561.3	1392.0	108.8	108.2	112.4
2008	23547	25925	10375	2.5	2025.5	1650.3	1550.7	106.3	105.7	111.4
2009	25757	28207	11917	2.4	2197.7	1782.3	1746.1	108.5	108.0	112.6
2010	28925	31560	13392	2.4	2386.7	1926.7	1899.8	108.6	108.1	108.8
2011	32364	35384	13659	2.6	2541.8	2055.8	1839.0	106.5	106.7	96.8
2012	35385	38698	14664	2.6	2709.6	2189.4	1962.2	106.6	106.5	106.7
2013	39516	42843	18649	2.3	2885.7	2314.2	2331.1	106.5	105.7	118.8
2014	42166	45590	20506	2.2	3041.5	2432.2	2538.6	105.4	105.1	108.9
2015	45653	49310	22315	2.2	3239.2	2587.9	2703.6	106.5	106.4	106.5
2016	48883	52721	24285	2.2	3440.0	2745.8	2903.7	106.2	106.1	107.4

2-15 社会劳动生产率(1978-2016年)
OVERALL LABOR PRODUCTIVITY (1978-2016)

单位：元/人 (yuan/person)

年份 Year	社会劳动生产率 Overall Labor Productivity	第一产业 Primary Industry	第二产业 Secondary Industry	第三产业 Tertiary Industry
1978	2504	444	4484	1911
1979	2626	421	4556	2033
1980	2914	510	4750	2391
1981	2795	561	4316	2420
1982	2959	878	4437	2467
1983	3368	1094	4799	2998
1984	3909	1287	5347	3646
1985	4580	1671	6040	4268
1986	5002	1932	6331	4783
1987	5669	2569	6917	5501
1988	7046	4084	8309	6745
1989	7742	4270	9432	7140
1990	8203	4810	9564	7941
1991	9498	5014	10351	10145
1992	11051	5556	12282	11549
1993	13878	7112	14909	14644
1994	17728	9660	18709	18682
1995	22679	10042	23697	24647
1996	27236	10479	26954	31147
1997	31866	10757	30273	37751
1998	37655	10928	34921	45526
1999	43738	10733	41258	52802
2000	51908	10753	49041	62842
2001	60405	11212	54117	74751
2002	67212	11879	55825	85062
2003	73839	12910	64969	89044
2004	79170	13749	81452	86432
2005	82459	14049	88191	87530
2006	92481	14232	97163	98592
2007	108160	16399	111758	115530
2008	118444	17977	121322	126650
2009	125496	18653	140386	130552
2010	142289	19877	168425	145358
2011	158263	22330	177919	163451
2012	168582	25491	188050	173646
2013	180848	28362	207452	184305
2014	191009	29530	221650	193563
2015	202200	27339	226963	206459
2016	213356	25984	251114	215372

注：1.本表数据按当年价格计算。
2.劳动生产率为增加值与本年及上年从业人员平均人数之比。

Note: a) Figures in this table are calculated at current year's prices.
b) Labor productivity refers to the ratio of the value added and the average number of practitioners in this year and last year.

2-16 三次产业贡献率(2001–2016年) CONTRIBUTION RATE OF THREE INDUSTRIES TO THE INCREASE OF GDP (2001-2016)

单位：% (%)

年 份 Year	地区生产总值 Gross Domestic Product	第一产业 Primary Industry	第二产业 Secondary Industry	第三产业 Tertiary Industry	#工 业 Industry	#建筑业 Construction
2001	100.0	0.7	25.4	73.8	22.4	3.4
2002	100.0	0.6	23.4	76.1	17.8	5.3
2003	100.0	-0.3	32.9	67.4	27.6	5.4
2004	100.0		36.8	63.2	34.7	2.5
2005	100.0	-0.2	26.3	73.9	23.7	2.8
2006	100.0	0.1	23.7	76.2	18.6	5.6
2007	100.0	0.1	24.3	75.6	20.9	3.5
2008	100.0	0.2	0.4	99.4	0.6	1.9
2009	100.0	0.4	25.1	74.5	19.0	7.8
2010	100.0	-0.1	33.2	67.0	30.2	3.7
2011	100.0	0.1	19.1	80.8	18.5	1.5
2012	100.0	0.3	21.3	78.4	17.9	5.0
2013	100.0	0.3	22.5	77.2	19.3	5.1
2014	100.0		21.8	78.2	16.2	5.9
2015	100.0	-1.1	10.5	90.6	3.0	7.8
2016	100.0	-0.8	18.3	82.4	12.1	4.7

注：1．本表数据按可比价格计算。
2．产业贡献率指各产业增加值增量与地区生产总值增量之比。

Note: a) Statistics in this table are calculated at comparable prices.
b) Share of the contributions of the three industries to the increase of the GDP refers to the proportion of the increment of the value-added of each industry to the increment of GDP.

2-17 三次产业对地区生产总值增长的拉动(2001-2016年)
IMPETUS OF THREE INDUSTRIES TO GDP GROWTH (2001-2016)

单位：百分点 (Percentage Points)

年 份 Year	地区生产总值 Gross Domestic Product	第一产业 Primary Industry	第二产业 Secondary Industry	第三产业 Tertiary Industry	#工 业 Industry
2001	11.8	0.1	3.0	8.7	2.6
2002	11.8	0.1	2.8	9.0	2.1
2003	11.1	…	3.7	7.5	3.1
2004	14.3	…	5.3	9.0	5.0
2005	12.3	…	3.2	9.1	2.9
2006	12.8	…	3.0	9.8	2.4
2007	14.4	…	3.5	10.9	3.0
2008	9.0	…		8.9	0.1
2009	10.0	…	2.5	7.5	1.9
2010	10.4	…	3.4	7.0	3.1
2011	8.1	…	1.5	6.5	1.5
2012	8.0	…	1.7	6.3	1.4
2013	7.7	…	1.7	5.9	1.5
2014	7.4	…	1.6	5.8	1.2
2015	6.9	-0.1	0.7	6.2	0.2
2016	6.8	-0.1	1.2	5.6	0.8

注：1．本表数据按可比价格计算。

2．地区生产总值数据为其增速。三次产业拉动百分点为地区生产总值增长速度与各产业贡献率之乘积。

Note: a) Statistics in this table are calculated at comparable prices.

b) The data of GDP is that of its growth rate. Contribution of the three industries to GDP growth refers to the growth rate of GDP multiplied by the industrial shares.

主要统计指标解释

地区生产总值 是按市场价格计算的地区生产总值的简称。它是一个地区所有常住单位在一定时期内生产活动的最终成果。地区生产总值有三种表现形式，即价值形态、收入形态和产品形态。从价值形态看，它是所有常住单位在一定时期内所生产的全部货物和服务价值与同期投入的全部非固定资产货物和服务价值的差额，即所有常住单位的增加值之和；从收入形态看，它是所有常住单位在一定时期内创造的各项收入之和，包括劳动者报酬、生产税净额、固定资产折旧和营业盈余；从产品形态看，它是所有常住单位在一定时期内最终使用的货物和服务价值与货物和服务净出口价值之和。在实际核算中，地区生产总值有三种计算方法，即生产法、收入法和支出法。三种方法分别从不同的方面反映地区生产总值及其构成。

三次产业 根据社会生产活动历史发展的顺序对产业结构的划分，产品直接取自自然界的部门称为第一产业，对初级产品进行再加工的部门称为第二产业，为生产和消费提供各种服务的部门称为第三产业。它是世界上通用的产业结构分类，但各国的划分不尽一致。我国 2011 年版国民经济行业分类标准：第一产业是指农、林、牧、渔业（不含农、林、牧、渔服务业）；第二产业是指采矿业（不含开采辅助活动），制造业（不含金属制品、机械和设备修理业），电力、热力、燃气及水生产和供应业，建筑业；第三产业是指除第一产业、第二产业以外的其他行业。

最终消费率(消费率) 通常指一定时期内最终消费支出占国内（地区）生产总值的比重，一般按现行价格计算。

$$\text{最终消费率（消费率）}=\frac{\text{最终消费支出}}{\text{国内（地区）生产总值}}\times 100\%$$

资本形成率(投资率) 通常指一定时期内资本形成总额占国内（地区）生产总值的比重，一般按现行价格计算。

$$\text{资本形成率（投资率）}=\frac{\text{资本形成总额}}{\text{国内（地区）生产总值}}\times 100\%$$

部分新兴产业统计划分标准

1.**文化创意产业** 北京市文化创意产业指以创作、创造、创新为根本手段，以文化内容和创意成果为核心价值，以知识产权实现或消费为交易特征，为社会公众提供文化体验的具有内在联系的行业集群。北京市文化创意产业标准是在《国民经济行业分类》(GB/T 4754-2011）的基础上，根据文化创意活动的特点将行业分类中相关的类别重新进行的组合。适用于统计及政策管理中对文化创意相关活动的分类。内容上主要包括 9 大类，分别是文化艺术服务，新闻出版及发行服务，广播电视电影服务，软件和信息技术服务，广告和会展服务，艺术品生产与销售服务，设计服务、文化休闲娱乐服务，文化用品设备生产销售及其他辅助服务。

2.**信息产业** 信息相关产业主要是指与电子信息相关联的各种活动的集合。信息产业标准是国家统计局在《国民经济行业分类》(GB/T 4754-2011）的基础上，参考了联合国的《全部经济活动的国际标准产业分类》，并结合我国的实际情况制定的。北京市从 2004 年开始执行国家信息产业统计标准。

3.**高技术产业** 高技术产业主要是指与高技术产品相关联的各种活动的集合。高技术产业标准是国家统计局在《国民经济行业分类》(GB/T 4754-2011）的基础上，根据高技术产业的特性，结合我国的实际情况制定的。北京市从 2013 年开始执行国家高技术产业统计标准。包括高技术制造业和高技术服务业。

4.**现代制造业** 现代制造业是指用现代科学技术武装起来的制造业，是现代科学技术与制造业相结合的产物。现代制造业是应用现代制造技术、现代生产组织系统和现代管理理念所进行的以现代集成制造为特征、知识密集为特色、高效制造为特点的技术含量高、附加值大、产业链长的产业组织体系。现代制造业产业标准是北京市统计局在《国民经济行业分类》(GB/T4754-2011）的基础上，根据现代制造业的特性，将符合基本要求的行业归并，结合北京市的实际情况制定的。北京市从 2005 年开始执行现代制造业统计标准。

5.**现代服务业** 现代服务业是相对于传统服务业而言，是适应现代人和现代城市发展的需求，而产生和发展起来的具有高技术含量和高文化含量的服务业。现代服务业有新服务领域、新服务模式、高文化品位和高技术含量的特征。现代服务业标准是北京市统计局在《国民经济行业分类》(GB/T4754-2011）的基础上，根据现代服务业的特性，将符合基本要求的行业归并，结合北京市的实际情况制定的。北京市从 2005 年开始执行现代服务业统计标准。

6. **生产性服务业** 生产性服务业是国家统计局在《国民经济行业分类》(GB/T 4754-2011）的基础上，是对国民经济行业分类中符合生产性服务业特征有关活动的再分类。北京市从 2016 年开始执行国家生产性服务业统计标准。内容上主要包括 10 大类，分别是研发设计与其他技术服务，货物运输、仓储和邮政快递服务，信息服务，金融服务，节能与环保服务，生产性租赁服务，商务服务，人力资源管理与培训服务，批发经纪代理服务，生产性支持服务。

7. **信息服务业** 指以信息资源为基础，利用现代信息技术，对信息进行生产、收集、处理、输送、存储、传播、使用并提供信息产品和服务的产业。本分类涉及《国民经济行业分类》(GB/T 4754-2011）中信息传输、软件和信息技术服务业，文化、体育和娱乐业 2 个行业门类。根据信息服务业的概念和活动性质，将信息服务业划分为信息传输服务、信息技术服务和信息内容服务三大领域。

Explanatory Notes on Main Statistical Indicators

Gross Regional Product (GRP) is calculated at market prices. It represents the final results of all resident units in an area from their productive activities over a given period of time. It is expressed from three different perspectives respectively, namely value, income, and product. GRP from the value perspective refers to the total value of all goods and services produced by all resident units during a certain period of time, minus the total value of input of goods and services of the nature of non-fixed assets; in other words, it is the sum of added value of all resident units. GRP from the income perspective is the sum of primary incomes created by all resident units and distributed to resident and non-resident units. GRP from the product perspective means the finally used goods and services minus the imported goods and services. In actual national accounting, gross regional product is calculated in three methods, namely production method, income method and expenditure method, which reflect the gross regional product and its composition from different angles.

Three Industries means the division of industrial structure according to the historical sequence of social productive activities. The sector which receives products directly from nature is called the primary industry. The sector which re-processes primary products is called the secondary industry. The sector which offers various services for production and consumption is called the tertiary industry. This is a universal classification of industrial structure. However, the classification of three industries may vary in different countries. As stated in China's standards on Classification of Sectors in National Economy Version 2011: The primary industry refers to agriculture, forestry, animal production and hunting, fishing (excluding service activities for agriculture, forestry, animal production and hunting, fishing); secondary industry refers to mining and quarrying (excluding mining support service activities), manufacturing (excluding repair of fabricated metal products, machinery and equipment), production and distribution of electricity, heating power, gas and water and construction; the tertiary industry refers to others excluding the primary and secondary industries.

Final Consumption Rate (Consumption Rate)

Final Consumption Rate (Consumption Rate) = Final Consumption / GRP × 100%

Capital Formation Rate (Investment Rate)

Capital Formation Rate (Investment Rate) = Total Capital Formation /GRP ×100%

Statistical Classification of Some New Industries

1. Cultural and Creative Industry The cultural and creative industry in Beijing refers to an internally correlated cluster of sectors with invention, creation and innovation as fundamental means, cultural content and creative fruits as core value, realization or consumption of intellectual property rights as transaction features, which provide cultural experience for the public. It is a new combination of related sectors in the industrial classification according to the characteristics of cultural and creative activities on the basis of Classification of Sectors in National Economy (GB/T 4754-2011). It consists of 9 sectors, namely culture & art; press & publishing; broadcasting, television and film; software, internet and computer services; advertising and exhibition; artwork trading; design services; culture leisure and recreation and other auxiliary services.

2. Information Industry Information industry mainly means the set of activities related to electronic information. It is classified by the National Bureau of Statistics on the basis of Classification of Sectors in National Economy (GB/T 4754-2011) by referring to the International Standard Classification of Industries for All Economic Activities of the United Nations and combining the actual situation of China. The national statistical standard for information industry was implemented in 2004 in Beijing.

3. High-tech Industry High-tech industry mainly means the set of activities related to high-tech products. It is classified by the National Bureau of Statistics on the basis of Classification of Sectors in National Economy (GB/T 4754-2011), taking into consideration the features of high-tech industry and combining the actual situation of China. The national statistical standard for information industry was implemented in 2013 in Beijing.

4. Modern Manufacturing Modern manufacturing industry mainly means the manufacturing industry equipped with modern science and technology. Modern manufacturing is an industrial organization system with large content of technology, great added value and long industrial chain, with features of modern integrated manufacturing, intensive knowledge, efficient manufacturing, using modern manufacturing technologies, modern production organization system and modern management concepts. It is a combination of modern science, technology and manufacturing. It is classified by the Beijing Municipal Bureau of Statistics on the basis of Classification of Sectors in National Economy (GB/T 4754-2011), taking into consideration the features of modern manufacturing industry, merging the sectors meeting basic requirements and combining the actual situation of Beijing. The statistical standard for information industry was implemented in 2005 in Beijing.

5. Modern Service Modern service is in contrast with conventional service. It is a service sector with great content of high technology and great content of culture, which has emerged and developed to meet the need of modern people and modern cities' development. Modern service industry has new service fields, new service modes, high cultural taste and great content of high technology. It is classified by the Beijing Municipal Bureau of Statistics on the basis of Classification of Sectors in National Economy (GB/T 4754-2011), taking into consideration the features of modern service industry, merging the sectors meeting basic requirements and combining the actual situation of Beijing. The statistical standard for modern service industry was implemented in 2005 in Beijing.

6. **Producer Service** means the sector dominated by intermediate input services. Producer service is operational and tradable. It offers intermediate input services for manufacturing industry, and for the primary and tertiary industries. The classification standard for producer service in Beijing involves 6 sectors in Classification of Sectors in National Economy (GB/T 4754-2011), namely transportation, warehousing and post; information transmission, software and information technical service; wholesale and retail trade; finance; leasing and business service; and scientific research and technical service. According to features of business activities, producer service is divided into 5 categories, namely circulation service, information service, financial service, business service and technical service.

7. **Information Service** means the sector producing, collecting, processing, delivering, storing, transmitting and using information, and providing information products and services on the basis of information resources and by using modern information technology. Information service involves two sectors in the Classification of Sectors in National Economy (GB/T 4754-2011), namely information transmission, software and information technical service; and culture, sports and recreation. According to the definition and features of activities of information service, it is divided into three areas, namely information transmission service, information technical service and information content service.

03

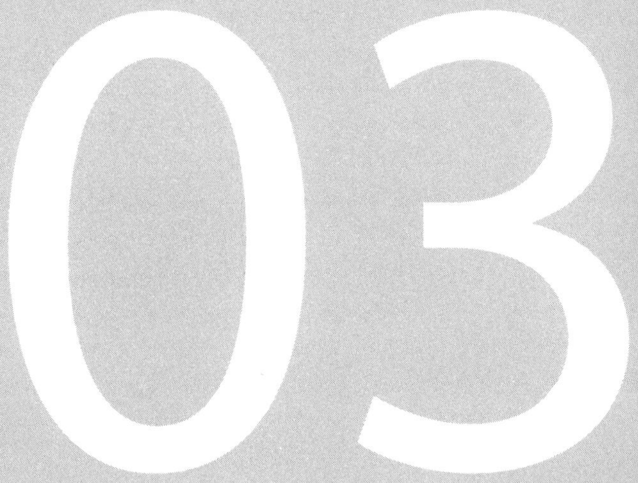

人口与就业
POPULATION AND EMPLOYMENT

简要说明

一、本章资料的主要内容

本章人口部分包括历年北京市常住人口和户籍人口的分组资料；建国以来已开展的六次人口普查的北京市人口数据；1990 年以后的人口变动情况抽样调查数据。

本章劳动力部分包括北京市三次产业从业人员情况；法人单位从业人员及平均工资情况；城镇单位在岗职工人数及工资的分组情况；城镇登记失业情况等。

二、本章数据资料的来源

本章人口部分中，“户籍人口”数据来自于北京市公安局；其余资料均来自北京市统计局。

本章劳动力部分中，城镇登记失业情况由北京市人力资源和社会保障局提供，其他资料来源于北京市统计局。

三、有关统计标准的变化说明

（一）关于行业划分。根据国家统计局规定，自 2012 年开始执行《国民经济行业分类》（GB/T 4754-2011）标准。

（二）关于三次产业划分。根据国家统计局《三次产业划分规定》（国统字[2012]108 号），该规定对三次产业的范围进行了调整。其中第一产业是指农、林、牧、渔业（不含农、林、牧、渔服务业）；第二产业是指采矿业（不含开采辅助活动），制造业（不含金属制品、机械和设备修理业），电力、热力、燃气及水生产和供应业，建筑业；第三产业是指除第一产业、第二产业以外的其他行业。2012 年及以后开始执行此标准。

（三）关于统计上城乡划分标准

2008 年 7 月，国务院批复了国家统计局与民政部、住房城乡建设部、公安部、财政部、国土资源部、农业部共同制定的《关于统计上划分城乡的规定》（国函[2008]60 号文件和国家统计局令第 14 号），以后每年国家统计局都会出台《统计用区划代码和城乡分类代码》。本章中“城镇人口”和“乡村人口”的确定均执行当年的城乡分类标准。

Brief Introduction

I. Main Content

Population statistics in this chapter include classified data for permanent population and registered population in Beijing in previous years; statistics of population in Beijing from six national population censuses since the founding of the People's Republic of China; statistics from National Sample Survey on Population Changes after 1990.

Employment statistics in this chapter include information on employed persons in three industries in Beijing; employees and average wages in business entities; classified statistics for the number and wage of fully employed staff and workers in urban entities; registered unemployment in urban areas.

II. Source of Statistics

In the population section of this chapter, statistics on "registered population" are from Beijing Municipal Bureau of Public Security; other statistics are from Beijing Municipal Bureau of Statistics.

In the employment section in this chapter, urban registered unemployment statistics are from Beijing Municipal Bureau of Human Resources and Social Security; other statistics are from Beijing Municipal Bureau of Statistics.

III. Changes in Relevant Statistical Standards

(I) Classification of Sectors. According to relevant provisions of the National Bureau of Statistics, the Standard for *Classification of National Economic Sectors* (GB/T 4754-2011) was implemented in 2012.

(II) Classification of Three Industries. According to the *Regulations on the Classification of the Three Industries (G.T.Z. [2012] No. 108)* issued by National Bureau of Statistics, the scope of three industries was changed. The primary industry refers to agriculture, forestry, animal production and hunting, fishing (excluding service for agriculture, forestry, animal production and hunting, fishing); the secondary industry refers to mining and quarrying (excluding mining support activities), manufacturing (excluding metal products, machinery and equipment repair), production and distribution of electricity, heating power, gas and water, and construction; the tertiary industry refers to sectors other than the primary and secondary industries. The *Regulations on the Classification of the Three Industries* (G.T.Z. [2012] No. 108) issued by National Bureau of Statistics came into effect in 2012.

(III) Urban-Rural Statistical Definition

In July 2008, the State Council approved the *Regulations on Urban-Rural Statistical Definition* (G.H. [2008] No. 60 and No. 14 Decree of National Bureau of Statistics) jointly developed by the National Bureau of Statistics, Ministry of Civil Affairs, Ministry of Housing and Urban-Rural Development, Ministry of Public Security, Ministry of Finance, Ministry of Land and Resources and Ministry of Agriculture. In the population section, new definition applies for the figures of "urban population" and "rural population".

3-1 六次人口普查人口基本情况
BASIC STATISTICS ON POPULATION CENSUS

项　　目		Item		1953	1964	1982	1990	2000	2010
常住人口	**(万人)**	**Permanent Population**	**(10000 persons)**	**276.8**	**759.7**	**923.1**	**1081.9**	**1356.9**	**1961.2**
按性别分		**By Sex**							
男		Male		159.8	391.1	467.1	559.3	707.4	1012.6
女		Female		117.0	368.6	456.0	522.6	649.5	948.6
性别比(女=100)		Sex Ratio (Female=100)		136.5	106.1	102.4	107.0	108.9	106.8
按城乡分		**By Urban Area and Rural Area**							
城镇人口		Urban Population		205.8	425.8	597.0	794.5	1052.2	1685.9
乡村人口		Rural Population		71.0	333.9	326.1	287.4	304.7	275.3
家庭户规模	**(人/户)**	**Average Family Size**	**(person/household)**			**3.7**	**3.2**	**2.9**	**2.5**
各年龄组人口比重	**(%)**	**Composition by Age Group**	**(%)**						
0-14		Age 0-14		30.1	41.5	22.4	20.2	13.6	8.6
15-59		Age 15-59		64.3	51.9	69.1	69.7	73.9	78.9
60岁及以上		Age 60 and Above		5.6	6.6	8.5	10.1	12.5	12.5
#65岁及以上		Age 65 and Above		3.3	4.1	5.6	6.3	8.4	8.7
总抚养比	**(%)**	**Gross Dependency Ratio**	**(%)**	**50.2**	**83.8**	**38.9**	**36.1**	**28.2**	**20.9**
老年抚养比		Old-age Dependency Ratio		5.0	7.5	7.8	8.6	10.8	10.5
少儿抚养比		Child Dependency Ratio		45.2	76.3	31.1	27.5	17.4	10.4
民族人口		**Population by Ethnic Group**							
汉　族	(万人)	Han Chinese	(10000 persons)	260.0	731.2	890.8	1040.5	1298.4	1881.1
占常住人口比重	(%)	Percentage in Permanent Population	(%)	93.9	96.2	96.5	96.2	95.7	95.9
少数民族	(万人)	Ethnic Minority	(10000 persons)	16.8	28.5	32.3	41.4	58.5	80.1
占常住人口比重	(%)	Percentage in Permanent Population	(%)	6.1	3.8	3.5	3.8	4.3	4.1
每十万人口拥有的各种受教育程度人口	**(人)**	**Population with Various Education Attainment Per 100000 Persons**	**(person)**						
大专及以上		Junior College and Above			4359	4866	9300	16839	31499
高中和中专		Senior Secondary/Secondary Technical School			4513	17646	18978	23165	21220
初　中		Junior Secondary School			11768	29086	30551	34380	31396
小　学		Primary School			31883	26197	22579	16963	9956
文盲人口及文盲率		**Illiterate Population and Illiteracy Rate**							
文盲人口	(万人)	Illiterate Population	(10000 persons)		168.9	114.7	94.3	57.8	33.3
文盲率	(%)	Illiteracy Rate	(%)		34.2	16.0	10.9	4.9	1.9
平均受教育年限	**(年)**	**Average Education Years**	**(year)**		**5.3**	**7.8**	**8.6**	**10.0**	**11.5**
平均预期寿命	**(岁)**	**Average Life Expectancy**	**(year old)**			**71.9**	**72.9**	**76.1**	**80.2**

注：1. 1964年的文盲人口数为12周岁及以上文盲和半文盲人口，1982年、1990年、2000年、2010年的文盲人口数为15周岁及以上文盲和半文盲人口。文盲率是指15周岁及以上人口中，文盲人口和半文盲人口所占比重。

2. 本表与表3-2相同的指标数据不同，是因为本表数据为普查时点数，表3-2为年末时点数。1953年普查时点为7月1日零时；1964年普查时点为7月1日零时；1982年普查时点为7月1日零时；1990年普查时点为7月1日零时；2000年普查时点为11月1日零时；2010年普查时点为11月1日零时。

Note: a) Statistics on illiterate population covered the illiterate and semi-illiterate people at 12 and above in 1964, and those at 15 and above in 1982, 1990, 2000, and 2010. Illiteracy rate means the share of illiterate and semi-illiterate people in the population at 15 and above.

b) This table has the same indicators but different figures from 3-2, because this table uses the data at the time point of the census, while 3-2 uses the year end as the time point. The time point of the census in 1953 was 12 o'clock midnight, July 1st; the time point in 1964 was 12 o'clock midnight, July 1st; the time point in 1982 was 12 o'clock midnight, July 1st; the time point in 1990 was 12 o'clock midnight,July 1st; the time point in 2000 was 12 o'clock midnight, November 1st; the time point in 2010 was 12 o'clock midnight, November 1st.

3-2 常住人口(1978-2016年)
PERMANENT POPULATION (1978-2016)

年份 Year	常住人口(万人) Permanent Population (10000 persons)	#常住外来人口 Permanent Migrant Population	按性别分 By Sex		按城乡分 By Urban Area and Rural Area		常住人口密度(人/平方公里) Permanent Population Density (person/sq.km)	常住人口出生率(‰) Birth Rate (‰)	常住人口死亡率(‰) Death Rate (‰)	常住人口自然增长率(‰) Natural Growth Rate (‰)
			男 Male	女 Female	城镇人口 Urban Population	乡村人口 Rural Population				
1978	871.5	21.8	443.2	428.3	479.0	392.5	519	12.93	6.12	6.81
1979	897.1	26.5	454.6	442.5	510.3	386.8	534	13.67	5.92	7.75
1980	904.3	18.6	457.8	446.5	521.1	383.2	538	15.56	6.30	9.26
1981	919.2	18.4	465.9	453.3	533.3	385.9	547	16.93	6.02	10.91
1982	935.0	17.2	474.0	461.0	544.0	391.0	556	20.04	5.68	14.36
1983	950.0	16.8	483.0	467.0	557.0	393.0	565	15.63	5.49	10.14
1984	965.0	19.8	491.0	474.0	570.0	395.0	574	16.74	5.53	11.21
1985	981.0	23.1	500.0	481.0	586.0	395.0	584	15.45	5.75	9.70
1986	1028.0	56.8	524.0	504.0	621.0	407.0	612	15.82	4.47	11.35
1987	1047.0	59.0	525.0	522.0	637.0	410.0	623	17.29	5.40	11.89
1988	1061.0	59.8	534.0	527.0	650.0	411.0	631	14.43	5.08	9.35
1989	1075.0	53.9	538.0	537.0	664.0	411.0	640	12.84	5.35	7.49
1990	1086.0	53.8	545.0	541.0	798.0	288.0	646	13.04	5.81	7.23
1991	1094.0	54.5	547.0	547.0	808.0	286.0	651	8.03	5.82	2.21
1992	1102.0	57.1	554.0	548.0	819.0	283.0	656	9.22	6.11	3.11
1993	1112.0	60.8	559.0	553.0	831.0	281.0	662	9.35	6.16	3.19
1994	1125.0	63.2	564.0	561.0	846.0	279.0	669	8.96	5.76	3.20
1995	1251.1	180.8	627.0	624.1	946.2	304.9	744	7.92	5.12	2.80
1996	1259.4	181.7	639.0	620.4	957.9	301.5	749	8.02	5.34	2.68
1997	1240.0	154.5	628.7	611.3	948.3	291.7	738	7.91	6.02	1.89
1998	1245.6	154.1	630.6	615.0	957.7	287.9	741	6.00	5.30	0.70
1999	1257.2	157.4	636.4	620.8	971.7	285.5	748	6.50	5.60	0.90
2000	1363.6	256.1	710.9	652.7	1057.4	306.2	811	6.20	5.30	0.90
2001	1385.1	262.8	722.1	663.0	1081.2	303.9	824	6.10	5.30	0.80
2002	1423.2	286.9	743.1	680.1	1118.0	305.2	847	6.60	5.73	0.87
2003	1456.4	307.6	761.2	695.2	1151.3	305.1	867	5.06	5.15	-0.09
2004	1492.7	329.8	779.9	712.8	1187.2	305.5	910	6.13	5.39	0.74
2005	1538.0	357.3	778.7	759.3	1286.1	251.9	937	6.29	5.20	1.09
2006	1601.0	403.4	817.6	783.4	1350.2	250.8	976	6.22	4.94	1.28
2007	1676.0	462.7	850.8	825.2	1416.2	259.8	1021	8.16	4.83	3.33
2008	1771.0	541.1	900.2	870.8	1503.6	267.4	1079	7.89	4.59	3.30
2009	1860.0	614.2	949.8	910.2	1581.1	278.9	1133	7.66	4.33	3.33
2010	1961.9	704.7	1013.0	948.9	1686.4	275.5	1196	7.27	4.29	2.98
2011	2018.6	742.2	1040.7	977.9	1740.7	277.9	1230	8.29	4.27	4.02
2012	2069.3	773.8	1068.1	1001.2	1783.7	285.6	1261	9.05	4.31	4.74
2013	2114.8	802.7	1090.7	1024.1	1825.1	289.7	1289	8.93	4.52	4.41
2014	2151.6	818.7	1106.5	1045.1	1859.0	292.6	1311	9.75	4.92	4.83
2015	2170.5	822.6	1113.4	1057.1	1877.7	292.8	1323	7.96	4.95	3.01
2016	2172.9	807.5	1112.7	1060.2	1879.6	293.3	1324	9.32	5.20	4.12

注：1. 1978—1981年为户籍统计数，含暂住人口；1982—1989年数据是根据1982年、1990年两次人口普查数据调整的；1990年以后数据为人口变动情况抽样调查推算数，其中1995年、2005年为1%人口抽样调查推算数；2000年为第五次人口普查快速汇总推算数；2010年为第六次人口普查推算数。2006—2009年常住人口、出生率、死亡率等数据根据2010年人口普查数据进行了调整。

2. “按城乡分”栏包括的“城镇人口”和“乡村人口”，1978—1989年数据为户籍管理统计中的“非农业人口”和“农业人口”口径；1990—1999年数据是根据1990年、2000年两次人口普查数据调整的；2000年数据为国家统计局1999年发布的《关于统计上划分城乡的规定(试行)》中的“城镇人口”和“乡村人口”口径，2001—2005年数据为该口径的推算数；2006—2008年数据为国家统计局2006年发布的《关于统计上划分城乡的暂行规定》中的“城镇人口”和“乡村人口”口径的推算数；2009年以后数据为《国务院关于统计上划分城乡规定的批复》中的“城镇人口”和“乡村人口”口径的推算数。

Note: a) Statistics for 1978-1981 were figures of registered residents, including temporary residents; statistics for 1982-1989 were adjusted from population censuses in 1982 and 1990. Data after 1990 were estimated from sample surveys on population changes; data for 1995 and 2005 were estimated from sample surveys on 1% of the population. Data for 2000 were estimated from fast summarizing of the fifth population census. Data for 2010 were estimated from fast summarizing of the 6th population census. Data of permanant population, birth rate and death rate, etc. from 2006 to 2009 were adjusted from population census in 2010.

b) In classification by rural and urban areas, the "urban population" and "rural population" from 1978 to 1989 were non-agricultural population and agricultural population respectively in household registration. Data from 1990-1999 were adjusted from the population censuses conducted in 1990 and 2000, and those in 2000 were on the basis of statistical classification of rural and urban population stated in the Regulations on the Statistical Division of Rural and Urban Population (trial) issued by the State Statistical Bureau in 1999. Statistics from 2001 to 2005 were estimated on the same basis. Figures from 2006 to 2008 were the estimated figures of "urban population" and "rural population", of which the statistical range was provided in Provisional Regulations on Statistical Division of Rural and Urban Areas issued by the State Statistics Bureau in 2006. Figures after 2009 were the estimated figures of "urban population" and "ruralpopulation", of which the statistical range was provided in the Official Reply of the State Council Concerning the Statistical Division of Rural and Urban Areas.

3-3 常住人口总量及人口密度(按区分)(2016年)
TOTAL NUMBER AND DENSITY OF PERMANENT POPULATION (BY DISTRICT) (2016)

地区	District	常住人口(万人) Permanent Population (10000 persons)	#常住外来人口 Permanent Migrant Population	城镇人口 Urban Population	乡村人口 Rural Population	常住人口密度(人/平方公里) Permanent Population Density (person/sq.km)
全市	**Total**	**2172.9**	**807.5**	**1879.6**	**293.3**	**1324**
首都功能核心区	**Core Funtional Area of the Capital**	**213.7**	**48.4**	**213.7**		**23130**
东城区	Dongcheng District	87.8	19.2	87.8		20975
西城区	Xicheng District	125.9	29.2	125.9		24916
城市功能拓展区	**Urban Function Extension Area**	**1033.8**	**413.0**	**1025.6**	**8.2**	**8102**
朝阳区	Chaoyang District	385.6	174.8	384.7	0.9	8473
丰台区	Fengtai District	225.5	79.9	224.8	0.7	7374
石景山区	Shijingshan District	63.4	19.0	63.4		7519
海淀区	Haidian District	359.3	139.3	352.7	6.6	8342
城市发展新区	**New Area of Urban Development**	**730.3**	**313.9**	**516.7**	**213.6**	**1160**
房山区	Fangshan District	109.6	28.0	78.4	31.2	551
通州区	Tongzhou District	142.8	57.0	93.0	49.8	1576
顺义区	Shunyi District	107.5	43.0	59.0	48.5	1054
昌平区	Changping District	201.0	103.8	164.5	36.5	1496
大兴区	Daxing District	169.4	82.1	121.8	47.6	1635
生态涵养发展区	**Ecological Conservation Area**	**195.1**	**32.2**	**123.6**	**71.5**	**223**
门头沟区	Mentougou District	31.1	5.0	27.2	3.9	214
怀柔区	Huairou District	39.3	10.6	26.6	12.7	185
平谷区	Pinggu District	43.7	5.5	24.5	19.2	460
密云区	Miyun District	48.3	7.2	27.6	20.7	217
延庆区	Yanqing District	32.7	3.9	17.7	15.0	164

注：本表数据为人口抽样调查推算数据，为年末数。

Note: Figures in this table are estimated figures from sample survey on population in the end of year.

3-4 常住人口自然变动(按区分)(2016年)
NATURAL CHANGE OF PERMANENT POPULATION (BY DISTRICT) (2016)

地 区	District	出生人数 (人) Number of Births (person)	死亡人数 (人) Number of Deaths (person)	自然增加人数 (人) Natural Increase of Population (person)	出生率 (‰) Birth Rate (‰)	死亡率 (‰) Death Rate (‰)	自然增长率 (‰) Natural Growth Rate (‰)
全 市	**Total**	**202349**	**113000**	**89349**	**9.32**	**5.20**	**4.12**
首都功能核心区	**Capital Core Functional Area**	**18334**	**15911**	**2423**	**8.45**	**7.33**	**1.12**
东 城 区	Dongcheng District	7199	7136	63	8.07	8.00	0.07
西 城 区	Xicheng District	11135	8775	2360	8.71	6.86	1.85
城市功能拓展区	**Urban Function Extension Area**	**93874**	**46018**	**47856**	**8.96**	**4.39**	**4.57**
朝 阳 区	Chaoyang District	33402	15517	17885	8.55	3.97	4.58
丰 台 区	Fengtai District	24175	11366	12809	10.56	4.96	5.60
石景山区	Shijingshan District	5681	3742	1939	8.84	5.82	3.02
海 淀 区	Haidian District	30616	15393	15223	8.40	4.22	4.18
城市发展新区	**Urban Development New Area**	**70285**	**36280**	**34005**	**9.85**	**5.08**	**4.77**
房 山 区	Fangshan District	11778	6722	5056	11.00	6.28	4.72
通 州 区	Tongzhou District	10794	7052	3742	7.69	5.03	2.66
顺 义 区	Shunyi District	10921	7500	3421	10.42	7.16	3.26
昌 平 区	Changping Ddistrict	19795	8097	11698	9.96	4.07	5.89
大 兴 区	Daxing District	16997	6909	10088	10.44	4.24	6.20
生态涵养发展区	**Ecological Conservation Area**	**19856**	**14791**	**5065**	**10.29**	**7.67**	**2.62**
门头沟区	Mentougou District	3385	2524	861	10.92	8.14	2.78
怀 柔 区	Huairou District	4690	2574	2116	12.06	6.62	5.44
平 谷 区	Pinggu District	4635	3378	1257	10.78	7.86	2.92
密 云 区	Miyun District	4284	4426	-142	8.91	9.20	-0.29
延 庆 区	Yanqing District	2862	1889	973	8.92	5.88	3.04

注：本表数据为人口抽样调查推算数据。
Note: Figures in this table are estimated figures from the sample survey on population.

3-5 常住人口年龄构成(2016年)
PERMANENT POPULATION BY AGE COMPOSITION (2016)

年龄组 Age Group	常住人口数(万人) Permanent Population (10000 persons)	比重(%) Percentage (%)
合计 Total	**2172.9**	**100.0**
0-4	96.4	4.5
5-9	75.5	3.5
10-14	51.9	2.4
15-19	59.2	2.7
20-24	191.6	8.8
25-29	256.9	11.8
30-34	236.8	10.9
35-39	187.9	8.7
40-44	171.0	7.9
45-49	175.9	8.1
50-54	177.8	8.2
55-59	143.6	6.6
60-64	118.0	5.4
65-69	80.4	3.7
70-74	52.9	2.4
75-79	44.3	2.0
80-84	33.2	1.5
85岁及以上 85 and above	19.6	0.9

注：本表数据为人口抽样调查推算数据，为年末数。
Note: Figures in this table are estimated figures from the sample survey on population in the end of year.

3-6 常住人口受教育程度(2016年)
EDUCATION ATTAINMENT OF PERMANENT POPULATION (2016)

单位：人 (person)

项目	Item	调查人口合计 Total	男 Male	女 Female
6岁及以上人口	**Population at 6 and above**	**400887**	**201599**	**199288**
#小学	Primary School	46729	21242	25487
初中	Junior Secondary School	115058	61623	53435
普通高中	Senior Secondary School	58313	29436	28877
中职	Vocational School	27971	14504	13467
大学专科	Junior College	53540	26450	27090
大学本科	4-year Unversity Education	72754	36728	36026
研究生	Postgraduate	18142	9497	8645

注：本表数据为人口抽样调查样本数据。
Note: Figures in this table are sample figures from the sample survey on population.

3-7 常住人口家庭户规模(2016年)
FAMILY SIZE OF PERMANENT POPULATION (2016)

地区	Area	调查家庭总户数(户) Total Number of Households (household)	家庭户规模所占比重(%) Percentage of Various Sized Family (%)				
			一人户 One Person	二人户 Two Persons	三人户 Three Persons	四人户 Four Persons	五人及以上户 Five Persons and above
全市	**Total**	**154028**	**20.1**	**31.3**	**27.8**	**10.8**	**10.1**
城镇	Urban	125300	20.3	31.0	29.2	10.5	9.0
乡村	Rural	28728	19.1	32.4	21.8	11.9	14.9

注：本表数据为人口抽样调查样本数据。
Note: Figures in this table are sample figures from the sample survey on population.

3-8 户籍人口(1978-2016年)
REGISTERED POPULATION (1978-2016)

单位：万人 (10000 persons)

年份 Year	户籍户数(万户) Registered Households (10000 households)	户籍人口 Registered Population	#60岁及以上人口 Population at 60 and obove	按性别分 By Sex		按户籍性质分 By Type of Household Register		户籍人口出生人数 Births of Registered Population	户籍人口死亡人数 Deaths of Registered Population	户籍人口自然增加人数 Natural Increase of Registered Population
				男 Male	女 Female	非农业户 Non-Agricultural	农业户 Agricultural			
1978	205.5	849.7		432.1	417.5	467.0	382.6	10.9	5.2	5.7
1979	214.6	870.6		441.1	429.4	495.2	375.4	11.8	5.1	6.7
1980	223.2	885.7		448.4	437.3	510.4	375.3	13.7	5.5	8.2
1981	234.8	900.8		456.6	444.2	522.6	378.2	15.1	5.4	9.7
1982	245.0	917.8		465.5	452.3	534.0	383.8	18.2	5.2	13.1
1983	255.1	933.2		474.7	458.5	547.1	386.0	14.5	5.1	9.4
1984	263.1	945.2		481.2	464.0	558.1	387.0	13.2	5.1	8.1
1985	274.1	957.9		488.0	469.9	572.5	385.4	11.8	5.2	6.6
1986	284.6	971.2		495.5	475.7	586.8	384.4	12.9	5.2	7.8
1987	299.4	988.0		504.1	483.9	601.0	387.0	16.9	5.3	11.6
1988	310.8	1001.2		510.4	490.8	614.3	387.0	15.3	5.5	9.8
1989	322.5	1021.1		520.3	500.8	630.6	390.5	19.0	5.7	13.3
1990	335.0	1032.2		525.3	507.0	640.2	392.1	14.0	6.3	7.7
1991	343.1	1039.5		528.5	511.1	648.4	391.2	9.2	5.7	3.5
1992	349.3	1044.9		530.8	514.1	656.3	388.6	8.3	6.2	2.2
1993	354.6	1051.2		533.9	517.3	668.7	382.5	7.9	6.3	1.6
1994	360.3	1061.8		538.9	522.8	683.8	377.9	8.5	6.3	2.2
1995	365.7	1070.3		543.0	527.3	696.9	373.5	8.5	6.2	2.3
1996	370.9	1077.7		546.8	530.9	709.7	368.0	7.8	6.7	1.2
1997	375.7	1085.5		550.4	535.1	722.7	362.9	7.6	6.7	0.9
1998	383.4	1091.5		552.6	538.9	733.6	357.8	6.7	7.5	-0.8
1999	390.3	1099.8		556.7	543.1	747.2	352.6	6.3	6.2	0.1
2000	397.9	1107.5		560.1	547.4	760.7	346.8	7.2	7.8	-0.5
2001	405.3	1122.3		567.3	555.0	780.2	342.2	6.0	5.3	0.7
2002	416.3	1136.3		574.7	561.6	806.9	329.4	6.0	5.2	0.8
2003	427.6	1148.8		581.0	567.9	830.8	318.0	4.5	5.8	-1.3
2004	439.8	1162.9		587.2	575.7	854.7	308.2	6.6	6.2	0.4
2005	451.7	1180.7		596.0	584.7	880.2	300.5	7.5	7.0	0.5
2006	463.7	1197.6		604.2	593.4	905.4	292.2	7.7	5.1	2.6
2007	473.0	1213.3	210.3	612.0	601.3	929.0	284.3	9.9	5.2	4.8
2008	481.2	1229.9	218.6	620.0	609.9	950.7	279.2	10.6	5.1	5.5
2009	488.7	1245.8	228.7	627.5	618.9	971.9	273.9	10.9	6.2	4.7
2010	496.1	1257.8	237.2	632.8	625.0	989.5	268.3	10.2	9.1	1.1
2011	503.1	1277.9	250.5	642.4	635.6	1013.8	264.2	12.5	5.3	7.2
2012	509.2	1297.5	266.1	651.7	645.8	1039.3	258.2	14.5	5.7	8.8
2013	516.2	1316.3	283.2	660.4	655.9	1065.0	251.4	13.6	5.7	7.9
2014	522.6	1333.4	301.0	668.3	665.1	1089.8	243.6	17.2	7.6	9.6
2015	529.2	1345.2	318.0	673.3	671.9	1111.3	233.8	12.3	7.3	4.9
2016	538.2	1362.9	334.4	681.5	681.4	1132.0	230.9	20.5	8.9	11.6

资料来源：北京市公安局。
Source: Beijing Municipal Bureau of Public Security.

3-9 户籍户数、人口数及性别比(按区分)(2016年)
REGISTERED HOUSEHOLDS AND SEX RATIO OF REGISTERED POPULATION (BY DISTRICT) (2016)

地区	District	户数(万户) Households (10000 households)	人口数(万人) Population (10000 persons)					性别比(女=100) Sex Ratio (female=100)
		合计 Total	合计 Total	非农业 Non-Agricultural	农业 Agricultural	男 Male	女 Female	
全市	**Total**	**538.2**	**1362.9**	**1132.0**	**230.9**	**681.5**	**681.4**	**100.0**
首都功能核心区	**Capital Core Functional Area**	**83.8**	**243.9**	**243.9**	**0.0**	**120.8**	**123.1**	**98.1**
东城区	Dongcheng District	34.7	97.4	97.4	0.0	47.9	49.5	96.8
西城区	Xicheng District	49.1	146.5	146.5	0.0	72.9	73.6	99.0
城市功能拓展区	**Urban Function Extension Area**	**218.7**	**605.1**	**583.0**	**22.2**	**303.8**	**301.4**	**100.8**
朝阳区	Chaoyang District	82.8	210.9	201.6	9.3	105.4	105.5	**100.0**
丰台区	Fengtai District	47.7	115.3	106.6	8.7	58.4	56.9	102.5
石景山区	Shijingshan District	14.9	38.7	38.7		19.9	18.8	105.5
海淀区	Haidian District	73.3	240.2	236.0	4.2	120.1	120.1	100.0
城市发展新区	**Urban Development New Area**	**142.6**	**348.2**	**216.9**	**131.4**	**173.7**	**174.5**	**99.5**
房山区	Fangshan District	12.1	81.3	48.9	32.4	40.8	40.5	100.6
通州区	Tongzhou District	38.4	74.7	47.5	27.1	37.1	37.6	98.6
顺义区	Shunyi District	37.6	62.7	37.6	25.2	31.1	31.6	98.4
昌平区	Changping District	27.2	61.1	43.3	17.8	30.7	30.4	101.0
大兴区	Daxing District	27.3	68.4	39.5	28.8	34.0	34.4	99.0
生态涵养发展区	**Ecological Conservation Area**	**93.1**	**165.6**	**88.3**	**77.4**	**83.2**	**82.4**	**101.0**
门头沟区	Mentougou District	27.6	25.1	20.6	4.5	12.8	12.3	103.8
怀柔区	Huairou District	13.6	28.3	13.7	14.6	14.1	14.2	99.8
平谷区	Pinggu District	17.1	40.2	21.9	18.3	20.2	20.0	101.2
密云区	Miyun District	20.7	43.6	18.9	24.7	21.8	21.8	99.8
延庆区	Yanqing District	14.2	28.4	13.1	15.3	14.3	14.1	101.5

资料来源：北京市公安局。
Source: Beijing Municipal Bureau of Public Security.

3-10 户籍人口年龄构成(2016年)
AGE COMPOSITION OF REGISTERED POPULATION (2016)

年龄组 Age Group	户籍人口(万人) Registered Population (10000 persons)			占人口比重(%) Percentage (%)		
	合计 Total	男 Male	女 Female	合计 Total	男 Male	女 Female
合计 Total	**1362.9**	**681.5**	**681.4**	**100.0**	**50.0**	**50.0**
0-4	74.7	38.5	36.1	5.5	2.8	2.7
5-9	54.3	28.1	26.3	4.0	2.1	1.9
10-14	35.7	18.4	17.3	2.6	1.4	1.3
15-19	44.8	22.5	22.3	3.3	1.7	1.6
20-24	69.7	34.7	35.0	5.1	2.5	2.6
25-29	105.0	53.3	51.7	7.7	3.9	3.8
30-34	117.9	59.2	58.6	8.6	4.3	4.3
35-39	100.6	50.7	49.9	7.4	3.7	3.7
40-44	86.4	43.8	42.6	6.3	3.2	3.1
45-49	106.2	53.4	52.8	7.8	3.9	3.9
50-54	124.8	63.7	61.1	9.2	4.7	4.5
55-59	108.3	54.4	53.9	7.9	4.0	4.0
60-64	109.9	53.7	56.3	8.1	3.9	4.1
65-69	70.1	34.2	35.9	5.1	2.5	2.6
70-74	46.3	21.8	24.5	3.4	1.6	1.8
75-79	43.4	19.9	23.5	3.2	1.5	1.7
80-84	36.5	17.5	19.0	2.7	1.3	1.4
85-89	18.6	9.0	9.5	1.4	0.7	0.7
90岁及以上 90 and above	9.6	4.6	5.0	0.7	0.3	0.4

资料来源：北京市公安局。
Source: Beijing Municipal Bureau of Public Security.

3-11 户籍人口变动情况
CHANGES OF REGISTERED POPULATION

单位：人 (person)

项　　目	Item	2016	2015
自然变动	**Natural Changes**		
自然增加	Natural Increase	116219	49366
非农业人口	Non-agricultural Population	115011	60071
农业人口	Agricultural Population	1208	-10705
出　生	Births	205153	122627
非农业人口	Non-agricultural Population	181374	112197
农业人口	Agricultural Population	23779	10430
死　亡	Deaths	88934	73261
非农业人口	Non-agricultural Population	66363	52126
农业人口	Agricultural Population	22571	21135
机械变动	**Non-natural Changes**		
机械增加	Non-natural Increase	60988	75497
非农业人口	Non-agricultural Population	52636	66282
农业人口	Agricultural Population	8352	9215
市外迁入	Inflow	160739	167506
非农业人口	Non-agricultural Population	151192	157074
农业人口	Agricultural Population	9547	10432
迁往市外	Outflow	99751	92009
非农业人口	Non-agricultural Population	98556	90792
农业人口	Agricultural Population	1195	1217

资料来源：北京市公安局。
Source: Beijing Municipal Bureau of Public Security.

3-12 户籍人口自然变动情况(按区分)
NATURAL CHANGES OF REGISTERED POPULATION (BY DISTRICT)

单位：人 (person)

地 区	District	出生人数 Number of Births		死亡人数 Number of Deaths		自然增加人数 Number of Natural Increase	
		2016	2015	2016	2015	2016	2015
全 市	**Total**	**205153**	**122627**	**88934**	**73261**	**116219**	**49366**
首都功能核心区	**Capital Core Functional Area**	**30572**	**22435**	**23814**	**22704**	**6758**	**-269**
东 城 区	Dongcheng District	11719	8814	13776	16645	-2057	-7831
西 城 区	Xicheng District	18853	13621	10038	6059	8815	7562
城市功能拓展区	**Urban Function Extension Area**	**83175**	**54822**	**31421**	**21420**	**51754**	**33402**
朝 阳 区	Chaoyang District	31800	21146	9246	8020	22554	13126
丰 台 区	Fengtai District	15575	9672	5078	4905	10497	4767
石景山区	Shijingshan District	5072	3236	1795	1580	3277	1656
海 淀 区	Haidian District	30728	20768	15302	6915	15426	13853
城市发展新区	**Urban Development New Area**	**66878**	**33093**	**20123**	**18376**	**46755**	**14717**
房 山 区	Fangshan District	13997	6630	4498	4392	9499	2238
通 州 区	Tongzhou District	14743	7193	5253	4267	9490	2926
顺 义 区	Shunyi District	11518	5655	3662	3660	7856	1995
昌 平 区	Changping District	11859	6443	3020	2928	8839	3515
大 兴 区	Daxing District	14761	7172	3690	3129	11071	4043
生态涵养发展区	**Ecological Conservation Area**	**24528**	**12277**	**13576**	**10761**	**10952**	**1516**
门头沟区	Mentougou District	3132	1635	1268	1448	1864	187
怀 柔 区	Huairou District	4365	2335	2548	1788	1817	547
平 谷 区	Pinggu District	6817	3157	4777	3030	2040	127
密 云 区	Miyun District	6095	3133	3109	2733	2986	400
延 庆 区	Yanqing District	4119	2017	1874	1762	2245	255

资料来源：北京市公安局。
Source: Beijing Municipal Bureau of Public Security.

3-13 户籍人口机械变动情况(按区分)
NON-NATURAL CHANGES OF REGISTERED POPULATION (BY DISTRICT)

单位：人 (person)

地　区	District	市外迁入 Inflow		迁往市外 Outflow		机械增加 Non-natural Increase	
		2016	2015	2016	2015	2016	2015
全　市	**Total**	**160739**	**167506**	**99751**	**92009**	**60988**	**75497**
首都功能核心区	**Capital Core Functional Area**	**18827**	**19803**	**4402**	**4221**	**14425**	**15582**
东 城 区	Dongcheng District	5939	5911	1063	1040	4876	4871
西 城 区	Xicheng District	12888	13892	3339	3181	9549	10711
城市功能拓展区	**Urban Function Extension Area**	**112908**	**118376**	**85258**	**77585**	**27650**	**40791**
朝 阳 区	Chaoyang District	24967	29162	15546	14754	9421	14408
丰 台 区	Fengtai District	8272	9818	2513	2594	5759	7224
石景山区	Shijingshan District	3172	3412	1215	1214	1957	2198
海 淀 区	Haidian District	76497	75984	65984	59023	10513	16961
城市发展新区	**Urban Development New Area**	**24236**	**23770**	**9162**	**9227**	**15074**	**14543**
房 山 区	Fangshan District	3464	3102	394	431	3070	2671
通 州 区	Tongzhou District	4269	3568	735	703	3534	2865
顺 义 区	Shunyi District	2660	2646	687	839	1973	1807
昌 平 区	Changping District	8349	8912	5574	5598	2775	3314
大 兴 区	Daxing District	5494	5542	1772	1656	3722	3886
生态涵养发展区	**Ecological Conservation Area**	**4768**	**5557**	**929**	**976**	**3839**	**4581**
门头沟区	Mentougou District	841	1029	107	135	734	894
怀 柔 区	Huairou District	878	986	164	173	714	813
平 谷 区	Pinggu District	1034	1150	233	251	801	899
密 云 区	Miyun District	1158	1480	253	253	905	1227
延 庆 区	Yanqing District	857	912	172	164	685	748

资料来源：北京市公安局。
Source: Beijing Municipal Bureau of Public Security.

3-14 三次产业从业人员年末人数及构成(1978-2016年)
EMPLOYED PERSONS IN THREE INDUSTRIES AND THEIR COMPOSITION (1978-2016)

年 份 Year	从业人员年末人数（万人） Year-end Employed Persons (10000 persons)				构 成(%) (合计=100) Composition (%) (Total=100)		
		第一产业 Primary Industry	第二产业 Secondary Industry	第三产业 Tertiary Industry	第一产业 Primary Industry	第二产业 Secondary Industry	第三产业 Tertiary Industry
1978	444.1	125.9	177.9	140.3	28.3	40.1	31.6
1979	470.5	121.4	195.2	153.9	25.8	41.5	32.7
1980	484.2	118.0	207.3	158.9	24.4	42.8	32.8
1981	511.7	117.2	220.4	174.1	22.9	43.1	34.0
1982	535.2	115.1	228.6	191.5	21.5	42.7	35.8
1983	552.0	117.1	240.2	194.7	21.2	43.5	35.3
1984	556.2	111.3	247.9	197.0	20.0	44.6	35.4
1985	566.5	100.6	260.4	205.5	17.7	46.0	36.3
1986	572.7	96.1	262.7	213.9	16.8	45.9	37.3
1987	580.2	92.3	264.1	223.8	15.9	45.5	38.6
1988	584.1	88.4	267.6	228.1	15.1	45.8	39.1
1989	593.9	91.0	266.3	236.6	15.3	44.9	39.8
1990	627.1	90.7	281.6	254.8	14.5	44.9	40.6
1991	634.0	90.8	279.7	263.5	14.3	44.1	41.6
1992	649.3	84.5	281.6	283.2	13.0	43.4	43.6
1993	627.8	65.1	279.4	283.3	10.4	44.5	45.1
1994	664.3	73.2	272.2	318.9	11.0	41.0	48.0
1995	665.3	70.6	271.0	323.7	10.6	40.7	48.7
1996	660.2	72.5	260.1	327.6	11.0	39.4	49.6
1997	655.8	71.0	257.6	327.2	10.8	39.2	50.0
1998	622.2	71.5	226.0	324.7	11.5	36.3	52.2
1999	618.6	74.5	216.2	327.9	12.1	34.9	53.0
2000	619.3	72.9	208.2	338.2	11.8	33.6	54.6
2001	628.9	71.2	215.9	341.8	11.3	34.3	54.4
2002	679.2	67.6	235.3	376.3	10.0	34.6	55.4
2003	703.3	62.7	225.8	414.8	8.9	32.1	59.0
2004	854.1	61.5	232.8	559.8	7.2	27.3	65.5
2005	878.0	62.2	231.1	584.7	7.1	26.3	66.6
2006	919.7	60.3	225.4	634.0	6.6	24.5	68.9
2007	942.7	60.9	228.1	653.7	6.5	24.2	69.3
2008	980.9	63.0	207.4	710.5	6.4	21.2	72.4
2009	998.3	62.2	199.6	736.5	6.2	20.0	73.8
2010	1031.6	61.4	202.7	767.5	6.0	19.6	74.4
2011	1069.7	59.1	219.2	791.4	5.5	20.5	74.0
2012	1107.3	57.3	212.6	837.4	5.2	19.2	75.6
2013	1141.0	55.4	210.9	874.7	4.8	18.5	76.7
2014	1156.7	52.4	209.9	894.4	4.5	18.2	77.3
2015	1186.1	50.3	200.8	935.0	4.2	17.0	78.8
2016	1220.1	49.6	193.0	977.5	4.1	15.8	80.1

注：1．2010年及以前，劳务派遣人员按照“谁发工资谁统计”的原则进行统计。2011年以后，劳务派遣人员按照“谁用工谁统计”的原则进行统计。
2．自2012年开始，三次产业划分执行国家统计局《三次产业划分规定》(国统字〔2012〕108号)。

Note: a) In 2010 and before, dispatched personnel of labor service were calculated by "wage payers". After 2011, dispatched personnel of labor service were calculated by "employers".
b) Since 2012, the three industries have been classified according to the Regulations on the Classification of the Three Industries (G.T.Z. [2012] No. 108) issued by National Bureau of Statistics.

3-15 按登记注册类型分从业人员年末人数(1978-2016年)
YEAR-END EMPLOYED PERSONS BY TYPE OF REGISTRATION (1978-2016)

单位：万人 (10000 persons)

年 份 Year	合 计 Total	#城 镇 Urban	#国有单位 State-owned Enterprises	#集体单位 Collectively-owned Enterprises	#联营单位 Associated Enterprises	#有限责任公司 Limited Liability Companies	#股份有限公司 Companies Limited by Shares	#外商投资 Foreign-invested	#港澳台商投资 Hong Kong, Macao and Taiwan-invested	#私 营 Private Enterprises	#个 体 Individual Economy
1978	444.1	291.6	240.9	50.7							
1979	470.5	311.9	254.2	57.8							
1980	484.2	326.8	269.4	57.1							0.3
1981	511.7	345.2	283.1	61.3							
1982	535.2	361.1	293.0	67.1							
1983	552.0	373.8	303.4	68.5							
1984	556.2	377.6	302.5	71.6				1.3			
1985	566.5	392.6	308.1	72.6				1.6			2.5
1986	572.7	400.5	324.4	71.1				2.4			2.6
1987	580.2	408.3	331.8	70.7				2.8			3.1
1988	584.1	413.9	336.4	69.9	0.2			3.4			3.5
1989	593.9	424.0	343.8	67.4	3.4			3.7			5.6
1990	627.1	461.2	357.9	86.8	5.1			4.6			6.3
1991	634.0	477.2	367.8	89.0	0.5			7.7	0.2		7.2
1992	649.3	490.6	371.5	90.5	0.4			11.4	0.2		14.0
1993	627.8	481.4	362.3	79.7	2.8			11.0	6.4		14.0
1994	664.3	492.7	363.5	73.3	3.5			15.0	9.4		20.9
1995	665.3	492.7	358.2	72.1	3.7			17.4	10.0		21.9
1996	660.2	495.7	355.1	68.6	3.4			20.7	10.1		22.9
1997	655.8	498.7	354.7	68.5	3.2			21.2	10.2		21.2
1998	622.2	463.2	308.1	51.0	5.2	13.7	10.8	21.2	13.1		20.1
1999	618.6	456.1	287.6	49.7	4.8	24.0	12.2	20.6	13.5		23.7
2000	619.3	456.3	266.2	48.3	4.0	34.2	14.0	23.8	14.2		24.4
2001	628.9	464.2	246.3	45.8	4.1	50.6	17.3	22.4	12.9		24.8
2002	679.2	513.6	224.8	36.8	4.1	85.0	27.1	29.2	17.0	4.8	33.1
2003	703.3	533.7	212.8	30.1	3.8	102.3	33.4	31.5	17.3	5.2	37.2
2004	854.1	682.7	199.5	28.2	3.5	134.5	37.9	45.0	18.3	134.2	45.7
2005	878.0	694.0	195.0	23.8	2.4	149.4	36.4	49.6	21.7	131.2	57.2
2006	919.7	734.2	189.3	18.8	2.1	165.1	35.5	57.3	23.5	154.8	65.6
2007	942.7	745.4	189.3	17.3	1.9	179.5	38.7	69.3	28.8	133.8	67.2
2008	980.9	813.7	187.8	24.8	2.2	196.4	46.4	72.9	33.5	159.6	65.1
2009	998.3	856.6	185.7	24.3	0.9	215.7	58.4	71.2	36.6	172.2	67.5
2010	1031.6	905.4	189.0	22.7	0.9	228.2	64.7	74.9	42.4	193.5	65.3
2011	1069.7	955.8	188.8	20.1	0.7	243.0	75.9	90.1	50.6	210.6	59.3
2012	1107.3	996.1	188.3	19.8	0.7	261.6	83.2	92.7	54.3	227.9	50.8
2013	1141.0	1073.0	189.5	17.5	0.7	278.0	85.4	96.1	56.1	265.9	64.8
2014	1156.7	1066.2	188.6	18.8	0.5	290.6	86.2	94.5	58.7	254.6	55.7
2015	1186.1	1107.1	182.9	16.9	0.4	300.3	103.5	90.6	59.7	273.3	56.4
2016	1220.1	1141.1	188.1	13.9	0.3	305.1	116.9	81.6	61.2	298.4	51.4

资料来源：表中2002-2013年私营从业人员数据来源于北京市工商行政管理局，2014-2016年数据根据劳动工资年报全面调查和抽样调查推算得到；个体从业人员数据来源于北京市工商行政管理局。

Source: Figures of employed persons in private enterprises from 2002 to 2013 in this table were from Beijing Administration for Industry and Commerce. Figures in 2014 were calculated based on comprehensive and sample surveys in annual report on employee salary; and figures on self-employed individuals were from Beijing Administration for Industry and Commerce.

3-16 全市法人单位从业人员年末人数和平均工资
YEAR-END EMPLOYED PERSONS IN LEGAL ENTITIES AND AVERAGE WAGES

项目	Item	从业人员年末人数（万人）Year-end Employed Persons (10000 persons)		从业人员平均工资（元）Average Wage (yuan)	
		2016	2015	2016	2015
合计	**Total**	**1089.7**	**1050.7**	**105161**	**97616**
按登记注册类型分	**By Registration Type**				
内资	Domestically-invested Enterprises	946.9	900.4	97665	89949
国有	State-owned Enterprises	188.1	182.9	125419	115098
集体	Collectively-owned Enterprises	13.9	16.9	59150	49717
股份合作	Joint-equity Cooperative Enterprises	5.2	5.2	47536	43749
联营	Associated Enterprises	0.3	0.4	75502	71428
有限责任公司	Limited Liability Companies	305.1	300.3	97340	89353
股份有限公司	Companies Limited by Shares	116.9	103.5	147798	140491
私营	Private Enterprises	298.2	273.3	65881	58689
其他	Others	19.2	17.9	60643	55352
港、澳、台商投资	Hong Kong, Macao and Taiwan-invested Enterprises	61.2	59.7	139304	127552
外商投资	Foreign-invested Enterprises	81.6	90.6	165761	157966
按国民经济行业分	**By Sector**				
农、林、牧、渔业	Agriculture, Forestry, Animal Production and Hunting, Fishing	4.9	5.1	48682	47210
采矿业	Mining and Quarrying	4.6	5.3	90575	87853
制造业	Manufacturing	110.7	119.0	89079	80634
电力、热力、燃气及水生产和供应业	Production and Distribution of Electricity, Heating Power, Gas and Water	9.5	8.6	130888	125813
建筑业	Construction	67.7	66.4	76055	70625
批发和零售业	Wholesale and Retail Trade	127.5	129.5	81940	75843
交通运输、仓储和邮政业	Transport, Storage and Post	64.1	66.8	86222	77542
住宿和餐饮业	Lodging and Catering Services	42.0	42.6	51327	48497
信息传输、软件和信息技术服务业	Information Transmission, Software and Information Technology Services	92.9	92.2	155638	141333
金融业	Financial Intermediation	53.8	50.9	233561	240844
房地产业	Real Estate	59.0	53.7	93353	82760
租赁和商务服务业	Leasing and Business Services	168.8	142.9	90682	88683
科学研究和技术服务业	Scientific Research and Development, Technical Services	99.8	88.5	119492	110659
水利、环境和公共设施管理业	Management of Water Conservancy, Environment and Public Facilities	12.8	12.4	72893	69042
居民服务、修理和其他服务业	Resident Service, Repair and Other Services	18.2	17.6	46230	44740
教育	Education	52.4	50.7	116588	107713
卫生和社会工作	Health Care and Social Works	30.6	28.8	142394	135008
文化、体育和娱乐业	Culture, Sports and Entertainment	23.4	23.0	124201	113632
公共管理、社会保障和社会组织	Public Management, Social Security and Social Organizations	47.0	46.7	101999	91030
国际组织	International Organizations				

3–17 城镇单位在岗职工年末人数及工资总额(1978–2016年)
YEAR-END NUMBER AND WAGES OF FULLY EMPLOYED STAFF AND WORKERS IN URBAN ENTITIES (1978-2016)

年 份 Year	在岗职工年末人数(万人) Year-end Fully Employed Staff and Workers (10000 persons)	国有单位 State-owned	集体单位 Collectively-owned	其他单位 Others	在岗职工工资总额(亿元) Total Wages of Fully Employed Staff and Workers (100 million yuan)	国有单位 State-owned	集体单位 Collectively-owned	其他单位 Others
1978	291.6	240.9	50.7		18.7	16.2	2.5	
1979	311.9	254.2	57.7		22.4	19.4	3.0	
1980	326.5	269.4	57.1		26.9	23.3	3.6	
1981–1985					**183.7**	**153.7**	**29.6**	**0.4**
1981	344.4	283.1	61.3		28.3	24.2	4.1	
1982	360.1	293.0	67.1		30.5	25.9	4.6	
1983	371.9	303.4	68.5		33.8	28.5	5.3	
1984	375.4	302.5	71.6	1.3	40.4	33.7	6.6	0.1
1985	382.3	308.1	72.6	1.6	50.7	41.5	9.0	0.3
1986–1990					**421.1**	**349.7**	**64.4**	**7.0**
1986	397.9	324.4	71.1	2.4	58.0	48.5	9.1	0.4
1987	405.2	331.8	70.7	2.7	66.7	56.0	10.1	0.6
1988	410.4	336.4	69.9	4.1	81.2	68.1	12.1	1.0
1989	418.4	343.8	67.4	7.2	96.3	81.0	13.4	1.9
1990	454.9	357.9	86.8	10.2	118.9	96.1	19.7	3.1
1991–1995					**1198.1**	**950.3**	**156.6**	**91.2**
1991	470.0	367.8	89.0	13.2	132.2	106.1	21.5	4.6
1992	476.6	371.5	90.5	14.6	158.5	128.6	23.9	6.0
1993	467.3	362.3	79.6	25.4	218.9	176.6	28.5	13.8
1994	471.8	363.5	73.4	34.9	306.5	243.4	36.2	26.9
1995	470.9	358.2	72.1	40.6	382.0	295.6	46.5	39.9
1996–2000					**2825.4**	**1988.5**	**236.5**	**600.4**
1996	460.6	349.0	64.8	46.8	442.4	339.4	46.2	56.8
1997	465.3	348.7	65.0	51.6	514.8	383.6	53.8	77.4
1998	450.1	321.7	50.8	77.6	558.2	391.9	45.0	121.3
1999	438.0	303.0	49.6	85.4	614.5	420.0	44.8	149.7
2000	434.2	283.0	46.0	105.2	695.5	453.6	46.7	195.2
2001–2005					**5662.3**	**2872.7**	**184.6**	**2605.0**
2001	400.3	235.9	40.0	124.4	777.3	477.8	44.8	254.7
2002	434.2	212.6	32.7	188.9	950.9	508.8	40.0	402.1
2003	436.3	197.6	26.1	212.6	1098.9	565.5	35.0	498.4
2004	446.4	183.7	24.8	237.9	1315.1	625.7	34.0	655.4
2005	448.4	178.5	20.7	249.2	1520.1	694.9	30.8	794.4
2006–2010					**13890.4**	**4904.7**	**219.9**	**8765.8**
2006	453.1	172.9	16.4	263.8	1805.5	738.0	30.5	1037.0
2007	478.9	172.7	15.4	290.8	2194.3	862.4	31.2	1300.7
2008	526.1	171.0	22.7	332.4	2874.3	1008.8	48.2	1817.3
2009	560.4	170.9	22.4	367.1	3227.2	1074.3	53.3	2099.6
2010	587.7	175.1	21.1	391.5	3789.1	1221.2	56.7	2511.2
2011–2015					**32457.0**	**8671.8**	**367.1**	**23418.1**
2011	640.3	177.1	18.7	444.5	4778.6	1421.1	62.3	3295.2
2012	670.4	177.3	18.6	474.5	5657.9	1582.5	71.6	4003.8
2013	695.5	178.4	16.5	500.6	6502.0	1724.7	70.2	4707.1
2014	708.8	177.7	17.8	513.3	7293.3	1884.5	81.5	5327.3
2015	724.8	172.8	16.0	536.0	8225.2	2059.0	81.5	6084.7
2016	733.5	178.0	13.1	542.4	9005.0	2299.0	80.1	6625.9

注：1．2007年及以前城镇单位是指乡及乡以上独立核算法人单位，不包括乡镇企业、私营单位和个体工商户。2008年及以后城镇单位是指不包括私营单位和个体工商户的独立核算法人单位(下表同)。

2．表中2000年及以前数据为职工口径，职工包括在岗职工和不在岗职工(下表同)。

Note: a) Urban entities in and before 2007 referred to legal entities with independent accounting at and above township level, excluding township enterprises, private entities and self-employed businesses. Urban entities in and after 2008 referred to legal entities with independent accounting excluding private entities and self-employed businesses (the same to the follow s).

b) Figures before 2001 were counted by the statistical range of employees including on-the-job and off-the-job ones (the same to the follow tables).

3-18 城镇单位在岗职工平均工资(1978-2016年)
AVERAGE WAGES OF FULLY EMPLOYED STAFF AND WORKERS IN URBAN ENTITIES (1978-2016)

单位：元 (yuan)

年份 Year	在岗职工平均工资 Average Wage of Fully Employed Staff and Workers	国有单位 State-owned Enterprises	集体单位 Collectively-owned Enterprises	其他单位 Others
1978	673	703	471	
1979	742	778	556	
1980	848	889	635	
1981	837	880	685	
1982	863	896	715	
1983	931	964	785	
1984	1086	1127	946	1170
1985	1343	1367	1231	1768
1986	1488	1530	1287	2080
1987	1670	1712	1449	2267
1988	2000	2048	1738	2661
1989	2312	2366	1992	2761
1990	2653	2713	2334	3243
1991	2877	2937	2504	3713
1992	3402	3500	2828	4289
1993	4780	4920	3834	5469
1994	6540	6695	5009	8179
1995	8144	8237	6516	10278
1996	9579	9645	7133	13851
1997	11019	10917	8259	15370
1998	12285	11971	8800	15989
1999	13778	13483	8928	17748
2000	15726	15483	9844	19165
2001	19155	19776	11063	20594
2002	21852	23754	11997	21432
2003	25312	28464	13580	23769
2004	29674	34009	13422	28026
2005	34191	39067	14695	32324
2006	40117	43298	17781	39513
2007	46507	50524	20379	45508
2008	54913	59361	20990	54983
2009	58140	63239	23553	57911
2010	65683	70320	26607	65755
2011	75834	81215	32469	75584
2012	85307	90456	38596	85234
2013	93997	97356	42482	94513
2014	103400	106097	45772	104473
2015	113073	119046	49969	113066
2016	122749	129542	59507	122096

3-19 城镇单位在岗职工年末人数
YEAR-END NUMBER OF FULLY EMPLOYED STAFF AND WORKERS IN URBAN ENTITIES

单位：人 (person)

项　　目	Item	2016	2015	2016年为2015年% 2016 as % of 2015
合　计	**Total**	**7335386**	**7247899**	**101.2**
按登记注册类型分	**By Registration Type**			
内　资	Domestically-invested Enterprises	6016239	5844677	102.9
国　有	State-owned Enterprises	1779807	1727534	103.0
集　体	Collectively-owned Enterprises	131296	160286	81.9
股份合作	Joint-equity Cooperative Enterprises	48746	48550	100.4
联　营	Associated Enterprises	3169	3475	91.2
有限责任公司	Limited Liability Companies	2832045	2816740	100.5
股份有限公司	Companies Limited By Shares	1055009	931042	113.3
其他	Others	166167	157050	105.8
港、澳、台商投资	Hong Kong, Macao and Taiwan-invested Enterprises	569228	561729	101.3
外商投资	Foreign-invested Enterprises	749919	841493	89.1
按国民经济行业分	**By Sector**			
农、林、牧、渔业	Agriculture, Forestry, Animal Production and Hunting, Fishing	35912	38024	94.4
#农　业	Agriculture	15128	14732	102.7
采矿业	Mining and Quarrying	45183	52733	85.7
制造业	Manufacturing	846574	898403	94.2
电力、热力、燃气及水生产和供应业	Production and Distribution of Electricity, Heating Power, Gas and Water	88864	80247	110.7
建筑业	Construction	429130	417942	102.7
批发和零售业	Wholesale and Retail Trade	699532	706228	99.1
批发业	Wholesale	396310	398156	99.5
零售业	Retail Trade	303222	308072	98.4
交通运输、仓储和邮政业	Transport, Storage and Post	566225	586448	96.6
#铁路运输业	Transport via Railway	108267	109304	99.1
道路运输业	Transport via Road	275093	284638	96.6
邮政业	Post	56342	66950	84.2
住宿和餐饮业	Lodging and Catering Services	245767	254728	96.5
住宿业	Lodging	113166	119626	94.6
餐饮业	Catering Services	132601	135102	98.1
信息传输、软件和信息技术服务业	Information Transmission, Software and Information Technology Services	680188	663216	102.6
金融业	Financial Intermediation	386621	374255	103.3
房地产业	Real Estate	410668	392353	104.7
租赁和商务服务业	Leasing and Business Services	768864	769553	99.9
租赁业	Leasing	19108	18688	102.2
商务服务业	Business Services	749756	750865	99.9
科学研究和技术服务业	Scientific Research and Development, Technical Services	637823	545017	117.0
水利、环境和公共设施管理业	Management of Water Conservancy, Environment and Public Facilities	98061	97439	100.6
居民服务、修理和其他服务业	Resident Services, Repair and Other Services	80172	83267	96.3
#居民服务业	Resident Services	26201	31230	83.9
教　育	Education	438709	429961	102.0
卫生和社会工作	Health Care and Social Works	269080	257088	104.7
#卫　生	Health Care	254559	244067	104.3
文化、体育和娱乐业	Culture, Sports and Entertainment	175405	171661	102.2
#文化艺术业	Cultures and Arts	43283	39014	110.9
体　育	Sports Activities	20735	21362	97.1
公共管理、社会保障和社会组织	Public Management, Social Security and Social Organizations	432608	429336	100.8
国际组织	International Organizations			

3-20 城镇单位在岗职工工资总额
TOTAL WAGES OF FULLY EMPLOYED STAFF AND WORKERS IN URBAN ENTITIES

单位：万元 (10000 yuan)

项目	Item	2016	2015	2016年为2015年% 2016 as % of 2015
合　计	**Total**	**90050421**	**82252242**	**109.5**
按登记注册类型分	**By Registration Type**			
内　资	Domestically-invested Enterprises	69803874	63050276	110.7
国　有	State-owned Enterprises	22990622	20589795	111.7
集　体	Collectively-owned Enterprises	800749	815449	98.2
股份合作	Joint-equity Cooperative Enterprises	225728	210797	107.1
联　营	Associated Enterprises	24464	24717	99.0
有限责任公司	Limited Liability Companies	28397518	25325700	112.1
股份有限公司	Companies Limited By Shares	16412830	15265116	107.5
其　他	Others	951963	818702	116.3
港、澳、台商投资	Hong Kong, Macao and Taiwan-invested Enterprises	7988806	7146947	111.8
外商投资	Foreign-invested Enterprises	12257741	12055019	101.7
按国民经济行业分	**By Sector**			
农、林、牧、渔业	Agriculture, Forestry, Animal Production and Hunting, Fishing	196444	204769	95.9
#农　业	Agriculture	73395	62568	117.3
采矿业	Mining and Quarrying	432294	496229	87.1
制造业	Manufacturing	8300535	8054195	103.1
电力、热力、燃气及水生产和供应业	Production and Distribution of Electricity, Heating Power, Gas and Water	1147481	1028999	111.5
建筑业	Construction	3885968	3566118	109.0
批发和零售业	Wholesale and Retail Trade	7290541	6785183	107.4
批发业	Wholesale	5161347	4796188	107.6
零售业	Retail Trade	2129194	1988995	107.0
交通运输、仓储和邮政业	Transport, Storage and Post	5136675	4816986	106.6
#铁路运输业	Transport via Railway	1047227	943273	111.0
道路运输业	Transport via Road	1816443	1627636	111.6
邮政业	Post	476607	601706	79.2
住宿和餐饮业	Accommodation and Restaurants	1452314	1404336	103.4
住宿业	Accommodation	727576	715018	101.8
餐饮业	Restaurants	724738	689318	105.1
信息传输、软件和信息技术服务业	Information Transmission, Software and Information Technology Services	11562039	10457415	110.6
金融业	Finance	11006935	10457828	105.3
房地产业	Real Estate	3881812	3419712	113.5
租赁和商务服务业	Renting and Leasing Activities and Business Services	8778348	7953059	110.4
租赁业	Renting and Leasing Activities	157000	156936	100.0
商务服务业	Business Services	8621348	7796123	110.6
科学研究和技术服务业	Scientific Research and Development, Technical Services	9154815	7475107	122.5
水利、环境和公共设施管理业	Management of Water Conservancy, Environment and Public Facilities	785678	717418	109.5
居民服务、修理和其他服务业	Resident Services, Repair and Other Services	420884	416799	101.0
#居民服务业	Resident Services	154776	155095	99.8
教　育	Education	5442322	4961049	109.7
卫生和社会工作	Health Care and Social Works	4041040	3609374	112.0
#卫　生	Health Care	3946794	3531283	111.8
文化、体育和娱乐业	Culture, Sports and Entertainment	2484206	2288357	108.6
#文化艺术业	Cultures and Arts	479365	380350	126.0
体　育	Sports Activities	189022	180087	105.0
公共管理、社会保障和社会组织	Public Management, Social Security and Social Organizations	4650090	4139309	112.3
国际组织	International Organizations			

注：行业划分执行2011年国民经济行业分类标准(GB/T 4754-2011)。
Note: Sectors in this table are classified in accordance with the Standard for Classification of National Economic Sectors 2011 (GB/T 4754-2011).

3-21 城镇单位在岗职工平均工资
AVERAGE WAGES OF FULLY EMPLOYED STAFF AND WORKERS IN URBAN ENTITIES

单位：元 (yuan)

项　　目	Item	2016	2015	2016年为2015年% 2016 as % of 2015
合　　计	**Total**	**122749**	**113073**	**108.6**
按登记注册类型分	**By Registration Type**			
内　资	Domestically-invested Enterprises	116189	106531	109.1
国　有	State-owned Enterprises	129542	119046	108.8
集　体	Collectively-owed Enterprises	59507	49969	119.1
股份合作	Joint-equity Cooperative Enterprises	46432	42692	108.8
联　营	Associated Enterprises	73620	70578	104.3
有限责任公司	Limited Liability Companies	100753	91233	110.4
股份有限公司	Companies Limited By Shares	154858	147294	105.1
其　他	Others	56627	50998	111.0
港、澳、台商投资	Hong Kong, Macao and Taiwan-invested Enterprises	139643	126537	110.4
外商投资	Foreign-invested Enterprises	162080	152406	106.3
按国民经济行业分	**By Sector**			
农、林、牧、渔业	Agriculture, Forestry, Animal Production and Hunting, Fishing	52325	51214	102.2
#农　业	Agriculture	46909	40761	115.1
采矿业	Mining and Quarrying	91144	88432	103.1
制造业	Manufacturing	96514	87581	110.2
电力、热力、燃气及水生产和供应业	Production and Distribution of Electricity, Heating Power, Gas and Water	136460	131438	103.8
建筑业	Construction	91301	84021	108.7
批发和零售业	Wholesale and Retail Trade	102420	94528	108.3
批发业	Wholesale	127553	119090	107.1
零售业	Retail Trade	69313	63131	109.8
交通运输、仓储和邮政业	Transport, Storage and Post	90640	81608	111.1
#铁路运输业	Transport via Railway	96892	86614	111.9
道路运输业	Transport via Road	65696	57364	114.5
邮政业	Post	84876	82963	102.3
住宿和餐饮业	Accommodation and Restaurants	58359	54731	106.6
住宿业	Accommodation	63471	59015	107.6
餐饮业	Restaurants	53993	50898	106.1
信息传输、软件和信息技术服务业	Information Transmission, Software and Information Technology Service	169695	158210	107.3
金融业	Finance	288638	285795	101.0
房地产业	Real Estate	94814	87044	108.9
租赁和商务服务业	Renting and Leasing Activities and Business Services	115053	104501	110.1
租赁业	Renting and Leasing Activities	82745	76918	107.6
商务服务业	Business Services	115876	105260	110.1
科学研究和技术服务业	Scientific Research and Development, Technical Services	144321	136687	105.6
水利、环境和公共设施管理业	Management of Water Conservancy, Environment and Public Facilities	78957	74242	106.4
居民服务、修理和其他服务业	Resident Services, Repair and Other Services	52858	49481	106.8
#居民服务业	Resident Services	58444	49241	118.7
教　育	Education	125260	115520	108.4
卫生和社会工作	Health Care and Social Works	152204	142971	106.5
#卫　生	Health Care	157183	147464	106.6
文化、体育和娱乐业	Culture, Sports and Entertainment	141797	132675	106.9
#文化艺术业	Cultures and Arts	109627	97398	112.6
体　育	Sports Activities	93998	83590	112.5
公共管理、社会保障和社会组织	Pulic Management,Social Security and Social Organizations	108069	96659	111.8
国际组织	International Organizations			

3-22 国民经济各行业城镇单位在岗职工平均工资(2016年)
AVERAGE WAGES OF URBAN ENTITIES FULLY EMPLOYED STAFF AND WORKERS IN DIFFERENT SECTORS OF NATIONAL ECONOMY (2016)

单位：元 (yuan)

项目	Item	平均工资 Average Wages	国有单位 State-owned	集体单位 Collectively-Owned	其他单位 Others
合计	**Total**	**122749**	**129542**	**59507**	**122096**
农、林、牧、渔业	**Agriculture, Forestry, Animal Production and Hunting,Fishing**	**52325**	**83330**	**39092**	**48476**
#农、林、牧、渔服务业	Service Activities for Agriculture, Forestry, Animal Production and Hunting, Fishing	54523	87573	46352	35209
采矿业	**Mining and Quarrying**	**91144**		**42131**	**91588**
煤炭开采和洗选业	Mining and Washing of Coal	75035			75035
石油和天然气开采业	Extraction of Petroleum and Natural Gas	140637			140637
黑色金属矿采选业	Mining and Processing of Ferrous Metal Ores	84809		44200	85646
有色金属矿采选业	Mining and Processing of Non-Ferrous Metal Ores				
非金属矿采选业	Mining and Processing of Nonmetal Ores	49064		26922	61611
开采辅助活动	Mining Support Service Activities	98351			98351
其他采矿业	Mining of Other Ores	83316			83316
制造业	**Manufacturing**	**96514**	**114749**	**47360**	**96566**
农副食品加工业	Processing of Food from Agricultural Products	65763	55702	31455	66845
食品制造业	Manufacture of Foods	78474	90657	36028	78533
酒、饮料和精制茶制造业	Manufacture of Wine, Beverage and Refined Tea	75663	73238	38929	77154
烟草制品业	Manufacture of Cigarettes and Tobacco	228741	228741		
纺织业	Manufacture of Textile	59491	44655	32992	60551
纺织服装、服饰业	Manufacture of Textile, Wearing Apparel and Ornament	54792	49000	45843	55199
皮革、毛皮、羽毛及其制品和制鞋业	Manufacture of Leather, Fur, Feather and Its Products, and Footwear	54276		103742	49330
木材加工和木、竹、藤、棕、草制品业	Processing of Timbers, Manufacture of Wood, Bamboo, Rattan, Palm and Straw Products	39280		44683	38739
家具制造业	Manufacture of Furniture	55158		37733	55294
造纸和纸制品业	Manufacture of Paper and Paper Products	62975	38020	38331	66912
印刷和记录媒介复制业	Printing, Reproduction of Recording Media	75396	93458	69980	71917
文教、工美、体育和娱乐用品制造业	Manufacture of Articles for Culture, Education, Artwork, Sport and Entertainment Activities	63599	46178	58664	64223
石油加工、炼焦和核燃料加工业	Processing of Petroleum, Coking, Processing of Nucleus Fuels	93198	79925	35917	93432
化学原料和化学制品制造业	Manufacture of Chemical Raw Materials and Chemical Products	81769	108775	41473	81110
医药制造业	Manufacture of Medicines	141496	117894	49672	142395
化学纤维制造业	Manufacture of Chemical Fibers	72448			72448
橡胶和塑料制品业	Manufacture of Rubber and Plastics Products	57991	81578	51473	58166
非金属矿物制品业	Manufacture of Non-metallic Mineral Products	71394	67896	41812	72681
黑色金属冶炼和压延加工业	Manufacture and Pressing of Ferrous Metals	77606	115000	34522	78444

3-22 续表 1 Continued 1

单位：元 (yuan)

行业	Sector	平均工资 Average Wages	国有单位 State-owned	集体单位 Collectively-Owned	其他单位 Others
有色金属冶炼和压延加工业	Manufacture and Pressing of Nonferrous Metals	87283	116436	32314	88759
金属制品业	Manufacture of Fabricated Metal Products	69494	53424	40250	71226
通用设备制造业	Manufacture of General-Purpose Machinery	92254	137196	38295	92372
专用设备制造业	Manufacture of Special-Purpose Machinery	97925	119864	45076	97604
汽车制造业	Manufacture of Motor Vehicles	99347	50696	44109	99580
铁路、船舶、航空航天和其他运输设备制造业	Manufacture of Railway Locomotives, Building of Ships and Boats, Manufacture of Air and Spacecrafts and Other Transportation Equipment	119174	161629	39617	101348
电气机械和器材制造业	Manufacture of Electrical Machinery and Equipment	106238	73669	46641	107256
计算机、通信和其他电子设备制造业	Manufacture of Computers, Communication Equipment and Other Electronic Equipment	119447	82491	49112	119975
仪器仪表制造业	Manufacture of Measuring Instruments and Meters	108728	87434	57810	109858
其他制造业	Other Manufacturing	122673	143546	29200	117367
废弃资源综合利用业	Waste Rrecycling and Recovery	77956		23000	78919
金属制品、机械和设备修理业	Repair of Fabricated Metal Products, Machinery and Equipment	139484	59094	51075	141167
电力、热力、燃气及水生产和供应业	**Production and Distribution of Electricity, Heating Power, Gas and Water**	**136460**	**166944**	**50607**	**129583**
电力、热力生产和供应业	Production and Distribution of Electricity and Heating Power	149824	179017	54784	141244
燃气生产和供应业	Production and Distribution of Gas	116369	92570		119886
水的生产和供应业	Production and Distribution of Water	94812	97611	42097	95285
建筑业	**Construction**	**91301**	**93557**	**74944**	**91752**
房屋建筑业	Construction of Buildings	94359	76117	59664	97103
土木工程建筑业	Civil Engineering Construction	101965	113893	82921	101137
建筑安装业	Construction Installation	82715	54791	116592	81768
建筑装饰和其他建筑业	Building Completion, Finishing and Other Constructions	66844	87807	49054	66307
批发和零售业	**Wholesale and Retail Trade**	**102420**	**138352**	**54145**	**101511**
批发业	Wholesale	127553	162681	57741	126498
零售业	Retail Trade	69313	88397	51132	68988
交通运输、仓储和邮政业	**Transport, Storage and Post**	**90640**	**95877**	**33730**	**90172**
铁路运输业	Transport via Railway	96892	99466		91317
道路运输业	Transport via Road	65696	34776	26214	66436
水上运输业	Water Transport	250819			250819
航空运输业	Air Transport	176983	299657		176745
管道运输业	Transport via Pipeline	141391			141391
装卸搬运和运输代理业	Loading, Unloading, Portage and Other Transport Services	98953	101932	66442	99511
仓储业	Storage	77217	82491	38476	78632
邮政业	Post	84876	88072		83346
住宿和餐饮业	**Accommodation and Restaurants**	**58359**	**63550**	**51367**	**57717**
住宿业	Accommodation	63471	63844	56273	63789
餐饮业	Restaurants	53993	60567	39046	54067
信息传输、软件和信息技术服务业	**Information Transmission, Software and Information Technology Services**	**169695**	**165516**	**57042**	**169848**
电信、广播电视和卫星传输服务	Telecommunications, Broadcasting, Television and Satellite Transmission Services	186354	180672	55711	186550
互联网和相关服务	Internet and Related Services	152000	168431	33667	151686
软件和信息技术服务业	Software and Information Technology Services	171031	161484	57536	171298

3-22 续表 2 Continued 2

单位：元 (yuan)

行业	Sector	平均工资 Average Wages	国有单位 State-owned	集体单位 Collectively-Owned	其他单位 Others
金融业	**Finance**	**288638**	**240719**	**82743**	**289937**
货币金融服务	Monetary Financial Services	297675	253597		299239
资本市场服务	Capital Market Services	375988	181698	64600	384034
保险业	Insurance	226262	294579		225622
其他金融业	Other Financial Services	255898	262144	191600	255878
房地产业	**Real Estate**	**94814**	**93426**	**53306**	**96808**
租赁和商务服务业	**Renting and Leasing Activities and Business Services**	**115053**	**96159**	**47277**	**123521**
租赁业	Renting and Leasing Activities	82745	104087	93805	81651
商务服务业	Business Services	115876	96134	45868	124857
科学研究和技术服务业	**Scientific Research and Development, Technical Services**	**144321**	**166611**	**100547**	**134302**
研究和试验发展	Research and Experimental Development	163815	166802	119947	155635
专业技术服务业	Professional Technique Services	141265	164637	92290	136239
科技推广和应用服务业	Technique Generalization and Application Services	130616	171603	79706	127004
水利、环境和公共设施管理业	**Management of Water Conservancy, Environment and Public Facilities**	**78957**	**81843**	**39104**	**77247**
水利管理业	Management of Water Conservancy	102880	104075	65555	104870
生态保护和环境治理业	Ecological Protection and Environmental Control	116509	115893		116656
公共设施管理业	Management of Public Facilities	72490	77646	35860	66604
居民服务、修理和其他服务业	**Resident Services, Repair and Other Services**	**52858**	**61513**	**39246**	**52491**
居民服务业	Resident Services	58444	61070	43858	59158
机动车、电子产品和日用产品修理业	Repair of Motor Vehicles, Electronics and Household Appliances	64158	75123	40937	65046
其他服务业	Other Services	40114	53223	33485	39695
教　育	**Education**	**125260**	**137922**	**76809**	**81119**
卫生和社会工作	**Health Care and Social Works**	**152204**	**168987**	**95272**	**84797**
卫　生	Health Care	157183	171572	105907	91039
社会工作	Social Works	65421	90638	36557	45464
文化、体育和娱乐业	**Culture, Sports and Entertainment**	**141797**	**161428**	**50445**	**117363**
新闻和出版业	Journalism and Publishing	161476	161073	92376	163592
广播、电视、电影和影视录音制作业	Radio Broadcasting, Television, Movies, Videos and Sound Recording	181676	215061	25191	133248
文化艺术业	Culture and Arts	109627	123023	50061	94286
体　育	Sports Activities	93998	120945	29214	83179
娱乐业	Entertainment	81971	105264	40591	80342
公共管理、社会保障和社会组织	**Public Management, Social Security and Social Organizations**	**108069**	**111904**	**73126**	**61739**
中国共产党机关	Organs of Communist Party of China	111986	111986		
国家机构	Organs of State	111046	111058		54726
人民政协、民主党派	Peole's Political Consultative Conference and Democratic Parties	134835	134835		
社会保障	Social Security	94149	95011	54776	120336
群众团体、社会团体和其他成员组织	Mass Communities, Social Organizations and Other Membership Organizations	127168	130525	79694	125075
基层群众自治组织	Grass Roots Self-Government Organization	31531		28316	31536
国际组织	**International Organizations**				

3-23 城镇登记失业率和城镇新增就业人数(1979-2016年)
REGISTERED UNEMPLOYED RATE IN URBAN AREA AND NEWLY EMPLOYED PERSONS IN URBAN AREA (1979-2016)

单位：万人 (10000 persons)

年 份 Year	年末实有登记失业人员 Year-end Number of Actual Registed Unemployed Persons	城镇登记失业率(%) Registered Unemployment Rate in Urban Area	城镇新增就业人数 Newly Employed Persons in Urban Area
1979	4.96	1.60	
1980	8.67	1.60	
1981	8.36	1.28	
1982	7.03	1.62	
1983	4.20	1.09	
1984	2.03	0.54	
1985	1.61	0.40	
1986	1.25	0.30	
1987	2.24	0.45	
1988	1.58	0.40	
1989	1.71	0.40	
1990	1.67	0.30	
1991	1.92	0.40	
1992	1.72	0.36	
1993	1.92	0.41	
1994	1.91	0.41	
1995	2.19	0.46	
1996	2.80	0.58	
1997	3.29	0.73	
1998	2.95	0.66	
1999	2.80	0.62	
2000	3.32	0.76	
2001	5.19	1.18	
2002	6.02	1.35	
2003	6.96	1.43	
2004	6.46	1.30	
2005	10.57	2.11	31.50
2006	10.40	1.98	34.39
2007	10.63	1.84	40.71
2008	10.33	1.82	41.97
2009	8.16	1.44	42.44
2010	7.73	1.37	44.64
2011	7.89	1.39	44.69
2012	7.20	1.27	43.89
2013	6.81	1.21	42.87
2014	8.77	1.31	42.65
2015	9.16	1.39	42.62
2016	9.14	1.41	42.80

注：2014年开始年末实有登记失业人员指标统计口径为全市口径，2014年以前为城镇口径。
资料来源：北京市人力资源和社会保障局。
Note: Since 2014, the year-end number of actual registered unemployed persons refers to the statistic of the whole city;while the number before 2014 refers to the statistic in urban and rural areas.
Source: Beijing Municipal Bureau of Human Resource and Social Security.

主要统计指标解释

户籍人口 指公民依照《中华人民共和国户口登记条例》已在其经常居住地的公安户籍管理机关登记了常住户口的人。

常住人口 指在某地区实际居住半年以上的人口。

常住外来人口 指不具有本市户籍户口，来自北京市行政区划以外的省、自治区、直辖市，且在京居住半年以上的人口。

出生率 指在一定时期内（通常为一年）出生人数与同期平均人数(或期中人数)之比，一般用千分比表示。计算公式：

$$出生率=\frac{年出生人数}{年平均人数}\times1000‰$$

出生人数是指活产，即脱离母体时（不管怀孕月数），有过呼吸或其他生命现象的活婴儿总和。年平均人数是年初、年末人口数的平均数，也可用年中人口数代替。

死亡率 指在一定时期内（通常为一年）死亡人数与同期平均人数（或期中人数）之比，一般用千分比表示。计算公式：

$$死亡率=\frac{年死亡人数}{年平均人数}\times1000‰$$

自然增长率 指在一定时期内（通常为一年）人口自然增加数（出生人数减死亡人数）与该时期内平均人数（或期中人数）之比，一般用千分比表示。计算公式：

$$自然增长率=\frac{年出生人数-年死亡人数}{年平均人数}\times1000‰$$

人口自然增长率=人口出生率－人口死亡率

从业人员 指在各级国家机关、党政机关、社会团体及企业、事业单位中工作，取得工资或其他形式的劳动报酬的全部人员。包括：在岗职工、聘用的离退休人员以及在单位中工作的港澳台及外籍人员、兼职人员、借用的外单位人员和第二职业者。不包括本单位的不在岗职工。

在岗职工 指在本单位工作并由单位支付工资的人员，以及有工作岗位，但由于学习、病伤产假（六个月以内）等原因暂未工作，仍由单位支付工资的人员。

在岗职工工资总额 与“在岗职工”指标相对应，根据1990年1月1日的国家统计局令（一号）修订，指单位在报告期内直接支付给本单位在岗职工的劳动报酬总额。包括基础工资、职务工资、级别工资、工龄工资、计件工资、奖金、各种津贴和补贴、交通补贴、洗理费、书报费、旅游费、过节费、伙食补助、住房补贴、住房提租补贴、由单位从个人工资中直接为其代扣或代缴的个人所得税、房水电费以及住房公积金和社会保险基金个人缴纳部分等。

在岗职工平均工资 指企业、事业、机关等单位的在岗职工在一定时期内的人均劳动报酬。它表明一定时期在岗职工工资收入的高低程度，是反映在岗职工工资水平的主要指标。计算公式为：

$$在岗职工平均工资=\frac{报告期实际支付的全部在岗职工工资总额}{报告期全部在岗职工平均人数}$$

从业人员平均工资 指企业、事业、机关等单位的从业人员在一定时期内的人均劳动报酬。计算公式为：

$$从业人员平均工资=\frac{报告期实际支付的全部从业人员劳动报酬总额}{报告期全部从业人员平均人数}$$

期末实有登记失业人员 指报告期末实有的登记失业人员总数，包括城镇登记失业人员和城市化建设地区的登记失业农民（失地农民）。

城镇登记失业率 指城镇登记失业人数与城镇从业人数和城镇登记失业人数二者之和的比。计算公式如下：

$$城镇登记失业率=\frac{年末实有登记失业人数}{城镇从业人数+年末实有登记失业人数}\times100\%$$

Explanatory Notes on Main Statistical Indicators

Registered Population refers to persons who have registered their permanent residence with the public security register authority of their habitual residence according to the Households Registration Regulations of PRC.

Permanent Population refers to persons actually living for more than half a year at a place.

Permanent Migrant Population refers to persons who have no permanent residence registration in Beijing, come from other provinces, autonomous regions and municipalities, and have stayed in Beijing for more than half a year.

Birth Rate refers to the ratio of the number of births to the average population (or mid-period population) during a certain period of time (usually a year), which is often expressed in ‰. The following formula is used:

Birth Rate = Annual Number of Births/Annual Average Number of Population×1,000‰

Number of births refers to live births i.e. the births when babies had shown any vital phenomena regardless of the length of pregnancy. Annual average number of population is the average of the number of population at the beginning of the year and that at the end of the year. Sometimes it is substituted with the mid-year population.

Death Rate refers to the ratio of the number of deaths to the average population (or mid-period population) during a certain period of time (usually a year), which is often expressed in ‰. The following formula is used:

Death Rate= Annual Number of Deaths/Annual Average Number of Population×1,000‰

Natural Growth Rate refers to the ratio of the natural growth of population (births minus deaths) to the average population (or mid-period population) during a certain period of time (usually a year), which is often expressed in ‰. The following formula is used:

Natural Growth Rate of Population = (Annual Number of Births - Annual Number of Deaths)/Annual Average Number of Population×1,000‰

Natural Growth Rate of Population = Birth Rate - Death Rate

Employed Persons refer to all persons working in government agencies, Party and political organs, social groups, enterprises and public institutions at all levels, and receiving wages or labor remuneration in other forms. They include: fully employed staff and workers, retired persons employed, persons from Hong Kong, Macao, Taiwan and foreign countries who are employed, part-time employees, employees transferred from other entities, and employees with a second job. They exclude employees that are not on the job in the entity.

Fully Employed Staff and Workers refer to persons working in the entity and paid by the entity, as well as persons having a job in the entity, but not working temporarily due to study, illness, injury or maternity leaves (less than 6 months) and other reasons, and still paid by the entity.

Total Wages of Full-time Staff and Workers corresponds to the indicator Full-time Staff and Workers. The indicator was revised in accordance with No. 1 Decree of the National Bureau of Statistics dated January 1, 1990, referring to the total wages directly paid by an entity to full-time staff and workers of the entity during the reporting period. It consists of basic wage, position-based wage, post wage, wage of a rank, piece rate wage, bonus, allowances and subsidies, traffic subsidy, washing and haircutting allowance, books and newspaper allowance, travel benefit, festival bonus, food subsidy, housing subsidy, subsidy for incremental house rent, as well as personal income tax, water and electricity fees and the personally payable portion of housing accumulation fund and social security fund withheld directly by the employer from the employee's wage.

Average Wage of Full-time Staff and Workers refers to the per-capita labor remuneration of full-time staff and workers in enterprises, public institutions and government agencies within a given period of time. It shows the level of wage income of fully employed staff and workers within a given period of time, serving as a main indicator reflecting the level of wage of fully employed staff and workers. The following formula is used:

Average Wage of Full-time Staff and Workers = Total Wages of Full-time Staff and Workers Actually Paid in the Reporting Period / Total Number of Full-time Staff and Workers in the Reporting Period

Average Wage of Employed Persons refers to the per-capita labor remuneration of employed persons in enterprises and government agencies within a given period of time. The following formula is used:

Average Wage of Employed Persons = Total Wages of All Employed Persons Actually Paid in the Reporting Period / Total Number of Employed Persons in the Reporting Period

Number of Actual Registered Unemployed Persons in Urban Area at Year-end refers to the actual number of unemployed persons registered at the year end (including all unemployed persons receiving unemployment insurance benefit).

Period-end Actual Registered Unemployed Persons refer to the total number of actual unemployed persons registered at the end period, including unemployed persons registered in urban regions and the unemployed peasants registered in urbanization regions (land-lost peasants).

Registered Unemployment Rate in Urban Area refers to the ratio of urban registered unemployed persons to the sum of urban staff and workers and urban registered unemployed persons. The following formula is used:

Registered Unemployment Rate in Urban Area =Number of Actual Registered Unemployed Persons at Year-end / (Urban Employed Persons + Number of Actual Registered Unemployed Persons at Year-end) × 100%

04

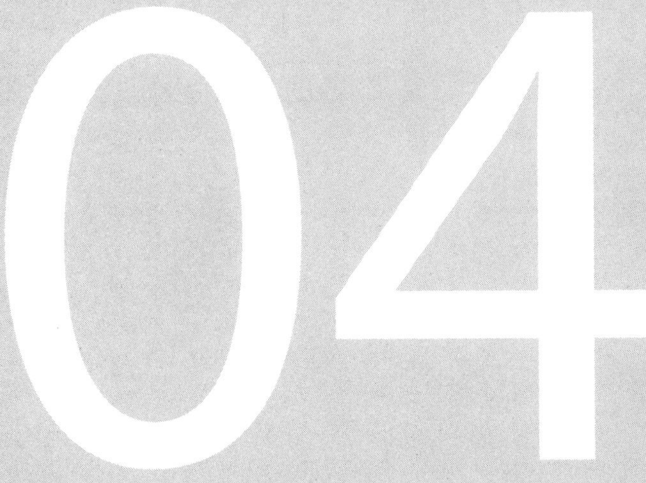

北京统计年鉴2017　BEIJING STATISTICAL YEARBOOK

财政与税收
GOVERNMENT FINANCE AND TAX REVENUES

简要说明

一、本章资料的主要内容

本章资料包括北京市政府预算收支情况，北京市国税、地税税收(费)收入情况。其中地方政府预算收支包括一般公共预算收支、政府性基金预算收支、国有资本经营预算收支和社会保险基金预算收支情况；税收（费）收入包括国税、地税税收（费）收入分组情况。

二、本章资料的数据来源

本章地方政府预算收支数据由北京市财政局提供；税收（费）数据由北京市国家税务局、北京市地方税务局提供。

Brief Introduction

I. Main Content

Statistics in this chapter include Local government budgetary revenue and expenditure, state and local tax revenues of Beijing Municipality. Local government budgetary revenue and expenditure include fiscal revenues, government fund budgetary revenue and expenditure, budgetary revenue and expenditure of state-owned capital operation, and social insurance fund budgetary revenue and expenditure; figures of tax revenues include the grouped figures of state and local tax revenues.

II. Source of Data

Data of local government budgetary revenue and expenditure are from Beijing Municipal Bureau of Finance; data of tax revenues are from Beijing Municipal Bureau of State Tax and Beijing Municipal Bureau of Local Tax.

4-1 地方政府预算收入(1978-2016年)

单位：亿元

年 份 Year	一般公共预算收入 Local Public Budgetary Revenue	税收收入 Tax Revenue	增值税 Value-added Tax	房产税 Housing Property Tax	土地增值税 Increment Tax On Land Value	契税 Deed Tax	营业税 Operation Tax
1978		18.25					
1979		19.41					
1980		21.22					
1981-1985		**191.96**					
1981		24.22					
1982		25.81	0.05				
1983		38.03	1.30				
1984		43.91	2.20				1.23
1985		59.99	4.79				10.23
1986-1990		**397.96**	**65.02**				**103.00**
1986		60.83	7.61				13.19
1987		67.77	9.09				15.42
1988		84.04	15.10				21.11
1989		91.09	16.75				25.33
1990		94.23	16.47				27.95
1991-1995		**643.24**	**136.88**				**228.80**
1991		100.58	19.53				30.78
1992		110.54	22.29				35.86
1993		148.19	42.30				52.07
1994		120.53	25.54				45.63
1995		163.40	27.22				64.46
1996-2000		**1397.26**	**185.46**				**570.06**
1996		201.32	29.53				81.61
1997	182.32	235.82	32.67				97.54
1998	229.45	272.23	37.58				113.00
1999	281.37	315.10	39.72				128.86
2000	345.00	372.79	45.96				149.05
2001-2005	**3244.40**	**3216.46**	**367.43**				**1389.75**
2001	454.17	475.00	59.00				181.35
2002	533.99	539.87	66.69				227.79
2003	592.54	588.96	75.26	30.79	3.07	20.40	263.69
2004	744.49	726.50	68.88	31.97	1.85	43.68	333.16
2005	919.21	886.13	97.60	35.21	2.38	60.68	383.76
2006-2010	**8827.85**	**8453.62**	**800.72**	**316.70**	**204.70**	**465.57**	**3321.83**
2006	1117.15	1076.82	117.80	43.29	5.67	64.87	460.99
2007	1492.64	1435.67	134.84	51.75	24.34	80.30	601.06
2008	1837.32	1775.58	158.34	63.84	34.67	82.97	651.78
2009	2026.81	1913.97	179.73	73.98	54.16	103.16	752.60
2010	2353.93	2251.59	210.01	83.83	85.86	134.27	855.40
2011-2015	**18733.34**	**17619.09**	**2489.47**	**624.94**	**829.78**	**843.00**	**5513.81**
2011	3006.28	2854.63	237.76	99.40	121.29	136.17	1071.51
2012	3314.93	3124.75	314.00	110.72	132.07	126.58	1152.74
2013	3661.11	3514.52	574.89	122.54	187.24	177.49	1034.79
2014	4027.16	3861.29	646.69	140.22	214.33	192.52	1068.64
2015	4723.86	4263.91	716.12	152.06	174.86	210.23	1186.13
2016	5081.26	4452.97	1214.34	198.22	177.35	254.29	584.41

注：1. 地方政府预算收入为决算数。
2. 地方政府预算收支包含四部分内容，即一般公共预算收支、政府性基金预算收支、国有资本经营预算收支和社会保险基金预算收支(下同)。

资料来源：北京市财政局。

LOCAL GOVERNMENT BUDGETARY REVENUE(1978-2016)

(100 million yuan)

			非税收入	政府性基金预算收入	国有资本经营预算收入	社会保险经营预算收入
个人所得税 Individual Income Tax	企业所得税 Company Income Tax	城市维护建设税 Urban Maintenance and Construction Tax	Non-tax Revenue	Governmental Fund Budgetary Revenue	Budgetary Revenue of State-owned Capital Operation	Social Insurance Fund Budgetary Revenue
0.61	**43.77**					
0.02	1.76					
0.05	1.43					
0.07	11.70					
0.13	12.70					
0.34	16.18	2.16				
7.29	**116.89**	**16.67**				
0.97	20.46	2.51				
1.54	21.87	2.70				
1.23	27.70	3.37				
1.53	24.31	3.74				
2.02	22.55	4.35				
35.46	**105.24**	**34.07**				
2.56	20.59	4.77				
3.15	19.08	5.13				
4.30	14.20	6.57				
9.24	21.70	7.18				
16.21	29.67	10.42				
190.18	**223.71**	**70.84**				
22.67	37.22	11.36				
28.76	41.05	12.74	-53.50	27.59		
36.49	41.42	14.12	-42.78	32.56		
45.88	45.99	15.27	-33.74	39.07		
56.38	58.03	17.35	-27.79	53.39		
355.88	**566.23**	**147.84**	**27.94**	**367.57**		
79.52	86.07	20.53	-20.83	53.51		
61.29	100.00	24.91	-5.88	66.97		
57.21	93.70	28.85	3.58	73.40		
73.34	121.70	34.72	17.99	85.55		
84.52	164.76	38.83	33.08	88.14		
801.97	**1965.28**	**317.03**	**374.23**	**3061.69**		
102.28	213.86	45.17	40.33	118.63		
135.20	309.34	56.63	56.97	389.40		
171.33	497.52	63.95	61.75	444.71		
177.84	430.42	71.28	112.84	651.96		
215.33	513.09	80.00	102.34	1456.98		
1749.87	**4178.87**	**875.00**	**1114.25**	**12074.97**		
272.90	683.71	145.65	151.65	1352.82		
281.49	752.47	160.34	190.18	1197.92		
333.84	802.12	177.41	146.59	1841.76	63.21	
383.52	915.84	187.24	165.87	3122.91	64.46	
478.12	1024.73	204.36	459.95	2028.37	61.60	
571.26	1095.23	221.64	628.29	1316.47	64.75	3446.83

Note: a) Local government Budgetary revenue are final accounts.

b) The budgetary revenue and expenditure of local governments includes four parts, i.e. general public budgetary revenue and expenditure, government fund budgetary revenue and expenditure, budgetary revenue and expenditure of state-owned capital operation and social insurance fund budgetary revenue and expenditure (the same below).

Source: Beijing Municipal Bureau of Finance.

4-2 地方政府预算支出(1978-2016年)

单位：亿元

年份 Year	一般公共预算支出 Local Public Budgetary Expenditures	一般公共服务 General Public Service	教育 Education	科学技术 Science and Technology	文化体育与传媒 Culture, Sports and Media	社会保障和就业 Social Security and Employment	医疗卫生与计划生育 Healthcare
1978							
1979							
1980							
1981-1985							
1981							
1982							
1983							
1984							
1985							
1986-1990							
1986							
1987							
1988							
1989							
1990							
1991-1995							
1991							
1992							
1993							
1994							
1995							
1996-2000							
1996							
1997	236.39						
1998	280.68						
1999	355.19						
2000	443.00						
2001-2005	**3878.85**						
2001	559.11						
2002	628.35						
2003	734.80						
2004	898.28						
2005	1058.31						
2006-2010	**9942.31**	**987.56**	**1604.40**	**578.30**	**309.36**	**1048.02**	**718.40**
2006	1296.84	159.95	209.21	70.14	40.51	149.22	100.95
2007	1649.50	179.56	263.00	90.74	53.62	179.28	118.95
2008	1959.29	196.27	316.30	112.19	61.11	209.33	145.05
2009	2319.37	212.21	365.67	126.31	74.75	234.29	166.63
2010	2717.32	239.57	450.22	178.92	79.36	275.90	186.82
2011-2015	**21366.56**	**1417.42**	**3427.63**	**1188.20**	**735.49**	**2457.82**	**1450.49**
2011	3245.23	261.38	520.08	183.07	87.01	354.88	225.49
2012	3685.31	286.57	628.65	199.94	141.37	424.31	256.06
2013	4173.66	297.12	681.18	234.67	154.71	469.13	276.13
2014	4524.67	272.23	742.05	282.71	163.90	509.01	322.29
2015	5737.70	300.12	855.67	287.80	188.50	700.48	370.52
2016	6406.77	367.20	887.38	285.78	198.35	716.21	397.95

注：地方政府预算支出为决算数。
资料来源：北京市财政局。

LOCAL GOVERNMENT BUDGETARY EXPENDITURE(1978-2016)

(100 million yuan)

节能环保 Energy Conservation and Environmental Protection	交通运输 Transportation	城乡社区事务 Urban and Rural Community Affairs	农林水 Agriculture Forestry and Water Conservancy	政府性基金预算支出 Governmental Fund Budgetary Expenditure	国有资本经营预算支出 Budgetary Expenditure of State-owned Capital Operation	社会保障基金预算支出 Social Security Fund Budgetary Expenditure
199.77	**422.53**	**1182.65**	**613.55**	**2823.69**		
20.14	7.05	153.26	88.62	114.74		
29.27	33.09	187.43	102.51	418.15		
35.47	80.35	199.84	121.77	441.64		
54.04	147.07	347.82	142.01	501.50		
60.85	154.99	294.30	158.64	1347.65		
862.83	**1184.86**	**2843.48**	**1476.10**	**10637.82**		
94.51	199.12	339.27	187.34	1329.71		
113.54	243.76	430.76	222.69	1118.45		
138.17	231.79	510.67	297.62	1798.81	66.95	
213.36	214.55	567.40	343.67	2559.09	63.99	
303.26	295.63	995.39	424.78	2281.30	61.72	
363.38	353.48	1120.37	443.55	1432.09	45.63	2497.23

Note: Local government Budgetary expenditure are final accounts.
Source: Beijing Municipal Bureau of Finance.

4-3 地方政府预算收入
LOCAL GOVERNMENT BUDGETARY REVENUE

项目	Item	绝对数(亿元) Absolute Value (100 million yuan) 2016	2015	2016年为2015年% 2016 as % of 2015
一般公共预算收入	**Local Public Budgetary Revenue**	**5081.26**	**4723.86**	**107.6**
增值税	Value-added Tax	1214.34	716.12	169.6
营业税	Business Tax	584.41	1186.13	49.3
房产税	House Property Tax	198.22	152.06	130.4
土地增值税	Increment Tax on Land Value	177.35	174.86	101.4
契税	Deed Tax	254.29	210.23	121.0
个人所得税	Personal Income Tax	571.26	478.12	119.5
企业所得税	Company Income Tax	1095.23	1024.73	106.9
城市维护建设税	Urban Maintenance and Construction Tax	221.64	204.36	108.5
耕地占用税	Arable Land Occupation Tax	3.34	4.54	73.7
罚没收入	Income of Fines and Confiscations	45.66	55.78	81.8
行政事业性收费收入	Administrative Fees	55.37	64.38	86.0
政府性基金预算收入	**Government Fund Budgetary Revenue**	**1316.47**	**2028.37**	**64.9**
国有资本经营预算收入	**Budgetary Revenue of State-owned Capital Operation**	**64.75**	**61.60**	**105.1**
社会保险基金预算收入	**Social Insurance Fund Budgetary Revenue**	**344.68**		

资料来源：北京市财政局。
Source: Beijing Finance Bureau.

4-4 地方政府预算支出
LOCAL GOVERNMENT BUDGETARY EXPENDITURE

项目	Item	绝对数(亿元) Absolute Value (100 million yuan) 2016	2015	2016年为2015年% 2016 as % of 2015
一般公共预算支出	**Local Public Budgetary Expenditures**	**6406.77**	**5737.70**	**111.7**
一般公共服务	General Public Service	367.20	300.12	122.3
教　育	Education	887.38	855.67	103.7
科学技术	Science and Technology	285.78	287.80	99.3
文化体育与传媒	Culture, Sports and Media	198.35	188.50	105.2
社会保障和就业	Social Security and Employment	716.21	700.48	102.2
医疗卫生与计划生育	Healthcare	397.95	370.52	107.4
节能环保	Energy Conservation and Environmental Protection	363.38	303.26	119.8
交通运输	Transportation	353.48	295.63	119.6
城乡社区事务	Urban and Rural Community Affairs	1120.37	995.39	112.6
农林水事务	Agriculture, Forestry and Water Conservancy	443.55	424.78	104.4
政府性基金支出合计	**Total Expenditures of Governmental Funds**	**1432.09**	**2281.30**	**62.8**
国有资本经营预算支出	**Budgetary Expenditure of State-owned Capital Operation**	**45.63**	**61.72**	**73.9**
社会保险基金预算支出	**Social Insurance Fund Budgetary Expenditure**	**2497.23**		

资料来源：北京市财政局。
Source: Beijing Municipal Bureau of Finance.

4–5 地税税费收入分税种、分行业完成情况(2010–2016年)
LOCAL TAX REVENUE BY CATEGORY AND INDUSTRY (2010-2016)

单位：亿元 (100 million yuan)

项　　目	Item	2010	2011	2012	2013	2014	2015	2016
地税税费收入	**Local Tax Revenue**	**2104.89**	**2666.62**	**2865.25**	**3061.65**	**3387.80**	**3868.24**	**3261.78**
按税种分	**By Category**							
#增值税	Business Tax	-	-	-	-	-	-	44.58
企业所得税	Coporate Income Tax	173.18	210.52	221.02	258.07	333.91	374.10	479.77
个人所得税	Personal Income Tax	536.27	681.27	703.48	834.47	958.79	1195.28	1428.15
按行业分	**By Sector**							
第一产业	Primary Industry	3.67	4.00	4.94	4.98	7.74	7.87	7.38
第二产业	Secondary Industry	235.22	303.14	326.20	348.54	388.51	408.74	345.50
#制造业	Manufacturing	101.75	138.36	150.45	160.70	179.36	206.27	219.50
电力、燃气及水的生产和供应业	Production and Distribution of Electricity, Gas and Water	15.69	19.37	21.18	25.20	28.94	29.17	35.12
建筑业	Construction	109.88	134.37	144.65	153.99	171.73	166.45	85.11
第三产业	Tertiary Industry	1866.00	2359.46	2534.11	2708.14	2991.56	3451.63	2908.90
#交通、运输、仓储及邮政业	Transport, Storage and Post	51.41	63.95	60.58	38.14	40.47	46.37	47.07
信息传输、计算机服务和软件业	Information Transmission, Computer Servicesand Software	98.02	125.48	132.76	123.65	141.82	147.05	171.14
批发和零售业	Wholesale and Retail Trade	111.40	159.35	169.30	188.84	206.15	230.14	244.20
金融业	Finance	276.40	366.35	446.67	477.99	599.52	762.95	392.48
房地产业	Real Estate	437.40	520.36	525.44	659.25	734.16	745.68	695.17

资料来源：北京市地方税务局。
Source: Beijing Municipal Bureau of Local Taxation.

4-6 国税税收收入分税种、分行业完成情况(2010-2016年) STATE TAX REVENUE BY CATEGORY AND INDUSTRY (2010-2016)

单位：亿元 (100 million yuan)

项目	Item	2010	2011	2012	2013	2014	2015	2016
国税税收收入	**State Tax Revenue**	**4346.8**	**5332.5**	**6339.4**	**7470.9**	**8325.2**	**8655.2**	**9378.5**
按税种分	**By Category**							
#增值税	Value-added Tax	868.3	961.7	1096.0	1456.3	1659.8	1710.5	2486.2
企业所得税	Corporate Income Tax	2642.0	3506.5	4252.0	5024.4	5757.3	5937.2	5976.0
按行业分	**By Sector**							
第一产业	Primary Industry	5.8	0.7	0.3	2.6	0.9	2.5	4.3
第二产业	Secondary Industry	779.1	881.1	843.8	1069.3	1159.4	1182.2	1198.0
#制造业	Manufacturing	623.2	709.2	764.6	832.0	889.5	963.2	960.7
电力、燃气及水的生产和供应业	Production and Distribution of Electricity, Gas and Water	105.2	103.5	131.0	261.4	194.1	171.2	169.2
建筑业	Construction	30.1	45.3	54.8	57.0	50.9	63.9	170.2
第三产业	Tertiary Industry	3561.9	4450.8	5495.3	6399.0	7164.8	7470.5	8176.1
#交通、运输、仓储及邮政业	Transport, Storage and Post	157.9	209.2	212.1	245.1	242.6	242.6	189.4
信息传输、计算机服务和软件业	Information Transmission, Computer Services and Software	30.8	105.9	245.9	373.2	296.2	285.0	306.3
批发和零售业	Wholesale and Retail Trade	1081.6	1410.8	1314.6	1451.0	1474.0	1420.6	1468.5
金融业	Finance	1831.2	2158.0	3034.0	3500.2	4153.2	4401.4	4828.6
房地产业	Real Estate	107.6	122.3	111.6	157.0	156.9	104.3	274.9

资料来源：北京市国家税务局。
Source: Beijing Municipal Bureau of State Taxation.

主要统计指标解释

财政部分

一般公共预算收入 是通过一定的形式和程序，由各级财政部门组织并纳入预算管理的各项收入。

政府性基金预算收入 是按规定收取，转入或通过当年财政安排，由财政管理并具有指定用途的政府性基金预算收入等。

国有资本经营预算收入 指国家以所有者身份依法取得国有资本收益，并对所得收益进行分配而发生的各项收支预算，是政府预算的重要组成部分。

社会保险基金预算收入 社会保险基金预算是指社会保险经办机构根据国家预算管理和社会保险相关法律法规编制的、经规定程序审批的具有法律效力的年度基金财务收支计划。

税收收入 包括增值税、营业税、企业所得税、个人所得税、资源税、城市维护建设税、房产税、印花税、城镇土地使用税、土地增值税、车船税、耕地占用税、契税等。

非税收收入 包括专项收入、行政事业性收费、罚没收入和其他收入。

一般公共预算支出 是各级财政部门对集中的一般预算收入有计划地分配和使用而安排的支出。

政府性基金预算支出 是各级财政部门用基金预算收入安排的支出。

一般公共服务支出 指政府提供基本公共管理与服务的支出，包括人大事务、政协事务、政府办公厅（室)及相关机构事务、发展与改革事务、统计信息事务、财政事务、税收事务、审计事务、海关事务、人力资源事务、纪检监察事务、人口与计划生育事务、 商贸事务、知识产权事务、工商行政管理事务、国土资源事务、 海洋管理事务、 测绘事务、地震事务、气象事务、民族事务、宗教事务、港澳台侨事务、档案事务、共产党事务、民主党派事务及工商联事务、群众团体事务、彩票事务等。

教育支出 指政府教育事务支出，包括教育行政管理、学前教育、小学教育、初中教育、普通高中教育、普通高等教育、初等职业教育、中专教育、技校教育、职业高中教育、高等职业教育、广播电视教育、留学生教育、特殊教育、干部继续教育、教育机关服务等。

科学技术支出 指用于科学技术方面的支出，包括科学技术管理事务、基础研究、应用研究、技术研究与开发、科技条件与服务、社会科学、科学技术普及、科技交流与合作等。

文化教育与传媒支出 指政府在文化、文物、体育、广播影视、新闻出版等方面的支出。

社会保障和就业支出 指政府在社会保障与就业方面的支出，包括社会保障和就业管理事务、民政管理事务、财政对社会保险基金的补助、补充全国社会保障基金、行政事业单位离退休、企业改革补助、就业补助、抚恤、退役安置、社会福利、残疾人事业、城市居民最低生活保障、其他城镇社会救济、农村社会救济、自然灾害生活救助、红十字事务等。

医疗卫生与计划生育支出 指政府医疗卫生与计划生育管理方面的支出。

节能环保支出 指政府环境保护支出，包括环境保护管理事务支出、环境监测与监察支出、污染治理支出、自然生态保护支出、天然林保护工程支出、退耕还林支出、风沙荒漠治理支出、退牧还草支出、已垦草原退耕还草、能源节约利用、污染减排、可再生能源和资源综合利用等支出。

交通运输支出 指政府交通运输和邮政业方面的支出，包括公路运输支出、水路运输支出、铁路运输支出、民用航空运输支出、邮政业支出等。

城乡社区事务支出 指政府城乡社区事务支出，包括城乡社区管理事务支出、城乡社区规划与管理支出、城乡社区公共设施支出、城乡社区住宅支出、城乡社区环境卫生支出、建设市场管理与监督支出等。

农林水事务支出 指政府农林水事务支出，包括农业支出、林业支出、水利支出、扶贫支出、农业综合开发支出等。

税收部分

税费收入 指由各级地方税务局征缴的各项税收收入和罚没收入。包括企业所得税、个人所得税、资源税、房产税、契税、城市维护建设税等。

税收收入 指由各级国家税务局征缴的各项税收收入。包括增值税、消费税、企业所得税、个人所得税、城市维护建设税等。

企业所得税 是对中国境内全部企业的生产经营所得和其他所得征收的一种税。

增值税 指以商品或劳务销售额为计税依据并实行扣除已征税款制度的一种流转税。

个人所得税 是对个人（自然人）取得的各项应税所得征收的一种税。

Explanatory Notes on Main Statistical Indicators

Finance

Local Public Budgetary Revenue refers to the revenue organized by finance authorities at all levels in certain form and through certain procedures and involved in budgetary management.

Governmental Fund Budgetary Revenue refers to governmental fund budgetary revenues collected, transferred or allocated by government finance in the current year in accordance with regulations, and regulated by government finance and used for specific purpose.

Budget of State-owned Capital Operation refers to the state-owned capital income of the country as the owner and all kinds of income and expenditure budgets resulted from the allocation of the income. It is an important part of governmental budget.

Social Insurance Fund Budget refers to a legally effective annual financial revenue and expenditure plan of fund formulated by social insurance agencies in accordance with relevant laws and regulations ofstate budget management and social insurance as well as specified approval procedures.

Tax Revenue includes value-added tax, business tax, corporate income tax, individual income tax, resource tax, urban maintenance and construction tax, house property tax, stamp tax, urban land use tax, land appreciation tax, tax on vehicles and boat operation, farm land occupation tax, deed tax, etc.

Non-tax Revenue includes special program receipts, charge of administrative and institutional units, income of fines and confiscation, and other non-tax revenues.

Local Public Budgetary Expenditure refers to the expenditure arranged by finance authorities at all levels from the general budgetary revenue according to the planned distribution .

Governmental Fund Budgetary Expenditure refers to the expenditure arranged by finance authorities at all levels according to the fund budget revenue.

Expenditure for General Public Services refers to the spending on the basic public management and services provided by the government, including the expenses on affairs of Beijing Municipal People's Congress, CPC Beijing Municipal Committee, General Office of Beijing Municipal Government and relative institutions, development and reform, statistical information, finance, taxation, audit, customs, human resources, discipline inspection and supervision, population and family planning, commerce and trade, intellectual property, administration for industry and commerce, land and resources, oceanic administration, surveying and mapping, earthquake, weather, ethnics, religions, Hong Kong, Macao, Taiwan, and Overseas Chinese, archive administration, Chinese Communist Party, democratic parties, federation of industry and commerce, mass organizations, and lottery, etc.

Expenditure for Education refers to the spending of government on education, including the expenses on the administration of education, pre-school education, primary education, junior high school education, senior high school education, general higher education, primary vocational education, secondary vocational education, technical school education, vocational senior high school education and higher vocational education, radio and television education, overseas student education, special education, continuing education for management personnel, and services for education authorities, etc.

Expenditure for Science and Technology refers to the spending on science and technology (S&T), including the expense on the administration of S&T, basic research, applied research, research and development, conditions and services of S&T, popularization of social science and S&T, exchanges and cooperation of S&T, etc.

Expenditure for Cultural Education and Media refers to the spending on culture, cultural relics, sports, radio, films, television, press and publication, etc.

Expenditure for Social Security and Employment refers to the spending on social security and employment, including the expenses on social security and employment administration affairs, civil affairs, budgetary subsidy on the social insurance funds, subsidy on National Social Security Fund, subsidy on retirees of administrative and institutional units, subsidy on enterprise reform, subsidy on employment, pension, reemployment of ex-serviceman, social welfare, the handicapped undertakings, subsistence allowances for urban residents, other urban social relief, rural social relief, relief for natural disasters, affairs of Red Cross, etc.

Expenditure for Health Care and Family Planning refers to the spending of government on health care and family planning.

Expenditure for Energy Conservation and Environmental Protection refers to the spending of government on environmental protection, including the expenses on administration of environmental protection, environment monitoring and supervision, pollution control, natural and ecological protection, projects of natural forest protection, reforestation, control of sand storms, returning pasture and grazing land to grassland, energy conservation and utilization, emission reduction, comprehensive utilization of renewable energy and resources, etc.

Expenditure for Transportation refers to the spending of government on transportation and postal services, including the expenses on highway transportation, waterway transportation, railway transportation, civil aviation transportation and postal services, etc.

Expenditure for Urban and Rural Community Affairs refers to the spending of government on urban and rural community affairs, including the expenses on administration of urban and rural communities, planning and management of urban and rural communities, public facilities in urban and rural communities, residential houses in urban and rural communities, sanitation in urban and rural communities, management and supervision of construction markets, etc.

Expenditure for Agriculture, Forestry and Water Conservancy Affairs refers to the spending of government on agriculture affairs, forestry affairs, water conservancy affairs, poverty alleviation and comprehensive agricultural development, etc.

Taxes

Local Tax Revenue refers to the revenue of taxes, fines and confiscations levied and collected by local tax bureaus at all levels, including, corporate income tax, personal income tax, resource tax, house property tax, deed tax, urban maintenance and construction tax, etc.

State Tax Revenue refers to the revenue of taxes levied and collected by state tax bureaus at all levels, including value-added tax, excise tax, corporate income tax, individual income tax, urban maintenance and construction tax, etc.

Corporate Income Tax is a sort of tax levied against income of China domestic enterprises from their production and operation and other income.

Value-Added Tax is a sort of commodity turnover tax based on commodity and service sales, with a system of deduction of tax levied.

Personal Income Tax is a sort of tax levied against taxable income earned by individuals (natural persons).

北京统计年鉴2017　BEIJING STATISTICAL YEARBOOK

能源、资源和环境
ENERGY, RESOURCES AND ENVIRONMENT

简要说明

一、本章资料的主要内容

本章包括的主要内容有：北京市能源生产量、能源消费量、万元地区生产总值能耗、能源消费的行业构成和品种构成、能源平衡表、能源消费弹性系数、人均及日均能源消费量和北京地区用电量情况；土地利用情况；气象情况、水资源情况、排水及节水情况；园林绿化及森林情况；大气环境、固体废物处置情况等环境保护资料。

二、本章资料的统计范围

本章能源部分统计范围为全社会口径。

三、本章资料的数据来源

本章能源部分由北京市统计局提供；土地利用情况由北京市规划和国土资源管理委员会提供；气象资料由北京市气象局提供；水资源、排水及节水情况由北京市水务局提供；城市环境卫生由北京市城市管理委员会提供；环境保护资料由北京市环境保护局提供。

四、本章中关于历史数据调整的问题

本章中 2008 年能源消费数据为第二次经济普查数据，1995-2007 年的能源消费数据已根据北京市第二次全国经济普查的数据结果进行了修正。1997-2007 年的万元地区生产总值能耗及下降率、万元地区生产总值水耗及下降率、能源消费弹性系数、平均每万元地区生产总值能源消费量中使用的地区生产总值数据，已根据北京市第二次全国经济普查和北京市第二次全国农业普查的数据结果进行了修正。

本章中人均生活用能、人均水资源按年平均常住人口计算；同时，根据北京市第六次全国人口普查的数据结果对 2006-2010 年的人均指标数据进行了修正。

2013 年能源消费数据为第三次全国经济普查数据。2005-2012 年的能源生产量、能源消费总量、万元地区生产总值能耗及下降率，以及 2010-2012 年的能源消费构成、能源消费弹性系数、平均每万元地区生产总值能源消费量、人均生活用能源、主要能源日均消费量数据已根据第三次全国经济普查的数据结果进行了修正。

2016 年万元地区生产总值能耗及下降率、万元地区生产总值水耗及下降率、能源消费弹性系数、平均每万元地区生产总值能源消费量中使用的地区生产总值数据包含研发支出，历史数据未按照新的地区生产总值核算口径进行修正。

五、有关统计标准的变化说明

（一）关于行业划分。根据国家统计局规定，自 2012 年开始执行《国民经济行业分类》GB/T 4754-2011 标准。

（二）关于三次产业划分。根据国家统计局《三次产业划分规定》（国统字[2012]108 号），对三次产业的范围进行了调整。其中第一产业是指农、林、牧、渔业（不含农、林、牧、渔服务业）；第二产业是指采矿业（不含开采辅助活动），制造业（不含金属制品、机械和设备修理业），电力、热力、燃气及水生产和供应业，建筑业；第三产业是指除第一产业、第二产业以外的其他行业。自 2012 年开始执行此规定。

六、全市能源统计的内容及能源消费量的测算方法

全市能源统计主要内容包括第二、三产业限额以上法人单位能源消费情况全面调查；限额以下法人单位能源消费情况抽样调查；农业生产能源消费统计；居民生活能源消费情况抽样调查；能源供应部门的能源供应情况等。

从全市范围看，各能源品种的生产量、供应量和消费量存在平衡关系。因此，在进行生产和居民生活的能源消费量测算时，根据全市各能源品种的生产量、供应量和供应结构进行平衡修正。

Brief Introduction

I. Main Content

This chapter consists of statistics for volume of energy production and energy consumption in Beijing, energy consumption in regions with RMB 10,000 GDP, energy consumption by sector and by type, energy balance sheet, energy consumption elasticity coefficient, per-capita and daily energy consumption and electricity consumption in Beijing; land utilization; meteorology, water resources, water drainage and water saving; landscaping and forest; atmospheric environment, solid waste disposal and other environmental protection data.

II. Scope of Statistics

In this chapter, statistics on energy cover the entire society.

III. Source of Statistics

Energy statistics are from Beijing Municipal Bureau of Statistics; statistics on land utilization are from Urban Planning, Land & Resources Administration Commission of Beijing Municipal; meteorology statistics are from Beijing Meteorological Service; water resources, water drainage and water saving statistics are from Beijing Water Authority; urban environment and sanitation statistics are from Beijing Municipal Commission of City Administration; other statistics on environmental protection are from Beijing Municipal Environmental Protection Bureau.

IV. Adjustment to Historical Statistics

Total energy consumption figures of 2008 in this chapter are the results from the "second economic census". Statistics on total energy consumption from 1995 to 2007 are corrected based on the second national economic census in Beijing. Figures of GDP of Beijing used in the 1997-2007 energy consumption and decrease rate in regions with RMB 10,000 GDP, water consumption and decrease rate in regions with RMB 10,000 GDP, energy consumption elasticity coefficient, and energy consumption in regions with per RMB 10,000 GDP by different energy have been corrected in accordance with results from the second economic census and the second agricultural census.

In this chapter, the per-capita energy consumption for living and per-capita water resources are calculated by average permanent population; at the same time, per-capita index figures from 2006 to 2010 have been corrected in accordance with the sixth national population census.

Energy consumption figures of 2013 are the results from the 3rd national economic census. Figures of energy production, total energy consumption, energy consumption and decrease rate in regions with RMB 10,000 GDP in the 2005-2012, as well as the energy consumption structure, energy consumption elasticity coefficient, energy consumption in regions with per RMB 10,000 GDP by different energy, per-capita energy consumption for living and average daily consumption of primary energy in the 2010-2012 have been corrected in accordance with results from the third national economic census.

GDP data used in 2016 Energy Consumption per 10000 yuan of GDP and its Decrease Rate, Water Consumption per 10000 yuan of GDP and its Decrease Rate, Elasticity Coefficient of Energy Consumption, Energy consumption per 10000 yuan of GDP contain the R&D expenditure but the historical data were not revised according to the new calculation coverage of GDP.

V. Changes in Relevant Statistical Standards

(I) Classification of Sectors. According to relevant provisions of the National Bureau of Statistics of the People's Republic of China, the *Classification of National Economic Sectors* (Standard GB/T 4754-2011) came into effect in 2012.

(II) Classification of Three Industries. According to the *Regulations on Three Industries Classification* (G.T.Z. [2012] No. 108) of National Bureau of Statistics, the scope of three industries has been adjusted. The primary industry refers to agriculture, forestry, animal production and hunting, fishing (excluding service activities for agriculture, forestry, animal production and hunting, fishing); secondary industry refers to mining and quarrying (excluding mining support service activities), manufacturing (excluding repair of fabricated metal products, machinery and equipment), production and distribution of electricity, heating power, gas and water and construction; the tertiary industry refers to others excluding the primary and secondary industries. The Provisions of the National Bureau of Statistics on *Regulations on Three Industries Classification* (G.T.Z. [2012] No. 108) came into effect in 2012.

VI. Content of Energy Statistics in Beijing and Calculation Method of Energy Consumption

Energy statistics in Beijing include complete survey on energy consumption in entities above designated size in the secondary and tertiary industries; sample survey on energy consumption in entities below designated size; statistics on energy consumption in agricultural production; sample survey on energy consumption in residents' living and energy supply in energy supply departments, etc.

In terms of the whole city, the volume of production, supply and consumption shall be balanced among all types of energy. Therefore, in the calculation of energy consumption in production and residents' living by using the above-mentioned method, a balanced correction shall be made according to the volume of production, supply and supply structure of all types of energy in the city.

5-1 能源生产量(2005-2016年)
ENERGY PRODUCTION (2005-2016)

项目		Item		2005	2006	2007	2008	2009	2010
一次能源	**(万吨标准煤)**	**Primary Energy**	**(10000 tons of SCE)**	**679.5**	**460.6**	**466.1**	**414.2**	**475.7**	**499.9**
#原煤	(万吨)	Raw Coal	(10000 tons)	945.2	642.1	648.8	578.5	641.3	500.1
二次能源	**(万吨标准煤)**	**Secondary Energy**	**(10000 tons of SCE)**	**2772.6**	**2632.9**	**2767.9**	**3104.9**	**3146.9**	**3418.3**
#汽油	(万吨)	Gasoline	(10000 tons)	142.2	145.6	160.4	202.3	242.1	247.7
煤油	(万吨)	Kerosene	(10000 tons)	12.4	11.6	36.4	85.2	111.6	116.1
柴油	(万吨)	Diesel Oil	(10000 tons)	154.7	167.1	244.7	354.8	314.8	314.5
燃料油	(万吨)	Fuel Oil	(10000 tons)	64.5	57.9	36.7	28.6	28.0	33.7
液化石油气	(万吨)	Liquefied Petroleum Gas	(10000 tons)	47.3	23.0	41.0	42.9	28.8	29.0
热力	(万百万千焦)	Heat	(10 billion kilo-joules)	11335.7	12181.6	12686.9	13650.5	14226.1	15345.0
电力	(亿千瓦时)	Electricity	(100 million kwh)	209.8	209.7	224.2	244.7	241.9	262.0

5-1 续表 Continued

项目		Item		2011	2012	2013	2014	2015	2016
一次能源	**(万吨标准煤)**	**Primary Energy**	**(10000 tons of SCE)**	**500.3**	**507.2**	**541.7**	**514.0**	**545.6**	**445.8**
#原煤	(万吨)	Raw Coal	(10000 tons)	500.1	493.1	500.1	457.5	450.1	317.6
二次能源	**(万吨标准煤)**	**Secondary Energy**	**(10000 tons of SCE)**	**3080.9**	**3155.5**	**3019.0**	**3333.2**	**3476.8**	**3281.5**
#汽油	(万吨)	Gasoline	(10000 tons)	245.3	255.2	223.9	287.4	296.3	260.5
煤油	(万吨)	Kerosene	(10000 tons)	126.4	132.9	99.4	152.3	160.0	149.8
柴油	(万吨)	Diesel Oil	(10000 tons)	309.3	274.5	194.7	219.8	180.4	152.5
燃料油	(万吨)	Fuel Oil	(10000 tons)	21.3	18.4	16.9	4.7	1.4	0.7
液化石油气	(万吨)	Liquefied Petroleum Gas	(10000 tons)	27.2	31.9	28.1	32.1	34.0	41.3
热力	(万百万千焦)	Heat	(10 billion kilo-joules)	14795.5	15400.5	14893.6	15055.4	15819.7	16091.9
电力	(亿千瓦时)	Electricity	(100 million kwh)	256.1	283.3	326.7	351.6	412.5	419.0

5-2 能源消费总量及构成情况(2010-2016年)
PRIMARY ENERGY CONSUMPTION AND ITS COMPOSITION(2010-2016)

年份 Year	能源消费总量(万吨标准煤) Total Energy Consumption (10,000 tons of SCE)	占能源消费总量的比重 (%) As Percentage of Primary Energy Production (%)					
		煤品 Coal	油品 Petroleum	天然气 Natural Gas	一次电力 Primary Electricity	电力净调入(+)、调出(-)量 Net Amount of Electricity Transferred in/out	其它能源 Other energy
2010	6359.49	29.59	30.94	14.58	0.45	24.35	0.09
2011	6397.30	26.66	32.92	14.02	0.45	25.62	0.33
2012	6564.10	25.22	31.61	17.11	0.42	25.38	0.26
2013	6723.90	23.31	32.19	18.20	0.35	24.99	0.96
2014	6831.23	20.37	32.56	21.09	0.41	24.03	1.54
2015	6852.55	13.68	33.54	28.97	0.40	21.55	1.86
2016	6961.70	9.81	32.93	31.68	0.66	23.20	1.72

5-3 能源消费总量及万元地区生产总值能耗(1980-2016年)
TOTAL ENERGY CONSUMPTION AND ENERGY CONSUMPTION PER 10000 YUAN OF GDP (1980-2016)

单位：万吨标准煤 (10000 tons of SCE)

年份 Year	能源消费总量 Total Energy Consumption	第一产业 Primary Industry	第二产业 Secondary Industry	第三产业 Tertiary Industry	生活消费 Residential Consumption	万元地区生产总值能耗（吨标准煤）Energy Consumption per 10000 yuan of GDP (ton of SCE)	万元地区生产总值能耗下降率(%) Decrease Rate of Energy Consumption per 10000 yuan GDP(%)
1980	1907.7	66.8	1400.3	297.6	143.0	13.715	
1981	1902.6	53.3	1339.4	334.9	175.0	13.668	-0.23
1982	1920.4	55.7	1346.2	338.0	180.5	12.398	6.02
1983	1984.7	73.4	1379.4	313.6	218.3	10.839	11.22
1984	2144.1	85.8	1470.9	347.3	240.1	9.899	7.98
1985	2211.4	90.7	1488.3	351.6	280.8	8.601	5.12
1986	2400.0	95.7	1612.0	380.4	311.9	8.424	-0.49
1987	2475.8	89.0	1647.8	424.7	314.3	7.576	5.88
1988	2612.6	111.7	1748.1	412.2	340.6	6.369	6.45
1989	2653.2	114.4	1735.9	427.0	375.9	5.818	2.73
1990	2709.7	105.7	1720.1	515.3	368.6	5.411	2.92
1991	2872.0	126.7	1807.6	542.0	395.7	4.795	3.56
1992	2987.5	143.6	1888.1	552.4	403.4	4.213	6.54
1993	3264.6	133.6	2150.9	561.0	419.1	3.684	2.69
1994	3385.9	143.6	2234.1	574.8	433.4	2.956	8.78
1995	3533.3	120.4	2328.4	632.7	451.8	2.344	6.83
1996	3734.5	110.8	2477.0	698.1	448.6	2.087	2.75
1997	3719.2	95.7	2369.6	799.8	454.1	1.792	9.55
1998	3808.1	96.2	2400.5	856.4	455.0	1.603	6.49
1999	3906.6	86.9	2370.7	971.8	477.2	1.459	7.49
2000	4144.0	104.8	2424.8	1080.9	533.5	1.311	5.12
2001	4229.2	105.4	2366.6	1196.2	561.0	1.198	8.62
2002	4436.1	103.0	2414.6	1334.5	584.0	1.127	5.93
2003	4648.2	99.9	2476.7	1391.0	680.6	1.062	5.73
2004	5139.6	85.6	2664.2	1638.0	751.8	1.029	3.09
2005	5049.8	85.4	2363.7	1771.7	829.0	0.902	4.17
						(0.725)	
2006	5399.3	91.1	2421.2	1962.8	924.2	0.686	5.37
2007	5747.7	95.1	2434.6	2198.4	1019.6	0.637	7.02
2008	5786.2	95.2	2215.6	2394.3	1081.1	0.588	7.74
2009	6008.6	97.1	2206.5	2527.3	1177.7	0.554	5.76
2010	6359.5	98.5	2364.1	2654.4	1242.5	0.532	4.04
						(0.451)	
2011	6397.3	98.3	2160.1	2818.9	1320.0	0.419	6.95
2012	6564.1	98.1	2082.1	2967.0	1416.9	0.399	4.75
2013	6723.9	97.3	2079.2	3109.1	1438.3	0.380	4.88
2014	6831.2	91.7	1998.4	3236.5	1504.6	0.360	5.29
2015	6852.6	84.6	1902.7	3312.6	1552.7	0.338	6.13
						(0.298)	
2016	6961.7	80.4	1870.8	3414.4	1596.1	0.275	4.87

注：1．本表能源消费量指标按等价值计算，万元地区生产总值能耗下降率按可比价格计算。
2．2000年及以前万元地区生产总值能耗按当年价格计算；2000年以后按可比价格计算，可比价格每五年调整一次基期，更换基期年份计算两个可比价数据，括号内数据按新基期价格计算。

Note: a) Enery consumption in this table is at equivalent prices. Decrease Rate of Energy Consumption per 10000 yuan of GDP is calculated at comparable prices.
b) Energy consumption per 10000 yuan of GDP before 2000 was calculated at the price of that year; figures after 2000 were calculated at comparable prices. The base period of comparable prices is changed every five years. Two figures at comparable prices were calculated for the year in which the base period is changed. Figures in brackets were calculated at the price of new base period.

5−4 按行业分能源消费总量
TOTAL ENERGY CONSUMPTION BY SECTOR

单位：万吨标准煤 (10000 tons of SCE)

项　　目	Item	2016	2015
能源消费总量	**Total Energy Consumption**	**6961.7**	**6852.6**
按产业分组	**By There Industies**		
第一产业	Primary Industry	80.4	84.6
第二产业	Secondary Industry	1870.8	1902.7
第三产业	Tertiary Industry	3414.4	3312.6
生活消费	Residential Consumption	1596.1	1552.7
按行业分组	**By Sector**		
#采矿业	Mining and Quarrying	14.6	17.2
制造业	Manufacturing	1197.4	1292.5
电力、热力、燃气及水生产和供应业	Production and Distribution of Electricity, Heating Pewer, Gas and Water	539.4	474.7
建筑业	Construction	119.5	118.3
批发和零售业	Wholesale and Retail Trade	211.8	198.5
交通运输、仓储和邮政业	Transport, Storage and Post	1312.7	1249.4
住宿和餐饮业	Accommodation and Restaurants	279.6	299.1
信息传输、软件和信息技术服务业	Information Transmission,Software and Information Technology Services	181.1	164.9
金融业	Finance	64.5	66.8
房地产业	Real Estate	384.4	376.9
租赁和商务服务业	Renting and Leasing Activities and Business Services	205.5	195.5
科学研究和技术服务业	Scientific Research and Development, Technical Services	191.5	170.9
水利、环境和公共设施管理业	Management of Water Conservancy, Environment and Public Facilities	62.5	60.3
居民服务、修理和其他服务业	Resident Services, Repair and Other Services	31.3	30.3
教　育	Education	218.6	228.7
卫生和社会工作	Healtlcare and Social Works	84.9	84.1
文化、体育和娱乐业	Culture, Sports and Entertainment	75.6	72.2
公共管理、社会保障和社会组织	Public Administration, Social Security and Social Organizations	110.4	115.0

5-5 按三次产业分万元地区生产总值能耗及能耗下降率(2001-2016年)
ENERGY CONSUMPTION PER 10000 YUAN OF GDP AND DECREASE RATE BY THREE INDUSTRIES (2001-2016)

单位：吨标准煤 (ton of SCE)

年 份 Year	万元地区生产总值能耗 Energy Consumption per 10000 yuan of GDP	按产业分组 By Three Industies			按主要行业分组 By Sector	
		第一产业 Primary Industry	第二产业 Secondary Industry	第三产业 Tertiary Industry	#工 业 Industry	#交通运输、仓储和邮政业 Transport, Storage and Post
2001	1.198	1.282	2.091	0.516	2.460	1.633
2002	1.127	1.220	1.968	0.508	2.318	1.675
2003	1.062	1.196	1.803	0.476	2.114	1.564
2004	1.029	1.031	1.658	0.496	1.898	1.929
2005	0.902	1.049	1.336	0.473	1.527	1.757
	(0.725)	(0.963)	(1.166)	(0.365)	(1.333)	(1.244)
2006	0.686	1.021	1.081	0.354	1.249	1.476
2007	0.637	1.044	0.965	0.343	1.108	1.588
2008	0.588	1.034	0.871	0.332	0.998	1.802
2009	0.554	1.008	0.785	0.319	0.902	1.801
2010	0.532	1.039	0.740	0.306	0.839	1.739
	(0.451)	(0.792)	(0.698)	(0.250)	(0.804)	(1.371)
2011	0.419	0.783	0.598	0.245	0.683	1.362
2012	0.399	0.757	0.536	0.239	0.616	1.336
2013	0.380	0.740	0.509	0.230	0.569	1.325
2014	0.360	0.697	0.458	0.223	0.516	1.304
2015	0.338	0.721	0.422	0.211	0.486	1.300
	(0.298)	(0.603)	(0.419)	(0.181)	(0.481)	(1.270)
2016	0.275	0.627	0.378	0.169	0.435	1.251

注：万元地区生产总值能耗按可比价格计算，可比价格每五年调整一次基期，更换基期年份计算两个可比价数据，括号内数据是按新基期价格计算。

Note: Energy consumption per 10000 yuan of GDP were calculated at comparable prices. The base period of comparable prices is changed every five years. Two figures at comparable prices were calculated for the year in which the base period is changed. Figures in brackets were calculated at the price of new base period.

5-5 续表 Continued

单位：% (%)

年 份 Year	万元地区生产总值能耗下降率 Decrease Rate of Energy Consumption per 10000 yuan GDP	按产业分组 By Three Industies			按主要行业分组 By Sector	
		第一产业 Primary Industry	第二产业 Secondary Industry	第三产业 Tertiary Industry	#工 业 Industry	#交通运输、仓储和邮政业 Transport, Storage and Post
2001	8.62	2.98	10.90	2.13	11.91	-14.90
2002	5.93	4.83	5.88	1.56	5.75	-2.60
2003	5.73	1.96	8.39	6.23	8.80	6.66
2004	3.09	13.79	8.04	-4.08	10.22	-23.40
2005	4.17	-2.80	7.89	-3.25	8.07	-2.24
2006	5.37	-6.08	7.31	3.04	6.32	-18.63
2007	7.02	-2.21	10.79	2.95	11.24	-7.63
2008	7.74	0.98	9.71	3.19	9.93	-13.43
2009	5.76	2.45	9.81	4.20	9.68	0.07
2010	4.04	-3.05	5.79	3.89	6.92	3.41
2011	6.95	1.07	14.35	2.31	15.07	0.64
2012	4.75	3.29	10.32	2.42	9.83	1.87
2013	4.88	3.87	7.50	2.90	7.72	0.36
2014	5.29	5.76	10.06	3.14	9.43	1.60
2015	6.13	-3.41	7.80	5.33	5.67	0.31
2016	4.87	-4.07	7.53	3.69	6.59	1.42

注：表内万元地区生产总值能耗下降率按可比价格计算。

Note: Energy consumption per 10000 yuan of GDP decrease rate is at comparable prices.

5-6 电力平衡表
ELECTRICITY BALANCE

单位：亿千瓦时 (100 million kwh)

项　　目	Item	2016	2015
可供本地区消费的能源量	**Total Energy Available for Local Consumption**	**601.25**	**541.44**
加工转换投入(-)产出(+)量	**Input(-) or Output(+) in Processing and Conversion**	**419.00**	**412.53**
火力发电	Thermal Power	419.00	412.53
供　热	Heating		
煤炭洗选	Washing of Coal		
炼　焦	Coking		
炼油及煤制油	Oil Refining and Coal to Liquid		
#油品再投入量(-)	Oil Product Re-input(-)		
制　气	Gas Production		
#焦炭再投入量(-)	Coke Re-input(-)		
煤制品加工	Coal Product Processing		
回收能	Energy Recycled		
损失量	**Losses**	**63.64**	**61.29**
#运输和输配损失	In Transportation and Transmission	63.64	61.29
终端消费量	**End-use Energy Consumption**	**956.61**	**889.96**
第一产业	Primary Industry	19.62	18.50
第二产业	Secondary Industry	258.35	249.65
工业	Industry	237.00	228.89
#用作原料、材料	Use as Materials		
建筑业	Construction	21.35	20.76
第三产业	Tertiary Industry	483.20	447.05
生活消费	Residential Consumption	195.43	174.76
城镇	Urban	166.45	149.61
乡村	Rural	28.98	25.15
平衡差额	**Balance**		**2.72**
消费量合计	**Total Energy Consumption**	**1020.25**	**951.25**

5-7 综合能源平衡表(标准量)
COMPREHENSIVE ENERGY BALANCE (STANDARD VOLUME)

单位：万吨标准煤 (10000 tons of SCE)

项　　目	Item	2016	2015
可供本地区消费的能源量	**Total Energy Available for Consumption**	**6961.68**	**6860.13**
加工转换投入(-)产出(+)量	**Input(-) or Output(+) in Processing and Conversion**	**-68.50**	**-73.90**
火力发电	Thermal Power		
供　热	Heating	-74.89	-81.24
煤炭洗选	Washing of Coal		-0.02
炼　焦	Coking		
炼油及煤制油	Oil Refining and Coal to Liquid	388.59	345.18
#油品再投入量(-)	Oil Product Re-input(-)	-396.05	-353.95
制　气	Gas Production		
#焦炭再投入量(-)	Coke Re-input(-)		
煤制品加工	Coal Product Processing	-0.01	-0.26
回收能	Energy Recycled	13.86	16.39
损失量	**Losses**	**276.90**	**217.64**
#运输和输配损失	In Transportation and Transmission	175.85	171.13
终端消费量	**End-use Energy Consumption**	**6616.30**	**6561.01**
第一产业	Primary Industry	80.43	84.56
第二产业	Secondary Industry	1525.40	1611.18
工　业	Industry	1405.93	1492.88
#用作原料、材料	Use as Materials	220.59	285.64
建筑业	Construction	119.47	118.30
第三产业	Tertiary Industry	3414.38	3312.56
生活消费	Residential Consumption	1596.08	1552.71
城　镇	Urban	1341.34	1297.69
乡　村	Rural	254.74	255.02
平衡差额	**Balance**	**-0.02**	**7.58**
消费量合计	**Total Energy Consumption**	**6961.70**	**6852.55**

5-8 能源平衡表(实物量简表)(2016年)
ENERGY BALANCE (PHYSICAL VOLUME) (SIMPLE EDITION) (2016)

单位：万吨 (10000 tons)

项　目	Item	原 煤 Coal	洗精煤 Washed Coal	其他洗煤 Other Washed Coal	煤制品 Coal Products	焦 炭 Coke	原 油 Crude Oil	汽 油 Gaso-line	煤 油 Kero-sene
可供本地区消费的能源量	**Total Energy Available for Local Consumption**	**841.81**	**0.02**	**1.16**	**4.63**	**0.21**	**821.00**	**209.90**	**444.48**
加工转换投入(-)产出(+)量	**Input(-) or Output(+) in Procesing and Conversion**	**-330.87**		**-1.14**	**-1.90**		**-820.05**	**260.47**	**149.79**
火力发电	Thermal Power	-93.40			-0.61				
供 热	Heating	-237.47			-2.89				
煤炭洗选	Washing of Coal								
炼 焦	Coking								
炼油及煤制油	Oil Refining and Coal to Liquid						-820.05	260.47	149.79
#油品再投入量(-)	Oil Product Re-input(-)								
制 气	Gas Production								
#焦炭再投入量(-)	Coke Re-input(-)								
煤制品加工	Coal Product Processing			-1.14	1.59				
回收能	Energy Recycled								
损失量	**Losses**						**0.96**		
#运输和输配损失	In Transportation and Transmission								
终端消费量	**End-use Energy Consumption**	**510.95**	**0.02**	**0.02**	**2.73**	**0.21**		**470.37**	**594.27**
第一产业	Primary Industry	24.20						3.27	
第二产业	Secondary Industry	120.93			0.41	0.19		26.11	0.05
工 业	Industry	118.29			0.04	0.19		17.73	0.05
#用作原料、材料	Use as Materials	0.10						0.02	0.02
建筑业	Construction	2.63			0.37			8.38	
第三产业	Tertiary Industry	125.21	0.02	0.02	2.32	0.02		126.58	594.21
生活消费	Residential Consumption	240.61						314.41	
城 镇	Urban	91.72						314.41	
乡 村	Rural	148.89							
平衡差额	**Balance**								
消费量合计	**Total Energy Consumption**	**841.81**	**0.02**	**1.16**	**6.22**	**0.21**	**821.00**	**470.37**	**594.27**

5-8 续表 1 Continued 1

单位：万吨 (10000 tons)

项目	Item	柴油 Diesel Oil	燃料油 Fuel Oil	石脑油 Naphtha	润滑油 Grease Oil	石蜡 Oilfin	溶剂油 Solvent Oil	石油沥青 Oil Asphalt	石油焦 Petroleum Coal
可供本地区消费的能源量	**Total Energy Available for Local Consumption**	**20.15**	**3.95**	**57.33**	**1.21**	**0.21**	**0.04**	**4.20**	**-15.64**
加工转换投入(-)产出(+)量	**Input(-) or Output(+) in Procesing and Conversion**	**151.81**	**-0.03**	**-6.43**				**11.59**	**15.72**
火力发电	Thermal Power	-0.30							-4.28
供　热	Heating	-0.44	-0.73						-17.11
煤炭洗选	Washing of Coal								
炼　焦	Coking								
炼油及煤制油	Oil Refining and Coal to Liquid	152.54	0.69	145.53				11.59	37.11
#油品再投入量(-)	Oil Product Re-input(-)			-151.96					
制　气	Gas Production								
#焦炭再投入量(-)	Coke Re-input(-)								
煤制品加工	Coal Product Processing								
回收能	Energy Recycled								
损失量	**Losses**								
#运输和输配损失	In Transportation and Transmission								
终端消费量	**End-use Energy Consumption**	**171.96**	**3.91**	**50.90**	**1.21**	**0.21**	**0.05**	**15.80**	**0.08**
第一产业	Primary Industry	2.65							
第二产业	Secondary Industry	38.01	2.17	50.90	1.21	0.21	0.05	15.80	0.08
工　业	Industry	15.39	2.17	50.90	1.21	0.21	0.05	15.80	0.08
#用作原料、材料	Use in Materials	0.14		50.90	1.21	0.21	0.05	15.80	
建筑业	Construction	22.62							
第三产业	Tertiary Industry	131.31	1.74						
生活消费	Residential Consumption								
城镇	Urban								
乡村	Rural								
平衡差额	**Balance**								
消费量合计	**Total Energy Consumption**	**172.69**	**4.64**	**202.87**	**1.21**	**0.21**	**0.05**	**15.80**	**21.47**

5-8 续表 2 Continued 2

单位：万吨 (10000 tons)

项目	Item	液化石油气 Liquefied Petroleum Gas	炼厂干气 Refinery Gas	其它石油制品 Other Petroleum Products	天然气（亿立方米）Natural Gas (100 million cu.m)	液化天然气 Liquefied Natural Gas	热力（万百万千焦）Heat (10000 million kilo-joule)	电力（亿千瓦时）Electricity (100 million kWh)	其它能源（万吨标准煤）Others (10000 tons of SCE)
可供本地区消费的能源量	**Total Energy Available for Local Consumption**	**8.20**		**23.42**	**160.30**	**14.60**	**567.92**	**601.25**	**100.44**
加工转换投入(-)产出(+)量	**Input(-) or Output(+) in Procesing and Conversion**	**40.16**	**64.68**	**83.64**	**-96.59**	**-0.17**	**16091.90**	**419.00**	**-40.25**
火力发电	Thermal Power	-0.13	-0.52	-0.93	-64.39			419.00	-54.11
供热	Heating	-0.97	-3.81	-7.52	-32.20	-0.17	16091.90		
煤炭洗选	Washing of Coal								
炼焦	Coking								
炼油及煤制油	Oil Refining and Coal to Liquid	41.26	69.01	232.18					
#油品再投入量(-)	Oil Product Re-input(-)			-140.09					
制气	Gas Production								
#焦炭再投入量(-)	Coke Re-input(-)								
煤制品加工	Coal Product Processing								
回收能	Energy Recycled								13.86
损失量	**Losses**				**8.39**			**63.64**	
#运输和输配损失	In Transportation and Transmission							63.64	
终端消费量	**Final Consumption Industry**	**48.37**	**64.68**	**107.06**	**55.32**	**14.43**	**16659.83**	**956.61**	**60.19**
第一产业	Primary Industry	0.05						19.62	
第二产业	Secondary Industry	2.37	64.68	107.06	12.48	0.70	3918.12	258.35	6.78
工业	Industry	1.96	64.68	107.06	11.79	0.70	3808.84	237.00	6.37
#用作原料、材料	Use in Materials	0.13	11.79	83.24					
建筑业	Construction	0.41			0.69		109.28	21.35	0.40
第三产业	Tertiary Industry	19.61			30.01	13.73	8265.23	483.20	35.91
生活消费	Residential Consumption	26.33			12.82		4476.48	195.43	17.50
城镇	Urban	15.88			12.82		4476.48	166.45	
乡村	Rural	10.45						28.98	17.50
平衡差额	**Balance**								
消费量合计	**Total Energy Consumption**	**49.47**	**69.01**	**255.60**	**160.30**	**14.60**	**16659.83**	**1020.25**	**114.30**

5-9 能源平衡表(标准量简表)(2016年)
ENERGY BALANCE (STANDARD VOLUME) (SIMPLE EDITION) (2016)

单位：万吨标准煤 (10000 tons of SCE)

项　　目	Item	合 计 Total	原 煤 Coal	洗精煤 Washed Coal	其他洗煤 Other Washed Coal	煤制品 Coal Products	焦 炭 Coke	原 油 Crude Oil	汽 油 Gasoline	煤 油 Kerosene
可供本地区消费的能源量	**Total Energy Available for Local Consumption**	**6961.68**	**678.87**	**0.02**	**1.04**	**2.61**	**0.20**	**1172.89**	**308.85**	**654.00**
加工转换投入(-)产出(+)量	**Input(-) or Output(+) in Processing and Transformation**	**-68.50**	**-256.95**		**-1.03**	**-1.11**		**-1171.52**	**383.25**	**220.40**
火力发电	Thermal Power		-74.42			-0.38				
供　热	Heating	-74.89	-182.53			-1.76				
煤炭洗选	Washing of Coal									
炼　焦	Coking									
炼油及煤制油	Oil Refining and Coal to Liquid	388.59						-1171.52	383.25	220.40
#油品再投入量(-)	Oil Product Re-input(-)	-396.05								
制　气	Gas Production									
#焦炭再投入量(-)	Coke Re-input(-)									
煤制品加工	Coal Product Processing	-0.01			-1.03	1.02				
回收能	Energy Recycled	13.86								
损失量	**Losses**	**276.90**						**1.36**		
#运输和输配损失	In Transportation and Transmission	175.85								
终端消费量	**Final Consumption Industry**	**6616.30**	**421.92**	**0.02**	**0.01**	**1.50**	**0.21**		**692.10**	**874.40**
第一产业	Primary Industry	80.43	17.40						4.81	
第二产业	Secondary Industry	1525.40	87.57			0.22	0.18		38.42	0.08
工　业	Industry	1405.93	85.64			0.02	0.18		26.09	0.08
#用作原料、材料	Use as Materials	220.59	0.05						0.03	0.02
建筑业	Construction	119.47	1.94			0.20			12.33	
第三产业	Tertiary Industry	3414.38	91.25	0.02	0.01	1.27	0.02		186.25	874.33
生活消费	Residential Consumption	1596.08	225.70						462.62	
城　镇	Urban	1341.34	86.48						462.62	
乡　村	Rural	254.74	139.22							
平衡差额	**Balance**	**-0.02**								
消费量合计	**Total Energy Consumption**	**6961.70**								

5-9 续表 1 Continued 1

单位：万吨标准煤 (10000 tons of SCE)

项目	Item	柴油 Diesel Oil	燃料油 Fuel Oil	石脑油 Naphtha	润滑油 Grease Oil	石蜡 Oilfin	溶剂油 Solvent Oil	石油沥青 Oil Asphalt	石油焦 Petroleum Coal
可供本地区消费的能源量	**Total Energy Available for Local Consumption**	**29.36**	**5.64**	**86.00**	**1.71**	**0.29**	**0.06**	**5.59**	**-17.98**
加工转换投入(-)产出(+)量	**Input(-) or Output(+) in Processing and Transformation**	**221.20**	**-0.05**	**-9.64**				**15.43**	**18.07**
火力发电	Thermal Power	-0.43							-4.72
供热	Heating	-0.63	-1.04						-18.90
煤炭洗选	Washing of Coal								
炼焦	Coking								
炼油及煤制油	Oil Refining and Coal to Liquid	222.27	0.99	218.30				15.43	41.68
#油品再投入量(-)	Oil Product Re-input(-)			-227.94					
制气	Gas Production								
#焦炭再投入量(-)	Coke Re-input(-)								
煤制品加工	Coal Product Processing								
回收能	Energy Recycled								
损失量	**Losses**								
#运输和输配损失	In Transportation and Transmission								
终端消费量	**Final Consumption Industry**	**250.56**	**5.59**	**76.36**	**1.72**	**0.28**	**0.07**	**21.02**	**0.09**
第一产业	Primary Industry	3.86							
第二产业	Secondary Industry	55.38	3.11	76.36	1.72	0.28	0.07	21.02	0.09
工业	Industry	22.42	3.11	76.36	1.72	0.28	0.07	21.02	0.09
#用作原料、材料	Use as Materials	0.20		76.36	1.72	0.28	0.07	21.02	
建筑业	Construction	32.95							
第三产业	Tertiary Industry	191.33	2.48						
生活消费	Residential Consumption								
城镇	Urban								
乡村	Rural								
平衡差额	**Balance**								
消费量合计	**Total Energy Consumption**								

5-9 续表 2 Continued 2

单位：万吨标准煤 (10000 tons of SCE)

项　　目	Item	液化石油气 Liquefied Petroleum Gas	炼厂干气 Refinery Gas	其它石油制品 Other Petroleum Products	天然气 Natural Gas (100 million cu.m)	液化天然气 Liquefied Natural Gas	热力 Heat	电力 Electricity	其它能源 Others
可供本地区消费的能源量	**Total Energy Available for Local Consumption**	**14.06**		**32.06**	**2179.59**	**25.65**	**19.37**	**1661.37**	**100.44**
加工转换投入(-)产出(+)量	**Input(-) or Output(+) in Processing and Transformation**	**68.85**	**101.64**	**99.25**	**-1422.27**	**-0.30**	**548.73**	**1157.79**	**-40.25**
火力发电	Thermal Power	-0.22	-0.81	-1.23	-1021.46			1157.79	-54.11
供　热	Heating	-1.67	-5.99	-10.02	-400.80	-0.30	548.73		
煤炭洗选	Washing of Coal								
炼　焦	Coking								
炼油及煤制油	Oil Refining and Coal to Liquid	70.74	108.45	278.62					
#油品再投入量(-)	Oil Product Re-input(-)			-168.11					
制　气	Gas Production								
#焦炭再投入量(-)	Coke Re-input(-)								
煤制品加工	Coal Product Processing								
回收能	Energy Recycled								13.86
损失量	**Losses**				**99.68**			**175.85**	
#运输和输配损失	In Transportation and Transmission							175.85	
终端消费量	**Final Consumption Industry**	**82.91**	**101.64**	**131.31**	**657.65**	**25.35**	**568.10**	**2643.31**	**60.19**
第一产业	Primary Industry	0.09			0.06			54.23	
第二产业	Secondary Industry	4.07	101.64	131.31	148.40	1.22	133.61	713.87	6.78
工　业	Industry	3.37	101.64	131.31	140.19	1.22	129.88	654.87	6.37
#用作原料、材料	Use as Materials	0.23	18.52	102.11					
建筑业	Construction	0.70			8.21		3.73	59.00	0.40
第三产业	Tertiary Industry	33.61			356.73	24.13	281.84	1335.19	35.91
生活消费	Residential Consumption	45.14			152.46		152.65	540.02	17.50
城　镇	Urban	27.23			152.43		152.65	459.95	
乡　村	Rural	17.92			0.03			80.07	17.50
平衡差额	**Balance**				**-0.01**				
消费量合计	**Total Energy Consumption**								

5-10 分行业能源消费总量和主要能源品种消费量(2016年)

单位：万吨

项　　目	Item	能源消费总量(万吨标准煤) Total Energy Consumption (10000 tons of SCE)	煤　炭 Coal
合　　计	**Total**	**6961.70**	**847.62**
农、林、牧、渔业	Agriculture, Forestry, Animal Production and Hunting, Fishing	80.43	24.20
采矿业	Mining and Quarrying	14.60	1.43
煤炭开采和洗选业	Mining and Washing of Coal	3.78	0.44
石油和天然气开采业	Extraction of Petroleum and Natural Gas	0.02	
黑色金属矿采选业	Mining of Ferrous Metal Ores	9.94	0.97
有色金属矿采选业	Mining of Non-ferrous Metal Ores	0.01	
非金属矿采选业	Mining and Processing of Nonmetal Ores	0.71	0.02
开采辅助活动	Mining Support Service Activities	0.16	
其他采矿业	Mining of Other Ores n.e.c		
制造业	Manufacturing	1197.35	110.26
农副食品加工业	Processing of Food from Agricultural Products	23.03	4.27
食品制造业	Manufacture of Foods	29.43	2.81
酒、饮料和精制茶制造业	Manufacture of Wine, Beverage and Refined Tea	25.35	9.52
烟草制品业	Manufacture of Cigarettes and Tobacco	***	
纺织业	Manufacture of Textile	3.61	1.13
纺织服装、服饰业	Manufacture of Textile Wearing Apparel and Ornament	11.66	2.22
皮革、毛皮、羽毛及其制品和制鞋业	Manufacture of Leather, Fur, Feather and Its Products, and Footwear	1.17	0.11
木材加工和木、竹、藤、棕、草制品业	Processing of Timbers, Manufacture of Wood, Bamboo, Rattan, Palm, and Straw Products	2.44	0.18
家具制造业	Manufacture of Furniture	7.47	0.63
造纸和纸制品业	Manufacture of Paper and Paper Products	10.02	1.72
印刷和记录媒介复制业	Printing, Reproduction of Recording Media	22.58	0.73
文教、工美、体育和娱乐用品制造业	Manufacture of Articles for Culture, Education, Artwork, Sport and Entertainment Activities	3.73	0.19
石油加工、炼焦和核燃料加工业	Processing of Petroleum, Coking, Processing of Nucleus Fuel	414.30	0.17
化学原料和化学制品制造业	Manufacture of Chemical Raw Materials and Chemical Products	89.98	2.09
医药制造业	Manufacture of Medicines	35.61	2.74
化学纤维制造业	Manufacture of Chemical Fibers	1.34	0.01
橡胶和塑料制品业	Manufacture of Rubber and Plastics Products	22.21	1.98
非金属矿物制品业	Manufacture of Non-Metallic Mineral Products	128.68	67.11

注：各行业能源消费总量为各行业终端消费量与各行业分摊的损失量和加工转换损失量之和，不等于分品种能源消费量(标准煤)的合计。

CONSUMPTION OF TOTAL ENERGY AND MAIN ENERGY VARIETIES BY SECTOR (2016)

(10000 tons)

汽 油 Gasoline	煤 油 Kerosene	柴 油 Diesel Oil	燃料油 Fuel Oil	液 化 石油气 Liquefied Petroleum Gas	液化 天然气 Liquefied Natural Gas	天然气 (亿立方米) Natural Gas (100 million cu.m)	热 力 (万百万千焦) Heat (10 billion kilo-joule)	电 力 (亿千瓦时) Electricity (100 million kwh)
470.37	**594.27**	**172.69**	**4.64**	**49.47**	**14.60**	**160.30**	**16659.83**	**1020.25**
3.27		2.65		0.05				19.62
0.09		0.93		0.01		0.01	11.98	4.18
0.01		0.03		0.01			2.96	1.17
								0.01
0.04		0.61				0.01	8.87	2.87
		0.28						0.10
0.04		0.01					0.15	0.03
16.64	0.05	13.98	2.03	1.85	0.68	10.44	3628.66	176.43
0.43		0.29		0.06	0.02	0.32	62.93	4.62
0.52		0.51		0.16	0.13	0.61	82.03	5.52
0.26		0.25		0.02	0.01	0.40	52.20	4.02
						***		***
0.15		0.02		0.02		0.03	3.00	0.76
0.71		0.12		0.05	0.01	0.08	31.70	2.35
0.07		0.02		0.01			3.02	0.29
0.22		0.07		0.02		0.01	0.09	0.64
0.54		0.10	0.01	0.03	0.01	0.04	9.40	1.86
0.34		0.18	0.01	0.03	0.09	0.13	6.65	2.13
0.82		0.20		0.03		0.19	57.13	5.86
0.21		0.05		0.02	0.02	0.02	15.59	0.84
0.08		0.12		0.17		2.27	1393.96	15.03
0.78		0.65	0.03	0.12	0.09	0.22	835.29	13.70
0.49		0.23		0.05	0.03	0.56	162.23	7.39
0.02						0.03		0.34
0.60		0.22		0.31	0.02	0.14	24.01	5.99
0.98		7.07	1.88	0.11	0.11	0.88	30.12	15.75

Note: Total energy consumption in each sector is the end consumption of each sector plus losses shared by each sector and losses from processing in each sector, but not equal to sum of consumption (SCE equivalent) of all sorts of energy.

5-10 续表

单位：万吨

项目	Item	能源消费总量(万吨标准煤) Total Energy Consumption (10000 tons of SCE)	煤炭 Coal
黑色金属冶炼及压延加工业	Manufacture and Pressing of Ferrous Metals	21.19	0.39
有色金属冶炼及压延加工业	Manufacture and Pressing of Non-Ferrous Metals	5.44	0.08
金属制品业	Manufacture of Fabricated Metal Products	29.69	2.13
通用设备制造业	Manufacture of General-purpose Machinery	28.30	1.24
专用设备制造业	Manufacture of Special-purpose Machinery	21.69	1.45
汽车制造业	Manufacture of Motor Vehicles	115.98	0.43
铁路、船舶、航空航天和其他运输设备制造业	Manufacture of Railway Locomotives, Building of Ships and Boats, Manufacture of Air and Spacecrafts and Other Transportation Equipment	15.99	2.25
电气机械和器材制造业	Manufacture of Electrical Machinery and Equipment	21.20	0.63
计算机、通讯和其他电子设备制造业	Manufacture of Computer, Communication Equipment and Other Electronic Equipment	82.89	0.30
仪器仪表制造业	Manufacture of Measuring Instruments and Meters	7.96	0.21
其他制造业	Other Manufacturing	6.79	3.15
废弃资源综合利用业	Waste recycling and recovery	1.40	0.36
金属制品、机械和设备修理业	Repair of Fabricated Metal Products, Machinery and Equipment	4.30	0.03
电力、燃气及水的生产和供应业	Production and Distribution of Electricity, Gas and Water	539.38	340.55
电力、热力生产和供应业	Production and Supply of Electric Power and Heat Power	388.49	340.33
燃气生产和供应业	Production and Distribution of Gas	104.62	0.01
水的生产和供应业	Production and Distribution of Water	46.27	0.21
建筑业	Construction	119.47	3.00
批发和零售业	Wholesale and Retail Trade	211.77	6.42
交通运输、仓储和邮政业	Transport, Storage and Post	1312.69	7.99
住宿和餐饮业	Accommodation and Restaurants	279.58	15.45
信息传输、软件和信息技术服务业	Information transmission,software and information technology services	181.05	0.58
金融业	Finance	64.52	0.61
房地产业	Real Estate Trade	384.41	29.28
租赁和商务服务业	Renting and Leasing Activities and Business Services	205.51	20.93
科学研究和技术服务业	Scientific Research and Development, Technical Services	191.55	8.67
水利、环境和公共设施管理业	Water, Environment and Municipal Engineering Conservancy	62.55	4.93
居民服务、修理和其他服务业	Resident services, repair and other services	31.34	8.04
教　育	Education	218.55	9.27
卫生和社会工作	Healthcare and Social Works	84.89	6.47
文化、体育和娱乐业	Culture, Sports and Entertainment	75.56	1.01
公共管理、社会保障和社会组织	Public Administration, Social Security and Social Organizations	110.42	7.92
生活消费	Residential Consumption	1596.08	240.61
城　镇	Urban	1341.34	91.72
乡　村	Rural	254.74	148.89

5-10 Continued

(10000 tons)

汽 油 Gasoline	煤 油 Kerosene	柴 油 Diesel Oil	燃料油 Fuel Oil	液 化 石油气 Liquefied Petroleum Gas	液化 天然气 Liquefied Natural Gas	天然气 (亿立方米) Natural Gas (100 million cu.m)	热 力 (万百万千焦) Heat (10 billion kilo-joule)	电 力 (亿千瓦时) Electricity (100 million kwh)
0.12		0.15	0.09	0.01	0.01	0.62	1.21	4.20
0.10		0.04		0.03	0.04	0.03	10.60	1.56
1.46		0.38		0.22	0.02	0.30	56.98	7.03
1.30	0.01	0.45		0.13	0.01	0.19	115.34	6.51
1.26		0.21		0.05	0.02	0.10	113.71	4.79
2.33		1.53		0.09	0.02	2.37	115.46	27.63
0.23		0.14				0.18	106.13	2.90
1.03		0.11		0.06	0.02	0.14	83.67	4.90
0.67		0.48		0.01		0.23	172.85	26.13
0.62		0.03	0.01	0.01		0.06	53.81	1.53
0.11		0.11		0.01		0.04	25.41	0.88
0.03		0.03		0.01		0.01	0.84	0.31
0.16	0.04	0.23		0.01		0.14	3.30	0.69
1.00		1.21	0.86	1.20	0.19	106.32	168.20	120.03
0.58		1.05	0.86	1.17	0.17	97.39	131.50	103.55
0.24		0.07		0.01	0.02	8.84	6.81	0.91
0.18		0.09		0.02		0.09	29.89	15.58
8.38		22.62		0.41		0.69	109.28	21.35
28.45		4.66	0.01	0.68		0.97	679.38	44.24
41.62	593.66	109.92	1.49	0.28	13.73	1.99	538.60	50.61
1.41		0.45	0.02	15.60		5.66	569.02	53.44
4.56		0.17		0.05		0.24	281.37	57.97
2.24		0.16		0.03		0.14	299.23	17.54
4.62		0.83	0.05	0.19		8.86	1220.25	73.41
15.21		5.64	0.04	0.59		2.43	773.35	36.61
13.49	0.55	1.35	0.12	0.34		2.81	753.92	36.86
1.94		4.27		0.18		0.48	46.50	15.04
1.86		0.77		0.10		0.41	63.27	5.19
2.93		1.58		0.50		3.73	1515.03	35.56
0.96		0.25		0.32		1.02	418.53	17.41
2.17		0.35		0.13		0.52	360.52	18.66
5.12		0.91	0.01	0.62		0.74	746.25	20.67
314.41				26.33		12.82	4476.48	195.43
314.41				15.88		12.82	4476.48	166.45
				10.45				28.98

5-11 能源消费弹性系数(2000-2016年)
ELASTICITY COEFFICIENT OF ENERGY CONSUMPTION (2000-2016)

项 目 Item	能源消费比上年增长 (%) Growth of Energy Consumption over the Previous Year	电力消费比上年增长 (%) Growth of Electricity Consumption over the Previous Year	地区生产总值比上年增长 (%) Growth of Gross Domestic Product(GDP) over the Previous Year	能源消费弹性系数 Elasticity Coefficient of Energy Consumption	电力消费弹性系数 Elasticity Coefficient of Electricity Consumption
2000	6.08	9.53	11.8	0.51	0.81
2001	2.06	5.68	11.7	0.18	0.49
2002	4.89	9.54	11.5	0.43	0.83
2003	4.78	5.71	11.1	0.43	0.51
2004	10.57	10.60	14.1	0.75	0.75
2005	7.44	11.16	12.1	0.61	0.92
2006	6.92	9.16	13.0	0.53	0.71
2007	6.45	9.06	14.5	0.45	0.63
2008	0.67	4.90	9.1	0.07	0.54
2009	3.84	7.15	10.2	0.38	0.70
2010	5.84	9.49	10.3	0.57	0.92
2011	0.59	2.21	8.1	0.07	0.27
2012	2.61	5.91	7.7	0.34	0.77
2013	2.44	4.42	7.7	0.32	0.57
2014	1.60	2.72	7.3	0.22	0.37
2015	0.31	1.91	6.9	0.05	0.28
2016	1.59	7.25	6.8	0.23	1.07

注：1. 地区生产总值增长速度按可比价计算。
2. 2013年数据为第三次全国经济普查数据。2005-2012年电力数据根据第三次全国经济普查的数据结果进行了修正。
3. 2016年地区生产总值增速及能源消费弹性系数中使用的地区生产总值数据均包含研发支出，历史数据未按照新的地区生产总值核算口径进行修正。

Note: a) The groth rates of GDP are calculated at comparable prices.
b) Data for 2013 were collected from the third national economic census.Data for 2005-2012 were revised acording to the third national economic census.
c) GDP data used in 2016 GDP Growth Rate and Elasticity Coefficient of Energy Consumption contain the R&D expenditure, but the historical data were not revised according to the new calculation coverage of GDP.

5-12 平均每万元地区生产总值能源消费量(2010-2016年)
ENERGY CONSUMPTION PER 10000 YUAN OF GROSS DOMESTIC PRODUCT (2010-2016)

项 目 Item	能源总消费量 (吨标准煤) Total (ton of SCE)	煤 炭 (吨) Coal (ton)	电 力 (千瓦时) Electricity (kwh)	石 油 (吨) Petroleum (ton)
2010	0.53	0.21	672.13	0.11
	(0.45)	(0.18)	(569.60)	(0.10)
2011	0.42	0.15	538.34	0.09
2012	0.40	0.13	529.22	0.09
2013	0.38	0.11	513.11	0.08
2014	0.36	0.09	491.30	0.08
2015	0.34	0.06	468.52	0.08
	(0.30)	(0.05)	(413.32)	(0.07)
2016	0.28	0.03	403.34	0.06

注：本表中每万元地区生产总值能源消费量按可比价格计算，可比价格每五年调整一次基期，更换基期年份计算两个可比价格数据，括号内数据是按新基期价格计算。

Note: Energy consumption per 10000 yuan of GDP were calculated at comparable prices. The base period of comparable prices is changed every five years. Two figures at comparable prices were calculated for the year in which the base period is changed. Figures in brackets were calculated at the price of new base period.

5－13 人均生活用能源(2010－2016年) PER CAPITA ENERGY CONSUMPTION FOR NON-PRODUCTIVE PURPOSE (2010-2016)

年 份 Year	合 计 (千克标准煤) Total (kg of SCE)	煤 炭 (千克) Coal (kg)	电 力 (千瓦时) Electricity (kwh)	液化石油气 (千克) Liquefied Petroleum Gas(kg)	天然气 (立方米) Natural Gas (cu.m)	汽 油 (升) Gasoline (liter)
2010	650.2	173.6	729.1	11.3	53.1	164.9
2011	663.2	167.1	727.2	10.7	52.7	167.6
2012	693.2	159.0	791.8	9.3	56.5	174.4
2013	687.5	147.7	750.6	9.9	57.1	180.7
2014	705.3	137.6	793.5	11.0	59.6	182.5
2015	718.5	126.3	808.7	11.6	63.7	194.3
2016	734.9	110.8	899.9	12.1	59.0	198.3

注：本表人均生活用能源按常住人口年平均数计算。2006—2010年数据根据全国第六次人口普查进行了修正。

Note：Per-capita energy consumption for non-productive prupose is calculated by average permanent population. Figures for 2006-2010 have been revised in accordance with the 6th national population census.

5–14 主要能源日均消费量(2010–2016年)
DAILY CONSUMPTION OF MAIN ENERGY VARIETIES(2010-2016)

年份 Year	合计 (万吨标准煤) Total (10000 tons of SCE)	煤炭 (吨) Coal (ton)	原油 (吨) Crude Oil (ton)	汽油 (吨) Gasoline (ton)	煤油 (吨) Kerosene (ton)	柴油 (吨) Diesel Oil (ton)	燃料油 (吨) Fuel Oil (ton)	电力 (万千瓦时) Electricity (10000 kwh)	天然气 (万立方米) Natural Gas (10000 cu.m)
2010	17.4	69315.4	30175.6	9935.4	10757.0	5333.0	442.3	22024.9	2048.9
2011	17.5	62056.8	29778.2	10418.6	11503.7	5366.2	340.3	22512.5	2014.0
2012	18.0	59714.8	29072.1	11116.6	12146.1	5166.4	302.4	23842.3	2522.4
2013	18.4	55321.3	23860.7	11605.7	13070.1	5312.2	227.3	24896.0	2707.2
2014	18.7	47576.5	28345.6	12071.7	13906.3	5382.5	154.3	25572.9	3115.0
2015	18.8	31922.7	27165.5	12678.2	14914.6	4995.9	134.5	26061.7	3982.9
2016	19.1	23222.5	22493.2	12886.8	16281.4	4731.2	127.1	27952.1	4391.8

5-15 全社会用电量情况(1978-2016年)
TOTAL ELECTRICITY CONSUMPTION IN BEIJING (1978-2016)

单位：万千瓦时 (10000 kwh)

年 份 Year	全社会用电量 Electricity Consumption	第一产业 Primary Industry	第二产业 Secondary Industry	工 业 Industry	建筑业 Construction	第三产业 Tertiary Industry	城乡居民生活用电 Residential Electricity Consumption	城 市 Urban	乡 村 Rural
1978	735000	48993	570621	570621		94555	20831	11022	9809
1979	802317	52134	620262	620262		107437	22484	11495	10989
1980	854638	65283	648496	648496		116947	23912	12441	11471
1981	867153	80027	643976	643976		121883	21267	9452	11815
1982	925700	104842	657060	657060		139403	24395	10820	13575
1983	956293	92601	687937	687937		151290	24465	12320	12145
1984	1029420	105234	716653	716653		177455	30078	16025	14053
1985	1106255	111110	746324	746324		210622	38199	22479	15720
1986	1181155	105688	851519	835725	15794	175090	48858	31008	17850
1987	1285023	77909	923797	899760	24037	224747	58570	35063	23507
1988	1378574	83809	970885	943383	27502	248446	75434	48624	26810
1989	1421817	100151	979216	949629	29587	258067	84383	56120	28263
1990	1504785	93049	1014037	986356	27681	302775	94924	65262	29662
1991	1613977	93256	1061207	1032064	29143	348769	110745	77575	33170
1992	1759611	101985	1155514	1123835	31679	375874	126238	88621	37617
1993	1924978	107010	1243115	1206001	37114	429835	145018	103579	41439
1994	2054504	101134	1307898	1262961	44937	479679	165791	119025	46766
1995	2225922	102099	1403864	1341398	62466	538936	181022	130897	50125
1996	2443709	111904	1496968	1422590	74378	617286	217551	158474	59077
1997	2636078	120444	1529201	1449129	80072	721774	264659	196641	68018
1998	2762080	108267	1548485	1457149	91336	811283	294045	220543	73502
1999	2972629	121242	1581977	1478523	103454	912834	356576	276642	79934
2000	3844266	130865	2172604	2066892	105712	1064322	476475	385396	91079
2001	3999415	131811	2105819	1978673	127146	1222471	539314	439058	100256
2002	4399637	137370	2293735	2145292	148443	1342490	626042	517386	108656
2003	4676056	107372	2418419	2250525	167894	1447344	702921	574623	128298
2004	5131804	104234	2593504	2391414	202090	1628731	805335	647474	157861
2005	5705364	114308	2795753	2605832	189921	1906093	889210	706405	182805
2006	6115719	122550	2943550	2744127	199423	2090888	958731	768884	189847
2007	6670089	133557	3091374	2881807	209567	2378399	1066759	862604	204155
2008	6897189	136065	2943893	2763399	180494	2654140	1163091	949878	213213
2009	7391465	157310	3027974	2853018	174956	2918229	1287952	982720	305232
2010	8099029	168992	3278682	3081364	197319	3258009	1393346	951811	441535
2011	8217055	170368	3109174	2894464	214708	3490143	1447370	945588	501782
2012	8742835	181391	3209078	2980645	228430	3734022	1618344	1370932	247412
2013	9131113	185749	3345854	3110626	235229	4029145	1570365	1347401	222964
2014	9370485	185633	3352904	3129060	223846	4139319	1692629	1457398	235231
2015	9527169	185031	3238220	3030638	207583	4356332	1747586	1496078	251508
2016	10202704	196243	3343189	3129675	213514	4708959	1954313	1664539	289774

注：1. 1985年以前农、林、牧、渔和水利业用电量中，只包含农业排灌、农副业和社队企业的用电量。
2. 1980年以前的城市居民用电量以全市市政用电量的 1/10计算。
3. 2000年以前工业用电量不包含输配损失和发电企业自产自用电量。

资料来源：北京市电力公司。

Note: a) Before 1985, electricity consumption by agriculture, forestry, animal production and hunting, fishing and water conservancy only included the electricity consumption by farming irrigation, agricultural and sideline products, and village enterprises.

b) Before 1980, electricity consumption by urban residents was one-tenth of the total electricity consumption by municipal administration in Beijing.

c) Before 2000, electricity consumption by industry excluded transmission and distribution losses and electricity generated and consumed by power generating enterprises.

Source: Beijing Electric Power Corporation.

5-16 主要土地利用状况(2009-2015年)
LAND UTILIZATION (2009-2015)

单位：公顷 (hectare)

年 份 Year	耕地面积 Arable Land	园地面积 Garden Plot	林地面积 Forest Land	草地面积 Grass Land	城镇村及工矿用地面积 Land for Urban, Rural,Industrial and Mining Use	交通运输用地面积 Land for Transportation	水域及水利设施用地面积 Water Areas and Land for Water Conservancy Facilities
2009	227170.43	141617.22	743696.19	84843.14	284791.79	44446.42	80235.85
2010	223779.38	139298.50	742018.50	85827.05	290782.01	45335.78	79774.99
2011	221956.16	138072.99	740730.87	85651.69	295116.72	45452.68	79380.05
2012	220856.16	137117.72	739633.48	85491.29	297758.79	46327.98	79088.32
2013	221157.28	135573.37	738036.45	85348.82	300847.83	46626.41	78739.52
2014	219948.76	135103.71	737542.89	85139.49	302939.17	47006.28	78378.65
2015	219326.49	134857.89	737078.88	85066.77	304393.05	47062.78	78304.28

注：表中2009年数据为第二次全国土地调查数据，2010—2015年为各年土地变更调查数据。

资料来源：北京市规划和国土资源管理委员会。

Note: Statistics for 2009 were from the 2nd National Land Survey, and statistics for 2010-2015 were survey data of land changed.

Source:Urban Planning, Land & Resources Administration Commission of Beijing Municipal.

5-17 水资源情况(2001-2016年)

单位：亿立方米

项　目	Item	2001	2002	2003	2004
全年水资源总量	**Total Volume of Water Resource in the Year**	**19.2**	**16.1**	**18.4**	**21.4**
地表水资源量	Volume of Surface Water Resource	7.8	5.3	6.1	8.2
地下水资源量	Volume of Underground Water Resource	15.7	14.7	14.8	16.5
人均水资源(立方米)	**Per-capita Water Resource(cu.m)**	**139.7**	**114.7**	**127.8**	**145.1**
全年供水(用水)总量	**Total Volume of Water Supplied (Consumed) in the Year**	**38.9**	**34.6**	**35.8**	**34.6**
按来源分	By Source				
地表水	Surface Water	11.7	10.4	8.3	5.7
地下水	Underground Water	27.2	24.2	25.4	26.8
外调水	Transferred Water				
其中：南水北调	Water Transit from South to North				
非常规水源	Unconventional Water Source				
其中：再生水	Recycled Water			2.1	2.0
应急供水	Emergent Water Supply				
按用途分	By Purpose				
农业用水	Water Used by Agriculture	17.4	15.5	13.8	13.5
工业用水	Water Used by Industry	9.2	7.5	8.4	7.7
生活用水	Domestic Water	12.0	10.8	13.0	12.8
环境用水	Water for the Environment	0.3	0.8	0.6	0.6
万元地区生产总值水耗(立方米)	**Water Consumption per 10000 yuan GDP (cu.m)**	**104.91**	**80.19**	**71.50**	**57.35**
万元地区生产总值水耗下降率(%)	**Decrease Rate of Water Consumption per 10000 yuan GDP (%)**	**13.79**	**20.22**	**6.91**	**15.29**

注：1. 万元地区生产总值水耗按现价计算，下降率按可比价计算，如按可比价计算，2016年万元地区生产总值水耗为15.34立方米。
2. 本表人均水资源按常住人口年平均数计算。2006-2010年数据根据全国第六次人口普查进行了修正。
3. 2013年万元地区生产总值水耗及下降率数据为第三次全国经济普查数据。
4. 2016年万元地区生产总值水耗及下降率中使用的地区生产总值数据包含研发支出，历史数据未按照新的地区生产总值核算口径进行修正。

资料来源：除人均数据和万元地区生产总值水耗以外其它数据来自北京市水务局。

STATISTICS FOR WATER RESOURCES (2001-2016)

(100 million cu.m)

2005	2006	2007	2008	2009	2010	2011	2012	2013	2014	2015	2016
23.2	**22.1**	**23.8**	**34.2**	**21.8**	**23.1**	**26.8**	**39.5**	**24.8**	**20.3**	**26.8**	**35.1**
7.6	6.7	7.6	12.8	6.8	7.2	9.2	18.0	9.4	6.5	9.3	14.0
15.6	15.4	16.2	21.4	15.1	15.9	17.6	21.6	15.4	13.8	17.4	21.1
153.1	**140.6**	**145.3**	**198.5**	**120.3**	**120.8**	**134.7**	**193.3**	**118.6**	**94.9**	**123.8**	**161.4**
34.5	**34.3**	**34.8**	**35.1**	**35.5**	**35.2**	**36.0**	**35.9**	**36.4**	**37.5**	**38.2**	**38.8**
6.4	5.7	5.0	4.7	3.8	3.9	4.8	4.4	3.9	7.7	2.2	2.1
23.1	22.2	21.6	20.5	19.7	19.1	18.8	18.3	17.9	17.5	16.7	16.5
			0.7	2.6	2.6	2.6	2.8	3.5	0.8	7.6	8.4
2.6	3.6	5.0	6.0	6.5	6.8	7.0	7.5	8.0	8.6	9.5	10.0
2.5	2.8	3.2	3.2	2.9	2.9	2.7	2.9	3.0	2.8	2.3	1.8
13.2	12.8	12.4	12.0	12.0	11.4	10.9	9.3	9.1	8.2	6.5	6.0
6.8	6.2	5.8	5.2	5.2	5.1	5.0	4.9	5.1	5.1	3.9	3.8
13.4	13.7	13.9	14.7	14.7	14.8	15.6	16.0	16.2	17.0	17.5	17.8
1.1	1.6	2.7	3.2	3.6	4.0	4.5	5.7	5.9	7.2	10.4	11.1
49.50	**42.25**	**35.34**	**31.58**	**29.92**	**24.94**	**22.13**	**20.07**	**18.37**	**17.58**	**16.60**	**15.12**
11.07	**12.01**	**11.38**	**7.56**	**8.12**	**10.14**	**5.49**	**7.38**	**5.87**	**3.93**	**4.65**	**4.87**

Note: a) Water consumption per 10000 yuan GDP is at current prices,and decrease rate is at comparable prices.Caculated at comparable prices, the water consumption per 10000 yuan GDP in 2016 is 15.34 cubic metres.

b) Per-capita water resource are calculated by average permanent population.Per-capita figures 2006-2010 have been corrected in accordance with the Sixth Population Census.

c) Water consumption per 10000 yuan GDP and Decrease Rate of Water Consumption for 2013 is were collected from the third national economic census.

d) GDP data used in 2016 Water Consumption per 10000 yuan of GDP and its Decrease Rate contain the R&D expenditure but the historical data were not revised according to the new calculation coverage of GDP.

Source: Except for per-capita figures and water consumption per 10000 yuan GDP,other figures are from Beijing Water Authority.

5-18 气象情况(1978-2016年)
METEOROLOGY (1978-2016)

年 份 Year	降水量 (毫米) Precipitation (mm)	平均气温(℃) Average Temperature (℃)	最高 Highest	最低 Lowest	日照时数(时) Hours of Sunshine (hours)	平均风速(米/秒) Average Wind Speed (meter/second)	平均气压(百帕) Average Air Pressure (100 pa)	大风日数(日) Days of Strong Wind (day)	雨日数(日) Days of Rain (day)
1978	664.8	11.6	37.5	-14.4	2865.4	2.6	1012.8	35	64
1979	718.4	11.1	35.9	-15.4	2667.4	2.5	1012.2	33	63
1980	380.7	11.0	35.1	-15.4	2920.8	2.5	1012.7	29	83
1981	393.2	12.3	38.1	-14.0	2803.9	2.5	1010.8	15	92
1982	544.4	12.8	37.3	-14.3	2825.1	2.6	1010.5	26	92
1983	489.9	13.0	37.2	-15.0	2844.3	2.4	1010.3	29	100
1984	488.8	11.9	36.1	-14.9	2767.6	2.4	1010.6	18	90
1985	721.0	11.5	35.1	-15.2	2511.9	2.2	1010.4	12	104
1986	665.3	12.1	38.5	-15.4	2804.1	2.3	1010.7	21	96
1987	683.9	12.3	36.1	-15.5	2631.9	2.4	1010.3	23	102
1988	673.3	12.7	38.1	-13.2	2558.1	2.4	1010.8	17	96
1989	442.2	13.2	35.8	-11.0	2626.2	1.9	1011.1	3	78
1990	697.3	12.7	37.5	-14.8	2325.0	1.9	1010.6	12	113
1991	747.9	12.5	35.7	-12.6	2536.6	2.1	1010.8	8	98
1992	541.5	12.8	37.5	-8.7	2712.5	2.2	1011.0	6	100
1993	506.7	13.0	35.8	-13.0	2669.8	2.6	1010.8	12	91
1994	813.2	13.7	37.2	-11.5	2470.5	2.5	1010.1	9	92
1995	572.5	13.3	35.0	-9.2	2519.1	2.6	1010.3	16	89
1996	700.9	12.7	36.0	-10.0	2418.7	2.6	1011.0	16	103
1997	430.9	13.1	38.2	-14.0	2596.5	2.5	1012.9	11	76
1998	731.7	13.1	37.2	-14.2	2420.7	2.3	1012.5	10	93
1999	266.9	13.1	41.9	-12.2	2594.0	2.4	1012.5	7	86
2000	371.1	12.8	39.4	-15.0	2667.2	2.5	1012.7	10	83
2001	338.9	12.9	39.6	-17.0	2611.7	2.4	1012.9	10	78
2002	370.4	13.2	41.1	-12.8	2588.4	2.3	1012.7	15	84
2003	444.9	12.9	37.6	-15.0	2260.2	2.5	1013.3	6	93
2004	483.5	13.5	38.9	-12.9	2515.4	2.4	1012.6	12	94
2005	410.7	13.2	38.9	-11.5	2576.1	2.4	1012.8	5	79
2006	318.0	13.4	37.3	-14.7	2192.7	2.2	1012.5	5	86
2007	483.9	14.0	37.3	-11.7	2351.1	2.2	1012.6	5	78
2008	626.3	13.4	36.3	-13.5	2391.4	2.2	1012.6	8	100
2009	480.6	13.3	39.6	-12.2	2511.8	2.2	1011.9	15	86
2010	522.5	12.6	40.6	-16.7	2382.9	2.3	1012.2	14	88
2011	720.6	13.4	35.9	-11.6	2485.7	2.2	1013.2	3	82
2012	733.2	12.9	38.0	-13.7	2450.2	2.2	1012.2	3	85
2013	578.9	12.8	38.2	-14.1	2371.1	2.1	1012.2	3	71
2014	461.5	14.1	41.1	-11.2	2344.1	2.1	1013.0	8	77
2015	458.6	13.7	38.9	-9.2	2420.2	2.1	1013.2	7	99
2016	669.1	13.8	37.8	-15.2	2502.1	2.1	1013.1	2	86

资料来源：北京市气象局。
Source: Beijing Municipal Bureau of Meteorology.

5-19 气　象(2016年)
METEOROLOGY (2016)

月　份 Month	降水量（毫米） Precipitation (mm)	平均气温(℃) Average Temperature (℃)	日照时数(时) Hours of Sunshine (hours)	平均风速(米/秒) Average Wind Speed (meter/second)	平均气压(百帕) Average Air Pressure (100 pa)	大风日数(日) Days of Strong Wind (day)	雨日数(日) Days of Rain (day)
全　年 Total	**669.1**	**13.8**	**2502.1**	**2.1**	**1013.1**	**2**	**86**
1	0.1	-4.2	210.9	2.2	1026.1		
2	8.1	1.4	240.5	2.5	1022.8		4
3		9.4	262.0	2.4	1017.1		
4	5.5	16.9	265.8	2.6	1008.1		6
5	24.0	21.5	281.9	2.6	1005.9	1	7
6	72.9	25.9	224.4	2.2	1001.0		14
7	344.3	27.4	153.4	1.9	1000.8		13
8	76.9	27.5	218.7	1.8	1003.9	1	12
9	59.0	22.2	201.5	1.7	1009.5		12
10	70.1	13.4	123.8	1.8	1017.3		13
11	8.2	4.3	154.4	1.8	1020.8		5
12		0.3	164.8	1.7	1023.7		

注：1．无霜期208天。
　　2．年极端最高气温37.8℃，出现日期6月25日。
　　3．年极端最低气温-15.2℃，出现日期1月23日。
资料来源：北京市气象局。
Note: a) Annual frost-free period is 208 days.
　　b) Annual utmost highest air temperature is 37.8℃, seen on the 25th of June.
　　c) Annual utmost lowest air temperature is -15.2℃, seen on the 23th of January .
Source: Beijing Municipal Bureau of Meteorology.

5-20 污水处理及环境卫生(1978-2016年)
SEWAGE DISPOSAL AND ENVIRONMENTAL SANITATION (1978-2016)

年份 Year	污水管道长度(公里) Length of Sewage Pipes (km)	污水处理能力(万立方米/日) Sewage Treatment Capacity (10000 cu.m/day)	污水处理率(%) Sewage Treatment Rate (%)	再生水利用量(万立方米) Volume of Recycled Water Used (10000 cu.m)	生活垃圾无害化处理能力(吨/日) Harmless Disposal Capacity of Domestic Waste (ton/day)	生活垃圾产生量(万吨) Output of Domestic Garbage (10000 tons)	生活垃圾清运量(万吨) Domestic Waste Removed and Transported (10000 tons)	生活垃圾无害化处理率(%) Rate of Harmless Disposal of Domestic Waste (%)	粪便清运量(万吨) Excrement Removed and Transported (10000 tons)
1978	290	23.2	7.6				107.20		88.9
1979	309	23.2	10.2				128.00		89.4
1980	334	23.2	9.4				147.00		95.1
1981	347	25.2	10.8				174.00		97.6
1982	365	25.2	10.9				204.70		99.3
1983	411	25.2	10.2				221.40		99.5
1984	568	25.2	10.0				235.40		98.8
1985	706	25.2	10.0				248.10		142.2
1986	747	26.4	8.9				274.40		167.5
1987	805	26.4	7.7				298.30		181.0
1988	770	26.4	7.4				319.90		190.0
1989	860	26.4	6.6				337.00		196.0
1990	904	30.4	7.3				384.10		210.0
1991	968	30.4	6.6				397.10		210.3
1992	1036	4.5	1.2				430.90		216.0
1993	1064	4.5	3.1				446.30		220.6
1994	1122	24.5	9.6				467.20		238.1
1995	1065	58.5	19.4				483.90		258.4
1996	1597	58.5	21.2				483.00		268.0
1997	1635	58.5	22.0				490.00		279.0
1998	1712	58.5	22.5				495.10		295.6
1999	1754	58.5	25.0				505.00		298.0
2000	1852	128.5	39.4		6550		295.56	56.4	274.0
2001	2163	143.5	42.0		6750		309.27	82.2	301.0
2002	2658	180.6	45.0		8750		321.35	86.4	311.7
2003	2903	215.0	50.1		9400		361.36	91.3	268.0
2004	2909	255.0	53.9		10050	495.46	405.86	93.8	175.0
2005	2521	324.0	62.4	23816	10350	536.93	454.59	96.0	171.7
2006	3398	331.0	73.2	36088	10350	585.13	538.32	92.5	175.7
2007	4357	348.0	76.2	49501	10350	619.49	600.93	95.7	189.1
2008	4458	329.4	78.9	60000	12148	672.82	656.61	97.7	206.8
2009	4495	356.0	80.3	64999	13680	669.13	656.12	98.2	211.2
2010	4479	365.0	81.0	68014	16680	634.86	632.98	96.9	194.4
2011	4765	369.4	82.0	71012	16930	634.35	634.35	98.2	207.5
2012	5735	388.5	83.0	75003	17530	648.31	648.31	99.1	207.2
2013	6363	393.0	84.6	80108	21971	671.69	671.69	99.3	220.7
2014	6536	425.0	86.1	86620	21971	733.84	733.84	99.6	216.1
2015	7157	439.5	87.9	94826	27321	790.33	790.33	99.8	204.7
2016	7889	612.0	90.0	100398	24341	872.61	872.61	99.8	204.0

注：1. 污水处理能力等指标1992年及以后为污水无害化处理情况，1992年以前为污水简易处理情况。
2. 生活垃圾无害化处理率按清运量计算。

资料来源：北京市水务局、北京市城市管理委员会。

Note: a) Disposal capacity and other indicators in and after 1992 were about harmless disposal, and those before 1992 were about simple disposal.
b) The harmless disposal rate of domestic waste is calculated with the volume of waste cleared and transported.

Source: Beijing Water Authority, Beijing Municipal Commission of City Administration.

5-21 排水及节水
WATER DRAINAGE AND SAVING

项　　目		Item		2016	2015
排　　水		**Water Drainage**			
污水处理能力	(万立方米/日)	Sewage Treatment Capacity	(10000cu.m/day)	612.0	439.5
污水年处理量	(万立方米)	Annual Treatment Volume of Sewage	(10000 cu.m)	152807	144453
#污水厂	(万立方米)	Treated by Sewage Treatment Plants	(10000 cu.m)	148396	140413
污水处理率	(%)	Sewage Treatment Rate	(%)	90.0	87.9
污水排放总量	(万立方米)	Total Volume of Sewage Drainage	(10000 cu.m)	169748	164217
排水管道长度	(公里)	Length of Drainage Pipelines	(km)	16901	15528
污水管	(公里)	Sewage Pipes	(km)	7889	7157
雨水管	(公里)	Rain Pipes	(km)	7317	6139
雨污合流管	(公里)	Rain-sewage Sewer	(km)	1695	2232
再生水利用量	(万立方米)	Volume of Recycled Water Used	(10000 cu.m)	100398	94826
节　　水		**Water Saving**			
节水量	(万立方米)	Volume Saved	(10000 cu.m)	12033	9878
节水措施	(项)	Water Saving Measures Implemented	(unit)	134	137

资料来源：北京市水务局。
Source: Beijing Water Authority.

5-22 环境卫生
MUNICIPAL ENVIRONMENT AND SANITATION

项　　目		Item		2016	2015
工作量		**Work Load**			
清扫街道面积	(万平方米／日)	Area of Cleaned Streets	(10000 sq.m/day)	14678	15122
生活垃圾无害化处理能力	(吨/日)	Harmless Disposal Capacity of Domestic Waste	(ton/day)	24341	27321
生活垃圾产生量	(万吨)	Output of Domestic Waste	(10000 tons)	872.6	790.3
生活垃圾清运量	(万吨)	Domestic Waste Removed and Transported	(10000 tons)	872.6	790.3
生活垃圾无害化处理量	(万吨)	Volume of Harmless Disposal of Domestic Waste	(10000 tons)	871.2	788.7
生活垃圾无害化处理率		Rate of Harmless Disposal of Domestic Waste			
(按清运量计算)	(%)	(Calculated by Volume of Waste Cleared and Transpo	(%)	99.8	99.8
餐余垃圾处理量	(万吨)	Kitchen Waste Removed and Transported	(10000 tons)	28.2	27.3
粪便清运量	(万吨)	Excrement Removed and Transported	(10000 tons)	204.0	204.7
环卫机械数量	**(辆)**	**Number of Environmental Sanitation Machinery**	**(unit)**	**11033**	**10747**
环卫设施		**Environmental Sanitation Facilities**			
公共厕所	(座)	Public Lavatories	(unit)	5398	5401

资料来源：北京市城市管理委员会。
Source: Beijing Municipal Commission of City Administration.

5-23 环境保护(2000-2016年)
ENVIRONMENTAL PROTECTION (2000-2016)

年 份 Year	可吸入颗粒物年日均值(毫克/立方米) Daily Average of Inspiratory Particulate Matter in the Year (mg/cu.m)	二氧化硫年日均值(毫克/立方米) Daily Average of Sulfur Dioxide in the Year (mg/cu.m)	二氧化氮年日均值(毫克/立方米) Daily Average of Nitrogen Dioxide (mg/cu.m)	化学需氧量(COD)排放量(万吨) COD Emission Volume (10000 tons)	二氧化硫(SO_2)排放量(万吨) SO_2 Emission Volume (10000 tons)	区域环境噪声平均值(分贝) Average Value of Noises in Regional Environment (db)	道路交通干线噪声平均值(分贝) Average Value of Noises in Road Transportation (db)
2000	0.162	0.071	0.071	17.9	22.4	53.9	71.0
2001	0.165	0.064	0.071	17.0	20.1	53.9	69.6
2002	0.166	0.067	0.076	15.3	19.2	53.5	69.5
2003	0.141	0.061	0.072	13.4	18.3	53.6	69.7
2004	0.149	0.055	0.071	13.0	19.1	53.8	69.6
2005	0.142	0.050	0.066	11.6	19.1	53.2	69.5
2006	0.161	0.053	0.066	11.0	17.6	53.9	69.7
2007	0.148	0.047	0.066	10.7	15.2	54.0	69.9
2008	0.122	0.036	0.049	10.1	12.3	53.6	69.6
2009	0.121	0.034	0.053	9.9	11.9	54.1	69.7
2010	0.121	0.032	0.057	9.2	11.5	54.1	70.0
2011	0.114	0.028	0.055	19.3	9.8	53.7	69.6
2012	0.109	0.028	0.052	18.7	9.4	54.0	69.2
2013	0.108	0.027	0.056	17.8	8.7	53.9	69.1
2014	0.116	0.022	0.057	16.9	7.9	53.6	69.1
2015	0.102	0.014	0.050	16.2	7.1	53.3	69.2
2016	0.092	0.010	0.048	8.7	3.3	54.3	69.3

注：化学需氧量(COD)排放量和二氧化硫排放量(SO_2)指标自2011年起调整统计口径和核算方法。
资料来源：北京市环境保护局。
Note: From 2011, statistical standard and calculation method are adjusted for COD emission volume and SO2 emission volume.
Source: Beijing Municipal Bureau of Environmental Protection.

5-24 环境保护
ENVIRONMENTAL PROTECTION

项　　目		Item		2016	2015
水环境		**Water Environment**			
废水排放总量	(万吨)	Total Discharge of Sewage	(10000 tons)	166419.28	151733.34
#工业废水排放量		Industrial Waste Water Discharge Volume		8515.44	8978.08
化学需氧量(COD)排放量	(吨)	COD Emission Volume	(ton)	87094	161536
#工业废水中COD排放量		Emission of COD in Industrial Waster Water		2381	4738
氨氮排放量	(吨)	Ammonia Nitrogen Discharge	(ton)	5576	16491
#工业废水中氨氮排放量		Ammonia Nitrogen Discharge in Industrial Waster Water		114	307
大气环境		**Atmosphere Environment**			
二氧化硫(SO_2)排放量	(吨)	SO_2 Emission Volume	(ton)	33210	71172
#工业二氧化硫排放量		Emission of Industrial SO_2		10257	22070
氮氧化物排放量	(吨)	Smoke and Dust Emission	(ton)	96119	137627
#工业氮氧化物排放量		Emission of Industrial Smoke and Dust		23412	26864
烟(粉)尘排放量	(吨)	Smoke and Dust Emission	(ton)	34535	49387
#工业烟(粉)尘排放量		Emission of Industrial Smoke and Dust		7874	12987
固体废物		**Solid Waste**			
一般工业固体废物产生量	(万吨)	General Industrial Solid Waste Generated	(10000 tons)	629.10	709.86
一般工业固体废物综合利用量	(万吨)	General Industrial Solid Waste Recycled	(10000 tons)	542.53	591.56
一般工业固体废物处置量	(万吨)	General Industrial Solid Waste Disposed	(10000 tons)	86.99	118.41
危险废物产生量	(吨)	Hazardous Wastes Generated	(ton)	178324	149939
危险废物综合利用量	(吨)	Hazardous Wastes Recycled	(ton)	82808	75886
危险废物处置量	(吨)	Hazardous Wastes Disposed	(ton)	94076	73728
生态环境		**Ecological Environment**			
自然保护区个数	(个)	Number of Nature Reserves	(unit)	20	20
#国家级自然保护区		State-level Nature Reserves		2	2
自然保护区面积	(万公顷)	Area of Nature Reserves	(10000 hectares)	13.66	13.79

数据来源：北京市环境保护局。
Source: Beijing Municipal Bureau of Environmental Protection.

5-25 园林绿化及森林情况(1978-2016年)

年 份 Year	年末公园绿地面积 (公顷) Green Land and Park (year-end) (hectare)	人均公园绿地面积 (平方米/人) Per Capita Green Land and Park (sq.m/person)	城市绿化覆盖率 (%) Green Land Coverage (%)	林木绿化率 (%) Forest Coverage (%)	年末园林绿地面积 (公顷) Green Area (year-end) (hectare)
1978	2693	5.07	22.30		
1979	2693	5.07	22.30		
1980	2746	5.14	20.10	16.6	
1981	2751	5.14	20.10	16.6	
1982	2779	5.14	20.10	16.6	
1983	2823	5.14	20.10	16.6	
1984	2878	5.14	20.10	16.6	
1985	3263	4.94	22.10	16.6	
1986	3606	5.07	22.86	16.6	
1987	3570	5.07	22.90	16.6	
1988	4074	5.80	25.00	16.6	
1989	6910	6.00	26.00	16.6	
1990	7110	6.14	28.00	28.3	
1991	4279	6.41	28.43	28.3	
1992	4213	6.65	30.33	28.3	
1993	4452	7.76	31.33	28.3	
1994	5221	7.89	32.39	28.3	
1995	5017	7.48	32.68	36.3	
1996	5147	7.54	33.24	36.3	
1997	5408	7.80	34.22	36.3	
1998	6351	9.00	35.60	36.3	
1999	6457	9.10	36.30	36.3	
2000	7140	9.66	36.50	42.0	26680
2001	7554	10.07	38.78	44.0	30224
2002	7907	10.66	40.57	45.5	32572
2003	9115	11.43	40.87	47.5	38475
2004	10446	11.45	41.91	49.5	36755
2005	11365	12.00	42.00	50.5	38877
2006	11788	12.00	42.50	51.0	45495
2007	12101	12.60	43.00	51.6	46320
2008	12316	13.60	43.50	52.1	46993
2009	18070	14.50	44.40	52.6	61695
2010	19020	15.00	45.00	53.0	62672
2011	19728	15.30	45.60	54.0	63541
2012	21178	15.50	46.20	55.5	65540
2013	22215	15.70	46.80	57.4	67048
2014	28798	15.90	47.40	58.4	80223
2015	29503	16.00	48.40	59.0	81305
2016	30069	16.10	48.40	59.3	82113

资料来源：北京市园林绿化局。

STATISTICS FOR LANDSCAPING AND FORESTS (1978-2016)

森林面积 (公顷) Forest Area (hectare)	森林覆盖率 (%) Forest Coverage Rate (%)	活立木蓄积量 (万立方米) Total Stock of Standing Trees (10000 cu.m)	森林蓄积量 (万立方米) Forest Stock (10000 cu.m)	森林火灾次数 (次) Number of Forest Fires (unit)	森林火灾经济损失 (万元) Economic Loss of Forest Fires (10000 yuan)
619243.2		1521.4	1295.3	9	11.4
626006.3	35.9	1521.4	1295.3	13	96.7
636565.7	36.5	1559.5	1368.9	8	28.1
641368.3	36.5	1574.0	1394.4		
658914.1	36.7	1810.3	1406.2	2	…
666050.7	37.0	1854.7	1435.4	4	1.4
673411.8	37.6	1899.4	1468.7	3	1.7
691341.1	38.6	1943.3	1499.0	1	
716456.1	40.1	1993.4	1536.8		
734530.6	41.0	2109.1	1669.9	1	
744956.1	41.6	2149.3	1701.1	3	29.7
756000.7	42.3	2180.0	1724.6	4	

Source: Beijing Municipal Bureau of Landscape and Forestry.

主要统计指标解释

能源生产量 能源生产量是反映能源生产规模、构成、生产成果的重要指标。按能源的成因分为一次能源（亦称天然能源）生产量和二次能源（亦称人工能源）生产量。

一次能源生产量 指报告期内生产一次能源的企业将自然界现存的能源资源经过开采而产出的合格产品，主要包括原煤、原油、天然气、水电等。

二次能源生产量 指报告期内将一次能源经过各种加工转换设备生产出的另一种形式的各种合格的能源产品。如火电、热力、洗煤、焦炭、各种石油制品、焦炉煤气、其他煤气等。

能源消费总量 指一定地域（行政或地理区域）内，国民经济各行业和居民家庭在一定时期所消费的各种能源的总和。能源消费总量包括终端能源消费量、能源加工转换损失量、能源运输和管理过程的损失量三部分。

能源消费总量（等价值） 是电力、热力按等价热值计算的能源消费总量。等价热值是能源统计中经常使用的一个热值概念，是指加工转换产出的某种二次能源所投入的一次能源的量，即获得一个度量单位的某种二次能源所消耗的以热值表示的一次能源。

能源加工转换投入产出量 能源具有由一种能量形式转换为另一种能量形式及耗用过程中可用一种能源替代另一种能源的特征。为提高能源的利用价值和效率，对能源进行加工、转换，产出适合生产和生活需要的更高级的能源产品。在加工转换投入(-)产出(+)量中，“-”表示能源加工转换的投入量，“+”表示二次能源的产出量。

投入量 是指为生产二次能源产品，所投入到能源加工转换设备的各种能源数量。在表中以负数表示。

产出量 是指各种能源（一次能源或少量再投入的二次能源）经过加工转换后，产出的各种二次能源产品（包括不作为能源使用的副产品，联产品）数量。

加工转换损失量 是指在能源加工、转换过程中损失的能量（能源），即能源加工、转换过程中投入的能源和产出的二次能源之间的差额。

损失量 指能源在经营管理和生产、输送、分配、储存等过程中发生的损失以及由于自然因素等原因造成的损失数量。不包括加工转换损失量。

终端消费量 是指能源消费环节的最后一个环节的能源消费，包括直接用作燃料、原材料和动力的各种能源的消费。它们的消费过程体现了能源消费的终止，不会再重新作为能源投入使用。终端消费量不包括用于能源加工转换投入量、加工转换损失量和损失量。

能源消费弹性系数 指能源消费总量增长率与地区生产总值增长率的比值。

电力消费弹性系数 指电力消费量增长率与地区生产总值增长率的比值。

平均每万元地区生产总值能源消费量 能源总消费量或分品种能源消费量与地区生产总值之比。

人均生活用能量 指用于生活消费的各种能源数量与人口总数之比。

日均能源消费量 指各品种能源消费量与当年实际天数之比。

垃圾无害化处理能力 指垃圾无害化处理场（厂）按工艺设计每天所能处理生活垃圾的数量。垃圾无害化处理场（厂）必须是按照有关技术、环境、卫生标准和规范进行设计、建设、运行、维护和管理的各种生活垃圾处理设施，主要包括卫生填埋场、堆肥厂和焚烧厂等。

水资源总量 指降水形成的地表和地下水总量，不包括过境水量。

排水管道长度 指所有排水总管、干管、支管、检查井及连接井进出口等长度之和。计算时应按单管计算，即在同一条街道上如有两条或两条以上并排的排水管道时，应按每条排水管道的长度相加计算。

污水处理能力 指污水处理厂（或处理装置）每昼夜处理污水量的设计能力。

污水处理量 指污水处理厂和处理装置实际处理的污水量。包括物理处理量、生物处理量和化学处理量。

污水处理率 指污水处理量与污水排放总量的比率。计算公式：

$$污水处理率 = \frac{污水处理量}{污水排放总量} \times 100\%$$

生活垃圾清运量 指报告期内收集和运送到各垃圾处理场（厂）的垃圾的数量。

粪便清运量 指报告期内收集和运送到各粪便处理场（厂）的粪便的数量。

生活垃圾无害化处理量 指报告期内简易处理场和各种垃圾无害化处理场（厂）处理垃圾的总量。垃圾简易处理量指垃圾简易填埋场所处理的垃圾总量。垃圾无害化处理量指垃圾无害化处理场（厂）所处理的垃圾总量。

生活垃圾无害化处理率 指报告期垃圾无害化处理量与垃圾产生量的比率。计算公式：

$$垃圾无害化处理率 = \frac{垃圾无害化处理量}{垃圾产生量} \times 100\%$$

在统计时，如果生活垃圾产生量不易取得，可用清运量代替。

化学需氧量（COD）排放量 指工业废水中 COD 排放量与生活污水中 COD 排放量之和。指用化学氧化剂氧化水中有机污染物时所需的氧量。COD 值越高，表示水中有机污染物污染越重。

二氧化硫（SO_2）排放量 指报告期内工业 SO_2 排放量与生活 SO_2 排放量之和。

工业固体废物综合利用量 指报告期内企业通过回收、加工、循环、交换等方式，从固体废物中提取或者使其转化为可以利用的资源、能源和其他原材料的固体废物量（包括当年利用的往年工业固体废物贮存量）。如用做农业肥料、生产建筑材料、筑路等。

公园绿地 指向公众开放，以游憩为主要功能，兼具生态、美化、防灾等作用，其绿地率达到 65%以上，配有多种乔灌木及地被植物，有一定设施和艺术布局的绿地。包括公园、社区公园、街旁绿地、其他公园绿地。人均公园绿地面积计算口径为户籍非农业人口。

绿化覆盖率 指报告期末区域内绿化覆盖面积与区域面积的比率。

计算公式：

$$绿化覆盖率 = \frac{区域内绿化覆盖面积}{区域面积} \times 100\%$$

森林面积 指由乔木树种构成，郁闭度 0.20 以上(含 0.20)的林地或冠幅宽度 10 米以上的林带的面积，即有林地面积。它是反映森林资源总面积的重要指标。森林面积包括天然起源和人工起源的针叶林面积、阔叶林面积、针阔混交林面积和竹林面积。

活立木蓄积量 指一定范围土地上全部树木蓄积的总量，包括森林蓄积、疏林蓄积、散生木蓄积和四旁树蓄积。

森林蓄积量 指一定森林面积上存在着的林木树干部分的总材积，以立方米为计量单位。

森林火灾次数 指发生在城市市区外的一切森林、林木和林地的火灾次数，包括森林火警、一般灾害、重大灾害和特大灾害。

Explanatory Notes on Main Statistical Indicators

Energy Production is an important indicator reflecting the size, composition and results of energy production. By the cause of formation, it consists of the production of primary energy (also known as natural energy) and that of secondary energy (also known as artificial energy).

Production of Primary Energy means up-to-grade products produced by primary energy producers in the reporting period through extraction of existing energy in the nature, mainly including raw coal, crude oil, natural gas, hydroelectricity, etc.

Production of Secondary Energy means various up-to-grade energy products in another form that are made from primary energy with various processing and converting equipment in the reporting period, including thermal power, heating power, washed coal, coke, various petroleum products, coke oven gas and other gases, etc.

Total Energy Consumption means the total consumption of various energies by national economic sectors and resident households in a specific region (administrative or geographic). Total energy consumption can be divided into three parts: end-use energy consumption, loss during energy processing and conversion and loss during energy transport and management.

Total Energy Consumption (in Equivalent Caloricity) means the total consumption of electric power and heating power calculated in equivalent caloricity. Equivalent caloricity is a caloricity concept frequently used in statistics of energy. It means the quantity of primary energy input for a secondary energy produced through processing and conversion, i.e. the primary energy in terms of caloricity which is consumed to produce one measuring unit of a secondary energy.

Input and Output of Energy Processing and Conversion One form of energy can be converted into another form of energy. And in consumption, one sort of energy can be replaced with another. In order to improve the energy use value and efficiency, energy is processed and converted to produce energy products at higher levels which are suitable for productive and living needs. In the processing and conversion input (-) and output (+), "-" means the input for energy processing and conversion. And "+" means the output from energy processing and conversion.

Input means the volume of energy put into the energy processing and converting equipment in order to produce secondary energy products.

Output means the volume of secondary energy products (including byproducts and multi-products that cannot be used as energy) from processing and conversion of energy sources (primary energy or a small amount of secondary energy re-input).

Loss during Processing and Conversion means the energy lost in the processing and conversion of energy, namely the difference between the energy input and the secondary energy output during energy processing and conversion.

Energy Loss means the loss of energy during operation, management, production, transportation, distribution and storage, as well as the loss due to natural factors and other reasons. It excludes the loss during processing and conversion.

End-use Energy Consumption means the energy consumption in the last section of energy consumption, including the consumption of various energy sources used as fuel, raw materials and power. Such consumption represents the end of energy consumption, and the energy will not be put into use again as energy. End-use energy consumption does not include the input for energy processing and conversion, loss during the processing and conversion of energy, and energy loss.

Elasticity Coefficient of Energy Consumption means the ratio of growth rate of total energy consumption to the growth rate of GDP.

Elasticity Coefficient of Electric Power Consumption means the ratio of growth rate of electric power consumption to the growth rate of GDP.

Average Energy Consumption per RMB 10000 of GDP means the ratio of total energy consumption or energy consumption by variety to GDP.

Per-capital Energy Consumption by Households means the ratio of quantity of energy consumed by households to the total population.

Daily Energy Consumption means the ratio of energy consumption to the actual days in the same year.

Harmless Disposal Capacity of Waste means the daily quantity of domestic waste that can be disposed at harmless disposal facilities (sites) according to the process designed. Harmless disposal facilities (sites) must be domestic waste disposal facilities, including landfills, manure yards, incineration facilities and so on, which are designed, built, operated and managed in accordance with relevant technological, environmental, and sanitary standards and criterion.

Total Water Resources means the total volume of surface water and underground water caused by rainfall, excluding passing-by water.

Length of Sewage Pipes means the total length of all main drainage pipes, trunk pipes, branch pipes, access manholes, and connector well entrances and exits, and so on. The length of single pipes shall be included, i.e. if there are two or more drainage pipes parallel on a street, the length of every pipe shall be included.

Sewage Treatment Capacity means the designed capacity of sewage disposal day and night for a sewage disposal plant (or facility).

Volume of Sewage Treated means the volume of sewage actually disposed by sewage disposal plants and facilities, consisting of physical volume, biological volume and chemical volume of waste water disposed.

Sewage Treatment Rate means the ratio of sewage disposed to the total discharge of sewage. The formula is:

Sewage Disposal Rate = Volume of Sewage Disposed / Total Discharge of Sewage × 100%

Domestic Waste Removed and Transported means the quantity of waste collected and transported to waste treatment sites (plants) in the reporting period.

Excrement Removed and Transported means the quantity of excrement collected and transported to waste treatment sites (plants) in the reporting period.

Volume of Harmless Disposal of Domestic Waste means the total volume of waste disposed by simple disposal sites and harmless waste disposal sits (plants) in the reporting period. Simple disposal of waste means the total volume of waste by simple landfills. Harmless waste disposal means the total volume of waste disposed by harmless waste disposal sites (plants).

Rate of Harmless Disposal of Domestic Waste means the ratio of harmless waste disposal to the waste produced in the reporting period. The formula is:

Rate of Harmless Disposal of Domestic Waste = Harmless Waste Disposal / Waste Produced × 100%

In practical statistics, if it is hard to get figures on the volume of domestic waste produced, the volume removed and transported may be used.

COD Emission Volume means the sum of COD emission in industrial sewage and in domestic waste water. It means the amount of oxygen required when chemical oxidants are used to oxidize organic pollutants in water. A higher value of COD corresponds to more serious pollution by organic pollutants.

SO_2 Emission Volume means the sum of industrial SO_2 emission and domestic SO_2 emission in the reporting period.

Industrial Solid Waste Utilized means the volume of solid wastes from which useful materials can be extracted or which can be converted into usable resources, energy or other materials by means of reclamation, processing, recycling and exchange (including utilizing in the year the stocks of industrial solid wastes of the previous year). Examples of such utilizations include fertilizers, building materials and road materials.

Green Land and Parks means the green land open to the public, with main function of recreation, together with ecological, landscaping and disaster preventing functions, and with more than 65% green coverage, provided with multiple arbors, shrubs and ground-cover plants, along with certain facilities and artistic layouts. They include parks, community parks, street-side green land and other green land in gardens. Per capita area of green land is calculated on the basis of non-agricultural household population.

Green Land Coverage means the ratio of area of green land in a region to the total area of the region in the reporting period. The formula is:

Green Land Coverage = Area of Green Land in a Region / Total Area of the Region × 100%

Forest Area means the area of forest where arbor trees grow with canopy density above 0.2 (and at 0.2) or forest area with crown width more than 10m, i.e. the area of land with forest. It is an important indicator reflecting the total area of forest resources. Forest Area includes the area of coniferous forest, broad leaf forest, mixed coniferous-broad-leaf forest and bamboo forest from both natural and artificial origins.

Total Stock of Standing Trees mean the total stock of all trees on specific area of land, including trees in forest, trees in sparse forest, scattered trees and trees planted by the side of villages, farm houses and along roads and rivers.

Forest Stock means the total volume of timber of forest tree trunks growing on specific area of forest, which are measured in cubic meters.

Number of Forest Fires means the number of all fires occurring in forests, woods, woodlands outside the urban districts, including forest fires, general fires, severe fires and fire disasters.

北京统计年鉴2017　BEIJING STATISTICAL YEARBOOK

全社会固定资产投资和房地产开发

TOTAL INVESTMENT IN FIXED ASSETS AND REAL ESTATE DEVELOPMENT

简要说明

一、本章资料的主要内容

本章资料包括历年北京市全社会固定资产投资、房地产开发的主要分组数据、保障性安居工程建设等情况。

二、本章资料的统计范围

1996 年及以前固定资产投资统计起点为 5 万元及以上，1996 年以后调整为 50 万元及以上，从 2011 年开始调整为 500 万元及以上。

三、有关统计标准的变化说明

（一）关于行业划分。根据国家统计局规定，自 2012 年开始执行《国民经济行业分类》（GB/T 4754-2011）标准。

（二）关于三次产业划分。根据国家统计局《三次产业划分规定》（国统字[2012]108 号），该规定对三次产业的范围进行了调整。其中第一产业是指农、林、牧、渔业（不含农、林、牧、渔服务业）；第二产业是指采矿业（不含开采辅助活动），制造业（不含金属制品、机械和设备修理业），电力、热力、燃气及水生产和供应业，建筑业；第三产业是指除第一产业、第二产业以外的其他行业。自 2012 年开始执行此规定。

四、本章资料的数据来源

本章资料来源于北京市统计局。

五、本章的统计调查方法

除农户固定资产投资统计采用抽样调查方法外，其他均为全面调查。

Brief Introduction

I. Main Content

Statistics in this chapter include figures on fixed assets investment in Beijing and its main grouped figures as well as figures on government-subsidized housing projects.

II. Scope of Statistics

Before and in 1996, the threshold of fixed assets statistics was RMB 50,000 or more; after 1996, it was increased to RMB 500,000 or more; since 2011, the figure has been set at RMB 5 million and above.

III. Changes in Relevant Statistical Standards

(I) Classification of Sectors. According to relevant provisions of the National Bureau of Statistics, the Standard for Classification of National Economic Sectors (GB/T 4754-2011) came into effect in 2012.

(II) Classification of Three Industries. According to the Regulations on the Classification of the Three Industries (G.T.Z. [2012] No. 108) issued by National Bureau of Statistics, the scope of three industries has been adjusted. The primary industry refers to agriculture, forestry, animal production and hunting, fishing (excluding services for a agriculture, forestry, animal production and hunting, fishing); the secondary industry refers to mining (excluding mining support activities), manufacturing (excluding metal products, machinery and equipment repair), production and distribution of electricity, heating power, gas and water, and construction; the tertiary industry refers to sectors other than the primary and secondary industries. The Regulations on the Classification of the Three Industries (G.T.Z. [2012] No. 108) issued by National Bureau of Statistics came into effect in 2012.

IV. Source of Statistics

Statistics in this chapter are from the Beijing Municipal Bureau of Statistics.

V. Method of Statistical Survey

Sample survey is used for the statistics on investment of rural households in fixed assets. For other statistics, the complete survey is conducted.

6–1 全社会固定资产投资和增长速度情况(1978–2016年)
TOTAL INVESTMENT IN FIXED ASSETS AND GROWTH RATE (1978-2016)

单位：亿元 (100 million yuan)

年份 Year	全社会固定资产投资 Total Investment in Fixed Assets	城镇固定资产投资 Investment in Urban Fixed Assets	#房地产开发投资 Investment in Real Estate Development	农村固定资产投资 Investment in Rural Fixed Assets	#基础设施投资 Infrastructure Investment	#建筑安装投资 Construction and Installation Investment	新增固定资产 Incremental Fixed Assets
1978	22.6	22.6			5.4		16.9
1979	26.5	26.5			5.8		21.2
1980	33.2	33.2			6.0		23.2
1981–1985	**286.8**	**234.4**		**50.8**	**40.6**		**184.4**
1981	36.6	31.4		5.2	5.8		30.9
1982	38.6	34.5		4.1	6.1		26.3
1983	51.3	38.5		12.8	6.7		32.5
1984	66.3	52.2		14.1	8.8		47.1
1985	94.0	77.8		14.6	13.2		47.6
1986–1990	**724.1**	**634.9**	**22.5**	**76.5**	**117.9**		**417.4**
1986	106.2	94.5		10.4	14.5		58.5
1987	136.2	121.4		12.7	22.1		79.9
1988	163.0	138.7		21.3	23.2		77.3
1989	139.5	122.2		14.7	26.5		79.6
1990	179.2	158.1	22.5	17.4	31.6		122.1
1991–1995	**2358.7**	**2181.5**	**568.4**	**154.1**	**494.9**	**1297.1**	**1229.1**
1991	192.0	168.4	24.0	21.0	35.2	107.3	139.0
1992	266.0	234.7	33.7	27.2	58.8	136.2	157.8
1993	410.4	376.6	58.4	30.0	91.4	232.0	201.6
1994	648.8	607.4	99.5	35.7	153.4	362.6	356.0
1995	841.5	794.4	352.8	40.2	156.1	459.0	374.7
1996–2000	**5461.7**	**5063.8**	**1979.5**	**322.7**	**1382.1**	**3069.5**	**4051.2**
1996	876.9	825.6	328.2	43.6	188.8	515.8	592.5
1997	961.2	912.4	330.3	40.6	218.3	546.2	637.9
1998	1155.6	1060.3	377.4	75.8	320.4	626.9	759.3
1999	1170.6	1072.9	421.5	78.2	302.7	679.1	949.5
2000	1297.4	1192.6	522.1	84.5	351.9	701.5	1112.0
2001–2005	**10857.4**	**10033.6**	**5974.0**	**755.4**	**2260.0**	**5926.2**	**6897.4**
2001	1530.5	1417.1	783.8	93.7	356.4	801.6	1177.0
2002	1814.3	1688.2	989.4	102.5	411.9	964.9	1251.0
2003	2157.1	1999.9	1202.5	132.1	417.8	1151.3	1165.9
2004	2528.3	2333.0	1473.3	195.3	463.2	1438.9	1455.1
2005	2827.2	2595.4	1525.0	231.8	610.7	1569.5	1848.4
2006–2010	**21538.5**	**19678.6**	**10863.2**	**1859.9**	**6137.3**	**9860.6**	**11666.8**
2006	3371.5	3086.3	1719.9	285.2	935.3	1836.0	1972.1
2007	3966.6	3656.7	1995.8	309.9	1175.8	2117.9	2004.9
2008	3848.5	3554.8	1908.7	293.7	1160.7	1798.8	2666.8
2009	4858.4	4378.2	2337.7	480.2	1462.0	1983.0	2457.2
2010	5493.5	5002.6	2901.1	490.9	1403.5	2124.9	2565.8
	(5218.3)						
2011–2015	**34958.8**	**31863.2**	**17810.7**	**3095.7**	**9167.7**	**15608.7**	**15996.7**
2011	5910.6	5463.9	3036.3	446.7	1400.2	2585.3	2382.0
2012	6462.8	5853.1	3153.4	609.8	1789.2	3076.6	2570.4
2013	7032.2	6352.6	3483.4	679.6	1785.7	3482.2	3163.8
2014	7562.3	6926.6	3911.3	635.7	2018.1	3468.1	3887.3
2015	7990.9	7267.0	4226.3	723.9	2174.5	2996.5	3993.2
2016	8461.7	7728.2	4045.4	733.5	2399.5	3132.8	3608.4

注：1．根据国家统计局有关规定，从2004年起，全社会固定资产投资中不包括零星购置投资（下同）。
2．2004年起、新增固定资产、基础设施投资、建筑安装投资中包含农村投资。
3．根据国家统计局有关规定，2011年起投资统计起点调整为500万元，为便于比较，2010年的相应数据也作了调整，未加括号的为原口径数，括号内为调整后的数据，当年固定资产投资增长速度及2011–2015年平均增长速度均按可比口径计算。

Note: a) According to related regulations of National Bureau of Statistics, since 2004, total investment in fixed assets has not included investment in acquiring minor items（the same below）.
b) Since 2004, rural investment has been counted in incremental fixed assets, infrastructure investment, construction and installation investment.
c) Since 2011, the statistical threshold of investment has been adjusted to RMB 5 million according to the related regulations of National Bureau of Statistics. For comparison, relevant figures in 2010 were adjusted accordingly. Figures with no brackets are based on the former standard. Figures in brackets are data after adjustment. Growth rates of fixed assets investment in respective years are calculated in comparable terms.

6-1 续表 Continued

单位：% (%)

年 份 Year	全社会固定资产投资比上年增长 Growth rate of Total Investment in Fixed Assets	城镇固定资产投资 Growth rate of Investment in Urban Fixed Assets	#房地产开发投资 Growth rate of Investment in Real Estate Development	农村固定资产投资 Growth rate of Investment in Rural Fixed Assets	#基础设施投资 Growth rate of Infrastructure Investment	#建筑安装投资 Growth rate of Construction and Installation Investment
1978						
1979	17.3	17.3			7.4	
1980	25.3	25.3			3.4	
1981-1985	**18.8**	**11.7**			**10.3**	
1981	10.2	-5.4			-3.3	
1982	5.5	9.9		-21.2	5.2	
1983	32.9	11.6		212.2	9.8	
1984	29.2	35.6		10.2	31.3	
1985	41.8	49.0		3.5	50.0	
1986-1990	**14.8**	**16.8**		**1.5**	**20.0**	
1986	13.0	21.5		-28.8	9.8	
1987	28.2	28.5		22.1	52.4	
1988	19.7	14.3		67.7	5.0	
1989	-14.4	-11.9		-31.0	14.2	
1990	28.5	29.4		18.4	19.2	
1991-1995	**34.2**	**36.0**	**59.9**	**19.7**	**40.8**	
1991	7.1	6.5	6.7	20.7	11.4	
1992	38.5	39.4	40.4	29.5	67.0	26.9
1993	54.3	60.5	73.3	10.3	55.4	70.3
1994	58.1	61.3	70.4	19.0	67.8	56.3
1995	29.7	30.8	254.6	12.6	1.8	26.6
1996-2000	**8.9**	**8.2**	**3.9**	**16.2**	**19.7**	**9.9**
1996	4.2	3.9	-7.0	8.5	20.9	12.4
1997	9.6	10.5	0.6	-6.9	15.6	5.9
1998	20.2	16.2	14.3	86.7	46.8	14.8
1999	1.3	1.2	11.7	3.2	-5.5	8.3
2000	10.8	11.2	23.9	8.1	16.3	3.3
2001-2005	**17.7**	**17.9**	**29.0**	**20.1**	**8.5**	**18.0**
2001	18.0	18.8	50.1	10.9	1.3	14.3
2002	18.5	19.1	26.2	9.4	15.6	20.4
2003	18.9	18.5	21.5	28.9	1.4	19.3
2004	17.2	16.7	22.5	47.8	10.9	25.0
2005	11.8	11.2	3.5	18.7	31.8	9.1
2006-2010	**14.4**	**14.2**	**12.0**	**16.2**	**24.2**	**7.7**
2006	19.3	18.9	12.8	23.0	53.2	17.0
2007	17.6	18.5	16.0	8.7	25.7	15.4
2008	-3.0	-2.8	-4.4	-5.2	-1.3	-15.1
2009	26.2	23.2	22.5	63.5	26.0	10.2
2010	13.1	14.3	24.1	2.2	-4.0	7.2
2011-2015	**9.9**	**9.9**	**8.7**	**10.1**	**9.0**	**13.3**
2011	13.3	14.8	10.1	-2.9	0.3	22.4
2012	9.3	7.1	3.9	36.5	27.8	19.0
2013	8.8	8.5	10.5	11.5	-0.2	13.2
2014	7.5	9.0	12.3	-6.5	13.0	-0.4
2015	5.7	4.9	8.1	13.9	7.7	-13.6
2016	5.9	6.3	-4.3	1.3	10.3	4.5

6-2 按登记注册类型分全社会固定资产投资(1978-2016年)
TOTAL INVESTMENT IN FIXED ASSETS BY REGISTRATION TYPE (1978-2016)

单位：亿元 (100 million yuan)

年 份 Year	全社会固定资产投资 Total Investment in Fixed Assets	国 有 State-owned	集 体 Collectively-owned	股份制 Joint-stock	港澳台商 Hong Kong, Macao and Taiwan	外 商 Foreign	私营个体 Private	其 他 Others
1978	22.6							
1979	26.5							
1980	33.2							
1981-1985	**286.8**	**223.8**	**22.6**				**40.4**	
1981	36.6	30.1	1.3				5.2	
1982	38.6	33.0	1.5				4.1	
1983	51.3	37.1	1.4				12.8	
1984	66.3	50.0	2.2				14.1	
1985	94.0	73.6	16.2				4.2	
1986-1990	**724.1**	**609.6**	**83.1**				**31.4**	
1986	106.2	88.7	13.3				4.2	
1987	136.2	115.8	15.2				5.2	
1988	163.0	133.2	21.4				8.4	
1989	139.5	117.7	15.1				6.7	
1990	179.2	154.2	18.1				6.9	
1991-1995	**2358.7**	**1764.2**	**188.7**				**24.8**	
1991	192.0	165.0	20.2				6.8	
1992	266.0	230.1	27.3				8.6	
1993	410.4	340.1	37.4				2.0	
1994	648.8	514.8	44.6				3.1	
1995	841.5	514.2	59.2				4.3	
1996-2000	**5461.7**	**3380.8**	**261.8**				**155.3**	
1996	876.9	545.7	57.6				4.8	
1997	961.2	605.7	54.7				4.0	
1998	1155.6	727.9	48.7				30.9	
1999	1170.6	735.7	55.8				36.1	
2000	1297.4	765.8	45.0				79.5	
2001-2005	**10857.4**	**3922.4**	**303.3**				**809.4**	
2001	1530.5	752.6	45.8				110.9	
2002	1814.3	771.5	53.9				150.6	
2003	2157.1	745.1	62.4				201.3	
2004	2528.3	755.5	69.5	1063.8	204.5	198.8	176.4	59.8
2005	2827.2	897.7	71.7	1211.8	164.1	274.1	170.2	37.6
2006-2010	**21538.5**	**8162.9**	**398.0**	**9206.8**	**903.8**	**1480.8**	**1121.2**	**265.0**
2006	3371.5	1207.2	69.3	1384.5	180.9	315.9	174.9	38.8
2007	3966.6	1343.0	80.4	1679.0	236.4	378.9	209.0	39.9
2008	3848.5	1388.6	66.8	1688.5	145.3	274.9	242.2	42.2
2009	4858.4	2316.8	68.9	1728.5	172.2	273.0	233.0	66.0
2010	5493.5	1907.3	112.6	2726.3	169.0	238.1	262.1	78.1
2011-2015	**34958.8**	**11452.2**	**635.5**	**17733.9**	**1525.3**	**1468.8**	**1707.3**	**435.7**
2011	5910.6	1903.3	99.4	3053.2	224.1	266.8	278.4	85.4
2012	6462.8	2248.2	106.8	3280.9	208.8	300.2	231.7	86.1
2013	7032.2	2382.0	151.4	3318.4	464.2	321.7	317.0	77.5
2014	7562.3	2389.5	151.4	3944.0	380.7	255.9	366.1	74.7
2015	7990.9	2529.2	126.5	4137.4	247.5	324.2	514.1	112.0
2016	8461.7	2588.0	61.7	4725.0	341.2	303.1	365.3	77.4

注：1.国有包括登记注册类型为国有、国有联营及国有独资公司的单位。
2.集体包括登记注册类型为集体和集体联营的单位。

Note: a) State-owned units include state-owned enterprises, state-owned associated enterprises and wholly state-owned enterprises.
b) Collectively-owned units include collectively-owned enterprises and collectively-owned associated enterprises.

6-3 按产业分全社会固定资产投资(1978-2016年)
INVESTMENT IN FIXED ASSETS BY INDUSTRY (1978-2016)

单位：亿元 (100 million yuan)

年份 Year	全社会固定资产投资 Total Investment in Fixed Assets	第一产业 Primary Industry	第二产业 Secondary Industry	第三产业 Tertiary Industry
1978	22.6	1.4	10.8	10.4
1979	26.5	1.0	12.0	13.5
1980	33.2	0.7	15.7	16.8
1981-1985	**286.8**	**5.9**	**98.1**	**130.4**
1981	36.6	0.6	13.6	17.2
1982	38.6	1.2	15.4	17.9
1983	51.3	1.2	16.4	20.9
1984	66.3	1.3	20.3	30.6
1985	94.0	1.6	32.4	43.8
1986-1990	**724.1**	**9.4**	**218.8**	**384.2**
1986	106.2	1.5	41.4	51.6
1987	136.2	1.6	46.9	72.9
1988	163.0	2.0	48.8	87.9
1989	139.5	1.9	38.4	81.9
1990	179.2	2.4	43.3	89.9
1991-1995	**2358.7**	**15.5**	**624.1**	**973.5**
1991	192.0	2.7	51.3	90.4
1992	266.0	3.9	82.9	114.2
1993	410.4	2.1	150.4	165.7
1994	648.8	3.7	185.8	318.4
1995	841.5	3.1	153.7	284.8
1996-2000	**5461.7**	**9.9**	**914.3**	**2160.2**
1996	876.9	2.8	174.9	319.7
1997	961.2	0.9	201.1	380.1
1998	1155.6	1.5	201.7	479.7
1999	1170.6	1.7	179.4	470.4
2000	1297.4	3.0	157.2	510.3
2001-2005	**10857.4**	**63.4**	**1410.6**	**9383.4**
2001	1530.5	8.4	154.2	1367.9
2002	1814.3	7.5	185.0	1621.8
2003	2157.1	21.0	260.7	1875.4
2004	2528.3	14.6	401.0	2112.7
2005	2827.2	11.9	409.7	2405.6
2006-2010	**21538.5**	**159.9**	**2172.8**	**19205.8**
2006	3371.5	14.5	363.2	2993.8
2007	3966.6	16.7	484.1	3465.8
2008	3848.5	28.1	386.0	3434.4
2009	4858.4	57.4	411.4	4389.5
2010	5493.5	43.2	528.1	4922.3
2011-2015	**34958.8**	**643.0**	**3630.9**	**30684.9**
2011	5910.6	47.2	762.2	5101.3
2012	6462.8	145.4	719.8	5597.5
2013	7032.2	175.5	755.0	6101.7
2014	7562.3	163.9	716.8	6681.6
2015	7990.9	111.0	677.1	7202.8
2016	8461.7	99.8	722.9	7639.0

注：1.2000年及以前按产业划分中，不含房地产开发投资及农村投资。2000年以后含房地产开发投资及农村固定资产投资。
2.自2012年起，三次产业划分执行国家统计局《三次产业划分规定》(国统字〔2012〕108号)。

Note: a) Data of investment in fixed assets grouped by industry excluded investment in real estate development and rural investment in 2000 and before. After 2000, data of investment in fixed assets included investment in real estate development and rural fixed assets.
b) Since 2012, the three industries have been classified according to the Regulations on the Classification of the Three Industries (G.T.Z. [2012] No. 108) issued by National Bureau of Statistics.

6-4 全社会固定资产投资资金来源情况(1978-2016年)
TOTAL INVESTMENT IN FIXED ASSETS BY SOURCE OF FUNDS (1978-2016)

单位：亿元 (100 million yuan)

年份 Year	上年末结余资金 Surplus Funds by the End of the Previous Year	本年资金来源小计 Subtotal of Funds at Current Year	国家预算内资金 State Budgets	国内贷款 Domestic Loans	债券 Bonds	利用外资 Foreign Investment	自筹资金 Self-raised Funds	其他资金 Others
1978		22.5	16.9					
1979		26.5	19.2					
1980		33.2	18.5					
1981		31.4	15.4					
1982		34.5	14.1					
1983		38.5	16.0					
1984		52.2	22.5					
1985		77.8	30.4					
1986		94.5	33.0					
1987		126.2	43.1					
1988		149.4	37.4					
1989		123.1	35.0	12.8		18.2	44.5	12.6
1990		136.2	34.4	22.8		15.2	52.3	11.5
1991		151.1	35.5	28.2		13.9	65.5	8.0
1992		216.7	42.2	40.1		14.9	109.9	9.6
1993	54.3	425.2	47.1	79.2	1.6	28.0	205.2	64.1
1994	71.1	695.7	64.1	91.5	0.8	96.9	331.2	111.2
1995	200.8	915.8	70.3	122.7	1.1	187.3	339.8	194.6
1996	204.9	926.1	76.7	152.8	1.0	161.2	330.5	203.9
1997	183.1	1016.7	86.3	194.3		139.2	383.4	213.5
1998	207.1	1140.1	98.4	223.8	17.0	132.1	450.2	218.6
1999	212.1	1183.8	136.2	262.2	1.4	82.7	461.3	240.0
2000	293.1	1439.1	107.0	373.8	0.6	51.5	505.6	400.6
2001	325.5	1796.8	136.7	429.4	2.5	35.6	595.6	597.0
2002	433.2	2075.3	108.5	543.8	1.9	41.5	672.8	706.8
2003	542.7	2674.0	78.4	755.2		52.6	887.9	899.9
2004	654.6	3712.8	118.6	804.7		120.5	1245.7	1423.3
2005	924.4	4553.7	128.8	1055.8		70.9	1452.8	1845.4
2006	1043.8	4927.3	126.4	1347.5	32.7	76.2	1532.2	1812.3
2007	1202.2	6193.0	102.2	1513.3	22.4	82.8	2195.6	2276.7
2008	1469.5	5184.7	104.2	1394.2	35.5	80.0	2016.4	1554.5
2009	1321.7	8702.2	118.1	3038.5	17.5	39.3	2441.3	3047.4
2010	2109.1	8327.8	99.5	2218.7	4.3	43.8	3209.1	2752.4
2011	2341.4	8235.4	71.7	1853.6	85.4	29.8	3588.6	2606.3
2012	2830.7	9156.0	156.1	2186.3	12.7	24.9	3478.4	3297.6
2013	3133.1	10580.3	159.6	2554.1	0.8	23.5	4295.2	3547.2
2014	3586.5	10208.7	161.7	2841.0	8.0	33.3	4347.9	2816.8
2015	4238.6	10773.9	184.9	2390.1	10.6	13.2	4853.6	3321.5
2016	4585.2	12065.0	107.9	2677.3	9.2	13.1	5047.8	4209.6

注：1978—1992年不含房地产开发和农村投资；1993—2003年不含农村投资。

Note: Figures from 1978 to 1992 did not include investment in real estate development and rural investment; figures from 1993 to 2003 did not include rural investment.

6-5 全社会基础设施投资(1978-2016年)

单位：亿元

年 份 Year	基础设施投资 Infrastructure Investment	#能 源 Energy	电 力 Electricity	供 热 Heating	供 气 Gas	供 水 Water	#公 共服务业 Public Services	#园林绿化 Landscaping	#环境卫生 Environmental Sanitation	#市政工程管理 Municipal Project Management
1978	5.4	1.4	0.7				0.6			
1979	5.8	1.1	0.4				1.3			
1980	6.0	0.9	0.6				2.3			
1981-1985	**40.6**	**9.4**	**5.4**				**11.2**			
1981	5.8	1.3	0.6				2.0			
1982	6.1	1.4	0.9				1.9			
1983	6.7	1.5	0.9				1.9			
1984	8.8	1.4	0.7				3.0			
1985	13.2	3.8	2.3				2.5			
1986-1990	**117.9**	**39.8**	**21.1**				**25.3**			
1986	14.5	4.8	2.3				2.1			
1987	22.1	8.0	4.1				3.1			
1988	23.2	8.8	4.1				5.3			
1989	26.5	9.2	5.2				6.6			
1990	31.6	9.0	5.3				8.3			
1991-1995	**494.9**	**134.1**	**84.6**	**12.3**	**15.2**	**22.0**	**62.9**	**2.9**		**57.3**
1991	35.2	12.4	6.4	2.0	1.3	2.7	7.5	0.3		6.8
1992	58.8	17.7	9.0	4.0	2.6	2.1	8.2	0.4		7.2
1993	91.4	19.3	11.4	1.4	2.6	3.9	4.1	1.6		1.7
1994	153.4	38.0	22.7	2.5	5.0	7.8	27.2	0.3		26.5
1995	156.1	46.7	35.1	2.4	3.7	5.5	15.9	0.3		15.1
1996-2000	**1382.1**	**363.4**	**239.7**	**45.2**	**41.4**	**37.1**	**321.0**	**14.2**	**27.1**	**275.9**
1996	188.8	59.2	48.2	3.4	4.1	3.5	29.1	2.3	0.1	25.4
1997	218.3	75.6	52.1	10.3	7.8	5.4	24.3	1.7	2.8	19.8
1998	320.4	85.1	54.2	14.2	6.7	10.0	38.0	3.0	1.9	33.1
1999	302.7	90.3	58.6	11.2	10.3	10.2	75.0	5.4	2.9	64.7
2000	351.9	53.2	26.6	6.1	12.5	8.0	154.6	1.8	19.4	132.9
2001-2005	**2260.0**	**301.7**	**165.2**	**52.7**	**53.9**	**29.9**	**668.6**	**23.1**	**79.9**	**511.4**
2001	356.4	40.8	19.3	7.2	11.0	3.3	114.6	6.7	22.4	85.4
2002	411.9	49.5	26.0	7.2	13.2	3.0	101.6	3.5	17.0	81.1
2003	417.8	36.1	10.6	11.3	10.8	3.4	152.8	1.9	17.0	103.6
2004	463.2	73.0	39.3	14.8	6.9	12.0	139.3	5.5	16.3	100.8
2005	610.7	102.3	70.0	12.2	12.0	8.1	160.3	5.5	7.2	140.6
2006-2010	**6137.3**	**780.3**	**443.6**	**176.9**	**57.6**	**102.1**	**1640.0**	**44.8**	**349.4**	**1117.7**
2006	935.3	113.4	72.8	18.7	11.0	10.9	265.3	3.4	55.4	194.8
2007	1175.8	200.2	121.0	43.0	11.2	25.0	289.5	8.0	75.7	187.3
2008	1160.7	144.1	88.4	25.9	8.1	21.7	291.6	8.0	82.2	188.7
2009	1462.0	165.4	88.9	40.1	10.5	25.8	434.5	15.9	77.7	314.0
2010	1403.5	157.2	72.5	49.2	16.8	18.7	359.1	9.5	58.4	232.9
2011-2015	**9167.7**	**1323.2**	**611.2**	**264.0**	**119.9**	**328.3**	**2335.7**	**125.6**	**236.9**	**1668.6**
2011	1400.2	171.1	90.1	25.3	17.0	38.8	379.4	8.1	40.5	267.8
2012	1789.2	231.9	106.3	64.8	27.3	33.5	508.1	22.0	23.5	361.6
2013	1785.7	270.2	133.7	53.6	38.1	44.8	451.3	18.2	53.6	318.3
2014	2018.1	352.7	149.1	81.4	21.3	100.9	502.5	67.7	35.9	366.6
2015	2174.5	297.3	132.0	38.9	16.2	110.3	494.4	9.6	83.4	354.3
2016	2399.5	332.0	150.9	37.0	37.3	106.8	643.8	29.1	211.6	362.0

注：2004年及以后基础设施投资包括农村基础设施投资。

TOTAL INVESTMENT IN INFRASTRUCTURE (1978-2016)

(100 million yuan)

#交通运输 Transportation	#铁路 Railway	#公路 Road	#城市公共交通业 Urban Public Transportation	#航空 Aviation	#邮政电信 Post & Telecommunications	邮政 Post	电信 Telecommunications	基础设施投资占全社会固定资产投资比重(%) Infrastructure Investment as Percentage of Total Investment in Fixed Assets (%)
1.7	0.8	0.4		0.5	0.4			23.9
1.7	0.4	0.4		0.8	0.4			21.9
2.3	1.1	0.7		0.5	0.5			17.9
11.1	**3.9**	**5.5**		**1.7**	**5.2**			
1.8	0.6	0.9		0.3	0.4			15.8
1.9	0.8	0.8		0.3	0.4			15.8
2.6	1.2	1.0		0.4	0.6			13.1
2.3	0.7	1.3		0.3	1.1			13.3
2.6	0.7	1.6		0.4	2.7			14.0
28.3	**5.0**	**19.3**		**4.0**	**20.3**			
3.1	1.0	1.5		0.6	3.5			13.7
6.6	1.2	4.0		1.3	3.2			16.2
4.7	1.4	3.0		0.4	3.0			14.2
5.2	0.7	3.9		0.6	5.2			19.0
8.7	0.7	6.9		1.1	5.4			17.6
123.0	**50.8**	**30.6**	**22.4**	**4.6**	**137.3**	**9.5**	**127.8**	
9.3	0.8	5.6	2.3	0.5	5.8	5.0	0.8	18.3
20.1	4.7	10.7	4.0	0.7	12.3	1.1	11.2	22.1
29.4	11.2	4.7	4.7	1.1	24.2	1.7	22.5	22.3
30.0	13.6	3.6	5.7	1.0	48.6	0.9	47.7	23.6
34.2	20.5	6.0	5.7	1.3	46.4	0.8	45.6	18.6
337.4	**26.0**	**131.3**	**80.0**	**3.2**	**299.6**	**6.0**	**293.6**	
54.0	11.7	15.8	6.0	1.2	44.1	0.9	43.2	21.5
51.2	6.0	11.1	9.1	0.2	60.3	2.1	58.2	22.7
104.6	8.0	42.1	24.4		77.5	1.8	75.7	27.7
63.0		30.1	20.7		54.0	0.4	53.6	25.9
64.6	0.3	32.2	19.8	1.8	63.7	0.8	62.9	27.1
766.2	**23.2**	**294.0**	**302.8**	**137.6**	**384.0**	**6.2**	**377.9**	
104.4	1.5	52.8	45.1	2.0	84.8	2.2	82.6	23.3
159.7	1.4	107.0	44.6	1.4	78.7	1.6	77.1	22.7
129.2	9.3	55.3	48.8	15.8	82.2	0.9	81.3	19.4
148.8	7.2	38.2	51.1	52.3	68.5	1.0	67.5	18.3
224.1	3.9	40.7	113.2	66.2	69.9	0.5	69.4	21.6
3010.9	**358.7**	**732.8**	**1456.7**	**457.7**	**462.9**	**8.2**	**454.4**	
439.6	25.1	140.6	201.0	72.2	72.3	1.2	71.1	27.7
548.0	65.7	189.6	202.4	87.5	84.8	…	84.7	29.6
604.2	75.9	170.5	215.8	141.8	86.7	0.3	86.3	30.2
698.6	114.9	134.8	426.7	21.9	124.9	3.3	121.5	30.1
720.5	77.1	97.3	410.8	134.3	94.2	3.4	90.8	25.5
3640.7	**191.8**	**506.8**	**1918.9**	**987.9**	**636.8**	**12.5**	**624.2**	
680.7	43.6	107.7	351.3	176.6	82.3	2.7	79.6	23.7
712.0	43.0	98.2	391.0	178.1	122.0	4.6	117.4	27.7
664.5	36.9	127.5	310.9	162.5	132.9	3.5	129.4	25.4
756.5	9.0	84.6	491.6	166.0	127.3	0.1	127.2	26.7
827.0	59.3	88.8	374.1	304.7	172.3	1.6	170.6	27.2
973.0	252.8	135.3	318.0	258.8	147.5	4.4	143.1	28.4

Note: Investment in infrastructure in and after 2004 includes that in rural infrastructure investment.

6-6 全社会基础设施投资(2016年)
TOTAL INVESTMENT IN INFRASTRUCTURE (2016)

项目	Item	投资额(万元) Investment (10000 yuan)		比重(%) Percentage (%)	
		全市 Beijing Municipality	#城镇 Urban	全市 Beijing Municipality	#城镇 Urban
合计	**Total**	**23994893**	**19649009**	**100.0**	**100.0**
能源	**Energy**	**3319814**	**2509431**	**13.8**	**12.8**
电力	Electricity	1509366	1195807	6.3	6.1
供热	Heating	369672	211589	1.5	1.1
供气	Gas	372851	194145	1.6	1.0
供水	Water	1067925	907890	4.5	4.6
公共服务业	**Public Services**	**6438139**	**4922092**	**26.8**	**25.1**
园林绿化	Landscaping	291224	140153	1.2	0.7
环境卫生	Environmental Sanitation	2115863	1468788	8.8	7.5
市政工程管理	Municipal Project Management	3620474	3174890	15.1	16.2
其他公共服务业	Others	410578	138261	1.7	0.7
交通运输	**Transportation**	**9730459**	**9560359**	**40.6**	**48.7**
铁路	Railway	2528266	2528266	10.5	12.9
公路	Road	1353389	1188741	5.6	6.0
管道运输	Pipeline	81710	81710	0.3	0.4
城市公共交通业	Urban Public Transportation	3179535	3174083	13.3	16.2
#公交电汽车客运	Buses and Electirc Cars	167903	167903	0.7	0.9
出租汽车	Taxis	269922	269922	1.1	1.4
航空	Aviation	2587559	2587559	10.8	13.2
其他	Others				
邮政电信	**Post and Telecommunications**	**1475427**	**1462928**	**6.1**	**7.4**
邮政	Post	44408	44408	0.2	0.2
电信	Telecommunications	1431019	1418520	6.0	7.2
其他	**Others**	**3031054**	**1194199**	**12.6**	**6.1**
#水利	Water Conservancy	1466842	722408	6.1	3.7

6-7 全社会固定资产投资及新增固定资产(按行业分)(2016年)
TOTAL INVESTMENT IN FIXED ASSETS AND ITS INCREMENTAL FIXED ASSETS (GROUPED BY SECTOR) (2016)

单位：万元 (10000 yuan)

项 目	Item	投 资 额 Investment			新增固定资产 Incremental Fixed Assets		
		合 计 Total	中 央 Central	地 方 Local	合 计 Total	中 央 Central	地 方 Local
合 计	**Total**	**84616861**	**10131887**	**74484974**	**36084024**	**6697826**	**29386198**
农、林、牧、渔业	**Agriculture, Forestry, Animal Production and Hunting, Fishing**	**1030884**	**1788**	**1029096**	**448874**	**1788**	**447086**
农 业	Agriculture	89978		89978	71961		71961
林 业	Forestry	880559	1788	878771	340512	1788	338724
畜牧业	Animal Production and Hunting	1554		1554	700		700
渔 业	Fishing	9418		9418	2332		2332
农、林、牧、渔服务业	Service Activities for Agriculture, Forestry, Animal Production and Hunting, Fishing	49375		49375	33369		33369
采矿业	**Mining and Quarrying**	**29345**		**29345**	**508**		**508**
煤炭开采和洗选业	Mining and Washing of Coal						
黑色金属矿采选业	Mining of Ferrous Metal Ores	29345		29345	508		508
制造业	**Manufacturing**	**3835706**	**444553**	**3391153**	**2855397**	**373248**	**2482149**
农副食品加工业	Processing of Food from Agricultural Products	51342		51342	57073		57073
食品制造业	Manufacture of Foods	69539		69539	78181		78181
酒、饮料和精制茶制造业	Manufacture of Wines, Beverage and Refined Tea	48506		48506	24354		24354
纺织业	Manufacture of Textile	1672		1672			
纺织服装、服饰业	Manufacture of Textile Wearing Apparel and Ornament	24280		24280			
皮革、毛皮、羽毛及其制品和制鞋业	Manufacture of Leather, Fur, Feather and Its Products, and Footwear	5400		5400			
木材加工及木、竹藤、棕、草制品	Processing of Timbers, Manufacture of Wood, Bamboo, Rattan, Palm and Straw Products	23818		23818			
家具制造业	Manufacture of Furniture	23059		23059	4595		4595
造纸及纸制品业	Manufacture of Paper and Paper Products	12428		12428	823		823
印刷和记录媒介复制业	Printing, Reproduction of Recording Media	54432		54432	18402		18402
文教、工美、体育和娱乐用品制造业	Manufacture of Articles for Culture, Education, Artwork, Sport and Entertainment Activities	1933		1933			
石油加工、炼焦及核燃料加工业	Processing of Petroleum, Coking, Processing of Nucleus Fuel	16886	5496	11390	1500		1500
化学原料及化学制品制造业	Manufacture of Chemical Raw Materials and Chemical Products	151792	127767	24025	159890	136871	23019
医药制造业	Manufacture of Medicines	313863	27933	285930	170819		170819
化学纤维制造业	Manufacture of Chemical Fibers	500		500	2000		2000
橡胶和塑料制品业	Manufacture of Rubber and Plastic Products	22038		22038	8486		8486
非金属矿物制品业	Manufacture of Non-metallic Mineral Products	25122	821	24301	3593	3593	
黑色金属冶炼及压延加工业	Manufacture and Pressing of Ferrous Metals	1816		1816			
有色金属冶炼及压延加工业	Manufacture and Pressing of Non-ferrous Metals	11392	8607	2785			
金属制品业	Manufacture of Fabricated Metal Products	24710		24710	4470		4470
通用设备制造业	Manufacture of General-Purpose Machinery	54702	19012	35690	22728		22728

注：本表分行业数据不含农户投资。
Note: The figures of grouping exclude investment of rural households.

6-7 续表 1 Continued 1

单位：万元 (10000 yuan)

项　目	Item	投资额 Investment			新增固定资产 Incremental Fixed Assets		
		合计 Total	中央 Central	地方 Local	合计 Total	中央 Central	地方 Local
专用设备制造业	Manufacture of Special-Purpose Machinery	156910	3940	152970	127944	2750	125194
汽车制造业	Manufacture of Motor Vehicles	1080379		1080379	1297952		1297952
铁路、船舶、航空航天和其他运输设备制造业	Manufacture of Railway Locomotives, Building of Ships and Boats, Manufacture of Air and Spacecrafts and Other Transportation Equipment	221010	204175	16835	226163	198230	27933
电气机械及器材制造业	Manufacture of Electrical Machinery and Equipment	108557		108557	62783		62783
计算机、通信和其他电子设备制造业	Manufacture of Computer, Communication Equipment and Other Electronic Equipment	1260622	15976	1244646	520170	978	519192
仪器仪表制造业	Manufacture of Measuring Instrument and Meter	34419		34419	26347		26347
其他制造业	Other Manufacturing	2480		2480	1500		1500
废弃资源综合利用业	Waste Recycling and Recovery	1273		1273	4798		4798
金属制品、机械和设备修理业	Repair of Fabricated Metal Products, Machinery and Equipment	30826	30826		30826	30826	
电力、热力、燃气及水生产和供应业	**Production and Distribution of Electricity, Heating Power, Gas and Water**	**3319814**	**265507**	**3054307**	**1785246**	**80263**	**1704983**
电力、热力的生产和供应业	Production and Supply of Electric Power and Heat Power	1879038	265207	1613831	1273393	80263	1193130
燃气生产和供应业	Production and Distribution of Gas	372851		372851	77768		77768
水的生产和供应业	Production and Distribution of Water	1067925	300	1067625	434085		434085
建筑业	**Construction**	**62622**	**10265**	**52357**	**12610**	**10265**	**2345**
房屋建筑业	Construction of Building	30662	9365	21297	9865	9365	500
土木工程建筑业	Civil Engineering Construction	11834		11834	1845		1845
建筑安装业	Construction Installation	19150	900	18250	900	900	
建筑装饰和其他建筑业	Building Completion, Finishing and Other Construction	976		976			
批发和零售业	**Wholesale and Retail Trade**	**295578**	**28204**	**267374**	**257760**	**781**	**256979**
批发业	Wholesale	145505	27949	117556	86602	781	85821
零售业	Retail Trade	150073	255	149818	171158		171158
交通运输、仓储和邮政业	**Transport, Storage and Post**	**9954028**	**3991632**	**5962396**	**4268940**	**3198262**	**1070678**
铁路运输业	Transport via Railway	2528266	1423366	1104900	1362598	1362598	
道路运输业	Transport via Road	4532924	39410	4493514	879181	39410	839771
水上运输业	Water Transport						
航空运输业	Air Transport	2589197	2397667	191530	1881941	1696632	185309
管道运输业	Transport via Pipeline	81710	79710	2000			
仓储业	Storage	177523	24890	152633	127401	99622	27779
邮政业	Post	44408	26589	17819	17819		17819
住宿和餐饮业	**Accommodation and Restaurants**	**458245**	**202625**	**255620**	**586091**	**19638**	**566453**
住宿业	Accommodation	447124	202372	244752	582905	19638	563267
餐饮业	Restaurants	11121	253	10868	3186		3186
信息传输、软件和信息技术服务业	**Information Transmission, Software and Information Technology Services**	**1988521**	**165818**	**1822703**	**1266459**	**267969**	**998490**
电信、广播电视和卫星传输服务	Telecommunications, Broadcasting, Television and Satellite Transmission Services	1092355	29696	1062659	557581	123550	434031
互联网和相关服务	Internet and Related Services	338664	12295	326369	362540	12295	350245
软件和信息技术服务业	Software and Information Technology Services	557502	123827	433675	346338	132124	214214
金融业	**Finance**	**506453**	**383449**	**123004**	**92960**	**62544**	**30416**
货币金融服务	Monetary Financial Services	218676	217000	1676	55612	53946	1666
资本市场服务	Capital Market Services	5492		5492			
保险业	Insurance	239039	147634	91405	1451		1451
其他金融业	Other Financial Services	43246	18815	24431	35897	8598	27299

6-7 续表 2 Continued 2

单位：万元 (10000 yuan)

项目	Item	投资额 Investment			新增固定资产 Incremental Fixed Assets		
		合计 Total	中央 Central	地方 Local	合计 Total	中央 Central	地方 Local
房地产业	**Real Estate**	**48057634**	**3421158**	**44636476**	**16222720**	**616755**	**15605965**
租赁和商务服务业	**Renting and Leasing Activities Business Services**	**1292314**	**192630**	**1099684**	**253655**	**44226**	**209429**
租赁业	Renting and Leasing Activities	200533	31494	169039	185744	21698	164046
商务服务业	Business Services	1091781	161136	930645	67911	22528	45383
科学研究和技术服务业	**Scientific Research and Ddevelopment, Technical Services**	**809699**	**428344**	**381355**	**1105565**	**749125**	**356440**
研究与试验发展	Research and Experimental Development	335285	204050	131235	659031	618950	40081
专业技术服务业	Professional Technique Services	172020	126041	45979	281943	112918	169025
科技推广和应用服务业	Technique Generalization and Application Services	302394	98253	204141	164591	17257	147334
水利、环境和公共设施管理业	**Management of Water Conservancy, Environment and Public Facilities**	**7744125**		**7744125**	**2642224**		**2642224**
水利管理业	Management of Water Conservancy	1466842		1466842	443705		443705
生态保护和环境治理业	Ecological Protection and Environmental Control	681271		681271	505156		505156
公共设施管理业	Management of Public Facilities	5596012		5596012	1693363		1693363
居民服务、修理和其他服务业	**Resident Services, Repair and Other Services**	**160731**		**160731**	**155753**		**155753**
居民服务业	Resident Services	57203		57203	24056		24056
机动车、电子产品和日用产品修理业	Repair of Motor Vehicles, Electronics and Household Applicances	621		621	6038		6038
其他服务业	Other Services	102907		102907	125659		125659
教育	**Education**	**1399305**	**409881**	**989424**	**907560**	**262475**	**645085**
卫生和社会工作	**Health Care and Social Works**	**582007**	**61348**	**520659**	**252749**	**44022**	**208727**
卫生	Health Care	509483	61348	448135	224634	44022	180612
社会工作	Social Work activities	72524		72524	28115		28115
文化、体育和娱乐业	**Culture, Sports and Entertainment**	**2144336**	**122101**	**2022235**	**2139222**	**966458**	**1172764**
新闻出版业	Journalism and Publishing	2355	2355		92127	92127	
广播、电视、电影和影视录音制作业	Radio Broadcasting, Television,Movies, Videos and Sound Recording	319608	82878	236730	868809	754082	114727
文化艺术业	Culture and Arts	215541	36616	178925	188102	120249	67853
体育	Sports Activities	59914	252	59662	23758		23758
娱乐业	Entertainment	1546918		1546918	966426		966426
公共管理、社会保障和社会组织	**Public Management, Social Security and Social Organizations**	**393470**	**2584**	**390886**	**302809**	**7**	**302802**
中国共产党机关	Organs of Communist Party of China	1095	1095				
国家机构	Organs of State	388616		388616	301847		301847
社会保障	Social Security	1186	406	780	530		530
群众团体、社会团体和其他成员组织	Mass Communities, Social Organizations and Other Membership Organizations	2101	1083	1018	7	7	
基层群众自治组织	Grass Roots Self-government Organizations	472		472	425		425

6-8 全社会房屋建筑施工及竣工面积(1978-2016年) FLOOR SPACE OF BUILDINGS UNDER CONSTRUCTION AND COMPLETED (1978-2016)

单位：万平方米 (10000 sq.m)

年 份 Year	施工面积 Floor Space of Buildings under Construction	#住 宅 Residential Buildings	竣工面积 Floor Space of Buildings Completed	#住 宅 Residential Buildings	中 央 Central	地 方 Local
1978	956.3	456.8	407.0	190.4	158.7	248.3
1979	1340.6	780.2	537.6	304.9	235.2	302.4
1980	1704.1	1037.0	648.4	396.9	315.8	332.6
1981-1985			**3941.6**	**2383.4**	**1723.2**	**2218.4**
1981	1875.8	1189.9	726.9	462.6	327.2	399.7
1982	1938.6	1210.1	728.3	463.8	303.7	424.6
1983	1952.1	1163.6	775.5	514.0	312.3	463.2
1984	2351.9	1327.1	818.7	437.6	352.7	466.0
1985	2802.7	1599.2	892.2	505.4	427.3	464.9
1986-1990			**5142.4**	**2939.9**	**2635.1**	**2507.3**
1986	2760.7	1557.4	906.5	532.7	424.5	482.0
1987	2578.0	1273.2	1042.2	608.9	507.8	534.4
1988	2642.2	1226.2	1065.6	623.5	499.6	566.0
1989	2450.8	1167.8	1046.9	601.8	565.8	481.1
1990	2864.9	1561.9	1081.2	573.0	637.4	443.8
1991-1995			**6206.7**	**3707.2**	**1869.2**	**4337.5**
1991	2818.0	1612.0	1036.4	601.8	396.2	640.2
1992	3126.8	1784.7	1111.4	681.2	399.3	712.1
1993	3607.5	1866.4	1158.0	654.8	320.5	837.5
1994	4460.9	2315.1	1370.7	832.1	366.8	1003.9
1995	5524.3	2897.6	1530.2	937.3	386.4	1143.8
1996-2000			**9644.3**	**5979.9**	**2726.7**	**6917.6**
1996	5633.2	2696.9	1517.5	870.4	452.0	1065.5
1997	5819.4	2881.3	1625.7	996.8	492.2	1133.5
1998	6496.1	3473.7	1821.5	1093.1	508.4	1313.1
1999	6556.5	3754.8	2321.4	1519.9	655.3	1666.1
2000	6995.9	4083.3	2358.2	1499.7	618.8	1739.4
2001-2005			**17781.6**	**11992.2**	**1733.0**	**16048.6**
2001	8203.3	5226.4	2554.6	1804.9	490.6	2064.0
2002	9697.7	6193.3	3121.8	2191.4	441.8	2680.0
2003	11262.2	7011.3	3222.8	2322.3	242.1	2980.7
2004	13121.9	7513.1	4203.2	2649.5	301.9	3901.3
2005	14096.2	8043.2	4679.2	3024.1	256.6	4422.6
2006-2010			**20059.1**	**10993.8**	**2002.6**	**18056.4**
2006	14069.2	7113.0	4191.0	2391.6	388.6	3802.4
2007	14146.7	6788.8	3866.4	2098.0	399.6	3466.8
2008	14145.3	6656.3	3840.7	1871.1	496.8	3343.9
2009	14380.6	7058.4	4252.6	2369.6	388.4	3864.2
2010	15572.1	7932.9	3908.4	2263.5	329.2	3579.1
2011-2015			**20883.8**	**10717.4**	**1919.2**	**18964.5**
2011	18065.2	8817.1	4032.9	2121.8	425.5	3607.4
2012	20045.4	9217.8	3723.5	1992.5	216.9	3506.6
2013	21526.0	9469.0	3989.7	2154.8	255.2	3734.4
2014	21677.7	8978.3	4967.5	2547.6	541.4	4426.1
2015	20009.1	7962.3	4170.2	1900.7	480.2	3690.0
2016	22721.4	7744.2	3594.0	1763.3	299.8	3294.2

注：2007年及以前，表中数据不包含农村农户房屋施工和竣工面积。

Note: Figures in and before 2007 excluded floor space of buildings under construction and completed in rural areas.

6-9 全社会房屋建筑施工及竣工面积
FLOOR SPACE OF BUILDINGS UNDER CONSTRUCTION AND COMPLETED

单位：万平方米 (10000 sq.m)

项　　目	Item	2016	2015	占竣工面积比重(%) Proportion in Completed Floor Space (%) 2016	2015
施工总面积	**Floor Space of Buildings under Construction**	**22721.4**	**20009.1**		
竣工总面积	**Floor Space of Buildings Completed**	**3594.0**	**4170.2**	**100.0**	**100.0**
按隶属关系分	**By Affiliation**				
中　央	Central	299.8	480.2	8.3	11.5
地　方	Local	3294.2	3690.0	91.7	88.5
#国　有	State-owned	413.3	696.7	11.5	16.7
集　体	Collectively-owned	40.1	191.7	1.1	4.6
按功能区分	**By Functional Zone**				
首都功能核心区	Core Functional Area of the Capital	37.9	195.0	1.1	4.7
城市功能拓展区	Urban Function Extension Area	1044.0	1064.3	29.0	25.5
城市发展新区	New Area of Urban Development	2090.1	2302.0	58.2	55.2
生态涵养发展区	Ecological Conservation Area	422.0	609.0	11.7	14.6

6-10 房地产开发面积(1990-2016年)

单位：万平方米

年份 Year	商品房施工面积 Floor Space of Commercial Buildings under Construction	#本年新开工面积 Floor Space of Buildings Newly Started Construction in Current Year	住宅 Residential Houses	#经济适用房 Affordable Houses	#公寓别墅 Apartments & Villas	办公楼(写字楼) Office Buildings	商业、非公益用房及其他 Buildings for Commercial Use, Non-public Buildings and Others	商品房竣工面积 Floor Space of Comnmercial Buildings Completed	住宅 Residential Houses	#经济适用房 Affordable Houses	#公寓别墅 Apartments & Villas
1990	774.0	249.1	643.4			17.4	41.2	271.6	226.5		
1991	815.1	317.6	692.1			2.1	57.6	275.2	240.4		
1992	1021.1	508.6	865.4			7.6	54.8	331.4	300.8		
1993	1262.0	524.8	887.6					356.4	280.6		
1994	1593.2	659.4	1107.6					445.7	385.6		
1995	2810.2	1012.2	1728.7		334.8	462.7	252.6	653.0	506.3		55.6
1996	2824.6	578.7	1520.7		316.8	638.7	283.9	663.4	470.8		43.3
1997	2869.6	848.4	1541.1		335.7	637.7	260.8	682.3	478.3		99.8
1998	3499.1	1193.4	2107.2		368.3	590.7	297.7	842.8	588.7		57.0
1999	3784.0	1061.8	2447.9	301.4	390.7	484.4	281.3	1208.5	908.3	114.1	93.2
2000	4455.0	1676.9	2971.6	296.6	537.8	449.1	281.3	1365.6	1013.7	184.9	164.2
2001	5966.7	2789.8	4349.6	563.1	494.4	495.5	330.6	1707.4	1393.4	214.0	150.8
2002	7510.7	3206.0	5397.5	660.2	550.8	672.5	400.3	2384.4	1926.2	228.4	161.9
2003	9070.7	3433.8	6352.9	802.5	705.0	901.3	557.7	2593.7	2080.8	322.8	127.9
2004	9931.3	3054.3	6759.4	793.2	776.0	1122.4	641.8	3067.0	2343.9	298.8	153.2
2005	10748.5	2965.9	7283.4	783.4	1023.5	1209.8	809.2	3770.9	2841.4	325.6	342.7
2006	10483.5	3179.4	6311.3	551.9	913.8	1245.8	1403.0	3193.9	2193.3	270.1	255.6
2007	10438.6	2557.4	5914.5	440.1	1009.2	1364.6	1482.1	2891.7	1854.0	188.6	239.6
2008	10014.3	2337.2	5538.2	544.9	954.7	1287.2	1429.8	2558.0	1399.3	101.1	233.0
2009	9719.1	2246.6	5551.9	628.7	840.9	1132.2	1323.4	2678.6	1613.2	98.2	213.7
2010	10300.9	2974.2	6176.0	572.7	830.0	1054.8	1229.3	2386.7	1498.5	144.6	183.2
2011	12065.4	4246.1	7168.1	444.8	754.8	1422.7	1187.5	2245.2	1316.1	74.6	133.0
2012	13122.5	3224.2	7510.4	435.1	642.2	1711.9	1236.9	2390.9	1522.7	188.5	135.1
2013	13886.9	3577.5	7406.9	310.5	530.1	2114.1	4365.9	2666.4	1692.0	95.7	133.5
2014	13641.5	2502.8	6999.7	328.0	485.4	2277.1	4364.7	3054.1	1804.3	101.4	52.5
2015	13095.0	2790.2	6314.6	150.0	508.5	2426.8	4353.6	2631.5	1378.2	17.0	92.5
2016	13089.8	2813.7	5927.6	180.7	486.8	2447.3	4714.9	2383.1	1275.2	22.5	97.2

注：1. 2005年及以前的商品房销售面积为竣工后的全部商品房销售面积，2006年及以后为期房与现房销售面积之和。
2. 2010年起，商品房销售面积中包含定向安置房数据。
3. 2012年及以前商业、非公益用房及其他只包括商业及服务性等营业性用房。自2013年起包括：厂房、仓库、商业营业用房、服务业用房、教育用房、文化体育用房、医疗用房、科研用房及其他用房(下同)。

STATISTICS FOR FLOOR SPACE OF REAL ESTATE DEVELOPENT (1990–2016)

(10000 sq.m)

办公楼（写字楼） Office Buildings	商业、非公益用房及其他 Buildings for Commercial Use, Non-public Buildings and Others	商品房销售面积 Floor Space of Commercial Buildings Sold	住宅 Residential Houses	#经济适用房 Affordable Houses	#公寓别墅 Apartments & Villas	办公楼（写字楼） Office Buildings	商业、非公益用房及其他 Buildings for Commercial Use, Non-public Buildings and Others	年末商品房待售面积 Floor Space of Vacant Commercial Buildings at the Year End	#住宅 Residential Houses	#一年以内 Less than One Year	#三年以上 Over Three Years
9.7	13.3	142.2									
0.9	10.9	154.0	152.5								
2.7	8.3	159.1	153.0								
		182.0	182.0								
		168.6	149.0			17.2	1.1				
27.9	43.5	191.9	180.0		16.7	4.0	4.5	81.5			
79.0	38.3	215.3	183.1		24.9	13.7	14.4	214.8	179.6		
80.9	42.4	290.9	256.2		53.5	18.8	8.0	298.3	258.9		
92.3	69.8	409.2	377.0		40.0	23.2	7.0	334.8	262.9		
108.8	43.1	544.4	484.7	45.8	55.1	48.0	6.8	624.3	529.1		
97.2	48.7	956.9	898.2	166.5	107.6	41.2	6.1	627.4	515.1		
98.0	48.2	1205.0	1127.5	185.2	120.8	49.8	17.4	774.0	634.1	429.4	84.6
97.4	82.9	1708.3	1604.4	220.7	153.6	44.0	32.9	919.0	763.2	557.9	96.4
94.0	117.5	1895.8	1771.1	320.0	131.9	38.1	50.8	1123.4	896.9	745.5	109.8
153.9	225.3	2472.0	2285.8	306.3	172.7	92.5	60.2	1044.1	723.8	744.4	72.9
287.8	180.9	2803.2	2566.0	304.0	302.1	131.2	66.9	1374.2	799.7	993.5	75.8
304.4	289.2	2607.6	2205.0	176.3	276.9	260.3	108.6	1039.7	494.1	628.3	106.9
314.8	315.1	2176.6	1731.5	100.1	319.3	265.7	134.8	1136.2	411.8	697.2	203.1
364.6	313.1	1335.4	1031.4	108.3	164.6	139.4	112.4	1438.3	522.7	945.1	209.8
316.6	322.4	2362.3	1880.5	82.2	339.8	255.8	157.1	1351.4	426.8	768.0	229.9
198.4	271.9	1639.5	1201.4	49.5	175.9	208.1	142.1	1482.7	511.9	810.4	239.7
245.2	232.4	1440.0	1035.0	39.4	93.3	211.4	108.7	1792.6	699.8	1021.5	298.3
226.8	240.1	1943.7	1483.4	85.9	116.9	253.5	114.0	1911.8	789.5	958.7	309.0
273.1	701.3	1903.1	1363.7	106.6	87.8	317.9	221.5	1861.4	829.3	922.3	337.7
387.5	862.3	1459.0	1141.3	56.2	48.2	136.8	180.9	2065.7	864.8	1121.4	374.2
385.4	867.8	1554.7	1127.3	37.7	72.0	243.0	184.4	2168.1	867.7	1151.7	436.9
343.7	764.2	1675.1	993.5	45.4	153.4	415.4	266.2	2160.8	845.8	1197.1	492.9

Note: a) Floor space of commercial buildings sold in 2005 and before was the floor space of completed commercial buildings, and after 2006, the figure is the sum of completed commercial buildings and those under construction.

b) Since 2010, the floor space of completed commercial buildings has included figures of targeted resettlement buildings.

c) In and Before 2012, buildings for commercial use, non-public buildings and others only included business and commercial buildings. Since 2013, it has included: factory buildings, warehouses, commercial buildings, buildings for service industy, education buildings, cultural and sports buildings, medical buildings, scientific research buildings and others(the same below).

6-11 房地产开发情况(1990-2016年)
STATISTICS FOR REAL ESTATE DEVELOPENT (1990-2016)

年份 Year	房地产开发企业个数(个) Number of Real Estate Development Enterprises (unit)	房地产开发投资额(亿元) Investment in Real Estate Development (100 million yuan)	#土地购置费 Land Purchase Cost	按用途分 By Purpose of Investment 住宅 Residential Buildings	写字楼(办公楼) Office Buildings	商业、非公益用房及其他 Buildings for Commercial Use, Non-public Buildings and Others	按投资构成分 By Investment Structure #建筑安装工程 Construction and Installation Projects	#设备工器具购置 Purchase of Equipment, Tools and Devices
1990		22.5		12.3			18.4	
1991-1995		**568.4**		**264.8**			**341.9**	
1991	40	24.0		14.0			16.8	
1992	42	33.7		20.0			20.7	
1993	74	58.4	2.5	38.1			43.4	0.4
1994	81	99.5	4.0	50.3			69.3	0.9
1995	623	352.8	52.4	142.4	71.5	35.2	191.7	8.4
1996-2000		**1979.5**	**161.5**	**950.7**	**351.5**	**161.3**	**1280.6**	**95.5**
1996	554	328.2	15.0	124.9	84.2	35.2	222.0	17.0
1997	601	330.3	23.9	132.9	91.1	29.2	208.0	19.8
1998	585	377.4	28.4	168.0	78.5	36.1	250.7	20.7
1999	716	421.5	36.6	236.6	52.5	30.2	278.6	16.8
2000	893	522.1	57.6	288.3	45.2	30.6	321.3	21.2
2001-2005		**5974.0**	**993.6**	**3239.5**	**696.1**	**368.3**	**3498.9**	**137.8**
2001	1142	783.8	115.6	464.2	72.0	41.7	438.0	22.3
2002	1508	989.4	149.2	586.7	97.3	57.6	572.7	31.5
2003	1546	1202.5	213.2	633.0	142.7	61.3	716.2	24.3
2004	2704	1473.3	275.8	776.0	187.9	94.8	872.1	35.4
2005	3123	1525.0	239.8	779.5	196.2	112.9	881.8	42.3
2006-2010		**10863.2**	**3642.0**	**5211.5**	**1055.2**	**1270.8**	**4550.5**	**255.0**
2006	2882	1719.9	477.9	863.6	216.7	226.0	953.2	55.5
2007	2688	1995.8	644.7	991.7	242.2	267.4	1015.3	58.9
2008	3433	1908.7	639.0	940.6	170.5	240.4	829.6	48.6
2009	3171	2337.7	587.7	906.6	166.7	200.7	841.6	45.7
2010	3190	2901.1	1292.7	1509.0	259.1	336.3	910.8	46.3
2011-2015		**17810.7**	**7264.1**	**9055.6**	**3017.1**	**4275.8**	**7037.8**	**227.5**
2011	3069	3036.3	1301.2	1778.3	363.8	296.7	1235.1	38.5
2012	2960	3153.4	1102.7	1628.0	384.8	275.9	1383.1	65.7
2013	2927	3483.4	1159.5	1724.6	611.7	1147.1	1510.0	53.0
2014	2810	3911.3	1561.2	1962.0	750.2	1199.1	1601.9	47.3
2015	2780	4226.3	2139.5	1962.7	906.6	1357.0	1307.7	23.0
2016	2654	4045.4	1953.6	1950.9	699.1	1395.5	1341.6	20.8

6-12 房地产开发企业经营情况(2016年)
REAL ESTATE DEVELOPMENT ENTERPRISES (2016)

项目	Item	企业单位个数(个) Number of Enterprises (unit)	实收资本合计(万元) Paid-in Capital (10000 yuan)	资产总计(万元) Total Assets (10000 yuan)	主营业务收入(万元) Main Business Income (10000 yuan)	利润总额(万元) Total Profits (10000 yuan)
合计	**Total**	**2654**	**70890065**	**556936607**	**46117023**	**8025536**
按企业登记注册类型分	**By Registration Type**					
内资企业	Domestically-Funded Enterprises	2431	59641187	489953430	42911547	7528957
国有企业	State-owned Enterprises	53	5077569	14376488	444719	75055
集体企业	Collectively-owned Enterprises	17	66448	2329318	319597	15396
私营企业	Private Enterprises	490	2708935	27777752	1619006	-31156
股份合作企业	Joint-equity Cooperative Enterprises	***	***	***	***	***
股份有限公司	Companies Limited by Shares	46	4956260	42414289	1297266	1680731
有限责任公司	Limited Liability Companies	1824	46826976	403045923	39230934	5791044
港澳台商投资企业	Hong Kong, Macao and Taiwan-invested Enterprises	129	7239587	38610800	2403611	274756
港澳台合资经营	Joint Ventures	43	2464590	10602942	728091	329454
港澳台合作经营	Cooperative	46	1228256	8066324	703483	133638
港澳台商独资企业	Solely-funded Enterprises	40	3546741	19941534	972037	-188336
港澳台商投资股份有限公司	Companies Limited by Shares					
外商投资企业	Foreign-invested Enterprises	94	4009291	28372377	801864	221822
中外合资经营	Joint Ventures	40	1979660	14475816	406885	31189
中外合作经营	Cooperative	31	581493	5748681	134515	74537
外资(独资)企业	Solely-funded Enterprises	21	1310356	7498858	249864	60629
外商投资股份有限公司	Companies Limited by Shares	***	***	***	***	***
按隶属关系分	**By Affiliation**					
中央	Central	101	6066860	40890928	2441954	1401287
地方	Local	2553	64823205	516045679	43675069	6624248
按资质等级分	**By Qualification Grade**					
一级	First-grade	105	12452288	120267875	7354936	3312514
二级	Second-grade	160	5966066	62672763	6070814	510344
三级	Third-grade	201	4703464	40939049	3891451	453296
四级	Fourth-grade	1182	20846624	181857096	15043431	2017030
暂定	Provisional	547	14826296	105247905	11656624	1213568
其他	Others	459	12095327	45951918	2099766	518784
按营业状况分	**By Operating Condition**					
营业	Operating	2526	70270742	554111243	46095177	8043984
停业	Closed	116	500715	2219403	21845	-12004
其他	Others	12	118608	605961		-6444

6-13 房地产开发企业开发建设情况(2016年)
DEVELOPMENT OF REAL ESTATE ENTERPRISES (2016)

单位：万元、平方米 (10000 yuan,sq.m)

项目	Item	全市合计 Total	#国有企业 State-owned	#三资企业 Foreign Funded	按隶属关系分 By Affiliation 中央 Central	地方 Local
计划总投资	**Total Planned Investment**	**253224352**	**15004386**	**14560185**	**16530494**	**236693858**
开始建设至本年度累计完成投资	**Accumulative Investment Completed from Beginning to the End of This Year**	**196346404**	**12250516**	**12099470**	**14046218**	**182300186**
本年完成投资合计	**Investment Completed in the Current Year**	**40454483**	**2510726**	**1132700**	**2674542**	**37779941**
#土地购置费	Land Purchase Cost	19535732	1216620	12510	1280310	18255422
本年完成投资按用途分	**Grouped by Purpose of Investment**					
住宅	Residential Buildings	19508886	1012976	426682	1587931	17920955
办公楼(写字楼)	Office Buildings	6990757	124632	219458	465357	6525400
商业、非公益用房及其他	Buildings for Commercial Use, Non-public Buildings and Others	13954840	1373118	486560	621254	13333586
本年购置土地面积	**Land Space Purchased in Current Year**	**2684998**			**52353**	**2632645**

6-14 保障性安居工程建设情况
CONSTRUCTION OF GOVERNMENT-SUBSIDIZED HOUSING PROJECTS

单位：亿元、万平方米 (100 million yuan,10000 sq.m)

项目	Item	2016	2015	2016年为2015年% 2016 as % of 2015
完成投资额	**Investment Completed**	**936.2**	**824.0**	**113.6**
经济适用房	Affordable Houses	22.6	24.5	92.1
限价房	Price-capped Houses	277.8	303.4	91.6
公租(廉租)房	Public Rental (Low-rent) Houses	213.0	73.6	289.5
定向安置房	Targeted Resettlement Houses	422.8	422.5	100.1
施工面积	**Floor Space Under Construction**	**3952.4**	**3870.5**	**102.1**
经济适用房	Affordable Housing	236.9	200.7	118.0
限价房	Price-capped Housing	606.7	578.3	104.9
公租(廉租)房	Public Rental (Low-rent) Housing	450.7	395.5	114.0
定向安置房	Resettlement Housing	2658.1	2696.0	98.6
竣工面积	**Floor Space Completed**	**663.9**	**881.8**	**75.3**
经济适用房	Affordable Houses	28.5	23.8	119.7
限价房	Price-capped Houses	95.3	164.6	57.9
公租(廉租)房	Public Rental (Low-rent) Houses	161.1	35.8	450.0
定向安置房	Targeted Resettlement Houses	379.0	657.6	57.6
本年新开工面积	**Floor Space Newly Started in the Year**	**1051.9**	**636.6**	**165.2**
经济适用房	Affordable Houses	62.1	18.9	328.6
限价房	Price-capped Houses	244.3	183.3	133.3
公租(廉租)房	Public Rental (Low-rent) Houses	122.5	63.3	193.5
定向安置房	Targeted Resettlement Houses	623.0	371.0	167.9

主要统计指标解释

全社会固定资产投资 包括城镇固定资产投资（含房地产开发投资）和农村固定资产投资。

城镇固定资产投资 是指城镇各种登记注册类型的企业、事业、行政单位及个体户进行的计划总投资在500万元及以上的建设项目投资。镇及镇以上各级政府及主管部门直接领导、管理的建设项目和企事业单位的投资均为城镇固定资产投资。

农村固定资产投资 农村投资统计以投资项目建设地址所在的地域为界定农村投资统计的范围，即农村投资是指各种投资主体建设的建设项目地址在农村区域范围内的、以满足农村居民生产、生活需要为主要目的的各种投资活动。农村固定资产投资包括农户和非农户固定资产投资。

新增固定资产投资 是指报告期内交付使用的固定资产价值。包括本年内建成投入生产或交付使用的工程投资和达到固定资产标准的设备、工具、器具的投资及有关应摊入的费用。属于增加固定资产价值的其他建设费用，应随同交付使用的工程一并计入新增固定资产。

基础设施投资 是指能够为企业提供作为中间投入用于生产的基本需求；能够为消费者提供所需的基本消费服务；能够为社区提供用于改善不利的外部环境的服务等建设的投资，包括固定资产投资中用于市政工程、电信工程、公共设施和水利环保等建设的投资。

上年末结余资金 是指上年资金来源中没有形成固定资产投资额而结余的资金。包括尚未用到工程上去的材料价值、未开始安装的需要安装设备价值及结存的现金和银行存款等。

本年资金来源小计 是指固定资产投资单位在报告期收到的，用于固定资产投资的各种货币资金。包括国家预算内资金、国内贷款、债券、利用外资、自筹资金和其他资金。

国家预算资金 指各级政府用于固定资产投资的财政资金，包括中央预算资金和地方预算资金。

国内贷款 是指报告期固定资产投资项目单位向银行及非银行金融机构借入的用于固定资产投资的各种国内借款，包括银行利用自有资金及吸收存款发放的贷款、上级主管部门拨入的国内贷款、国家专项贷款(包括煤代油贷款、劳改煤矿专项贷款等)，地方财政专项资金安排的贷款、国内储备贷款、周转贷款等。

利用外资 是指报告期收到的用于固定资产建造和购置投资的境外资金(包括设备、材料、技术在内)。包括外商直接投资、对外借款(外国政府贷款、国际金融组织贷款、出口信贷、外国银行商业贷款、对外发行债券和股票)及外商其他投资(包括利用外商投资收益在国内进行固定资产再投资活动的资金)。不包括我国自有外汇资金(包括国家外汇、地方外汇、留成外汇、调剂外汇和国内银行自有资金发行的外汇贷款等)。

自筹资金 指固定资产投资单位报告期收到的，由各地区、各部门及企业、事业单位筹集用于固定资产投资的预算外资金，包括中央各部门、各级地方和企业、事业单位的自有资金。

其他资金来源 是指在报告期收到的除以上各种资金之外其他用于固定资产投资的资金。包括社会集资、个人资金、无偿捐赠的资金及其他单位拨入的资金等。

建筑安装投资（建筑安装工作量） 是指各种房屋、建筑物的建造工程，各种设备、装置的安装工程，又称建筑安装工作量。建筑工程投资必须经过兴工动料，通过施工活动才能实现。在安装工程中，不包括被安装设备本身价值。

设备工器具购置 是指建设单位或企、事业单位购置或自制的，达到固定资产标准的设备、工具、器具的价值。

房地产开发投资 指从本年1月1日起至本年最后一天止完成的全部用于房屋建设工程和土地开发工程的投资额，以及公益性建筑和土地购置费等投资。

土地购置费 通过各种方式取得土地使用权而支付的费用（包括开发补偿费）。土地购置费包括：(1)通过“划拨”方式取得的土地使用权所支付的土地补偿费、附着物和青苗补偿费、安置补偿费及土地征收管理费等；竣工后计入新增固定资产。(2)通过“出让”方式（包括协议出让、招、拍、挂出让）取得的土地使用权所支付的费用；竣工后不计入新增固定资产。

经济适用住房 指政府提供政策优惠，限定套型面积和销售价格，按照合理标准建设，面向城镇低收入住房困难家庭供应的具有保障性质的政策性住房。

限价商品住房（限价房） 指政府控制土地出让价格，限定销售价格和套型面积，向城镇中等收入家庭供应的普通商品住房。

公共租赁住房（公租房） 指政府提供财政投入和政策支持，限定套型建筑面积标准，按照合理标准组织建设，或通过长期租赁等方式筹集，按照当地政府规定的供应标准，面向城镇中等偏下收入住房困难家庭、新就业职工和有稳定职业并在城镇居住一定年限的外来务工人员供应的保障性住房。

廉租住房（廉租房） 指政府提供财政投入和政策支持，限定套型建筑面积标准，按照合理标准组织建设，或通过购买、改建和租赁等方式筹集，按照当地政府规定的供应标准，面向城镇低收入住房困难家庭供应的具有保障性质的住房。

房屋施工面积 是指报告期内施工的全部房屋建筑面积。包括本期新开工的面积和上年开工跨入本期继续施工房屋面积，以及上期已停建在本期恢复施工的房屋面积。本期竣工和本期施工后又停建、缓建的房屋面积仍包括在施工面积中，多层建筑应填各层建筑面积之和。

房屋竣工面积 是指报告期内房屋建筑按照设计要求已全部完工，达到住人和使用条件，经验收鉴定合格（或达到竣工验收标准)，可正式移交使用的各栋房屋建筑面积的总和。

待售面积 指报告期末已竣工的可供销售或出租的商品房屋建筑面积中，尚未销售或出租的商品房屋建筑面积，包括以前年度竣工和本期竣工的房屋面积，但不包括报告期已竣工的拆迁还建，统建代建，公共配套建筑、房地产公司自用及周转房等不可销售或出租的房屋面积。

Explanatory Notes on Main Statistical Indicators

Total Investment in Fixed Assets includes urban investment in fixed assets (including the investment in real estate development) and rural investment in fixed assets.

Investment in Urban Fixed Assets refers to investment in construction projects with a total planned investment over RMB 5,000,000 (inclusive) by enterprises with various types of registration, institutions, administrative units and individuals in urban areas. The investment in construction projects under the direct leadership and management of government agencies at and above town levels and investment by enterprises and public institutions are also calculated in investment in urban fixed assets.

Investment in Rural Fixed Assets refers to all investment activities that are conducted in rural areas to meet the production and living needs of the rural residents. Investment in rural fixed assets consists of investment in fixed assets by rural and non-rural households.

Incremental Fixed Assets Investment means the value of fixed assets put into use in the reporting period, including investment in projects completed and put into use within the year, and investment in equipment, tools and appliances that reach the standard of fixed assets, together with expenses incurred in these activities. Other construction costs adding value to fixed assets shall be calculated in the incremental fixed assets together with the projects put into use.

Infrastructure Investment refers to investment that provides intermediate inputs for enterprise to meet their basic production needs, provides consumers with basic consumer services needed, or provides communities with services for improving external environment, which includes the investment in municipal projects, telecom projects, public facilities, water conservancy and environmental protection.

Surplus Funds by the Year End of the Previous Year refers to the fund in the previous year that was not included in the investment in fixed assets, including the value of materials not yet used for projects, value of equipment to be installed, and balance of cash and bank deposits.

Subtotal of Funds at Current Year refers to monetary capital received by investors that was used for investment in fixed assets, including funds from state budgetary funds, domestic loans, bonds, foreign investment, self-raised funds and other funds.

National Budget Funds refers to the financial funds used by governments at all levels for investment in fixed assets, including budget funds of central and local government .

Domestic Loans refer to loans of various forms borrowed by fixed assets investment project entities from banks and non-bank financial institutions for the purpose of investment in fixed assets during the reporting period, including loans issued by banks from their equity funds and deposits, loans appropriated by higher authorities, special loans allocated by the central government (including loans for replacing oil with coal, and special loans for labor camp coal mines), loans arranged by local government from special funds, domestic reserve loans and revolving loans.

Foreign Investment refers to foreign funds received during the reporting period for the investment in construction and purchase of fixed assets (including equipment, materials and technologies), including foreign direct investment, foreign loans (loans from foreign governments and international financial institutions, export credit, commercial loans from foreign banks, issued bonds and stocks overseas), and other foreign investments (including funds for domestic re-investment in fixed assets by earnings from foreign investment). It does not include foreign exchanges owned by China (foreign exchanges owned by the central and local governments, foreign exchanges retained, foreign exchange swap, loans in foreign exchanges issued by the domestic banks with their own funds, etc.).

Self-raised Funds refer to non-budgetary funds for investment in fixed assets received during the reporting period by different regions, departments, enterprises and public institutions, including self-owned funds of central departments, local authorities, enterprises and public institutions.

Other Funds refer to funds for investment in fixed assets received from sources other than those listed above, including social funds, personal funds, donated funds and funds transferred from other institutions.

Investment in Construction and Installation (Workload of Construction and Installation) refers to the investment in construction projects of various houses and buildings, and installation projects of various equipment and devices, also known as the workload of construction and installation. It can only be realized through construction work and consumption of materials. For installation projects, the value of equipment installed is not included.

Purchase of Equipment, Tools and Devices refers to the value of equipment, tools and devices purchased or made by construction companies, enterprises or public institutions, which reach the specified amount of fixed assets.

Real Estate Development Investment refers to all investment used for housing projects and land development projects, together with public welfare buildings and land purchase costs spent from January 1st to the last day of the year.

Land Purchase Cost refers to expenses on acquiring the land use right, including development compensation. It includes: (1) Expenses on land use right by allocation, including land compensation fees, compensation fees for its attached objects and crops; after completion, these expanses will be included in incremental fixed assets. (2) Expenses on land use right by transfer, including fees for agreement transfer, bid invitation, auction and listing; after completion, these expanses will not be included in incremental fixed assets.

Affordable Houses refer to government-subsidized houses that are supplied to urban low-income households and built in line with reasonable standards, limited size and fixed pricing.

Price-capped Houses refer to ordinary commercial houses with limited size and fixed pricing that are supplied to middle-income urban households, and their land transfer price is controlled by the government.

Public Rental Houses refer to government-subsidized houses that are built in line with reasonable standards and limited size, and can be rented by lower middle-income urban households with housing difficulties, new employees and migrant workers with stable jobs and have lived in the urban area for a certain period.

Low-rent Houses refer to government-subsidized houses that are built in line with reasonable standards and limited size, with funds raised by purchasing, reconstruction or leasing, and can be rented by low-income urban households with housing difficulties.

Floor Space of Buildings under Construction refers to the total floor space of all houses and buildings under construction during the reference period, including floor space of newly started buildings in current period, floor space of construction extended from the previous period to the current period, and floor space of construction suspended during the previous period and resumed in the current period. Floor space of construction completed in the current period, and floor space of construction started and then suspended in the current period are also included in the floor space under construction. For multi-storey buildings, the sum of floor space of all floors shall be calculated.

Floor Space of Buildings Completed refers to the total floor space of all houses and buildings fully completed as required in the design plan during the reference period, which have been examined as qualified for living and use, and can be handed over and put into use.

Floor Space of Vacant Commercial Buildings refers to total floor space of commercial buildings for sale or for renting by the end of the reference period. It consists of the floor space of completed buildings in previous years and in the current year, but does not include relocated houses or buildings of unified construction or agent contract, as well as houses not for sale or renting such as public facilities, houses used by real estate companies and temporary houses.

07

北京统计年鉴2017　BEIJING STATISTICAL YEARBOOK

对外经济贸易
FOREIGN ECONOMY AND TRADE

简要说明

一、本章资料的主要内容

本章资料主要反映北京市对外经济贸易的发展状况，包括对外贸易、利用外资、对外经济合作的历年概况，以及对外友好交往情况。

二、本章资料的统计范围和数据来源

1.对外贸易情况

对外贸易统计的范围是凡能引起北京市海关境内物质资源存量增加或减少的进出口货物，除制度另有规定者外，均列入该项统计，调查方法采用全面调查。主要内容包括北京地区进出口总值；主要产品进出口数量等。数据来源于中华人民共和国北京海关。

2.口岸运营情况

口岸运营情况的统计范围是北京首都国际机场空港口岸、北京丰台货运口岸、北京朝阳口岸、北京西站铁路口岸、北京平谷国际陆港、北京天竺综合保税区。主要内容包括旅客吞吐量、货邮吞吐量、监管货物的数量、征收关税等。数据来源于北京市人民政府口岸办公室。

3.利用外资情况

利用外资情况的统计范围是凡经工商行政管理机关核准登记，在中华人民共和国北京地域内所有使用外资（包括港澳台地区投资）的单位和部门，经批准设立的中外合资经营企业、合作经营企业、外资企业、外商投资股份制企业、合作开发项目等具有法人资格的独立核算企业(包括港澳台地区投资企业)，在华从事经营活动的外国及港澳台地区企业及外国公司在中国境内设立的分支机构。主要内容包括实际利用外商直接投资，外商投资企业经营情况，调查方法采用全面调查。数据来源于北京市商务委员会和北京市统计局。

4.对外经济合作

对外经济合作的统计范围是经各级商务部门批准的从事对外承包、劳务合作和设计咨询业务并具有法人资格的对外承包劳务企业；调查方法采用全面调查。主要内容包括对外承包工程、劳务合作和设计咨询。数据来源于北京市商务委员会。

5.友好城市

主要内容包括与北京市建立友好关系的城市名录。数据来源于北京市人民政府外事办公室。

Brief Introduction

I. Main Content

Data in this chapter show the development of foreign economic relations and trade in Beijing, including foreign trade, foreign capital utilization, and foreign economic cooperation in Beijing over the years, as well as friendly exchanges.

II. Scope of Statistical and Source of Data

1. Foreign trade

Foreign trade statistics apply for: any imports and exports that lead to increase or decrease in the stock of physical resources at Beijing customs, except for those otherwise stated in regulations, and were obtained through comprehensive survey. Foreign trade data include: total volume of import and export in Beijing, and quantity of main import and export products, and so on.. Foreign trade data are from Beijing Customs, P.R.C..

2. Statistics for Port Operation

The statistical scope of port operation covers the Port of Beijing Capital International Airport, Beijing Fengtai Cargo Transport Port, Beijing Chaoyang Transport Port, Railway Port at Beijing West Railway Station, Beijing Pinggu International Land Port, and Beijing Tianzhu Comprehensive Bonded Zone. Statistics in this chapter, which is sourced from Port Administration Office of the People's Government of Beijing Municipality, mainly include passenger throughput, cargo throughput, cargos under customs regulation and duties levied.

3. Foreign capital utilization

Scope of statistics: all entities and organizations registered with administration for industry and commerce upon approval, and using foreign capital (including investment from Hong Kong, Macao and Taiwan region) within the jurisdiction of Beijing, P.R.C, enterprises with legal person statues and independent accounting system (including enterprises invested by companies from Hong Kong, Macao and Taiwan region), including joint ventures, cooperative enterprises and foreign-invested enterprises, foreign-invested joint-stock enterprises, and cooperative development projects, and enterprises of foreign countries and Hong Kong, Macao and Taiwan region conducting operations in China as well as branch offices opened by foreign companies in China. Foreign capital utilization data include foreign direct investment, operation of foreign-invested enterprises, and were obtained through comprehensive survey. Data are sourced from Beijing Municipal Commission of Commerce (former Beijing Municipal Bureau of Commerce) and Beijing Municipal Bureau of Statistics.

4. Foreign economic cooperation

Statistics cover foreign labor service enterprises with legal person statues that are engaged in foreign contracting, labor service cooperation and design consulting with approval from departments of commerce at different levels. Comprehensive survey was used. Foreign economic cooperation statistics apply for: foreign contracting projects, labor service cooperation and design consulting. Data are sourced from Beijing Municipal Commission of Commerce (former Beijing Municipal Bureau of Commerce).

5. Sister cities

Data showing the detailed list of sister cities of Beijing are from Foreign Affairs Office of the People's Government of Beijing Municipality.

7-1 北京地区对外经济贸易(1980-2016年)
FOREIGN ECONOMIC RELATIONS AND TRADE (1980-2016)

年 份 Year	进出口总值(万美元) Total Value of Imports and Exports (USD 10000)	出 口 Exports	#高新技术产品 High-tech Products	#机电产品 Mechanical and Electrical Products	进 口 Imports	#高新技术产品 High-tech Products	#机电产品 Mechanical and Electrical Products
1980							
1981-1985							
1981							
1982							
1983	3059926	1468740			1591186		
1984	3559284	1751704			1807580		
1985	3254341	437398			2816943		
1986-1990	**13945243**	**1865234**			**12080009**		
1986	3060236	371282			2688954		
1987	2670466	354374			2316092		
1988	2988576	395887			2592689		
1989	2861489	302343			2559146		
1990	2364476	441348			1923128		
1991-1995	**14305670**	**3547263**			**10758405**		
1991	2424137	457114			1967023		
1992	2498241	561037		157835	1937204	271005	731359
1993	2791700	669930		151133	2121769	302965	885074
1994	2888079	834205		194937	2053873	421071	1121082
1995	3703513	1024977		281810	2678536	407176	1225200
1996-2000	**17397285**	**5011639**		**1609152**	**12385646**	**2242338**	**5049210**
1996	2931833	811975		254450	2119858	240903	733641
1997	3038852	961103		271119	2077749	346166	766288
1998	3050608	1051293		325390	1999315	347556	909222
1999	3435951	990352		320852	2445599	567687	1213857
2000	4940041	1196916	226549	437341	3743125	740026	1426202
2001-2005	**39258570**	**9270820**	**2525916**	**4291246**	**29987748**	**5318558**	**10501427**
2001	5149809	1177236	263382	477568	3972572	992797	1883151
2002	5250529	1261386	314174	570971	3989142	916363	1701504
2003	6850017	1688682	396489	715359	5161335	990357	1949077
2004	9457572	2056926	580929	970117	7400647	1053395	2271805
2005	12550643	3086590	970942	1557231	9464052	1365646	2695890
2006-2010	**113918161**	**24817747**	**8781469**	**14861935**	**89100414**	**11589524**	**25107110**
2006	15803663	3795398	1388925	2170700	12008265	1704997	3786847
2007	19299976	4892639	1797751	2862301	14407337	2360093	4477646
2008	27169290	5749961	1906381	3354179	21419329	2417936	4987666
2009	21479103	4835807	1751571	3080447	16643296	2357239	5194072
2010	30166129	5543942	1936840	3394308	24622187	2749258	6660878
2011-2015	**196258645**	**29872913**	**9027650**	**18089490**	**166385732**	**14606903**	**36430695**
2011	38958314	5899770	1811744	3523452	33058544	3145224	7667795
2012	40810735	5963212	1901750	3737918	34847523	2987939	7217809
2013	42994169	6309757	2035695	3894782	36684413	2923787	7167539
2014	41553810	6233597	1874973	3789748	35320213	2937309	7785199
2015	31941616	5466577	1403488	3143590	26475039	2612644	6592353
2016	28237935	5201982	1131875	2728167	23035954	2549528	6552686

注：进出口总值为海关统计的北京地区进出口数据(包括中央单位)。
资料来源：北京市商务委员会、中华人民共和国北京海关。
Note: Figures of "total value of imports and exports" were imports and exports of Beijing counted by Beijing Customs (including central entities).
Source: Beijing Municipal Commission of Commerce and Beijing Customs of People's Republic of China.

7-1 续表 Continued

年 份 Year	外商直接投资项目(合同)个数 (个) Number of Foreign Direct Investment Projects (Contracts) (unit)	实际利用外商直接投资额 (万美元) Actal Use of Foreign Direct Investment (USD10000)
1980	4	
1981-1985	**124**	
1981	3	
1982	4	
1983	5	
1984	29	
1985	83	
1986-1990	**709**	
1986	63	
1987	72	9534
1988	148	50278
1989	185	31846
1990	241	27696
1991-1995	**10912**	**410896**
1991	724	24482
1992	2208	34984
1993	3753	66693
1994	2675	144460
1995	1552	140277
1996-2000	**4100**	**989794**
1996	868	155290
1997	790	159286
1998	651	206415
1999	644	223004
2000	1147	245799
2001-2005	**7821**	**1231631**
2001	1147	177000
2002	1370	178964
2003	1362	214675
2004	1806	308354
2005	2136	352638
2006-2010	**9232**	**2818387**
2006	2106	455191
2007	2177	506572
2008	1897	608172
2009	1423	612094
2010	1629	636358
2011-2015	**6599**	**4565745**
2011	1345	705447
2012	1360	804160
2013	1190	852418
2014	1318	904085
2015	1386	1299635
2016	1073	1302858

7-2 北京地区海关进出口贸易总值(按企业性质、贸易方式分)
TOTAL VALUE OF IMPORTS AND EXPORTS AT BEIJING CUSTOMS (BY ENTERPRISE TYPE AND COMPOSITION)

项　目	Item	金额(万美元) Value (USD 10000)		金额(万元) Value (10000 Yuan)	
		2016	2015	2016	2015
出口	**Local Exports**	**5201982**	**5466577**	**34302431**	**33949862**
按企业性质分	**By Enterprise Type**				
国有企业	State-owned Enterprises	3040377	3023535	20015317	18758656
外商投资企业	Foreign-invested Enterprises	1233211	1475572	8135172	9165544
中外合资	Joint Ventures	452496	668911	2985389	4157912
中外合作	Cooperatives	3226	4571	21129	28409
外商独资	Solely-funded Enterprises	777489	802091	5128654	4979218
民营企业	Private Enterprises	912522	963142	6034581	5998977
集体企业	Collectively-owned Enterprises	2174	3211	14315	19850
私营企业	Privately-owned Enterprises	909874	959269	6017158	5975034
个体工商户	Privately or Individually-owned Business	473	663	3107	4098
报关企业	Customs Declaration Enterprises	7649		63143	
其　他	Others	8223	4327	54218	26706
按贸易方式分	**By Composition**				
#一般贸易	General Trade	2677746	2994745	17658762	18611248
来料加工装配贸易	Trade of Processing & Assembling Supplied Materials	901172	597712	5921024	3707339
进料加工贸易	Trade of Processing Imported Materials	633595	931221	4176903	5786611
对外承包工程货物	Contracted Foreign Goods and Projects	578167	630388	3818544	3903915
出料加工贸易	Trade of Processing Exported Materials	2278	2416	14996	15007
进口	**Imports**	**23035954**	**26475039**	**152208582**	**164319770**
按企业性质分	**By Enterprise Type**				
国有企业	State-owned Enterprises	16112223	19863530	106421693	123203915
外商投资企业	Foreign-invested Enterprises	5204585	5040741	34428087	31341740
中外合资	Joint Ventures	1065198	1011323	7035886	6299387
中外合作	Cooperatives	6068	5405	39915	33746
外商独资	Solely-funded Enterprises	4133320	4024016	27352286	25008628
民营企业	Private Enterprises	1664047	1535192	10988145	9549005
集体企业	Collectively-owned Enterprises	63572	98113	419316	610514
私营企业	Privately-owned Enterprises	1600286	1436920	10567584	8937500
个体工商户	Privately or Individually-owned Business	189	159	1245	986
报关企业	Customs Declaration Enterprises	5664		46787	
其　他	Others	49434	35574	323871	225118
按贸易方式分	**By Composition**				
#一般贸易	General Trade	19701596	22696536	130160841	140862290
来料加工装配贸易	Trade of Processing and Assembling Supplied Materials	1606178	1563598	10619456	9716991
进料加工贸易	Trade of Processing Imported Materials	319043	468247	2104718	2911947
外商投资企业进口设备、物品	Equipment and Goods Imported by Foreign-invested Enterprises	17443	5823	114670	36121
租赁贸易	Leasing Trade	21233	160431	140814	991114

注：报关企业为2016年新增指标。
资料来源：中华人民共和国北京海关。
Note: The indicator of "Customs Declaration Enterprises" is newly added in 2016.
Source: Beijing Customs of People's Republic of China.

7-3 北京地区海关进出口贸易总值(按国别、地区分)
TOTAL VALUE OF IMPORTS AND EXPORTS AT BEIJING CUSTOMS (BY COUNTRY AND REGION)

项目	Item	金额(万美元) Value (USD 10000)		金额(万元) Value (10000 YUAN)	
		2016	2015	2016	2015
出口合计	**Total Exports**	**5201982**	**5466577**	**34302431**	**33949862**
按国别(地区)分	**By Country (Region)**				
#中国香港	Hong Kong, China	443046	486582	2925389	3021144
中国澳门	Macao, China	23888	28654	156930	176865
中国台湾	Taiwan, China	106136	125470	699361	777794
日本	Japan	398209	449913	2627027	2794558
新加坡	Singapore	323395	190938	2123849	1182992
韩国	Korea	196324	207698	1292045	1287462
越南	Vietnam	173480	191578	1145072	1186330
伊朗	Iran	103708	162444	686609	1006407
印度	India	115721	197150	759715	1219405
印度尼西亚	Indonesia	88936	108460	585892	671845
英国	United Kingdom	82371	120832	544978	756572
德国	Germany	87331	112499	576873	698804
法国	France	49415	59704	326072	371732
意大利	Italy	36806	42467	243737	263588
匈牙利	Hungary	9871	7840	65336	48558
俄罗斯联邦	Russian Federation	123342	126334	814286	789682
美国	United States	489067	495661	3234025	3082472
澳大利亚	Australia	141092	119496	930157	747440
进口合计	**Total Imports**	**23035954**	**26475039**	**152208582**	**164319770**
按国别(地区)分	**By Country (Region)**				
#中国香港	Hong Kong, China	631482	184397	4130350	1151462
日本	Japan	1159325	957100	7670020	5956922
新加坡	Singapore	262514	203079	1738556	1260535
韩国	Korea	780952	923731	5152357	5742874
沙特阿拉伯	Saudi Arabia	1094632	1477198	7223871	9144233
英国	United Kingdom	378133	359137	2500454	2234148
德国	Germany	1878294	1916550	12422680	11910196
法国	France	217811	299372	1438866	1865041
意大利	Italy	188517	200815	1247676	1248451
瑞士	Switzerland	1526015	1679705	10111480	10475547
比利时	Belgium	62093	72970	409850	451806
俄罗斯联邦	Russian Federation	881725	1099626	5817525	6828610
加拿大	Canada	243350	922538	1604847	5726463
美国	United States	2379959	2686606	15737643	16686151
澳大利亚	Australia	1185295	1120257	7850847	6944426
阿曼	Oman	607668	882155	4014743	5463997
安哥拉	Angola	1013934	1379771	6685417	8545335

资料来源：中华人民共和国北京海关。
Source: Beijing Customs of People's Republic of China.

7-4 北京地区海关主要商品进口量及金额(2016年) VOLUME & VALUE OF MAJOR COMMODITIES IMPORTED AT BEIJING CUSTOMS (2016)

项 目		Item		进口数量 Import Volume	进口金额（万美元） Import Value (USD 10000)
粮 食	(吨)	Grain	(tons)	15818	557198
食用植物油	(吨)	Edible Vegetable Oil	(tons)	926	72321
食 糖	(吨)	Sugar	(tons)	1054	42017
酒 类	(万升)	Alcohol	(10000 liters)	67	62862
合成橡胶(包括胶乳)	(吨)	Synthetic Rubber (Including Latex)	(tons)	54	8254
纸 浆	(吨)	Paper Pulp	(tons)	1025	55569
羊 毛	(吨)	Wool	(tons)	36	23253
棉 花	(吨)	Cotton	(tons)	131	21260
纺织用合成纤维	(吨)	Synthetic Fiber for Textile	(tons)	16	2784
铁矿砂及其精矿	(吨)	Iron Sand and Iron Ore Concentrates	(tons)	136439	755925
原 油	(吨)	Crude Oil	(tons)	242590	7369392
成品油	(吨)	Product Oil	(tons)	9257	342988
医药品	(吨)	Medicines	(tons)	17	479553
肥 料	(吨)	Fertilizers	(tons)	3426	88459
非泡沫塑料的板、片、膜、箔	(吨)	Non-foam Plastic Plates, Sheets, Films and Foi	(tons)	14	9391
纸及纸板(未切成形的)	(吨)	Paper and Pressboard (Not Shaped by Cutting)	(tons)	164	25548
纺织纱线、织物及制品		Textile Yarn, Fabric and Products		236540	62269
服装及衣着附件		Clothes and Clothing Accessories		20298	35464
钢 材	(吨)	Steel Products	(tons)	283	63473
建筑及采矿用机械及零件		Building and Mining Machinery and Parts		2123	14705
印刷、装订机械及零件		Printing and Binding Machinery and Parts		6410	77769
自动数据处理设备及其部件	(吨)	Automatic Data Processing Equipment and Their Components		1	22007
电动机及发电机	(台)	Electromotors and Generators	(sets)	9782	31929
变压、整流、电感器及零件		Voltage Transformer, Rectifier, Inductor and Parts		7003062	73575
电视摄像机、数字照相机及视频摄录一体机	(台)	Television Cameras, Digital Cameras and Integrated Video Cameras and Recorders	(sets)	2443	117826
印刷电路	(万块)	Printed Circuits	(10000 pieces)	152	6880
集成电路	(万个)	Integrated Circuits	(10000 units)	999	248404
电线和电缆	(吨)	Wires and Cables		7	19192
汽 车		Automobiles		618	2348965
汽车零件		Auto Parts		229564	433783
飞机及其他航空器		Aircrafts			153883
船 舶		Ships and Boats			26855
医疗仪器及器械		Medical Instruments and Devices		207765	204380
计量检测分析自控仪器及器具		Automatically-controlled Measuring, Testing and Analyzing Instruments		83448	500093

资料来源：中华人民共和国北京海关。
Source: Beijing Customs of People's Republic of China.

7-5 北京地区海关主要商品出口量及金额(2016年)
VOLUME & VALUE OF MAIN COMMODITIES EXPORTED AT BEIJING CUSTOMS (2016)

项目		Item		出口数量 Export Volume	出口金额 Export Value (万美元) (USD 10000)
粮食	(吨)	Grain	(tons)	395	26738
果蔬汁	(吨)	Fruit and Vegetable Juice	(tons)	104	10808
肥料	(吨)	Fertilizers	(tons)	2591	61254
煤及褐煤	(吨)	Coal	(tons)	3533	26378
焦炭、半焦炭	(吨)	Coke and Semi-coke	(tons)	1399	19235
成品油	(吨)	Product Oil	(tons)	26072	1120797
医药品	(吨)	Medicines	(tons)	22	38437
纺织纱线、织物及制品		Textile Yarn, Fabric and Products		294172	64660
铁合金	(吨)	Ferroalloy	(tons)	8	6417
钢材	(吨)	Steel Products	(tons)	4992	260781
未锻造的铝及铝材	(吨)	Non-forged Aluminum and Aluminum Products	(tons)	91	29575
纺织机械及零件		Textile Machinery and Parts		4689	13190
金属加工机床	(台)	Metal Processing Lathe	(sets)	16	8995
自动数据处理设备及其部件		Automatic Data Processing Equipment and Their Components		3188	34495
液晶显示板	(个)	LCD Plates	(units)	14538	49203
电动机及发电机	(台)	Electromotors and Generators	(sets)	2277	11928
变压器	(个)	Voltage Transformers	(units)	862	21118
蓄电池	(个)	Storage Cells	(units)	3421	3526
电话机	(台)	Telephone Sets	(sets)	15618	265664
二极管及类似半导体器件	(万个)	Diode and Similar Semiconductor Devices	(10000 units)	121	19781
集成电路	(万个)	Integrated Circuits	(10000 units)	725	192713
电线和电缆	(吨)	Wires and Cables	(tons)	38	37143
汽车(包括整套散件)	(辆)	Automobiles (Including Complete Sets of Spare Parts)	(sets)	54	104216
汽车零件		Auto Parts		248205	176160
船舶		Boats and Ships			83460
医疗仪器及器械		Medical Instruments and Devices		373167	55220
家具及其零件		Furnitures and Their Parts		8131	24163
服装及衣着附件		Clothes and Clothing Accessories		367995	179563
鞋类	(吨)	Footwear	(tons)	18	26229
塑料制品	(吨)	Plastic Products	(tons)	64	35948

资料来源：中华人民共和国北京海关。
Source: Beijing Customs of People's Republic of China.

7-6 北京口岸运营情况
STATISTICS FOR PORT OPERATION IN BEIJING

项　目		Item		2016	2015	2016年为2015年% 2016 as % of 2015
北京首都国际机场空港口岸		**Port of Beijing Capital International Airport**				
旅客吞吐量	(万人次)	Passenger Throughput	(10000 person-times)	9439	8994	105.0
进出境人员	(万人次)	Inbound/Outbound Visitors	(10000 person-times)	2425	2323	104.4
#外籍人员进出境	(万人次)	Inbound/Outbound Foreign Visitors	(10000 person-times)	700	712	98.3
货邮吞吐量	(万吨)	Cargos Carried	(10000 tons)	194	189	102.8
飞机起降	(架次)	Takeoff and Landing of Airplanes	(unit)	606086	590169	102.7
#进出境飞机起降	(架次)	Takeoff and Landing of Airplanes Inbound/Outbound	(unit)	139973	132613	105.5
海关监管货物	(万吨)	Cargos under Customs Regulation	(10000 tons)	5750	4160	138.2
北京丰台货运口岸		**Beijing Fengtai Cargo Transport Port**				
海关监管货物	(吨)	Cargos under Customs Regulation	(ton)	15547	17767	87.5
北京朝阳口岸		**Beijing Chaoyang Transport Port**				
海关监管货物	(吨)	Cargos under Customs Regulation	(ton)	1007374	937912	107.4
北京西站铁路口岸		**Railway Port at Beijing West Railway Station**				
进出境人员	(人次)	Inbound/Outbound Visitors	(person-times)	53787	66548	80.8
#外籍人员进出境	(人次)	Inbound/Outbound Foreign Visitors	(person-times)	3388	4196	80.7
北京平谷国际陆港		**Beijing Pinggu International Land Port**				
海关监管货物	(吨)	Cargos under Customs Regulation	(ton)	184904	189997	97.3
北京天竺综合保税区		**Beijing Tianzhu Comprehensive Bonded Zone**				
实际进出货物	(吨)	Cargos under Customs Regulation	(ton)	55404	62133	89.2
海关征收税款净入库税额	**(亿元)**	**Net Paid-in Duties Levied and Collecte**	**(100 million yuan)**	**610**		

注：取消指标“海关监管货物（标箱）”和“海关征收关税及代征税”，新增指标“海关征收税款净入库税额”。
资料来源：北京市人民政府口岸办公室。
Note: The indicator of " Cargos under Customs Regulation(TEU)" and "Duties Levied and Collected by Customs (on behalf of others)"
Source: Port Administration Office of the People's Government of Beijing Municipality.

7-7 外商投资企业实际利用外资情况(2006-2016年)

单位：万美元

项　　目	Item	2006	2007
实际利用外商直接投资额	**Actual Use of Foreign Direct Investment**	**455191**	**506572**
按登记注册类型分	**By Registration Type**		
合资经营	Joint Ventures	80570	77887
合作经营	Cooperatives	33039	18037
独资经营	Solely-funded Enterprises	341367	408754
外商投资股份制	Companies Limited by Shares	215	1894
按产业分	**By Industry**		
第一产业	Primary Industry	544	4774
第二产业	Secondary Industry	109380	93391
第三产业	Tertiary Industry	345267	408407
按行业分	**By Sector**		
农、林、牧、渔业	Agriculture, Forestry, Animal Production and Hunting, Fishing	544	4774
制造业	Manufacturing	105590	89618
建筑业	Construction	1254	878
信息传输、计算机服务和软件业	Information Transmission, Computer Services and Software	44341	78470
批发与零售业	Wholesale and Retail Trade	24378	33318
住宿和餐饮业	Accommodation and Restaurants	1882	5824
房地产业	Real Estate	72242	119476
租赁和商务服务业	Renting and Leasing Activities, Business Services	174342	92896
其他行业	Other Sectors	30618	81318
按外商国别(地区)分	**By Country (Region) of Foreign Investors**		
#中国香港	Hongkong,China	86600	149291
英属维尔京群岛	Virgin Islands	78445	104154
开曼群岛	Cayman Islands	27596	68646
日　本	Japan	67580	30386
韩　国	Korea	35357	24420
美　国	United States	20043	18280
新加坡	Singapore	17616	15328
巴巴多斯	Barbados	7278	13789
德　国	Germany	47797	11476
毛里求斯	Mauritius	10166	8068
百慕大	Bermuda	1658	7540
萨摩亚	Samoan	1483	6189
荷　兰	Netherlands	4610	4876
法　国	France	3578	3824
英　国	United Kingdom	2977	3304

资料来源：北京市商务委员会。

ACTUAL USE OF FOREIGN CAPITAL BY FOREIGN INVESTED ENTERPRISES (2006-2016)

(USD 10000)

2008	2009	2010	2011	2012	2013	2014	2015	2016
608172	**612094**	**636358**	**705447**	**804160**	**852418**	**904085**	**1299635**	**1302858**
90916	91049	91335	78983	191944	190667	154808	268500	792030
21372	32249	22890	15068	14184	22887	5166	202	4021
490252	448912	516766	594890	592310	593258	704367	995202	487714
5632	39884	5367	16506	5722	45606	39744	35731	19093
2032	3833	1246	214	733	1717	13947	7620	2303
162515	88536	71899	80798	112326	149687	97254	59528	68266
443625	519725	563213	624435	691101	701014	792884	1232487	1232289
2032	3833	1246	214	733	1717	13947	7620	2303
150056	75364	68496	63303	86378	106848	84226	59397	63806
1715	2493	411	2343	383	193	703	131	113
105396	94752	95453	109246	135121	119547	115292	48611	113490
34677	55411	66032	115437	74311	92739	54792	242167	584292
3357	8427	3525	1705	2877	1822	2047	549	3010
78787	79682	141728	112539	87739	148057	136822	27541	66160
132541	225888	175580	190363	161595	171079	339759	71199	120407
99611	66244	83887	110297	255023	210416	156497	842420	349277
173292	270295	312863	323041	440357	360481	541495	993199	561687
125045	123201	76255	112981	28882	51111	37592	189644	210649
75463	41389	45209	35982	59320	43982	36835	5774	269682
47174	23905	40692	77196	59022	44781	31125	12193	12449
27841	17601	14725	22372	70959	21029	18584	8143	37807
17888	18628	21370	30221	21097	38882	15634	3677	10182
10520	12600	24888	12898	31656	19383	35631	16468	54266
15803	2384	941	821	200	2839	3000	3	
26654	14308	22344	17939	25763	107467	99968	35761	95500
7780	5615	7179	1311	1392	3297	3586	275	774
1699	4441	4860	813	1483	265	2005		150
2468	1310	1705	893	1163	589	311	1463	95
28520	4906	10639	3677	8542	14619	12119	508	845
2583	6349	3700	6642	2286	1409	6284	16054	13446
4897	4242	1120	6245	3828	2387	1738	2010	1741

Source: Beijing Municipal Commission of Commerce.

7-8 外商投资企业基本情况

项 目	Item	企业单位数（个） Number of Enterprises (unit) 2016	2015
合 计	**Total**	**3764**	**3835**
按登记注册类型分	**By Registration Type**		
港澳台商投资企业	Hong Kong, Macao and Taiwan-invested Enterprises	1487	1481
与港澳台商合资	Joint Ventures	461	467
与港澳台商合作	Cooperatives	99	104
港澳台商独资	Solely-funded Enterprises	895	879
港澳台商投资股份有限公司	Companies Limited by Shares	30	30
其他港澳台投资企业	Others	***	***
外商投资企业	Foreign-invested Enterprises	2277	2354
中外合资	Joint Ventures	660	689
中外合作	Cooperatives	85	97
外商独资	Solely-funded Enterprises	1479	1521
外商投资股份有限公司	Companies Limited by Shares	39	38
其他外商投资企业	Others	14	9
按国民经济行业分	**By Sector**		
农、林、牧、渔业	Agriculture, Forestry, Animal Production and Hunting, Fishing		
制造业	Manufacturing	733	789
建筑业	Construction	80	82
批发与零售业	Wholesale and Retail Trade	500	490
住宿和餐饮业	Accommodation and Restaurants	178	190
信息传输、软件和信息技术服务业	Information Transmission, Software and Information Technology Services	525	522
房地产业	Real Estate	365	381
租赁和商务服务业	Renting and Leasing Activities, Business Services	593	589
其他行业	Other Sectors	790	792
按三次产业分	**By Industry**		
第一产业	Primary Industry		
第二产业	Secondary Industry	819	877
第三产业	Tertiary Industry	2945	2958

注：1．本表统计范围为限额以上法人企业。
2．行业划分执行2011年国民经济行业分类标准(GB/T 4754—2011)。

STATISTICS FOR FOREIGN-INVESTED ENTERPRISES

从业人员平均人数(人) Average Number of Persons Employed (person)		主营业务收入(万元) Revenue from Main Businesses (10000 yuan)		利润总额(万元) Total Profits (10000 yuan)		应交税金合计(万元) Total Taxes Paid (10000 yuan)	
2016	2015	2016	2015	2016	2015	2016	2015
1335774	**1354764**	**278872030**	**258960457**	**32364452**	**37024049**	**14186866**	**9134588**
585945	556649	105777550	92266827	8128491	8320533	4305911	2340965
145850	140317	15394514	14670402	2686305	2800611	1275100	648346
18505	18554	1940775	1617303	404436	238192	387162	156906
358202	336678	79250071	66802264	3992186	4384180	2326469	1506092
57838	56511	8844506	8881942	999651	843905	302657	15577
***	***	***	***	***	***	***	***
749829	798115	173094480	166693631	24235961	28703516	9880955	6793623
268739	281641	62104352	57082878	7840295	8113541	4707750	3391631
15276	17361	1095946	1626346	140971	158371	90885	126468
441794	471914	108754149	106781150	15184132	19998067	4945725	3189767
22602	25982	919456	1058275	1041257	396681	117132	76029
1418	1217	220576	144982	29306	36855	19462	9728
321948	354557	78070314	73467769	5955432	5149087	5130179	3794873
10090	11175	1859300	1731944	66475	42687	62258	52786
202168	206262	119132200	108725266	4223522	4604341	3130458	2242543
102685	102159	3243968	3143053	261362	141742	214516	199444
248246	243850	27055779	24385008	8167814	12750113	1725758	891656
64862	62677	5539228	4665419	921764	909663	1021801	511314
121579	120820	17437341	16932333	3870342	4005597	776092	468248
264196	253264	26533900	25909665	8897742	9420821	2125805	973724
330760	368969	83063234	78771509	6715821	5865349	5344878	3942968
1005014	985795	195808795	180188949	25648632	31158701	8841988	5191619

Note: a) Statistics in this table cover corporate enterprises above designated size.
b) Sectors in this table are classified in accordance with the Standard for Classification of National Economic Sectors 2011 (GB/T 4754-2011).

7-9 境外投资情况(2003-2015年)
STATISTICS FOR OVERSEAS INVESTMENT (2003-2015)

单位：万美元 (USD 10000)

年 份 Year	中方投资额 Amount of Investment by China	截至到各年期末直接投资存量 Diret Investment Stock by the Year End
2003	30054	44844
2004	15739	70086
2005	11306	92940
2006	5612	91873
2007	15295	159195
2008	47299	251019
2009	45185	375865
2010	76614	480882
2011	117503	603380
2012	168900	757800
2013	413010	1276456
2014	727353	2848870
2015	1228033	3879895

资料来源：北京市商务委员会。
Source: Beijing Municipal Commission of Commerce.

7-10 对外经济合作(1984-2016年)
STATISTICS FOR FOREIGN ECONOMIC COOPERATION (1984-2016)

年 份 Year	合同数 (份) Number of Contracts (unit)	#对外承包工程 Foreign Contracted Works	合同额 (万美元) Contract Value (USD 10000)	#对外承包工程 Foreign Contracted Works	完成营业额 (万美元) Turnover (USD 10000)	#对外承包工程 Foreign Contracted Works	年末在外人数 (人) Year-end Workers Staying Abroad (person)	对外承包工程 Foreign Contracted Works	对外劳务合作 Foreign Labor Service Cooperation
1984	9	2	2801	2768	502	331	541	163	378
1985	12	2	852	736	2083	355	2401	18	2383
1986	30	7	446	319	1535	90	837	71	766
1987	37	5	547	354	696	186	690	20	670
1988	46	5	885	344	802	281	819	104	715
1989	111	7	1685	235	1018	459	600	83	517
1990	105	16	3756	2253	1056	625	336	25	311
1991	114	9	3202	1671	1897	1469	980	306	674
1992	130	16	8889	7762	3140	2543	952	264	688
1993	143	48	29397	27625	9748	8871	1555	532	1023
1994	114	34	15715	15089	18783	17822	2720	1694	1026
1995	116	35	15613	14014	12789	12156	2604	1297	1307
1996	116	49	67689	62945	43057	38124	2516	1559	957
1997	107	37	35640	23374	29629	17945	3122	1993	1129
1998	180	48	25526	19292	31009	24930	3647	2239	1408
1999	90	28	25232	18715	26167	19690	3476	2199	1277
2000	104	54	16285	9936	19799	13543	3205	1660	1545
2001	105	54	21439	14758	18628	11680	3494	2141	1353
2002	73	42	27949	19376	23160	14453	2134	1112	1022
2003	117	99	48271	30761	34926	17334	2097	1270	827
2004	128	116	81185	51136	59630	29241	2552	1629	923
2005	272	238	93732	56709	71281	35554	4424	2528	1896
2006	232	166	176752	160328	83518	70062	8962	6760	2202
2007	317	143	236881	211560	94077	71727	11299	7060	4239
2008	486	197	558714	520973	168416	131686	11422	6366	5056
2009	190	182	336223	296851	226893	185017	17121	11805	5316
2010	199	170	286179	251114	259794	222514	22499	17145	5354
2011	229	229	264019	262078	252951	249146	17821	12393	5428
2012	340	340	405885	403475	295639	289902	16747	12143	4604
2013	349	349	564383	562440	341046	335854	21036	16549	4487
2014	283	283	437463	429369	365358	357432	29457	21683	7774
2015	208	208	471988	464808	370880	354868	34183	19287	14896
2016	229	229	515670	514151	260173	249642	20436	13176	7260

注：1984—2008年，对外承包工程统计中含对外设计咨询统计数据。
资料来源：北京市商务委员会。
Note: In 1984-2008, statistics for foreign contracted projects included statistics for consultation on foreign design.
Source: Beijing Municipal Commission of Commerce.

7-11 北京市市级友好城市
MUNICIPAL-LEVEL SISTER CITIES OF BEIJING

顺序 No.	城市	City	所在国家	Contury	所属洲	Continent	缔结日期 Date of Conclusion
1	东京都	Tokyo	日本	Japan	亚洲	Asia	1979.03.14
2	纽约市	New York	美国	USA	北美洲	North America	1980.02.25
3	贝尔格莱德市	Belgrade	塞尔维亚	Serbia	欧洲	Europe	1980.10.14
4	利马市	Lima	秘鲁	Peru	南美洲	South America	1983.11.21
5	华盛顿特区	Washington, DC	美国	USA	北美洲	North America	1984.05.15
6	马德里市	Madrid	西班牙	Spain	欧洲	Europe	1985.09.16
7	里约热内卢市	Rio De Janeiro	巴西	Brazil	南美洲	South America	1986.11.24
8	巴黎大区	Greater Parisian Region	法国	France	欧洲	Europe	1987.07.02
9	科隆市	Cologne	德国	Germany	欧洲	Europe	1987.09.14
10	安卡拉市	Ankara	土耳其	Turkey	亚洲	Asia	1990.06.20
11	开罗省	Cairo	埃及	Egypt	非洲	Africa	1990.10.28
12	雅加达省	Jakarta	印度尼西亚	Indonesia	亚洲	Asia	1992.08.04
13	伊斯兰堡市	Islamabad	巴基斯坦	Pakistan	亚洲	Asia	1992.10.08
14	曼谷市	Bangkok	泰国	Thailand	亚洲	Asia	1993.05.26
15	布宜诺斯艾利斯市	Buenos Aires	阿根廷	Argentina	南美洲	South America	1993.07.13
16	首尔特别市	Seoul Special City	韩国	South Korea	亚洲	Asia	1993.10.23
17	基辅市	Kiev	乌克兰	Ukraine	欧洲	Europe	1993.12.13
18	柏林市	Berlin	德国	Germany	欧洲	Europe	1994.04.05
19	布鲁塞尔大区	Greater Brussels Region	比利时	Belgium	欧洲	Europe	1994.09.22
20	河内市	Hanoi	越南	Viet Nam	亚洲	Asia	1994.10.06
21	阿姆斯特丹市	Amsterdam	荷兰	Holland	欧洲	Europe	1994.10.29
22	莫斯科市	Moscow	俄罗斯	Russia	欧洲	Europe	1995.05.16
23	巴黎市	Paris	法国	France	欧洲	Europe	1997.10.23
24	罗马市	Rome	意大利	Italy	欧洲	Europe	1998.05.28
25	豪登省	Gauteng	南非	South Africa	非洲	Africa	1998.12.06
26	渥太华市	Ottawa	加拿大	Canada	北美洲	North America	1999.10.18
27	首都地区	The Capital Region	澳大利亚	Australia	大洋洲	Oceania	2000.09.14
28	马德里自治区	Madrid Autonomous Region	西班牙	Spain	欧洲	Europe	2005.01.17
29	雅典市	Athens	希腊	Greece	欧洲	Europe	2005.05.10
30	布达佩斯市	Budapest	匈牙利	Hungary	欧洲	Europe	2005.06.16
31	布加勒斯特市	Bucharest	罗马尼亚	Rumania	欧洲	Europe	2005.06.21
32	哈瓦那市	Havana	古巴	Cuba	南美洲	South America	2005.09.24
33	马尼拉市	Manila	菲律宾	Philippines	亚洲	Asia	2005.11.14
34	伦敦市	London	英国	UK	欧洲	Europe	2006.04.11
35	亚的斯亚贝巴市	Addis Abeba	埃塞俄比亚	Ethiopia	非洲	Africa	2006.04.17
36	惠灵顿市	Wellington	新西兰	New Zealand	大洋洲	Oceania	2006.05.10
37	赫尔辛基市	Helsinki	芬兰	Finland	欧洲	Europe	2006.07.14
38	阿斯塔纳市	Astana	哈萨克斯坦	Kazakstan	亚洲	Asia	2006.11.16
39	特拉维夫市	Tel Aviv	以色列	Israel	亚洲	Asia	2006.11.21
40	首都大区	The Greater Capital Region	智利	Chile	南美洲	South America	2007.08.06
41	里斯本市	Lisbon	葡萄牙	Portugal	欧洲	Europe	2007.10.22
42	地拉那市	Tirana	阿尔巴尼亚	Albania	欧洲	Europe	2008.03.21
43	多哈市	Doha	卡塔尔	Qatar	亚洲	Asia	2008.06.23
44	圣何塞市	San Jose	哥斯达黎加	Costarica	北美洲	North America	2009.10.17
45	墨西哥城	Mexican City	墨西哥	Mexico	北美洲	North America	2009.10.19
46	都柏林市	Dublin	爱尔兰	Ireland	欧洲	Europe	2011.06.02
47	哥本哈根市	Copenhagen	丹麦	Denmark	欧洲	Europe	2012.06.28
48	新南威尔士州	New South Wales	澳大利亚	Australia	大洋洲	Oceania	2012.08.03
49	德里邦	Delhi	印度	India	亚洲	Asia	2013.10.23
50	德黑兰	Teheran	伊朗	Iran	亚洲	Asia	2014.02.27
51	乌兰巴托	Ulaanbaatar	蒙古国	Mongolia	亚洲	Asia	2014.08.17
52	万象市	Vientiane	老挝	Laos	亚洲	Asia	2015.04.24
53	布拉格市	Prague	捷克	Czech	欧洲	Europe	2016.03.29
54	明斯克市	Minsk	白俄罗斯	Belarus	欧洲	Europe	2016.04.26

资料来源：北京市人民政府外事办公室。
Sourse: Foreign Affairs Office of the People's Government of Beijing Municipality.

主要统计指标解释

进出口总值 指实际进、出我国海关并能引起我国境内物质资源增加或减少的进出口货物总金额。包括我国境内法人和其他组织以一般贸易、易货贸易、加工贸易、补偿贸易、寄售代销贸易等方式进出口的货物、租赁期一年及以上的租赁进出口货物、边境小额贸易货物、国际援助物资或捐赠品、保税区和保税仓库进出口货物等的金额合计。进出口总值用以观察一个国家在对外贸易方面的总规模。我国规定出口货物按离岸价格统计，进口货物按到岸价格统计。

一般贸易 指我国境内有进出口经营权的企业单边进口或单边出口的货物。

来料加工装配贸易 指由外商提供全部或部分原材料、辅料、零部件、元器件、配套件和包装物料，必要时提供设备，由我方按对方的要求进行加工装配，成品交对方销售，我方收取工缴费；或对方提供的作价设备价款，我方用工缴费偿还的交易形式。

进料加工贸易 指我方用外汇购买进口的原料、材料、辅料、元器件、零部件、配套件和包装物料，加工成品或半成品后再外销出口的交易形式。

旅客吞吐量 指经乘航班进出北京民用运输机场的中国公民、港澳台同胞、华侨及外国人等旅客数量的总和。

货邮吞吐量 指通过民用运输机场的航班运输的货物、邮寄物品和随身携带的行李物品重量总和。

飞机起降架次 指进出民用运输机场的正常航班架次，不包括包机和其他非正常航班。

海关征收税款净入库税额 指北京海关征收的税款合计，包含进出口关税和进口环节税。

批准外商直接投资企业项目个数 指外商直接投资中批准设立的外商投资企业个数、批准的合作开发项目个数。

实际利用外商直接投资额 指批准的合同外资金额的实际执行数，外国投资者根据批准外商投资企业的合同（章程）的规定实际缴付的出资额和企业投资总额内外国投资者以自己的境外自有资金实际直接向企业提供的贷款。

对外承包工程 指企业按照国际通行做法，在国（境）外承揽和实施各类工程项目的经济活动。企业承揽的我国对外经济援助项目、我国驻外使（领）馆等建设项目视同对外承包工程项目。

对外劳务合作 指企业按照与国（境）外政府有关机构、团体、企业、私人雇主所签合同规定，向国（境）外派遣各类劳务人员的经济活动。企业自带设备以提供技术服务的形式在国（境）外承揽的项目视同对外劳务合作项目。

对外设计咨询 指企业在国（境）外承揽的工程设计、工程监理、技术咨询和人员培训等经济活动。

Explanatory Notes on Main Statistical Indicators

Total Value of Imports and Exports refer to the total value of goods actually imported and exported at China's customs, which lead to increase or decrease in the physical resources in China, including goods imported/exported by China domestic legal persons and other organizations in such manners as general trade, barter trade, processing trade, compensation trade, commission-based sales trade, leasing imports/exports with a lease period of one year and more, small-sum border trade goods, international aid goods and donations, imports/exports in bonded zones and bonded warehouses. The indicator of the Total Value of Imports and Exports can be used to observe the total size of foreign trade in a country. In accordance with the stipulation of the Chinese government, imports are calculated at CIF, while exports are calculated at FOB.

General Trade means goods imported and exported unilaterally by domestic enterprises with import/export rights.

Trade of Processing and Assembling Supplied Materials is a form of transaction in which all or part of raw materials, auxiliary materials, parts and components, elements, fittings, and packaging materials, and equipment if necessary are provided by the foreign party, processed or assemble by Chinese party according to requirements of the foreign party, and the finished products are sold by the foreign party. The Chinese party charges processing fees and pays back the money of priced equipment provided by the foreign party with processing charges.

Trade of Processing Imported Materials is a form of transaction in which the Chinese party purchases raw materials, auxiliary materials, parts and components, elements, fittings, and packaging materials with foreign exchange, processing them into finished or semi-finished products and export them.

Passenger Throughput means the total number of Chinese citizens, compatriots form Hong Kong, Macao and Taiwan, oversea Chinese and foreigners that take off and land at civil airports in Beijing by flights.

Cargos Throughput means the sum of goods, mailed articles and luggage transported by flights taking off from and landing at civil airports in Beijing.

Takeoff and Landing of Airplanes means the number of regular flights taking off from and landing at civil airports in Beijing, excluding chartered flights and other non-regular flights.

Net Paid-in Duties Levied and Collected by Customs mean the sum of duties actually levied by customs in Beijing, including import and export duties and import linkage taxs.

Number of Direct Foreign-invested Enterprises Approved means the number of foreign-invested enterprises and joint development projects approved in foreign direct investment (FDI).

Actual Use of Foreign Capital means the value of approved contractual foreign investment actually used, the amount of actual capital contribution by foreign investors according to the contract (articles of incorporation) of the foreign-invested enterprise approved and, in the total investment of an enterprise, the amount of loans provided directly by foreign investor with its own overseas money.

Foreign Contracted Projects refer to economic activities in which enterprises undertake and implement various projects in foreign (overseas) countries in line with international practices. Foreign economic aid projects and construction projects of Chinese Embassies (Consulates) undertaken by enterprises are deemed as foreign contracted projects.

Foreign Labor Service Cooperation means any economic activity in which enterprises dispatch labors to foreign (overseas) countries as stated in contracts signed with foreign (overseas) government agencies, groups, enterprises, and private employers. Projects undertaken by enterprises in foreign (overseas) countries in a manner of providing technical service with their own equipment are deemed as foreign labor service cooperation projects.

Foreign Design Consulting means any economic activity of project design, project supervision, technical consulting and personnel training undertaken in foreign (overseas) countries by enterprises.

北京统计年鉴2017　BEIJING STATISTICAL YEARBOOK

价格指数
PRICE INDEX

简要说明

一、本章资料的主要内容

本章价格指数资料，反映生产、流通、消费与投资的价格变动趋势和变动幅度。主要包括居民消费价格指数；商品零售价格指数；农产品生产者价格指数；工业生产者出厂价格指数；工业生产者购进价格指数；固定资产投资价格指数；住宅销售价格指数。

二、本章资料的数据来源

本章资料由国家统计局北京调查总队、北京市统计局提供。

三、调查方法

（一）居民消费价格指数和商品零售价格指数

编制居民消费价格指数、商品零售价格指数的资料采用抽样调查和重点调查相结合的方法取得，即在全市选择不同的区域，按照布局合理的原则抽选价格调查点，由国家确定调查商品和服务项目，在此基础上按照消费量大、价格变动趋势有较强代表性的原则选择调查样本，对其市场价格进行定期调查，以样本推算总体。现将指数编制过程按下列几个步骤进行说明。

抽选价格调查点。按照布局合理等原则，将不同区域各种类型的商场、农贸市场、服务网点分别按销售额、成交额和经营规模为标志，从高到低排队，依据所需调查点的数量进行等距抽样。

选择代表规格品。代表商品和服务项目由国家确定，代表规格品由各省市按照有关原则选择。选择原则：（1）消费量较大；（2）价格变动趋势和变动程度有较强的代表性，即选中规格品的价格变动特征与未选中规格品之间价格变动的相关性愈高愈好；（3）选中的规格品之间，性质相隔愈远愈好，价格变动特征的相关性愈低愈好；选中的工业消费品必须是合格产品，产品包装上有注册商标、产地、规格等级等标识。

目前，居民消费价格调查按用途划分为 8 个大类，262 个基本分类，国家规定大城市调查规格品数量应在 600 种左右，北京市由于编制分收入层居民消费价格指数，代表规格品数量增加到 1848 种。商品零售价格指数划分为 16 个大类，197 个基本分类，北京市代表规格品数量为 1385 种。

价格资料的采集。采取定人、定点、定时直接调查的方法采集价格资料。

权数资料来源与计算。居民消费价格指数的权数根据城市居民家庭生活消费支出调查资料整理计算。商品零售价格指数的权数根据商业统计中社会消费品零售总额计算。

按照国家统计局统一要求，自 2016 年 1 月起，北京流通消费价格统计专业执行新的《流通和消费价格统计报表制度》，其中居民消费价格和商品零售价格调查项目目录均重新进行了修订调整，具体变化详见 2017 年年鉴中《居民消费价格分类指数(2016 年)》表和《商品零售价格分类指数(2016 年)》表。

（二）工业生产者出厂价格指数和工业生产者购进价格指数

工业生产者出厂价格是工业品第一次出售时的出厂价格。该项调查采用重点调查与典型调查相结合的调查方法。重点调查对象为选中的全年主营业务收入 2000 万元及以上的工业法人样本单位及部分生产特定产品的全年主营业务收入 2000 万元以下的工业法人样本单位。

工业生产者购进价格是工业企业作为中间投入的价格。调查对象从填报工业生产者出厂价格的企业中选择。

选择代表企业的原则：（1）按工业行业选择调查企业，各中类行业原则上都要有调查企业；（2）大型（或占相当大比重）企业应尽量都选作调查企业；（3）选择生产正常、稳定的企业作为调查对象；（4）选择企业时要兼顾不同所有制形式。

选择代表产品的原则：（1）按工业行业选择代表产品；（2）选择对国计民生影响大的产品；（3）选择生产较为稳定的产品；（4）选择有发展前景的产品；（5）选择具有地方特色的产品。

除了以上原则及方法外，工业生产者购进价格调查还要考虑到特殊性，即调查企业要填报其生产中消耗的主要原材料、燃料、动力，不填报消耗较少、在生产投入中比重较小的原材料、燃料、动力。

权数的确定。编制工业生产者出厂价格小类及以上的权数资料来源于工业统计中分行业工业销售产值数据资料；基本分类的权数资料来源于独立的工业企业产品权数调查。购进价格权数资料主要来源于独立的工业企业产品权数调查，中类及以上的权数还要参考分行业的投入产出数据资料和相应行业的出厂权数资料。权数五年更换一次。

根据国家统计制度要求，2016 年开始使用 2015 年作为新一轮的对比基期，同时在按行业分组的工业生产者出厂价格指数中新增加“开采辅助活动”行业。

（三）固定资产投资价格指数

固定资产投资价格调查采用重点调查与典型调查相结合的方法。固定资产投资价格调查所涉及的价格是构成固定资产投资额实体的实际购进价格（或结算价格）。调查的内容包括构成当年建筑工程实体的钢材、木材、水泥、地方建筑材料、电料、化工材料等主要建筑材料价格，投入的劳动力价格（单位工资）和各种施工机械使用费用；设备工器具购置和其他费用投资价格。

选择建筑安装工程调查点的原则：（1）样本单位应具有

一定覆盖面；(2) 投资经济活动代表性强；(3) 兼顾不同经济类型；(4) 选择重点工程；(5) 兼顾不同工程类别。

选择其他费用调查点的原则：在选择其他费用调查点时，所遵循的原则与建筑安装工程调查点的原则基本相同，特别是要注意选择那些投资额大的工程。但由于其他费用不易取得，所以在实际操作过程中，应同时在建设单位、施工单位开展重点调查，并辅以典型调查（从有关管理部门取得资料）。

权数的确定。固定资产投资价格指数的计算权数是建筑安装工程、设备工器具购置和其他费用三者前三年投资完成额的平均比重。

（四）住宅销售价格指数是反映住宅销售价格总水平变动趋势和程度的相对数。包括新建住宅销售价格指数和二手住宅销售价格指数。

新建住宅销售价格的调查方法：目前我国住宅销售价格调查在 70 个大中城市开展。新建住宅销售价格、面积、金额等资料直接采用当地房地产管理部门的网签数据。新建住宅的网签数据内容主要包括：住宅在建项目（楼盘）名称、项目地址、幢号、总层数、所在层数、住宅结构、建筑面积、成交总价（合同金额）、签约时间等。

二手住宅销售价格的调查方法：二手住宅销售价格调查为非全面调查，采用重点调查与典型调查相结合的方法，按照房地产经纪机构上报的方式收集基础数据。

（五）农产品生产者价格指数

农产品生产者价格调查采取抽样调查和重点调查相结合的调查方法。抽取 360 个农产品生产和出售的农业生产经营单位及行政村作为调查对象。对一些区域性比较强的农产品采取在主产区主观选样的方法选择农业生产经营单位及行政村作为调查对象。

被调查单位及行政村在辅助调查员的指导下将在报告期出售的农产品的名称、出售数量、价格、金额即时记入农产品生产者价格调查台账，并上报，由市级超级汇总。

由于北京市林业产品（树苗）产值比重较少，不足 1%，根据国家统计局统计制度要求，不需要进行林业产品生产者价格调查。

Brief Introduction

I. Main Content

Price indexes in this chapter reflect the trend and rate of changes in prices of production, circulation, consumption and investment, mainly consisting of consumer price index (CPI), retail price index (RPI), producer price index for farm products, producer price index for industrial products (PPI); purchasing price index for industrial products; price index for investment in fixed assets; and selling price index for residential houses.

II. Source of Statistics

Statistics in this chapter are from NBS Survey Office in Beijing and Beijing Municipal Bureau of Statistics.

III. Survey Methods

1. Consumer Price Index (CPI) and Retail Price Index (RPI)

Data for compilation of the consumer price index and retail price index are collected through a combination of sample surveys and surveys of key units. Different areas are selected across the city as the sample areas and representative commodities with large amount of consumption and price changes are selected as the sample commodities in reasonable layout. Commodity and service items are identified by the central government. Regular surveys are conducted to collect data on their market prices. General indexes are inferred on the basis of the sample data. The process of CPI development is described as the following steps.

The selection of price survey sites: By adopting the principle of reasonable layout, an equidistant sampling is conducted for department stores, agricultural product trade markets and service outlets in different types and in different areas by their sales value, transaction value and operational scale, which will be ranked in a descending order based on the number of survey sites required.

The selection of representative commodities: Representative commodity and service items are determined by the country. Representative commodities are selected by provinces and cities according to relevant principles. Principles for selection: (1) large quantity of consumption; (2) strongly representative trend and extent of price changes, which means the characteristics of price changes of selected commodities shall be highly correlated with price changes of those that are not selected; (3) selected commodities shall be different in their nature and least correlated in the characteristics of price changes between each other; the selected industrial products must be qualified products, with registered trademark, origin, specifications, grade and other marks on the their package.

At present, data are collected over 600 specifications each month under 262 basic headings in 8 categories in the consumer price surveys. In Beijing, due to the development of CPI by income class, representative commodities have increased to 1848 specifications. Retail price index consists of 16 categories, 197 basic headings and 1385 specifications of representative commodities.

Method of data collection: Price data are collected through direct surveys by designated personnel at designated sites on periodic basis.

Source and calculation of the weights: CPI weights are calculated according to survey information on living expenditures of urban residents. RPI weights are calculated according to the total retail sales of commodities.

According to the uniform requirement of the National Bureau of Statistics, since January 2016, the new Circulation and Consumption Price Statistical Reporting System has been implemented for statistics of circulation and consumption price in Beijing, of which the survey catalogues of consumer prices of household and retail prices of commodities have been revised and adjusted. See the tables of *Consumer Price Index by Category (2016)* and the *Retail Price Index by Category (2016)* in the *China Statistical Yearbook 2017* for change details.

2. Producer Price Index for Industrial Products (PPI); Purchasing Price Index for Industrial Products

The producer price index for industrial products refers to the producer's price of industrial products when sold for the first time. The survey program is a combination of the key units' survey and typical units' survey methods. Key units refer to industrial enterprises with annual turnover from primary activities at and above RMB 20 million. Typical units refer to the industrial enterprises with annual revenue from the primary activities below RMB 20 million.

Purchasing price for Industrial Products refers to the price of intermediate inputs of industrial enterprise. Enterprises for survey are selected among those that have submitted the ex-factory prices of industrial products.

Principles for selecting the representative enterprises: (1) enterprises to be covered in the survey are selected by industrial sectors. In principle, every branch should have enterprises selected; (2) Large-sized enterprises (or enterprises accounting for large proportion) should be selected; (3) enterprises selected should be those with normal and stable production; (4) enterprises selected should include those with different ownerships.

Principles for selecting representative products: (1) representative products are be selected by industrial sectors; (2) the selected products should have significant impact on the national economy and people's livelihood; (3) the production of the goods selected should be relatively more stable; (4) the prospects of the goods selected should be promising; (5) the products selected shall represent the localities.

In addition to the above-mentioned principles, a special

condition shall be taken into account in the survey of producer price index for industrial products. Namely, enterprises under survey shall report main raw materials, fuel and power consumed in production.

Determination of weights: Materials of weights used for compiling producer price index for industrial products (PPI) of small class and above come from data of industrial sales value collected by sectors in industrial statistics. Materials of weights in basic classification come from independent survey on industrial enterprise product weights. Materials of purchase price weights mainly come from independent survey on industrial enterprise product weights. Weights of medium class and above shall also take reference to input and output data collected by sectors and materials of factory weights in relevant sectors. The weights are changed every five years.

3. Price Index for Investment in Fixed Assets

A combined method of key survey and typical survey is used for the collection of data on prices of investment in fixed assets. The prices collected in the surveys of investment in fixed assets are the actual purchasing prices (or settlement prices) of entities of investment in fixed assets. The survey covers the prices of main construction materials that constitute the architectural engineering entities in the year, such as steel, timber, cement, local construction materials, electric parts and chemical materials in construction projects; prices of labor input (wages) and costs of use of construction machines; purchasing price of equipment, tools and devices as well as other expenditures.

Principles for selecting survey sites of construction and installation projects: (1) the sample unit shall have certain coverage; (2) the economic activity of investment should have strong representativeness; (3) different types of registration should be considered; (4) key projects shall be selected; (5) attention should be given to various types of projects.

Principles for selecting survey sites of other expenditures: in the selection of survey sites of other expenditures, the same principles shall be followed as in the selection of survey sites of building and installation projects. Especially projects with larger amount of investment shall be selected. Since it is not easy to obtain data on other expenditures, during the actual data operations, survey on key builders and construction units is to be conducted concurrently with survey on typical units (with information from administration units).

Determination of weights. Weights used for calculating the fixed assets investment price index are determined according to the average proportion of investment amount of construction and installation projects, purchase of equipment, tools and instruments and other expenditures completed in the previous three years.

4. Selling Price Index for Residential Houses is a relative number reflecting the trend and extent of overall level of house selling prices. It includes selling price index for new houses and second-hand houses.

Survey method of new house selling price:

At present, real estate price survey is conducted in 70 medium and large-sized cities across the country. For new houses, selling price, area, amount and other data are taken directly from the online data recorded by local real estate authorities. Online data of new house transaction mainly consist of the name of construction project in process, project location, building number, total number of floors, floor number, house structure, building area, total price of transaction (contractual amount), and date of contract signing, etc.

Survey method of second-hand house selling price: Survey of second-house selling price is incomplete survey conducted with the combined method of key survey and typical survey. Basic data are collected in a combined manner of reporting by real estate broker agencies, providing by real estate authorities and field survey by investigators.

5. Producer Price Index for Farm Products

A combined method of sample survey and key survey was used for the survey of producer prices of farm products. 300 entities and administrative villages producing and selling agricultural products are sampled. For some regional agricultural products, data on farm entities and administrative villages are collected with the method of subjective sampling in main production areas.

Under the instruction of assistant investigators, the surveyed entities and administrative villages will record the name, quantity, price and amount of farm products sold during the reporting period onto the log book and report them for summarization at the municipal level.

As the production of forestry products (saplings) in Beijing is relatively small, taking no more than 1%, so no survey on producer price for forestry products is conducted according to statistical requirements of National Bureau of Statistics.

8-1 各种价格指数(1978-2016年) PRICE INDEXES (1978-2016)

(上年=100) (preceding year=100)

年份 Year	居民消费价格指数 Consumer Price Index	商品零售价格指数 Retail Price Index	农产品生产者价格指数 Producer Price Index for Farm Products	工业生产者出厂价格指数 Producer Price Index for Industrial Products (PPI)	工业生产者购进价格指数 Purchasing Price Index for Industrial Products	固定资产投资价格指数 Price Index for Investment in Fixed Assets
1978	100.6	100.6				
1979	101.8	101.8	109.5			
1980	106.0	106.7	105.5			
1981	101.3	101.4	109.4			
1982	101.8	102.0	101.9			
1983	100.5	100.6	101.8			
1984	102.2	102.1	102.3			
1985	117.6	118.6	117.6			
1986	106.8	106.7	108.1			
1987	108.6	108.7	116.1			
1988	120.4	121.9	123.2			
1989	117.2	118.5	106.8			
1990	105.4	104.1	101.9	107.9	114.8	
1991	111.9	108.5	101.7	105.8	111.7	107.3
1992	109.9	108.3	102.4	100.9	103.3	112.2
1993	119.0	116.9	107.0	121.8	133.2	126.6
1994	124.9	117.9	133.4	112.9	118.7	116.2
1995	117.3	112.6	130.6	107.3	106.7	113.9
1996	111.6	107.3	101.5	100.7	100.3	108.2
1997	105.3	103.8	92.8	101.1	103.4	102.7
1998	102.4	98.3	93.6	95.1	98.1	100.8
1999	100.6	98.8	97.5	97.7	95.8	99.9
2000	103.5	98.9	95.0	102.5	100.0	101.0
2001	103.1	98.8	102.0	99.4	100.5	100.6
2002	98.2	98.4	92.4	96.6	97.1	100.4
2003	100.2	98.2	102.5	101.5	104.7	102.2
2004	101.0	99.2	106.2	103.0	114.2	104.3
2005	101.5	99.7	102.9	101.3	111.4	100.7
2006	100.9	100.2	99.1	99.1	105.5	100.4
2007	102.4	100.8	114.4	99.7	105.0	102.8
2008	105.1	104.4	112.3	103.3	115.8	107.8
2009	98.5	97.8	98.3	94.4	88.6	97.1
2010	102.4	100.4	106.5	102.2	110.5	102.5
2011	105.6	103.2	110.7	102.3	108.4	105.7
2012	103.3	100.6	104.7	98.4	98.7	101.3
2013	103.3	99.8	104.7	97.4	97.8	99.9
2014	101.6	99.1	99.7	99.1	98.8	100.0
2015	101.8	98.5	99.8	96.9	93.7	97.6
2016	101.4	98.1	99.7	98.1	98.5	99.7

注：1．从2011年开始“工业品出厂价格指数”更名为“工业生产者出厂价格指数”，“原材料、燃料、动力购进价格指数”更名为“工业生产者购进价格指数”(下同)。

2．从2013年起，农产品生产价格指数调整为农产品生产者价格指数。

Note: a) From 2011 ,the "Ex-factory Price Index for Manufactured Products" has been renamed as "Producer Price Index for Industrial Products (PPI), and the "Purchasing Price Index for Raw Materials, Fuels and Power" has been renamed as "Purchasing Price Index for Industrial Products" (the same below).

b) From 2013,the "Producer Price Index For Agricultural Products" has been renamed as "Producer Price Index For Farm Products".

8-2 各种价格定基指数(1978-2016年)
FIXED-BASE PRICE INDEXES (1978-2016)

年份 Year	居民消费价格指数 Consumer Price Index (1978=100)	商品零售价格指数 Retail Price Index (1978=100)	工业生产者出厂价格指数 Producer Price Index for Industrial Products (1990=100)	工业生产者购进价格指数 Purchasing Price Index for Industrial Products (1990=100)	固定资产投资价格指数 Price Index for Investment in Fixed Assets (1990=100)
1978	100.0	100.0			
1979	101.8	101.8			
1980	107.9	108.6			
1981	109.3	110.1			
1982	111.3	112.3			
1983	111.8	113.0			
1984	114.3	115.4			
1985	134.4	136.8			
1986	143.5	145.9			
1987	155.8	158.6			
1988	187.6	193.3			
1989	219.9	229.1			
1990	231.8	238.5	100.0	100.0	100.0
1991	259.4	258.8	105.8	111.7	107.3
1992	285.1	280.3	106.8	115.4	120.4
1993	339.3	327.7	130.0	153.7	152.4
1994	423.8	386.4	146.8	182.4	177.1
1995	497.1	435.1	157.5	194.7	201.7
1996	554.8	466.9	158.6	195.2	218.3
1997	584.2	484.6	160.4	201.9	224.2
1998	598.2	476.4	152.5	198.0	226.0
1999	601.8	470.7	149.0	189.7	225.7
2000	622.9	465.5	152.7	189.7	228.0
2001	642.2	459.9	151.8	190.7	229.4
2002	630.6	452.5	146.6	185.1	230.3
2003	631.9	444.4	148.8	193.8	235.3
2004	638.2	440.8	153.3	221.4	245.5
2005	647.8	439.5	155.3	246.6	247.2
2006	653.6	440.4	153.9	260.2	248.2
2007	669.3	443.9	153.5	273.3	255.1
2008	703.4	463.4	158.6	316.3	275.0
2009	692.8	453.2	149.8	280.3	266.9
2010	709.4	455.0	153.1	309.7	273.6
2011	749.1	469.6	156.6	335.7	289.2
2012	773.8	472.4	154.1	331.3	293.0
2013	799.3	471.5	150.1	324.0	292.7
2014	812.1	467.3	148.7	320.1	292.7
2015	826.7	460.3	144.1	299.9	285.7
2016	838.3	451.6	141.4	295.4	284.8

8-3 居民消费价格分类指数(2016年)
CONSUMER PRICE INDEX BY CATEGORY (2016)

项　目	Item	2015 =100
居民消费价格指数	**Consumer Price Index**	**101.4**
#非食品价格指数	Non-food Price Index	101.0
#服务项目价格指数	Price Index for Services	102.7
#消费品价格指数	Price Index for Consumer Goods	100.5
食品烟酒	**Food, Tobacco and Liquor**	**103.0**
食品	Food	103.3
粮食	Grain	99.1
薯	Tubers	109.9
豆	Beans	101.0
食用油	Edible Oil	99.5
菜	Vegetables	109.9
#鲜菜	Fresh Vegetables	110.3
畜肉	Livestock Meat	106.5
禽肉	Poultry Meat	101.3
水产品	Aquatic Products	103.9
蛋	Eggs	96.7
奶	Milk	102.1
干鲜瓜果	Dried and Fresh Melons and Fruits	98.2
#鲜瓜果	Fresh Fruits	97.9
糖果糕点	Confectionery	103.2
调味品	Condiment	105.2
其他食品	Other Dood	105.1
茶及饮料	Tea and Drinks	100.4
烟酒	Tobacco and Liquor	101.0
烟　草	Tobacco	101.2
酒	Liquor	100.7
在外餐饮	Outside Food and Drinks	102.8
衣　着	**Clothing**	**100.2**
服　装	Garments	99.6
服装材料	Clothing Materials	100.7
其他衣着及配件	Other Clothing and Accessories	98.1
衣着加工服务费	Clothing Processing Fee	101.7
鞋	Shoes	102.0
居　住	**Living**	**103.7**
租赁房房租	Rental	103.8
住房保养维修及管理	Housing Maintenance and Management	101.2
水电燃料	Utilities and Fuels	100.2
自有住房	Own Housing	104.9
生活用品及服务	**Daily Necessities and Services**	**99.2**
家具及室内装饰品	Furniture and Interior Decorations	101.2
家具	Furniture	101.3
室内装饰品	Interior Decorations	100.6
家用器具	Domestic Appliances	93.1
大型家用器具	Large Domestic Appliances	92.2
小家电	Small Domestic Appliances	96.0
家用纺织品	Home Textiles	95.7
家庭日用杂品	Daily Groceries for Households	100.2
个人护理用品	Personal Care Products	102.5
家庭服务	Home Service	103.4
交通和通信	**Traffic and Communication**	**96.6**
交通	Traffic	97.9
交通工具	Vehicles	95.3
交通工具用燃料	Fuels for Vehicles	96.3
交通工具使用和维修	Vehicle Use and Maintenance	103.1
交通费	Transportation Fee	101.3
通信	Communication	93.5
通信工具	Communication Devices	82.5
通信服务	Communication Services	98.0
邮递服务	Mail Service	100.0
教育文化和娱乐	**Education,Culture and Entertainment**	**98.3**
教育	Education	101.2
教育用品	Educational Supplies	100.8
教育服务	Education Services	101.2
文化娱乐	Culture and Entertainment	96.5
文娱耐用消费品	Durable Consumer Goods for Cultural and Recreation Use	92.4
其他文娱用品	Other Recreational Supplies	101.0
文化娱乐服务	Cultural and Recreational Services	101.1
旅游	Tourism	97.6
医疗保健	**Medical Care**	**102.6**
药品及医疗器具	Medicine and Medical Equipment	103.7
中药	Traditional Chinese Medicine	101.3
西药	Western Medicine	105.0
滋补保健品	Nourishing Health Care Products	105.5
医疗卫生器具	Medical and Health Equipment	101.1
保健器具	Health Care Equipment	100.3
医疗服务	Medical Service	100.0
其他用品和服务	**Other Supplies and Services**	**104.3**
其他用品	Other Supplies	106.1
首饰手表	Jewelry and Watches	107.8
其他杂项用品	Other Miscellaneous	96.7
其他服务	Other Services	103.0
旅馆住宿	Hotel Accommodation	102.3
美容美发洗浴	Beauty Salon and Bath	106.6
养老服务	Pension Services	102.8
金融保险	Financial Insurance	100.3
其他服务	Other Services	99.8

注：按照国家统计局统一要求，自2016年1月起，北京流通消费价格统计专业执行新的《流通和消费价格统计报表制度》，居民消费价格调查项目目录重新进行了修订调整。

Note: In accordance with the unified requirements of the National Bureau of Statistics of the People's Republic of China (NBS), since January 2016, a new Circulation and Consumer Price Statistical Form System has been implemented by the circulation and consumer price statistics sector in Beijing, of which the survey item directory for consumer price was revised.

8-4 商品零售价格分类指数(2016年)
RETAIL PRICE INDEX BY CATEGORY (2016)

项　目	Item	2015 =100	项　目	Item	2015 =100
商品零售价格指数	**Retail Price Index**	**98.1**	专业音像器材	Professional Audio Equipment	100.8
食　品	**Food**	**103.2**	**文化办公用品**	**Cultural Office Supplies**	**95.1**
粮　食	Grain	99.1	**日用品**	**Daily Necessities**	**99.1**
薯	Tubers	109.9	日用百货	Articles of Daily Use	100.0
豆	Beans	101.0	厨具餐具茶具	Kitchen Utensils, Tableware and Teaware	100.5
食用油	Edible Oil	99.5	清洗用品	Cleaning Supplies	100.8
菜	Vegetables	109.9	其他日用品	Other Daily Necessities	95.8
畜肉	Livestock Meat	106.5	**体育娱乐用品**	**Sports and Entertainment Supplies**	**100.5**
禽肉	Poultry Meat	101.3	体育户外用品	Sports and Outdoor Supplies	100.4
水产品	Aquatic Products	103.9	娱乐用品	Entertainment Supplies	100.5
蛋	Eggs	96.7	**交通、通信用品**	**Transportation and Communication Supplies**	**90.9**
奶	Milk	102.1			
干鲜瓜果	Dried and Fresh Melons and Fruits	98.2	交通运输机械	Transportation Machinery	95.3
			通信器材	Communication Equipment	82.5
糖果糕点	Confectionery	103.2	**家具**	**Furniture**	**101.3**
调味品	Condiment	105.2	**化妆品**	**Cosmetic**	**103.4**
其他食品	Other Food	105.1	**金银饰品**	**Gold and Silver Jewelry**	**111.2**
在外餐饮	Outside Food and Drinks	102.8	**中西药品及医疗保健用品**	**Chinese Traditional Medicine, Western Medicines and Health Care Products**	**104.0**
饮料、烟酒	**Drinks, Tobacco and Liquor**	**100.8**			
茶及饮料	Tea and Drinks	100.4	医疗卫生器具	Medical and Health Equipment	101.1
烟草	Tobacco	101.2	中药	Traditional Chinese Medicine	101.3
酒	Liquor	100.7	西药	Western Medicine	105.0
服装、鞋帽	**Clothing, Shoes and Hats**	**100.2**	保健器具及用品	Health Care Equipment and Supplies	105.1
服装	Garments	99.6	**书报杂志及电子出版物**	**Books, Newspapers, Magazines and Electronic Publications**	**101.3**
鞋袜帽	Footgear and Hats	101.9			
其他衣着配件	Other Clothing Accessories	95.8	教材及参考书	Teaching Materials and Reference Books	100.8
纺织品	**Textile**	**95.5**	书报杂志	Books, Newspapers and Magazines	102.3
服装材料	Clothing Materials	100.7	计算机办公软件	Computer Office Software	98.9
床上用品	Bedding	94.8	**燃　料**	**Fuel**	**96.7**
家用电器及音像器材	**Domestic Appliances, Audio & Video Equipment**	**94.0**	煤炭及制品	Coal and Coal Products	103.3
			石油及制品	Petroleum and Oil Products	96.7
家庭设备	Home Equipment	93.1	**建筑材料及五金电料**	**Building Materials and Hardware**	**101.0**
文娱用耐用消费品	Durable Consumer Goods for Cultural and Recreation Use	91.5	建筑装潢材料	Building Decoration Materials	100.4
			五金水暖	Hardware and Plumbing	102.1

注：按照国家统计局统一要求，自2016年1月起，北京流通消费价格统计专业执行新的《流通和消费价格统计报表制度》，商品零售价格调查项目目录重新进行了修订调整。

Note: In accordance with the unified requirements of the National Bureau of Statistics of the People's Republic of China (NBS), since January 2016, a new Circulation and Consumer Price Statistical Form System has been implemented by the circulation and consumer price statistics sector in Beijing, of which the survey item directory for retail price was revised.

8-5 农产品生产者价格指数
PRODUCER PRICE INDEX FOR FARM PRODUCTS

(上年=100) (preceding year=100)

项目	Item	2016	2015
总指数	**General Index**	**99.7**	**99.8**
农业产品	Agricultural Products	94.7	97.5
#粮食	Grain	85.3	92.4
蔬菜及食用菌	Vegetable and Edible Fungus	103.2	101.9
林业产品	Forestry Products		
畜牧业产品	Animal Husbandry Products	104.7	101.9
#肉牛	Beef Cattle	98.8	100.7
肉羊	Mutton Sheep	90.0	90.4
奶产品	Milk Products	93.1	90.7
猪	Hogs	121.0	111.2
肉禽(毛重)	Poultry (Gross Weight)	98.4	100.4
禽蛋	Eggs	96.2	99.3
渔业产品	Fishing	99.0	101.0

8-6 工业生产者出厂价格及购进价格指数(2000-2016年)

(上年=100)

年份 Year	工业生产者出厂价格指数 Producer Price Index for Industrial Products (PPI)	轻工业 Light Industry	重工业 Heavy Industry	生产资料 Means of Production	生活资料 Comsumer Goods	工业生产者购进价格指数 Purchasing Price Index for Industrial Products	燃料、动力类 Fuels and Power
2000	102.5	98.0	104.2	103.4	98.8	100.0	104.3
2001	99.4	99.6	99.4	99.4	99.6	100.5	101.7
2002	96.6	97.6	96.4	96.4	97.9	97.1	102.3
2003	101.5	98.0	104.5	102.2	99.1	104.7	109.6
2004	103.0	100.2	105.3	103.7	100.6	114.2	120.0
2005	101.3	98.7	103.3	101.9	99.1	111.4	117.1
2006	99.1	97.9	99.6	99.0	99.3	105.5	113.1
2007	99.7	100.7	99.2	99.3	101.3	105.0	105.1
2008	103.3	101.8	104.0	103.8	101.3	115.8	132.3
2009	94.4	96.2	93.6	93.3	99.1	88.6	85.1
2010	102.2	98.7	103.8	102.7	100.3	110.5	121.3
2011	102.3	104.6	102.0	102.5	101.6	108.4	117.8
2012	98.4	101.1	98.0	97.8	101.0	98.7	99.0
2013	97.4	100.7	96.9	96.7	100.5	97.8	96.4
2014	99.1	100.8	98.8	98.7	100.9	98.8	99.4
2015	96.9	100.0	96.4	96.1	99.9	93.7	85.6
2016	98.1	101.8	97.6	98.0	98.3	98.5	98.0

PRODUCER PRICE INDEX AND PURCHASING PRICE INDEX FOR INDUSTRIAL PRODUCTS (2000-2016)

(preceding year=100)

黑色金属材料类 Ferrous Metal Materials	有色金属材料和电线类 Nonferrous Metal Materials and Electric Wires	化工原料类 Chemical Raw Materials	木材及纸浆类 Timber and Paper Pulp	建筑材料及非金属矿类 Construction Materials and Nonmetal Ores	其他工业原材料及半成品类 Other Industrial Materials and Semi-finished Products	农副产品类 Agricultural Products	纺织原料类 Textile Raw Materials
100.5	106.9	103.4	94.8	101.9	98.4	94.5	91.5
100.3	97.9	97.6	98.3	99.5	98.8	103.5	100.6
96.4	96.1	99.3	102.5	97.6	92.3	93.6	97.8
110.9	101.4	107.3	100.6	99.0	95.2	114.3	98.1
124.5	120.9	111.1	100.7	105.8	103.8	122.3	102.8
108.3	123.3	114.9	103.6	101.8	102.8	96.3	106.2
96.7	138.3	104.1	100.3	99.4	98.0	101.3	100.9
115.6	112.2	106.7	101.7	103.5	95.3	138.6	99.2
128.5	97.9	108.3	108.5	115.2	94.9	132.6	101.5
79.8	81.1	82.3	97.0	99.4	95.3	88.2	97.6
115.4	121.6	111.7	104.2	102.7	99.0	106.6	102.8
112.7	115.2	112.7	105.7	103.0	98.9	128.8	108.2
92.2	96.7	102.5	99.0	93.9	98.8	98.5	100.8
94.6	92.1	98.6	98.4	94.2	98.9	102.2	99.6
95.3	95.3	99.2	99.9	96.8	98.9	97.5	100.7
87.2	93.7	94.1	99.0	95.7	98.4	103.1	99.8
99.7	97.2	96.6	99.1	100.6	98.3	112.8	99.8

8-7 工业生产者出厂价格指数
PRODUCER PRICE INDEX FOR INDUSTRIAL PRODUCTS

(上年=100) (preceding year=100)

项 目	Item	2016	2015
总 指 数	**General Index**	**98.1**	**96.9**
按轻、重工业分	**By Light Industry and Heavy Industry**		
轻工业	Light Industry	101.8	100.0
以农产品为原料	Using Farming Products as Raw Materials	102.3	100.3
以非农产品为原料	Using Non-agricultural Products as Raw Materials	101.1	99.6
重工业	Heavy Industry	97.6	96.4
采 掘	Excavation	97.1	88.5
原 料	Raw Materials	97.4	95.8
加 工	Processing	97.7	97.0
按生产、生活资料分	**By Capital Goods and Living Goods**		
生产资料	Means of Production	98.0	96.1
采 掘	Excavation	97.1	88.5
原 料	Raw Materials	97.4	95.8
加 工	Processing	98.6	96.8
生活资料	Living Goods	98.3	99.9
食 品	Foods	103.5	101.8
衣 着	Clothing	99.1	100.1
一般日用品	Articles for Daily Use	100.6	100.0
耐用消费品	Durable Consumer Goods	96.1	97.9

8-8 工业生产者出厂价格指数(按行业分)
PRODUCER PRICE INDEX FOR INDUSTRIAL PRODUCTS (BY SECTOR)

(上年=100) (preceding year=100)

项目	Item	2016	2015
总指数	**General Index**	**98.1**	**96.9**
煤炭开采和洗选业	Mining and Washing of Coal	96.0	89.7
黑色金属矿采选业	Mining and Processing of Ferrous Metal Ores	96.9	64.8
非金属矿采选业	Mining and Processing of Nonmetal Ores	99.7	114.0
开采辅助活动		100.2	
农副食品加工业	Processing of Food from Agriculture Products	107.7	101.5
食品制造业	Manufacture of Foods	99.4	99.0
酒、饮料和精制茶制造业	Manufacture of Wines, Beverage and Refined Tea	99.4	101.7
烟草制品业	Manufacture of Cigarettes and Tobacco	100.2	100.0
纺织业	Manufacture of Textile	97.3	99.4
纺织服装、服饰业	Manufacture of Textile Wearing Apparel and Ornament	98.9	100.4
皮革、毛皮、羽毛及其制品和制鞋业	Manufacture of Leather, Fur, Feather and Its Products, and Footwear	100.6	100.3
木材加工和木、竹、藤、棕、草制品业	Processing of Timbers, Manufacture of Wood, Bamboo, Rattan, Palm and Straw Products	100.0	98.3
家具制造业	Manufacture of Furniture	100.3	99.5
造纸和纸制品业	Manufacture of Paper and Paper Products	98.5	96.8
印刷和记录媒介复制业	Printing, Reproduction of Recording Media	98.9	100.2
文教、工美、体育和娱乐用品制造业	Manufacture of Articles for Culture, Education, Artwork, Sports and Entertainment Activity	114.9	100.1
石油加工、炼焦和核燃料加工业	Processing of Petroleum, Coking, Processing of Nucleus Fuel	91.9	84.8
化学原料和化学制品制造业	Manufacture of Chemical Raw Material and Chemical Products	98.1	91.9
医药制造业	Manufacture of Medicines	101.2	102.0
化学纤维制造业	Manufacture of Chemical Fibres	100.2	99.9
橡胶和塑料制品业	Manufacture of Rubber and Plastics Products	98.8	97.8
非金属矿物制品业	Manufacture of Non-Metallic Mineral Products	98.6	97.8
黑色金属冶炼和压延加工业	Manufacture and Processing of Ferrous Metals	101.9	81.5
有色金属冶炼和压延加工业	Manufacture and processing of Non-Ferrous Metals	87.0	90.8
金属制品业	Manufacture of Fabricated Metal Products	94.6	97.2
通用设备制造业	Manufacture of General-Purpose Machinery	99.7	99.1
专用设备制造业	Manufacture of Special Purpose Machinery	99.8	99.0
汽车制造业	Manufacture of Motor Vehicles	97.4	98.4
铁路、船舶、航空航天和其他运输设备制造业	Manufacture of Railway Locomotives, Building of Ships and Boats, Manufacture of Air and Spacecrafts and Other Transportation Equipments	98.2	99.6
电气机械和器材制造业	Manufacture of Electrical Machinery and Equipment	98.6	99.5
计算机、通信和其他电子设备制造业	Manufacture of Computer, Communication Equipment and Other Electronic Equipment	96.3	95.5
仪器仪表制造业	Manufacture of Measuring Instrument and Meter	99.9	100.3
其他制造业	Other Manufacturing	94.8	99.9
废弃资源综合利用业	Waste Recycling and Recovery	88.8	97.4
金属制品、机械和设备修理业	Repair of Fabricated Metal Products, Machinery and Equipment	100.2	100.9
电力、热力生产和供应业	Production and Supply of Electricity and Heating Power	99.6	101.1
燃气生产和供应业	Production and Distribution of Gas	87.8	106.3
水的生产和供应业	Production and Distribution of Water	102.8	105.1

注：根据国家统计局规定，2012年起执行2011年国民经济行业分类标准(GB/T 4754—2011)。

Note: According to provisions of the National Bureau of Statistics, since 2012, sectors have been classified in accordance with the Standard for Classification of National Economic Sectors 2011(GB/T 4754-2011).

8-9 工业生产者购进价格指数
PURCHASING PRICE INDEX FOR INDUSTRIAL PRODUCTS

(上年=100) (preceding year=100)

项目	Item	2016	2015
总指数	**General Index**	**98.5**	**93.7**
燃料、动力类	Fuels and Power	98.0	85.6
黑色金属材料类	Ferrous Metal Materials	99.7	87.2
#钢材	Steel Products	100.0	85.4
其他	Others	97.1	94.2
有色金属材料和电线类	Nonferrous Metal Materials and Electric Wires	97.2	93.7
化工原料类	Chemical Raw Materials	96.6	94.1
木材及纸浆类	Timber and Paper Pulp	99.1	99.0
建筑材料及非金属矿类	Construction Materials and Nonmetal Ores	100.6	95.7
其他工业原材料及半成品类	Other Industrial Materials and Semi-finished Products	98.3	98.4
农副产品类	Agricultural Products	112.8	103.1
纺织原料类	Textile Raw Materials	99.8	99.8

8-10 固定资产投资价格指数(2016年)
PRICE INDEX FOR INVESTMENT IN FIXED ASSETS (2016)

项目	Item	1992 =100	1993 =100	1994 =100	2000 =100	2004 =100	2005 =100	2006 =100	2007 =100	2008 =100	2009 =100	2010 =100	2011 =100	2012 =100	2013 =100	2014 =100	2015 =100
总指数	**General Index**	**236.6**	**187.0**	**160.8**	**124.9**	**116.1**	**115.2**	**114.8**	**111.7**	**103.6**	**106.6**	**104.1**	**98.5**	**97.2**	**97.3**	**97.3**	**99.7**
建筑安装、装饰工程	Construction, Installation and Decoration Projects	274.8	209.5	174.8	128.1	111.1	110.4	110.9	106.4	95.2	101.0	97.1	88.5	89.4	91.9	93.3	98.8
人工费	Labor Cost	1111.4	785.8	543.2	238.4	205.2	197.3	189.6	178.6	163.7	157.0	147.6	132.3	120.6	113.3	107.6	103.4
材料费	Cost of Materials	208.3	154.4	131.3	113.0	96.8	97.0	98.4	94.6	83.8	91.3	87.9	79.9	82.8	87.1	89.8	97.7
机械使用费	Cost of Machinery Use				126.2	122.6	122.6	121.0	119.1	113.2	112.4	110.6	106.9	103.7	102.4	101.5	100.9
设备、工器具购置	Purchase of Equipment, Tools and Instruments	102.0	88.7	86.9	69.6	84.0	85.3	85.7	86.7	88.3	91.3	92.1	93.2	95.7	97.9	98.5	99.0
其他费用	Others	214.3	175.6	142.2	134.5	130.7	128.3	126.1	123.4	117.7	116.8	114.6	110.1	105.9	102.9	101.2	100.7

8-11 住宅销售价格指数(2016年各月)
SELLING PRICE INDEX OF RESIDENTIAL HOUSES (EACH MONTH OF 2016)

(上年同月=100) (same month of previous year=100)

项 目	Item	1月 Jan.	2月 Feb.	3月 Mar.	4月 Apr.	5月 May	6月 Jun.
新建住宅	**New Residential Houses**	**110.3**	**112.9**	**116.0**	**118.3**	**119.5**	**120.3**
#新建商品住宅	New Commercial Residential Houses	111.3	114.2	117.6	120.2	121.4	122.3
90平方米及以下	90sq.m and below	100.0	102.4	103.8	107.9	109.2	110.1
90-144平方米	90-144sq.m	114.5	116.9	120.9	122.7	124.1	124.6
144平方米以上	Above 144sq.m	117.4	121.1	125.7	127.5	128.6	129.7
二手住宅	**Second-hand Residential Houses**	**123.7**	**127.7**	**135.1**	**137.2**	**134.5**	**133.4**
90平方米及以下	90sq.m and below	123.7	127.6	134.6	136.9	134.7	133.5
90-144平方米	90-144sq.m	123.6	127.5	135.2	137.2	134.2	132.8
144平方米以上	Above 144sq.m	124.0	128.4	136.3	137.9	134.7	134.3

8-11 续表 Continued

(上年同月=100) (same month of previous year=100)

项 目	Item	7月 Jul.	8月 Aug.	9月 Sep.	10月 Oct.	11月 Nov.	12月 Dec.
新建住宅	**New Residential Houses**	**120.7**	**123.5**	**127.8**	**127.5**	**126.4**	**125.9**
#新建商品住宅	New Commercial Residential Houses	122.7	125.8	130.4	130.2	128.9	128.4
90平方米及以下	90sq.m and below	110.8	113.6	118.0	119.5	119.5	123.3
90-144平方米	90-144sq.m	125.0	128.1	132.8	132.3	131.3	129.2
144平方米以上	Above 144sq.m	129.9	133.0	137.9	136.4	133.9	131.3
二手住宅	**Second-hand Residential Houses**	**132.2**	**134.8**	**140.5**	**140.4**	**138.7**	**136.7**
90平方米及以下	90sq.m and below	132.4	135.0	140.7	140.5	139.0	137.0
90-144平方米	90-144sq.m	131.5	134.0	139.6	139.7	137.9	135.9
144平方米以上	Above 144sq.m	133.0	135.5	141.2	141.3	139.6	137.3

主要统计指标解释

居民消费价格指数 是度量消费商品及服务项目价格水平随着时间而变动的相对数，反映一定时期内居民家庭购买的消费品及服务价格水平的变动趋势和变动程度。居民消费价格指数变动率通常被用来作为反映通货膨胀（或紧缩）程度的指标。

商品零售价格指数 是度量工业、商业、餐饮业和其他零售企业向城乡居民、机关团体出售生活消费品和办公用品价格水平随着时间而变动的相对数，反映市场商品零售价格的变动趋势和变动程度。

工业生产者出厂价格指数 是反映全部工业产品出厂价格总水平变动程度的相对数。其中包括工业企业售给商业、外贸、物资部门的产品，还包括售给工业和其他部门的生产资料以及直接售给居民的生活消费品。通过工业生产者价格指数能观察工业产品出厂价格变动对工业总产值的影响。

工业生产者购进价格指数 是反映全部工业原材料、燃料、动力购进价格总水平变动程度的相对数。用其可以观察和研究工业企业原材料价格变动对生产的影响，以及企业对原材料涨价的消化能力和承受能力，为制定价格政策提供依据。

固定资产投资价格指数 是反映固定资产投资额价格变动程度的相对数。固定资产投资额由建筑安装装饰工程投资完成额，设备、工器具购置投资完成额和其他费用投资完成额三部分组成。编制固定资产投资价格指数可以准确地反映固定资产投资中涉及的各类商品和取费项目价格变动幅度，消除按现价计算的固定资产投资指标中的价格变动因素，真实地反映固定资产投资的规模、速度、结构和效益，为国家科学地制定、检查固定资产投资计划，提高宏观调控水平，为完善国民经济核算体系提供科学、可靠的依据。

住宅销售价格指数 是反映住宅销售价格总水平变动趋势和程度的相对数。包括新建住宅销售价格指数和二手住宅销售价格指数。

农产品生产者价格指数 是指农产品生产者价格总水平变动程度的相对数。农产品生产者价格是指农产品生产者第一次出售其产品时的单位产品价格。

Explanatory Notes on Main Statistical Indicators

Consumer Price Index (CPI) is a relative number measuring the changes in prices of consumer goods and service over time, reflecting the trend and degree of changes in prices of consumer goods and service purchased by households over a period of time. CPI is usually used for reflecting the level of inflation (or deflation).

Retail Price Index is a relative number measuring the changes in prices of consumer goods and office supplies provided by industry, commerce, restaurants and other retail businesses for urban and rural residents and government agencies and organizations over time. It reflects the trend and degree of changes in retail price of commodities in the market.

Producer Price Index for Industrial Products (PPI) is a relative number reflecting the degree of changes in general producer prices of all industrial products, including products sold by industrial enterprises to commercial, foreign trade and materials companies, as well as production materials sold to industrial and other enterprises, and consumer goods directly sold to consumers. It can be used to analyze the impact of producer prices of industrial products on gross industrial output value.

Purchasing Price Index for Industrial Products is a relative number reflecting the degree of changes in the overall level of prices of all industrial materials, fuels and power. It can be used to observe and analyze the effect of changes in prices of raw materials in industrial enterprises on their production, as well as the enterprises' capacity of digesting and bearing the rising prices of raw materials, thus providing basis for formulating price policies.

Price Index for Investment in Fixed Assets is a relative number reflecting the degree of changes in prices of investment in fixed assets. The investment in fixed assets consists of three components, i.e. the investment in construction and installation, the investment in purchasing equipment and instrument, and the investment in other items. Removing the factor of price change in the aggregates of investment at current prices, this indicator shows the changes in the prices of commodities and fees involved in the investment of fixed assets, and can be used to observe the actual size, growth, structure, and efficiency of investment in fixed assets and provides reliable and scientific basis for government planning on and examination of fixed assets investment, thus to improve overall adjustment and controlling skill, and further improve the national accounting system.

Selling Price Index of Residential Houses is a relative number reflecting the trend and degree of changes in the overall level of house selling prices, including newly built residential house selling price index and second-hand house selling price index.

Producer Price Index for Farm **Products** is a relative number reflecting the degree of changes in the overall production prices of farm products. Producer price of farm products refers to the price of unit product at which the producers of farm products sell their products for the first time.

人民生活
PEOPLE'S LIFE

简要说明

一、本章资料的主要内容

本章资料反映北京市居民生活现状及变化情况，分为全市居民生活、城镇居民生活和农村居民生活三部分。调查内容主要包括家庭基本情况、家庭收入和消费支出情况、主要商品购买数量及支出金额、居住状况和耐用消费品拥有量等。

二、本章资料的数据来源

城乡居民生活状况的数据来源于国家统计局北京调查总队、北京市统计局。

三、本章资料的调查方法

城乡居民生活状况调查方法和方案由国家统计局统一制定，采用抽样调查的方法，按对全市及分区居民主要收支指标有代表性的原则在全市城乡住户中抽取样本，并按一定的周期对样本进行轮换以保证其代表性。对抽中的住户采用日记账和问卷相结合的方式采集数据。

四、本章资料的调查范围

城镇住户调查的口径范围：2000–2003 年为 1000 户城市居民，覆盖城八区；2004–2006 年为 2000 户城市居民，覆盖城八区；2007 年为 3000 户城镇居民，覆盖所有区县；2008– 2012 年为 5000 户城镇居民，覆盖所有区县。

农村住户调查的口径范围：2000–2002 年为 2710 户，覆盖 14 个郊区县；2003 年为 2670 户（石景山区全部农民转居民，40 个样本取消），覆盖 13 个郊区县；2004–2012 年为 3000 户，覆盖 13 个郊区县。

城乡住户调查一体化：2013 年，根据国家统计局实施城乡住户调查一体化改革的要求和《住户收支与生活状况调查方案》的有关规定，国家统计局北京调查总队、北京市统计局对全市城乡住户进行了统一的样本抽取，城乡住户调查样本量共计 10000 户。

按照国家统计局要求，自 2015 年起，我市按照改革后的新口径发布全市和分城乡的居民收支数据。与老口径相比，新口径的差异主要体现在三个方面：一是对居民收支指标口径进行了调整，将反映居民收入的核心指标由原来的城镇居民“人均可支配收入”和农村居民“人均纯收入”统一为“人均可支配收入”；二是按照国家城乡划分标准，将城镇地区的村委会由原来的农村划入城镇进行统计；三是在分城乡的居民收支数据基础上，增加了全体居民的人均可支配收入、人均消费支出数据。

五、五等分组的含义

要客观的反映不同收入层次家庭的收支及生活状况，必须按不同收入水平进行分组来观察和分析。“五等分组”即住户按人均可支配收入从低到高排队分别分成五等份，即低收入组、中低收入组、中等收入组、中高收入组和高收入组五部分，各组的户数均占总户数的 20%。通过对调查户的分组，分别加权后计算各组人均可支配收入、消费支出的情况，以观察不同收入组之间的差距和存在的问题。

Brief Introduction

I. Main Content

Statistics in this chapter reflect the living conditions of residents in Beijing and their changes, consisting of three parts, including the living conditions of the residents of the whole city, urban residents and rural residents. Figures include the basic family situation, household income and expenditures in cash, purchase quantity and expenditures of main commodities, housing conditions and number of durable consumer goods in possession.

II. Source of Statistics

Statistics on the living conditions of urban and rural residents are from NBS Survey Office in Beijing, and Beijing Municipal Bureau of Statistics.

III. Method of Survey

Methods and plans of survey for living conditions of urban and rural residents are designated by National Bureau of Statistics. The method of sampling survey is adopted to take samples across Beijing Municipality following the principle of selecting representative residents in terms of major income and expenditure indicators. Samples are changed in certain periods to ensure their representativeness. For selected residents, statistics are gathered through journals and questionnaires.

IV. Scope of Survey

Scope of survey for urban residents: In 2000-2003, the survey covered 1,000 urban households in 8 urban districts; in 2004-2006, covered 2,000 urban households in 8 urban districts; in 2007 covered 3,000 urban households in all districts and counties; in 2008-2012, covered 5,000 households in all districts and counties.

Scope of survey for rural residents: In 2000-2002, the survey covered 2,710 households in 14 suburban districts and counties; in 2003, covered 2,670 households (All rural residents became urban residents in Shijingshan District, so 40 samples were cancelled.) in 13 suburban districts and counties; in 2004-2012 covered 3,000 households in 13 suburban districts and counties.

Integration of survey on urban and rural residents: in 2013, according to the requirements of the National Bureau of Statistics on carrying out integrated reforms of urban and rural resident survey, and *Survey Plan on Income and Expenditure, and Living Conditions of Households*, the NBS Survey Office in Beijing and Beijing Municipal Bureau of Statistics took a total of 10,000 samples of urban and rural residents in an integrated way.

According to requirements of National Bureau of Statistics, since 2015, Beijing has started to issue data on income and expense of residents in the city and residents in urban and rural areas according to new standards after the reform. As compared with former standards, the new standards mainly show differences in the following 3 aspects: first, according to national standards on division of urban and rural areas, village committees in urban areas that were classified into rural areas are now classified into urban areas; second, standards on resident income and expense indicators are adjusted. Core indicators reflecting resident income are unified from original "per capita disposable income" of urban residents and "per capita net income" of rural residents to "per capita disposable income"; third, based on data on resident income and expense in urban and rural areas, data on per capita disposable income and per capita consumption expense of residents in Beijing are added.

V. Meaning of Five-level Grouping

It is necessary to have groups at different income levels for observation and analysis to objectively reflect the income and expenditure and living conditions of households at different income levels. "Five-level grouping" means that households are divided into five groups in a low-to-high order regarding the per capita disposable income. These five groups are the low-income, middle-low-income, middle-income, middle-high-income and high-income groups. The number of households in each group accounts for 20% of the total. Through grouping of the households under survey, we can calculate the per capita income and consumption expenditures of each group respectively so as to observe the differences between different income groups and existing problems.

9-1 全市居民家庭生活基本情况(2016年)
BASIC LIVING CONDITIONS OF THE WHOLE HOUSEHOLDS (2016)

单位：元 (yuan)

项目	Item	2016	2016年为2015年% 2016 as % of 2015
全市居民家庭生活基本情况	**Basic Living Conditions of Residents**		
人均可支配收入	Per capita disposable income	52530	108.4
人均消费支出	Per capita consumption expenditure	35416	104.8
居民家庭恩格尔系数(%)	Engel's coefficient of households (%)	21.5	
人均住房建筑面积(平方米)	Per capita floor space of houses (sq.m)	34.02	102.4
城镇居民家庭生活基本情况	**Basic Living Conditions of Urban Households**		
人均可支配收入	Per capita disposable income	57275	108.4
人均消费支出	Per capita consumption expenditure	38256	104.4
居民家庭恩格尔系数(%)	Engel's coefficient of households (%)	21.1	
人均住房建筑面积(平方米)	Per capita floor space of houses (sq.m)	32.38	102.2
农村居民家庭生活基本情况	**Basic Living Conditions of Rural Households**		
人均可支配收入	Per capita disposable income	22310	108.5
人均消费支出	Per capita consumption expenditure	17329	109.6
居民家庭恩格尔系数(%)	Engel's coefficient of households (%)	26.9	
人均住房建筑面积(平方米)	Per capita floor space of houses (sq.m)	44.50	103.4

注：按照国家统计局要求，自2015年起北京按照改革后新口径发布全市和分城乡的居民收支数据，增长速度为同口径增速(下表同)。
Note: According to the requirements of National Bureau of Statistics, Beijing released data on income and expenses of urban and rural residents based on the reformed standard since 2015 and the growth rate was calculated under the same standard (the same to the follows).

9-2 全市居民家庭基本情况(按收入水平分)(2016年)
BASIC DATA ON URBAN HOUSEHOLDS(BY INCOME LEVEL) (2016)

项目	Item	全市平均 Average	低收入户20% Low Income 20% 20%	中低收入户20% Medium-Low Income 20%	中等收入户20% Medium Income 20%	中高收入户20% Medium-High Income 20%	高收入户20% High Income 20%
平均每户常住人口 (人)	Permanent Population Per Household (person)	2.7	3.1	2.9	2.6	2.6	2.3
平均每户就业人口数 (人)	Average Employee Per Household (person)	1.3	1.6	1.5	1.2	1.2	1.2
平均每一就业者负担人数(人)	Dependents Per Employee (person)	1.6	1.9	1.6	1.5	1.4	1.3
平均每人年可支配收入 (元)	Per Capita Annual Disposable Income (yuan)	52530	20204	36277	49342	65555	105425
平均每人年消费支出 (元)	Per Capita Annual Consumption Expenditures (yuan)	35416	16848	26223	33181	43944	64717

9-3 全市居民家庭人均可支配收入(2016年)

单位：元

项目	Item	全市平均 Average
可支配收入	**Disposable Income**	**52530**
工资性收入	**Wage Income**	**33114**
工　资	Wage	30234
实物福利	Benefit in Kind	174
其　他	Other Income from Work	2706
经营净收入	**Net Income from Operations**	**1396**
第一产业经营净收入	Net Income from Operations in the Primary Industry	68
第二产业经营净收入	Net Income from Operations in the Secondary Industry	158
第三产业经营净收入	Net Income from Operations in the Tertiary Industry	1170
财产净收入	**Net Property Income**	**8230**
利息净收入	Net Interest Income	-24
红利收入	Dividend Income	307
集体分配的红利	Dividend Distributed by the Collective	260
其他红利收入	Other Dividend Income	47
储蓄性保险净收益	Net Income from Saving Insurance	5
转让承包土地经营权租金净收入	Net Rent from Transfer of Contracted Land Management Right	43
出租房屋净收入	Net Income from House Rent	1281
出租机械专利版权等资产的收入	Income from Lease of Assets such as Mechanical Patent Copyright	13
其他财产净收入	Other Net Property Income	-31
自有住房折算净租金	Converted Net Rent from Owner-Occupied Housing	6636
转移净收入	**Net Transfer Income**	**9790**
转移性收入	Transfer Income	13745
养老金或离退休金	Pensions or Retirement Payments	12663
社会救济和补助	Social Relief and Subsidies	48
政策性生活补贴	Policy-type Living Allowances	80
报销医疗费	Reimbursement of Medical Fees	668
家庭外出从业人员寄回带回收入	Income from Family Members Going out for a Job	21
赡养收入	Alimony Income	115
其他经常转移收入	Other Current Transfer Income	122
从政府和组织得到的实物产品和服务折价	Converted Income from Physical Products and Services Obtained from the Government and Organizations	18
现金政策性惠农补贴	Subsidies Benefiting Peasants under Cash Policy	11
转移性支出	Transfer Expenditures	3955

注：1.全市居民人均可支配收入实际增长6.9%。
2.收支数据细项及构成数据均未做机械配平(下表同)。

PER DISPOSABLE INCOME OF THE WHOLE HOUSEHOLDS (2016)

(yuan)

低 收 入 户 20% Low Income 20%	中 低 收入户 20% Medium- Low Income 20%	中 等 收入户 20% Medium Income 20%	中 高 收入户 20% Medium- High Income 20%	高 收 入 户 20% High Income 20%	2016年为 2015年% 2016 as % of 2015
20204	**36277**	**49342**	**65555**	**105425**	**108.4**
14400	**23394**	**28777**	**36597**	**71532**	**109.5**
13728	21658	26183	32999	64700	109.1
50	148	284	140	285	120.6
622	1587	2310	3458	6547	113.4
1664	**1443**	**1299**	**967**	**1524**	**98.3**
195	67	29	13	…	85.4
151	84	123	196	257	158.5
1318	1292	1147	758	1266	94.2
2188	**5511**	**7413**	**11055**	**17561**	**109.7**
-31	13	-18	-120	39	-41.3
382	347	224	131	435	147.5
380	334	222	103	213	151.2
3	12	3	28	222	129.8
	2	11	6	4	58.0
82	39	11	40	34	111.0
592	1334	1314	1413	1941	124.3
		67			648.4
-2	-33	-24	-30	-78	3123.3
1164	3808	5827	9614	15186	107.9
1952	**5929**	**11853**	**16935**	**14808**	**105.3**
3498	8385	15008	21165	24513	108.9
2758	7665	14115	19815	22612	107.2
96	37	19	3	78	119.6
133	120	30	66	23	126.5
141	267	603	1042	1540	146.4
36	31	27	6		97.6
93	64	93	131	214	129.2
159	174	113	97	41	112.2
50	17	6	5	3	105.6
30	11	2	1	2	95.6
1546	2457	3154	4229	9705	118.9

Note: a)Real growth rate of the per capita annual disposable income is 6.9%.

b)No mechanical trim for both detailed revenue & expenditure data and compositional data (the same below).

9-4 全市居民家庭人均总支出(2016年)

单位：元

项　目	Item	全市平均 Average
家庭总支出	**Total Expenditures of Households**	**44293**
消费支出	**Consumption Expenditures**	**35416**
生产经营费用支出	**Expenditures of Production and Operating Costs**	**550**
第一产业经营费用支出	Operating Cost Expenditures in the Primary Industry	98
第二产业经营费用支出	Operating Cost Expenditures in the Secondary Industry	137
第三产业经营费用支出	Operating Cost Expenditures in the Tertiary Industry	315
财产性支出	**Property Expenditures**	**176**
转移性支出	**Transfer Expenditures**	**3955**
个人所得税	Individual Income Tax	778
社会保障支出	Social Security Expenditures	2700
个人缴纳的养老保险	Pensions Paid by Individual	2031
个人缴纳的医疗保险	Medical Funds Paid by Individual	606
个人缴纳的失业保险	Unemployment Funds Paid by Individual	56
其他社会保障支出	Other Social Security Expenditures	7
外来从业人员寄给家人的支出	Expenditures of Outside Employees for Their Family	113
赡养支出	Alimony Expenditures	252
其他转移性支出	Other Transfer Expenditures	113
部分商业保险支出	**Partially Commercial Insurance Expenditures**	**223**
意外伤害保险	Accident Insurance	23
商业医疗保险(含大病保险)	Commercial Medical Insurance (including Critical Illness Insurance)	124
其他非储蓄性商业保险	Other Non-saving Commercial Insurance	9
其他储蓄性商业保险	Other Saving Commercial Insurance	67
购置资产及非经常性转移支出	**Expenditures of Acquisition Assets and Non-recurrent Transfer**	**2496**
购置资产支出	Acquisition Asset Expenditures	1083
#建造住房支出	Expenditures of Building Houses	133
购买住房支出	Expenditures of Purchasing Houses	874
非经常性转移支出	Non-recurrent Transfer Expenditures	1413
#一次性馈赠支出	Disposable Donation Expenditures	633
借贷性支出	**Credit Expenditures**	**1476**
#存入储蓄款	Saving Deposits	595
归还借款	Repayment of Loans	75
购买有价证券	Purchase of Securities	51
归还住房贷款	Repayment of Housing Loan	612
归还汽车贷款	Repayment of Automobile Loans	49

PER CAPITA ANNUAL EXPENDITURES OF URBAN HOUSEHOLDS (2016)

(yuan)

低 收 入 户 20% Low Income 20%	中 低 收入户 20% Medium- Low Income 20%	中 等 收入户 20% Medium Income 20%	中 高 收入户 20% Medium- High Income 20%	高 收 入 户 20% High Income 20%	2016年为 2015年% 2016 as % of 2015
22150	**32083**	**40262**	**53188**	**83794**	**99.5**
16848	**26223**	**33181**	**43944**	**64717**	**104.8**
1356	**374**	**236**	**498**	**58**	**130.0**
331	39	35	25	…	95.2
254	26		369	6	268.6
771	309	201	104	53	117.1
74	**94**	**119**	**260**	**388**	**143.1**
1546	**2457**	**3154**	**4229**	**9706**	**118.9**
23	110	264	709	3328	140.2
1262	1975	2320	3225	5379	113.1
901	1446	1735	2461	4135	113.5
329	480	535	687	1122	111.4
24	41	47	68	113	116.7
8	8	3	8	8	140.0
118	79	310	44	1	163.8
118	210	202	171	632	97.7
25	84	60	81	367	198.3
92	**121**	**163**	**200**	**625**	**116.8**
13	28	11	12	55	104.6
48	65	76	135	347	130.5
2	1	17	15	10	180.0
28	27	59	38	213	97.1
1673	**1870**	**2198**	**2582**	**4609**	**53.3**
563	717	1011	981	2442	31.6
454	59	69		…	103.1
34	567	879	909	2363	28.4
1110	1153	1186	1601	2167	113.1
322	464	556	683	1291	121.0
561	**945**	**1210**	**1474**	**3691**	**75.6**
305	466	508	721	1098	50.0
30	44	44	54	237	111.9
37	4	6	6	234	76.1
151	311	496	556	1813	120.0
4	77	39	17	123	153.1

9-5 全市居民家庭人均消费支出(2016年)
PER CAPITA CONSUMPTION EXPENDITURES OF THE WHOLE HOUSEHOLDS (2016)

单位：元 (yuan)

项目	Item	全市平均 Average	低收入户20% Low Income 20%	中低收入户20% Medium-Low Income 20%	中等收入户20% Medium Income 20%	中高收入户20% Medium-High Income 20%	高收入户20% High Income 20%	2016年为2015年% 2016 as % of 2015
人均消费支出	**Per Capita Consumption Expenditures**	**35416**	**16848**	**26223**	**33181**	**43944**	**64717**	**104.8**
食品烟酒支出	Expenditures of Foods, Tobacco and Liquor	7609	4619	6605	7896	8958	10940	100.3
衣着支出	Clothing Expenditures	2433	1147	1926	2410	2885	4305	100.3
居住支出	Housing Expenditures	11188	4621	7457	9545	14390	22971	108.1
生活用品及服务支出	Expenditures of Living Articles and Services	2327	1097	1648	2107	2985	4336	110.9
交通和通信支出	Expenditures of Transportation and Communication	4702	2186	3532	4619	5423	8821	104.7
教育、文化和娱乐支出	Educational, Cultural and Recreational Expenditures	3687	1785	2678	3254	4694	6853	101.4
医疗保健支出	Healthcare Expenditures	2456	1071	1851	2312	3250	4336	110.2
其他用品及服务支出	Expenditures of Other Goods and Services	1015	323	526	1038	1358	2156	102.4

注：全市居民人均消费支出实际增长3.4%。

Note: Real growth rate of the per capita consumption expenditures of the whole residents is 3.4%.

9-6 全市居民家庭人均消费支出构成(2016年)
COMPOSITION OF PER CAPITA CONSUMPTION EXPENDITURES OF THE WHOLE HOUSEHOLDS (2016)

单位：% (%)

项目	Item	全市平均 Average	低收入户20% Low Income 20%	中低收入户20% Medium-Low Income 20%	中等收入户20% Medium Income 20%	中高收入户20% Medium-High Income 20%	高收入户20% High Income 20%
人均消费支出	**Per Capita Consumption Expenditures**	**100.0**	**100.0**	**100.0**	**100.0**	**100.0**	**100.0**
食品烟酒支出(恩格尔系数)	Expenditures of Foods, Tobacco and Liquor (Engel Coefficient)	21.5	27.4	25.2	23.8	20.4	16.9
衣着支出	Clothing Expenditures	6.9	6.8	7.3	7.3	6.6	6.7
居住支出	Housing Expenditures	31.6	27.4	28.4	28.8	32.7	35.5
生活用品及服务支出	Expenditures of Living Articles and Services	6.6	6.5	6.3	6.4	6.8	6.7
交通和通信支出	Expenditures of Transportation and Communication	13.3	13.0	13.5	13.9	12.3	13.6
教育、文化和娱乐支出	Educational, Cultural and Recreational Expenditures	10.4	10.6	10.2	9.8	10.7	10.6
医疗保健支出	Healthcare Expenditures	6.9	6.4	7.1	7.0	7.4	6.7
其他用品及服务支出	Expenditures of Other Goods and Services	2.9	1.9	2.0	3.1	3.1	3.3

9–7 全市居民家庭人均食品烟酒支出(2016年)
PER CAPITA EXPENDITURES ON FOODS, TOBACCO AND LIQUOR OF THE WHOLE HOUSEHOLDS (2016)

单位：元 (yuan)

项 目	Item	全市平均 Average	低收入户20% Low Income 20%	中低收入户20% Medium-Low Income 20%	中等收入户20% Medium Income 20%	中高收入户20% Medium-High Income 20%	高收入户20% High Income 20%
食品烟酒支出	**Expenditures of Foods, Tobacco and Liquor**	**7609**	**4619**	**6605**	**7896**	**8958**	**10940**
食 品	Foods	4556	3151	4185	4836	5234	5748
谷 物	Grain	530	398	470	586	514	730
薯 类	Potatoes	62	49	60	61	71	69
豆 类	Beans	62	50	57	62	71	73
食用油	Edible Oil	211	166	222	234	224	212
蔬菜和食用菌	Vegetables and Edible Mushrooms	579	445	562	593	660	660
肉 类	Meat	924	705	912	980	1051	1006
禽 类	Poultry	146	101	132	157	173	178
水产品	Aquatic Products	303	152	256	333	393	425
蛋 类	Eggs	131	105	125	129	150	152
奶 类	Milk	368	224	317	398	437	511
干鲜瓜果类	Nuts, Fresh Melons and Fruits	708	437	608	743	867	968
糖果糕点类	Sweets and Cakes	268	137	218	285	331	414
其他食品	Other Foods	263	181	245	273	292	349
烟 酒	Tobacco and Liquor	606	487	595	625	653	690
烟 草	Tobacco	334	296	344	345	356	327
酒 类	Liquor	272	191	251	280	297	363
饮 料	Beverages	335	187	314	370	405	437
饮食服务	Catering Services	2112	795	1512	2066	2666	4066

9-8 全市居民家庭人均衣着、居住支出(2016年)
PER CAPITA ANNUAL EXPENDIATURES ON CLOTHING AND HOUSING OF URBAN HOUSEHOLDS (2016)

单位：元 (yuan)

项目	Item	全市平均 Average	低收入户20% Low Income 20%	中低收入户20% Medium-Low Income 20%	中等收入户20% Medium Income 20%	中高收入户20% Medium-High Income 20%	高收入户20% High Income 20%
衣着支出	**Clothing Expenditures**	**2433**	**1147**	**1926**	**2410**	**2885**	**4305**
衣类	Clothes	1763	792	1351	1737	2096	3236
服装	Garments	1623	733	1237	1564	1958	2991
服装材料	Clothing Materials	8	6	8	6	9	11
其他衣类及配件	Other Clothes and Accessories	93	42	76	89	109	171
衣着加工服务费	Service Fees for Clothing Processing	7	3	4	10	9	11
鞋类	Footwear	670	355	575	672	789	1069
居住支出	**Housing Expenditures**	**11188**	**4621**	**7457**	**9545**	**14390**	**22971**
租赁房房租	House Rent	475	317	503	508	427	661
住房维修及管理	Housing Maintenance and Management	882	405	579	508	1255	1908
#住房装潢	Housing Decoration	615	245	401	290	952	1369
住房维修	Housing Maintenance	114	140	102	100	91	132
物业管理费	Property Management Fees	143	16	68	115	198	382
水电燃料及其他	Water, Electricity, Fuels and Others	1185	958	1084	1241	1268	1433
#水费	Water	132	54	104	139	178	212
电费	Electricity	423	385	404	411	465	456
燃料	Fuels	278	411	308	213	202	208
自有住房折算租金	Converted Rent from Owner-Occupied Housing	8646	2942	5292	7288	11440	18969

9–9 全市居民家庭人均生活用品及服务、交通和通信支出(2016年)
PER CAPITA EXPENDITURE ON LIVING ARTICLES AND SERVICES, TRANSPORTATION AND COMMUNICATION OF THE WHOLE HOUSEHOLDS (2016)

单位：元 (yuan)

项　目	Item	全市平均 Average	低收入户20% Low Income 20%	中低收入户20% Medium-Low Income 20%	中等收入户20% Medium Income 20%	中高收入户20% Medium-High Income 20%	高收入户20% High Income 20%
生活用品及服务支出	**Expenditures of Living Articles and Services**	**2327**	**1097**	**1648**	**2107**	**2985**	**4336**
家具及室内装饰品	Furniture and Interior Decorations	439	133	183	282	770	980
家　具	Furniture	393	119	159	257	718	848
家具材料	Furniture Materials	5	2	3	2	5	12
室内装饰品	Interior Decorations	41	11	21	23	46	120
家用器具	Household Appliances	547	318	479	467	669	887
耐用消费品	Durable Consumer Goods	434	271	391	367	527	671
小家电	Small Appliance	113	47	86	99	143	215
家用纺织品	Household Textile	178	83	140	177	229	298
#床上用品	Bedding	156	69	125	157	205	258
家庭日用杂品	Daily Groceries for Households	517	314	412	511	567	865
个人用品	Personal Articles	460	211	372	476	530	805
家庭服务	Domestic Services	187	37	62	195	219	501
交通和通信支出	**Expenditures of Transportation and Communication**	**4702**	**2186**	**3532**	**4619**	**5423**	**8821**
交　通	Transportation	3439	1409	2396	3382	3955	6964
#交通工具	Vehicles	1091	352	726	1229	1136	2344
交通费	Transportation Expenses	818	271	497	746	937	1914
通　信	Communication	1263	776	1136	1238	1468	1857
通信工具	Communication Devices	378	188	342	352	469	602
通信服务	Communication Services	885	589	794	886	999	1255

9-10 全市居民家庭人均教育文化和娱乐、医疗保健、其他用品及服务支出(2016年)

PER CAPITA EXPENDITURES ON EDUCATION, CULTURE, RECREATION, HEALTHCARE, OTHER GOODS AND SERVICES OF THE WHOLE HOUSEHOLDS (2016)

单位：元 (yuan)

项目	Item	全市平均 Average	低收入户20% Low Income 20%	中低收入户20% Medium-Low Income 20%	中等收入户20% Medium Income 20%	中高收入户20% Medium-High Income 20%	高收入户20% High Income 20%
教育、文化和娱乐支出	**Educational, Cultural and Recreational Expenditures**	**3687**	**1785**	**2678**	**3254**	**4694**	**6853**
教育	Education	1335	1108	1286	1051	1428	1892
#学杂费	Tuition for Compulsory Education	332	298	350	232	375	410
培训费	Training Fees	547	231	478	526	576	1050
一揽子教育服务(含食宿)	A Package of Education Services (including Accommodation)	327	480	305	196	325	288
学前教育	Pre-school Education	457	306	390	330	640	678
小学教育	Primary Education	290	119	280	277	317	517
初中教育	Junior Secondary Education	98	78	126	65	80	145
高中教育	Senior Secondary Education	137	142	120	156	91	177
中专职高教育	Secondary Vocational Education	11	31	3	4	10	1
大专及以上教育	Education for Junior College and Above	245	374	278	143	198	185
成人教育	Adult Education	97	58	88	77	92	190
文化和娱乐	Culture and Recreation	2351	677	1393	2202	3266	4961
文娱耐用消费品	Durable Consumer Goods for Cultural Recreation	344	157	189	311	427	738
其他文娱用品	Other Cultural and Recreational Articles	410	168	274	414	526	768
文化娱乐服务	Cultural and Recreational Services	1597	352	930	1477	2312	3455
医疗保健支出	**Healthcare Expenditures**	**2456**	**1071**	**1851**	**2312**	**3250**	**4336**
医疗器具及药品	Medical Apparatus and Medicine	824	448	589	831	945	1475
药品	Medicine	489	378	427	475	544	661
滋补保健品	Nutritious Healthcare Products	262	45	130	260	335	642
医疗卫生器具	Medical and Hygienic Apparatus	30	9	19	29	39	65
保健器具	Healthcare Apparatus	39	15	9	54	28	105
医疗服务	Medical Services	1632	622	1262	1482	2305	2861
其他用品及服务支出	**Expenditures of Other Goods and Services**	**1015**	**323**	**526**	**1038**	**1358**	**2156**
其他用品	Other Goods	542	190	258	546	797	1084
其他服务	Services	473	133	268	491	561	1072

9-11 全市居民家庭每百户主要耐用消费品拥有量(2016年)
NUMBER OF MAIN DURABLE CONSUMER GOODS PER 100 URBAN HOUSEHOLDS (2016)

项目		Item		全市平均 Average	低收入户20% Low Income 20%	中低收入户20% Medium-Low Income 20%	中等收入户20% Medium Income 20%	中高收入户20% Medium-High Income 20%	高收入户20% High Income 20%
家用汽车	(辆)	Household Cars	(unit)	47	35	42	41	57	62
摩托车	(辆)	Motorcycles	(unit)	3	6	4	2	4	1
助力车	(台)	Powered Bicycles	(unit)	26	54	29	19	16	12
洗衣机	(台)	Washing Machines	(unit)	95	94	93	89	99	100
电冰箱(柜)	(台)	Refrigerators	(unit)	98	99	96	90	100	103
微波炉	(台)	Microwave Ovens	(unit)	77	59	75	76	88	88
彩色电视机	(台)	Color TV Sets	(unit)	128	128	123	118	135	136
#接入有线电视网络的电视机	(台)	TV Sets Accessed to Cable TV Network	(unit)	113	113	109	103	121	118
空调	(台)	Air Conditioners	(unit)	163	130	149	154	180	199
热水器	(台)	Water Heaters	(unit)	94	93	93	88	98	97
消毒碗柜	(台)	Disinfection cabinets	(unit)	5	2	3	3	7	10
洗碗机	(台)	Dishwashers	(unit)	1	…	1	2	2	3
移动电话	(部)	Mobile Phones	(unit)	226	237	229	216	231	216
#接入互联网的移动电话	(部)	Mobile Phones Accessed to the Internet	(unit)	157	132	161	154	171	169
计算机	(台)	Computers	(unit)	100	80	90	94	109	125
#接入互联网的计算机	(台)	Computers Accessed to the Internet	(unit)	92	71	83	88	102	114
摄像机	(台)	Video Cameras	(unit)	17	5	9	16	23	31
照相机	(台)	Cameras	(unit)	54	25	41	52	69	81
中高档乐器	(架)	Musical Instruments of M	(unit)	8	3	5	7	10	14
健身器材	(台)	Fitness Equipment	(unit)	7	2	5	7	7	12
组合音响	(套)	Audio Systems	(set)	6	4	5	6	8	10

9-12 全市居民家庭居住构成情况(2016)
COMPOSITION OF HOUSING CONDITIONS FOR URBAN HOUSEHOLDS (2016)

单位：% (%)

项　目	Item	全市居民 Residents	城镇居民 Urban Residents	农村居民 Rural Residents
居住空间样式	**Style of Living Space**	**100.0**	**100.0**	**100.0**
单栋楼房占比重	Individual Storied Buildings	3.1	2.9	4.4
单栋平房占比重	Individual Single-storey Buildings	22.3	13.6	84.3
四居室及以上单元房占比重	Four-bedroom and above Flat	1.9	2.2	
三居室单元房占比重	Three-bedroom Flat	15.6	17.5	2.1
二居室单元房占比重	Two-bedroom Flat	39.4	44.7	1.9
一居室单元房占比重	One-bedroom Flat	6.5	7.4	0.1
筒子楼或连片平房占比重	Tube-shaped Apartment or Closely Grouped Single-storey Buildings	11.2	11.7	7.2
其他占比重	Others	0.1	0.1	
房屋来源	**Housing Property Right**	**100.0**	**100.0**	**100.0**
租赁公房占比重	Public Houses Rented	7.0	7.9	0.2
租赁私房占比重	Private Houses Rented	7.5	8.2	2.6
自建住房占比重	Self-building Houses	23.6	14.7	87.1
购买商品房占比重	Purchased Commercial Houses	25.9	29.1	3.0
购买房改住房占比重	Purchased Houses from Housing Reform	19.5	22.1	0.9
购买保障性住房占比重	Purchase of Indemnificatory Housing	4.9	5.6	
拆迁安置房占比重	Resettlement Housing	5.7	6.5	0.5
继承或获赠住房占比重	Housing under Inheritance or Donation	0.6	0.6	0.4
免费借用房占比重	Free Borrowed Houses	1.9	1.9	1.3
雇主提供免费住房占比重	Free Housing Supplied by Employers	3.3	3.2	4.1
其他来源占比重	Others	0.1	0.1	
住宅有管道供水情况	**Water Supply Conditions of Housing with Pipes**	**100.0**	**100.0**	**100.0**
管道供水入户	Water Supply to Households through Pipes	96.5	96.6	96.3
管道供水至公共取水点	Water Supply to Public Water-taking Location through Pipes	3.5	3.4	3.7
没有管道设施	Without Pipelines			
饮用水来源情况	**Source of Drinking Water**	**100.0**	**100.0**	**100.0**
经过净化处理的自来水占比重	Tap Water via Purification Treatment	92.8	94.1	83.2
受保护的井水和泉水占比重	Protected Well Water and Spring Water	5.4	3.8	16.7
不受保护的井水和泉水占比重	Unprotected Well Water and Spring Water			

9-12 续表 continued

单位：% (%)

项　　目	Item	全市居民 Residents	城镇居民 Urban Residents	农村居民 Rural Residents
江河湖泊水占比重	Water from Rivers and Lakes			
收集雨水占比重	Collecting Rainwater			
桶装水占比重	Barreled Water	1.8	2.1	0.1
其他占比重	Others			
住户厕所类型	**Toilet Type of Households**	**100.0**	**100.0**	**100.0**
水冲式卫生厕所占比重	Water-flushing Sanitary Toilets	88.8	89.9	80.8
水冲式非卫生厕所占比重	Water-flushing Non-sanitary Toilets	0.3	0.2	0.9
卫生旱厕占比重	Sanitary Pit Toilet	2.3	1.6	7.2
普通旱厕占比重	Common Pit Toilet	3.1	2.0	10.6
无厕所占比重	Households Without Toilet	5.6	6.3	0.6
住户厕所使用情况	**Toilet Use Conditions of Households**	**100.0**	**100.0**	**100.0**
本住户独用占比重	Exclusive Use by One Household	87.4	86.6	92.7
几户合用占比重	One Toilet Shared by Several Households	1.4	1.3	2.0
公用厕所占比重	Communal Toilet	11.2	12.1	5.3
主要炊用能源状况	**Main Cooking Energy Conditions**	**100.0**	**100.0**	**100.0**
柴草占比重	Firewood	0.2	0.0	1.9
煤炭占比重	Coal	0.1	0.1	0.1
罐装液化石油气占比重	Bottled LPG	31.9	24.0	88.3
管道液化石油气占比重	Pipeline LPG	0.4	0.5	
管道煤气占比重	Pipeline Gas			
管道天然气占比重	Pipeline Natural Gas	62.0	70.2	3.6
电占比重	Electricity	2.2	2.2	2.2
燃料用油占比重	Oil Used in Fuel			
沼气占比重	Marsh Gas	0.2	0.2	
其他占比重	Others			
无炊用行为占比重	Non-cooking Behaviors	3.0	2.8	4.0
住宅外道路路面状况	**Pavement Conditions of Roads Outside Houses**	**100.0**	**100.0**	**100.0**
水泥或柏油路面的户数占比重	Cement or Tar-coated Surface	96.2	96.2	96.3
沙石或石板等硬质路面的户数占比重	Hard Surface Paved with Sand and Stones or Slates	3.3	3.2	3.5
其它路面的户数占比重	Other Pavements	0.6	0.6	0.2

9-13 城镇居民家庭生活基本情况(1978-2016年)
BASIC LIVING CONDITIONS OF URBAN HOUSEHOLDS (1978-2016)

年份 Year	人均家庭总收入(元) Per Capita Total Income (Yuan)	人均可支配收入(元) Per Capita Disposable Income (Yuan)	人均可支配收入实际增长(%) Actual Growth Rate of Per Capita Disposable Income (%)	人均消费支出(元) Per Capita Living Expenditures (Yuan)	#食品烟酒 Foods Tobacco and Liquor	城镇居民家庭恩格尔系数(%) Engel Coefficient of Urban Households (%)	每一城镇就业者负担人数(人) Dependents Per Urban Employee (person)	城镇居民人均住房建筑面积(平方米) Per Capita Floor Space of Houses in Urban Areas (sq.m)
1978	450.2	365.4		359.9	211.2	58.7	1.86	
1979	491.5	415.0	11.6	408.7	236.7	57.9	1.83	
1980	599.4	501.4	14.0	490.4	271.0	55.3	1.80	
1981	619.6	514.1	1.2	511.4	295.1	57.7	1.72	
1982	668.1	561.1	7.2	534.8	317.6	59.3	1.66	
1983	716.6	590.5	4.7	574.1	337.7	58.8	1.65	
1984	837.7	693.7	15.0	666.8	379.1	56.8	1.63	
1985	1158.8	907.7	11.3	923.3	466.9	50.6	1.66	
1986	1317.3	1067.5	10.1	1067.4	543.4	50.9	1.66	
1987	1413.2	1181.9	1.9	1147.6	605.0	52.7	1.65	
1988	1767.7	1437.0	1.0	1455.6	743.4	51.1	1.71	
1989	1899.6	1597.1	-5.2	1520.4	841.3	55.3	1.52	
1990	2067.3	1787.1	6.2	1646.1	892.2	54.2	1.52	
1991	2359.9	2040.4	2.1	1860.2	1016.8	54.7	1.47	
1992	2813.1	2363.7	5.4	2134.7	1126.3	52.8	1.43	
1993	3935.4	3296.0	17.1	2939.6	1404.7	47.8	1.42	
1994	5585.9	4731.2	14.9	4134.1	1919.0	46.4	1.41	
1995	6748.7	5868.4	5.7	5019.8	2436.5	48.5	1.41	
1996	7945.8	6885.5	5.1	5729.5	2671.5	46.6	1.41	
1997	8741.7	7813.1	7.8	6531.8	2854.4	43.7	1.43	
1998	10098.2	8472.0	5.9	6970.8	2865.7	41.1	1.40	
1999	10654.8	9182.8	7.8	7498.5	2959.2	39.5	1.41	
2000	12560.3	10349.7	8.9	8493.5	3083.4	36.3	1.41	
2001	13768.8	11577.8	8.5	8922.7	3229.3	36.2	1.39	
2002	13253.3	12463.9	15.6	10285.8	3472.5	33.8	1.41	19.22
2003	14959.3	13882.6	11.2	11123.8	3522.7	31.7	1.39	19.71
2004	17116.5	15637.8	11.5	12200.4	3925.5	32.2	1.44	21.49
2005	19533.3	17653.0	11.2	13244.2	4215.6	31.8	1.39	22.03
2006	22417.0	19978.0	12.2	14825.0	4561.0	30.8	1.40	23.65
2007	24576.0	21989.0	11.2	15330.0	4934.0	32.2	1.40	24.77
2008	27678.0	24725.0	7.0	16460.0	5562.0	33.8	1.40	26.90
2009	30674.0	26738.0	9.7	17893.0	5936.0	33.2	1.40	27.69
2010	33360.0	29073.0	6.2	19934.0	6393.0	32.1	1.40	28.94
2011	37124.0	32903.0	7.2	21984.0	6905.0	31.4	1.50	29.38
2012	41103.0	36469.0	7.3	24046.0	7535.0	31.3	1.40	29.26
2013	45274.0	40321.0	7.1	26275.0	8170.0	31.1	1.50	31.31
2014	49730.0	43910.0	7.2	28009.0	8632.0	30.8	1.50	31.54
2015		52859.0	7.0	36642.0	8091.0	22.1	1.50	31.69
2016		57275.0	6.9	38256.0	8070.0	21.1	1.56	32.38

9-14 城镇居民家庭基本情况(按收入水平分)(2016年)
BASIC DATA ON URBAN HOUSEHOLDS (BY INCOME LEVEL) (2016)

项　　目	Item	全市平均 Average	低收入户20% Low Income 20%	中低收入户20% Medium-Low Income 20%	中等收入户20% Medium Income 20%	中高收入户20% Medium-High Income 20%	高收入户20% High Income 20%
平均每户常住人口 (人)	Permanent Population Per Household (person)	2.6	3.2	2.8	2.6	2.5	2.3
平均每户就业人口数 (人)	Average Employee Per Household (person)	1.3	1.4	1.4	1.2	1.2	1.2
平均每一就业者负担人数 (人)	Dependents Per Employee (person)	1.6	2.0	1.6	1.5	1.4	1.2
平均每人年可支配收入 (元)	Per Capita Annual Disposable Income (yuan)	57275	25812	41555	53829	69501	109429
平均每人年消费支出 (元)	Per Capita Annual Consumption Expenditures (yuan)	38256	20476	28909	36156	46586	66743

9–15 城镇居民家庭人均可支配收入(2016年)

单位：元

项目	Item	全市平均 Average
可支配收入	**Disposable Income**	**57275**
工资性收入	**Wage Income**	**35701**
工资	Wage	32502
实物福利	Benefit in Kind	179
其他	Other Income from Work	3020
经营净收入	**Net Income from Operations**	**1292**
第一产业经营净收入	Net Income from Operations in the Primary Industry	3
第二产业经营净收入	Net Income from Operations in the Secondary Industry	168
第三产业经营净收入	Net Income from Operations in the Tertiary Industry	1120
财产净收入	**Net Property Income**	**9310**
利息净收入	Net Interest Income	-32
红利收入	Dividend Income	288
储蓄性保险净收益	Net Income from Saving Insurance	5
转让承包土地经营权租金净收入	Net Rent from Transfer of Contracted Land Management Right	15
出租房屋净收入	Net Income from House Rent	1377
出租机械专利版权等资产的收入	Income from Lease of Assets such as Mechanical Patent Copyright	15
其他财产净收入	Other Net Property Income	-36
自有住房折算净租金	Converted Net Rent from Owner-Occupied Housing	7678
转移净收入	**Net Transfer Income**	**10972**
转移性收入	Transfer Income	15285
#养老金或离退休金	Pensions or Retirement Payments	14225
社会救济和补助	Social Relief and Subsidies	36
赡养收入	Alimony Income	109
其他经常转移收入	Other Current Transfer Income	107
#失业保险金	Unemployment Insurance Benefits	13
经常性捐赠收入	Recurrent Donation Income	1
其他转移性收入	Other Transfer Income	93
转移性支出	Transfer Expenditures	4313
非收入所得	**Non-revenue Proceeds**	**1605**
出售资产所得	Proceeds from assets sales	363
#出售住房本金所得	Proceeds from Selling Housing Principal	152
出售住房溢价所得(含亏损)	Proceeds from Selling Housing Premium (including losses)	12
出售其他财物和收回其他投资本金所得	Proceeds from Property Sales and Taking other Investment Principal back	36
非经常性转移所得	Non-recurrent Transfer Proceeds	1239
#提取住房公积金	Withdrawing Public Reserve Fund for Housing	242
调查补贴	Survey Subsidy	709
其他非收入所得	Other Non-revenue Proceeds	3
借贷性所得	**Loan Proceeds**	**1632**

注：城镇居民人均可支配收入实际增长6.9%。

PER CAPITA DISPOSABLE INCOME OF URBAN HOUSEHOLDS (2016)

(yuan)

低 收 入 户 20% Low Income 20%	中 低 收入户 20% Medium- Low Income 20%	中 等 收入户 20% Medium Income 20%	中 高 收入户 20% Medium- High Income 20%	高 收 入 户 20% High Income 20%	2016年为 2015年% 2016 as % of 2015
25812	**41555**	**53829**	**69501**	**109429**	**108.4**
17478	**25102**	**31079**	**38770**	**75156**	**109.6**
16529	22932	28149	34957	68007	109.1
45	216	218	140	317	128.1
903	1954	2712	3673	6832	114.1
1194	**1283**	**1468**	**846**	**1705**	**96.6**
7	4	…	2		50.7
146	69	176	200	275	163.5
1041	1210	1293	645	1430	91.2
3979	**6705**	**8447**	**11726**	**18015**	**109.6**
-53	12	-27	-108	24	-50.8
371	283	194	98	490	162.6
2		13	7	5	59.7
16	16	4	35		81.6
825	1382	1769	1103	1967	124.4
	72				1500.5
-8	-40	-44	-20	-78	516.1
2827	4980	6538	10611	15608	107.8
3160	**8465**	**12834**	**18159**	**14553**	**104.9**
5054	11175	16331	22598	24896	108.7
4492	10580	15247	21274	22917	107.0
59	27	2	2	89	118.8
65	47	124	117	217	132.5
166	96	188	18	46	108.5
35	13	2		10	327.6
2		3			43.6
129	81	184	18	36	100.2
1893	2710	3497	4439	10344	119.7
1323	**992**	**1133**	**1676**	**3173**	**81.5**
398	7	30	211	1292	57.4
17			79	778	
51					
10	6	4	77	98	137.0
918	979	1102	1465	1880	94.4
59	137	87	390	630	113.9
573	660	725	755	874	108.6
7	6	1		1	13.5
950	**1151**	**1138**	**1621**	**3715**	**48.9**

Note: Real growth rate of the per capita annual disposable income is 6.9%.

9-16 城镇居民家庭人均总支出(2016年)

单位：元

项目	Item	全市平均 Average
家庭总支出	**Total Expenditures of Households**	**47370**
消费支出	**Consumption Expenditures**	**38256**
#车辆保险支出	Expenditures of Automotive Insurance	175
生产经营费用支出	**Expenditures of Production and Operating Costs**	**274**
第一产业经营费用支出	Operating Cost Expenditures in the Primary Industry	3
第二产业经营费用支出	Operating Cost Expenditures in the Secondary Industry	83
第三产业经营费用支出	Operating Cost Expenditures in the Tertiary Industry	188
财产性支出	**Property Expenditures**	**200**
转移性支出	**Transfer Expenditures**	**4313**
个人所得税	Individual Income Tax	893
社会保障支出	Social Security Expenditures	2921
个人缴纳的养老保险	Pensions Paid by Individual	2202
个人缴纳的医疗保险	Medical Funds Paid by Individual	653
个人缴纳的失业保险	Unemployment Funds Paid by Individual	62
其他社会保障支出	Other Social Security Expenditures	5
外来从业人员寄给家人的支出	Expenditures of Outside Employees for Their Family	95
赡养支出	Alimony Expenditures	277
其他转移性支出	Other Transfer Expenditures	127
部分商业保险支出	**Partially Commercial Insurance Expenditures**	**244**
意外伤害保险	Accident Insurance	24
商业医疗保险(含大病保险)	Commercial Medical Insurance (including Critical Illness Insurance)	136
其他非储蓄性商业保险	Other Non-saving Commercial Insurance	10
其他储蓄性商业保险	Other Saving Commercial Insurance	74
购置资产及非经常性转移支出	**Expenditures of Acquisition Assets and Non-recurrent Transfer**	**2464**
购置资产支出	Acquisition Asset Expenditures	1098
#建造住房支出	Expenditures of Building Houses	71
购买住房支出	Expenditures of Purchasing Houses	957
非经常性转移支出	Non-recurrent Transfer Expenditures	1367
#一次性馈赠支出	Disposable Donation Expenditures	664
借贷性支出	**Credit Expenditures**	**1620**
#存入储蓄款	Saving Deposits	624
归还借款	Repayment of Loans	82
购买有价证券	Purchase of Securities	59
归还住房贷款	Repayment of Housing Loan	697
归还汽车贷款	Repayment of Automobile Loans	53

PER CAPITA ANNUAL EXPENDITURES OF URBAN HOUSEHOLDS (2016)

(yuan)

低收入户 20% Low Income 20%	中低收入户 20% Medium-Low Income 20%	中等收入户 20% Medium Income 20%	中高收入户 20% Medium-High Income 20%	高收入户 20% High Income 20%	2016年为2015年% 2016 as % of 2015
25112	**34602**	**43817**	**56573**	**86775**	**98.9**
20476	**28909**	**36156**	**46586**	**66743**	**104.4**
118	135	151	189	313	106.1
306	**245**	**214**	**546**	**25**	**145.0**
8	2	…	5		50.0
11	2		419		1037.5
287	241	213	122	25	107.4
111	**112**	**132**	**300**	**391**	**142.9**
1893	**2710**	**3497**	**4439**	**10345**	**119.7**
53	165	358	779	3672	140.0
1609	2023	2661	3387	5564	112.9
1146	1505	1986	2598	4280	113.0
420	476	613	712	1157	112.0
36	41	58	69	118	117.0
7	1	4	7	8	125.0
14	208	202	44	1	279.4
188	207	195	172	694	98.2
29	107	81	58	415	204.8
112	**105**	**210**	**205**	**676**	**117.3**
24	17	12	11	63	104.4
51	66	100	137	375	134.7
3	2	29	8	10	166.7
35	21	70	49	228	94.9
1498	**1493**	**2341**	**2778**	**4733**	**49.7**
528	554	1164	1039	2523	29.2
233	73			…	76.3
271	372	1093	975	2433	28.0
970	940	1178	1740	2210	114.1
396	402	569	750	1355	122.1
716	**1027**	**1267**	**1718**	**3862**	**74.4**
259	552	486	823	1144	47.5
32	33	56	109	208	122.4
46		12	3	267	76.6
328	311	523	663	1902	118.7
19	58	56	17	130	143.2

9-17 城镇居民家庭人均消费支出(2016年)
PER CAPITA CONSUMPTION EXPENDITURES OF URBAN HOUSEHOLDS (2016)

单位：元 (yuan)

项　目	Item	全市平均 Average	低收入户20% Low Income 20%	中低收入户20% Medium-Low Income 20%	中等收入户20% Medium Income 20%	中高收入户20% Medium-High Income 20%	高收入户20% High Income 20%	2016年为2015年% 2016 as % of 2015
人均消费支出	**Per Capita Consumption Expenditures**	**38256**	**20476**	**28909**	**36156**	**46586**	**66743**	**104.4**
食品烟酒支出	Expenditures of Foods, Tobacco and Liquor	8070	5430	7193	8350	9165	11106	99.7
衣着支出	Clothing Expenditures	2643	1481	2112	2709	2924	4465	99.7
居住支出	Housing Expenditures	12128	5548	8303	10313	15880	23604	107.8
生活用品及服务支出	Expenditures of Living Articles and Services	2511	1250	1862	2333	3128	4524	110.5
交通和通信支出	Expenditures of Transportation and Communication	5078	2771	3751	4880	5933	9077	104.5
教育、文化和娱乐支出	Educational, Cultural and Recreational Expenditures	4055	2378	2886	3771	4843	7178	100.7
医疗保健支出	Healthcare Expenditures	2630	1163	2108	2619	3307	4514	111.0
其他用品及服务支出	Expenditures of Other Goods and Services	1141	456	694	1181	1405	2275	102.1

注：城镇居民人均消费支出实际增长3.0%。

Note: Real growth rate of the per capita consumption expenditures of urban residents is 3.0%.

9-18 城镇居民家庭人均消费支出构成(2016年)
COMPOSITION OF PER CAPITA CONSUMPTION EXPENDITURES OF URBAN HOUSEHOLDS (2016)

单位：% (%)

项目	Item	全市平均 Average	低收入户20% Low Income 20%	中低收入户20% Medium-Low Income 20%	中等收入户20% Medium Income 20%	中高收入户20% Medium-High Income 20%	高收入户20% High Income 20%
人均消费支出	**Per Capita Consumption Expenditures**	**100.0**	**100.0**	**100.0**	**100.0**	**100.0**	**100.0**
食品烟酒支出	Expenditures of Foods, Tobacco and Liquor	21.1	26.5	24.9	23.1	19.7	16.6
(恩格尔系数)	(Engel Coefficient)						
衣着支出	Clothing Expenditures	6.9	7.2	7.3	7.5	6.3	6.7
居住支出	Housing Expenditures	31.7	27.1	28.7	28.5	34.1	35.4
生活用品及服务支出	Expenditures of Living Articles and Services	6.6	6.1	6.4	6.5	6.7	6.8
交通和通信支出	Expenditures of Transportation and Communication	13.3	13.5	13.0	13.5	12.7	13.6
教育、文化和娱乐支出	Educational, Cultural and Recreational Expenditures	10.6	11.6	10.0	10.4	10.4	10.8
医疗保健支出	Healthcare Expenditures	6.9	5.7	7.3	7.2	7.1	6.8
其他用品及服务支出	Expenditures of Other Goods and Services	3.0	2.2	2.4	3.3	3.0	3.4

9-19 城镇居民家庭人均食品烟酒支出(2016年)
PER CAPITA EXPENDITURES ON FOODS, TOBACCO AND LIQUOR OF URBAN HOUSEHOLDS (2016)

单位：元 (yuan)

项 目	Item	全市平均 Average	低收入户20% Low Income 20%	中低收入户20% Medium-Low Income 20%	中等收入户20% Medium Income 20%	中高收入户20% Medium-High Income 20%	高收入户20% High Income 20%
食品烟酒支出	**Expenditures of Foods, Tobacco and Liquor**	**8070**	**5430**	**7193**	**8350**	**9165**	**11106**
食 品	Foods	4778	3585	4490	5010	5350	5781
谷 物	Grain	543	396	533	557	521	756
薯 类	Potatoes	64	55	60	61	75	69
豆 类	Beans	64	51	59	65	74	72
食用油	Edible Oil	219	191	223	244	226	209
蔬菜和食用菌	Vegetables and Edible Mushrooms	604	517	564	620	678	661
肉 类	Meat	949	760	959	996	1066	997
禽 类	Poultry	155	121	145	163	175	178
水产品	Aquatic Products	330	204	292	367	397	426
蛋 类	Eggs	135	110	124	139	154	151
奶 类	Milk	394	263	359	427	448	512
干鲜瓜果类	Nuts, Fresh Melons and Fruits	754	527	665	772	900	978
糖果糕点类	Sweets and Cakes	291	178	247	312	341	415
食 糖	Sugar	14	12	13	14	15	14
糖 果	Sweets	32	19	26	35	38	49
糕 点	Cakes	162	99	142	176	187	226
其他糖果糕点	Other Sweets and Cakes	81	47	65	85	99	122
其他食品	Other Foods	278	211	259	287	296	356
#调味品	Flavoring	145	110	139	152	168	167
烟 酒	Tobacco and Liquor	609	490	584	667	634	696
烟 草	Tobacco	328	287	327	378	322	329
酒 类	Liquor	281	202	258	289	313	367
饮 料	Beverages	358	235	339	418	393	436
饮食服务	Catering Services	2326	1120	1780	2254	2788	4193

9–20 城镇居民家庭人均衣着、居住支出(2016年)
PER CAPITA EXPENDITURES ON FOODS, TOBACCO AND LIQUOR OF URBAN HOUSEHOLDS (2016)

单位：元 (yuan)

项 目	Item	全市平均 Average	低收入户20% Low Income 20%	中低收入户20% Medium-Low Income 20%	中等收入户20% Medium Income 20%	中高收入户20% Medium-High Income 20%	高收入户20% High Income 20%
衣着支出	**Clothing Expenditures**	**2643**	**1481**	**2112**	**2709**	**2924**	**4465**
衣 类	Clothes	1922	1026	1511	1949	2134	3361
服 装	Garments	1770	952	1359	1798	1985	3104
服装材料	Clothing Materials	8	6	9	6	11	11
其他衣类及配件	Other Clothes and Accessories	102	55	83	96	118	177
衣着加工服务费	Service Fees for Clothing Processing	8	3	6	11	10	12
鞋 类	Footwear	721	455	602	759	790	1104
居住支出	**Housing Expenditures**	**12128**	**5548**	**8303**	**10313**	**15880**	**23604**
租赁房房租	House Rent	535	496	554	492	439	714
住房维修及管理	Housing Maintenance and Management	942	471	496	505	1545	1949
#住房装潢	Housing Decoration	668	326	328	283	1192	1400
住房维修	Housing Maintenance	99	108	59	92	107	130
物业管理费	Property Management Fees	164	32	101	121	235	391
水电燃料及其他	Water, Electricity, Fuels and Others	1191	923	1126	1282	1251	1448
#水 费	Water	151	94	126	152	189	214
电 费	Electricity	415	359	375	466	426	461
燃 料	Fuels	233	291	235	218	195	202
自有住房折算租金	Converted Rent from Owner-Occupied Housing	9460	3659	6127	8035	12646	19493

9-21 城镇居民家庭人均生活用品及服务、交通和通信支出(2016年)
PER CAPITA EXPENDITURES ON LIVING ARTICLES AND SERVICES, TRANSPORTATION AND COMMUNICATION OF URBAN HOUSEHOLDS (2016)

单位：元 (yuan)

项目	Item	全市平均 Average	低收入户20% Low Income 20%	中低收入户20% Medium-Low Income 20%	中等收入户20% Medium Income 20%	中高收入户20% Medium-High Income 20%	高收入户20% High Income 20%
生活用品及服务支出	**Expenditures of Living Articles and Services**	**2511**	**1250**	**1862**	**2333**	**3128**	**4524**
家具及室内装饰品	Furniture and Interior Decorations	484	147	238	308	852	1036
家具	Furniture	434	130	216	271	798	897
家具材料	Furniture Materials	5	3	3	2	6	12
室内装饰品	Interior Decorations	45	14	19	34	48	127
家用器具	Household Appliances	568	330	477	513	725	887
耐用消费品	Durable Consumer Goods	445	267	375	410	580	657
小家电	Small Appliance	123	63	100	101	146	230
家用纺织品	Household Textile	191	96	151	208	240	297
#床上用品	Bedding	169	85	135	185	215	254
家庭日用杂品	Daily Groceries for Households	551	347	472	543	577	898
个人用品	Personal Articles	505	277	447	524	513	848
家庭服务	Domestic Services	212	53	77	237	221	558
交通和通信支出	**Expenditures of Transportation and Communication**	**5078**	**2771**	**3751**	**4880**	**5933**	**9077**
交通	Transportation	3741	1875	2578	3489	4433	7199
#交通工具	Vehicles	1206	601	743	1065	1568	2350
交通费	Transportation Expenses	914	375	610	869	988	1985
通信	Communication	1337	896	1173	1391	1501	1878
通信工具	Communication Devices	408	231	362	422	481	606
通信服务	Communication Services	929	665	811	969	1020	1272

9-22 城镇居民家庭人均教育文化和娱乐、医疗保健、其他用品及服务支出(2016年)

PER CAPITA EXPENDITURES ON EDUCATION, CULTURE, RECREATION, HEALTHCARE, OTHER GOODS AND SERVICES OF URBAN HOUSEHOLDS (2016)

单位：元 (yuan)

项目	Item	全市平均 Average	低收入户20% Low Income 20%	中低收入户20% Medium-Low Income 20%	中等收入户20% Medium Income 20%	中高收入户20% Medium-High Income 20%	高收入户20% High Income 20%
教育、文化和娱乐支出	**Educational, Cultural and Recreational Expenditures**	**4055**	**2378**	**2886**	**3771**	**4843**	**7178**
教育	Education	1420	1371	1166	1189	1436	2013
#学杂费	Tuition for Compulsory Education	356	434	262	304	312	458
培训费	Training Fees	611	340	549	532	647	1104
一揽子教育服务(含食宿)	A Package of Education Services (including Accommodation)	314	462	213	246	312	304
学前教育	Pre-school Education	510	494	342	453	574	720
小学教育	Primary Education	327	195	288	298	377	531
初中教育	Junior Secondary Education	102	90	129	58	76	165
高中教育	Senior Secondary Education	137	114	165	121	102	188
中专职高教育	Secondary Vocational Education	7	13	4	8	6	1
大专及以上教育	Education for Junior College and Above	234	392	158	173	207	197
成人教育	Adult Education	103	72	81	77	94	210
文化和娱乐	Culture and Recreation	2635	1007	1720	2582	3407	5165
文娱耐用消费品	Durable Consumer Goods for Cultural Recreation	376	166	251	364	441	756
其他文娱用品	Other Cultural and Recreational Articles	451	224	326	473	530	796
文化娱乐服务	Cultural and Recreational Services	1808	617	1143	1746	2437	3612
医疗保健支出	**Healthcare Expenditures**	**2630**	**1163**	**2108**	**2619**	**3307**	**4514**
医疗器具及药品	Medical Apparatus and Medicine	871	466	635	914	963	1557
药品	Medicine	493	357	435	473	579	669
滋补保健品	Nutritious Healthcare Products	298	83	151	347	311	700
医疗卫生器具	Medical and Hygienic Apparatus	33	11	21	33	43	68
保健器具	Healthcare Apparatus	43	14	13	58	29	118
医疗服务	Medical Services	1758	697	1473	1705	2344	2957
其他用品及服务支出	**Expenditures of Other Goods and Services**	**1141**	**456**	**694**	**1181**	**1405**	**2275**
其他用品	Other Goods	609	244	361	655	796	1147
其他服务	Services	532	212	333	527	609	1129

9-23 城镇居民家庭每百户主要耐用消费品拥有量(1978-2016年) NUMBER OF MAIN DURABLE CONSUMER GOODS PER 100 URBAN HOUSEHOLDS (1978-2016)

年份 Year	热水器 (台) Water Heaters (unit)	洗衣机 (台) Washing Machines (unit)	彩色电视机 (台) Color TV Sets (unit)	电冰箱 (台) Refrigerators (unit)	照相机 (台) Cameras (unit)	空调器 (台) Air Conditioners (unit)	计算机 (台) Computers (unit)	移动电话 (部) Mobile Phones (unit)	家用汽车 (辆) Household Cars (unit)
1978					8				
1979		…			10				
1980		2		…	11				
1981		12	2	2	13				
1982		19	2	3	17				
1983		29	4	7	21				
1984		42	8	15	29				
1985		58	32	42	35				
1986		76	51	62	47				
1987		83	58	72	56				
1988		86	70	81	60				
1989		90	81	89	62				
1990		93	91	96	67				
1991		93	97	102	73	…			
1992	17	96	101	101	77	1			
1993	23	100	107	101	82	2			
1994	39	103	112	104	85	5			
1995	45	100	114	104	87	12			
1996	52	101	119	105	87	14			
1997	58	101	124	104	88	27	12	1	1
1998	65	102	133	105	95	34	15	3	1
1999	67	100	141	103	95	50	24	13	3
2000	74	103	146	107	96	70	32	28	3
2001	78	102	149	107	101	90	45	62	3
2002	84	99	148	102	100	107	56	94	4
2003	85	99	147	100	103	119	68	134	7
2004	94	102	151	103	100	136	79	165	13
2005	97	105	153	104	109	147	89	190	14
2006	98	107	155	105	113	157	96	206	18
2007	99	102	147	108	99	157	92	207	20
2008	95	99	134	103	82	152	86	191	23
2009	98	100	138	104	89	163	97	213	30
2010	98	100	140	103	92	169	104	221	34
2011	97	100	138	103	85	171	104	215	38
2012	99	101	141	103	90	179	112	226	42
2013	99	100	140	103	85	180	110	225	43
2014	99	101	141	104	88	186	114	229	45
2015	93	96	130	98	65	161	107	220	47
2016	93	95	127	97	58	166	103	223	49

9-24 城镇居民家庭每百户主要耐用消费品拥有量(2016年) NUMBER OF MAIN DURABLE CONSUMER GOODS PER 100 URBAN HOUSEHOLDS (2016)

项目		Item		全市平均 Average	低收入户20% Low Income 20%	中低收入户20% Medium-Low Income 20%	中等收入户20% Medium Income 20%	中高收入户20% Medium-High Income 20%	高收入户20% High Income 20%
家用汽车	(辆)	Household Cars	(unit)	49	37	42	45	57	63
摩托车	(辆)	Motorcycles	(unit)	2	3	3	2	3	1
助力车	(台)	Powered Bicycles	(unit)	19	32	20	18	15	12
洗衣机	(台)	Washing Machines	(unit)	95	95	88	94	99	100
电冰箱(柜)	(台)	Refrigerators	(unit)	97	97	91	94	101	103
微波炉	(台)	Microwave Ovens	(unit)	80	71	74	81	88	88
彩色电视机	(台)	Color TV Sets	(unit)	127	119	119	123	135	137
#接入有线电视网络的电视机	(台)	TV Sets Accessed to Cable TV Network	(unit)	112	105	105	108	121	120
空调	(台)	Air Conditioners	(unit)	166	137	150	160	186	200
热水器	(台)	Water Heaters	(unit)	93	92	87	93	96	98
消毒碗柜	(台)	Disinfection cabinets	(unit)	5	2	4	3	8	10
洗碗机	(台)	Dishwashers	(unit)	2	…	1	2	2	3
移动电话	(部)	Mobile Phones	(unit)	223	228	224	220	231	214
#接入互联网的移动电话	(部)	Mobile Phones Accessed to the Internet	(unit)	162	149	163	157	171	169
计算机	(台)	Computers	(unit)	103	89	91	102	112	124
#接入互联网的计算机	(台)	Computers Accessed to the Internet	(unit)	95	80	84	94	103	115
摄像机	(台)	Video Cameras	(unit)	19	6	14	16	25	32
照相机	(台)	Cameras	(unit)	58	35	47	58	70	83
中高档乐器	(架)	Musical Instruments of Middle and High-grade	(unit)	9	3	6	8	11	14
健身器材	(台)	Fitness Equipment	(unit)	7	4	4	8	8	13
组合音响	(套)	Audio Systems	(set)	6	2	5	6	8	11

9–25 农村居民家庭基本情况(1978–2016年)
BASIC LIVING CONDITIONS OF RURAL HOUSEHOLDS (1978-2016)

年份 Year	人均可支配收入(元) Per Capita Disposable Income (yuan)	人均可支配收入实际增长(%) Actual Growth Rate of Per Capita Disposable Income (%)	人均总支出(元) Per Capita Total Expen-ditures (yuan)	人均消费支出(元) Per Capita Consumption Expen-ditures (yuan)	#食品烟酒 Foods Tobacco and Liquor	农村居民家庭恩格尔系数(%) Engel Coefficient of Rural Households (%)	每一农村劳动力负担人数(人) Dependents Per Rural Labor Force (person)	农村居民人均住房面积(平方米) Per Capita Living Space of Rural Residents (sq.m)
1978	224.8		219.0	185.4	116.7	63.2	2.15	9.20
1979	250.0	10.9	235.0	204.7	131.1	63.9	2.16	9.67
1980	308.1	22.1	290.0	256.8	140.2	54.1	2.13	10.09
1981	361.4	17.1	350.5	307.2	160.6	52.3	2.14	12.35
1982	430.2	17.3	411.2	345.5	181.1	52.4	1.97	13.01
1983	519.5	20.9	498.5	384.4	193.8	50.4	1.82	14.24
1984	664.2	25.7	559.3	435.0	222.5	51.1	1.79	14.22
1985	775.1	14.5	726.0	510.0	240.5	47.1	1.64	16.48
1986	823.1	3.7	857.0	645.3	292.4	45.3	1.66	17.41
1987	916.4	6.5	943.0	705.5	340.9	48.3	1.64	18.38
1988	1062.6	3.1	1246.0	883.3	407.9	46.2	1.63	19.23
1989	1230.7	2.2	1356.0	976.3	484.3	49.6	1.62	20.09
1990	1297.1	2.1	1372.0	980.7	497.0	50.7	1.61	20.62
1991	1422.3	1.7	1585.0	1100.1	537.0	48.8	1.59	21.92
1992	1568.8	2.0	1684.0	1179.0	573.8	48.7	1.58	22.67
1993	1854.8	5.1	1714.0	1308.9	611.7	46.8	1.51	23.70
1994	2422.1	9.1	2175.0	1676.5	824.8	49.2	1.49	24.42
1995	3208.5	6.3	3080.0	2433.0	1206.0	49.6	1.47	24.74
1996	3562.7	4.8	3272.0	2655.5	1233.1	46.4	1.45	25.74
1997	3762.4	5.1	3379.0	2795.4	1248.4	44.7	1.48	27.39
1998	4028.9	6.7	3617.0	2945.5	1241.9	42.2	1.44	27.64
1999	4316.4	7.2	3938.0	3132.5	1253.5	40.0	1.43	28.65
2000	4687.0	7.3	4517.9	3441.4	1263.6	36.7	1.51	28.91
2001	5274.3	8.7	5098.8	3871.5	1353.2	34.9	1.52	31.01
2002	5880.1	12.3	5548.7	4206.0	1386.6	33.0	1.48	32.58
2003	6496.3	11.5	5886.6	4655.3	1475.6	31.7	1.45	33.95
2004	7172.1	9.2	6275.2	4886.4	1592.3	32.6	1.46	34.21
2005	7860.0	8.1	7181.2	5515.0	1807.0	32.8	1.45	36.94
2006	8620.0	8.7	7935.0	6061.0	1937.0	32.0	1.42	39.10
2007	9559.0	8.2	8866.0	6828.0	2190.0	32.1	1.40	39.54
2008	10747.0	6.5	10166.0	7656.0	2629.0	34.3	1.40	39.40
2009	11986.0	13.4	11814.0	9141.0	2961.0	32.4	1.39	39.42
2010	13262.0	8.1	12805.0	10109.0	3121.0	30.9	1.39	40.62
2011	14736.0	7.6	14503.0	11078.0	3593.0	32.4	1.38	48.63
2012	16476.0	8.2	15196.0	11879.0	3945.0	33.2	1.40	49.08
2013	18337.0	7.7	16994.0	13553.0	4696.0	34.6	1.49	51.35
2014	20226.0	8.6	18011.0	14529.0	5043.0	34.7	1.50	52.42
2015	20569.0	7.1	22823.0	15811.0	4372.0	27.7	1.60	43.03
2016	22310.0	7.0	24696.0	17329.0	4667.0	26.9	1.62	44.50

注：2015年开始，根据国家统计局城乡居民统计新口径要求，“农村居民人均纯收入”统一改为“人均可支配收入”。

Note: According to the requirements of the National Bureau of Statistics on the new statistical range for urban and rural residents, "per capita net income of rural residents" shall be modified as "per capita disposable income" since 2015.

9-26 农村居民家庭基本情况(按收入水平分)(2016年) BASIC DATA ON RURAL HOUSEHOLDS (BY INCOME LEVEL) (2016)

项目	Item	全市平均 Average	低收入户20% Low Income 20%	中低收入户20% Medium-Low Income 20%	中等收入户20% Medium Income 20%	中高收入户20% Medium-High Income 20%	高收入户20% High Income 20%
平均每户常住人口 (人)	Permanent Population Per Household (person)	3.0	2.9	3.1	3.2	2.9	2.6
平均每户整半劳动力 (个)	Full/Semi Labor Force Per Household (person)	2.4	2.2	2.5	2.6	2.5	2.2
平均每一劳动力负担人口 (人)	Dependents Per Labor Force (person)	1.6	2.0	1.8	1.6	1.5	1.3
人均住房面积 (平方米)	Per Capita Living Space (sq.m)	44.50	46.11	38.99	41.85	47.47	51.53
人均可支配收入 (元)	Per Capita Disposable Income (yuan)	22310	9359	17029	21903	27609	39008
人均消费支出 (元)	Per Capita Consumption Expenditures (yuan)	17329	14061	14203	16418	20005	23803
农村居民家庭恩格尔系数 (%)	Engel Coefficient of Rural Households (%)	26.9	25.6	28.0	27.2	27.3	26.6

9-27 农村居民家庭人均可支配收入(2016年)

单位：元

项目	Item	全市平均 Average
人均可支配收入	**Per Capita Disposable Income**	**22310**
生产性收入	**Productive Income**	**18699**
工资性收入	**Wage Income**	**16637**
工资	Wage	15789
实物福利	Benefit in Kind	138
其他	Other Income from Work	711
经营净收入	**Net Income from Operations**	**2062**
第一产业净收入	Net Income from the Primary Industry	484
#农业收入	Agricultural Income	456
牧业收入	Animal Husbandry Income	54
第二产业净收入	Net Income from the Secondary Industry	95
#工业收入	Industrial Income	34
第三产业净收入	Net Income from the Tertiary Industry	1483
#交通运输业收入	Transportation Income	793
非生产性收入	**Non-productive Income**	**3610**
财产净收入	**Net Property Income**	**1350**
利息净收入	Net Interest Income	24
红利收入	Dividend Income	427
#集体分配的红利	Dividend Distributed by the Collective	427
储蓄性保险净收益	Net Income from Saving Insurance	
转让承包土地经营权租金净收入	Net Rent from Transfer of Contracted Land Management Right	225
出租房屋净收入	Net Income from House Rent	673
出租机械专利版权等资产的收入	Income from Lease of Assets such as Mechanical Patent Copyright	
其他财产净收入	Other Net Property Income	…
自有住房折算净租金	Converted Net Rent from Owner-Occupied Housing	
转移净收入	**Net Transfer Income**	**2260**
转移性收入	**Transfer Income**	**3940**
#养老金或离退休金	Pensions or Retirement Payments	2715
家庭外出从业人员寄回带回收入	Income from Family Members Going out for a Job	123
其他经常转移收入	Other Current Transfer Income	217
#经常性捐赠收入	Recurrent Donation Income	
现金政策性惠农补贴	Subsidies Benefiting Peasants under Cash Policy	54
转移性支出	**Transfer Expenditures**	**1680**

注：农村居民人均可支配收入实际增长7.0%。

PER CAPITA DISPOSABLE INCOME OF RURAL HOUSEHOLDS (2016)

(yuan)

低收入户 20% Low Income 20%	中低收入户 20% Medium-Low Income 20%	中等收入户 20% Medium Income 20%	中高收入户 20% Medium-High Income 20%	高收入户 20% High Income 20%	2016年为2015年% 2016 as % of 2015
9359	**17029**	**21903**	**27609**	**39008**	**108.5**
7143	**14292**	**19612**	**22621**	**32493**	**107.2**
6403	**11766**	**17428**	**20534**	**29578**	**107.4**
6215	11248	16651	19600	27542	108.2
12	40	138	153	391	84.2
176	478	638	781	1645	97.0
740	**2526**	**2185**	**2087**	**2915**	**105.3**
1	413	654	603	795	88.7
348	255	594	601	506	105.9
-96	152	58	3	157	58.9
-181	206	99	134	229	118.8
-111	128		16	149	180.4
920	1908	1432	1350	1891	111.2
552	1505	673	623	582	124.3
2216	**2737**	**2290**	**4988**	**6515**	**115.7**
523	**1062**	**1259**	**1595**	**2542**	**112.1**
25	5	22	53	18	71.1
288	367	465	635	397	106.3
287	367	464	635	397	106.2
140	187	195	124	533	128.8
70	482	562	808	1610	122.2
1	21	14	-26	-16	
1694	**1674**	**1032**	**3393**	**3973**	**118.0**
2579	**2917**	**3060**	**5149**	**6646**	**113.3**
1714	2011	1999	3773	4536	111.8
19	99	73	154	301	92.2
102	198	272	246	279	128.4
61	37	57	58	60	81.3
885	**1243**	**2028**	**1756**	**2673**	**107.5**

Note: Real growth rate of the per capita disposable income of rural residents is 7.0%.

9–28 农村居民家庭人均消费支出(2016年)
PER CAPITA CONSUMPTION EXPENDITURE OF RURAL HOUSEHOLDS (2016)

单位：元 (Yuan)

项目	Item	全市平均 Average	低收入户20% Low Income 20%	中低收入户20% Medium-Low Income 20%	中等收入户20% Medium Income 20%	中高收入户20% Medium-High Income 20%	高收入户20% High Income 20%	2016年为2015年% 2016 as % of 2015
人均消费支出	**Per Capita Consumption Expenditures**	**17329**	**14061**	**14203**	**16418**	**20005**	**23803**	**109.6**
食品烟酒支出	Expenditures of Foods, Tobacco and Liquor	4667	3594	3978	4458	5451	6325	106.7
衣着支出	Clothing Expenditures	1095	668	912	1059	1384	1573	109.9
居住支出	Housing Expenditures	5199	4787	4178	4457	5889	7311	112.1
生活用品及服务支出	Expenditures of Living Articles and Services	1157	819	1001	1040	1419	1633	116.5
交通和通信支出	Expenditures of Transportation and Communication	2306	1650	1718	2392	2800	3213	107.8
教育、文化和娱乐支出	Educational, Cultural and Recreational Expenditures	1342	1329	1314	1361	1335	1442	117.2
医疗保健支出	Healthcare Expenditures	1347	1090	895	1480	1456	1966	100.8
其他用品及服务支出	Expenditures of Other Goods and Services	217	123	207	171	273	341	112.5

注：农村居民人均消费支出实际增长8.1%。
Note: Real growth rate of the per capita consumption expenditures of rural residents is 8.1%.

9–29 农村居民家庭人均消费支出构成(2016年)
COMPOSITION OF PER CAPITA CONSUMPTION EXPENDITURES OF RURAL HOUSEHOLDS (2016)

单位：% (%)

项目	Item	全市平均 Average	低收入户20% Low Income 20%	中低收入户20% Medium-Low Income 20%	中等收入户20% Medium Income 20%	中高收入户20% Medium-High Income 20%	高收入户20% High Income 20%
人均消费支出	**Per Capita Consumption Expenditures**	**100.0**	**100.0**	**100.0**	**100.0**	**100.0**	**100.0**
食品烟酒支出(恩格尔系数)	Expenditures of Foods, Tobacco and Liquor (Engel Coefficient)	26.9	25.6	28.0	27.2	27.3	26.6
衣着支出	Clothing Expenditures	6.3	4.8	6.4	6.4	6.9	6.6
居住支出	Housing Expenditures	30.0	34.0	29.4	27.1	29.4	30.7
生活用品及服务支出	Expenditures of Living Articles and Services	6.7	5.8	7.0	6.3	7.1	6.9
交通和通信支出	Expenditures of Transportation and Communication	13.3	11.7	12.1	14.6	14.0	13.5
教育、文化和娱乐支出	Educational, Cultural and Recreational Expenditures	7.7	9.5	9.2	8.3	6.7	6.1
医疗保健支出	Healthcare Expenditures	7.8	7.8	6.3	9.0	7.3	8.3
其他用品及服务支出	Expenditures of Other Goods and Services	1.3	0.9	1.5	1.0	1.4	1.4

9–30 农村居民家庭人均食品烟酒、衣着支出(2016年)
PER CAPITA EXPENDITURES ON FOOD, TOBACCO, LIQUOR AND CLOTHING OF RURAL HOUSEHOLDS (2016)

单位：元 (yuan)

项目	Item	全市平均 Average	低收入户20% Low Income 20%	中低收入户20% Medium-Low Income 20%	中等收入户20% Medium Income 20%	中高收入户20% Medium-High Income 20%	高收入户20% High Income 20%
食品烟酒支出	**Expenditures of Foods, Tobacco and Liquor**	**4667**	**3594**	**3978**	**4458**	**5451**	**6325**
食品	Foods	3144	2606	2867	2885	3687	3956
谷物	Grain	452	405	406	394	484	620
薯类	Potatoes	49	48	45	44	55	58
豆类	Beans	53	55	53	45	57	59
食用油	Edible Oil	166	150	145	146	207	194
蔬菜和食用菌	Vegetables and Edible Mushrooms	417	356	393	376	494	499
肉类	Meat	763	619	703	690	917	955
禽类	Poultry	91	73	81	86	108	114
水产品	Aquatic Products	131	98	121	109	169	174
蛋类	Eggs	110	105	101	103	120	128
奶类	Milk	205	128	190	242	241	233
干鲜瓜果类	Nuts, Fresh Melons and Fruits	414	328	367	377	495	541
糖果糕点类	Sweets and Cakes	121	90	101	118	147	158
其他食品	Other Foods	173	151	161	154	193	223
烟酒	Tobacco and Liquor	586	416	528	577	622	850
烟草	Tobacco	373	259	338	357	389	568
酒类	Liquor	213	157	190	220	233	282
饮料	Beverages	189	156	157	169	220	268
饮食服务	Catering Services	747	417	425	827	923	1251
#其他在外饮食	Other Meals at a Restaurant	637	389	377	673	753	1092
衣着支出	**Clothing Expenditures**	**1095**	**668**	**912**	**1059**	**1384**	**1573**
衣类	Clothes	755	434	598	730	966	1140
服装	Garments	687	399	546	672	898	995
服装材料	Clothing Materials	6	5	6	6	7	6
其他衣类及配件	Other Clothes and Accessories	41	27	43	39	45	54
衣着加工服务费	Service Fees for Clothing Processing	3	2	2	4	2	3
鞋类	Footwear	340	234	313	329	418	434

9-31 农村居民家庭人均居住、生活用品及服务、交通和通信支出(2016年)

PER CAPITA EXPENDITURES ON HOUSING, LIVING ARTICLES AND SERVICES, TRANSPORTATION AND COMMUNICATION OF RURAL HOUSEHOLDS (2016)

单位：元 (yuan)

项目	Item	全市平均 Average	低收入户20% Low Income 20%	中低收入户20% Medium-Low Income 20%	中等收入户20% Medium Income 20%	中高收入户20% Medium-High Income 20%	高收入户20% High Income 20%
居住支出	**Housing Expenditures**	**5199**	**4787**	**4178**	**4457**	**5889**	**7311**
租赁房房租	House Rent	91	96	80	52	103	136
住房维修及管理	Housing Maintenance and Management	499	474	410	363	475	859
#住房装潢	Housing Decoration	274	299	273	162	251	428
住房维修	Housing Maintenance	211	171	128	193	213	387
物业管理费	Property Management Fees	9	2	4	5	6	32
水电燃料及其他	Water, Electricity, Fuels and Others	1145	1048	1053	1070	1263	1381
#水　费	Water	12	10	9	12	15	15
电　费	Electricity	478	403	415	457	552	605
燃　料	Fuels	567	570	549	538	611	597
#生活用煤	Living Coals	389	393	362	372	434	406
自有住房折算租金	Converted Rent from Owner-Occupied Housing	3464	3168	2636	2972	4048	4935
生活用品及服务支出	**Expenditures of Living Articles and Services**	**1157**	**819**	**1001**	**1040**	**1419**	**1633**
家具及室内装饰品	Furniture and Interior Decorations	150	121	105	116	177	256
家　具	Furniture	131	105	94	101	160	220
家具材料	Furniture Materials	4	4	1	4	3	7
室内装饰品	Interior Decorations	15	12	9	11	15	30
家用器具	Household Appliances	414	256	381	366	517	594
耐用消费品	Durable Consumer Goods	365	220	337	327	457	524
小家电	Small Appliance	48	36	44	39	59	69
家用纺织品	Household Textile	97	69	83	81	113	155
#床上用品	Bedding	75	50	68	59	96	111
家庭日用杂品	Daily Groceries for Households	300	245	274	280	362	362
个人用品	Personal Articles	174	111	137	186	222	230
家庭服务	Domestic Services	22	16	22	11	27	36
交通和通信支出	**Expenditures of Transportation and Communication**	**2306**	**1650**	**1718**	**2392**	**2800**	**3213**
交　通	Transportation	1513	1027	975	1563	1958	2228
#交通工具	Vehicles	357	265	147	458	524	421
交通费	Transportation Expenses	211	122	172	221	264	297
通　信	Communication	793	623	743	829	842	985
通讯工具	Communication Devices	184	125	179	211	212	202
通信服务	Communication Services	609	498	564	618	631	783

9-32 农村居民家庭人均教育文化和娱乐、医疗保健、其他用品及服务支出(2016年)

PER CAPITA EXPENDITURES ON EDUCATION, CULTURE, RECREATION, HEALTHCARE, OTHER GOODS AND SERVICES OF RURAL HOUSEHOLDS (2016)

单位：元 (yuan)

项目	Item	全市平均 Average	低收入户20% Low Income 20%	中低收入户20% Medium-Low Income 20%	中等收入户20% Medium Income 20%	中高收入户20% Medium-High Income 20%	高收入户20% High Income 20%
教育、文化和娱乐支出	**Educational, Cultural and Recreational Expenditures**	**1342**	**1329**	**1314**	**1361**	**1335**	**1442**
教育	Education	795	962	878	866	663	608
学杂费	Tuition for Compulsory Education	181	197	237	189	129	153
培训费	Training Fees	139	80	99	135	219	175
一揽子教育服务(含食宿)	A Package of Education Services (including Accommodation)	412	612	470	485	252	226
学前教育	Pre-school Education	123	148	162	108	72	127
小学教育	Primary Education	54	36	54	63	76	40
初中教育	Junior Secondary Education	69	78	66	59	120	23
高中教育	Senior Secondary Education	139	197	113	147	130	110
中专职高教育	Secondary Vocational Education	35	73	66	27	6	…
大专及以上教育	Education for Junior College and Above	316	406	366	393	183	224
成人教育	Adult Education	60	24	51	70	76	83
文化和娱乐	Cultural and Recreational Articles	546	367	435	495	672	834
文娱耐用消费品	Durable Consumer Goods for Cultural Recreation	143	98	112	132	179	208
其他文娱用品	Other Cultural and Recreational Articles	148	140	114	127	181	194
文化娱乐服务	Cultural and Recreational Services	256	128	209	236	312	431
#团体旅游	Group Tour	130	38	86	120	173	261
医疗保健支出	**Healthcare Expenditures**	**1347**	**1090**	**895**	**1480**	**1456**	**1966**
医疗器具及药品	Medical Apparatus and Medicine	521	562	469	514	508	588
药品	Medicine	462	522	421	466	452	474
滋补保健品	Nutritious Healthcare Products	33	23	18	33	35	62
医疗卫生器具	Medical and Hygienic Apparatus	10	10	5	9	16	13
保健器具	Healthcare Apparatus	14	5	25	4	4	36
医疗服务	Medical Services	826	528	426	967	947	1378
其他用品及服务支出	**Expenditures of Other Goods and Services**	**217**	**123**	**207**	**171**	**273**	**341**
其他用品	Other Goods	118	57	134	98	144	166
其他服务	Services	99	66	73	73	128	175

9-33 农村居民家庭人均粮食收支情况(2016年)
PER CAPITA GRAIN BALANCE OF RURAL HOUSEHOLDS (2016)

单位：公斤 (kg)

项目	Item	全市平均 Average	低收入户 20% Low Income 20%	中低收入户 20% Medium-Low Income 20%	中等收入户 20% Medium Income 20%	中高收入户 20% Medium-High Income 20%	高收入户 20% High Income 20%
年内粮食收入实物量	**Grain Collected in the Year**	**219.2**	**241.5**	**253.5**	**221.5**	**223.4**	**155.2**
家庭经营生产	Household-based Production	132.2	152.9	165.9	145.4	124.0	66.9
购买	Purchased	87.0	88.6	87.7	76.0	99.4	88.3
年内粮食消费量	**Grain Consumed in the Year**	**102.1**	**107.1**	**102.6**	**90.0**	**116.0**	**100.2**
#稻谷	Rice	32.0	34.2	32.6	26.0	37.8	31.4
小麦	Wheat	54.7	57.4	55.0	50.3	61.2	52.3
年内粮食出售量	**Grain Sold in the Year**	**102.8**	**159.3**	**145.9**	**98.4**	**61.7**	**43.6**
出售谷物	Cereal Sold	102.6	158.5	145.9	98.4	61.7	43.6
#小麦	Wheat	20.0	29.9	21.7	16.0	29.2	2.2

9-34 农村居民家庭主要食品人均消费量(2016年)
PER CAPITA CONSUMPTION OF MAJOR FOODS OF RURAL HOUSEHOLDS (2016)

单位：公斤 (kg)

项目	Item	全市平均 Average	低收入户 20% Low Income 20%	中低收入户 20% Medium-Low Income 20%	中等收入户 20% Medium Income 20%	中高收入户 20% Medium-High Income 20%	高收入户 20% High Income 20%
粮食	Grain	102.1	107.1	102.6	90.0	116.0	100.2
豆类	Beans	7.7	7.9	7.9	6.8	8.1	8.3
蔬菜及菜制品	Vegetables and Vegetable Products	92.7	90.4	90.2	84.0	101.9	103.4
植物油	Vegetable Oil	9.7	9.9	9.2	8.4	11.6	10.1
猪肉	Pork	14.9	12.9	14.7	13.5	17.1	17.2
牛羊肉	Beef and Mutton	4.7	3.7	4.1	4.2	5.9	6.0
禽类	Poultry	4.4	3.8	4.1	4.1	5.2	5.1
蛋类及其制品	Eggs and Egg Products	11.8	11.7	11.2	11.2	12.8	13.0
奶及奶制品	Milk and Dairy Products	13.3	10.3	11.8	13.9	14.6	16.9
水产品	Aquatic Products	5.7	4.7	5.6	4.8	6.8	6.9
食糖	Sugar	1.3	1.6	1.2	1.0	1.5	1.3
酒类	Liquor	16.9	15.3	15.0	19.0	16.5	19.6
茶叶	Tea	0.5	0.5	0.5	0.4	0.6	0.7
干鲜瓜果类	Nuts, Fresh Melons and Fruits	51.5	45.0	47.7	48.1	58.7	62.0

9-35 农村居民家庭每百户主要耐用消费品拥有量(1985-2016年) NUMBER OF MAIN DURABLE CONSUMER GOODS PER 100 RURAL HOUSEHOLDS (1985-2016)

年 份 Year	移动电话 (部) Mobile Phones (unit)	空调机 (台) Air Conditioners (unit)	彩 色 电视机 (台) Color TV Sets (unit)	家 用 计算机 (台) Computers (unit)	照相机 (架) Cameras (unit)	洗衣机 (台) Washing Machines (unit)	电冰箱 (台) Refrige-rators (unit)	家用汽车 (辆) Household Cars (unit)
1985			7		2	23	2	
1986			12		4	39	5	
1987			15		5	48	9	
1988			20		7	56	14	
1989			25		8	61	19	
1990			29		8	63	23	
1991			42		11	69	36	
1992			46		14	73	40	
1993			56		15	76	47	
1994		1	65		17	80	53	
1995		2	74		21	81	63	
1996		2	79		21	83	67	
1997		3	85		25	84	72	
1998		5	92		26	85	75	
1999		9	101		29	86	81	
2000	14	20	107	7	26	85	84	3
2001	30	27	112	12	29	91	86	5
2002	52	35	116	16	32	94	91	6
2003	77	39	116	22	32	94	94	6
2004	102	47	119	27	35	96	96	8
2005	139	63	129	36	37	97	100	10
2006	161	72	131	41	38	97	100	10
2007	182	78	134	46	37	99	104	11
2008	201	89	137	52	39	101	104	12
2009	212	98	138	58	42	101	105	12
2010	224	107	139	64	42	103	107	16
2011	231	108	134	63	37	99	104	19
2012	235	113	136	67	37	99	103	21
2013	221	123	132	74	32	95	102	34
2014	222	127	132	75	32	97	103	35
2015	230	118	131	69	21	90	95	32
2016	243	135	138	74	20	94	101	38

9-36 农村居民家庭每百户主要耐用消费品拥有量(2016年)
NUMBER OF MAIN DURABLE CONSUMER GOODS PER 100 RURAL HOUSEHOLDS (2016)

项目		Item		全市平均 Average	低收入户20% Low Income 20%	中低收入户20% Low-Medium Income 20%	中等收入户20% Medium Income 20%	中高收入户20% Medium-High Income 20%	高收入户20% High Income 20%
家用汽车	(辆)	Household Cars	(unit)	38	27	30	40	46	47
摩托车	(辆)	Motorcycles	(unit)	10	7	10	12	11	8
助力车	(台)	Powered Bicycles	(unit)	74	65	86	77	78	62
洗衣机	(台)	Washing Machines	(unit)	94	89	98	94	100	89
电冰箱(柜)	(台)	Refrigerators	(unit)	101	102	105	98	106	93
微波炉	(台)	Microwave Ovens	(unit)	55	41	53	58	62	61
彩色电视机	(台)	Color TV Sets	(unit)	138	136	139	139	142	136
#接入有线电视网络的电视机	(台)	TV Sets Accessed to Cable TV Network	(unit)	123	123	127	123	124	117
空调	(台)	Air Conditioners	(unit)	135	112	124	136	161	144
热水器	(台)	Water Heaters	(unit)	99	94	100	98	105	98
消毒碗柜	(台)	Disinfection Cabinets	(unit)	1	1	2	1	1	…
洗碗机	(台)	Dishwashers	(unit)	1			1	…	1
移动电话	(部)	Mobile Phones	(unit)	243	229	253	256	244	234
#接入互联网的移动电话	(部)	Mobile Phones Accessed to the Internet	(unit)	124	109	134	124	118	137
计算机	(台)	Computers	(unit)	74	60	69	81	79	80
#接入互联网的计算机	(台)	Computers Accessed to the Internet	(unit)	65	52	62	71	71	71
摄像机	(台)	Video Cameras	(unit)	3	1	3	3	5	6
照相机	(台)	Cameras	(unit)	20	11	14	18	29	26
中高档乐器	(架)	Musical Instruments of Middle and High-grade	(set)	2	1	…	4	3	1
健身器材	(台)	Fitness Equipment	(set)	2	1	1	2	2	4
组合音响	(套)	Audio Systems	(set)	7	5	4	7	7	9

主要统计指标解释

按照国家统计局要求，自2015年起，我市按照改革后的新口径发布全市和分城乡的居民收支数据。与老口径相比，新口径的差异主要体现在三个方面：一是按照国家城乡划分标准，将城镇地区的村委会由原来的农村划入城镇进行统计；二是对居民收支指标口径进行了调整，将反映居民收入的核心指标由原来的城镇居民“人均可支配收入”和农村居民“人均纯收入”统一为“人均可支配收入”；三是在分城乡的居民收支数据基础上，增加了全体居民的人均可支配收入、人均消费支出数据。

可支配收入 指调查户在调查期内获得的、可用于最终消费支出和储蓄的总和，即调查户可以用来自由支配的收入。可支配收入既包括现金，也包括实物收入。按照收入的来源，可支配收入包含四项，分别为：工资性收入、经营净收入、财产净收入和转移净收入。计算公式为：

可支配收入＝工资性收入+经营净收入+财产净收入+转移净收入

其中：经营净收入=经营收入-经营费用-生产性固定资产折旧-生产税

财产净收入=财产性收入-财产性支出

转移净收入=转移性收入-转移性支出。

工资性收入 指就业人员通过各种途径得到的全部劳动报酬和各种福利，包括受雇于单位或个人、从事各种自由职业、兼职和零星劳动得到的全部劳动报酬和福利。

工资 指就业人员通过劳动从单位或雇主获取的各种现金报酬。

实物福利 指单位或雇主免费或低价提供给员工的各种实物产品和服务折价。

其他 指就业人员获取的、除工资以外的其他现金劳动报酬以及单位缴纳的各种社会保障费。

经营净收入 指住户或住户成员从事生产经营活动所获得的净收入，是全部经营收入中扣除经营费用、生产性固定资产折旧和生产税之后得到的净收入。计算公式为：

经营净收入=经营收入-经营费用-生产性固定资产折旧-生产税

财产净收入 指住户或住户成员将其所拥有的金融资产、住房等非金融资产和自然资源交由其他机构单位、住户或个人支配而获得的回报并扣除相关的费用之后得到的净收入。财产净收入不包括转让资产所有权的溢价所得，计入“非收入所得”。

红利收入 指住户或个人作为股东将其资金交由公司支配或处置而有权获得的收益。包括股票发行公司按入股数量定期分配的股息、年终分红以及从集体财产入股或其他投资分配得到的股息和红利。股票买卖结算后获得的收益（含亏损）不包含在内，计入“非收入所得”。

储蓄性保险净收益 指住户或住户成员参加商业性的储蓄性保险，扣除缴纳的保险本金及相关费用后所获得的保险净收益。不包括保险责任人对保险受益人给予的保险理赔收入。

转移性收入 指国家、单位、社会团体对住户的各种经常性转移支付和住户之间的经常性收入转移。包括养老金或退休金、社会救济和补助、政策性生产补贴、政策性生活补贴、救灾款、经常性捐赠和赔偿、报销医疗费、住户之间的赡养收入，以及本住户非常住成员寄回带回的收入等。转移性收入不包括住户之间的实物馈赠。

其他经常转移收入 指住户从除上述各项转移性收入以外得到的其他经常性转移收入。如经常性捐赠收入、经常性赔偿收入、失业保险金、亲友搭伙费等。

转移净收入 指国家、单位、社会团体对住户的各种经常性转移支付和住户之间的经常性收入转移，在扣减调查户对国家、单位、住户或者个人的经常性或义务性转移支付后的净收入。

计算公式为：转移净收入=转移性收入-转移性支出。

转移性支出 指调查户对国家、单位、住户或个人的经常性或义务性转移支付。包括缴纳的税款、各项社会保障支出、赡养支出、经常性捐赠和赔偿支出以及其他经常转移支出等。

出售资产所得 指调查户出售家庭财物所得到的收入。由于出售财物是家庭财产从实物形态转为货币形态，家庭财产总量不变，因此不计入可支配收入中。

记账补贴 指调查户因承担记账工作从统计部门、工作单位和其他途径所得到的现金和实物折价收入。

借贷性所得 指家庭资产不发生增减的周转性非生产经营性收入。包括提取银行存款、借入款、收回借出款等。

家庭总支出 指包括借贷性支出的全部实际支出。包括消费支出、生产经营费用支出、财产性支出、转移性支出、部分商业保险支出、购置资产及非经常性转移支出、借贷性支出。

消费支出 指住户用于满足家庭日常生活消费需要的全部支出，包括用于消费品的支出和用于服务性消费的支出。根据用途不同，消费支出可划分为食品烟酒、衣着、居住、生活用品及服务、交通和通信、教育文化娱乐、医疗保健、其他用品及服务八大类。根据来源不同，消费支出可划分为现金消费支出、实物消费支出（含自产自用、来自单位或雇主、来自政府和其他社会组织）。

生产经营费用支出 包括农业生产经营费用和非农业生产经营费用。

财产性支出 指家庭购买或维护财产所支付的利息等有关费用。

转移性支出 指调查户对国家、单位、住户或个人的经常性或义务性转移支付。包括缴纳的税款、各项社会保障支出、赡养支出、经常性捐赠和赔偿支出以及其他经常转移支出等。

部分商业保险支出 包括意外伤害保险、商业医疗保险（含大病保险）、其他非储蓄性商业保险、其他储蓄性商业保险。

购置资产及非经常性转移支出 购置资产支出包括建造住房、购买住房的全部支出，以及购建生产性固定资产支出；非经常性转移支出包括博采支出、婚丧嫁娶（礼金、宴请等）支出、一次性赔偿支出、一次性馈赠支出等。

借贷性支出 指包括所有权没有变化的周转性非生产经营性支付，如存入储蓄款、借出款；资金归还，如归还借款、归还各类贷款等。

平均每一劳动力负担人口 是由调查户常住人口除以整半劳动力计算得到的。计算公式为：

$$平均每一劳动力负担人口=\frac{调查户常住人口}{整半劳动力}$$

农村居民家庭整半劳动力 指农村常住居民家庭成员中有劳动能力并经常参加实际劳动的人员。是生产的基本要素指标之一，是发展生产增加农民家庭收入的重要源泉。按规定，农村男18周岁至50周岁、女18周岁至45周岁为整劳动力；男16周岁至17周岁、51周岁到60周岁，女16周岁到17周岁、46周岁至55周岁为半劳动力。农民家庭整半劳动力既包括在上述规定劳动年龄内和在劳动年龄以外有劳动能力并经常参加实际劳动的男女整半劳动力，也包括农民家庭常住人员中属于职工的劳动力。但不包括在劳动年龄内已丧失劳动能力的人员。

现住房总建筑面积 指调查户现住房的总建筑面积。现住房计算总建筑面积时以房屋产权证或租赁证为准，建筑面积也可按使用面积×1.333计算得出。应扣除住房中专门用于出租的建筑面积。

恩格尔系数 随着家庭和个人收入增加，收入中用于食品方面的支出比例将逐渐减小，这一定律被称为恩格尔定律，反映这一定律的系数被称为恩格尔系数。计算公式为：

$$恩格尔系数=\frac{食品支出总额}{家庭或个人消费支出总额}\times 100\%$$

Explanatory Notes on Main Statistical Indicators

According to requirements of National Bureau of Statistics, since 2015, Beijing has started to issue data on income and expense of residents in the city and residents in urban and rural areas according to new standards after the reform. As compared with former standards, the new standards mainly show differences in the following 3 aspects: first, according to national standards on division of urban and rural areas, village committees in urban areas that were classified into rural areas are now classified into urban areas; second, standards on resident income and expense indicators are adjusted. Core indicators reflecting resident income are unified from original "per capita disposable income" of urban residents and "per capita net income" of rural residents to "per capita disposable income"; third, based on data on resident income and expense in urban and rural areas, data on per capita disposable income and per capita consumption expense of residents in Beijing are added.

Disposable Income refers to the total income at the disposal of sampled households gained during the survey, which can be used for final consumption expenditures and savings. Disposable income includes cash and income in kind. By income source, disposable income can be divided into 4 types, namely wage income, net business income, net property income and net transfer income. The following formula is used:

Disposable Income = wage income + net business income + net property income + net transfer income

Of which: Net business income = business income - business expense - depreciation of productive fixed assets - production tax

Net property income = property income - property expenditure

Net transfer income = transfer income - transfer expenditure

Wage Income refers to all payments of labour and various welfares earned by employed persons through all channels, including all payments of labour and welfare gained from institutional or individual employers, various freelance work, part-time job, and scattered work.

Wages refer to all cash rewards received by an employee from institutional or individual employer.

Physical Welfare refers to various physical products and service discounts provided by an institutional or individual employer to the employee for free or at a low price.

Other Income from Work refers to other cash compensation gained by an employed person except wages and various social security benefits paid by the employer.

Net Business Income refers to the net income of a family or family members from productive and operating activities. It is the net income of all operating income deducting business cost, depreciation of productive fixed assets and production tax. The following formula is used:

Net business income = business income - business cost - depreciation of productive fixed assets - production tax

Net Property Income refers to the net income of a family or family members earned by deducting relevant expenses from returns of their financial assets, non-financial assets (such as house) and natural resource delivered to other institutions, families or individuals for management. Net property income does not include income from premium of property ownership transfer and it shall be regarded as "non-revenue proceeds".

Dividend Income refers to legal benefits of households or individuals who deliver their capitals as shareholders to the company for management or disposal. It includes stock dividend regularly distributed by stock issuance company according to share amount, annual bonus and stock dividend and bonus gained from shares in collective properties or other investments. Benefits (including losses) gained from stock trading settlement are not included and shall be regarded as "non-revenue proceeds".

Net Proceeds from Saving Insurance refer to the net proceeds of insurance gained by households or members for participating in commercial saving insurance after the paid insurance principal and relevant fees are deducted, excluding the income of insurance claim paid by the responsible person to insurance beneficiary.

Transfer Income refers to various recurrent transfer payment from the nation, institutions and social groups to households, along with recurrent income transfer among households, including retirement pension, social relief and allowance, policy production subsidiary, policy living subsidiary, disaster relief fund, recurrent donation and compensations, medical expense reimbursement, alimony income among households and income mailed or brought by non-permanent members of such household, etc. Transfer income does not include physical donation among households.

Other Recurrent Transfer Income refers to other recurrent transfer income of households excluding the various transfer income stated above. It includes recurrent donation income, recurrent compensation income, unemployment insurance benefits and relative boarding expense, etc.

Net Transfer Income refers to net income after deducting recurrent or compulsory transfer payment of sampled households to the nation, institutions, households or individuals from various recurrent transfer payments by the nation, institutions, social groups to households and recurrent income transfer among households.

Net Transfer Income the following formula is used: Net transfer income = transfer income - transfer expenditure

Transfer Expenditure refers to the recurrent or

compulsory transfer payment made by the sampled households to the nation, institutions, households or individuals, including tax payment, various social security expenditures, alimony expenditure, recurrent donation and compensation expenditure and other recurrent transfer expenditure, etc.

Income from Asset Sales refers to the income received by the sampled household for selling any household properties. As the sale of household property is a conversion of physical form of household property to monetary form, and the total amount of household properties remains unchanged, the income from selling property is not included in the disposable income.

Account Subsidy refers to the cash paid by authorities of statistics, employers and other channels to the sampled household for its responsibility of accounts keeping, excluding any allowance in kind.

Loan Proceeds refer to the non-productive and non-operating income which causes no change in the amount of household asset, including withdrawal of bank deposits, borrowings and lending repaid, etc.

Total Household Expenditures refer to all actual expenditures including credit expenditures. It includes consumption expenditure, production and operation expenditure, properties expenditure, transfer expenditure, partial commercial insurance expenditure, property purchase and non-recurrent transfer expenditure, and loan expenditure.

Consumption Expenditure refers to total expenditures of households for consumption in daily life, including expenditures on consumer goods and services. By usage, it includes 8 categories, i.e. expenditures on food, tobacco and liquor, clothing, housing, living articles and services, transportation and communication, educational, cultural and recreational services, healthcare and medical services, and other goods and services. By source, it includes cash consumption and physical consumption (including self-produced and self-used products and those from institutions or employers, government and other social organizations).

Production and Operation Expenditure includes expenditure for agricultural production and operation and for non-agricultural production and operation.

Property Expenditure refers to relevant costs including interest paid by the sampled households for purchasing or maintaining properties.

Transfer Expenditure refers to the recurrent or compulsory transfer payment made by the sampled households to the nation, institutions, households or individuals, including tax payment, various social security expenditures, alimony expenditure, recurrent donation and compensation expenditure and other recurrent transfer expenditure, etc.

Partial Commercial Insurance Expenditure includes accident insurance, commercial medical insurance (including critical illness insurance), other non-saving commercial insurance and other saving commercial insurance.

Expenditures for Asset Purchase and Non-recurrent Transfer Payment Asset purchase expenditure refers to all expenditures for building and purchasing houses and expenditure on purchase and construction of productive fixed assets; non-recurrent transfer expenditure includes gaming expense, weddings and funerals (cash gift and entertaining, etc.) expense, lump-sum compensation and lump-sum gifting, etc.

Loan Expenditure refers to the revolving non-productive and non-operating expenditure which causes no change in ownership, including saving deposits, borrowings; capitals repayment, such as repayment of borrowings and various loans, etc.

Dependents Per Labour Force refers to the number of permanent population in the sampled household divided by the number of full/semi labourers. The following formula is used:

Dependents Per Laborer = Number of Permanent Population in the Sampled Households / Number of Full/Semi laborers

Full/Semi Labour Force in Rural Households refers to persons among permanent family members in rural households who are capable of working and work frequently. This is one of the indicators for basic production elements, and an important source for production development and increase of farmer's household income. As stated in regulations, rural males aged 18-50 and females aged 18-45 are full labours. Males aged 16-17 and 51-60 and females aged 16-17 and 46-55 are semi labor force. Full/Semi Labour Force in Rural Households includes the male and female full/semi labour force within the above-mentioned range age as well as those beyond such range of ages who are capable of working and work frequently; also include labourers among permanent members in rural households who are employees. But it excludes persons who are within the range of labour age but incapable of working.

Total Building Area of Current Houses refers to the total building area of house resided by the surveyed households, which is calculated on the basis of the property ownership certificate or lease certificate. The building area can also be calculated as the usable floor space multiplied by 1.333, which shall deduct the building area of the house specially used for lease.

Engel's Coefficient Along with the increase in household and personal income, a gradually smaller proportion of income is used for purchase of food. This law is called Engel's law, and the coefficient reflecting such law is called Engel's Coefficient. The following formula is used:

$$\text{Engels Coefficient} = \frac{\text{expenditure on food}}{\text{total consumption expenditure}} \times 100\%$$

北京统计年鉴2017 BEIJING STATISTICAL YEARBOOK

城市公用事业
PUBLIC UTILITIES

简要说明

一、本章资料的主要内容

本章资料反映北京市城市公用事业的综合水平，主要内容包括四部分：

1. 历年城市公用事业基本情况；
2. 水、气、热等供应及消费情况；
3. 城市公交、出租车情况；
4. 市政主要设施情况。

二、本章资料的数据来源

本章城市供热、供气情况由北京市城市管理委员会提供；自来水情况由北京市水务局提供；城市公交、出租车情况由北京市交通委员会提供；道路及市政主要设施情况由北京市交通委员会、北京市公安交通管理局、北京市路灯管理中心提供。

Brief Introduction

I. Main Content

Statistics in this chapter show the overall level of urban public utilities in Beijing, which consist of four parts:

1. Basic statistics for urban public utilities in previous years;
2. Water, gas and heating supply and consumption;
3. Urban public transport and taxi services;
4. Main public facilities.

II. Source of Data

Data on urban heating and gas supply were provided by Beijing Municipal Commission of City Administration; data on tap water were provided by Beijing Water Authority; data on urban public transport and taxi services were provided by Beijing Municipal Commission of Transport; data on roads and main public facilities were provided by Beijing Municipal Commission of Transport, Beijing Traffic Management Bureau and Street Lighting Administration Center Of Beijing.

10-1 公路、城市道路及桥梁(1978-2016年)
HIGHWAYS, URBAN ROADS AND BRIDGES (1978-2016)

年 份 Year	境内道路总里程(公里) Total Length of Highways and Roads (km)	公路里程(公里) Total Length of Highways (km)	#高速公路 Express-ways	城市道路里程(公里) Length of Urban Roads (km)	#快速路 Rapid Roads	#主干路 Trunk Roads	城市道路面积(万平方米) Area of Urban Roads (10000 sq.m)	城市道路桥梁(座) Number of Bridges (unit)	#立交桥 Overpasses
1978		6562		2078			1611	351	2
1979		7278		2131			1618	348	2
1980		7487		2185			1664	351	6
1981		7566		2234			1742	342	8
1982		7683		2671			2098	408	9
1983		8058		2820			2265	431	10
1984		8271		2928			2393	440	11
1985		8482		2979			2485	460	16
1986		8995		3038			2559	479	16
1987		9103		3087			2631	510	22
1988		9124		3151			2701	522	23
1989		9371		3235			2815	552	27
1990		9648	35	3276			2905	562	33
1991		10259	63	3308			3134	569	40
1992		10827	71	3189			3212	595	55
1993		11260	99	3285			3398	596	64
1994		11532	112	3316			3470	616	75
1995		11811	113	3194			3494	582	84
1996		12084	114	3665			3807	646	133
1997		12306	144	3637			4061	693	140
1998		12498	190	3721			4214	715	138
1999		12825	230	3753			4353	787	141
2000		13600	268	4126			4921	834	149
2001		13891	335	4312			6062	891	160
2002		14359	463	5444			7645	1051	180
2003	18942	14453	499	3055			5345	848	119
2004	19010	14630	525	4067	219	834	6417	949	271
2005	19015	14696	548	4073	239	922	7437	964	304
2006	25377	20503	625	4419	232	955	7258	1079	376
2007	25765	20754	628	4460	236	960	7632	1230	377
2008	26921	20340	777	6186	242	755	8941	1738	381
2009	27436	20755	884	6247	242	805	9179	1765	393
2010	27907	21114	903	6355	263	874	9395	1855	411
2011	28446	21347	912	6258	263	861	9164	1885	418
2012	28585	21492	923	6271	263	865	9236	1950	413
2013	28808	21673	923	6295	269	953	9611	1998	414
2014	29209	21849	982	6426	383	965	10002	2042	422
2015	29069	21885	982	6423	383	969	10029	2069	427
2016	29282	22026	1013	6373	390	970	10275	2088	431

注：1．境内道路总里程为全市道路和公路里程之和(剔除道路、公路交叉重复部分)。

2．道路及桥梁1978年—1981年统计范围为城八区及通县；1982年—2002年统计范围为城八区及14个县城；2003年—2010年统计范围为城八区和北京经济技术开发区。2011年起城市道路及其附属设施统计范围为城六区。

3．2008年道路数据为北京市城市道路普查数据。

资料来源：北京市交通委员会。

Note: a) Total length of highways and roads means the sum of roads and highways across the city (excluding intersections of roads and highways)

b) Statistics for roads and bridges covered 8 urban districts and Tongzhou County in 1978-1981; the coverage was extended to 8 urban districts and 14 counties in 1982-2002; in 2003-2010, the coverage included 8 central urban districts and Beijing Economic-Technological Development Zone; since 2011, statistics for urban roads and the auxiliary facilities have been confined to 6 urban districts.

c) Statistics for roads and highways in 2008 were from Beijing Urban Road Census.

Source: Beijing Municipal Commission of Transport.

10-2 城市公共交通(1978-2016年)

年份 Year	公共交通运营线路条数(条) Number of Operating Public Transport Routes (line)	公共电汽车 Buses and Trolley Buses	轨道交通 Rail Transit	公共交通运营线路长度(公里) Length of Operating Public Transport Lines (km)	公共电汽车 Buses and Trolley Buses	轨道交通 Rail Transit	公共交通运营车辆(辆) Number of Operating Public Transport Vehicles in Operation (vehicle)
1978	119	118	1	1427	1403	24	2743
1979	121	120	1	1469	1446	24	2997
1980	123	122	1	1479	1455	24	3113
1981	127	126	1	1525	1501	24	3375
1982	139	138	1	1678	1654	24	3620
1983	151	150	1	1820	1797	24	3907
1984	164	162	2	1939	1899	40	4221
1985	191	189	2	2312	2272	40	4583
1986	200	198	2	2574	2534	40	4576
1987	194	192	2	2382	2342	40	4776
1988	199	197	2	2445	2405	40	4787
1989	207	205	2	2525	2485	40	4890
1990	216	214	2	2654	2614	40	5160
1991	223	221	2	2755	2715	40	5182
1992	262	260	2	3379	3338	42	5223
1993	268	266	2	3532	3491	42	5213
1994	284	282	2	4117	4075	42	5319
1995	300	298	2	4538	4497	42	5367
1996	399	397	2	7317	7276	42	6828
1997	667	665	2	14011	13969	42	10479
1998	690	688	2	14929	14888	42	10819
1999	750	748	2	16566	16513	54	12509
2000	682	680	2	15639	15585	54	14191
2001	555	553	2	13180	13126	54	15420
2002	592	589	3	15835	15760	75	17580
2003	620	616	4	16131	16017	114	17445
2004	621	617	4	15247	15133	114	19343
2005	626	622	4	18328	18214	114	19471
2006	624	620	4	18582	18468	114	20489
2007	649	644	5	17495	17353	142	20525
2008	679	671	8	18057	17857	200	23221
2009	701	692	9	18498	18270	228	23730
2010	727	713	14	19079	18743	336	24011
2011	764	749	15	19832	19460	372	24478
2012	795	779	16	19989	19547	442	25831
2013	830	813	17	20153	19688	465	27590
2014	895	877	18	20776	20249	527	28331
2015	894	876	18	20740	20186	554	28311
2016	895	876	19	20392	19818	574	27892

注：自2006年5月1日起，公共电汽车、轨道交通售票采取刷卡方式，并陆续进行了票制票价改革，客运量统计口径方法相应调整，因此与历史数据不可比。

资料来源：本表2005年及以后数据来源于北京市交通委员会。

URBAN PUBLIC TRANSPORT (1978-2016)

		公共交通			出租小汽车 Taxis Service	
公共电汽车 Buses and Trolley Buses	轨道交通 Rail Transit	客运量(万人次) Passengers Carried by Public Transport (10000 person-times)	公共电汽车 Buses and Trolley Buses	轨道交通 Rail Transit	运营车辆(辆) Operating Vehicles (vehicle)	客运量(万人次) Passenger Traffic (10000 persons)
2627	116	172559	169465	3094		
2889	108	205703	200918	4785		
3001	112	236998	231477	5521		
3259	116	263944	257478	6466		
3500	120	284175	276922	7253		
3753	154	302501	294301	8200		
4037	184	324437	314132	10305		
4398	185	335227	321264	13963		
4371	205	328770	312990	15780		
4524	252	330417	311190	19227		
4535	252	337094	306396	30698		
4587	303	306435	275383	31052		
4857	303	334673	296495	38178		
4877	305	344525	307438	37087		
4900	323	348770	305959	42811		
4890	323	335378	286268	49110		
4984	335	353289	299993	53296		
4984	383	371579	315777	55802		
6427	401	349847	305433	44414		
10044	435	391182	346676	44507		
10382	437	418825	372494	46331		
12018	491	426706	378483	48223		
13604	587	406691	363213	43478		
14803	617	449720	402850	46870		
16939	641	492122	443880	48242		
16753	692	426628	379380	47248		
18451	892	499830	439130	60700		
18503	968	517769	449793	67976	66000	65000
19522	967	468225	397919	70306	66646	64121
19395	1130	488138	422645	65493	66646	64111
21507	1714	592523	470863	121660	66646	69000
21716	2014	658785	516517	142268	66646	68000
21548	2463	689788	505144	184645	66646	69000
21628	2850	722552	503272	219280	66646	69600
22146	3685	761578	515416	246162	66646	69862
23592	3998	804775	484306	320469	67046	69946
23667	4664	815849	477180	338668	67546	66828
23287	5024	738384	406003	332381	68284	58750
22688	5204	734953	369019	365934	68484	47665

Note: Since May 1, 2006, buses, trolley buses and rail transit tickets were sold by card swiping. Ticket system and prices were also reformed successively. The statistical coverage and methods for passenger traffic were adjusted accordingly, so these figures were incomparable with historical data.

Source: Since 2005, data in this table were provided by Beijing Municipal Commission of Transport.

10-3 城市供水、供气及供热(1978-2016年)
URBAN WATER SUPPLY, GAS SUPPLY AND HEAT SUPPLY (1978-2016)

年 份 Year	全市集中供热管道长度(公里) Total Length of Pipelines for Centralized Heating (km)	全市集中供热面积(万平方米) Centralized Heating Area in Beijing (10000 sq.m)	#住 宅 Residence	煤 气 销售量(万立方米) Sales Volume of Coal Gas (10000 cu.m)	液化石油气销售量(吨) Sales Volume of Liquefied Petroleum Gas (ton)	天然气销售量(万立方米) Sales Volume of Natural Gas (10000 cu.m)
1978				32687	97255	
1979				32113	114350	
1980				34935	128990	
1981				36309	134771	
1982				36748	149805	
1983				37319	150058	
1984				38710	156421	
1985				41678	169720	
1986				44542	182239	
1987				47594	178205	
1988				49595	177112	287
1989				56056	175814	1805
1990		3702		59508	172688	3544
1991		4560		66111	174326	5062
1992		5281		73615	174694	6040
1993		5730		80163	177065	6702
1994		7056		80409	173105	7623
1995		7537		85201	177637	11003
1996		7838		88356	185304	13504
1997		8399		76429	172879	16565
1998		9102		68998	174464	32619
1999		9992		61846	188450	64833
2000		10860		46719	190571	95919
2001		14729		33960	182188	150585
2002		18172		21077	234680	176504
2003		25108		23991	311657	208837
2004		28150	18962	17714	431660	250326
2005	6272	31736	22218	16776	356551	294279
2006	7013	34977	23158	9763	415268	389202
2007	10424	37203	23697		319631	441327
2008	11948	42501	26738		289576	578626
2009	12156	44240	27694		332693	645356
2010	12224	46715	32305		299392	677009
2011	11734	50794	34563		394437	726229
2012	11031	52555	35104		379371	883385
2013	11192	54591	36806		453546	956852
2014	12038	56786	38085		531556	1088999
2015	12207	58465	39031		523391	1400441
2016	13545	61136	41084		480873	1505882

注：1. 2006年6月开始全市煤气家庭用户已全部置换为天然气用户，因此2007年以后煤气销售量无数据。
2. 自2012年起，自来水数据口径调整为城镇公共供水。
资料来源：北京市城市管理委员会、北京市水务局。
Note: a) Since June 2006, all households using coal gas have started to use natual gas. Therefore, there are no data on coal gas sales volume since 2007
b) Since 2012, Relevant figures of tap water were changed to cover urban public water supply.
Source: Beijing Municipal Commission of City Administration、Beijing Water Authority.

10-3 续表 Continued

年 份 Year	居 民 燃气用户 (万户) Gas Using Households (10000 households)	自来水综合 生产能力 (万立方米/日) Gereral Production Capacity of Tap Water (10000 cu.m/day)	自来水供水 管线长度 (公里) Length of Tap Water Supply Pipelines (km)	自 来 水 销售总量 (万立方米) Total Sales Volume of Tap Water (10000 cu.m)
1978	65.2	134	2926	32664
1979	76.7	151	3083	36232
1980	80.3	163	3272	38933
1981	85.1	167	3435	41634
1982	88.0	164	4216	41136
1983	90.9	166	4452	42778
1984	96.9	167	4622	43716
1985	102.3	176	4927	45601
1986	153.6	188	5079	46695
1987	160.9	185	5257	47680
1988	165.4	189	5550	50059
1989	172.6	206	5647	50145
1990	176.1	215	5770	52718
1991	184.7	221	5947	56107
1992	192.4	226	6130	58704
1993	197.5	234	6367	60794
1994	210.3	242	6727	67977
1995	219.8	264	6907	67877
1996	188.1	266	6907	69684
1997	243.0	302	6339	79046
1998	254.4	330	6989	75969
1999	259.8	357	7179	78098
2000	291.9	367	7610	75364
2001	310.0	371	8146	69807
2002	336.4	428	8555	79322
2003	406.0	429	9278	71583
2004	438.6	399	9981	82986
2005	462.6	348	9831	71600
2006	540.2	373	11899	74970
2007	556.4	391	13133	77778
2008	591.0	404	14118	80792
2009	600.0	424	14791	86881
2010	634.2	445	16144	89185
2011	644.1	473	16963	94622
2012	713.5	411	14029	93826
2013	737.4	444	14495	98178
2014	846.0	503	14994	103402
2015	885.7	506	15421	103929
2016	900.7	504	15742	108386

10-4 全市集中供热
CENTRALIZED HEATING SUPPLY

项目	Item	2016	2015	2016年为2015年% 2016 as % of 2015
供热面积 (万平方米)	**Total Area of Heating Supply (10000 sq.m)**	**61136**	**58465**	**104.6**
#住宅	Residence	41084	39031	105.3
供热能力 (兆瓦)	**Heating Supply Capacity (megawatt)**	**42951**	**41451**	**103.6**
热电厂供热	Heating from Thermal Power Plants	7744	7590	102.0
锅炉房供热	Heating from Boiler Houses	35207	33861	104.0
供热总量 (万吉焦)	**Total Heating Supply (10000 giga joules)**	**37568**	**35857**	**104.8**
热电厂供热	Heating from Thermal Power Plants	5763	5551	103.8
锅炉房供热	Heating from Boiler Houses	31805	30306	104.9
供热管道长度 (公里)	**Length of Pipelines (km)**	**13545**	**12207**	**111.0**

资料来源：北京市城市管理委员会。
Source: Beijing Municipal Commission of City Administration.

10-5 液化石油气及天然气
LIQUEFIED PETROLEUM GAS AND NATURAL GAS

项目	Item	2016	2015	2016年为2015年% 2016 as % of 2015
液化石油气	**Liquefied Petroleum Gas**			
供气总量 (吨)	Gas Supply (ton)	500213	576306	86.8
销售气量 (吨)	Gas Sales (ton)	480873	523391	91.9
#家庭用量 (吨)	Domestic Consumption (ton)	195226	189188	103.2
家庭用户 (万户)	Domestic Consumers (10000 households)	302.7	296.9	101.9
天然气	**Natural Gas**			
供气总量 (万立方米)	Gas Supply (10000 cu.m)	1622393	1444924	112.3
销售气量 (万立方米)	Gas Sales (10000 cu.m)	1538425	1427808	107.7
#家庭用量 (万立方米)	Domestic Consumption (10000 cu.m)	127723	137199	93.1
家庭用户 (万户)	Domestic Consumers (10000 households)	598.1	588.8	101.6
居民燃气用户 (万户)	**Household Gas Users (10000 households)**	**900.7**	**885.7**	**101.7**

注：本表天然气、液化石油气用量中包含燕山石化用气量。
资料来源：北京市城市管理委员会、中国石化集团北京燕山石化有限公司。
Note: Data on natural gas consumption and liquefied petroleum gas consumption in this table include the consumption of Yanshan Petrochemical.
Source: Beijing Municipal Commission of City Administration, and SINOPEC Beijing Yanshan Petrochemical Co., Ltd.

10-6 自来水及自备水源
TAP WATER AND SELF-PROVIDED SOURCES OF WATER

项 目		Item		2016	2015
自来水		**Tap Water**			
综合生产能力	(万立方米/日)	General Production Capacity	(10000cu.m/day)	504.4	506.0
供水管道长度	(公里)	Length of Water Supply Pipelines	(km)	15742	15421
销售总量	(万立方米)	Total Sales Volume	(10000 cu.m)	108386	103929
#生产用水	(万立方米)	For Production Use	(10000 cu.m)	13724	12905
生活用水	(万立方米)	For Public Service Use	(10000 cu.m)	91965	88047
生态环境用水	(万立方米)	For Domestic Use	(10000 cu.m)	2698	2977
自备井水		**Self-provided Well Water**			
用水量	(万立方米)	Consumption	(10000 cu.m)	56104	58110
#生产用水	(万立方米)	For Production Use	(10000 cu.m)	14491	15103
生活用水	(万立方米)	For Public Service Use	(10000 cu.m)	34620	35980
生态环境用水	(万立方米)	For Domestic Use	(10000 cu.m)	6993	7026

注：自来水数据口径为城镇公共供水。自备井水数据口径为城镇范围。
资料来源：北京市水务局。
Note: Statistical basis for tap water is urban public water supply. Since 2013, statistical scope for the data on self-provided well water were changed to cover urban area, satellite city, central town, town with general organizational structure, except agriculture.
Source: Beijing Water Authority.

10-7 公共交通及客运出租小轿车
PUBLIC TRANSPORT AND TAXI SERVICES

项 目		Item		2016	2015
公共交通		**Public Transportation**			
运营车辆	(辆)	Operating Vehicles	(unit)	27892	28311
公共电汽车	(辆)	Buses and Trolley Buses	(unit)	22688	23287
轨道交通	(辆)	Rail Transit	(unit)	5204	5024
运营线路条数	(条)	Number of Operating Routes	(line)	895	894
公共电汽车	(条)	Buses and Trolley Buses	(line)	876	876
轨道交通	(条)	Rail Transit	(line)	19	18
运营线路长度	(公里)	Length of Operating Routes	(km)	20392	20740
公共电汽车	(公里)	Buses and Trolley Buses	(km)	19818	20186
轨道交通	(公里)	Rail Transit	(km)	574	554
客运量	(万人次)	Passenger Traffic	(10000 person-times)	734953	738384
公共电汽车	(万人次)	Buses and Trolley Buses	(10000 person-times)	369019	406003
轨道交通	(万人次)	Rail Transit	(10000 person-times)	365934	332381
客运出租小轿车		**Taxi Services**			
年末运营车辆	(辆)	Vehicles in Operation (year-end)	(unit)	68484	68284
客运量	(万人次)	Passenger Traffic	(10000 person-times)	47665	58750

资料来源：北京市交通委员会。
Source: Beijing Municipal Commission of Transport.

10-8 市政设施情况
BASIC STATISTICS FOR MUNICIPAL FACILITIES

项目	Item	2016	2015
境内道路总里程 (公里)	Total Length of Highways and Roads (km)	29282	29069
高速公路里程 (公里)	Length of Expressways (km)	1013	982
城市道路里程 (公里)	Length of Urban Roads (km)	6373	6423
#快速路 (公里)	Rapid Roads (km)	390	383
#主干路 (公里)	Trunk Roads (km)	970	969
城市道路面积 (万平方米)	Coverage of Urban Roads (10000 sq.m)	10275	10029
#铺装步道 (万平方米)	Paved Roads (10000 sq.m)	1713	1676
城市道路立交桥数 (座)	Number of Overpasses in City (unit)	431	427
城市过街天桥数 (座)	Number of Pedestrain Overpasses in City (unit)	544	531
城市地下通道数 (座)	Number of Underpasses in City (unit)	213	213
备案停车场个数 (个)	Number of Parking Lots Recorded (unit)	6676	6690
备案停车场车位总数 (个)	Total Capacity of Parking Lots Recorded (unit)	1931479	1905949
路口电视监视点位 (台)	TV Monitors at Crossings (unit)	1231	1224
城六区照明线路长度 (公里)	Length of Lighting Lines in 6 Urban Districts (km)	8402	6500

注：1．本表统计范围为城六区。

2．表中“备案停车场个数”和“备案停车场车位总数”为原指标“经营性停车场个数”和“经营性停车场车位总数”。

资料来源：北京市交通委员会、北京市公安局公安交通管理局、北京市路灯管理中心。

Note: a) Data in this table covers 6 urban districts .

b) In the table, the "Parking Lots Recorded" and "Total Capacity of Parking Lots Recorded" are the original indicators "Operational Parking Lots" and "Total Capacity of Operational Parking Lots".

Source: Beijing Municipal Communission of Transport, Beijing Traffic Management Bureau., Beijing Street Lamp Administration Center.

主要统计指标解释

自来水综合生产能力 指按供水设施取水、净化、送水、出厂输水干管等环节实际测定计算的综合生产能力。不包括供水高峰阶段，超负荷增加的生产能力。计算时，以四个环节中最薄弱的环节为主确定能力。

自来水供水管道长度 指从送水泵至用户水表之间所有管道的长度。不包括新安装尚未使用的管道。

生产用水 指在生产活动中取用的水量，包含工业用水量和农业用水量两个部分。

生活用水 指城乡居民家庭日常生活及除工业企业外的建筑业、商业、饮食业、宾馆业、服务业、机关团体、医院、学校部队等范围的用水。

生态环境用水 指通过认为措施补充给河湖、湿地的水量及园林绿化、环境卫生（公厕冲洗、道路喷洒等）等用水。

公共交通年末运营车辆 指公交企业（单位）用于运营业务的全部车辆数。

运营线路总长度 指全部运营线路长度之和。计算公式：

$$\text{运营线路长度} = \sum \text{各条运营线路长度}$$

$$= \sum\left[\begin{pmatrix}\text{上行起点至终点里程} + \text{下行起点至终点里程} \\ + \text{上下行终点掉头里程}\end{pmatrix}\right]$$

公路里程 指公路的长度，凡达到《公路工程技术标准（JTGB01-2003）》规定的技术等级的公路，均统计公路里程，包括大、中城市的郊区公路里程，公路通过城镇（指县城、集镇）街道的里程和公路桥梁长度、隧道长度、渡口的宽度以及分期修建的公路已验收交付使用的里程。国道、省道、县道、乡道和专用公路中新增的人工修建的、路基宽度在 4.5 米以上的等外路里程也纳入公路里程统计。按技术等级公路可分为高速公路、一级公路、二级公路、三级公路、四级公路和等外公路。

道路里程 指道路长度和与道路相通的桥梁、隧道的长度，按车行道中心线计算。城市道路由车行道和人行道两部分组成。在统计时只统计路面宽度在 3.5 米（含 3.5 米）以上的各种铺装道路，包括开放型工业区和住宅区道路在内。

道路面积 指道路面积和与道路相通的广场、桥梁、隧道的面积（统计时，将人行道面积单独统计）。人行道面积按道路两侧面积相加计算。包括步行街和广场，不含人车混行的道路。

Explanatory Notes on Main Statistical Indicators

General Production Capacity of Tap Water means the comprehensive production capacity of water facilities calculated by on-site measurement, including capacity of the water in-taking, treatment, transmission and delivery; while overloaded capacity during water supply peak hours are not included. Calculation of the capacity was mainly dependent upon the weakest link of the whole production process.

Length of Tap Water Supply Pipelines means the length of all pipes linking between the water outlet pumps and users' water meters, excluding the ones newly installed and not yet put into use.

Water for Production Use means the water used for production and operation of business entities within the city, covering sectors including agriculture, forestry, animal production and hunting, fishing, industry, construction, transportation, etc.

Water for Public Service Use means the water used for urban public services, including water supply for administrative and public institutions, military units, public facilities, social services, wholesale and retail trades, hotels and catering, and social service organizations.

Water for Domestic Use means the water used for daily life of all households in urban area, including the water used for urban residents, rural households, and public water supply stations.

Year-end Public Transport Vehicles in Operation means the number of all vehicles used for operational businesses in public transit enterprises (institutions).

Total Length of Public Transport Routes means the sum of all lines in operation. It is calculated with the formula:

Length of Public Transit Lines = ∑ Length of all lines in operation = ∑ [(mileage from the upward starting point to the end point + mileage from the downward starting point to the end point + mileage of double back from upward and downward end points)]

Total Length of Highways means the length of highways. Such statistics apply for any highway reaching the technical grade stated in *Highway Engineering Technical Standards (JTGB01-2003)*, including the mileage of highways in suburbs of middle and large cities, mileage of highways passing through streets in towns (counties and townships), length of highway bridges, length of tunnels, width of ferries, and mileage of highways constructed in several phases and put into use. The mileage of non-graded new highways built manually onto national highways, provincial highways, county highways, township highways and special highways, with roadbed width of 4.5m and above, are also incorporated. In terms of technical grade, highways fall into expressways, first-grade highways, second-grade highways, third-grade highways, fourth-grade highways, and non-graded highways.

Length of Highways and Roads means the length of roads and bridges and tunnels connecting with roads, calculated by the central lines of carriage ways. Urban roads consist of carriageways and sidewalks. Statistics only cover paved roads with width of pavement above 3.5m (including 3.5m), roads in open industrial zones and residential zones included.

Area of Roads means the area of roads and the area of squares, bridges and tunnels connecting to the roads (the area of sidewalks is calculated separately). The area of sidewalks is the sum of area on both sides of roads, including pedestrian streets and squares, excluding roads passable for both pedestrians and vehicles.

11

农业及农村经济
AGRICULTURE AND RURAL ECONOMY

简要说明

一、本章资料的主要内容

本章资料反映北京市农业生产和农村经济基本情况，主要包括农村基层组织情况、农村地区人口、从业人员、耕地、农林牧渔业产值及主要农产品生产情况、设施农业、农业观光园、民俗旅游、农村固定资产投资、乡镇企业情况、农村经济收入与分配情况等。

二、本章资料的统计范围

农林牧渔业统计范围包括辖区内全部农林牧渔业生产单位、非农行业单位附属的农林牧渔业生产活动单位以及农户的农业生产活动。军委系统的农林牧渔业生产（除军马外）也应包括在内，但不包括农业科学试验机构进行的农业生产。

1．农业：指各种农作物的种植活动。包括谷物、豆类、薯类、棉花、油料、糖料、麻类、烟叶、蔬菜、食用菌及花卉盆景园艺产品、水果、坚果、饲料和香料作物、药材及其它作物的种植。

2．林业：包括林木的栽培(不包括茶园、桑园和果园的栽培、管理和收获等活动)、木材和竹材的采运、林产品的采集。

3．畜牧业：包括牲畜饲养和放牧、家禽饲养以及野生动物的捕猎和饲养。

4．渔业：分为淡水养殖和海水养殖，包括水生动物和海藻类植物的养殖和捕捞。

农村社会经济统计范围包括所有乡镇辖区内的社会经济活动。

三、本章资料的数据来源

乡镇企业数据由北京市经济和信息化委员会提供。农村经济收入分配数据由北京市农村经济研究中心农村合作经济经营管理站提供，耕地数据由北京市规划和国土资源管理委员会提供，林业数据由北京市园林绿化局提供，水产品数据由北京市农业局提供，农村基层组织资料由北京市民政局提供。其余资料均由北京市统计局、国家统计局北京调查总队提供。

四、本章资料的调查方法和核算方法

根据农业生产特点，农林牧渔业总产值的核算采用“产品法”计算，即用产品产量乘以价格求出各种产品的产值，按产品产值类别分别汇总，计算出农林牧渔各业的产值，各业相加为农林牧渔业总产值。

(1)农业：包括谷物和其他作物；蔬菜、食用菌及花卉盆景园艺产品；水果、坚果、饲料、香料；中药材。

(2)林业：包括林木的培育和种植；木材、竹材采运；林产品的采集。

(3)牧业：包括除渔业养殖以外的一切动物饲养和放牧以及野生动物的捕猎和饲养。

(4)渔业：包括水生动物和海藻类植物的养殖和捕捞。

(5)服务业：产值等于农林牧渔服务业营业收入。

1957 年以前的农业总产值中包括了厩肥和农民自给性手工业（如农民自制衣服、鞋、袜，自己从事粮食初步加工等）。1958 年及以后的林业产值中增加了村及村以下竹木采伐产值；牧业中取消了厩肥产值；副业中取消了农民自给性手工业产值；渔业中增加了海洋捕捞水产品产值。1980 年及以后的农业总产值，在副业中增加了农民家庭兼营工业商品部分的产值。从 1984 年起村及村以下办工业产值划归工业。从 1993 年起，取消副业，将野生动物的捕猎划入牧业，野生植物采集和农民家庭兼营商品性工业划归农业。从 2003 年起按照新的《国民经济行业分类》标准取消了“其它农业”；将农林牧渔服务业产值纳入农林牧渔业总产值中；从农林牧渔业总产值中取消了“家庭兼营商品性工业”；将村以上木材和竹材的采运划入了林业；产值计算采用生产者价格，即生产者第一次出售农产品的价格。2004 年国家统计局报表制度规定农林牧渔业总产值增加按可比价计算的产值及发展速度（计算方法：用现价产值的中类数据除以中类缩减指数求得各中类的可比价产值，各中类相加得大类的可比价产值，最后用大类数据相加得农业可比价总产值，可比价产值除以上年现价产值得发展速度）。从2005年起，取消了按1990年价格计算的农业产值。由于 2006 年农业普查后对农业生产历史数据进行了修订，新修订的农业产值数据只到大类，如果按大类缩减计算农业可比价总产值不符合国家报表制度要求，故 2005 年及以前年度没有按可比价计算的发展速度。2010 年起，根据新的《统计用产品分类目录》将原林业产值中的核桃、栗子、白果、松子等干果产值调整至农业产值中，为同口径对比，将 2009 年年报数据也作了相应调整。

主要粮食播种面积数据通过卫星遥感测量方法取得,粮食产量数据通过抽样调查方法取得。农林牧渔业生产统计采取全面调查方法，村级起报。

五、本章中关于历史数据调整的问题

根据 2006 年第二次农业普查结果，北京市统计局、国家统计局北京调查总队按照国务院农普办要求，依照国际通用做法，已对 1997—2005 年的相关指标历史数据进行了修订。

Brief Introduction

I. Main Content

Statistics in this chapter show basic situation of agricultural production and rural economy in Beijing, mainly consisting of statistics for rural grass-root organizations, population and employment, arable land, output of agriculture, forestry, animal production and hunting, fishing, production of main agricultural products, facility agriculture, agricultural sightseeing gardens, folk-custom tourism, investment in fixed assets in rural areas, township enterprises, income and distribution of rural economy.

II. Scope of Statistics

Statistics on agriculture, forestry, animal production and hunting, fishing cover all related producing entities, producers affiliated to non-agricultural departments, as well as farmers' agricultural production activities. Production by the military commission system shall also be included (except for army horse breeding), but the production by scientific testing agencies is not included.

1. Agriculture: It refers to the growing of various agricultural crops, including grains, beans, potatoes, cotton, oil plants, sugar plants, fiber plants, tobacco leaves, vegetables, edible fungus, flower bonsai and gardening products, fruits, nuts, feedstuff, and spice crops, herbs, and other crops.

2. Forestry: It includes tree planting (except for the cultivation, management and harvest of tea gardens, mulberry fields, and orchards), the logging of timber and bamboo, and the collection of forestry products.

3. Animal production and hunting: It includes the breeding and grazing of livestock, poultry agriculture, as well as hunting and breeding of wildlife.

4. Fishing: It falls into two parts: freshwater agriculture and mariculture, including the cultivation and fishing for aquatic animals and algae.

Statistics for social and economic development in rural areas cover social and economic activities of all villages and towns within the jurisdiction.

III. Source of Statistics

Statistics on township enterprises were provided by Beijing Municipal Commission of Economy and Information Technology. Statistics on income distribution in rural economy were provided by the Operation and Management Station of Rural Cooperative Economy, Beijing Research Center for Rural Economy. Statistics on arable land were provided by Beijing Municipal Bureau of Land and Resources. Forestry statistics were provided by Beijing Municipal Bureau of Landscape and Forestry. Statistics on aquatic products were provided by Beijing Municipal Bureau of Agriculture. Statistics on rural basic organization were provided by Beijing Municipal Bureau of civil Affairs. All other statistics were provided by Beijing Municipal Bureau of Statistics and National Bureau of Statistics Survey Office in Beijing.

IV. Method for Survey and Counting

Based on agricultural production characteristics, the gross output value of agriculture, forestry, animal production and hunting, fishing was calculated by the "product approach"--that is to multiply production volume by the unit price, so as to get output value of each product, then sum it up by category, namely agriculture, forestry, animal production and hunting, fishing; and the sum total of these categories will be gross output value of the whole sector.

(1) Agriculture: including cereal and other crops; vegetables, edible mushrooms, flower bonsai and gardening products; fruits, nuts, beverage, spices, and herbs.

(2) Forestry: including the cultivation and planting of forest trees; logging of timber and bamboo; and collection of forestry products.

(3) Animal production and hunting: including the breeding and grazing of animals other than fish breeding, as well as hunting and breeding of wildlife.

(4) Fishing: including cultivation and catching of aquatic animals and seaweed plants.

(5) Service: the output value equals the operating income of services in support of agriculture, forestry, animal production and hunting, fishing.

Prior to 1957, China's gross agricultural output value included the output of barnyard manure and handicraft products for self-consumption (e.g. clothes, shoes, socks, and primary grain processing by peasants). Since 1958, output value of bamboo and timber logging by villages and units subordinated to villages has been included in the statistics of forestry; output value of barnyard manure has been excluded from animal production and hunting statistics; subsistence handicrafts has been excluded from sideline products output value; and the output value of aquatic products by marine fishing has been added to fishing. Since 1980, the output value of industrial commodities operated by rural households has been included in the output value of sideline products. Since 1984, industrial output value produced by villages and units subordinated to villages has been added in the sector of industry. In 1993, the group "sideline products" was cancelled; the hunting of wild animals has been classified as animal production and hunting, and the gathering of wild plants and commercial industrial businesses run by rural households have been included in agriculture. A new Standard for *Classification of National Economic Sectors* was introduced in 2003. According to the new classification, the group "other agricultural activities" was cancelled; the output value of services in support of agriculture, forestry, animal production and hunting, fishing is included in the gross output value of agriculture; the value of industrial output by households is excluded; output value of wood and bamboo logging is included in forestry statistics; the output value is calculated at the producer's price, namely the price at which producers sell their agricultural products for the first time; the 2004 Reporting System of National Bureau of Statistics states that, for incremental gross output value of agriculture, forestry, animal production and hunting, fishing, the output value and growth rate shall be calculated at comparable prices (calculation method: use the output value of groups at present prices to divide the groups' deflator, so as to get the output value at comparable prices; then add up the groups' output value to get the whole division's output value at comparable prices; in the end, add up all divisions' output value to get the gross output value at comparable prices for agriculture sector and divide the output value at comparable prices by the output value at current prices in the previous year to get the growth rate). Since 2005, the practice of using prices of 1990 as reference numbers to calculate agricultural output value has been cancelled. As historical data of agricultural production were revised after the agricultural census in 2006, revised agricultural production output value figures were presented only in divisions; and it does not meet the requirements of national reporting system to calculate the gross agricultural output value at comparable prices by divisions' deflator. Therefore, there were no figures of growth rate at comparable prices in and prior to 2005. Since 2010, the output value of nuts such as walnuts, chestnuts, gingkoes and pine nuts formerly included in forestry has been added in the output value of framing according to the new *Catalog on Statistical Product Classification*. In order to conduct same-caliber comparison, data in the 2009 annual report have also been adjusted accordingly.

Data on the sown area of major grain were collected by satellite remote sensing; data on grain yield were gathered through sampling survey; and the production figures on agriculture, forestry, animal production and hunting, fishing sectors were added up by complete survey, starting from the village level.

V. Adjustments to Historical Statistics

Based on results of the second agricultural census 2006, Beijing Municipal Bureau of Statistics and NBS Survey Office in Beijing revised related historical statistics during 1997-2005 as required by the Agricultural Census Office of the State Council and in accordance with the international practice.

11-1 农村基本情况(1978-2016年)
BASIC STATISTICS FOR RURAL AREAS (1978-2016)

年份 Year	乡政府 (个) Township Governments (unit)	镇政府 (个) Town Governments (unit)	村民委员会 (个) Villagers' Committees (unit)	乡镇及行政村常住户数 (万户) Number of Permanent Households in Towns and Administrative Villages (10000 households)	乡镇及行政村常住人口 (万人) Permanent Population in Towns and Administrative Villages (10000 persons)	乡镇及行政村从业人员 (万人) Employed Persons in Towns and Administrative Villages (10000 persons)
1978				91.9	382.1	165.3
1979				92.9	374.7	165.1
1980				95.0	374.3	167.4
1981				98.9	377.6	172.9
1982				103.2	381.8	179.4
1983				106.6	384.0	184.6
1984				108.9	385.6	188.9
1985	350	15	4394	111.8	387.2	190.0
1986	327	15	4400	113.1	386.9	189.5
1987	324	14	4326	115.7	388.9	189.8
1988	321	13	4111	118.6	389.6	189.2
1989	322	14	4483	121.5	390.0	186.1
1990	252	77	4481	124.5	392.0	184.3
1991	209	77	4480	125.5	390.7	182.1
1992	209	77	4229	126.2	387.6	178.7
1993	192	81	4476	126.5	382.4	176.0
1994	174	92	4464	124.9	376.0	171.6
1995	166	100	4355	125.0	371.5	163.6
1996	166	100	4357	124.6	368.9	164.2
1997	132	108	4348	124.6	365.3	161.2
1998	126	105	4032	125.9	364.4	161.0
1999	125	103	4040	125.9	363.9	165.3
2000	70	142	4039	126.8	363.7	165.8
2001	52	139	4010	127.6	361.6	165.3
2002	51	141	4005	128.0	357.6	165.6
2003	45	142	3985	131.1	360.6	169.6
2004	42	142	3985	132.8	359.9	171.4
2005	43	142	3953	142.2	381.8	184.0
2006	41	142	3957	143.6	501.6	316.9
2007	41	142	3955	176.9	510.0	313.4
2008	40	142	3951	189.8	547.4	321.3
2009	40	142	3950	203.8	572.5	338.7
2010	40	142	3943	216.0	589.4	347.8
2011	38	144	3941	212.4	574.8	338.3
2012	38	144	3940	215.2	582.5	341.7
2013	38	144	3938	221.9	599.5	353.5
2014	38	144	3937	225.2	606.9	357.0
2015	38	144	3936	221.4	593.5	348.0
2016	38	143	3941	232.6	612.6	385.9

注：1．从业人员指标1998年以前为乡村劳动力。
2．乡政府个数、镇政府个数、村民委员会个数由北京市民政局提供。
3．2006年乡镇及行政村人口和从业人员为农业普查数据；2007年以后乡镇及行政村人口和从业人员为农业普查口径，包含居住半年以上外来人口。
4．2006年乡镇及行政村户数为农业普查数据，为自然户口径；2007年以后为居住一年以上的户口径。

Note: a) Employed persons before 1998 were rural labor force.
b) Numbers of township governments, town governments, villagers' committees are provided by Beijing Municipal Bureau of Civil Affairs.
c) Population and employed persons in towns and administrative villages were agriculture census data in 2006. Statistical range of agriculture census data have covered population and employed persons in towns and administrative villages since 2007 including migrant population residing for over 6 months.
d) Number of households in towns and administrative villages in 2006 was from agricultural census, using natural households as the caliber; since 2007, the caliber was changed into households residing for over a year.

11-2 农业生产条件(1978-2016年)
CONDITIONS FOR AGRICULTURAL PRODUCTION (1978-2016)

年 份 Year	年末实有耕地面积(万公顷) Actual Area of Arable Land (year-end) (10000 hectares)	农业机械总动力(万千瓦) Total Power of Agricultural Machinery (10000 kW)	农村用电量(万千瓦小时) Rural Electricity Consumption (10000 kWh)	化肥施用量(万吨) Consumption of Chemical Fertilizers (10000 tons)
1978	42.9	189.4	58802	11.6
1979	42.7	212.2	63124	11.3
1980	42.6	234.6	76753	12.3
1981	42.5	244.8	91844	11.2
1982	42.4	242.2	96961	12.0
1983	42.3	261.8	104608	12.0
1984	42.2	290.8	119289	10.7
1985	42.1	320.4	126830	8.2
1986	41.9	345.5	180640	9.1
1987	41.8	388.4	159450	10.0
1988	41.6	399.7	163986	10.6
1989	41.4	423.9	128414	11.8
1990	41.3	416.2	122711	14.4
1991	41.1	384.8	111347	14.4
1992	40.9	399.8	143963	14.4
1993	40.6	450.5	169911	14.9
1994	40.2	459.2	172042	19.8
1995	39.4	468.1	201731	18.8
1996	34.4	468.4	275871	18.9
1997	34.2	433.2	301655	19.7
1998	34.1	415.5	290859	19.3
1999	33.8	410.4	330069	19.0
2000	32.9	399.2	572257	17.9
2001	29.2	394.9	619806	15.7
2002	27.5	381.8	414248	14.9
2003	26.0	366.9	427266	14.3
2004	23.6	340.3	383954	14.5
2005	23.3	337.7	421680	14.8
2006	23.3	325.5	416459	14.8
2007	23.2	300.5	411238	14.0
2008	23.2	267.0	427377	13.6
2009	22.7	271.5	439099	13.8
2010	22.4	276.0	443774	13.7
2011	22.2	265.2	454009	13.8
2012	22.1	241.1	473121	13.7
2013	22.1	207.7	485320	12.8
2014	22.0	195.8	505559	11.6
2015	21.9	185.9	516705	10.5
2016		144.4	547099	9.7

注：1．化肥施用量为折纯量。
2．2003年以前农村用电量由原北京市供电局提供。
3．农业机械总动力数据由北京市农业局提供。

Note: a) Data on consumption of chemical fertilizers were net amount.
b) Figures of rural electricity consumption before 2003 were provided by the former Beijing Electric Power Supply Bureau.
c) Figures of total power of agricultural machinery were provided by Beijing Municipal Bureau of Agriculture.

11-3 农作物播种面积和造林面积(1978-2016年)
SOWN AND AFFORESTATION AREA (1978-2016)

年 份 Year	农作物播种面积(万公顷) Sown Area (10000 hectares)	#粮食作物 Grain Crops	#玉米 Corn	#小麦 Wheat	#油料 Oil-bearing Crops	#蔬菜及食用菌 Vegetables and Edible Mushrooms	#瓜类及草莓 Melons & Strawberries	#饲料 Forage	造林面积(万公顷) Afforestation Area (10000 hectares)
1978	69.1	56.1	16.9	19.2	3.3	5.6	0.2	2.0	1.4
1979	67.7	56.0	18.2	19.7	3.0	5.4	0.3	2.0	1.6
1980	65.7	54.9	19.7	18.8	2.8	5.1	0.4	1.8	2.4
1981	64.4	53.0	19.8	18.4	2.7	5.5	0.6	1.7	2.7
1982	64.2	52.7	19.7	18.1	2.4	5.9	0.8	1.6	2.8
1983	63.8	53.0	20.1	18.7	1.9	5.7	0.5	1.5	3.3
1984	63.3	52.3	20.6	19.5	1.8	5.8	0.7	1.5	3.2
1985	61.8	51.1	21.7	19.1	2.0	5.4	0.9	1.3	3.0
1986	60.5	49.9	21.6	18.5	2.0	5.8	1.1	1.0	1.5
1987	59.8	49.5	22.3	18.3	1.6	6.0	0.9	1.1	2.0
1988	59.5	48.8	22.2	18.6	1.5	6.3	1.0	1.2	1.6
1989	58.9	48.3	21.9	18.5	1.3	6.8	0.8	1.1	0.8
1990	59.0	48.4	22.4	18.8	1.2	7.0	0.6	1.1	1.3
1991	59.0	48.3	22.3	19.2	1.2	7.3	0.5	1.0	1.5
1992	58.5	47.7	22.4	19.2	1.2	7.5	0.5	0.8	1.5
1993	56.5	45.6	21.8	17.8	1.3	7.8	0.5	0.7	4.8
1994	55.1	43.0	20.6	16.4	1.2	9.1	0.6	0.6	5.5
1995	55.3	43.4	20.8	17.2	1.2	9.1	0.5		4.7
1996	53.8	42.7	20.8	17.1	1.1	8.8	0.5	0.5	4.0
1997	53.6	42.5	20.6	17.1	1.0	8.9	0.5	0.5	3.8
1998	53.5	42.3	20.8	17.1	1.0	9.0	0.5	0.5	3.7
1999	52.6	41.0	19.8	16.8	1.0	9.2	0.5	0.5	3.0
2000	45.4	30.8	13.6	12.2	1.5	10.4	0.8	1.2	2.6
2001	38.0	21.4	10.0	7.3	1.4	11.3	0.9	1.9	3.2
2002	33.5	16.9	8.7	4.7	1.6	11.5	0.9	1.8	4.8
2003	30.1	14.1	7.5	3.6	1.4	10.8	0.9	1.9	4.7
2004	30.4	15.4	9.4	3.9	1.1	9.1	0.8	2.8	3.2
2005	30.8	19.2	12.0	5.3	0.9	7.9	0.8	1.5	1.2
2006	32.0	22.0	13.6	6.3	0.7	7.1	0.9	0.6	1.3
2007	29.5	19.7	13.9	4.1	0.7	7.0	0.9	0.4	1.1
2008	32.2	22.6	14.6	6.4	0.7	6.8	0.8	0.4	0.9
2009	32.0	22.6	15.1	6.1	0.6	6.8	0.8	0.4	1.8
2010	31.7	22.3	15.0	6.2	0.5	6.8	0.8	0.5	1.4
2011	30.3	20.9	14.1	5.8	0.5	6.7	0.8	0.5	2.1
2012	28.3	19.4	13.2	5.2	0.5	6.4	0.8	0.3	3.6
2013	24.2	15.9	11.4	3.6	0.3	6.2	0.7	0.2	4.4
2014	20.0	12.0	8.9	2.4	0.3	5.7	0.6	0.3	2.3
2015	17.7	10.4	7.6	2.1	0.2	5.4	0.5	0.2	0.8
2016	15.1	8.7	6.5	1.6	0.2	4.7	0.4	0.3	1.0

注：1．蔬菜播种面积2006年为农业普查衔接数据，1997年—2005年为历史修订数据。
2．造林面积2009年以前为人工造林面积，2009年起调整为荒山荒(沙)地造林面积，包括人工造林、无林地和疏林地新封面积。

Note: a) Figures of vegetable sown area in 2006 were from agricultural census, and figures in 1997-2005 were historically revised data.
b) Afforestation area before 2009 was artificial afforestation area, and after 2009 it became barren mountains and barren (sand) afforestation area, including the area of artificial forests, non-forest land and newly enclosed forest land.

11-4 农林牧渔业总产值(1978-2016年)
GROSS OUTPUT VALUE OF AGRICULTURE, FORESTRY, ANIMAL PRODUCTION AND HUNTING, FISHING (1978-2016)

年 份 Year	农林牧渔业总产值(亿元) Gross Output Value of Agriculture, Forestry, Animal Production and Hunting, Fishing (100 million yuan)	农 业 Agriculture	林 业 Forestry	牧 业 Animal Production and Hunting	渔 业 Fishing	农林牧渔服务业 Related Service Industry	农林牧渔业总产值比上年增长(%) Growth Rate (%) 按现价计算 Calculated at Current Price	按可比价计算 Calculated at Comparable Price
1978	11.5	8.9	0.2	2.4	0.01			
1979	12.3	8.8	0.2	3.3	0.02		7.0	
1980	14.3	9.8	0.5	3.9	0.05		16.3	
1981-1985	**99.4**	**64.6**	**3.9**	**30.1**	**0.8**			
1981	14.9	10.1	0.7	4.1	0.05		4.2	
1982	16.8	11.3	0.7	4.7	0.05		12.8	
1983	19.6	12.7	0.8	6.0	0.1		16.7	
1984	22.2	14.4	0.9	6.7	0.2		13.3	
1985	25.9	16.1	0.8	8.6	0.4		16.7	
1986-1990	**245.7**	**142.1**	**4.1**	**91.6**	**7.9**			
1986	28.1	17.2	0.8	9.4	0.7		8.5	
1987	34.4	20.3	0.8	12.3	1.0		22.4	
1988	52.6	31.4	0.9	18.6	1.7		52.9	
1989	60.4	34.2	0.7	23.3	2.2		14.8	
1990	70.2	39.0	0.9	28.0	2.3		16.2	
1991-1995	**570.1**	**293.2**	**11.2**	**244.6**	**21.1**			
1991	76.5	39.6	1.5	32.8	2.6		9.0	
1992	84.5	43.2	1.6	36.3	3.4		10.5	
1993	100.4	51.1	2.3	42.7	4.3		18.8	
1994	144.3	72.5	3.1	64.0	4.7		43.7	
1995	164.4	86.8	2.7	68.8	6.1		13.9	
1996-2000	**883.4**	**441.8**	**18.2**	**388.5**	**34.9**			
1996	168.9	89.2	2.8	71.1	5.8		2.7	
1997	170.5	86.8	2.9	74.6	6.2		0.9	
1998	174.8	88.3	3.2	75.8	7.5		2.5	
1999	180.6	89.4	4.1	79.5	7.6		3.3	
2000	188.6	88.1	5.2	87.5	7.8		4.4	
2001-2005	**1114.6**	**423.2**	**57.0**	**567.3**	**45.6**			
2001	202.2	84.7	9.0	99.3	9.2		7.2	
2002	213.5	83.5	11.9	108.6	9.5		5.6	
2003	224.7	80.9	12.3	114.3	9.3	7.9	5.2	
2004	234.9	83.1	11.4	124.3	8.9	7.2	4.5	
2005	239.3	91.0	12.4	120.8	8.7	6.4	1.9	
2006-2010	**1459.4**	**648.4**	**87.1**	**643.7**	**51.5**	**28.7**		
2006	240.2	104.5	14.8	105.1	9.8	6.0	0.4	0.9
2007	272.3	115.5	17.8	122.4	10.1	6.5	13.4	0.8
2008	303.9	128.1	20.5	140.5	9.8	5.0	11.6	0.8
2009	315.0	146.1	17.2	136.1	10.3	5.3	3.6	5.5
2010	328.0	154.2	16.8	139.6	11.5	5.9	4.1	-1.7
2011-2015	**1968.9**	**809.7**	**297.6**	**760.2**	**62.4**	**39.2**		
2011	363.1	163.4	18.9	162.7	11.5	6.6	10.7	0.9
2012	395.7	166.3	54.8	154.2	13.0	7.5	9.0	2.9
2013	421.8	170.4	75.9	154.8	12.8	8.0	6.6	2.1
2014	420.1	155.1	90.7	152.7	13.2	8.4	-0.4	…
2015	368.2	154.5	57.3	135.9	11.9	8.7	-12.3	-11.7
2016	338.1	145.2	52.2	122.7	9.2	8.7	-8.2	-9.9

注：1.农林牧渔业总产值绝对数按现价计算，从2003年起执行新《国民经济行业分类标准》，农林牧渔业总产值中含农林牧渔服务业产值。

2.2003年以后，计算农林牧渔业总产值使用的价格从农产品综合平均价调整为农产品生产价格。

3.2006年为与农业普查衔接的数据，1997-2005年为历史修订数据。

4.2010年按照新的《统计用产品分类目录》，将原归属林业产值的核桃、板栗等林产品调整至农业产值，并对2009年数据作了调整。

Note: a) The absolute number of agricultural gross output value are calculated at current prices. In the year of 2003, new Standard for Classification of National Economic Sectors was implemented, and gross output value of agriculture, forestry, animal production and hunting, fishing has included the output value of services for agriculture, forestry, animal production and hunting, fishing.

b) After 2003, the prices used for calculating the output value of agriculture, forestry, animal production and hunting, fishing have been changed from comprehensive average price of agricultural products to production price of agricultural products.

c) Figures for 2006 were from agricultural census, and figures in 1997-2005 were historically revised data.

d) Output value of forestry productions such as walnuts and chestnuts was transferred to that of the agriculture sector in 2010 according to the new Catalog of Product Classification Used for Statistics. Figures of 2009 were adjusted accordingly.

11–5 主要农业产品产量(1978–2016年)
OUTPUT OF MAJOR AGRICULTURAL PRODUCTS (1978-2016)

单位：万吨 (10000 tons)

年 份 Year	粮 食 Grain	油 料 Oil-bearing Crops	蔬菜及食用菌 Vegetables and Edible Mushroom	干鲜果品 Nuts and Fresh Fruits	牛 奶 Milk	肉 类 Meat	#猪牛羊肉 Pork, Beef and Mutton	禽蛋产量 Poultry and Eggs	水产品 Aquatic Products
1978	186.0	2.6	164.5	17.5	5.4	11.9	11.9	2.1	0.2
1979	172.8	2.6	181.3	15.8	6.0	13.1	13.1	3.1	0.3
1980	186.0	3.1	175.9	15.9	6.8	15.1	15.1	3.4	0.4
1981–1985	**1004.8**	**13.1**	**1002.2**	**86.7**	**53.3**	**69.0**	**69.0**	**44.3**	**4.0**
1981	180.7	2.2	172.8	15.6	7.6	13.2	13.2	3.7	0.4
1982	185.5	2.3	208.3	13.8	8.9	13.9	13.9	5.4	0.4
1983	201.5	2.1	199.1	18.2	10.6	14.9	14.9	8.9	0.6
1984	217.4	2.6	218.0	20.2	12.6	13.4	13.4	12.2	1.0
1985	219.7	3.9	204.0	18.9	13.5	13.6	13.6	14.1	1.6
1986–1990	**1181.9**	**15.2**	**1422.2**	**119.3**	**89.7**	**90.8**	**78.3**	**103.8**	**18.8**
1986	216.5	3.0	222.7	18.7	14.6	13.3	13.3	14.7	2.2
1987	227.0	3.3	241.1	22.5	15.5	12.9	12.9	16.8	3.0
1988	234.6	3.0	271.3	23.8	18.0	14.5	14.5	21.8	3.9
1989	239.2	2.8	331.0	26.7	19.9	23.3	17.2	24.7	4.6
1990	264.6	3.1	356.1	27.6	21.7	26.8	20.4	25.8	5.1
1991–1995	**1354.7**	**17.6**	**1915.9**	**198.5**	**113.7**	**180.7**	**134.0**	**139.3**	**34.7**
1991	279.7	3.3	368.4	29.3	23.9	33.9	24.8	27.9	5.6
1992	281.9	3.4	381.4	34.0	24.5	35.9	27.3	30.0	6.4
1993	284.1	3.8	418.8	39.6	22.5	36.7	28.2	31.4	7.0
1994	249.2	3.8	350.0	48.8	22.2	34.4	24.8	31.2	7.6
1995	259.8	3.3	397.3	46.8	20.6	39.8	28.9	28.5	8.1
1996–2000	**1059.4**	**15.0**	**2101.9**	**291.8**	**120.2**	**218.1**	**146.5**	**98.2**	**38.2**
1996	237.4	2.9	403.2	51.3	21.0	38.2	27.3	24.7	7.8
1997	237.5	2.7	408.8	54.8	22.2	39.9	27.8	23.8	7.7
1998	239.3	2.8	403.8	59.5	22.7	43.4	30.3	17.9	7.6
1999	201.0	2.8	419.8	60.2	24.0	46.1	30.2	15.8	7.6
2000	144.2	3.8	466.3	66.0	30.3	50.5	30.9	16.0	7.5
2001–2005	**410.3**	**18.5**	**2302.3**	**419.5**	**295.5**	**287.8**	**169.1**	**78.9**	**35.0**
2001	104.9	4.3	491.0	71.9	42.9	55.9	33.0	15.6	7.4
2002	82.3	4.6	507.4	78.7	55.1	60.9	35.2	15.2	7.4
2003	58.0	3.3	486.7	84.1	63.3	60.6	35.2	16.2	7.1
2004	70.2	2.9	444.1	90.9	70.0	57.4	34.0	15.9	6.7
2005	94.9	2.5	373.1	93.9	64.2	53.3	31.7	16.0	6.4
2006–2010	**577.3**	**10.0**	**1622.7**	**445.3**	**322.1**	**231.7**	**135.0**	**76.5**	**29.6**
2006	109.2	2.2	341.2	88.7	61.9	45.3	26.9	15.2	5.4
2007	102.1	2.2	340.1	91.1	62.2	47.9	27.1	15.6	6.0
2008	125.5	2.2	321.3	89.8	66.4	45.1	25.9	15.2	6.1
2009	124.8	1.8	317.1	90.3	67.4	47.2	27.6	15.4	5.8
2010	115.7	1.6	303.0	85.4	64.1	46.3	27.5	15.1	6.3
2011–2015	**458.3**	**4.9**	**1285.0**	**397.5**	**307.3**	**205.1**	**134.9**	**87.1**	**33.9**
2011	121.8	1.4	296.9	87.8	64.0	44.4	27.6	15.1	6.1
2012	113.8	1.3	279.9	84.3	65.1	43.2	27.3	15.2	6.4
2013	96.1	1.0	266.9	79.5	61.5	41.8	27.9	17.5	6.4
2014	63.9	0.7	236.2	74.5	59.5	39.3	26.9	19.7	6.8
2015	62.6	0.6	205.1	71.4	57.2	36.4	25.2	19.6	6.6
2016	53.7	0.6	183.6	66.1	45.7	30.4	24.4	18.3	5.4

注：1．蔬菜、干鲜果品、猪牛羊肉产量2006年为农业普查衔接数据，1997年—2005年为历史修订数据。
2．肉类产量1988年及以前为猪牛羊肉产量。
3．2006年及以前水产品产量为淡水鱼产量，2007年以后含远洋捕捞量。水产品数据由北京市农业局提供。

Note: a) Figures of output for vegetables, nuts and fresh fruits, pork, beef and mutton in 2006 were from agricultural census, and figures in 1997-2005 were historically revised data.
b) Output of meat in and before 1988 was the output of pork, beef and mutton.
c) Output of aquatic products was output of fresh water fish in and before 2006, and long-range fishing has been included since 2007. Figures of aquatic products were provided by Beijing Municipal Bureau of Agriculture.

11-6 平均每一从业人员创造农、林、牧、渔业产值(1990-2016年)
AVERAGE OUTPUT VALUE OF AGRICULTURE, FORESTRY, ANIMAL PRODUCTION AND HUNTING, FISHING CREATED BY EACH PERSON (1990-2016)

单位：元 (Yuan)

年份 Year	农林牧渔业总产值 Total Output Value of Agriculture, Forestry, Animal Production and Hunting, Fishing	#农业 Agriculture	#林业 Forestry	#畜牧业 Animal Production and Hunting	#渔业 Fishing
1990	8507	5537	1540	54837	22729
1991	9523	5722	2807	68268	26442
1992	11329	6678	3826	78905	33689
1993	13859	8271	4558	92901	39518
1994	21002	12461	6507	139136	39182
1995	25110	15760	5750	156332	47266
1996	25250	15504	6741	173404	53133
1997	26101	15605	6886	169541	56211
1998	25817	15653	7724	124279	68379
1999	25396	15621	8398	101869	63684
2000	27061	16454	8416	99481	65223
2001	29772	16838	12287	109151	76321
2002	33313	18193	15209	116799	86784
2003	37770	19579	14634	129862	92879
2004	40569	20934	12376	153518	98619
2005	40834	22700	12496	156911	96184
2006	36559	21147	17398	166889	195867
2007	44276	25892	19324	177359	126998
2008	49175	28405	22031	212910	122318
2009	51750	33061	18507	215008	128750
2010	54579	35130	17886	228814	164441
2011	62556	38613	20344	285988	155637
2012	70258	40585	59852	282916	175234
2013	77516	43643	81323	294659	179937
2014	81816	42790	98094	313314	199704
2015	74570	45000	60007	292513	183929
2016	66069	38680	69071	308089	168466

注：1. 2006年从业人员为农业普查数据，2007年以后为农业普查口径，含居住半年以上的外来人口。
2. 2006年农林牧渔业总产值及分行业产值为与农业普查衔接的数据，1997-2005年为历史修订数据。
3. 2010年按照新的《统计用产品分类目录》，将原归属林业产值的核桃、板栗等林产品调整至农业产值，并对2009年数据作了调整。

Note: a) Figures of employed persons in 2006 were from agriculture census. These figures are from agriculture census and include migrant population who have resided for over half a year since 2007.

b) Figures of output value for agriculture, forestry, animal production and hunting, fishing in 2006 were from agricultural census, and figures in 1997-2005 were historically revised data.

c) Output value of forestry, such as walnuts and chestnuts, was transferred to the agriculture sector in 2010 according to the new Catalog of Product Classification Used for Statistics. Figures in 2009 were adjusted accordingly.

11-7 耕地面积(2014-2015年) ARABLE LAND AREA (2014-2015)

单位：公顷 (hectare)

项　　目	Item	2015	2014
年初耕地总资源	**Total Arable Land Resources at the Beginning of the Year**	**219948.76**	**221157.28**
年内增加	**Increase in the Year**	**173.61**	**53.54**
土地综合整治	Comprehensive Land Improvement	134.16	44.49
农业结构调整	Agricultural Structure Adjustment	39.45	9.05
年内减少	**Decrease in the Year**	**795.88**	**1262.06**
建设占用	Occupied by Construction	686.79	911.63
灾害损毁	Disaster Damage		
生态退耕	Farmland Converted for EcologicalPreservation		
农业结构调整	Agricultural Structure Adjustment	109.09	350.43
年末耕地面积	**Total Arable Land Resources at the End of the Year**	**219326.49**	**219948.76**
水　田	Paddy Field	1970.51	1992.75
水浇地	Irrigable Land	165881.70	166347.22
其　他	Others	51474.28	51608.79

资料来源：北京市规划和国土资源管理委员会。
Source: Urban Planning, Land & Resources Administration Commission of Beijing Municipal.

11-8 农业观光园、民俗旅游、种业和设施农业(2005-2016年)

项目		Item		2005	2006
农业观光园		**Agricultural Sightseeing Gardens**			
农业观光园个数	(个)	Number of Agricultural Sightseeing Gardens	(unit)	1012	1230
高峰期从业人员	(人)	Employed Persons in Peak Production Period	(person)	40729	52828
接待人次	(万人次)	Visits Received	(10000 person-times)	892.5	1210.6
经营总收入	(亿元)	Total Operating Income	(100 million yuan)	7.88	10.49
民俗旅游		**Folk-Custom Tourism Receiption**			
从事民俗旅游实际经营		Number of Actual Operating Households in			
接待户	(户)	Folk-Custom Tourism Receiption	(household)	7268	8726
高峰期从业人员	(人)	Employed Persons in Peak Production Period		14070	18253
		of the Term	(person)		
民俗旅游接待人次	(万人次)	Number of Visits Received by Folk-Custom		758.9	982.5
		Tourism	(10000 person-times)		
民俗旅游总收入	(亿元)	Total Income of Folk-Custom Tourism	(100 million yuan)	3.14	3.65
种　业		**Seed Industry**			
种业收入	(亿元)	Income	(100 million yuan)	5.94	7.75
#销往外埠收入	(亿元)	Sales to Other Areas	(100 million yuan)		
#牧业收入	(亿元)	Income from Animal Production and Hunting	(100 million yuan)		
设施农业		**Facility Agriculture**			
设施农业实际利用占		Actual Area Utilized by Facility Agriculture	(hectare)		
地面积	(公顷)			15645	17832
设施农业播种面积	(公顷)	Sown Area of Facility Agriculture	(hectare)		
设施农业收入	(亿元)	Income of Facility Agriculture	(100 million yuan)	18.62	21.11

AGRICULTURAL SIGHTSEEING GARDENS, FOLK-CUSTOM TOURISM, BREEDING OF SEEDS AND FACILITY AGRICULTURE (2005-2016)

2007	2008	2009	2010	2011	2012	2013	2014	2015	2016
1302	1332	1294	1303	1300	1283	1299	1301	1328	1258
51392	49366	49504	42561	46038	48906	50406	47088	42617	40349
1446.8	1498.2	1597.4	1774.9	1842.9	1939.9	1944.4	1911.2	1903.3	2250.5
13.15	13.58	15.24	17.80	21.72	26.88	27.36	24.92	26.31	27.98
10323	9151	8705	7979	8396	8367	8530	8863	8941	9026
20750	19421	19790	16856	18232	18705	19578	21493	22313	22215
1167.6	1205.6	1393.1	1553.6	1668.9	1695.8	1806.5	1914.2	2139.7	2297.4
4.96	5.29	6.09	7.35	8.68	9.05	10.20	11.25	12.86	14.35
9.91	10.93	12.84	14.57	18.12	16.09	13.98	14.04	12.67	13.99
3.99	5.78	7.28	8.05	11.68	9.70	8.23	7.95	6.64	7.72
8.27	9.27	10.56	12.13	15.09	13.63	12.59	12.51	11.23	12.91
18022	17051	18762	18323	18616	19059	18852	18232	17397	15404
30331	33889	36203	36811	38006	37797	38763	38115	41088	37666
28.12	28.17	33.91	40.72	45.58	51.98	57.32	51.27	55.50	54.37

11-9 农业生产条件
PRODUCTIVE CONDITIONS OF AGRICULTURE

项　目		Item		2016	2015	2016年为2015年% 2016 as % of 2015
主要农业机械拥有量		**Possession of Major Agricultural Machinery**				
农业机械总动力	(万千瓦)	Total Power of Agricultural Machinery	(10000 kw)	144.4	185.9	77.7
大中型拖拉机	(混合台)	Large and Medium-sized Tractors	(unit)	7286	6998	104.1
小型拖拉机	(台)	Mini Tractors	(unit)	1309	1445	90.6
机引农具	(台)	Tractor-propelled Farm Tools	(unit)	12418	12348	100.6
机动喷雾器	(部)	Motorized Sprayers	(unit)	19433	19946	97.4
联合收割机	(台)	Combine Harvesters	(unit)	1667	1783	93.5
机动脱粒机	(台)	Motorized Shellers	(unit)	3791	3947	96.0
米面加工机	(台)	Processing Machines of Rice and Flour	(unit)	3957	3762	105.2
机动挤奶器	(台)	Motorized Milkers	(unit)	1875	1873	100.1
饲料粉碎机	(台)	Fodder Grinders	(unit)	3702	3796	97.5
农业机械作业面积		**Operation Area of Agricultural Machinery**				
机耕面积	(公顷)	Cultivated Area by Machinery	(hectare)	10833	12553	86.3
占全部耕地面积比重	(%)	Share in the Total Arable Land	(%)	90.3	89.6	
机播面积	(公顷)	Sown Area by Machinery	(hectare)	81444	94229	86.4
占播种面积比重	(%)	Share in the Total Sown Area	(%)	94.7	93.8	
机收面积	(公顷)	Harvest Area by Machinery	(hectare)	72736	80979	89.8
占收获面积比重	(%)	Share in the Total Harvest Area	(%)	81.9	78.9	
农村用电量及小水电		**Rural Electricity Consumption and Small Hydropower Stations**				
农村用电量	(万千瓦小时)	Rural Electricity Consumption	(10000 kwh)	547099	516705	105.9
农田水利		**Irrigation and Water Conservancy**				
排灌用动力机械	(台)	Irrigation Machinery	(unit)	35956	39449	91.1
排灌用动力机械动力	(万千瓦)	Power of Irrigation Machinery	(10000 kw)	42.4	45.6	92.9
机(电)井	(眼)	Motor-pumped Wells	(unit)	32586	32586	100.0
#已配套	(眼)	Completed Sets	(unit)	30645	30645	100.0
固定机电排灌站	(处)	Drainage and Irrigation Stations with Fixed Machinery	(unit)	782	1573	49.7
有效灌溉面积	(公顷)	Effective Irrigation Area	(hectare)	128470	137360	93.5
化肥施用量(折纯)		**Consumption of Chemical Fertilizers (converted into net amount)**				
化肥施用量	(吨)	Consumption of Chemical Fertilizers	(ton)	**96530**	**105284**	**91.7**
#氮　肥	(吨)	Nitrogenous Fertilizers	(ton)	43855	48524	90.4
磷　肥	(吨)	Phosphate Fertilizers	(ton)	5423	5981	90.7
钾　肥	(吨)	Potash Fertilizers	(ton)	5070	5373	94.4

注：1．农村小水电站是指乡村两级小水电站实有数。
2．主要农业机械拥有量、农业机械作业面积、排灌动力机械数据由北京市农业局提供。
3．机(电)井、固定机电排灌站数据由北京市水务局提供。

Note: a) Figures of rural small hydropower stations refer to actual number of small hydropower stations at township and village level.
b) Figures of possession of major agricultural machinery, operation area of agricultural machinery and irrigation machinery are provided by Beijing Municipal Bureau of Agriculture.
c) Figures of motor-pumped wells and Drainage and Irrigation Stations with Fixed Machinery are provided by Beijing Water Authority.

11-10 农林牧渔业总产值
GROSS OUTPUT VALUE OF AGRICULTURE, FORESTRY, ANIMAL PRODUCTION AND HUNTING, FISHING

单位：万元 (10000 yuan)

项目	Item	总产值 Gross Output Value 2016	2015	2016年为2015年% 2016 as % of 2015
合计	**Total**	**3380635.1**	**3682372.2**	**91.8**
农业	**Agriclture**	**1452011.5**	**1544776.6**	**94.0**
谷物	Cereal	97019.8	124551.0	77.9
豆类	Beans	3324.2	4645.7	71.6
经济作物	Cash Crops	4996.4	5021.8	99.5
蔬菜、食用菌	Vegetables and Edible Mushromms	699433.9	709806.4	98.5
水果（含瓜果类）	Fruits (including melons)	450386.6	506714.3	88.9
其他	Others	196850.6	194037.4	101.4
林业	**Forestry**	**522090.4**	**573278.6**	**91.1**
牧业	**Animal Production and Hunting**	**1226873.9**	**1358578.1**	**90.3**
牲畜饲养	Animal Breeding	318713.8	392526.8	81.2
养猪	Hogs	542999.9	465125.5	116.7
家禽饲养	Poultry	338993.4	463283.6	73.2
#禽蛋	Poultry Eggs	210723.6	248813.5	84.7
其他	Others	26166.8	37642.2	69.5
渔业	**Fishing**	**92269.0**	**118689.5**	**77.7**
农林牧渔服务业	**Services for Farming, Forestry, Animal Production and Hunting, Fishing**	**87390.3**	**87049.4**	**100.4**

11-11 主要农作物播种面积及产量
SOWN AREA AND OUTPUT OF MAJOR CROPS

项目	Item	2016 播种面积(公顷) Sown Areas (hectare)	2016 单产(公斤/公顷) Output Per Unit (kg/hectare)	2016 总产量(吨) Total Output (ton)	2015 播种面积(公顷) Sown Areas (hectare)	2015 单产(公斤/公顷) Output Per Unit (kg/hectare)	2015 总产量(吨) Total Output (ton)
粮食	**Grain**	**87328.7**	**6148.3**	**536917.2**	**104453.5**	**5996.6**	**626362.4**
按季节分	By Season						
夏粮	Summer Grain	15952.7	5366.3	85607.1	20863.9	5343.1	111478.3
秋粮	Autumn Grain	71376.0	6323.0	451310.1	83589.5	6159.7	514884.1
按品种分	Grouped by Variety						
稻谷	Rice	172.3	6721.1	1157.8	199.6	6971.4	1391.5
冬小麦	Winter Wheat	15889.3	5376.8	85433.0	20697.6	5356.8	110872.9
玉米	Corn	65236.8	6620.6	431903.5	76290.0	6481.7	494485.1
薯类	Tubers	1378.4	6347.0	8748.7	1404.9	5952.6	8362.9
大豆	Soybeans	2310.4	1894.8	4377.9	3477.6	1877.2	6528.3
棉花	**Cotton**	**53.4**	**1.1**	**58.2**	**96.2**	**1044.7**	**100.5**
油料	**Oil-bearing Crops**	**2207.8**	**2.6**	**5570.4**	**2115.7**	**2674.3**	**5657.9**
#花生	Peanuts	1490.0	3.0	4442.9	1779.1	2904.5	5167.3
中草药材	**Chinese medicine herbs**	**2520.3**	**1.4**	**3262.5**	**2252.7**	**1047.9**	**2360.6**
蔬菜及食用菌	**Vegetables and Edible Mushrooms**	**47450.2**	**38688.4**	**1835771.2**	**54270.7**	**37800.2**	**2051446.8**
瓜类及草莓	**Melons & Strawberries**	**4248.5**	**39524.6**	**167920.3**	**5203.3**	**39427.5**	**205154.6**
#西瓜	Watermelons	3485.7	43767.2	152559.5	4355.4	42886.5	186787.7
饲料	**Forage**	**2528.8**			**2250.5**		
#牧草	Forage Grass	104.5			366.9		
花卉	**Flowers**	**2682.4**			**2825.1**		

11－12 林业及干鲜果品生产
FORESTRY, NUTS AND FRESH FRUIT PRODUCTION

项目		Item		2016	2015	2016年为2015年% 2016 as % of 2015
林业生产		**Forestry**				
造林面积	(公顷)	Afforestation Area	(hectare)	99048	89707	110.4
#人工造林面积	(公顷)	Artificial Afforestation Area	(hectare)	10012	8133	123.1
育苗面积	(公顷)	Seedling Growing Area	(hectare)	14925	15161	98.4
果类生产		**Fruits**				
干鲜果总产量	(吨)	Output of Nuts and Fresh Fruit	(ton)	660910	713827	92.6
干　果	(吨)	Nuts	(ton)	39117	39558	98.9
#核　桃	(吨)	Walnuts	(ton)	11156	10473	106.5
板　栗	(吨)	Chinese Chestnuts	(ton)	24001	25220	95.2
鲜　果	(吨)	Fresh Fruits	(ton)	621793	674270	92.2
#苹　果	(吨)	Apples	(ton)	72542	80357	90.3
梨	(吨)	Pears	(ton)	101273	126637	80.0
葡　萄	(吨)	Grapes	(ton)	28414	32697	86.9
柿　子	(吨)	Persimmons	(ton)	34508	35541	97.1
桃	(吨)	Peaches	(ton)	325643	340771	95.6
年末实有果园面积	**(公顷)**	**Actual Orchard Area (year-end)**	**(hectare)**	**52512**	**57137**	**91.9**

资料来源：林业生产数据由北京市园林绿化局提供。
Source: Figures of forestry are from Beijing Municipal Bureau of Landscape and Forestry.

11－13 牲畜饲养及畜产品产量
LIVESTOCK BREEDING AND OUTPUT

项目		Item		2016	2015	2016年为2015年% 2016as % of 2015
畜禽存栏		**Amount of Livestock and Poultry on Hand**				
大牲畜	(万头)	Large Animals	(10000 heads)	16.71	18.08	92.5
#牛	(万头)	Cattle and Buffaloes	(10000 heads)	16.16	17.48	92.4
猪	(万头)	Hogs	(10000 heads)	165.31	165.61	99.8
羊	(万只)	Sheep	(10000 units)	59.62	69.35	86.0
山　羊	(万只)	Goats	(10000 units)	17.77	18.97	93.7
绵　羊	(万只)	Sheep	(10000 units)	41.85	50.38	83.1
家　禽	(万只)	Poultry	(10000 units)	1838.05	2128.44	86.4
#产蛋鸡	(万只)	Hens	(10000 units)	1507.99	1533.80	98.3
肉　鸡	(万只)	Chickens	(10000 units)	194.41	420.43	46.2
鸭	(万只)	Ducks	(10000 units)	133.51	163.35	81.7
兔	(万只)	Rabbits	(10000 units)	3.44	4.32	79.8
畜禽出栏		**Amount of Livestock and Poultry Marketed**				
牛	(万头)	Cattle	(10000 heads)	7.38	8.44	87.5
猪	(万头)	Hogs	(10000 heads)	275.34	284.42	96.8
羊	(万只)	Sheep	(10000 units)	69.64	70.99	98.1
畜禽产品产量		**Output of Livestock and Poultry Products**				
肉类产量	(万吨)	Output of Meat	(10000 tons)	30.37	36.42	83.4
#猪　肉	(万吨)	Pork	(10000 tons)	21.84	22.48	97.1
牛　肉	(万吨)	Beef	(10000 tons)	1.36	1.55	88.0
羊　肉	(万吨)	Mutton	(10000 tons)	1.16	1.20	97.4
牛奶产量	(万吨)	Output of Milk	(10000 tons)	45.70	57.22	79.9
禽　蛋	(万吨)	Poultry Eggs	(10000 tons)	18.33	19.58	93.6
#鸡　蛋	(万吨)	Eggs	(10000 tons)	18.09	19.28	93.9
蜂　蜜	(吨)	Honey	(ton)	2039.55	1631.30	125.0

11-14 水产品生产 AQUATIC PRODUCTS

项　　目	Item	2016	2015	2016年为2015年% 2016 as % of 2015
渔业水域面积 (公顷)	**Area of Fishery Waters (hectare)**	**23724**	**24986**	**94.9**
#淡水养殖面积 (公顷)	Freshwater Agriculture (hectare)	3456	3633	95.1
#池　塘 (公顷)	Puddles and Ponds (hectare)	3397	3563	95.3
水产品产量 (吨)	**Output of Aquatic Products (ton)**	**54288**	**65813**	**82.5**
#淡水鱼产量 (吨)	Output of Freshwater Fish (ton)	40774	49146	83.0
#大水库 (吨)	Large Reservoirs (ton)	2353	2405	97.8
中、小水库 (吨)	Medium and Small Reservoirs (ton)	998	1699	58.7
池　塘 (吨)	Puddles and Ponds (ton)	33308	39728	83.8

资料来源：北京市农业局。
Source: Beijing Municipal Bureau of Agriculture.

11-15 农业观光园 STATISTICS FOR AGRICULTURAL SIGHTSEEING GARDENS

项　　目	Item	2016	2015	2016年为2015年% 2016 as % of 2015
农业观光园个数 (个)	Number of Agricultural Sightseeing Gardens (unit)	1258	1328	94.7
高峰期从业人员 (人)	Employed Persons in Peak Production Period (person)	40349	42617	94.7
接待人次 (万人次)	Visits Received (10000 person-times)	2250.5	1903.3	118.2
经营总收入 (万元)	Total Operating Income (10000 yuan)	279770.9	263138.9	106.3

11−16 民俗旅游
STATISTICS FOR FOLK-CUSTOM TOURISM

项目	Item	2016	2015	2016年为2015年% 2016 as % of 2015
从事民俗旅游实际经营接待户 (户)	Number of Actual Operating Households in Folk-Custom Tourism Receiption (household)	9026	8941	101.0
高峰期从业人员 (人)	Number of Employed Persons at the End of the Term (person)	22215	22313	99.6
民俗旅游接待人次(万人次)	Number of Visits Received by Folk-Custom Tourism (10000 person-times)	2297.4	2139.7	107.4
民俗旅游总收入 (万元)	Total Income of Folk-Custom Tourism (10000 yuan)	143540.6	128550.1	111.7

注：从2014年起，将民俗旅游中期末从业人员调整为高峰期从业人员。
Note: From 2014, employed persons of folk-custom tourism in late period are changed as the persons in peak production period.

11−17 种业生产
STATISTICS FOR PRODUCTION OF SEED INDUSTRY

项目	Item	产量 Output			收入(万元) Income (10000 yuan)		
		2016	2015	2016年为2015年% 2016 as % of 2015	2016	2015	2016年为2015年% 2016 as % of 2015
合 计	**Total**				**139867.7**	**126733.7**	**110.4**
农 业	**Agriculture**				**5884.4**	**6825.5**	**86.2**
#小麦种 (公斤)	Wheat Seeds (kg)	1175900	1197400	98.2	282.9	294	96.2
玉米种 (公斤)	Corn Seeds (kg)	582138	542838	107.2	418.6	384.6	108.8
蔬菜种 (公斤)	Vegetable Seeds (kg)	174435	241020	72.4	1748.7	1382.1	126.5
林 业	**Forestry**				**1121.2**	**3270.3**	**34.3**
#树 苗 (百株)	Saplings (100 units)	1086.0	6082.0	17.9	1121.2	3240.2	34.6
牧 业	**Animal Production and Hunting**				**129068.7**	**112331.3**	**114.9**
#种 猪 (头)	Boars (head)	152625	134832	113.2	36047.1	29022.0	124.2
种雏禽 (万只)	Breeding Birds (10000 units)	2926.7	2830.3	103.4	41881.1	19672.2	212.9
种 蛋 (万枚)	Breeding Eggs (10000 units)	34434.4	39311.4	87.6	40801.8	53502.1	76.3
渔 业	**Fishing**				**3793.4**	**4306.6**	**88.1**
#种鱼苗 (万尾)	Breeding Fish Fry (10000 units)	7317.4	9155.0	79.9	3251.4	3560.6	91.3

11-18 设施农业(2016年)
FACILITY AGRICULTURE (2016)

项 目	Item	设施农业播种面积 (公顷) Sown Area of Facility Agriculture (hectare)	设施农业产量 (吨) Output of Facility Agriculture (ton)	设施农业收入 (万元) Income of Facility Agriculture (10000 yuan)
合 计	**Total**	**37666**		**543706.9**
温 室	**Greenhousse**	**21195**		**385097.5**
蔬菜及食用菌	Vegetables and Edible Mushrooms	18932	720370	295885.3
花卉苗木	Flowers and Saplings	873		30014.6
#切 花	Cut Flowers	206	2304	5205.1
盆 花	Potted Flowers	648	8496	24314.9
瓜果类	Melons	789	17496	42526.8
园林水果	Fruits	529	4584	13199.2
其 它	Others	72		3471.6
大 棚	**Greenhouse Garden**	**14329**		**140024.2**
蔬菜及食用菌	Vegetables and Edible Mushrooms	11324	418373	107130.0
花卉苗木	Flowers and Sapling	235		6556.7
#切 花	Cut Flowers	39	753	1153.5
盆 花	Potted Flowers	187	2055	5383.2
瓜果类	Melons	2431	111018	22302.6
园林水果	Fruits	315	1864	2840.3
其 它	Other	25		1194.6
中小棚	**Medium and Small Shed**	**2142**		**18585.2**
蔬菜及食用菌	Vegetables and Edible Mushrooms	1378	39273	11947.5
花卉苗木	Flowers and Sapling	42		1234.3
#切 花	Cut Flowers	2	15	4.5
盆 花	Potted Flowers	27	470	1087.8
瓜果类	Melons	695	25143	5148.1
园林水果	Fruits	2	17	83.3
其 它	Other	25		172.0

注：切花产量的计量单位是万枝，盆花产量的计量单位是万盆。

Note: Cut flowers output are measured in 10000 ones; and potted flowers, 10000 pots.

11－19 乡镇企业各业基本情况(2016年)
BASIC STATISTICS FOR TOWN AND TOWNSHIP ENTERPRISES IN DIFFERENT SECTORS (2016)

项目	Item	企业个数(个) Number of Enterprises (unit)		从业人员(人) Employed Persons (person)		总收入(万元) Total Income (10000 yuan)		利润总额(万元) Total Profits (10000 yuan)	
		数量 Number	构成(%) Composition (%)	数量 Number	构成(%) Composition (%)	数量 Number	构成(%) Composition (%)	数量 Number	构成(%) Composition (%)
合计	**Total**	**124487**	**100.0**	**862308**	**100.0**	**48869621**	**100.0**	**2929370**	**100.0**
农业	Agriculture	8341	6.7	21558	2.5	381914	0.8	11748	0.4
工业	Industry	35805	28.8	481520	55.8	26966894	55.2	2052149	70.1
建筑业	Construction	4653	3.7	66908	7.8	3830010	7.8	46693	1.6
交通运输业	Transportation	17711	14.2	37125	4.3	1167593	2.4	109228	3.6
批发零售业	Wholesale and Retail Trade	33151	26.6	59341	6.9	8121018	16.6	105127	3.6
住宿及餐饮业	Lodging and Catering Services	11202	9.0	41217	4.8	619178	1.3	34315	1.2
居民服务、其它服务和娱乐业	Household Services, Other Services and Entertainment	11883	9.5	112544	13.1	4810959	9.8	396100	13.5
其他	Others	1741	1.4	42095	4.9	2972055	6.1	174010	5.9

资料来源：北京市经济和信息化委员会。
Source: Beijing Municipal Commission of Economy and Information Technology.

11-20 乡镇企业出口供货情况
GOODS SUPPLIES FOR EXPORT OF TOWN AND TOWNSHIP ENTERPRISES

单位：万元 (10000 yuan)

项　　目	Item	2016	2015
合　　计	**Total**	**841769**	**931928**
化　　工	Chemical Products	39674	43923
机　　械	Machinery	14171	15689
矿　　产	Mineral Products	7847	8687
轻　　工	Light Industry	127282	140915
食　　品	Food	91245	101018
土产畜产	Local and Livestock Products	19640	21744
纺织服装	Textile and Garments	286185	316837
工 艺 品	Artworks	20535	22734
其　　他	Others	235190	260380

资料来源：北京市经济和信息化委员会。
Source: Beijing Municipal Commission of Economy and Information Technology.

11−21 双层经营主要指标情况(2016年)
MAIN INDICATORS OF DOUBLE-LAYER MANAGEMENT SYSTEM(2016)

项目		Item		2016
集体经济组织情况		**Organizations of Collective Economy**		
乡镇级集体经济组织数	(个)	Number of Township-level Collective Economic Organizations	(Unit)	195
村级集体经济组织数	(个)	Number of Village-level Collective Economic Organizations	(Unit)	3945
汇总农户数	(户)	Total Number of Peasant Households	(Household)	1324653
汇总人口数	(人)	Total Number of Population	(Person)	3103097
劳动力总人数	(人)	Total Number of Labor Force	(Person)	1854661
就业率	(%)	Employment Rate	(%)	93
集体经济经营情况		**Operation of Collective Economy**		
集体经济总收入	(万元)	Gross Income of Collective Economy	(10000 Yuan)	7461984.2
其中：主营业务收入	(万元)	Of which: Main Business Income	(10000 Yuan)	5073149.4
利润总额	(万元)	Total Profit	(10000 Yuan)	558418.8
净利润	(万元)	Net Profit	(10000 Yuan)	437076.1
可供分配的利润	(万元)	Profit Available for Distribution	(10000 Yuan)	124283.6
未分配利润	(万元)	Undistributed Profit	(10000 Yuan)	-259770.5
资产总计	(万元)	Total Assets	(10000 Yuan)	60364888.8
乡镇级	(万元)	Township Level	(10000 Yuan)	22540854.9
村级	(万元)	Village Level	(10000 Yuan)	37824033.9
所有者权益合计	(万元)	Total Owner's Equity	(10000 Yuan)	21300644
乡镇级	(万元)	Township Level	(10000 Yuan)	5334349.6
村级	(万元)	Village Level	(10000 Yuan)	15966294.4
人均所有者权益	(元)	Per-capita Owner's Equity	(Yuan)	68638
农户收入情况		**Income of Peasant Households**		
农户总收入	(万元)	Total Income	(10000 Yuan)	14500559
农户所得总额	(万元)	Total Earnings	(10000 Yuan)	6564676.4
人均所得	(元)	Per-capita Earnings	(Yuan)	21155
农户从集体经济获取的所得总额	(万元)	Total Earnings of Peasant Household from Collective Economy	(10000 Yuan)	1557602.3
农户经营休闲农业及乡村旅游收入	(万元)	Income of Peasant Household from Operating Leisure Agriculture and Rural Tourism	(10000 Yuan)	112291.3

资料来源：北京市农村合作经济经营管理办公室

Source: Beijing Municipal Office of Operation and Management on Rural Cooperative Economy

主要统计指标解释

农林牧渔业总产值 是以货币表现的农林牧渔业的全部产品总量和对农林牧渔业生产活动进行的各种支持性服务活动的价值。

耕地 指种植农作物的土地，包括熟地，新开发、复垦、整理地，休闲地（含轮歇地、轮作地）；以种植农作物（含蔬菜）为主，间有零星果树、桑树或其他树木的土地；平均每年能保证收获一季的已垦滩地和海涂。耕地中包括南方宽度<1.0米、北方宽度<小于2.0米固定的沟、渠、路和地坎(埂)；临时种植药材、草皮、花卉、苗木等的耕地，以及其他临时改变用途的耕地。

农作物播种面积 指实际播种或移植有农作物的面积。凡是实际种植有农作物的面积，不论种植在耕地上还是种植在非耕地上，均包括在农作物播种面积中。在播种季节基本结束后，因遭灾而重新改种和补种的农作物面积，也包括在内。

设施农业 指以工厂化生产方式，建造人工设施，改变气候条件，提高农作物抵御自然灾害的能力，改良生物特性，使作物实现错季或反季节生产，达到农作物均衡生产的目的。

农业机械总动力 指主要用于农、林、牧、渔业的各种动力机械的动力总和。包括耕作机械、排灌机械、收获机械、农用运输机械、植物保护机械、牧业机械、渔业机械和其他农用机械[内燃机按引擎马力折成瓦（特）计算，电动机按功率折成瓦（特）计算]。不包括专门用于乡、镇、村、组办工业、基本建设、非农业运输、科学实验和教学等非农业生产方面用的动力机械与作业机械。

农村用电量 指本年度内，扣除在农村中的国有经济工业交通、基建等单位的用电量以后的农村生产和生活的全年用电总量（计量单位千瓦小时，按全年累计数统计），即包括国家电网供电，也包括农村自办电站供电量。

农用化肥施用量 指本年度内实际用于农业生产的化学肥料数量，包括氮肥、磷肥、钾肥和复合肥。施用量要求按折纯量计算数量，即各类化学肥料的实际施用数量按其含氮、含五氧化二磷、含氧化钾的比例折成百分之百计算。

折纯量＝实物量×某种化肥有效成份含量的百分比

乡镇及行政村单位常住户数 指长期（一年以上）居住在乡镇（不包括城关镇）行政管理区域内的住户，还包括居住在城关镇所辖行政村范围内的农村住户。户口不在本地而在本地居住一年及以上的住户也包括在本地农村住户内；有本地户口，但举家外出谋生一年以上的住户，无论是否保留承包耕地都不包括在本地农村住户范围内。不包括乡村地区内的国有经济的机关、团体、学校、企业、事业单位的集体户。

乡镇及行政村常住人口 指乡村地区常住居民户数中的常住人口数，即经常在家或在家居住6个月以上，而且经济和生活与本户连成一体的人口。外出从业人员在外居住时间虽然在6个月以上，但收入主要带回家中，经济与本户连为一体，仍视为家庭常住人口；在家居住，生活和本户连成一体的国家职工、退休人员也为家庭常住人口。但是现役军人、中专及以上（走读生除外）的在校学生、以及常年在外（不包括探亲、看病等）且已有稳定的职业与居住场所的外出从业人员，不应当作家庭常住人口。

乡镇及行政村从业人员 指全部乡镇及行政村人口中16岁以上实际参加生产经营活动并取得实物或货币收入的人员，既包括劳动年龄内经常参加劳动的人员，也包括超过劳动年龄但经常参加劳动的人员。但不包括户口在家的在外学生、现役军人和丧失劳动能力的人，也不包括待业人员和家务劳动者。从业人员按从事主业时间最长（时间相同按收入）分为农业从业人员，工业从业人员，建筑业从业人员，交通运输仓储及邮政业从业人员，信息传输、计算机服务和软件业，批发与零售业从业人员，住宿和餐饮业从业人员，其它从业人员。

双层经营 指农民家庭分散经营和集体统一经营相结合。

Explanatory Notes on Main Statistical Indicators

Gross Output Value of Agriculture, Forestry, Animal Production and Hunting, Fishing refers to the monetary value of all products of agriculture, forestry, animal production and hunting, fishing, as well as the monetary value of services provided in support of all the above-mentioned sectors.

Arable Land refers to the land suitable for growing crops, including cultivated land; any land newly opened up, reclaimed and cultivated; fallow land (including swidden and rotated land); land mostly for growing crops (including vegetables), supplemented by mulberry trees, fruit trees, and other trees; cultivated bottomland and shallows that can secure an average of one harvest annually. Arable land includes furrows, ditches, paths and field ridges less than 1m wide in the southern part of China, or less than 2m wide in the northern part. It also covers arable land that is temporarily for growing medicinal materials, turf, flowers, nursery stock and other uses.

Sown Area refers to the area of all lands actually sown or transplanted with crops, including both the cultivated and non-cultivated land. Area of lands re-planted after seedtime has passed due to natural disasters is also included.

Facility Agriculture means to produce in an industrialized manner, put in place facilities of manual intervention, change climate conditions, increase the crops' capability to resist natural disasters, and improve the crops' biological property, so as to stagger harvest seasons, create anti-season production, and achieve balanced production of crops.

Total Power of Agricultural Machinery refers to the total power of motive power machines used in agriculture, forestry, animal production and hunting, fishing sectors, including machinery for ploughing, irrigation and drainage, harvesting, agricultural transport, plant protection, animal production and hunting, fishing and other farm machinery (The horsepower of internal combustion engines is converted into watts, and the output of electric motors is also converted into watts). Motive power machines and operating machines exclusively used for non-agricultural production activities, such as industrial operations run by counties, towns, villages and teams, capital construction, non-agricultural transport, scientific experiments and teaching, are not included.

Rural Electricity Consumption refers to the total rural production and rural residents' electricity consumption in the whole year (unit of measurement: kilowatt-hour; the data representing accumulative usage of the year), deducting the consumption by entities like state-owned industry, transport, and infrastructure construction. The data cover both power supplies by the State Grid and by the rural self-run power stations.

Consumption of Chemical Fertilizers refers to the total quantity of chemical fertilizers applied in agricultural production within the year, including nitrogenous fertilizer, phosphate fertilizer, potash fertilizer, and compound fertilizer. The amount of chemical fertilizers applied is calculated in terms of net amount, that is, to use the gross weight of the respective fertilizers in calculating the quantity of effective ingredients (e.g. nitrogen content in nitrogenous fertilizer, phosphorous pent oxide content in phosphate fertilizer, and potassium oxide content in potash fertilizer).

Net Amount = Physical Quantity× Content (%) of Effective Ingredients in Certain Chemical Fertilizer

Number of Resident Households in Towns and Administrative Villages refers to households living in the administrative areas of towns and villages (excluding township government premises) on a long-term basis (more than one year), including those living in administrative villages within township government premises. Households with non-local household registration but having been living locally for more than one year are also counted as local rural households; while households with local household registration but left to make a living elsewhere for more than one year, with or without contract lands, are not counted as local rural households. Collective households of state-owned organs, groups, schools, enterprises, and public institutions, as well as households living in grouped commercial residential quarters in rural areas are not included.

Permanent Population in Towns and Administrative Villages refers to the population of permanent households in rural areas, namely those who stay home regularly or live at home for more than 6 months with their economic life and livelihood incorporated into the household. Migrant workers who live away from home for more than 6 months but taking most of their earnings back home, with their economic life still incorporated into the household, are also counted as permanent population of the household; state employees and retirees who live locally with their life incorporated into the household are also considered permanent population. But soldiers in active service, enrolled students (externs excluded) in technical secondary schools or above, as well as migrant workers who lived away from home for years (excluding those who travel to visit their families or to seek medical care) with a stable job and residence elsewhere, are not regarded as permanent population.

Employ Persons in Towns and Administrative Villages refer to persons aged above 16 in all towns and administrative villages, who actually participate in productive and operating activities and earn incomes in kind or cash, including persons within the range of labor age and regularly participating in labor, and persons beyond the range of labor age but regularly participating in labor; while local registered students who left home for education, soldiers in active service, and people who lost the ability to work are not included, neither are the people waiting for employment or domestic workers. In terms of the length of employment period (or in terms of income if the employment periods are identical), employment falls into the following categories: agriculture, industry, construction, transportation, storage and post, information transmission, software and information technology services, wholesale and retail trade, accommodation and restaurants, and other sectors.

Two-tiered System of Rural Land Management refers to a system with integration of decentralized manage model and collective unified management by rural households.

北京统计年鉴2017　　BEIJING STATISTICAL YEARBOOK

工 业
INDUSTRY

简要说明

一、本章统计的主要内容

本章资料反映北京市工业方面的基本情况，主要包括按登记注册类型、轻重工业、企业规模、工业行业大类等分组的主要经济指标数据，还包括国有控股工业企业、股份制工业企业、港澳台及外商投资工业企业、大中型工业企业的主要经济指标数据。

具体指标包括单位数、工业总产值、工业增加值、资产总计、负债合计、主营业务收入、主营业务成本、主营业务税金及附加、利润总额、应交增值税、总资产贡献率、资产负债率、成本费用利润率、主要工业产品产量等。

二、本章资料的统计范围

1984 年以前农村的村及村以下办工业归属农业，1984 年以后划归工业。

1999 年及以前，工业的统计范围按隶属关系划分为乡及乡以上独立核算工业企业和非独立核算生产单位、村办工业、城镇合作工业、农村合作工业、城镇个体工业、农村个体工业六大部分（1984 年以前村办工业不在工业统计范围内）。

2000 年-2006 年，工业统计调查范围由按隶属关系划分，改变为按企业规模划分。2000 年至 2006 年，分为全部国有及年主营业务收入在 500 万元及以上非国有工业企业（简称“规模以上”）和年主营业务收入在 500 万元以下非国有工业企业和全部个体经营工业单位（简称“规模以下”）两部分。

2007 年-2010 年，分为年主营业务收入在 500 万元及以上法人工业企业（简称“规模以上”）和年主营业务收入在 500 万元以下法人工业企业和全部个体经营工业单位（简称“规模以下”）两部分。

2011 年及以后，分为年主营业务收入在 2000 万元及以上法人工业企业（简称“规模以上”）和年主营业务收入在 2000 万元以下法人工业企业和全部个体经营工业单位（简称“规模以下”）两部分。

三、数据来源和调查方法

本章工业企业统计数据来源于北京市统计局、国家统计局北京调查总队。其中，规模以上数据为全面调查，规模以下数据为抽样调查。

四、有关统计标准的变化说明

（一）关于行业划分：本章资料中工业行业分类 2002-2011 年期间执行 2002 年《国民经济行业分类标准》(GB/T 4754-2002)划分标准，2012 年开始执行 2011 年《国民经济行业分类》(GB/T 4754-2011)划分标准。

（二）关于企业标准划分：2010 年以前企业大中小型划分执行《统计上大中小型企业划分办法（暂行）》标准，自 2011 年开始，大中小微型企业划分标准执行国家统计局《关于统计上大中小微型企业划分办法》（国统字[2011]75 号）。

五、本章中关于历史数据调整的问题

1993-2003 年规模以上工业总产值及增加值历史资料根据“北京市第一次全国经济普查”的结果采用“趋势离差法”进行了修正，2004 年为第一次经济普查数据，2008 年为第二次经济普查数据，2013 年为第三次经济普查数据。

Brief Introduction

I. Main Content

Data in this chapter show the basic situation of industry in Beijing, including: major economic indicators grouped by type of registration, light or heavy industry, enterprise scale, and industrial sector. and also includes main economic indicators for state-holding industrial enterprises, industrial enterprises limited by shares, Hong Kong, Macao, Taiwan and foreign-invested enterprises, and the large and medium-sized industrial enterprises.

Indicators include: unit number, gross industrial output value, industrial added value, total assets, total liabilities, main business income, main business cost, main business tax and surtax, total profits, payable VAT, contribution rate to total assets, asset-liability ratio, cost-profit ratio, and output of main industrial products, etc.

II. Scope of Statistics

Prior to 1984, the rural industrial production run by villages and units subordinated to villages was classified as agriculture. Since 1984, it has been grouped into industry.

Before 1999, industrial statistics coverage was divided into six parts by registration type, i.e. industrial enterprises at the township-level and above with and without independent accounting, village-run industry, urban cooperative industry, rural cooperative industry, urban individual operated industry, and rural individual operated industry (village-run industry was not included in the industrial statistics before 1984).

2000-2006, the scope of industrial statistics was grouped by enterprise scale instead of registration type. From 2000 to 2006, industrial enterprises fell into two classes. One class includes all state-owned enterprises and non-state-owned ones with annual main business income of RMB 5 million and above ("above designated size"), while the other class covers all individual operations and non-state-owned enterprises with annual main business income below RMB 5 million ("below designated size").

2007-2010, industrial enterprises fell into two classes. One includes corporate industrial enterprises with main business income of RMB 5 million and above ("above designated size"), the other includes corporate industrial enterprises with main business income below RMB 5 million and all individual operations ("below designated size").

In and after 2011, industrial enterprises fell into two classes. One includes corporate industrial enterprises with main business income of RMB 20 million and above ("above designated size"), the other includes corporate industrial enterprises with main business income below RMB 20 million and all individual operations ("below designated size").

III. Source of Data and Methods of Survey

Data on industrial enterprises in this chapter were provided by Beijing Municipal Bureau of Statistics and NBS Survey Office in Beijing. Data on industrial enterprises above designated size were gathered through complete survey, and data on those below designated size were obtained through sampling survey.

IV. Changes in Relevant Statistical Standards

(I) Classification of Industrial Sectors: In this chapter, classification of industrial sectors during 2002-2011 was based on the *Standard for Classification of National Economic Sectors 2002* (GB/T 4754-2002). *Standard for Classification of National Economic Sectors 2011* (GB/T 4754-2011) began to be enforced in 2012;

(II) Classification of Enterprises: Before 2010, small, medium and large-sized enterprises were classified by standards of *Measures for Statistical Classification of Small, Medium and Large-sized Enterprises (Temporary)*. Since 2011, the classification of micro, small, medium and large-sized enterprises has been in line with standards of Circular by National Bureau of Statistics on Printing and Issuing the *Measures for Statistical Classification of Micro, Small, Medium and Large-sized Enterprises* (G.T.Z. [2011] No. 75).

V. About the Adjustment to Historical Data

In accordance with the unified requirements and methods of the National Bureau of Statistics, data on total output value and added value of industrial enterprises above designated size were based on results from the "first national economic census in Beijing" after revision through the "trend deviation method". The time span of the revised data is from 1993 to 2003. The first economic census was carried out in 2004 and the second in 2008, and the third in 2013.

12-1 规模以上工业总产值(1984-2016年) GROSS OUTPUT VALUE OF INDUSTRY ABOVE DESIGNATED SIZE (1984-2016)

单位：亿元 (100 million yuan)

年 份 Year	合 计 Total	轻工业 Light Industry	重工业 Heavy Industry	#大中型工业 Medium and Large-sized Industry
1984	276.2	118.0	158.2	178.7
1985	324.2	135.8	188.4	213.7
1986-1990	**2448.3**	**1039.7**	**1408.6**	**1691.2**
1986	336.5	140.8	195.7	231.6
1987	387.6	160.1	227.5	272.1
1988	495.6	212.5	283.1	345.4
1989	602.7	264.1	338.6	408.3
1990	625.9	262.2	363.7	433.8
1991-1995	**5826.7**	**1936.6**	**3890.1**	**3770.8**
1991	730.2	298.1	432.1	507.4
1992	860.0	306.5	553.5	587.4
1993	1166.6	361.9	804.7	747.6
1994	1576.6	497.9	1078.7	990.7
1995	1493.3	472.2	1021.1	937.7
1996-2000	**10382.8**	**3026.2**	**7356.6**	**5765.7**
1996	1590.6	509.1	1081.5	962.3
1997	1819.7	577.8	1241.9	999.6
1998	1947.0	598.2	1348.8	1059.8
1999	2183.5	621.8	1561.7	1090.9
2000	2842.0	719.3	2122.7	1653.1
2001-2005	**23980.6**	**4911.1**	**19069.5**	**16858.4**
2001	3270.1	842.4	2427.7	2298.4
2002	3620.2	882.4	2737.8	2434.7
2003	4410.8	936.7	3474.1	3183.9
2004	5733.3	1084.7	4648.6	3699.3
2005	6946.2	1164.9	5781.3	5242.1
2006-2010	**53010.4**	**8204.7**	**44805.7**	**40357.2**
2006	8210.0	1258.2	6951.8	6237.9
2007	9648.4	1505.5	8142.9	7365.9
2008	10413.1	1674.3	8738.8	7898.9
2009	11039.1	1766.7	9272.4	8349.3
2010	13699.8	2000.0	11699.8	10505.3
2011-2015	**83383.2**	**12349.7**	**71033.5**	**66759.9**
2011	14513.6	2227.2	12286.4	11289.3
2012	15596.2	2402.1	13194.1	12239.6
2013	17370.9	2541.5	14829.4	13941.3
2014	18452.9	2568.0	15884.9	15039.5
2015	17449.6	2610.8	14838.8	14250.3
2016	18087.3	2731.6	15355.7	15053.2

注：1. 工业总产值按现价计算。
2. 规模以上工业：2000年以前各年为乡及乡以上工业口径；2000-2006年调整为全部国有及年主营业务收入在500万元及以上非国有工业口径；2007年-2010年调整为年主营业务收入500万元及以上的全部法人工业企业；2011年及以后调整为年主营业务收入2000万元及以上的全部法人工业企业(下同)。

Note: a) Gross output value is calculated at current prices.
b) Data on industry above designated size covered enterprises at and above the township level before 2000, 2000-2006 covered all State-owned enterprises and non-State-owned enterprises with main business income of over RMB 5 million annually, 2007-2010 covered all corporate industrial enterprises with main business income of over RMB 5 million annually, and from 2011 covered all corporate industrial enterprises with main business income over RMB 20 million (the same below) .

12-2 规模以上工业企业主要指标(1978-2016年)
MAIN INDICATORS FOR INDUSTRIAL ENTERPRISES ABOVE DESIGNATED SIZE (1978-2016)

年 份 Year	企业单位个数(个) Number of Enterprises (unit)	从业人员平均人数(万人) Average Number of Employed Persons (10000 persons)	资产总计(万元) Total Assets (10000 yuan)	负债合计(万元) Total Liabilities (10000 yuan)	固定资产原价(万元) Original Value of Fixed Assets (10000 yuan)	主营业务收入(万元) Main Business Income (10000 yuan)	利润总额(万元) Total Profits (10000 yuan)	利税总额(万元) Total Taxes & Profits (10000 yuan)
1978	4225	114.8			1305271	1098279	370551	501588
1979	3746	116.8	1417223		1371335	1186497	414344	554895
1980	3733	140.9	1547267		1495083	1987967	453147	604241
1981-1985						**12561630**	**2404751**	**3383077**
1981	3778	152.9	1650869		1622035	2054862	440753	599452
1982	3867	158.7	1748915		1750727	2183458	440000	604372
1983	4011	162.0	1846698		1886857	2408893	469364	642437
1984	4291	165.5	2003625		2045344	2728866	505249	707360
1985	4458	165.6	2338194		2337082	3175551	549385	829456
1986-1990						**24054442**	**2924045**	**4825016**
1986	5461	169.9	2720485		2627346	3385055	523961	813979
1987	5746	170.5	3147157		3008917	3935004	570760	885303
1988	5932	170.5	3607173		3412765	5032042	701574	1081370
1989	6175		4343353		3890267	5597829	638385	1087017
1990	6272	173.5	4982746		4382462	6104512	489365	957347
1991-1995						**57731437**	**4241285**	**8051832**
1991	6344	172.4	5672894		5052285	7271529	583381	1106009
1992	6205	175.5	6409037		5754181	8526860	748098	1347058
1993	10320	167.9	15209851		9986886	12822058	1095165	1811556
1994	10889	179.5	19692285		9648050	13207344	961715	1857476
1995	10712	176.2	25826309	15287699	13900296	15903646	852926	1929733
1996-2000						**103617473**	**3188809**	**8655552**
1996	16905	166.6	28755517	17220941	16319878	15801389	330539	1225314
1997	19387	157.5	34083006	20496564	18503218	17070867	405129	1405499
1998	18089	167.1	40129028	24839166	22213387	20345380	484460	1617338
1999	19682	161.1	42540707	25863159	23121446	22186280	697807	1846310
2000	16027	145.6	46127325	26763977	25316408	28213557	1270874	2561091
2001-2005						**233471075**	**13486920**	**23453788**
2001	4356	108.0	44482243	24595592	25036546	30068965	1369794	2795203
2002	4551	107.6	47429487	25278299	26554117	31827790	1655153	3219863
2003	4019	100.8	51779832	27511740	27559571	38856527	2352909	4189859
2004	6872	113.6	120495094	41430793	39221838	59926564	3974076	6417537
2005	6301	117.1	128298350	47067350	44340413	72791229	4134988	6831326
2006-2010						**576103251**	**35550064**	**57599572**
2006	6400	117.4	142444009	55423362	50306165	89141630	5311453	8479249
2007	6398	119.3	162155043	65083476	58148433	104401683	6956067	10552194
2008	7206	123.4	168024206	80850104	65745860	112758173	5569968	9379138
2009	6891	120.4	195407033	98746128	70836396	121730618	7429216	12699472
2010	6885	124.2	227505774	115480740	79360648	148071147	10283360	16489519
2011-2015						**899886856**	**67937345**	**108777212**
2011	3740	117.9	253217462	126486073	86208174	157533565	11294991	18061726
2012	3692	120.2	286131557	148372202	102771932	169051357	12678868	20104385
2013	3641	116.1	308007299	162079598	107885887	186886314	12828840	21252443
2014	3686	116.6	335570497	171375654	115329380	197766666	15157524	24078630
2015	3548	110.4	386097637	181024377	122654798	188648954	15977122	25280028
2016	3340	104.4	430936843	197981343	129779692	197469575	16082648	25215765

12-3 规模以上工业增加值(1993-2016年)

单位：亿元

年 份 Year	增加值 Added Value of Industry	轻工业 Light Industry	重工业 Heavy Industry	#计算机、通信和其他电子设备制造业 Manufacture of Computers, Communication Equipment and Other Electronic Equipment	#汽车制造业 Manufacture of Motor Vehicles	#电力、热力生产和供应业 Production and Supply of Electricity and Heating Power	#铁路、船舶、航空航天和其他运输设备制造业 Manufacture of Railway Locomotives, Building of Ships Manufacture Air and Spacecrafts and Other Transportation Equipment
1993	304.1	98.3	205.8	22.6	28.4	4.6	
1994	374.6	138.0	236.6	30.9	29.7	9.5	
1995	473.1	112.3	360.8	46.7	44.4	33.0	
1996-2000	**3058.8**	**981.7**	**2077.1**	**622.0**	**180.7**	**170.4**	
1996	500.2	168.8	331.4	66.6	38.1	-12.1	
1997	558.0	170.1	387.9	75.7	58.0	45.8	
1998	588.2	197.2	391.0	133.8	30.0	41.5	
1999	636.5	200.6	435.9	154.5	25.6	45.4	
2000	776.0	245.0	531.0	191.4	29.0	49.8	
2001-2005	**6153.4**	**1549.4**	**4604.0**	**1078.7**	**505.4**	**564.2**	
2001	866.3	265.2	601.0	203.6	39.0	52.4	
2002	960.7	306.6	654.1	177.8	54.8	66.6	
2003	1174.7	304.8	869.9	228.3	126.0	78.3	
2004	1524.7	332.6	1192.1	197.5	144.2	174.4	
2005	1627.0	340.2	1286.8	271.5	141.4	192.5	
2006-2010	**11071.1**	**2366.2**	**8704.9**	**1423.7**	**1329.5**	**1705.0**	
2006	1840.2	370.1	1470.1	329.7	155.1	254.6	
2007	2159.4	427.6	1731.9	363.6	194.9	355.2	
2008	2037.6	482.3	1555.3	289.4	211.1	358.4	
2009	2282.2	529.4	1752.8	201.2	310.6	327.3	
2010	2751.7	556.8	2194.8	239.8	457.8	409.5	
2011-2015	**16653.2**	**3591.0**	**13062.1**	**1342.0**	**3333.2**	**2931.3**	
2011	2899.1	619.2	2279.9	204.5	562.1	448.8	
2012	3033.3	681.3	2352.0	243.6	512.6	536.0	53.5
2013	3432.1	749.7	2682.4	304.4	732.3	602.3	71.7
2014	3612.0	766.6	2845.3	305.1	726.2	682.0	96.9
2015	3676.6	774.2	2902.5	284.4	799.9	662.1	97.5
2016	3748.7	810.7	2938.0	185.2	949.5	728.3	136.1

注：1. 本表增加值均按生产法计算，2004年以前数据为根据全国第一次经济普查数据调整后的数据。
2. 2012年开始行业划分执行2011年国民经济行业分类标准(GB/T 4754-2011)；表中2012年前，汽车制造业为原“交通运输设备制造业”数据，计算机、通信和其它电子设备制造业为原“通信设备、计算机及其他电子设备制造业”的数据。

ADDED VALUE OF INDUSTRY ABOVE DESIGNATED SIZE (1993-2016)

(100 million yuan)

#化学原料和化学制品制造业 Manufacture of Chemical Raw Materials and Chemical Products	#通用设备制造业 Manufacture of General-Purpose Machinery	#专用设备制造业 Manufacture of Special-Purpose Machinery	#电气机械和器材制造业 Manufacture of Electrical Machinery and Equipment	#仪器仪表制造业 Manufacture of Measuring Instruments and Meters	#医药制造业 Manufacture of Medicines	#非金属矿物制品业 Manufacture of Non-Metallic Mineral Products	#石油加工、炼焦和核燃料加工业 Processing of Petroleum, Coking, Processing of Nuclear Fuel
15.5	13.0	10.0	10.1	3.2	5.5	14.8	12.5
19.7	15.9	26.4	11.6	4.5	5.3	21.2	14.2
28.9	17.2	12.1	9.8	9.0	7.5	17.7	45.9
136.2	**73.1**	**114.5**	**99.5**	**52.6**	**90.3**	**139.4**	**194.5**
26.0	18.1	16.9	15.4	10.6	11.8	28.4	37.9
21.4	13.2	19.3	17.3	7.5	15.6	25.7	42.3
25.3	17.5	22.9	21.0	10.9	12.6	30.9	31.4
24.0	8.2	22.9	19.0	11.1	22.7	19.6	42.3
39.5	16.1	32.5	26.8	12.4	27.6	34.8	40.6
381.2	**200.8**	**263.7**	**257.8**	**142.2**	**225.4**	**230.1**	**215.6**
44.1	25.7	29.2	36.5	17.0	31.0	34.4	35.8
55.3	25.5	56.3	38.7	19.0	47.2	47.2	53.9
76.3	36.6	49.8	54.9	21.6	53.2	48.5	29.6
141.8	56.5	67.7	65.1	38.3	44.7	52.0	19.7
63.7	56.5	60.7	62.6	46.4	49.3	48.0	76.6
331.2	**495.2**	**526.7**	**497.0**	**313.6**	**543.0**	**333.5**	**461.6**
56.9	72.6	86.6	57.1	57.2	57.0	53.5	49.6
72.6	84.7	84.7	85.8	70.6	81.6	52.7	56.9
60.5	99.1	111.9	92.9	58.7	115.3	55.2	-2.3
57.1	97.4	112.3	126.4	61.0	135.8	85.8	172.5
84.1	141.4	131.2	134.8	66.1	153.3	86.3	184.9
322.6	**685.2**	**708.1**	**692.5**	**332.9**	**1246.0**	**383.0**	**680.0**
77.7	153.1	139.8	137.1	63.6	184.2	80.7	122.8
56.1	130.2	130.4	124.8	59.6	222.2	79.5	126.2
55.8	125.0	158.1	135.4	64.9	254.2	80.5	98.2
62.3	147.3	132.6	145.5	68.2	283.1	75.0	151.3
70.6	129.6	147.3	149.7	76.7	302.3	67.3	181.5
77.9	122.4	129.8	118.5	75.5	336.2	83.1	157.5

Note: a) Added value in this table is calculated with production method. Figures before 2004 are adjusted according to the national first economic census.

b) The Standard for Classification of National Economic Sectors 2011 (GB/T 4754-2011) became effective in 2012; in this table,figures of " manufacture of motor vehicles" in 2012 were figures of the former "manufacture of transportation equipment", and figures of "manufacture of computers, communication equipment and other electronic equipment" were figures of the former "manufacture of communication equipment, computers and other electronic equipment".

12-4 规模以上工业产品产量(1978-2016年)
OUTPUT OF INDUSTRIAL PRODUCTS ABOVE DESIGNATED SIZE (1978-2016)

年份 Year	布 (万米) Cloth (10000 m)	机制纸及纸板 (万吨) Machine-made Paper and Paperboard (10000 tons)	饮料酒 (万千升) Alcoholic Beverage (10000 kL)	乳制品 (万吨) Dairy Products (10000 tons)	家用电冰箱 (万台) Household Refrigerators (10000 units)	照相机 (万台) Camera (10000 units)	家具 (万件) Furniture (10000 pieces)	原煤 (万吨) Raw Coal (10000 tons)	原油加工量 (万吨) Crude Oil Processed (10000 tons)	乙稀 (万吨) Ethylene (10000 tons)	发电量 (万千瓦时) Electricity Generation (10000 kWh)
1978	25436	12.1	8.4			0.5	137.8	818.7			990750
1979	27297	13.9	9.9		2.0	0.7	171.3	711.1			1042870
1980	28940	14.0	11.6		2.6	1.0	200.2	791.0	591.1		1065060
1981-1985	**142080**	**86.9**	**87.3**	**2.0**	**41.6**	**25.7**	**1348.4**	**4269.1**	**2811.3**	**132.3**	**5101356**
1981	28635	14.5	13.4		3.1	4.2	217.7	788.7	533.5	24.7	993071
1982	29758	15.8	14.9	0.2	4.5	0.9	243.5	811.3	533.5	25.6	1003446
1983	30068	17.1	17.4	0.3	6.4	2.8	254.2	840.5	563.8	27.3	1028826
1984	27621	18.9	20.3	0.6	10.3	5.3	297.9	884.3	589.4	26.9	1038842
1985	25998	20.6	21.3	0.9	17.3	12.5	335.1	944.3	591.1	27.8	1037171
1986-1990	**153032**	**120.5**	**131.4**	**4.7**	**96.4**	**74.6**	**2096.6**	**4745.3**	**3210.5**	**141.8**	**5656282**
1986	27503	21.9	21.5	0.7	18.1	15.9	303.8	917.2	619.0	25.3	1043208
1987	29738	24.1	22.7	0.8	19.4	16.5	283.0	899.8	640.2	27.0	1057493
1988	32262	23.3	23.9	1.0	23.6	15.8	347.1	906.0	645.0	30.3	1110758
1989	32271	25.8	28.7	1.0	24.7	13.5	572.1	1016.8	651.9	29.1	1191269
1990	31258	25.4	34.6	1.2	10.7	12.9	590.6	1005.5	654.4	30.1	1253554
1991-1995	**133994**	**116.5**	**347.3**	**5.9**	**27.0**	**450.8**	**3261**	**4851.0**	**3269.9**	**172.2**	**6772732**
1991	31497	27.2	43.8	1.3	7.1	5.4	602.0	996.5	653.4	31.1	1318000
1992	29717	22.6	56.6	1.2	9.1	4.2	570.0	1015.2	662.5	32.8	1423000
1993	26816	19.1	72.6	1.6	4.2	39.3	729.0	835.4	664.0	27.2	1410900
1994	21440	21.0	83.1	0.3	6.6	158.8	605.0	1008.5	642.0	28.1	1298718
1995	24524	26.6	91.2	1.5		243.1	755.0	995.4	648.0	53.0	1322114
1996-2000	**96005**	**70.0**	**436.6**	**7.3**	**15.9**	**706.5**	**1986.8**	**4360.0**	**3336.5**	**306.0**	**7330814**
1996	22585	15.3	102.2	1.2	6.3	234.3	510.6	1013.7	633.6	57.5	1415555
1997	25185	18.1	…	1.7	…	157.7	469.4	1011.7	657.0	58.0	1464302
1998	21299	13.1		0.9	0.3	177.7	348.5	989.5	602.3	57.0	1566621
1999	14753	13.0	148.8	1.4	5.8	81.6	386.2	792.1	701.9	68.0	1431772
2000	12183	10.6	185.6	2.1	3.6	55.2	272.1	553.0	741.7	65.5	1452564
2001-2005	**38411**	**59.5**	**700.9**	**119.7**	**189.7**	**685.0**	**2036.9**	**4359.5**	**3624.5**	**430.7**	**8369923**
2001	11353	8.8	135.8	3.7	5.9	61.3	370.6	690.2	647.9	54.3	1326588
2002	10314	6.2	138.7	1.4	16.2	220.7	368.3	880.9	695.2	90.4	1419754
2003	8393	7.9	132.8	1.3	22.8	238.3	323.8	822.6	701.1	88.8	1451197
2004	4081	19.6	148.0	56.4	63.1	116.8	567.7	1067.9	783.4	98.2	2038933
2005	4270	17.0	145.6	56.9	81.7	47.9	406.5	897.9	796.9	99.0	2133451
2006-2010	**4508**	**64.0**	**906.9**	**270.8**	**447.0**	**189.1**	**3765.4**	**2971.5**	**5143.2**	**455.6**	**11960020**
2006	930	14.0	170.8	63.5	74.1	49.2	893.4	629.2	828.9	99.1	2136918
2007	536	10.4	189.1	57.9	73.1	34.7	638.8	633.3	915.0	90.9	2278658
2008	1583	14.9	180.0	44.9	79.0	49.0	690.9	567.7	1114.6	85.4	2431255
2009	965	14.1	181.1	52.2	128.7	27.1	719.4	641.3	1161.3	84.1	2424839
2010	495	10.6	185.8	52.3	92.1	29.2	822.8	500.0	1123.4	96.2	2688350
2011-2015	**1586**	**42.9**	**931.2**	**296.4**	**237.6**	**70.9**	**3841.4**	**2400.9**	**5110.9**	**402.1**	**16408207**
2011	339	10.0	187.0	58.6	73.5	26.6	750.2	500.1	1103.1	89.6	2628331
2012	351	11.3	191.7	56.6	80.4	18.2	720.1	493.1	1075.0	84.0	2908214
2013	361	10.0	198.0	58.5	83.7	17.9	995.9	500.1	881.6	72.3	3312116
2014	361	6.6	187.4	60.6		6.6	674.7	457.5	1051.1	77.6	3385699
2015	174	5.0	167.1	62.1		1.6	700.5	450.1	1000.1	78.6	4173847
2016		6.1	167.5	62.2		0.1	776.2	317.6	844.8	69.6	4336690

12-4 续表 Continued

年 份 Year	粗 钢 (万吨) Crude Steel (10000 tons)	钢 材 (万吨) Rolled Steel (10000 tons)	水 泥 (万吨) Cement (10000 tons)	交 流 电动机 (万千瓦) Alternator (10000 kW)	汽 车 (万辆) Motor Vehicles (10000 units)	#轿 车 Sedan Cars	移动通信手持机 (万台) Mobile Phones (10000 units)	微型计算机设 备 (万台) Micro-Computers (10000 units)	数控金属切削机床 (台) CNC Metal Cutting Lathe (unit)	显示器 (万台) Displays (10000 units)	集 成 电 路 (亿块) IC (100 million units)
1978	191.0	116.8	191.5	152.5	1.8						
1979	196.5	137.5	196.9	179.7	2.4						
1980	200.9	152.1	217.4	142.7	2.8						
1981–1985	**1114.2**	**907.9**	**1355.7**	**713.0**	**17.2**			**2.0**			
1981	190.3	149.5	225.7	104.0	2.7						
1982	200.4	159.4	249.1	123.3	2.8						
1983	214.1	177.9	270.8	148.3	3.1			0.3			
1984	241.7	200.1	291.6	165.4	3.6			1.2			
1985	267.7	221.0	318.5	172.0	5.0			0.5			
1986–1990	**1837.8**	**1556.7**	**1649.3**	**889.7**	**39.5**			**6.9**			
1986	303.6	255.5	310.5	178.4	5.8			0.5			
1987	335.5	283.4	319.6	196.4	7.4			0.9			
1988	369.0	314.9	334.3	199.5	9.0			3.0			
1989	386.0	327.9	345.9	163.8	8.5			1.3			
1990	443.7	375.0	339.0	151.6	8.8			1.2			
1991–1995	**3411.0**	**2613.9**	**2364.7**	**824.3**	**70.8**			**32.3**			
1991	499.7	402.9	377.6	156.7	11.0			1.7			
1992	575.0	438.3	403.0	174.9	13.8			3.0			
1993	702.7	525.3	477.9	162.3	13.4			4.1			
1994	828.7	617.6	531.7	165.0	14.7			4.3			
1995	804.9	629.8	574.2	165.4	17.9			19.2			
1996–2000	**3937.5**	**3343.3**	**3758.9**	**753.3**	**57.7**			**686.6**	**2238**		**5.4**
1996	794.7	654.3	666.0	151.9	13.4			28.1	326		0.5
1997	801.7	652.4	700.9	148.7	11.0			59.8	433		0.6
1998	803.2	676.1	762.0	149.7	8.5			160.9	430		0.6
1999	734.5	663.8	803.0	142.0	12.3	1.0		180.0	481		1.3
2000	803.4	696.7	827.0	161.0	12.5	0.5	1549.6	257.8	568		2.4
2001–2005	**4113.3**	**4096.9**	**4963.3**	**1169.8**	**179.6**	**45.7**	**21081.2**	**2407.0**	**5783**		**33.0**
2001	824.9	727.3	809.0	175.1	14.3	0.5	2163.4	339.7	1004		2.1
2002	816.9	750.0	884.0	199.3	18.1	0.7	2280.1	415.7	912		2.5
2003	816.4	785.0	882.0	253.1	34.7	7.3	3334.5	469.3	1188		4.7
2004	827.5	868.3	1204.5	279.4	53.9	15.0	4172.1	532.7	1024		11.1
2005	827.6	966.3	1183.8	262.9	58.6	22.2	9131.1	649.6	1655		12.6
2006–2010	**2988.1**	**4267.1**	**5443.8**	**1160.6**	**492.9**	**191.6**	**106256.6**	**4052.3**	**23256**	**3205.7**	**90.2**
2006	818.1	1016.3	1269.4	269.0	68.3	27.0	14068.0	736.1	1875	680.7	11.8
2007	810.8	1030.4	1167.3	281.9	70.7	20.3	22719.9	843.3	2382	513.6	15.7
2008	466.8	656.8	880.8	259.7	76.6	28.3	20725.5	691.7	3108	478.1	19.1
2009	464.9	769.6	1077.4	159.0	127.1	53.8	21355.3	842.7	6125	655.6	18.3
2010	427.5	794.0	1049.0	191.1	150.3	62.2	27388.0	938.6	9766	877.8	25.3
2011–2015	**11.4**	**1132.6**	**3911.0**	**563.8**	**959.9**	**477.6**	**92219.5**	**5166.3**	**59213**	**3020.7**	**219.3**
2011	2.9	287.0	911.5	146.0	150.5	67.1	25962.3	1083.7	12537	851.4	32.0
2012	2.6	253.8	874.5	117.1	167.0	78.5	19949.3	1074.5	13332	796.9	31.9
2013	2.3	221.8	868.4	145.4	203.8	94.5	18783.4	1106.9	6983	305.3	38.4
2014	2.1	195.0	703.1	115.0	216.7	118.6	17983.6	1015.6	13890	548.1	54.3
2015	1.5	175.0	553.5	40.3	221.9	118.9	9540.8	885.6	12471	519.0	62.7
2016		162.8	510.3	46.1	260.4	120.7	6923.9	684.1	12420	503.5	80.5

12-5 规模以上工业企业主要经济指标(2016年)

单位：万元

项目	Item	企业单位个数(个) Number of Enterprises (unit)	#亏损企业 Loss-Suffering Enterprises	工业总产值(当年价格) Gross Output Value of Industry (at current year's prices)	工业增加值 Added Value of Industry	工业销售产值(当年价格) Sales Value of Industry (at current)	#出口交货值 Delivery Value of Exports
合计	**Total**	**3340**	**636**	**180872720**	**37486564**	**178374996**	**9568018**
按隶属关系分组	**By Affiliation**						
中央企业	Central Enterprises	219	34	58161978	12943242	57898807	287898
地方企业	Local Enterprises	3121	602	122710742	24543322	120476189	9280120
按登记注册类型分组	**By Registration Type**						
内资企业	Domestically-Invested Enterprises	2594	465	108071575	22457719	106709424	3094469
国有企业	State-owned Enterprises	62	10	33658576	6241773	33663750	13263
集体企业	Collectively-owned Enterprises	29	9	213801	58795	213519	3872
股份合作企业	Joint-equity Cooperative Enterprises	49	8	666237	152171	599576	12632
有限责任公司	Limited Liability Companies	1157	243	41486285	8449533	40930108	1797564
股份有限公司	Companies Limited by Shares	249	38	22336948	5251156	21864149	832194
私营企业	Private Enterprises	1047	157	9707793	2303983	9436242	434945
其他企业	Others	***	***	***	***	***	***
港澳台商投资企业	Hong Kong, Macao and Taiwan-invested Enterprises	181	48	16802997	1646995	16508798	2073284
港澳台合资经营	Joint Ventures	83	18	4023387	1103383	3948935	634237
港澳台合作经营	Cooperatives	***	***	***	***	***	***
港澳台商独资企业	Solely-funded Enterprises	84	29	12226789	654775	12029416	1374289
港澳台商投资股份有限公司	Companies Limited by Shares	11	1	534383	-120893	509522	64759
外商投资企业	Foreign-invested Enterprises	565	123	55998148	13381850	55156774	4400265
中外合资经营	Joint Ventures	213	36	37339241	9566393	36552257	2233063
中外合作经营	Cooperatives	8	3	211098	103449	209651	13841
外资(独资)企业	Solely-funded Enterprises	331	82	18000184	3664049	17929033	2107840
外商投资股份有限公司	Companies Limited by Shares	12	2	423204	38745	441778	45367
按城乡分组	**By urban and rural regions**						
#农村企业	Rural Enterprises	21	6	181745	33883	179714	435
按控股类型分组	**By holding types**						
#国有控股	State-holding Enterprises	697	140	107041993	23778616	105896130	2401046
集体控股	Collectively-holding Enterprises	92	19	3207092	637306	3081833	131126
私人控股	Private-holding Enterprises	1887	318	26215217	5511594	25430595	1098573
港澳台控股	Hong Kong, Macao, and Taiwan-holding Enterprises	136	39	14596651	1056102	14352684	1667327
外商控股	Foreign-Investor-holding Enterprises	490	111	28521318	6201254	28344371	4222244
按轻重工业分组	**By light and heavy industries**						
轻工业	Light Industry	1163	234	27315733	8106706	26699678	1404988
重工业	Heavy Industry	2177	402	153556988	29379858	151675317	8163030
按规模分组	**By size**						
#大中型企业	Medium and Large-sized Enterprises	676	111	150532406	31009228	148568616	8032114

注：1. 工业增加值按生产法计算(下表同)。
2. 应交税金合计包括应交增值税、所得税费用、营业税金及附加和管理费用中的税金，计算应交增值税时企业应交增值税为负数的按实际计算(下表同)。

MAIN ECONOMIC INDICATORS OF INDUSTRIAL ENTERPRISES ABOVE DESIGNATED SIZE (2016)

(10000 yuan)

平均用工人数（人） Average Number of Employed Persons (person)	资产负债 Assets and Liabilities						
	资产总计 Total Assets	流动资产合计 Total Current Assets	#存货 Inventories	#产成品 Finished Products	#应收账款 Accounts Receivable (Net)	固定资产合计 Total Fixed Assets	固定资产原价 Total Original Value of Fixed Assets
1044464	**430936843**	**166431586**	**23494977**	**8008211**	**43925283**	**68330561**	**129779692**
181035	200006375	41503770	4129499	971540	7873948	28291034	64658352
863429	230930468	124927816	19365478	7036671	36051335	40039527	65121340
705390	345051761	114505963	15346226	5093234	29624424	54080328	102342763
41185	164270214	26135533	1047456	171486	2843110	19213261	41271568
4908	353434	245679	62196	35125	40025	59128	129397
6336	545156	434434	122258	61270	120440	81859	136674
356515	104078537	47141318	7545615	2526019	14867168	27245031	47097452
157752	60353813	29661162	3993731	1317276	7975627	5534167	10597016
138664	15447187	10886321	2574173	981975	3777823	1944982	3108616
***	***	***	***	***	***	***	***
84534	24428253	15171577	2171898	763193	4272111	3201283	6545239
33880	5724683	3793294	460054	174851	1267682	1089843	3266135
***	***	***	***	***	***	***	***
44965	14833192	9223405	1298098	524794	2221277	2030294	3082434
5318	3835527	2123977	409940	61151	765103	78444	189461
254540	61456829	36754046	5976853	2151784	10028748	11048951	20891691
131730	37318708	21500185	3249987	1185686	4856778	7209167	11652057
5621	296034	242536	-13396	2450	42202	47842	135869
110487	19292137	13816034	2679250	940956	5000855	3535300	8408602
6617	4534963	1184617	57989	22366	124309	254871	691202
3499	396461	354980	70082	31781	77085	37447	74633
453629	314811115	92382040	10264820	3323591	20004099	54542152	104410451
22349	4010383	2943084	607451	197796	1089957	354807	639475
310853	58793660	35938941	6841182	2489208	11547501	5057702	8147052
65114	19886022	12605055	1796793	670973	3436602	2424743	3953347
182401	31145735	20876756	3816404	1276468	7153522	5768563	12326463
323275	43944384	26334732	5856808	2501802	5836202	7949885	13755179
721189	386992459	140096855	17638170	5506408	38089081	60380677	116024514
741043	368912813	128926836	15835100	5332020	31706454	60490908	116099257

Note: a) Added value of industry is calculated with production method (the same to the following tables).
b) Total tax payable mainly includes VAT payable, income tax expense, business tax and surtax, and tax in management expenses. The negative VAT payable of enterprises should be calculated by the actual value when calculating the VAT payable (the same to the following tables).

12-5 续表

单位：万元

项目	Item	资产负债 Assets and Liabilities 负债合计 Total Liabilities	#流动负债合计 Total Current Liabilities	#应付账款 Accounts Receivable	所有者权益合计 Total Owner's Equity	#实收资本 Paid-up Capital
合计	**Total**	**197981343**	**140505878**	**45118348**	**232724512**	**136610708**
按隶属关系分组	**By Affiliation**					
中央企业	Central Enterprises	75344736	40485166	9694606	124661639	89575796
地方企业	Local Enterprises	122636607	100020712	35423741	108062873	47034912
按登记注册类型分组	**By Registration Type**					
内资企业	Domestially-Invested Enterprises	150923957	98793034	27287186	193916491	118428794
国有企业	State-owned Enterprises	55989334	24513177	3776304	108182233	79814562
集体企业	Collectively-owned Enterprises	196232	162083	40961	157171	26951
股份合作企业	Joint-equity Cooperative Enterprises	333936	314884	150254	211160	82031
有限责任公司	Limited Liability Companies	60812310	46723241	14847485	43198067	25502189
股份有限公司	Companies Limited by Shares	25337996	19508396	5453471	35015817	9876661
私营企业	Private Enterprises	8252132	7569866	3018367	7150641	3126106
其他企业	Others	***	***	***	***	***
港澳台商投资企业	Hong Kong, Macao and Taiwan-invested Enterprises	14384832	12873478	5355853	10043125	4140201
港澳台合资经营	Joint Ventures	2577746	2476572	883871	3146938	1665075
港澳台合作经营	Cooperatives	***	***	***	***	***
港澳台商独资企业	Solely-funded Enterprises	9426814	8904769	3860883	5406083	1531749
港澳台商投资股份有限公司	Companies Limited by Shares	2376104	1487968	609980	1459423	936709
外商投资企业	Foreign-invested Enterprises	32672553	28839367	12475310	28764896	14041712
中外合资经营	Joint Ventures	20112246	17768106	7818893	17197982	8048783
中外合作经营	Cooperatives	137302	127406	65695	158732	166065
外资(独资)企业	Solely-funded Enterprises	10904775	9553911	4479618	8376463	4483500
外商投资股份有限公司	Companies Limited by Shares	1511594	1383307	104882	3023369	1336886
按城乡分组	**By urban and rural regions**					
#农村企业	Rural Enterprises	304306	118768	41487	92155	37750
按控股类型分组	**By holding types**					
#国有控股	State-holding Enterprises	136231832	87235623	24168208	178475871	114011349
集体控股	Collectively-holding Enterprises	2197330	1836176	618659	1812894	517740
私人控股	Private-holding Enterprises	28841616	24370533	8131938	29841629	10809172
港澳台控股	Hong Kong, Macao, and Taiwan-holding Enterprises	12451041	11278991	4825796	7434686	2868633
外商控股	Foreign-Investor-holding Enterprises	16842658	14531177	6813662	14286371	8017624
按轻重工业分组	**By light and heavy industries**					
轻工业	Light Industry	20400272	17348395	4149528	23532824	9728687
重工业	Heavy Industry	177581071	123157484	40968819	209191687	126882021
按规模分组	**By size**					
#大中型企业	Medium and Large-sized Enterprises	167689239	113745128	35740300	201223174	121999885

12-5 Continued

(10000 yuan)

损益 Profits and Losses								应交			
营业收入 Business Income	#主营业务收入 Main Business Income	营业成本 Business Cost	#主营业务成本 Main Business Cost	销售费用 Sales Expenses	管理费用 Management Expenses	财务费用 Financial Expenses	利润总额 Total Profits	税金合计 Total Tax	#营业税金及附加 Business Tax and Surtax	#主营业务税金及附加 Main Business Tax and Surtax	#应交增值税 Value Added Tax Payable
202138149	**197469575**	**167507152**	**163956085**	**10249966**	**10444149**	**2153834**	**16082648**	**11956830**	**3221330**	**3198907**	**5667337**
60216365	59354540	53482896	52776655	434795	1814071	604520	5578509	3809898	1270702	1258907	1735022
141921784	138115036	114024256	111179430	9815171	8630078	1549315	10504139	8146932	1950629	1940000	3932315
118155516	115494782	100649441	98559811	3878862	6723227	1541681	9438598	6641214	1759591	1741884	3342602
33937185	33829587	31016508	30951319	141308	314365	424122	4350229	1720690	373305	371860	824063
220986	215245	195430	192266	9038	24330	-918	4586	13054	1369	1325	9664
747381	734115	654311	652487	35365	32330	1670	27532	24849	2360	2360	15752
46924084	45891924	40886124	40093240	1591134	3248520	757357	1574399	2005546	220999	210185	1269551
25777946	24480271	19865284	18759646	1341204	2045208	279486	2690929	2330493	1113692	1108640	856641
10545645	10341351	8029787	7908856	760766	1058316	79934	790826	546520	47860	47509	366874
***	***	***	***	***	***	***	***	***	***	***	***
23952381	23323340	20663259	20302392	1677805	1032719	154565	1314963	672838	46792	46588	401827
4443323	4281361	3460946	3326783	243767	281281	1912	484815	272612	26718	26603	143251
***	***	***	***	***	***	***	***	***	***	***	***
18733459	18373320	16583093	16454219	1226567	655025	97283	748642	352861	13564	13476	228900
746702	640056	600295	502727	206189	91619	55414	77786	44251	6254	6254	27501
60030252	58651453	46194452	45093882	4693299	2688203	457588	5329086	4642778	1414948	1410435	1922908
37862595	37235208	29018533	28521468	2415651	1559367	239457	3720369	3465058	1307749	1305556	1194490
382895	378454	296520	292820	48133	19925	-2037	19835	28535	2153	2153	18712
21122834	20472059	16411262	15859015	2139439	1039343	166146	1331276	1104320	98861	98815	682467
620891	525771	438635	391078	89653	65256	53504	251464	41210	5956	3683	25440
192573	189641	175370	173009	2446	11475	1532	3368	7559	557	557	5836
113528698	111229887	96957102	95094140	3049032	4631979	1371339	10202731	7935842	2878942	2861062	3190817
3169539	3105482	2619734	2591892	145217	232364	7892	226217	118039	13606	13248	75253
29153156	28440115	22141001	21620442	2356439	2798656	370046	2366431	1449912	130684	128880	906735
21544128	21016636	18797499	18524850	1555350	847805	129310	781099	528149	30433	30346	327924
33370397	32380372	25991660	25160637	3028577	1779529	268916	2389335	1864079	161269	159116	1130844
32256727	31306351	21489015	20783520	4879858	2556482	260190	3062637	2759104	615607	611538	1539227
169881422	166163224	146018137	143172565	5370108	7887667	1893644	13020010	9197726	2605723	2587370	4128110
167025847	163561330	139702551	137042722	8170953	7331752	1835427	13650599	10104736	3049156	3034059	4501926

12-6 规模以上工业企业主要经济指标(按行业分)(2016年)

单位：万元

项目	Item	企业单位个数(个) Number of Enterprises (unit)	#亏损企业 Loss-Suffering Enterprises	工业总产值(当年价格) Gross Output Value of Industry (at current year's prices)	工业增加值 Added Value of Industry
合计	**Total**	**3340**	**636**	**180872720**	**37486564**
煤炭开采和洗选业	Mining and Washing of Coal	***	***	***	***
石油和天然气开采业	Extraction of Petroleum and Natural Gas	***	***	***	***
黑色金属矿采选业	Mining and Processing of Ferrous Metal Ores	7	6	726227	
非金属矿采选业	Mining and Processing of Nonmetal Ores	***	***	***	***
开采辅助活动	Mining Support Service Activities	6	4	1186103	583226
农副食品加工业	Processing of Food from Agricultural Products	133	32	3914735	503928
食品制造业	Manufacture of Foods	124	22	2935615	435229
酒、饮料和精制茶制造业	Manufacture of Wines, Beverage and Refined Tea	42	17	1656865	520998
烟草制品业	Manufacture of Cigarettes and Tobacco	***	***	***	***
纺织业	Manufacture of Textile	19	4	116381	22791
纺织服装、服饰业	Manufacture of Textile Wearing Apparel and Ornament	117	31	1125851	460942
皮革、毛皮、羽毛及其制品和制鞋业	Manufacture of Leather, Fur, Feather and Its Products, and Footwear	8	2	87532	18575
木材加工和木、竹、藤、棕、草制品业	Processing of Timbers, Manufacture of Wood, Bamboo, Rattan, Palm, and Straw Products	12	2	143469	23800
家具制造业	Manufacture of Furniture	60	12	786420	179995
造纸和纸制品业	Manufacture of Paper and Paper Products	41	8	580145	194590
印刷和记录媒介复制业	Printing, Reproduction of Recording Media	99	21	1115474	468085
文教、工美、体育和娱乐用品制造业	Manufacture of Articles for Culture, Education, Artwork, Sport and Entertainment Activities	30	8	1378445	25903
石油加工、炼焦和核燃料加工业	Processing of Petroleum, Coking, Processing of Mucleus Fuels	16	1	4943850	1575454
化学原料和化学制品制造业	Manufacture of Chemical Raw Materials and Chemical Products	184	34	3022624	778720
医药制造业	Manufacture of Medicines	209	28	8143946	3361704
化学纤维制造业	Manufacture of Chemical Fibres	***	***	***	***
橡胶和塑料制品业	Manufacture of Rubber and Plastics Products	108	26	828985	205805
非金属矿物制品业	Manufacture of Non-metallic Mineral Products	219	55	4320951	831298
黑色金属冶炼和压延加工业	Manufacture and Pressing of Ferrous Metals	20	5	1035339	47349
有色金属冶炼和压延加工业	Manufacture and Pressing of Non-ferrous Metals	35	6	723528	140050
金属制品业	Manufacture of Fabricated Metal Products	182	36	2801816	687433
通用设备制造业	Manufacture of General-purpose Machinery	213	52	4900143	1224225
专用设备制造业	Manufacture of Special-purpose Machinery	287	42	5121326	1297891
汽车制造业	Manufacture of Motor Vehicles	240	39	47715999	9494661
铁路、船舶、航空航天和其他运输设备制造业	Manufacture of Railway Locomotives, Building of Ships and Boats, Manufacture of Air and Spacecrafts and Other Transportation Equipment	78	13	3915137	1360543
电气机械和器材制造业	Manufacture of Electrical Machinery and Equipment	233	36	6786451	1184713
计算机、通信和其他电子设备制造业	Manufacture of Computers, Communication Equipment and Other Electronic Equipment	284	43	20198717	1852496
仪器仪表制造业	Manufacture of Measuring Instruments and Meters	158	23	2549480	755098
其他制造业	Other Manufacturing	24	6	672646	199499
废弃资源综合利用业	Waste Recycling and Recovery	9	3	60344	16297
金属制品、机械和设备修理业	Repair of Fabricated Metal Products, Machinery and Equipment	16	1	821637	343045
电力、热力生产和供应业	Production and Distribution of Electricity and Heating Power	74	14	41055448	7283035
燃气生产和供应业	Production and Distribution of Gas	20	1	3823347	518372
水的生产和供应业	Production and Distribution of Water	23	2	752533	335065

MAIN ECONOMIC INDICATORS OF INDUSTRIAL ENTERPRISES ABOVE DESIGNATED SIZE (BY SECTOR) (2016)

(10000 yuan)

工业销售产值(当年价格) Sales Value of Industry (at current year's prices)	#出口交货值 Delivery Value of Exports	平均用工人数(人) Average Number of Employed Persons (person)	资产负债 Assets and Liabilities 资产总计 Total Assets	流动资产合计 Total Current Assets	#存货 Inventories	#产成品 Finished Products	#应收账款 Accounts Receivable	固定资产合计 Total Fixed Assets	固定资产原价 Total Original Value of Fixed Assets
178374996	**9568018**	**1044464**	**430936843**	**166431586**	**23494977**	**8008211**	**43925283**	**68330561**	**129779692**
***	***	***	***	***	***	***	***	***	***
***	***	***	***	***	***	***	***	***	***
728089		18900	24835519	8094588	229495	42506	1830143	3895578	5593901
***	***	***	***	***	***	***	***	***	***
1186103	24617	19071	4391549	1986852	193354	9100	792062	1077011	2639200
3842996	63502	31322	4712738	3092763	547622	315571	388488	611483	936370
2914982	132948	46569	4112470	2279438	420128	188569	561445	784410	1466650
1646141	18693	25007	4183459	1835129	243061	60120	192805	1439020	1345083
***	***	***	***	***	***	***	***	***	***
121818	20092	3280	468381	284547	37842	18735	46012	82243	136462
1022641	181974	35051	1673197	1261283	557577	318225	225538	215223	378402
81121	11479	1592	95897	81780	39656	27287	23617	8613	15278
144023	2428	1766	118623	82000	16341	4777	21999	10994	17709
771260	41920	13011	971581	692072	188224	67051	169115	143435	220626
578764	47724	5147	541536	342141	89102	32840	97964	144249	361381
1110545	4824	21288	2106924	1309587	244746	94510	337285	563667	1480642
1366527	49155	5736	837636	668662	332051	194369	112075	62401	151508
4944220		9936	2636509	1040127	491315	108732	196370	1075246	3239902
2943567	120191	30583	4428620	2871857	537852	196886	626774	858239	2378360
7850785	131712	74795	12901078	7881276	2071291	797729	2055067	1713576	2828245
***	***	***	***	***	***	***	***	***	***
843119	76969	14782	1074817	723760	160022	74663	248119	239836	482951
4256791	73321	44024	10443676	7037211	997512	257067	3089622	893421	1924966
1042303	67583	4531	1106525	476034	183632	57735	160558	447306	808125
707237	122113	5209	984031	624550	162946	67336	187725	85392	188370
2754234	130317	32549	6291409	3841945	675245	211226	979699	810924	1428747
4737960	801219	51505	11002013	7526702	1976098	511907	1676214	1146776	2107329
4990914	688257	61641	18326086	11653316	1785454	542096	3322487	1072952	1923717
46784580	566154	151712	46070264	26386042	3466631	1598483	8463242	8560320	13023056
3812294	54777	37418	6957857	5083963	1534582	263380	1696061	879839	1461009
6698383	313287	46903	11838439	8867884	1397513	412140	4202379	718485	1362494
19836241	5500967	106931	39319148	23187171	3460561	1256348	6444524	4681375	10096155
2538299	126466	30475	5514047	4082049	859363	169040	1344194	441687	726142
663652	11432	6547	1392316	819423	179995	50481	290759	289130	523621
59620	201	836	222677	73707	3364	2163	31634	79847	107865
815251	46603	13803	3364872	976683	152339	6950	264876	201483	789499
41039606		57476	178545807	26516558	125680	11709	2949975	27482992	58745847
3823339		12025	5500676	1242511	13663	6703	333035	1635132	2405673
751397		11919	10530233	2426072	13467	2987	486054	5330293	7379325

12-6 续表

单位：万元

项目	Item	资产负债 Assets and Liabilities 负债合计 Total Liabilities	#流动负债合计 Total Current Liabilities	#应付账款 Accounts Payable	所有者权益合计 Total Owner's Equity
合计	**Total**	**197981343**	**140505878**	**45118348**	**232724512**
煤炭开采和洗选业	Mining and Washing of Coal	***	***	***	***
石油和天然气开采业	Extraction of Petroleum and Natural Gas	***	***	***	***
黑色金属矿采选业	Mining and Processing of Ferrous Metal Ores	14752334	8644899	792253	10083186
非金属矿采选业	Mining and Processing of Nonmetal Ores	***	***	***	***
开采辅助活动	Mining Support Service Activities	1266666	1188973	433720	3124883
农副食品加工业	Processing of Food from Agricultural Products	2547306	2088667	361499	2165432
食品制造业	Manufacture of Foods	2118453	1940954	-320541	1994016
酒、饮料和精制茶制造业	Manufacture of Wines, Beverage and Refined Tea	1691297	1580269	405019	2492162
烟草制品业	Manufacture of Cigarettes and Tobacco	***	***	***	***
纺织业	Manufacture of Textile	231971	134247	26998	232192
纺织服装、服饰业	Manufacture of Textile Wearing Apparel and Ornament	954245	846005	277014	702457
皮革、毛皮、羽毛及其制品和制鞋业	Manufacture of Leather, Fur, Feather and Its Products, and Footwear	54282	52895	15601	41615
木材加工和木、竹、藤、棕、草制品业	Processing of Timbers, Manufacture of Wood, Bamboo, Rattan, Palm, and Straw Products	82136	81671	24766	36487
家具制造业	Manufacture of Furniture	518638	497526	112219	452943
造纸和纸制品业	Manufacture of Paper and Paper Products	262282	237700	93762	279254
印刷和记录媒介复制业	Printing, Reproduction of Recording Media	896383	764489	341025	1210541
文教、工美、体育和娱乐用品制造业	Manufacture of Articles for Culture, Education, Artwork, Sport and Entertainment Activities	516394	472617	192434	321243
石油加工、炼焦和核燃料加工业	Processing of Petroleum, Coking, Processing of Mucleus Fuels	1302867	1251142	500623	1333642
化学原料和化学制品制造业	Manufacture of Chemical Raw Materials and Chemical Products	2425721	2254206	584926	2002900
医药制造业	Manufacture of Medicines	5360216	4572420	1479689	7540862
化学纤维制造业	Manufacture of Chemical Fibres	***	***	***	***
橡胶和塑料制品业	Manufacture of Rubber and Plastics Products	556924	519747	204261	506851
非金属矿物制品业	Manufacture of Non-metallic Mineral Products	6271372	5551335	2326492	4132007
黑色金属冶炼和压延加工业	Manufacture and Pressing of Ferrous Metals	1079959	514998	335367	27369
有色金属冶炼和压延加工业	Manufacture and Pressing of Non-ferrous Metals	480594	415833	148635	502530
金属制品业	Manufacture of Fabricated Metal Products	3235936	2678390	779753	3040443
通用设备制造业	Manufacture of General-purpose Machinery	5100732	4208476	1203426	5905057
专用设备制造业	Manufacture of Special-purpose Machinery	9577290	7559912	2408617	8716249
汽车制造业	Manufacture of Motor Vehicles	27640084	24547236	12180611	18421411
铁路、船舶、航空航天和其他运输设备制造业	Manufacture of Railway Locomotives, Building of Ships and Boats, Manufacture of Air and Spacecrafts and Other Transportation Equipment	4240267	3838918	1412341	2714917
电气机械和器材制造业	Manufacture of Electrical Machinery and Equipment	6980478	6379907	2697469	4853189
计算机、通信和其他电子设备制造业	Manufacture of Computers, Communication Equipment and Other Electronic Equipment	20749008	17929819	7847144	18569844
仪器仪表制造业	Manufacture of Measuring Instruments and Meters	2454343	2255798	937564	3059704
其他制造业	Other Manufacturing	567270	437860	176822	825046
废弃资源综合利用业	Waste Recycling and Recovery	151913	114588	10757	70893
金属制品、机械和设备修理业	Repair of Fabricated Metal Products, Machinery and Equipment	1031235	650858	97030	2333637
电力、热力生产和供应业	Production and Distribution of Electricity and Heating Power	64912199	31092142	5716247	113534961
燃气生产和供应业	Production and Distribution of Gas	1746881	1355330	269118	3753796
水的生产和供应业	Production and Distribution of Water	4826088	3351616	934261	5704144

12-6 Continued

(10000 yuan)

#实收资本 Paid-up Capital	损益 Profits and Losses								应交税金合计 Total Tax Payable	#营业税金及附加 Business Tax and Surtax	#主营业务税金及附加 Main Business Tax and Surtax	#应交增值税 Value Added Tax Payable
	营业收入 Business Income	#主营业务收入 Main Business Income	营业成本 Business Cost	#主营业务成本 Main Business Cost	销售费用 Sales Expenses	管理费用 Management Expenses	财务费用 Financial Expenses	利润总额 Total Profits				
136610708	**202138149**	**197469575**	**167507152**	**163956085**	**10249966**	**10444149**	**2153834**	**16082648**	**11956830**	**3221330**	**3198907**	**5667337**
***	***	***	***	***	***	***	***	***	***	***	***	***
***	***	***	***	***	***	***	***	***	***	***	***	***
2912404	2107219	2019294	2102350	1968127	2727	156888	348736	-216335	59641	13903	12432	39853
***	***	***	***	***	***	***	***	***	***	***	***	***
2829484	1234060	1229609	1183041	1181629	5035	64191	-17357	-18689	24015	7238	6814	12821
970659	4578845	4539612	3795178	3777160	301781	203673	32835	221171	225816	124201	124188	61493
1233792	5236406	5110865	3306621	3194213	1272881	291330	11086	348439	412337	33180	33027	286456
871745	1998203	1852154	1401922	1274101	326825	140946	1134	60035	205478	68312	68174	109229
***	***	***	***	***	***	***	***	***	***	***	***	***
183243	228211	219480	179214	175534	5792	29801	3795	9134	10129	2116	1718	5035
277923	1240483	1195441	833378	797105	214209	122264	9417	71813	87601	8587	8474	63140
9642	110948	106437	94728	91269	4068	5233	378	6096	6386	478	478	4101
20081	194015	192642	156563	155708	16490	12481	109	6932	8761	703	703	6859
232577	758247	742630	600497	588878	51514	68284	5521	45542	40425	3016	3002	27856
172675	654165	635343	510083	495550	19055	38373	380	60634	52533	3820	3757	27366
706467	1368149	1291009	1070026	1017447	40700	159869	-22	92747	103749	10687	9414	68506
229924	1507757	1480849	1416252	1408164	28305	46143	8422	9576	16338	2421	1954	10355
44740	5475436	5268769	4168788	3954993	48947	226409	16472	204777	1060922	740119	739824	259050
1758323	3418305	3282094	2607226	2489649	289291	360937	48753	101369	215536	20688	20507	154932
2195954	8354413	8090285	4019550	3794932	2065128	806366	129639	1534829	927949	75361	74163	602633
***	***	***	***	***	***	***	***	***	***	***	***	***
292354	1088700	1031018	939625	890726	38847	82014	8152	21277	44331	4382	4333	30851
1914357	4774075	4627674	4075897	3966029	200747	360099	60815	135836	199783	18046	17247	150776
337749	1113368	1101337	1054467	1044147	41150	32956	15042	-19807	18448	2876	2843	8400
169820	989093	761063	893247	674090	12095	53038	2821	28102	14950	1625	1524	8865
1448575	3371537	3208088	2761296	2639433	96336	294248	32458	234328	135864	15001	14397	78206
2271752	5383310	5278214	4155222	4099796	329493	483180	57124	679437	300617	28459	28148	163838
3233070	6276168	6083462	4436943	4336439	431312	742589	114345	810695	360607	33797	33684	216142
7651721	49431258	48019950	40978796	39779304	1904422	1776332	251630	3801345	3557736	1440544	1436021	1179473
1086969	4115960	4055436	3300570	3257368	72763	369739	32440	348013	214475	16284	15318	131171
2890679	7603553	7387798	5941612	5796915	586948	643930	50822	355851	413819	34726	34550	254989
8707351	27677109	27151370	24454334	24213536	1454079	1712368	188676	886452	525683	74789	73478	219224
997675	3103576	3046281	2180155	2159743	232649	364942	12405	373719	217870	21008	20316	143329
380637	699275	694419	518970	516438	23672	82550	3939	76618	36383	3985	3981	20987
55680	63333	62757	52986	52796	513	9884	2170	507	3487	296	296	2584
886778	922543	914563	759154	756701	9216	101758	31491	213640	58236	7775	7731	34915
83857686	41312811	41123363	38843914	38735284	12095	257962	609034	4905949	1798731	126720	121829	1066217
804248	3869689	3827087	3525874	3500849	36629	156909	28189	388122	122709	3999	3586	79629
4512573	948988	932445	710826	704470	48677	75937	34597	210300	79140	9457	8870	29975

12-7 规模以上工业企业主要经济效益指标(2016年)

单位：%

项　　目	Item	工业经济效益综合指数 Aggregate Index of Industrial Economic Efficiency	企业亏损面 Loss-Suffering Enterprises as % of Total	总资产贡献率 Contribution Rate of Total Assets	资产保值增值率 Rate of Assets Preservation and Appreciation
合　计	**Total**	**313.42**	**19.04**	**6.19**	**113.63**
按隶属关系分组	**By Affiliation**				
中央企业	Central Enterprises	534.42	15.53	4.58	115.52
地方企业	Local Enterprises	267.44	19.29	7.58	111.53
按登记注册类型分组	**By Registration Type**				
内资企业	Domestically-funded Enterprises	283.96	17.93	4.63	114.24
国有企业	State-owned Enterprises	1030.67	16.13	3.61	116.72
集体企业	Collectively-Owned Enterprises	136.88	31.03	4.15	108.98
股份合作企业	Joint-equity Cooperative Enterprises	227.99	16.33	8.67	80.49
有限责任公司	Limited Liability Companies	212.29	21.00	3.62	103.96
股份有限公司	Company Limited by Shares	310.33	15.26	8.17	122.27
私营企业	Private Enterprises	195.71	15.00	8.27	110.81
其他企业	Others	155.85		5.57	189.64
港澳台商投资企业	Hong Kong, Macao and Taiwan-invested Enterprises	208.67	26.52	7.52	109.05
港澳台合资经营	Joint Ventures	315.41	21.69	11.61	102.02
港澳台合作经营	Cooperatives	298.72		17.53	105.70
港澳台商独资企业	Solely-funded Enterprises	176.86	34.52	6.70	116.40
港澳台商投资股份有限公司	Companies Limited by Shares	-56.79	9.09	4.50	100.58
外商投资企业	Foreign-invested Enterprises	439.10	21.77	14.45	111.28
中外合资经营	Joint Ventures	572.63	16.90	17.01	118.92
中外合作经营	Cooperatives	212.40	37.50	13.57	103.60
外资(独资)企业	Solely-funded Enterprises	301.70	24.77	11.16	103.73
外商投资股份有限公司	Companies Limited by Shares	239.87	16.67	7.34	95.67
按城乡分组	**By urban and rural regions**				
#农村企业	Rural Enterprises	114.65	28.57	2.83	99.52
按控股类型分组	**By holding types**				
#国有控股	State-holding Enterprises	417.26	20.09	5.58	114.75
集体控股	Collectively-holding Enterprises	264.56	20.65	8.09	93.95
私人控股	Private-holding Enterprises	199.21	16.85	6.30	109.40
港澳台控股	Hong Kong, Macao, and Taiwan-holding Enterprises	180.22	28.68	5.89	111.85
外商控股	Foreign-Investor-holding Enterprises	313.64	22.65	12.06	110.91
按轻重工业分组	**By light and heavy industries**				
轻工业	Light Industry	266.10	20.12	12.21	108.30
重工业	Heavy Industry	340.24	18.47	5.51	114.27
按规模分组	**By size**				
#大中型企业	Medium and Large-sized Enterprises	351.38	16.42	6.14	114.79

MAIN INDICATORS OF ECONOMIC BENEFITS OF INDUSTRIAL ENTERPRISES ABOVE DESIGNATED SIZE (2016)

(%)

资 产 负债率 Assets-Liabilities Ratio	流动资产 周转率 (次) Turnover of Current Assets (times)	成 本 费 用 利润率 Ratio of Profits to Costs	全员劳动 生 产 率 (元/人) Overall Labor Productivity (yuan/person)	产 品 销售率 Sales Rate of Products	增 加 值 率 Value-added Rate	人均销售 收 入 (元/人) Sales Revenue Per Capita (yuan)	流动比率 (倍) Liquidity Ratio (times)	速动比率 (倍) Quick Ratio (times)
45.94	**1.21**	**8.45**	**358907**	**98.62**	**20.73**	**1890631**	**1.18**	**1.02**
37.67	1.45	9.90	714958	99.55	22.25	3278622	1.03	0.92
53.11	1.14	7.84	284254	98.18	20.00	1599611	1.25	1.06
43.74	1.03	8.37	318373	98.74	20.78	1637318	1.16	1.00
34.08	1.30	13.64	1515545	100.02	18.54	8214055	1.07	1.02
55.52	0.90	2.01	119795	99.87	27.50	438560	1.52	1.13
61.26	1.72	3.80	240169	89.99	22.84	1158640	1.38	0.99
58.43	1.00	3.39	237004	98.66	20.37	1287237	1.01	0.85
41.98	0.87	11.44	332874	97.88	23.51	1551820	1.52	1.32
53.42	0.97	7.96	166156	97.20	23.73	745785	1.44	1.10
59.01	1.51	4.36	102694	107.49	15.91	763333	1.09	0.52
58.89	1.58	5.59	194832	98.25	9.80	2759048	1.18	1.01
45.03	1.17	12.16	325674	98.15	27.42	1263684	1.53	1.35
11.96	0.94	14.91	262271	113.49	52.77	770978	7.41	6.50
63.55	2.03	4.03	145619	98.39	5.36	4086138	1.04	0.89
61.95	0.35	8.16	-227327	95.35	-22.62	1203565	1.43	1.15
53.16	1.63	9.86	525727	98.50	23.90	2304214	1.27	1.07
53.89	1.76	11.19	726212	97.89	25.62	2826631	1.21	1.03
46.38	1.58	5.47	184039	99.31	49.01	673286	1.90	2.01
56.52	1.53	6.74	331627	99.60	20.36	1852893	1.45	1.17
33.33	0.52	38.86	58553	104.39	9.16	794575	0.86	0.81
76.76	0.54	1.77	96837	98.88	18.64	541985	2.99	2.40
43.27	1.23	9.62	524186	98.93	22.21	2452001	1.06	0.94
54.79	1.08	7.53	285161	96.09	19.87	1389539	1.60	1.27
49.06	0.81	8.55	177305	97.01	21.02	914906	1.47	1.19
62.61	1.71	3.66	162193	98.33	7.24	3227668	1.12	0.96
54.08	1.60	7.69	339979	99.38	21.74	1775230	1.44	1.17
46.42	1.22	10.49	250768	97.74	29.68	968412	1.52	1.18
45.89	1.21	8.08	407381	98.77	19.13	2304018	1.14	0.99
45.45	1.30	8.69	418454	98.70	20.60	2207177	1.13	0.99

12-8 规模以上国有控股工业企业主要经济指标(2016年)

单位：万元

项 目	Item	企业单位个数(个) Number of Enterprises (unit)	#亏损企业 Loss-Suffering Enterprises	工业总产值(当年价格) Gross Output Value of Industry (at current year's prices)	工业增加值 Added Value of Industry	工业销售产值(当年价格) Sales Value of Industry (at current year's prices)
合 计	**Total**	**697**	**140**	**107041993**	**23778616**	**105896130**
按隶属关系分组	**By Affiliation**					
中央企业	Central Enterprises	215	34	58010651	12944844	57748299
地方企业	Local Enterprises	482	106	49031343	10833772	48147830
按轻重工业分组	**By light and heavy industries**					
轻工业	Light Industry	170	33	7080505	2437929	6966820
重工业	Heavy Industry	527	107	99961488	21340687	98929309
按规模分组	**By size**					
#大中型企业	Medium and Large-sized Enterprises	254	55	98918477	22004223	97914268

12-8 续表

单位：万元

项 目	Item	资产负债 Assets and Liabilities					营业收入 Business Income
		负债合计 Total Liabilities	#流动负债合计 Total Current Liabilities	#应付账款 Accounts Payable	所有者权益合计 Total Owner's Equity	#实收资本 Paid-up Capital	
合 计	**Total**	**136231832**	**87235623**	**24168208**	**178475871**	**114011349**	**113528698**
按隶属关系分组	**By Affiliation**						
中央企业	Central Enterprises	74686969	40156743	9583582	124301536	89491074	59912299
地方企业	Local Enterprises	61544864	47078880	14584626	54174335	24520275	53616399
按轻重工业分组	**By light and heavy industries**						
轻工业	Light Industry	6342368	4634775	1121049	9657223	3492028	8208062
重工业	Heavy Industry	129889464	82600849	23047159	168818648	110519321	105320636
按规模分组	**By size**						
#大中型企业	Medium and Large-sized Enterprises	126634119	79043762	21326972	167791748	108615739	103609885

MAIN ECONOMIC INDICATORS OF STATE-HOLDING INDUSTRIAL ENTERPRISES ABOVE DESIGNATED SIZE (2016)

(10000 yuan)

#出口交货值 Delivery Value of Exports	平均用工人数(人) Average Number of Employed Persons (person)	资产负债 Assets and Liabilities 资产总计 Total Assets	流动资产合计 Total Current Assets	#存货 Inventories	#产成品 Finished Products	#应收账款 Accounts Receivable	固定资产合计 Total Fixed Assets	固定资产原价 Total Original Value of Fixed Assets
2401046	**453629**	**314811115**	**92382040**	**10264820**	**3323591**	**20004099**	**54542152**	**104410451**
272673	178640	198988505	41045852	4101344	954958	7777341	28254323	64579657
2128373	274989	115822611	51336188	6163476	2368632	12226758	26287828	39830794
92928	80863	16003809	8428325	1697828	727273	1267370	3848833	6240832
2308118	372766	298807306	83953715	8566992	2596318	18736729	50693319	98169618
2242409	391593	294425867	82481829	8379644	2740912	17064376	50917994	98521202

12-8 Continued

(10000 yuan)

损益 Profits and Losses #主营业务收入 Main Business Income	营业成本 Business Cost	#主营业务成本 Main Business Cost	销售费用 Sales Expenses	管理费用 Management Expenses	财务费用 Financial Expenses	利润总额 Total Profits	应交税金合计 Total Tax Payable	#营业税金及附加 Business Tax and Surtax	#主营业务税金及附加 Main Business Tax and Surtax	#应交增值税 Value Added Tax Payable
111229887	**96957102**	**95094140**	**3049032**	**4631979**	**1371339**	**10202731**	**7935842**	**2878942**	**2861062**	**3190817**
59089928	53217607	52546900	427180	1789303	587367	5563317	3803116	1269782	1257988	1731771
52139960	43739495	42547240	2621852	2842676	783972	4639414	4132726	1609159	1603074	1459047
8011100	5873388	5752622	740175	677725	36999	697581	965128	459569	456336	368205
103218788	91083714	89341518	2308857	3954254	1334340	9505150	6970714	2419372	2404727	2822613
101836746	88786757	87312850	2732271	3801615	1244970	9186564	7376166	2823086	2811317	2856624

12-9 规模以上国有控股工业企业主要经济指标(按行业分)(2016年)

单位：万元

项目	Item	企业单位个数(个) Number of Enterprises (unit)	#亏损企业 Loss-Suffering Enterprises	工业总产值(当年价格) Gross Output Value of Industry (at current year's prices)	工业增加值 Added Value of Industry
合计	**Total**	**697**	**140**	**107041993**	**23778616**
煤炭开采和洗选业	Mining and Washing of Coal	***	***	***	***
石油和天然气开采业	Extraction of Petroleum and Natural Gas	***	***	***	***
黑色金属矿采选业	Mining and Processing of Ferrous Metal Ores	4	3	698112	-176558
非金属矿采选业	Mining and processing of nonmetal ores	***	***	***	***
开采辅助活动	Mining Support Service Activities	***	***	***	***
农副食品加工业	Processing of Food from Agricultural Products	22	7	1957756	303140
食品制造业	Manufacture of Foods	15	2	566843	131828
酒、饮料和精制茶制造业	Manufacture of Wines, Beverage and Refined Tea	9	6	527272	251681
烟草制品业	Manufacture of Cigarettes and Tobacco	***	***	***	***
纺织业	Manufacture of Textile	8	2	29779	3882
纺织服装、服饰业	Manufacture of Textile Wearing Apparel and Ornament	6		56185	8502
皮革、毛皮、羽毛及其制品和制鞋业	Manufacture of Leather, Fur, Feather and Its Products, and Footwear	***	***	***	***
木材加工和木、竹、藤、棕、草制品业	Processing of Timbers, Manufacture of Wood, Bamboo, Rattan, Palm, and Straw Products				
家具制造业	Manufacture of Furniture	***	***	***	***
造纸和纸制品业	Manufacture of Paper and Paper Products	***	***	***	***
印刷和记录媒介复制业	Printing, Reproduction of Recording Media	31	7	547728	261672
文教、工美、体育和娱乐用品制造业	Manufacture of Articles for Culture, Education, Artwork, Sport and Entertainment Activities	7	1	224334	12434
石油加工、炼焦和核燃料加工业	Processing of Petroleum, Coking, Processing of Mucleus Fuels	6	1	4389432	1494236
化学原料和化学制品制造业	Manufacture of Chemical Raw Materials and Chemical Products	31	7	1127446	138849
医药制造业	Manufacture of Medicines	30	2	1547441	738060
化学纤维制造业	Manufacture of Chemical Fibres	***	***	***	***
橡胶和塑料制品业	Manufacture of Rubber and Plastics Products	7	2	57467	16354
非金属矿物制品业	Manufacture of Non-metallic Mineral Products	52	18	1441308	262056
黑色金属冶炼和压延加工业	Manufacture and Pressing of Ferrous Metals	***	***	***	***
有色金属冶炼和压延加工业	Manufacture and Pressing of Non-ferrous Metals	9		432544	95954
金属制品业	Manufacture of Fabricated Metal Products	27	6	1024153	223316
通用设备制造业	Manufacture of General-purpose Machinery	41	14	917329	193568
专用设备制造业	Manufacture of Special-purpose Machinery	55	10	1362210	279960
汽车制造业	Manufacture of Motor Vehicles	43	4	34383837	7513530
铁路、船舶、航空航天和其他运输设备制造业	Manufacture of Railway Locomotives, Building of Ships and Boats, Manufacture of Air and Spacecrafts and Other Transportation Equipment	36	5	3320329	1129201
电气机械和器材制造业	Manufacture of Electrical Machinery and Equipment	25	5	1193694	155775
计算机、通信和其他电子设备制造业	Manufacture of Computers, Communication Equipment and Other Electronic Equipment	68	12	4260665	926624
仪器仪表制造业	Manufacture of Measuring Instruments and Meters	46	6	836838	210165
其他制造业	Other Manufacturing	10	1	589568	183969
废弃资源综合利用业	Waste Recycling and Recovery	***	***	***	***
金属制品、机械和设备修理业	Repair of Fabricated Metal Products, Machinery and Equipment	5		749118	307972
电力、热力生产和供应业	Production and Distribution of Electricity and Heating Power	53	11	40817852	7253877
燃气生产和供应业	Production and Distribution of Gas	13	1	559216	105221
水的生产和供应业	Production and Distribution of Water	19	1	725641	327593

MAIN ECONOMIC INDICATORS OF STATE-OWNED AND STATE-CONTROLLED INDUSTIRAL ENTERPRISES ABOVE DESIGNATED SIZE (BY SECTOR) (2016)

(10000 yuan)

工业销售产值(当年价格) Sales Value of Industry (at current year's prices)	#出口交货值 Delivery Value of Exports	平均用工人数(人) Average Number of Employed Persons (person)	资产负债 Assets and Liabilities						
			资产总计 Total Assets	流动资产合计 Total Current Assets	#存货 Inventories	#产成品 Finished Products	#应收账款 Accounts Receivable	固定资产合计 Total Fixed Assets	固定资产原价 Total Original Value of Fixed Assets
105896130	**2401046**	**453629**	**314811115**	**92382040**	**10264820**	**3323591**	**20004099**	**54542152**	**104410451**
***	***	***	***	***	***	***	***	***	***
***	***	***	***	***	***	***	***	***	***
700976		18060	24768246	8062088	221732	39326	1824153	3865448	5537503
***	***	***	***	***	***	***	***	***	***
***	***	***	***	***	***	***	***	***	***
1938374	888	11984	2473919	1876887	282204	209447	119111	333408	457153
592038	7383	8279	1054743	444826	50839	16940	128924	137440	244808
514798	4307	11220	2556799	955929	121375	25295	32825	1063364	547386
***	***	***	***	***	***	***	***	***	***
32039	2037	1699	339220	187471	17331	11353	9065	61947	83918
55477	29974	1171	81144	58940	36361	15125	7282	15144	26509
***	***	***	***	***	***	***	***	***	***
***	***	***	***	***	***	***	***	***	***
***	***	***	***	***	***	***	***	***	***
551141		10353	1159589	736632	120577	56810	221679	289608	877973
222821	4827	1775	406478	324156	196591	121280	78579	34403	61779
4384448		8704	2412775	853056	441794	101690	147454	1047283	3187596
1138553	33037	9184	1741020	1005235	203997	62215	177667	432585	1554409
1437531	4228	17296	3424092	1831214	588228	210954	251294	422279	805380
***	***	***	***	***	***	***	***	***	***
60076	23017	1975	174223	100424	14227	6965	25966	37171	65036
1425234	16127	15506	4040845	2489157	217028	84162	1095405	436329	921360
***	***	***	***	***	***	***	***	***	***
420257	97758	3085	650710	423059	117368	37734	94993	52435	125776
1003015	58701	11582	2630141	1283735	195923	49415	283720	461620	748805
937913	26362	13636	2641646	1891152	793886	108673	335191	251804	501129
1284419	43426	18917	3929565	2919075	734198	251886	1116669	446249	805209
33613022	360905	92721	35875439	19666611	2357679	1161451	5140892	6718828	9823685
3223857	46735	31030	5662675	4153827	1337991	207615	1359949	802261	1328669
1201593	8054	6189	2418972	1595591	179916	19913	832350	122969	244486
4128632	1368024	31709	13686596	7017895	998722	343784	1692216	1979784	4433820
854840	7309	9105	1316752	1057584	261758	57093	298674	91434	191833
585386	5	5346	1224691	721186	152730	34393	263219	270084	495066
***	***	***	***	***	***	***	***	***	***
743926	44247	12912	3209058	856508	131585	255	224501	184567	755611
40817304		53048	177989382	26255825	104101	8876	2911381	27295905	58458551
559216		3662	642438	367604	11209	6348	41663	238790	375246
722060		11532	10283137	2360608	8518	2572	468838	5311610	7357607

12-9 续表

单位：万元

项目	Item	负债合计 Total Liabilities	#流动负债合计 Total Current Liabilities	#应付账款 Accounts Payable	所有者权益合计 Total Owner's Equity
		资产负债 Assets and Liabilities			
合计	**Total**	**136231832**	**87235623**	**24168208**	**178475871**
煤炭开采和洗选业	Mining and Washing of Coal	***	***	***	***
石油和天然气开采业	Extraction of Petroleum and Natural Gas	***	***	***	***
黑色金属矿采选业	Mining and Processing of Ferrous Metal Ores	14711303	8606314	783594	10056943
非金属矿采选业	Mining and processing of nonmetal ores	***	***	***	***
开采辅助活动	Mining Support Service Activities	***	***	***	***
农副食品加工业	Processing of Food from Agricultural Products	1464067	1149945	96570	1009852
食品制造业	Manufacture of Foods	327557	288861	142426	727187
酒、饮料和精制茶制造业	Manufacture of Wines, Beverage and Refined Tea	670084	587526	35576	1886715
烟草制品业	Manufacture of Cigarettes and Tobacco	***	***	***	***
纺织业	Manufacture of Textile	164876	67261	5170	170126
纺织服装、服饰业	Manufacture of Textile Wearing Apparel and Ornament	62790	48319	13350	18354
皮革、毛皮、羽毛及其制品和制鞋业	Manufacture of Leather, Fur, Feather and Its Products, and Footwear	***	***	***	***
木材加工和木、竹、藤、棕、草制品业	Processing of Timbers, Manufacture of Wood, Bamboo, Rattan, Palm, and Straw Products				
家具制造业	Manufacture of Furniture	***	***	***	***
造纸和纸制品业	Manufacture of Paper and Paper Products	***	***	***	***
印刷和记录媒介复制业	Printing, Reproduction of Recording Media	467730	405851	195945	691859
文教、工美、体育和娱乐用品制造业	Manufacture of Articles for Culture, Education, Artwork, Sport and Entertainment Activities	273621	246634	151195	132856
石油加工、炼焦和核燃料加工业	Processing of Petroleum, Coking, Processing of Mucleus Fuels	1176259	1124638	469923	1236517
化学原料和化学制品制造业	Manufacture of Chemical Raw Materials and Chemical Products	1202377	1111389	256818	538643
医药制造业	Manufacture of Medicines	933673	653745	210843	2490419
化学纤维制造业	Manufacture of Chemical Fibres	***	***	***	***
橡胶和塑料制品业	Manufacture of Rubber and Plastics Products	49339	46924	12812	124884
非金属矿物制品业	Manufacture of Non-metallic Mineral Products	2135497	2037778	719141	1905348
黑色金属冶炼和压延加工业	Manufacture and Pressing of Ferrous Metals	***	***	***	***
有色金属冶炼和压延加工业	Manufacture and Pressing of Non-ferrous Metals	250681	204629	50991	399181
金属制品业	Manufacture of Fabricated Metal Products	1254952	1095299	330989	1375189
通用设备制造业	Manufacture of General-purpose Machinery	1600472	1496665	328172	1041174
专用设备制造业	Manufacture of Special-purpose Machinery	2619135	2194606	856727	1310430
汽车制造业	Manufacture of Motor Vehicles	21622434	19310888	8660389	14252504
铁路、船舶、航空航天和其他运输设备制造业	Manufacture of Railway Locomotives, Building of Ships and Boats, Manufacture of Air and Spacecrafts and Other Transportation Equipment	3689432	3342507	1187474	1973243
电气机械和器材制造业	Manufacture of Electrical Machinery and Equipment	1645218	1525386	569766	773755
计算机、通信和其他电子设备制造业	Manufacture of Computers, Communication Equipment and Other Electronic Equipment	5166728	4243389	1373782	8519869
仪器仪表制造业	Manufacture of Measuring Instruments and Meters	707597	607039	197640	609155
其他制造业	Other Manufacturing	458188	332335	151286	766503
废弃资源综合利用业	Waste Recycling and Recovery	***	***	***	***
金属制品、机械和设备修理业	Repair of Fabricated Metal Products, Machinery and Equipment	994579	614548	83062	2214479
电力、热力生产和供应业	Production and Distribution of Electricity and Heating Power	64499581	30798791	5658919	113391154
燃气生产和供应业	Production and Distribution of Gas	321560	274271	40970	320877
水的生产和供应业	Production and Distribution of Water	4647640	3260726	886044	5635498

12-9 Continued

(10000 yuan)

#实收资本 Paid-up Capital	损益 Profits and Losses								应交税金合计 Total Tax Payable	#营业税金及附加 Business Tax and Surtax	#主营业务税金及附加 Main Business Tax and Surtax	#应交增值税 Value Added Tax Payable
	营业收入 Business Income	#主营业务收入 Main Business Income	营业成本 Business Cost	#主营业务成本 Main Business Cost	销售费用 Sales Expenses	管理费用 Management Expenses	财务费用 Financial Expenses	利润总额 Total Profits				
114011349	**113528698**	**111229887**	**96957102**	**95094140**	**3049032**	**4631979**	**1371339**	**10202731**	**7935842**	**2878942**	**2861062**	**3190817**
***	***	***	***	***	***	***	***	***	***	***	***	***
***	***	***	***	***	***	***	***	***	***	***	***	***
2910339	2076890	1994030	2075351	1946883	2508	150873	348285	-212504	56703	13089	11617	37837
***	***	***	***	***	***	***	***	***	***	***	***	***
***	***	***	***	***	***	***	***	***	***	***	***	***
249306	2408310	2398923	1966625	1963945	178287	85387	12039	88317	193136	122117	122110	51042
361405	708448	679527	514559	488847	119050	39275	-1402	44701	42863	4402	4344	28873
152667	637411	599576	436479	409572	72022	44145	-6711	46554	105661	52194	52056	42358
***	***	***	***	***	***	***	***	***	***	***	***	***
140624	100654	95476	74369	73116	1432	21338	2131	1115	4504	1558	1159	1665
49305	98149	96905	89282	88815	2428	4274	1417	437	1119	410	403	493
***	***	***	***	***	***	***	***	***	***	***	***	***
***	***	***	***	***	***	***	***	***	***	***	***	***
***	***	***	***	***	***	***	***	***	***	***	***	***
444860	749369	693968	566553	530770	13758	103401	-1444	63551	62960	7093	5832	38426
142821	238137	231096	200834	198075	16681	14358	4636	927	6757	1084	919	4685
26669	4759629	4554163	3536146	3323161	31445	213702	16148	155714	1028045	736639	736344	242393
1123003	1264374	1211215	1073549	1031258	28963	195896	30764	-61053	67747	3525	3373	55591
655368	1516391	1496826	826394	819399	250750	168291	11581	318127	168985	16947	15879	105188
***	***	***	***	***	***	***	***	***	***	***	***	***
42667	127903	114099	104922	94816	3542	12618	-453	6931	6576	644	644	3809
880225	1605695	1535617	1367027	1314501	65631	145219	19026	60546	78686	10149	9352	61192
***	***	***	***	***	***	***	***	***	***	***	***	***
102448	653065	435845	586153	376430	6461	32891	724	26077	10051	1188	1096	5243
609932	1332792	1275521	1152712	1119484	22127	103362	6188	57964	30460	4084	3792	12202
589167	1088145	1063056	902704	885681	34415	123646	5968	14311	47230	7304	7041	28665
793487	1752209	1722736	1369629	1351780	73144	191811	15100	45592	81650	7979	7885	55072
6098196	34898881	33998987	27983952	27240946	1656777	1250994	154258	3112932	3032052	1406615	1404186	855891
890649	3465943	3409925	2897734	2857723	33687	284963	27575	212567	152480	12078	11112	97457
692512	1307683	1300948	1095919	1092267	73379	115193	17331	23919	64463	6775	6606	46503
3799534	5013516	4893372	4131741	4041338	185340	548624	35109	672353	235773	36635	35933	96818
242185	973697	956851	768844	761565	40455	108271	2030	55685	55390	6442	6299	40210
344763	610898	606694	454553	452445	16372	69712	266	76992	31603	3642	3638	17950
***	***	***	***	***	***	***	***	***	***	***	***	***
829645	839841	832446	712040	709835	5299	86184	31538	193505	48317	6972	6927	28818
83773370	41048253	40861237	38604346	38497847	6574	231573	602166	4879888	1788526	125775	120884	1062107
194292	586232	557932	536639	523273	8172	38298	-3011	40417	27872	2418	2092	16104
4456943	919360	903055	691893	685632	46273	70661	33645	208826	79752	9527	8940	30937

12-10 规模以上港澳台及外商投资工业企业主要经济指标(2016年)

单位：万元

项目	Item	企业单位个数(个) Number of Enterprises (unit)	#亏损企业 Loss-Suffering Enterprises	工业总产值(当年价格) Gross Output Value of Industry (at current year's prices)	工业增加值 Added Value of Industry	工业销售产值(当年价格) Sales Value of Industry (at current year's prices)	#出口交货值 Delivery Value of Exports
合　计	**Total**	**746**	**171**	**72801145**	**15028845**	**71665571**	**6473549**
按隶属关系分组	**By Affiliation**						
中央企业	Central Enterprises	10	1	1327153	510873	1327180	58609
地方企业	Local Enterprises	736	170	71473992	14517972	70338391	6414940
按轻重工业分组	**By Light and Heavy Industries**						
轻工业	Light Industry	279	72	10921530	3083823	10760858	1017475
重工业	Heavy Industry	467	99	61879615	11945022	60904713	5456074
按规模分组	**By Size**						
#大中型企业	Medium and Large-sized Enterprises	220	33	64048799	13262753	63046165	5617814

12-10 续表

单位：万元

项目	Item	资产负债 Assets and Liabilities					
		固定资产原价 Total Original Value of Fixed Assets	负债合计 Total Liabilities	#流动负债合计 Total Current Liabilities	#应付账款 Accounts Payable	所有者权益合计 Total Owner's Equity	#实收资本 Paid-up Capital
合　计	**Total**	**27436929**	**47057385**	**41712844**	**17831162**	**38808021**	**18181914**
按隶属关系分组	**By Affiliation**						
中央企业	Central Enterprises	1839936	1197854	834698	196701	1708026	983002
地方企业	Local Enterprises	25596993	45859532	40878146	17634462	37099995	17198912
按轻重工业分组	**By Light and Heavy Industries**						
轻工业	Light Industry	4267127	7032370	6424788	2342135	7043393	3631470
重工业	Heavy Industry	23169802	40025015	35288056	15489027	31764627	14550444
按规模分组	**By Size**						
#大中型企业	Medium and Large-sized Enterprises	23430389	39286445	34588712	15012206	30363829	13281464

MAIN ECONOMIC INDICATORS OF HONGKONG, MACAO, TAIWAN AND FOREIGN-INVESTED INDUSTRIAL ENTERPRISES ABOVE DESIGNATED SIZE (2016)

(10000 yuan)

平均用工人数（人） Average Number of Employed Persons	资产负债 Assets and Liabilities					
	资产总计 Total Assets	流动资产合计 Total Current Assets	#存货 Inventories	#产成品 Finished Products	#应收账款 Accounts Receivable	固定资产合计 Total Fixed Assets
339074	**85885081**	**51925623**	**8148751**	**2914976**	**14300859**	**14250234**
15987	2905880	1028789	161729	30005	390962	592043
323087	82979201	50896834	7987022	2884971	13909897	13658190
114252	14064605	9072940	2033846	875289	2410243	2046141
224822	71820477	42852683	6114905	2039688	11890616	12204093
271228	69650675	41434677	6350491	2306340	10962320	12444549

12—10 Continued

(10000 yuan)

损益 Profits and Losses								应交税金合计 Total Tax Payable			
营业收入 Business Income	#主营业务收入 Main Business Income	营业成本 Business Cost	#主营业务成本 Main Business Cost	销售费用 Sales Expenses	管理费用 Management Expenses	财务费用 Financial Expenses	利润总额 Total Profits		#营业税金及附加 Business Tax and Surtax	#主营业务税金及附加 Main Business Tax and Surtax	#应交增值税 Value Added Tax Payable
83982634	**81974793**	**66857711**	**65396274**	**6371104**	**3720922**	**612153**	**6644049**	**5315616**	**1461739**	**1457023**	**2324735**
1569022	1462796	1265939	1201951	16090	127783	24169	209186	108069	11737	9464	51490
82413611	80511998	65591772	64194323	6355014	3593140	587984	6434863	5207547	1450003	1447560	2273245
14132022	13530592	8703709	8210120	3059808	1009873	140012	1160401	1165565	107327	107203	764292
69850612	68444201	58154002	57186154	3311296	2711050	472142	5483648	4150051	1354413	1349820	1560443
73743754	72182684	58849728	57715298	5517890	2896980	495924	6000798	4715846	1411039	1408738	1954756

12-11 规模以上港澳台及外商投资工业企业主要经济指标(按行业分)(2016年)

单位：万元

项目	Item	企业单位个数(个) Number of Enterprises (unit)	#亏损企业 Loss-Suffering Enterprises	工业总产值(当年价格) Gross Output Value of Industry (at current year's prices)	工业增加值 Added Value of Industry
合计	**Total**	**746**	**171**	**72801145**	**15028845**
开采辅助活动	Mining Support Service Activities	***	***	***	***
农副食品加工业	Processing of Food from Agricultural Products	20	8	565294	71359
食品制造业	Manufacture of Foods	41	10	1835466	105774
酒、饮料和精制茶制造业	Manufacture of Wines, Beverage and Refined Tea	25	10	1100243	263835
纺织业	Manufacture of Textile	***	***	***	***
纺织服装、服饰业	Manufacture of Textile Wearing Apparel and Ornament	23	11	208690	67084
皮革、毛皮、羽毛及其制品和制鞋业	Manufacture of Leather, Fur, Feather and Its Products, and Footwear	***	***	***	***
木材加工和木、竹、藤、棕、草制品业	Processing of Timbers, Manufacture of Wood, Bamboo, Rattan, Palm, and Straw Products				
家具制造业	Manufacture of Furniture	9	3	290251	41625
造纸和纸制品业	Manufacture of Paper and Paper Products	13	1	409478	166662
印刷和记录媒介复制业	Printing, Reproduction of Recording Media	17	5	187774	77494
文教、工美、体育和娱乐用品制造业	Manufacture of Articles for Culture, Education, Artwork, Sport and Entertainment Activities	9	1	56163	19055
石油加工、炼焦和核燃料加工业	Processing of Petroleum, Coking, Processing of Mucleus Fuels	***	***	***	***
化学原料和化学制品制造业	Manufacture of Chemical Raw Materials and Chemical Products	36	4	994605	374275
医药制造业	Manufacture of Medicines	39	8	3964825	1579235
橡胶和塑料制品业	Manufacture of Rubber and Plastics Products	21	6	352054	104755
非金属矿物制品业	Manufacture of Non-metallic Mineral Products	21	6	360287	153195
黑色金属冶炼和压延加工业	Manufacture and Pressing of Ferrous Metals	***	***	***	***
有色金属冶炼和压延加工业	Manufacture and Pressing of Non-ferrous Metals	***	***	***	***
金属制品业	Manufacture of Fabricated Metal Products	31	9	326829	82507
通用设备制造业	Manufacture of General-purpose Machinery	70	19	2998201	698974
专用设备制造业	Manufacture of Special-purpose Machinery	74	10	1479579	386656
汽车制造业	Manufacture of Motor Vehicles	118	20	37127974	8223625
铁路、船舶、航空航天和其他运输设备制造业	Manufacture of Railway Locomotives, Building of Ships and Boats, Manufacture of Air and Spacecrafts and Other Transportation Equipment	7	4	193627	72285
电气机械和器材制造业	Manufacture of Electrical Machinery and Equipment	38	10	1931598	333429
计算机、通信和其他电子设备制造业	Manufacture of Computers, Communication Equipment and Other Electronic Equipment	63	13	12502977	1116751
仪器仪表制造业	Manufacture of Measuring Instruments and Meters	33	4	684938	133674
其他制造业	Other Manufacturing	6	2	24758	9071
废弃资源综合利用业	Waste recycling and recovery	***	***	***	***
金属制品、机械和设备修理业	Repair of Fabricated Metal Products, Machinery and Equipment	5		710220	326610
电力、热力生产和供应业	Production and Distribution of Electricity and Heating Power	5		542331	187996
燃气生产和供应业	Production and Distribution of Gas	5		3257067	414824
水的生产和供应业	Production and Distribution of Water	***	***	***	***

FOREIGN-INVESTED INDUSTRIAL ENTERPRISES ABOVE DESIGNATED SIZE (BY SECTOR) (2016)

(10000 yuan)

工业销售产值(当年价格) Sales Value of Industry (at current year's prices)	#出口交货值 Delivery Value of Exports	平均用工人数(人) Average Number of Employed Persons (person)	资产负债 Assets and Liabilities: 资产总计 Total Assets	流动资产合计 Total Current Assets	#存货 Inventories	#产成品 Finished Products	#应收账款 Accounts Receivable	固定资产合计 Total Fixed Assets
71665571	**6473549**	**339074**	**85885081**	**51925623**	**8148751**	**2914976**	**14300859**	**14250234**
***	***	***	***	***	***	***	***	***
553626	42717	6622	356482	213912	76424	21850	67348	99979
1879425	84544	26824	2640616	1402010	180543	100368	347984	545217
1101021	14386	13572	1554708	869102	103590	28725	149439	325676
***	***	***	***	***	***	***	***	***
188199	111669	7241	264666	233177	106722	46641	50364	16793
***	***	***	***	***	***	***	***	***
282868	21937	3408	270688	198401	71463	30376	56721	43127
410422	42644	2514	355032	235127	57950	15786	72471	92369
184414	4695	3700	294653	195834	31480	16436	42462	82611
54344	34099	1556	120111	110929	41547	29414	13315	7083
***	***	***	***	***	***	***	***	***
938219	45459	8598	1296580	761272	119676	45009	179845	331324
3866620	91549	27362	4526054	3077660	1010213	438018	870509	498971
360392	39260	6102	413529	284960	52327	22563	112318	104998
355582	23315	5652	458760	298472	48838	20771	128718	108966
***	***	***	***	***	***	***	***	***
***	***	***	***	***	***	***	***	***
331238	42797	4909	663941	450856	111742	32973	145751	98692
2984878	668909	22776	5391698	3936962	1130812	213694	752932	530159
1443621	432938	16097	3944453	2505357	336365	88456	698969	239013
36406613	246970	86081	31535726	18215760	2254513	1074540	5023457	6251034
192977	2323	830	151458	141049	21826	5378	46258	8066
1949779	276857	11554	2751788	2354382	367804	106229	982171	143531
12276622	4082720	50428	16785969	12364879	1594038	500486	3288280	2443003
676111	81453	6773	1279459	1058337	179386	37375	403662	59883
24254	11427	514	17307	14907	4643	2170	2146	1922
***	***	***	***	***	***	***	***	***
710220	46351	11576	561159	376295	113144	3756	202501	169900
532749		1426	4273434	943781	9647	8321	106399	567665
3257059		8241	4834776	867930	3575	230	290393	1391068
***	***	***	***	***	***	***	***	***

12-11 续表

单位：万元

项目	Item	资产负债 Assets and Liabilities 固定资产原价 Total Original Value of Fixed Assets	负债合计 Total Liabilities	#流动负债合计 Total Current Liabilities	#应付账款 Accounts Payable	所有者权益合计 Total Owner's Equity
合计	**Total**	**27436929**	**47057385**	**41712844**	**17831162**	**38808021**
开采辅助活动	Mining Support Service Activities	***	***	***	***	***
农副食品加工业	Processing of Food from Agricultural Products	210899	245684	216829	77077	110798
食品制造业	Manufacture of Foods	1073385	1239025	1178277	439663	1401591
酒、饮料和精制茶制造业	Manufacture of Wines, Beverage and Refined Tea	746083	989144	960041	363678	565564
纺织业	Manufacture of Textile	***	***	***	***	***
纺织服装、服饰业	Manufacture of Textile Wearing Apparel and Ornament	55224	192377	189718	57401	71889
皮革、毛皮、羽毛及其制品和制鞋业	Manufacture of Leather, Fur, Feather and Its Products, and Footwear	***	***	***	***	***
木材加工和木、竹、藤、棕、草制品业	Processing of Timbers, Manufacture of Wood, Bamboo, Rattan, Palm, and Straw Products					
家具制造业	Manufacture of Furniture	67849	169038	166430	25956	101650
造纸和纸制品业	Manufacture of Paper and Paper Products	271232	133178	129868	57977	221854
印刷和记录媒介复制业	Printing, Reproduction of Recording Media	217203	96712	84588	32830	197941
文教、工美、体育和娱乐用品制造业	Manufacture of Articles for Culture, Education, Artwork, Sport and Entertainment Activities	14604	56243	56025	21451	63868
石油加工、炼焦和核燃料加工业	Processing of Petroleum, Coking, Processing of Mucleus Fuels	***	***	***	***	***
化学原料和化学制品制造业	Manufacture of Chemical Raw Materials and Chemical Products	690309	453072	402408	172344	843508
医药制造业	Manufacture of Medicines	846775	2300486	2014279	684407	2225568
橡胶和塑料制品业	Manufacture of Rubber and Plastics Products	239730	191150	173260	91028	222379
非金属矿物制品业	Manufacture of Non-metallic Mineral Products	322172	218248	214078	77448	240512
黑色金属冶炼和压延加工业	Manufacture and Pressing of Ferrous Metals	***	***	***	***	***
有色金属冶炼和压延加工业	Manufacture and Pressing of Non-ferrous Metals	***	***	***	***	***
金属制品业	Manufacture of Fabricated Metal Products	265781	284796	254104	70876	379145
通用设备制造业	Manufacture of General-purpose Machinery	1117813	2463926	2072541	604765	2931707
专用设备制造业	Manufacture of Special-purpose Machinery	481700	2216615	1719105	558647	1717564
汽车制造业	Manufacture of Motor Vehicles	9931852	17969052	16067649	8173576	13561479
铁路、船舶、航空航天和其他运输设备制造业	Manufacture of Railway Locomotives, Building of Ships and Boats, Manufacture of Air and Spacecrafts and Other Transportation Equipment	21025	99160	82058	18987	49625
电气机械和器材制造业	Manufacture of Electrical Machinery and Equipment	432706	1707252	1428600	749129	1039764
计算机、通信和其他电子设备制造业	Manufacture of Computers, Communication Equipment and Other Electronic Equipment	5938923	11355191	10132405	4682766	5430483
仪器仪表制造业	Manufacture of Measuring Instruments and Meters	157918	718551	682064	345144	560908
其他制造业	Other Manufacturing	5392	9379	9378	2710	7928
废弃资源综合利用业	Waste recycling and recovery	***	***	***	***	***
金属制品、机械和设备修理业	Repair of Fabricated Metal Products, Machinery and Equipment	349206	333347	305028	51136	227812
电力、热力生产和供应业	Production and Distribution of Electricity and Heating Power	1711393	1473454	1399930	33513	2799980
燃气生产和供应业	Production and Distribution of Gas	2023630	1418410	1074149	221801	3416367
水的生产和供应业	Production and Distribution of Water	***	***	***	***	***

12-11 Continued

(10000 yuan)

#实收资本 Paid-up Capital	损益 Profits and Losses 营业收入 Business Income	#主营业务收入 Main Business Income	营业成本 Business Cost	#主营业务成本 Main Business Cost	销售费用 Sales Expenses	管理费用 Management Expenses	财务费用 Financial Expenses	利润总额 Total Profits	应交税金合计 Total Tax Payable	#营业税金及附加 Business Tax and Surtax	#主营业务税金及附加 Main Business Tax and Surtax	#应交增值税 Value Added Tax Payable
18181914	**83982634**	**81974793**	**66857711**	**65396274**	**6371104**	**3720922**	**612153**	**6644049**	**5315616**	**1461739**	**1457023**	**2324735**
***	***	***	***	***	***	***	***	***	***	***	***	***
169774	666699	660498	578344	574944	44812	28379	4652	9449	11002	959	959	5157
882464	4060685	3949936	2472939	2371641	1141203	210538	3796	222698	322985	26774	26774	231236
731691	1324665	1221275	943375	845379	250335	91677	7691	4738	97833	16692	16692	65396
***	***	***	***	***	***	***	***	***	***	***	***	***
50599	247567	211220	204817	170999	25660	22690	2959	5043	8175	995	888	4751
***	***	***	***	***	***	***	***	***	***	***	***	***
29934	209364	197042	150595	140846	29438	23942	1868	3744	8111	580	580	6640
132130	469339	458104	345630	336372	14720	24916	-1284	59601	47522	3273	3273	23697
121914	221294	217358	174279	172905	11493	20375	-528	13548	17085	1479	1479	11910
10975	54975	54668	43781	43599	3601	4705	-175	2922	1951	357	357	1116
***	***	***	***	***	***	***	***	***	***	***	***	***
459117	1008506	984795	647311	626007	168118	68687	10035	99137	97427	11990	11956	64488
741438	4213526	4008012	1971830	1780741	1271460	314908	107380	544176	467469	37080	37068	308274
121330	427782	399311	351713	324466	20339	41385	4228	11850	26016	2376	2372	18290
158820	387275	379622	287590	283666	17083	32605	1658	47961	41918	3336	3336	28502
***	***	***	***	***	***	***	***	***	***	***	***	***
***	***	***	***	***	***	***	***	***	***	***	***	***
207472	457007	436580	381518	363927	28882	35512	4301	6674	21942	1970	1924	14370
890557	3322563	3296033	2648658	2635340	183025	223878	38675	538731	171840	16669	16669	75866
623585	1853932	1734990	1286557	1239158	137215	247013	33071	179947	107170	9691	9684	58995
5167930	37216495	36504075	30100825	29491007	1668661	1092234	206248	3274305	3119017	1267003	1264910	1006974
14507	205376	203657	146035	144986	8360	11718	524	37544	23448	1158	1158	10141
920178	2371187	2273016	1784024	1695773	280879	157104	1892	50166	175510	11058	11058	93725
4029215	18736583	18368225	16785145	16649348	905670	718446	77287	653621	224377	24570	24530	109898
214054	1003403	992097	747770	744676	98017	74192	9394	100188	59417	5019	5017	35801
8848	25276	25171	18278	18245	1833	3485	-29	1473	1670	210	210	861
***	***	***	***	***	***	***	***	***	***	***	***	***
198163	716291	711072	618331	616178	1628	69238	5793	22824	31953	4487	4487	18498
1442199	608278	535950	418864	392753	30	37970	53924	364814	83284	7513	5240	38192
599896	3273302	3257692	2980081	2967434	27276	118584	30793	348356	95026	1582	1485	63548
***	***	***	***	***	***	***	***	***	***	***	***	***

12-12 大中型工业企业主要经济指标(2016年)

单位：万元

项 目	Item	企业单位个数(个) Number of Enterprises (unit)	#亏损企业 Loss-Suffering Enterprises	工业总产值(当年价格) Gross Output Value of Industry (at current year's prices)	工业增加值 Added Value of Industry
合 计	**Total**	**676**	**111**	**150532406**	**31009228**
按隶属关系分组	**By Affiliation**				
中央工业	Central Enterprises	97	17	55889006	12318526
地方工业	Local Enterprises	579	94	94643401	18690703
按登记注册类型分组	**By Registration Type**				
内资企业	Domestially-Invested Enterprises	456	78	86483608	17746475
国有企业	State-owned Enterprises	27	5	33323991	6100208
集体企业	Collectively-owned Enterprises	4	1	61594	28658
股份合作企业	Joint-equity Cooperative Enterprises	***	***	***	***
有限责任公司	Limited Liability Companies	242	54	29926917	5940714
股份有限公司	Companies Limited by Shares	98	10	20205263	4732911
私营企业	Private Enterprises	83	7	2848656	862924
港澳台商投资企业	Hong Kong, Macao and Taiwan-invested Enterprises	54	8	14752039	1373106
港澳台合资经营	Joint Ventures	27	3	3091789	807850
港澳台合作经营	Cooperatives				
港澳台商独资企业	Solely-funded Enterprises	22	5	11307769	531107
港澳台商投资股份有限公司	Companies Limited by Shares	5		352481	34149
外商投资企业	Foreign-invested Enterprises	166	25	49296760	11889647
中外合资经营	Joint Ventures	70	7	35012440	8968056
中外合作经营	Cooperatives	4	2	195647	97772
外资(独资)企业	Solely-funded Enterprises	89	15	13736845	2767631
外商投资股份有限公司	Companies Limited by Shares	***	***	***	***
按城乡分组	**By Urban and Rural Regions**				
#农村企业	Rural Enterprises	***	***	***	***
按轻重工业分组	**By Light and Heavy Industries**				
轻工业	Light Industry	251	43	18712303	6013233
重工业	Heavy Industry	425	68	131820103	24995995
按规模分组	**By Size**				
#大型企业	Large-sized Enterprises	137	23	115988999	23698787

MAIN ECONOMIC INDICATORS OF LOCAL MEDIUM AND LARGE-SIZED INDUSTRIAL ENTERPRISES (2016)

(10000 yuan)

工业销售产值(当年价格) Sales Value of Industry (at current year's prices)	#出口交货值 Delivery Value of Exports	平均用工人数(人) Average Number of Employed Persons (person)	资产负债 Assets and Liabilities 资产总计 Total Assets	流动资产合计 Total Current Assets	#存货 Inventories	#产成品 Finished Products	#应收账款 Accounts Receivable	固定资产合计 Total Fixed Assets
148568616	**8032114**	**741043**	**368912813**	**128926836**	**15835100**	**5332020**	**31706454**	**60490908**
55691151	244280	163224	194975451	38568084	3328341	708557	7072592	27563303
92877465	7787835	577819	173937362	90358752	12506759	4623463	24633861	32927606
85522451	2414301	469815	299262139	87492159	9484609	3025680	20744134	48046359
33336170	10584	36096	163356565	25630818	953298	152271	2773817	19044631
61719		2503	97252	65154	19386	8828	8417	19737
***	***	***	***	***	***	***	***	***
29553772	1549354	249879	83210598	33839274	4593566	1509757	10320004	23170183
19802828	676088	133980	47508768	24737686	3201336	1065440	6592182	5050477
2715761	175211	45313	4940395	3101238	685467	263451	1034560	734909
14500705	1853719	67176	19487425	11268945	1591215	552119	2999943	2828173
3035091	523873	25699	3749371	2258246	270100	87655	860115	907127
11124391	1278867	37253	13175358	7903565	1074472	408674	1867282	1858762
341223	50979	4224	2562696	1107133	246643	55790	272546	62284
48545460	3764094	204052	50163250	30165732	4759276	1754221	7962376	9616376
34229257	2119201	113106	34313237	19379201	2820754	1031971	4154024	6661700
193293	8948	5251	274529	229357	-16897	271	39963	43059
13751455	1598616	80905	14747141	10289526	1921207	708317	3706005	2807231
***	***	***	***	***	***	***	***	***
***	***	***	***	***	***	***	***	***
18276632	870345	213107	29805600	16819932	3502937	1542739	3561060	5808147
130291985	7161769	527936	339107214	112106904	12332163	3789281	28145394	54682761
114594094	6048695	442535	306858286	91658217	9814362	3309924	19507404	51895283

12-12 续表

单位：万元

项目	Item	资产负债 Assets and Liabilities 固定资产原价 Total Original Value of Fixed Assets	负债合计 Total Liabilities	#流动负债合计 Total Current Liabilities	#应付账款 Accounts Payable	所有者权益合计 Total Owner's Equity	#实收资本 Paid-up Capital
合计	**Total**	**116099257**	**167689239**	**113745128**	**35740300**	**201223174**	**121999885**
按隶属关系分组	**By Affiliation**						
中央工业	Central Enterprises	62994722	72868260	38303575	8927218	122107191	88091783
地方工业	Local Enterprises	53104535	94820979	75441553	26813082	79115983	33908103
按登记注册类型分组	**By Registration Type**						
内资企业	Domestially-Invested Enterprises	92668868	128402794	79156417	20728094	170859345	108718422
国有企业	State-owned Enterprises	40916280	55597593	24297668	3723297	107758972	79667436
集体企业	Collectively-owned Enterprises	64979	28785	26287	9258	68467	12880
股份合作企业	Joint-equity Cooperative Enterprises	***	***	***	***	***	***
有限责任公司	Limited Liability Companies	40766891	48149889	35733461	10499878	35060709	20412818
股份有限公司	Companies Limited by Shares	9803864	22206281	17013623	5750683	25302486	7781476
私营企业	Private Enterprises	1075308	2362747	2031624	711066	2577648	829812
港澳台商投资企业	Hong Kong, Macao and Taiwan-invested Enterprises	5750479	11855073	10639581	4370183	7632352	2655673
港澳台合资经营	Joint Ventures	2884101	1785766	1724483	666635	1963605	1314548
港澳台合作经营	Cooperatives						
港澳台商独资企业	Solely-funded Enterprises	2717358	8642869	8146498	3533743	4532489	1081198
港澳台商投资股份有限公司	Companies Limited by Shares	149020	1426438	768600	169806	1136258	259927
外商投资企业	Foreign-invested Enterprises	17679910	27431372	23949131	10642023	22731478	10625790
中外合资经营	Joint Ventures	10506129	18435934	16246176	7102975	15877303	7108885
中外合作经营	Cooperatives	123173	130827	120931	63358	143702	157446
外资(独资)企业	Solely-funded Enterprises	6830808	8656814	7422850	3392257	6089926	3163886
外商投资股份有限公司	Companies Limited by Shares	***	***	***	***	***	***
按城乡分组	**By Urban and Rural Regions**						
#农村企业	Rural Enterprises	***	***	***	***	***	***
按轻重工业分组	**By Light and Heavy Industries**						
轻工业	Light Industry	9724248	13392172	10935579	3102380	16413027	5785885
重工业	Heavy Industry	106375008	154297066	102809549	32637920	184810147	116214000
按规模分组	**By Size**						
#大型企业	Large-sized Enterprises	99387744	135073904	87266982	25379932	171784382	109406952

12-12 Continued

(10000 yuan)

损益 Profits and Losses								应交税金合计			
营业收入 Business Income	#主营业务收入 Main Business Income	营业成本 Business Cost	#主营业务成本 Main Business Cost	销售费用 Sales Expenses	管理费用 Management Expenses	财务费用 Financial Expenses	利润总额 Total Profits	应交税金合计 Total Tax Payable	#营业税金及附加 Business Tax and Surtax	#主营业务税金及附加 Main Business Tax and Surtax	#应交增值税 Value Added Tax Payable
167025847	**163561330**	**139702551**	**137042722**	**8170953**	**7331752**	**1835427**	**13650599**	**10104736**	**3049156**	**3034059**	**4501926**
57207815	56657814	51146936	50690411	325799	1518165	578001	5253470	3613847	1251236	1243983	1618607
109818032	106903516	88555614	86352311	7845154	5813587	1257426	8397129	6490889	1797920	1790076	2883320
93282093	91378646	80852822	79327424	2653063	4434772	1339503	7649801	5388890	1638117	1625321	2547170
33546875	33459930	30780383	30721057	98645	247374	424069	4298827	1686781	369867	368520	806358
63490	61013	50842	48087	2381	12832	-396	-2231	6213	807	807	5057
***	***	***	***	***	***	***	***	***	***	***	***
33568368	32904233	30024148	29503154	1053848	2164577	652187	575936	1308938	154086	146682	839498
22929359	21860047	17764714	16859570	1158572	1666390	243655	2413707	2188975	1096956	1092925	767571
3097671	3017837	2193755	2156632	318112	334573	19426	357615	191881	15960	15945	124384
21315850	20802202	18732084	18460742	1224461	788619	142795	1368306	495988	31950	31758	285860
3432138	3308537	2743841	2641292	170335	180982	2939	334467	196814	20173	20068	98153
17377831	17040752	15596837	15475600	1035394	543298	88211	708096	269224	5977	5889	172822
505880	452913	391405	343850	18732	64338	51644	325743	29950	5800	5800	14885
52427904	51380482	40117645	39254556	4293129	2108361	353129	4632492	4219858	1379089	1376980	1668896
35245058	34728318	26952565	26552636	2286244	1338136	214858	3552069	3294749	1294561	1292455	1089272
366938	362497	284669	280969	47351	17023	-1970	19280	27266	2075	2075	17870
16365921	15860358	12534121	12093190	1878712	730865	139863	1054561	878017	79556	79554	548255
***	***	***	***	***	***	***	***	***	***	***	***
***	***	***	***	***	***	***	***	***	***	***	***
22392217	21628254	14239905	13661616	3942082	1668384	185293	2283554	2182046	560290	557645	1172328
144633629	141933076	125462645	123381106	4228871	5663369	1650134	11367045	7922690	2488866	2476413	3329598
126990262	124529151	107738630	105779668	5823539	4323910	1398650	10357573	7727618	2603395	2591429	3263349

12-13 大中型工业企业主要经济指标(按行业分)(2016年)

单位：万元

项目	Item	企业单位个数(个) Number of Enterprises (unit)	#亏损企业 Loss-Suffering Enterprises	工业总产值(当年价格) Gross Output Value of Industry (at current year's prices)	工业增加值 Added Value of Industry
合计	**Total**	**676**	**111**	**150532406**	**31009228**
煤炭开采和洗选业	Mining and Washing of Coal	***	***	***	***
石油和天然气开采业	Extraction of Petroleum and Natural Gas	***	***	***	***
黑色金属矿采选业	Mining and Processing of Ferrous Metal Ores	5	4	705401	-174804
开采辅助活动	Mining Support Service Activities	4	3	1171272	582772
农副食品加工业	Processing of Food from Agricultural Products	27	5	2470488	432265
食品制造业	Manufacture of Foods	38	7	2084367	283957
酒、饮料和精制茶制造业	Manufacture of Wines, Beverage and Refined Tea	13	7	1329117	413950
烟草制品业	Manufacture of Cigarettes and Tobacco	***	***	***	***
纺织业	Manufacture of Textile	***	***	***	***
纺织服装、服饰业	Manufacture of Textile Wearing Apparel and Ornament	32	9	713173	369269.3
皮革、毛皮、羽毛及其制品和制鞋业	Manufacture of Leather, Fur, Feather and Its Products, and Footwear	***	***	***	***
木材加工和木、竹、藤、棕、草制品业	Processing of Timbers, Manufacture of Wood, Bamboo, Rattan, Palm, and Straw Products	***	***	***	***
家具制造业	Manufacture of Furniture	8		480163	117354
造纸和纸制品业	Manufacture of Paper and Paper Products	6	1	344413	146078
印刷和记录媒介复制业	Printing, Reproduction of Recording Media	16	3	648234	288346
文教、工美、体育和娱乐用品制造业	Manufacture of Articles for Culture, Education, Artwork, Sport and Entertainment Activities	***	***	***	***
石油加工、炼焦和核燃料加工业	Processing of Petroleum, Coking, Processing of Mucleus Fuels	4	1	4462340	1543776
化学原料和化学制品制造业	Manufacture of Chemical Raw Materials and Chemical Products	19	4	1348345	386468
医药制造业	Manufacture of Medicines	54	4	6291016	2689097
化学纤维制造业	Manufacture of Chemical fibres	***	***	***	***
橡胶和塑料制品业	Manufacture of Rubber and Plastics Products	6	2	238551	70231
非金属矿物制品业	Manufacture of Non-metallic Mineral Products	31	8	2540275	481336
黑色金属冶炼和压延加工业	Manufacture and Pressing of Ferrous Metals	5	2	651752	23109
有色金属冶炼和压延加工业	Manufacture and Pressing of Non-ferrous Metals	4		300002	80666
金属制品业	Manufacture of Fabricated Metal Products	19	3	1398793	356034
通用设备制造业	Manufacture of General-purpose Machinery	37	8	3344799	864346
专用设备制造业	Manufacture of Special-purpose Machinery	49	7	2984268	721645
汽车制造业	Manufacture of Motor Vehicles	73	8	43893479	8794627
铁路、船舶、航空航天和其他运输设备制造业	Manufacture of Railway Locomotives, Building of Ships and Boats, Manufacture of Air and Spacecrafts and Other Transportation Equipment	25	5	3371090	1153085
电气机械和器材制造业	Manufacture of Electrical Machinery and Equipment	39	2	4738811	967622
计算机、通信和其他电子设备制造业	Manufacture of Computers, Communication Equipment and Other Electronic Equipment	76	7	17184689	1140340
仪器仪表制造业	Manufacture of Measuring Instrument and Meter	26	2	1095148	416057
其他制造业	Other Manufacturing	7	1	576722	182533
金属制品、机械和设备修理业	Repair of Fabricated Metal Products, Machinery and Equipment	***	***	***	***
电力、热力生产和供应业	Production and Distribution of Electricity and Heating Power	27	6	39320165	6901963
燃气生产和供应业	Production and Distribution of Gas	***	***	***	***
水的生产和供应业	Production and Distribution of Water	5		632496	279428

MAIN ECONOMIC INDICATORS OF MEDIUM AND LARGE-SIZED INDUSTRIAL ENTERPRISES (BY SECTOR) (2016)

(10000 yuan)

工业销售产值(当年价格) Sales Value of Industry (at current year's prices)	#出口交货值 Delivery Value of Exports	平均用工人数(人) Average Number of Employed Persons (person)	资产负债 Assets and Liabilities						
			资产总计 Total Assets	流动资产合计 Total Current Assets	#存货 Inventories	#产成品 Finished Products	#应收账款 Accounts Receivable	固定资产合计 Total Fixed Assets	固定资产原价 Total Original Value of Fixed Assets
148568616	**8032114**	**741043**	**368912813**	**128926836**	**15835100**	**5332020**	**31706454**	**60490908**	**116099257**
***	***	***	***	***	***	***	***	***	***
***	***	***	***	***	***	***	***	***	***
708022		18435	24792331	8072486	224432	41087	1826735	3878409	5561487
1171272	24617	18821	4344805	1968454	191535	7280	779068	1050921	2597516
2439733	24578	19565	3690711	2404077	336959	234465	207991	424007	635633
2085873	88214	34849	2654448	1338773	219480	108744	305837	586526	1048679
1331758	18470	21176	3222062	1194328	148984	36705	120579	1275254	1019120
***	***	***	***	***	***	***	***	***	***
***	***	***	***	***	***	***	***	***	***
605605	94734	23909	945819	674007	261694	179088	129873	147984	230071
***	***	***	***	***	***	***	***	***	***
***	***	***	***	***	***	***	***	***	***
473367	13154	7405	537231	368009	83647	30098	89808	93508	136509
343454	15531	2341	257369	159493	52364	14265	43343	67705	204940
650575	2327	11768	1194341	764837	126065	54676	246787	307693	863768
***	***	***	***	***	***	***	***	***	***
4465012		9264	2485964	944952	422781	88034	185337	1044154	3191029
1290662	37819	17375	2047343	1343797	214778	72215	211111	379669	1467741
6067944	95146	52438	9697325	5868867	1655852	675269	1502024	1172307	1955492
***	***	***	***	***	***	***	***	***	***
247440	40833	4734	245188	164816	24337	8902	69391	66546	150379
2488127	28637	25057	6838132	4305715	652263	113496	1664829	503667	1050942
654414	61574	3302	843474	240617	114358	45520	69588	434933	763238
299224	89091	2416	514217	316134	84329	30529	77936	31621	90330
1342341	81704	14413	3701429	2070375	246958	45675	427996	475983	771664
3166071	639068	30224	6638786	4486659	1351801	331628	909539	783015	1462967
2936184	473824	34608	13106249	7743151	1029671	349312	1855889	656019	1253603
43049657	498915	129729	42847474	23876510	3015398	1421079	7260973	8144778	12289415
3282705	42915	30930	5547584	4051902	1333072	202631	1277628	778308	1282769
4640209	257300	27708	6990329	5039465	610034	147816	2591604	450520	912632
16956337	5154598	81027	28120910	18661463	2566976	891795	5255161	4349070	9510697
1115898	50056	13682	2254901	1686010	307145	75736	559266	166939	284049
572662		5174	1213523	710943	150999	33839	260872	269271	492622
***	***	***	***	***	***	***	***	***	***
39314687		51693	172204899	25051201	93119	9836	2680991	25491744	55673411
***	***	***	***	***	***	***	***	***	***
630954		9232	9839580	2150385	7607	2540	456608	5139960	7072877

12-13 续表

单位：万元

项目	Item	资产负债 Assets and Liabilities			
		负债合计 Total Liabilities	#流动负债合计 Total Current Liabilities	#应付账款 Accounts Payable	所有者权益合计 Total Owner's Equity
合计	**Total**	**167689239**	**113745128**	**35740300**	**201223174**
煤炭开采和洗选业	Mining and Washing of Coal	***	***	***	***
石油和天然气开采业	Extraction of Petroleum and Natural Gas	***	***	***	***
黑色金属矿采选业	Mining and Processing of Ferrous Metal Ores	14725358	8617923	786950	10066973
开采辅助活动	Mining Support Service Activities	1250485	1179169	430673	3094320
农副食品加工业	Processing of Food from Agricultural Products	1853179	1445492	162587	1837532
食品制造业	Manufacture of Foods	1269960	1198261	449312	1384488
酒、饮料和精制茶制造业	Manufacture of Wines, Beverage and Refined Tea	1289752	1199205	303165	1932310
烟草制品业	Manufacture of Cigarettes and Tobacco	***	***	***	***
纺织业	Manufacture of Textile	***	***	***	***
纺织服装、服饰业	Manufacture of Textile Wearing Apparel and Ornament	448499	396094	154428	496919
皮革、毛皮、羽毛及其制品和制鞋业	Manufacture of Leather, Fur, Feather and Its Products, and Footwear	***	***	***	***
木材加工和木、竹、藤、棕、草制品业	Processing of Timbers, Manufacture of Wood, Bamboo, Rattan, Palm, and Straw Products	***	***	***	***
家具制造业	Manufacture of Furniture	269553	263299	48615	267678
造纸和纸制品业	Manufacture of Paper and Paper Products	123846	123202	53510	133523
印刷和记录媒介复制业	Printing, Reproduction of Recording Media	458102	417979	213908	736240
文教、工美、体育和娱乐用品制造业	Manufacture of Articles for Culture, Education, Artwork, Sport and Entertainment Activities	***	***	***	***
石油加工、炼焦和核燃料加工业	Processing of Petroleum, Coking, Processing of Mucleus Fuels	1221431	1169810	477335	1264534
化学原料和化学制品制造业	Manufacture of Chemical Raw Materials and Chemical Products	1346719	1256692	254115	700624
医药制造业	Manufacture of Medicines	4202202	3514090	1083890	5495123
化学纤维制造业	Manufacture of Chemical fibres	***	***	***	***
橡胶和塑料制品业	Manufacture of Rubber and Plastics Products	116913	96837	59893	128276
非金属矿物制品业	Manufacture of Non-metallic Mineral Products	3731277	3225609	1124592	3106854
黑色金属冶炼和压延加工业	Manufacture and Pressing of Ferrous Metals	924651	370026	241861	-81177
有色金属冶炼和压延加工业	Manufacture and Pressing of Non-ferrous Metals	197162	155856	38165	317055
金属制品业	Manufacture of Fabricated Metal Products	1929276	1446557	372462	1772153
通用设备制造业	Manufacture of General-purpose Machinery	2843612	2433900	687539	3795174
专用设备制造业	Manufacture of Special-purpose Machinery	6636762	4968441	1416910	6469487
汽车制造业	Manufacture of Motor Vehicles	25689370	22690491	10891206	17158104
铁路、船舶、航空航天和其他运输设备制造业	Manufacture of Railway Locomotives, Building of Ships and Boats, Manufacture of Air and Spacecrafts and Other Transportation Equipment	3650898	3300635	1120237	1896686
电气机械和器材制造业	Manufacture of Electrical Machinery and Equipment	4049573	3772878	1408273	2940756
计算机、通信和其他电子设备制造业	Manufacture of Computers, Communication Equipment and Other Electronic Equipment	17554707	15068929	6814287	10566203
仪器仪表制造业	Manufacture of Measuring Instrument and Meter	876309	798198	336013	1378592
其他制造业	Other Manufacturing	453971	328117	151065	759552
金属制品、机械和设备修理业	Repair of Fabricated Metal Products, Machinery and Equipment	***	***	***	***
电力、热力生产和供应业	Production and Distribution of Electricity and Heating Power	61936241	28784290	5362092	110268658
燃气生产和供应业	Production and Distribution of Gas	***	***	***	***
水的生产和供应业	Production and Distribution of Water	4488951	3134575	860261	5350629

12-13 Continued

(10000 yuan)

	损益 Profits and Losses								应交税金合计			
#实收资本 Paid-up Capital	营业收入 Business Income	#主营业务收入 Main Business Income	营业成本 Business Cost	#主营业务成本 Main Business Cost	销售费用 Sales Expenses	管理费用 Management Expenses	财务费用 Financial Expenses	利润总额 Total Profits	应交税金合计 Total Tax Payable	#营业税金及附加 Business Tax and Surtax	#主营业务税金及附加 Main Business Tax and Surtax	#应交增值税 Value Added Tax Payable
121999885	**167025847**	**163561330**	**139702551**	**137042722**	**8170953**	**7331752**	**1835427**	**13650599**	**10104736**	**3049156**	**3034059**	**4501926**
***	***	***	***	***	***	***	***	***	***	***	***	***
***	***	***	***	***	***	***	***	***	***	***	***	***
2910689	2084974	2000370	2082222	1951626	2597	154480	348482	-215310	57711	13378	11907	38507
2791197	1218359	1214778	1167846	1166434	4399	58213	-18101	-11521	22991	7202	6778	12980
777059	2950289	2924698	2336848	2325080	224946	134067	24123	193434	209861	123003	122991	55221
698771	4170417	4051953	2601661	2494110	1083144	208992	4726	267128	321676	25655	25561	224577
521245	1543783	1432696	1081579	983424	286818	109320	-29	6286	167850	61530	61432	86521
***	***	***	***	***	***	***	***	***	***	***	***	***
***	***	***	***	***	***	***	***	***	***	***	***	***
137883	747992	709699	426937	395727	165303	79586	4339	67414	68763	6224	6119	49845
***	***	***	***	***	***	***	***	***	***	***	***	***
***	***	***	***	***	***	***	***	***	***	***	***	***
84592	396612	385732	298814	289044	33032	36077	2691	39135	25594	1864	1864	17296
52812	396688	382200	281997	269417	13613	21472	-139	54390	44264	3067	3067	22612
416188	800548	762484	632768	609789	17928	90103	-672	58538	62032	6599	5361	42524
***	***	***	***	***	***	***	***	***	***	***	***	***
8776	4911102	4706247	3633696	3421418	43145	214898	15464	196415	1051437	737648	737352	254590
985055	1494237	1445681	1089398	1047873	185880	216691	29845	-35962	111810	12127	12039	86546
1341039	6494151	6252698	2998440	2788452	1745992	562876	111216	1251704	753989	60385	60139	489484
***	***	***	***	***	***	***	***	***	***	***	***	***
43288	294368	265509	244534	216756	10533	28170	2591	8377	16866	1610	1610	11993
1203982	2888463	2777507	2474816	2380544	107911	213438	37707	112063	111161	8708	8271	83742
311352	707033	697067	672256	662500	36432	24052	14675	-42848	7471	2236	2216	3356
68916	324849	312629	281229	270722	4583	19320	655	18472	6349	802	802	3295
795734	1722723	1618033	1361086	1282766	38467	163645	21988	176443	67422	7725	7456	32755
1206388	3458233	3397745	2695150	2664611	197620	240294	38413	597775	181858	17627	17606	85368
2082036	3650072	3506140	2614171	2539592	243170	410172	91565	551901	201307	18150	18123	117316
7183647	45341010	44144259	37477744	36465767	1813969	1554753	227029	3554526	3380068	1428341	1423826	1069491
801513	3515425	3469495	2911391	2879554	41567	281234	27860	243673	164667	12158	11378	100782
1276448	5137077	4988314	3948085	3861834	310893	402107	29214	483845	266269	23403	23396	148783
7047072	23959161	23519552	21538984	21351140	1296392	1293097	169723	561431	375730	57005	56299	137641
406459	1366651	1351689	902128	895877	116801	147907	6303	229056	121120	11057	10588	77224
342785	591234	587168	438498	436390	15606	67675	175	76445	31026	3581	3581	17596
***	***	***	***	***	***	***	***	***	***	***	***	***
82107228	39502018	39389669	37297337	37216633	8527	167591	527771	4357604	1634348	114490	112568	984749
***	***	***	***	***	***	***	***	***	***	***	***	***
4298258	816123	803578	610890	605981	41501	50982	35042	199228	74189	8886	8476	28254

12-14 规模以上工业企业主要工业产品生产能力
PRODUCTION CAPACITY OF MAIN INDUSTRIAL PRODUCTS IN INDUSTRIAL ENTERPRISES ABOVE DESIGNATED SIZE

主要工业产品名称		Name of Main Industrial Products		2016	2015
原油加工能力	(吨)	Crude Oil Processing Capacity	(ton)	11500000	11500000
硅酸盐水泥熟料	(吨)	Portland Cement Chamotte	(ton)	4400000	5870000
发电设备容量总计	(万千瓦)	Total Capacity of Power Generation Equipment	(10000 kW)	1106	1122
#火电设备容量	(万千瓦)	Capacity of Thermal Power Equipment	(10000 kW)	966	983
水电设备容量	(万千瓦)	Capacity of Hydropower Equipment	(10000 kW)	98	98
风电设备容量	(万千瓦)	Capacity of Wind Power Equipment	(10000 kW)	19	15
原　煤	(吨)	Raw Coal	(ton)	4200000	5200000
卷　烟	(万支)	Cigarette	(10000 units)	4185000	3996000
气流纺锭	(头)	Air Spinning Spindles (Rotating-cup Spinning)	(unit)		1656
棉布织机	(台)	Cotton Cloth Weaver	(unit)		66
水　泥	(吨)	Cement	(ton)	5500000	7350000
钢　材	(吨)	Rolled Steel	(ton)	1749047	1758410
金属切削机床	(台)	Metal-Cutting Machine Tools	(unit)	21572	21995
汽　车	(辆)	Motor Vehicles	(unit)	2497500	2266600
#基本型乘用车(轿车)	(辆)	Basic-type Passenger Vehicles (Sedans)	(unit)	1918160	1142000
移动通信手持机(手机)	(台)	Mobile Communication Handsets (Mobile Phones)	(unit)	23968342	25093019
微型计算机设备	(台)	Micro-computers	(unit)	18318000	20068000

12−15 主要工业产品产量
OUTPUT OF MAIN INDUSTRIAL PRODUCTS

工业产品名称		Name of Main Industrial Product		2016	2015
单晶硅	(千克)	Monocrystalline Silicon	(kg)	85814.4	90872.0
中成药	(万吨)	Finished Traditional Chinese Herbal Medicines	(10000 tons)	4.2	4.6
沥青和改性沥青防水卷材	(万平方米)	Asphalt and Modified Asphalt Waterproof Roll Mater	(10000 sq.m)	3949.5	5063.6
纤维增强塑料制品	(万吨)	Fiber-reinforced Plastic Products	(10000 tons)	9.5	3.5
耐火材料制品	(万吨)	Products Made from Fire-resistant Materials	(10000 tons)	44.8	48.7
冷轧薄宽钢带	(万吨)	Cold-rolled Thin Broad Steel Bands	(10000 tons)	69.9	92.5
单一稀土金属	(千克)	Single Rare Earth Metals	(kg)	151491.0	120729.0
发动机	(万千瓦)	Engines	(10000 kW)	20001.8	15065.1
气动元件	(万件)	Pneumatic Components	(10000 units)	25662.5	22427.3
数控金属切削机床	(台)	Digital Metal Cutting Tools	(unit)	12420	12471
机床数控装置	(套)	CNC Units of Lathe	(unit)	54086	39187
工业电炉	(台)	Industrial Electric Cookers	(unit)	192	40
环境污染防治专用设备	(台套)	Special Equipment for Prevention and Control of Environmental Pollution	(set)	95343	109378
汽　车	(万辆)	Automobiles	(10000 units)	260.4	221.9
#基本型成用车(轿车)	(万辆)	Including: Basic-type Passenger Vehicles (Sedans)	(10000 units)	120.7	118.9
运动型多用途乘用车(SUV)	(万辆)	Sport Utility Vehicles (SUV)	(10000 units)	72.8	42.1
载货汽车	(万辆)	Freight Trucks	(10000 units)	43.2	42.1
改装汽车	(万辆)	Refitted Automobiles	(10000 units)	1.0	1.3
风力发电机组	(万千瓦)	Wind Power Generator Units	(10000 kW)	338.3	421.9
锂离子电池	(万只)	Lithiums Ion Batteries	(10000 units)	598.4	2305.3
移动通信手持机(手机)	(万台)	Mobile Communication Handsets (Mobile Phones)	(10000 units)	6923.9	9540.8
微型计算机设备	(万台)	Micro-computer Equipment	(10000 units)	684.1	885.6
服务器	(台)	Servers	(unit)	214682	259353
液晶显示模组	(万套)	Liquid Crystal Display Modules	(10000 sets)	12173.1	6510.6
显示器	(万台)	Displays	(10000 units)	503.5	519.0
集成电路	(亿块)	Integrated Circuits	(100 million pieces)	80.5	62.7
彩色电视机	(万台)	Color TV Sets	(10000 units)	304.6	222.4

12-16 规模以上高技术制造业主要经济指标(2016年)
MAIN ECONOMIC INDICATORS OF HIGH-TECH MANUFACTURING ENTERPRISES ABOVE DESIGNATED SIZE (2016)

单位：亿元 (100 million yuan)

项目	Item	工业总产值 Gross Output Value of Industry	主营业务收入 Main Business Income	利润总额 Total Profits	应交税金 Tax Payable
合计	**Total**	**3563.6**	**4308.5**	**321.0**	**185.5**
按登记注册类型分组	**By Registration Type**				
内资	Domestically-Invested Enterprises	1679.2	1803.7	176.8	102.7
国有	State-owned Enterprises	61.6	60.8	5.8	3.0
集体	Collectively-owned Enterprises	0.9	1.0	0.0	0.0
股份合作企业	Joint-equity Cooperative Enterprises	1.6	2.3	0.1	0.2
有限责任公司	Limited Liability Companies	1011.5	1068.2	23.4	42.0
股份有限公司	Companies Limited by Shares	368.7	420.9	114.0	40.9
私营企业	Private Enterprises	234.9	250.5	33.4	16.6
其他	Others				
港澳台商投资	Hong Kong, Macao and Taiwan-invested Enterprises	970.3	1543.6	65.1	23.2
外商投资	Foreign-invested Enterprises	914.1	961.3	79.1	59.6
按高技术领域分组	**By Field of High Technology**				
信息化学品制造	Information Chemical Manufacturing	10.7	10.9	0.2	0.1
医药制造业	Manufacture of Medicines	814.4	809.0	153.5	92.8
航空、航天器及设备制造业	Manufacture of Aircrafts and Spacecrafts	288.4	284.2	16.9	7.5
电子及通信设备制造业	Manufacture of Electronic Equipment and Communication Equipment	1743.8	2063.7	21.4	40.4
计算机及办公设备制造业	Manufacture of Computers and Office Equipments	326.6	710.1	68.5	12.7
医疗仪器设备及仪器仪表制造业	Manufacture of Medical Equipments and Meters	379.8	430.6	60.5	31.8

12-17 规模以上工业战略性新兴产业总产值(2016年)
TOTAL OUTPUT VALUE OF STRATEGIC EMERGING INDUSTRIES AMONG INDUSTRIAL ENTERPRISES ABOVE DESIGNATED SIZE(2016)

单位：亿元 (100 million yuan)

项目	Item	2016
合计	**Total**	**3566.4**
节能环保产业	Energy Conservation and Environmental Protection Industry	293.5
新一代信息技术产业	New Generation IT Industry	1433.5
生物产业	Bioindustry	744.5
高端装备制造业	High-end Equipment Manufacturing	419.3
新能源产业	New Energy Industry	153.8
新材料产业	New Material Industry	259.0
新能源汽车	New Energy Automobiles	262.8

主要统计指标解释

工业　指从事自然资源的开采，对采掘品和农产品进行加工和再加工的物质生产部门。具体包括：(1) 对自然资源的开采，如采矿、晒盐、森林采伐等（但不包括禽兽捕猎和水产捕捞）；(2) 对农副产品的加工、再加工，如粮油加工、食品加工、扎花、纺织、制革等；(3) 对采掘品的加工、再加工，如炼铁、炼钢、化工生产、石油加工、机器制造、木材加工等，以及电力、自来水、煤气的生产和供应等；(4) 对工业品的修理、翻新，如机器设备的修理。

轻工业　指主要提供生活消费品和制作手工工具的工业。按其所使用的原料不同，可分为两大类：(1) 以农业为原料的轻工业，是指直接或间接以农产品为基本原料的轻工业。主要包括食品制造、饮料制造、烟草加工、纺织、缝纫、皮革和毛皮制作、造纸以及印刷等工业；(2) 以非农产品为原料的轻工业，是指以工业品为原料的轻工业。主要包括文教体育用品、化学药品制造、合成纤维制造、日用化学制品、日用玻璃制品、日用金属制品、手工工具制造、医疗器械制造、文化和办公用机械制造等工业。

重工业　是指为国民经济各部门提供物质技术基础的主要生产资料的工业。按其生产性质和产品用途，可以分为下列三类：(1) 采掘（伐）工业，是指对自然资源的开采，包括石油开采、煤炭开采、金属矿开采、非金属矿开采和木材采伐等工业；(2) 原材料工业，指向国民经济各部门提供基本材料、动力和燃料的工业。包括金属冶炼及加工、炼焦及焦炭化学、化工原料、水泥、人造板以及电力、石油和煤炭加工等工业；(3) 加工工业，是指对工业原材料进行再加工制造的工业。包括装备国民经济各部门的机械设备制造工业、金属结构、水泥制品等工业，以及为农业提供的生产资料如化肥、农药等工业。

根据上述划分原则，修理业中以重工业产品为修理作业对象的划为重工业，反之划为轻工业。

工业总产值　指工业企业在报告期内生产的以货币形式表现的工业最终产品和提供工业劳务活动的总价值量。它包括：在本企业内不再进行加工，经检验、包装入库（规定不需包装的产品除外）的成品价值，对外加工费收入，自制半成品、在制品期末期初差额价值。工业总产值采用“工厂法”计算，即以工业企业作为一个整体，按企业生产活动的最终成果来计算。

工业增加值　是指工业企业在报告期内以货币形式表现的工业生产活动的最终成果，反映企业生产过程中新创造的价值。

工业销售产值　是以货币形式表现的，工业企业在报告期内销售的本企业生产的工业产品或提供工业性劳务价值的总价值量。包括企业在报告期内实际销售（包括本期生产和非本期生产）的全部成品、半成品的总价值，报告期内完成的对外承接的工业品加工的加工费收入，对外工业品修理作业可获取的加工费收入和对内非工业部门提供的加工修理、设备安装等收入。已销售的成品、半成品不论是本期生产的、还是非本期生产的，只要是本期销售出去的均包括在内。企业为本单位基本建设部门、生活福利部门等提供的产品和工业性作业及自制设备也应视同销售，这部分也应作为销售统计。

资产总计　指企业过去的交易或者事项形成的、由企业拥有或者控制的、预期会给企业带来经济利益的资源。资产一般按流动性分为流动资产和非流动资产。其中流动资产可分为货币资金、交易性金融资产、应收票据、应收账款、预付款项、其他应收款、存货等；非流动资产可分为长期股权投资、固定资产、无形资产及其他非流动资产等。

(1) 流动资产合计　资产满足以下条件之一应归为流动资产：①预计在一个正常营业周期中变现、出售或耗用，主要包括存货、应收账款等；②主要为交易目的而持有；③预计在资产负债表日起一年内（含一年）变现；④自资产负债表日起一年内，交换其他资产或清偿负债的能力不受限制的现金或现金等价物。包括货币资金、应收票据、应收账款、存货等项目。

(2) 固定资产合计　指企业为生产商品、提供劳务、出租或经营管理而持有的，使用寿命超过一个会计年度的有形资产。包括使用期限超过一年的房屋、建筑物、机器、机械、运输工具以及其他与生产、经营有关的设备、器具、工具等。固定资产合计是时点指标，表示固定资产经过扣减折旧、减值准备等后的期末余额。

负债合计　指企业过去的交易或者事项形成的，预期会导致经济利益流出企业的现时义务。负债一般按偿还期长短分为流动负债和非流动负债。

(1) 流动负债合计　负债满足下列条件之一的应归为流动负债：①预计在一个正常营业周期中清偿；②主要为交易目的而持有；③自资产负债表日起一年内到期应予清偿；④企业无权自主地将清偿推迟至资产负债表日后一年以上。包括短期借款、应付票据、应付账款、应付职工薪酬、应交税费等项目。

(2) 非流动负债合计　指流动负债之外的负债。包括长期借款、应付债券等。

所有者权益合计　指企业资产扣除负债后由所有者享有的剩余权益。公司的所有者权益又称股东权益。包括实收资本、资本公积、盈余公积、未分配利润等。

实收资本 指企业各投资者实际投入的资本（或股本）总额，包括货币、实物、无形资产等各种形式的投入。实收资本按投资主体可分为国家资本、集体资本、法人资本、个人资本、港澳台资本和外商资本。

主营业务收入 指企业确认的销售商品、提供劳务等主营业务的收入。

主营业务成本 指企业经营主要业务所发生的成本总额。

主营业务税金及附加 指企业经营主要业务应负担的营业税、消费税、城市维护建设税、教育费附加等。

营业利润 指企业从事生产经营活动所取得的利润。

利润总额 指企业在一定会计期间的经营成果，是生产经营过程中各种收入扣除各种耗费后的盈余，反映企业在报告期内实现的亏盈总额。

应交增值税 指企业按税法规定，从事货物销售或提供加工、修理修配劳务等增加货物价值的活动本期应交纳的税金。

应交增值税=销项税额-（进项税额-进项税额转出）-出口抵减内销产品应纳税额-减免税款+出口退税

应交增值税不含期初未抵扣税额。

工业产品销售率 指报告期工业销售产值与工业总产值之比。计算公式：

$$工业产品销售率(\%)=\frac{报告期现价工业销售产值}{报告期现价工业总产值}\times100\%$$

工业增加值率 指报告期工业增加值占工业总产值的比重，反映降低中间消耗的经济效益。计算公式：

$$工业增加率(\%)=\frac{报告期现价工业增加值}{报告期现价工业总产值}\times100\%$$

工业成本费用利润率 指在一定时期内实现的利润与成本费用之比，是反映工业生产成本及费用投入的经济效益指标，同时也是反映降低成本的经济效益的指标。计算公式：

$$工业成本费用利润率(\%)=\frac{利润总额}{成本费用总额}\times100\%$$

工业全员劳动生产率 指根据产品的价值量指标计算的平均每一个职工在单位时间内创造的工业生产最终成果。是考核企业经济活动的重要指标，是企业生产技术水平、经济管理水平、职工技术熟练程度和劳动积极性的综合表现。

$$工业全员劳动生产率（元/人）=\frac{工业增加值（现价）}{平均用工人数}$$

平均用工人数 指报告期企业平均实际拥有的、参与本企业生产经营活动的人员数。

流动资产周转率 指在一定时期内流动资产完成的周转次数，反映流动资产的周转速度。计算公式：

$$流动资产周转率(次)=\frac{产品销售收入}{流动资产平均余额}$$

流动比率 是反映企业每百元流动负债中，有多少元流动资产作后盾。计算公式：

$$流动比率(倍)=\frac{流动资产总额}{流动负债总额}$$

速动比率 是衡量企业流动资产中可以立即用于偿付流动负债的能力。计算公式：

$$速动比率(倍)=\frac{流动资产总额-存货}{流动负债总额}$$

资产负债率 反映在企业资产总额中有多少资产是通过借债而得的，也可以用于衡量企业利用债权人提供资金进行经营活动的能力以及企业在清算时保护债权人利益的程度。计算公式：

$$资产负债率=\frac{负债总额}{资产总额}\times100\%$$

总资产贡献率 反映企业全部资产的获利能力，是企业经营业绩和管理水平的集中体现，是评价和考核企业盈利能力的核心指标。计算公式为：

$$总资产贡献率=(利润总额+税金总额+利息支出)\div平均资产总额\times100\%$$

其中：税金总额为主营业务税金及附加、管理费用中的税金与应交增值税之和；平均资产总额为期初期末资产总计的算术平均值。

资产保值增值率 反映企业净资产的变动状况，是企业发展能力的集中体现。计算公式为：

$$资产保值增值率=\frac{报告期期末所有者权益}{上年同期期末所有者权益}\times100\%$$

高技术制造业 是指国民经济行业中R&D投入强度相对较高的制造业行业，根据国家统计局《高技术产业（制造业）分类（2013)》标准界定。

Explanatory Notes on Main Statistical Indicators

Industry refers to the material production sector which is engaged in extraction of natural resources and processing and reprocessing of minerals and agricultural products, including (1) extraction of natural resources, such as mining, salt production, logging (but not including animal hunting and fishing); (2) processing and reprocessing of agricultural products, such as grain and oil processing, food processing, embroidery, textile manufacturing and leather making; (3) processing and reprocessing of mining products, such as iron making, steel making, chemical production, petroleum processing, machine building, timber processing; and production and supply of electric power, tap water and gas; (4) repair and refurbishment of industrial products, such as the repair of machinery equipment.

Light Industry refers to the industries that produce consumer goods and hand tools. It falls into two categories, based on different raw materials:

(1) Industries basing the raw materials on agriculture, which directly or indirectly use farm products as basic raw materials, mainly include the manufacture of foods and beverages, tobacco processing, textile manufacturing, tailoring, fur and leather manufacturing, paper making, printing, etc.

(2) Industries using non-agricultural products as raw materials, which means the manufactured goods are used as raw materials, mainly include the manufacture of cultural, educational articles and sports goods, chemical medicines, synthetic fiber, daily chemical products, glass products for daily use, metal products for daily use, hand tools, medical appliances and instruments, as well as stationery and office machinery.

Heavy Industry refers to the industries that provide material and technical foundation as key means of production for various sectors of the national economy. It falls into the following three categories according to the purpose of production or the use of products:

(1) Mining, quarrying and logging industry refers to the industry that extracts natural resources, including the extraction of petroleum, coal, metal and non-metal ores and logging.

(2) Raw material industry refers to the industry that provides various sectors of the national economy with basic materials, fuels and power. It includes smelting and processing of metals, coking and coke chemistry, chemical materials, cement, artificial boards, as well as power generation, petroleum refining and coal processing.

(3) Processing industry refers to the industry that reprocesses raw materials. It includes machine manufacturing, which equips various sectors of the national economy, metal structure, cement products, and chemical fertilizer and pesticide industry that provide means of production for agriculture.

According to the above principle of classification, the repair services for products of heavy industry are classified as heavy industry, while the repair services for products of light industry are classified as light industry.

Gross Output Value of Industry is the total value in monetary terms for final industrial products and industrial labor service provided by industrial enterprises during the reporting period. It includes the value of the finished products, which will not be further processed in the enterprises and have been inspected, packed and put in storage (except for products required not to be packed), the revenue from processing products for others, the value of semi-finished products, and the price spread between the finished products and products at the initial stage. The gross industrial output value is calculated with "factory method"; that is, to take an industrial enterprise as a whole. It calculates the final products created by the enterprise.

Added Value of Industry refers to the final results of industrial production by industrial enterprises in monetary terms during the reporting period. It shows the newly created value generated in production by the enterprises.

Sales Value of Industry refers to the total value of industrial products sold or labor service provided by an industrial enterprise during the reporting period in monetary terms. It includes the total value of all finished and semi-finished products actually sold by the enterprise (including products produced in current period and noncurrent period), revenue from processing products for others, repairing industrial products for others, as well as processing, repairing, and installing equipment for internal non-industrial departments in the reporting period. All finished and semi-finished products sold in the current period will be counted, regardless of whether they were produced in the current period or not. The value of products, industrial work and home-built equipment provided by the enterprise for its capital construction department and welfare department will also be included in the industrial sales value.

Total Assets refer to resources formed by previous transactions or matters of an enterprise, owned or controlled by the enterprise, and expected to bring economic benefits to the enterprise. Classified by the liquidity, assets fall into current assets and non-current assets. Current assets include monetary capital, tradable financial assets, notes receivable, accounts receivable, prepayment, other receivables, and inventory, etc.; while non-current assets include long-term equity investment, fixed assets, intangible assets, and other non-current assets, etc.

(1) Total Current Assets Assets that meet any of the following requirements are considered current assets: a. assets expected to be cashed in, sold or consumed in a normal operating cycle, which mainly includes inventory and accounts receivable, etc.; b. assets held mainly for transaction; c. assets expected to be cashed in within one year (including one year) from the balance sheet date; d. cash or cash equivalents with unrestricted capacity of exchanging for other assets or paying off debts within one year from the balance sheet date, which include monetary capital, notes receivable, accounts receivable, inventory, etc.

(2) Total Fixed Assets refer to tangible assets held by an enterprise for producing commodities, rendering labor services, leasing or management, with service life exceeding one fiscal year, which include houses and buildings, apparatus, machinery, means of transport, as well as other equipment, instruments and tools related to production and operation, which have a service life exceeding one year. Total Fixed Assets is a time point indicator, showing the ending balance of fixed assets after deduction and discount, and impairment provision, etc.

Total Liabilities refer to the present obligations formed by previous transactions or matters of an enterprise, expected to lead the flow of economic benefits out of the enterprise. By the term of payment, liabilities generally include current liabilities and non-current liabilities.

(1) Total Current liabilities Liabilities that meet any of the following requirements are considered current liabilities: a. assets expected to be paid off within one normal operating cycle; b. assets held mostly for the purpose of transaction; c. assets expected to be due and paid off within one year from the balance sheet date; d. assets that the enterprise has no right to delay the payment to more than one year after the balance sheet date on its own. They include short-term loans, notes payable, accounts payable, wages payable, taxes and fees payable, etc.

(2) Total Non-current Liabilities refer to liabilities other than current liabilities, including long-term borrowings and bonds payable, etc.

Total Owner's Equity refers to the remaining equity of assets in an enterprise held by owners after deducting the liabilities. Owner's equity of a company is also called shareholders' equity, including paid-up capital, capital reserves, operating surplus reserves and non-distributed profits, etc.

Paid-up Capital refers to the total capital (or equity) actually contributed by investors to an enterprise, including input in various forms, such as monetary investment, physical investment and intangible assets. Categorized by investors, paid-up capital includes state capital, collective capital, legal person's capital, personal capital, capital from Hong Kong, Macao and Taiwan, and foreign capital.

Main Business Income refers to the income from main business of selling commodities and rendering services recognized by the enterprise.

Main Business Cost refers to the total cost incurred by the enterprise during its operation of main business.

Main Business Tax and Surtax refers to the business tax, excise tax, urban maintenance and construction tax, educational surcharge to be levied against the main business operated by an enterprise.

Operating Profits refer to the profits reaped by an enterprise from its productive and operating activities.

Total Profits refer to the operating results of an enterprise during certain accounting period, representing the surplus of various incomes from production and operation deducting various expenses, reflecting the total gains and losses realized by the enterprise during the reporting period.

VAT Payable refer to the tax payable by an enterprise in current period according to provisions in Law of Tax for its activities of adding value to goods, such as selling the goods, providing labor service for processing, repair and replacement.

VAT Payable = Output Tax – (Input Tax – Transfer-out of Input Tax) – Tax Payable Deducted by Export from Output Tax of Domestically Sold Products – Tax Concession + Export Rebate

VAT Payable excludes the taxes not deducted at the beginning of the period.

Sales Rate of Industrial Products refers to the ratio of industrial sales output to the gross output value of industry during the reporting period. The following formula is used:

Sales Rate of Industrial Products (%) = Sales Value of Industry at Present Value During the Reporting Period / Gross Output Value of Industry at Present Value During the Reporting Period × 100%

Rate of Industrial Added Value refers to the ratio of added value of industry to the gross output value of industry during the reporting period. It indicates the economic benefits from reduction of intermediate consumption. The following formula is used:

Rate of Industrial Added Value = Added Value of Industry at Present Value During the Reporting Period / Gross Output Value of Industry at Present Value During the Reporting Period × 100%

Rate of Profits to Total Industrial Costs refers to the ratio of profits realized in a given period to the total costs in the same period, which reflects the economic efficiency of industrial production input. The following formula is used:

Rate of Profits to Total Industrial Cost (%) = (Total Profits/ Total Costs) ×100%

Overall Labor Productivity of Industry refers to the average final result of industrial production created by each employee within a unit time, measured with the value of products. It is an important indicator evaluating the economic activities of an enterprise, and it reflects the level of production technology and economic management of the enterprise, employees' skills, as well as enthusiasm for work.

Overall Labor Productivity of Industry (RMB/person) = Added Value of Industry (at present value) / Average Number of Employees

Average Number of Employees refers to the average number of employees actually in the enterprise and engaged in its production and operation activities during the reporting period.

Turnover of Current Assets refers to the number of times for current assets turnover within a period of time. It reflects the turnover velocity of current assets. Calculation formula is listed below:

Turnover of Current Assets (No. of times) = Product Sales revenue / Average Balance of Current Assets

Liquidity Ratio reflects how many current assets are backing up every RMB 100 of current liabilities in an enterprise. The following formula is used:

Liquidity Ratio (times) = Total Current Assets / Total Current Liabilities

Quick Ratio indicates the capacity of an enterprise's current assets for paying off current liabilities immediately. The following formula is used:

Quick Ratio (times) = (Total Current Assets – Inventory) / Total Current Liabilities

Assets-liabilities Ratio reflects how many assets—out of the total assets of the enterprise, are obtained by borrowing. It can be used to evaluate the enterprise's capability of operating by using the funds provided by creditors, and to what extent the enterprise will be able to protect the creditors' interests in the case of liquidation. The following formula is used:

Assets-liabilities Ratio = Total Liabilities / Total Assets × 100%

Contribution Rate of Total Assets indicates the profitability of all assets in an enterprise, reflecting the operating performance and management of the enterprise. It serves as a core indicator evaluating the enterprise's profitability. The following formula is used:

Total Assets Contribution rate = (Total Profit + Total Tax + Total Interest Expenses) / Average Total Assets × 100%

Note: the total tax is the sum of main business tax and surtax, tax in management expenses, and VAT payable; average total assets are represented by the arithmetic average of total assets at the beginning and the end of the period.

Assets Maintenance and Appreciation Rate reflects the changes in the net assets of an enterprise. It embodies the development ability of the enterprise. Calculation formula is listed below:

Assets Maintenance and Appreciation Rate = Owner's Equity at the End of the Reporting Period / Owner's Equity at the End of the Same Period in the Previous Year × 100%

High-tech Manufacturing Sector refers to all sectors in the high-tech industry other than software development.

13

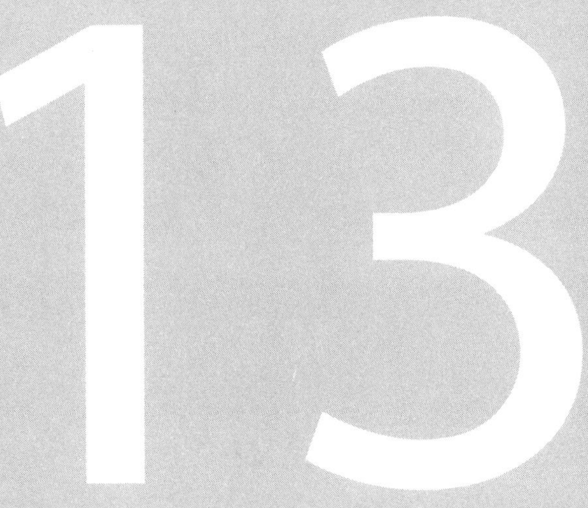

北京统计年鉴2017　BEIJING STATISTICAL YEARBOOK

建筑业
CONSTRUCTION

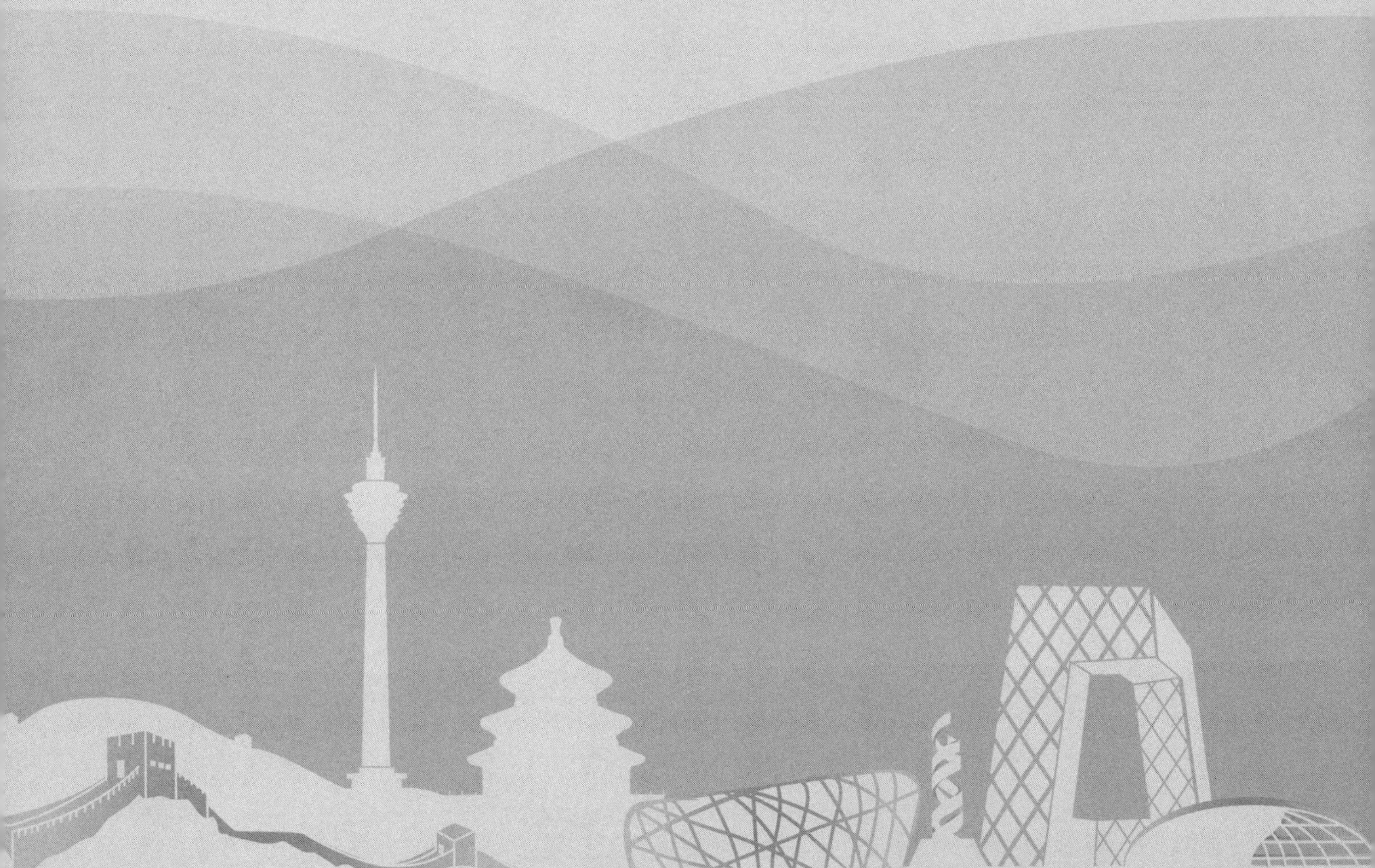

简要说明

一、本章资料的主要内容

本章资料主要反映北京市建筑业企业基本情况和生产经营情况。主要指标包括企业个数、从业人员、建筑业总产值、建筑业企业房屋建筑面积、利润、税金等。

二、本章资料的统计范围

建筑业统计范围从 2004 年起，由原具有建筑业资质等级四级及四级以上的独立核算的建筑业企业调整为具有施工总承包、专业承包资质的所有法人建筑业企业。

三、本章资料的数据来源及调查方法

本章建筑业企业统计数据根据国家统计局制定的《建筑业统计报表制度》整理汇总。建筑业统计数据采取全面调查的方法。资料由北京市统计局提供。

四、有关统计标准的变化说明

本章资料中建筑业行业分类2002-2011年期间执行2002年《国民经济行业分类标准》(GB/T 4754-2002)划分标准，2012 年开始执行 2011 年《国民经济行业分类》(GB/T 4754-2011)划分标准。

五、本章中关于历史数据调整的问题

由于2004年开展了“北京市第一次全国经济普查”，按照国家统计局统一要求和统一方法，历史资料要根据普查结果进行修正。本章中1993至2003年的建筑业总产值数据采用“趋势离差法”进行了调整，2004年为第一次经济普查数据，2008 年为第二次经济普查数据，2013 年为第三次经济普查数据。

Brief Introduction

I. Main Content

Data in this chapter reflect the basic situation and operation of construction enterprises in Beijing. Main indicators include number of enterprises, employees, total output value of the construction sector, as well as floor space, profits, and tax of construction enterprises.

II. Scope of Statistics

Since 2004, data on construction sector, which previously covered construction enterprises with independent accounting at or above Level-4 in construction qualifications, have been adjusted to cover all construction enterprises with qualifications of general and specialized contracting.

III. Source of Data and Methods of Survey

Data on construction enterprises in this chapter were gathered based on *Statistical Statement System for Construction Sector* developed by the National Bureau of Statistics. The figures were gained through complete survey, and were provided by Beijing Municipal Bureau of Statistics.

IV. Changes in Relevant Statistical Standards

In this chapter, classification of construction sectors during 2002-2011 was based on the *Standard for Classification of National Economic Sectors 2002* (GB/T 4754-2002). *Standard for Classification of National Economic Sectors 2011* (GB/T 4754-2011) began to be enforced in 2012.

V. About the Adjustment to Historical Data

As “The First National Economic Census in Beijing” was conducted in 2004, in accordance with the principles of unified requirements and methods by the National Bureau of Statistics, historical data must be revised on basis of the census result. Data of total output value of construction sector during 1993-2003 were revised by “trend deviation method”. The first economic census was in 2004, and the second was in 2008, and the third was in 2013.

13-1 建筑业企业基本情况(1978-2016年)
BASIC STATISTICS FOR ENTERPRISES IN THE CONSTRUCTION INDUSTRY (1978-2016)

年 份 Year	建筑业企业单位数(个) Construction Enterprises (unit)	建筑业企业年末从业人员(万人) Employed Persons (year-end) (10000 persons)	建筑业总产值(亿元) Gross Output Value (100 million yuan)	建筑业企业利润总额(亿元) Total Profits (100 million yuan)	建筑业企业房屋建筑面积(万平方米) Floor Space of Buildings (10000 sq.m)	
					施工面积 Floor Space under Construction	竣工面积 Floor Space Completed
1978	64	25.4	10.5	0.7		
1979	70	26.4	12.7	0.9		
1980	71	27.8	14.7	1.5		
1981	71	27.0	14.5	1.6		
1982	91	30.7	17.3	1.7		
1983	116	37.2	22.6	2.5		
1984	2765	53.0	33.4	3.2		
1985	2549	63.9	43.9	3.9		
1986	2361	61.3	51.3	3.3		
1987	2292	64.4	67.0	4.1		
1988	1659	64.2	81.6	3.9		
1989	1545	60.0	89.0	3.8		
1990	994	60.2	94.7	3.4		
1991	922	60.3	99.6	2.8	2495	1172
1992	976	62.7	122.6	3.1	2774	1227
1993	1098	75.9	215.5	6.1	3499	1428
1994	1259	73.4	336.0	9.4	4035	1437
1995	1332	82.6	426.6	7.8	4602	1593
1996	1292	82.5	494.7	8.9	5328	1967
1997	1297	80.3	556.4	10.4	5801	2117
1998	1482	75.6	678.6	12.4	6525	2225
1999	1588	62.0	750.6	13.6	6824	2632
2000	1697	56.6	812.5	16.4	7247	2809
2001	1811	57.8	1055.4	18.7	8919	3198
2002	2122	57.0	1211.3	24.7	10241	3827
2003	2419	59.1	1521.2	31.5	12160	4486
2004	2623	51.2	1659.8	40.0	14424	5258
2005	2752	67.2	1894.0	67.3	15418	4862
2006	2800	66.9	2167.9	112.8	16202	4786
2007	2845	51.7	2576.8	115.7	18225	4946
2008	3527	47.0	3066.2	84.5	19537	4803
2009	3556	56.2	4059.7	217.4	22721	5225
2010	3594	59.9	5196.0	265.2	29440	5933
2011	3667	49.6	6046.3	219.6	36507	6456
2012	3572	49.2	6588.3	293.0	41660	8414
2013	3522	49.3	7459.6	385.8	49259	8950
2014	3426	51.0	8209.8	473.2	56477	9275
2015	3369	59.0	8436.7	520.1	59777	9886
2016	3218	59.2	8841.2	725.7	61098	10703

注：1. 1996-2003年全部指标的统计口径为四级及四级以上的法人建筑施工企业。
2. 2004年开始全部指标的统计口径为建筑施工总承包、专业承包的建筑业企业。
3. 建筑业企业房屋建筑面积包括在本市和外省完成的施工、竣工面积。

Note: a) Data from 1996 to 2003 covers the corporate construction enterprises at Grade IV and above.
b) Data from 2004 covers general contracting and specialized contracting construction enterprises.
c) Data on floor space covers buildings under construction and completed in Beijing and other provinces.and outside the city.

13-2 建筑业施工企业基本情况(2016年)
BASIC STATISTICS FOR CONSTRUCTION ENTERPRISES (2016)

项　　目	Item	建筑业总产值（万元）Gross Output Value (10000 yuan)	年末从业人员（人）Employed Persons (year-end) (person)	签订合同额（万元）Value of Contract Signed (10000 yuan)	竣工产值（万元）Output Value of Completion (10000 yuan)
合　计	**Total**	**88411905**	**591563**	**265287415**	**43240147**
按企业登记注册类型分	**By Registration Type**				
内资企业	Domestically-funded Enterprises	87335502	579020	262351296	42507927
国有企业	State-owned Enterprises	2334431	21067	8604715	1578539
集体企业	Collectively-owned Enterprises	974365	11934	1999711	675259
股份合作企业	Joint-equity Cooperative Enterprises	427589	10736	561240	238901
联营企业	Associate Enterprises	***	***	***	***
有限责任公司	Limited Liability Companies	71531030	402306	215949370	35419094
股份有限公司	Companies Limited by Shares	5579934	15351	24682912	634585
私营企业	Private Enterprises	6488147	117624	10553342	3961544
港、澳、台商投资企业	Hong Kong, Macao and Taiwan-invested Enterprises	692777	7842	1332952	604248
外商投资企业	Foreign-invested Enterprises	383626	4701	1603167	127972
按隶属关系分	**By Affiliation**				
中　央	Central	51850247	222859	186026385	23497581
地　方	Local	36561658	368704	79261030	19742566
按行业分	**By Sector**				
房屋建筑业	Construction of Buildings	45397731	233692	149186167	27778890
土木工程建筑业	Civil Engineering Construction	28631685	160110	91210447	7854256
建筑安装业	Construction Installation	7045583	95776	14348642	3508942
建筑装饰和其他建筑业	Building Decoration and Other Construction	7336905	101985	10542160	4098059

注：1．统计范围为施工总承包、专业承包的法人建筑业企业（下表同）。
2．行业划分执行2011年国民经济行业分类标准(GB/T 4754-2011)。

Note: a)Statistics covers general contracting and specialized contracting corporate construction enterprises(same as the following table).
b)Sectors in this table are classified in accordance with the Standard for Classification of National Economic Sectors in 2011(GB/T 4754-2011).

13-3 建筑业施工企业主要财务指标(2016年)

单位：万元

项目	Item	企业单位数(个) Number of Enterprises (unit)	资产负债 Assets and Liabilities 资产总计 Total Assets	流动资产合计 Total Current Assets	#应收账款 Accounts Receivable	固定资产合计 Total Fixed Assets	固定资产原价 Total Original Value of Fixed Assets	负债合计 Total Liabilities	#流动负债合计 Total Current Liabilities
合　计	**Total**	**3218**	**224057029**	**151356459**	**35603608**	**4907026**	**8621996**	**151100156**	**135140104**
按企业登记注册类型分	**By Registration Type**								
内资企业	Domestically-funded Enterprises	3140	222024433	149512773	34920519	4848712	8507820	149560359	133634921
国有企业	State-owned Enterprises	71	4995181	4261847	846420	180152	376434	3842136	3463890
集体企业	Collectively-owned Enterprises	75	1765407	1385054	167458	57540	99779	1299508	1292136
股份合作企业	Joint-Equity Cooperative Enterprises	55	556886	491487	79168	36336	72382	374518	372880
联营企业	Associate Enterprises	***	***	***	***	***	***	***	***
有限责任公司	Limited Liability Companies	1159	137259229	110598568	28057808	3489248	6229987	109725326	102778529
股份有限公司	Companies Limited by Shares	50	65371064	22333068	2331969	468393	729544	26219352	17937705
私营企业	Private Enterprises	1729	12075936	10442021	3437067	617042	999656	8099258	7789521
港、澳、台商投资企业	Hong Kong, Macao and Taiwan- invested Enterprises	40	992887	920393	295721	18962	43277	798631	768226
外商投资企业	Foreign-invested Enterprises	38	1039709	923294	387369	39353	70899	741167	736956
按隶属关系分	**By Affiliation**								
中　央	Central	186	158285671	96045184	19783864	2245834	4367230	100889462	87255960
地　方	Local	3032	65771358	55311275	15819745	2661192	4254766	50210694	47884144
按国民经济行业分	**By Sector**								
房屋建筑业	Construction of Buildings	617	93115197	66320225	17369943	1938210	3425818	67249378	59435411
土木工程建筑业	Civil Engineering Construction	556	103878377	62493484	11457337	1677658	3398290	64688612	56964967
建筑安装业	Construction Installation	785	15074669	12024916	3228931	723673	949608	10187254	9940170
建筑装饰和其他建筑业	Building Decoration and Other Construction	1260	11988785	10517835	3547397	567486	848279	8974912	8799556

注：1．行业划分执行2011年国民经济行业分类标准(GB/T 4754—2011)。

2．应交税金合计包括应交增值税、应交所得税、营业税金及附加和管理费用中的税金。

MAIN FINANCIAL INDICATORS OF CONSTRUCTION ENTERPRISES (2016)

(10000 yuan)

#应付账款 Accounts Payable	所有者权益合计 Total Owner's Equity	#实收资本 Paid-up Capital	损益 Profits and Loss 营业收入 Business Income	#主营业务收入 Main Business Income	营业成本 Business Cost	#主营业务成本 Main Business Cost	管理费用 Management Expenses	财务费用 Financial Expenses	利润总额 Total Profits	应交税金合计 Total Taxes Payable	#营业税金及附加 Business Tax and Surtax	#主营业务税金及附加 Main Business Tax and Surtax
54036108	**72956873**	**30815217**	**119743328**	**119153640**	**110949026**	**110523043**	**4547049**	**681975**	**7257358**	**2829116**	**987146**	**974161**
53421333	72464074	30490554	117852188	117294340	109262740	108859976	4449629	670988	7190883	2766858	973776	960990
1279453	1153046	764748	3291101	3263571	3077178	3058331	135589	24360	95016	74796	14148	13791
363535	465898	164208	1138372	1131152	1007524	1005837	73809	-783	45903	50288	16866	16832
38220	182368	100609	500797	468724	454687	425124	19410	775	11672	27044	11424	11048
***	***	***	***	***	***	***	***	***	***	***	***	***
44591425	27533903	17060423	94726979	94371347	88413085	88141232	3266009	298776	2937035	2069431	772759	765477
4056875	39151712	9238189	9117028	9084239	8399356	8384669	304104	313139	3970802	209437	21128	17436
3091825	3976678	3161878	9077905	8975302	7910908	7844780	650691	34720	130468	335862	137453	136407
262672	194256	154193	906103	892123	819357	810345	48535	9589	13306	28356	6973	6914
352102	298542	170470	985037	967177	866929	852723	48886	1399	53169	33902	6397	6257
36455347	57396209	20760650	73526075	73308075	69035892	68875848	2280758	409942	6283026	1262025	401835	394227
17580761	15560663	10054567	46217253	45845565	41913134	41647196	2266292	272033	974332	1567091	585312	579933
27243974	25865819	11838351	54165306	53970992	50862142	50705009	1597191	440419	3626152	1109519	421681	416858
19799766	39189766	14284179	44432244	44233916	41253671	41114217	1721225	193380	2954268	1015182	312314	306037
3713033	4887415	2591116	11542246	11421829	10379052	10290751	643413	2146	481470	328784	130708	129476
3279335	3013873	2101572	9603531	9526904	8454160	8413066	585221	46030	195467	375630	122443	121790

Note: a) Sectors in this table are classified in accordance with the Standard for Classification of National Economic Sectors 2011 (GB/T 4754-2011).
b) Total tax payable mainly includes VAT payable, income tax payable, business tax and surtax, and tax in management expenses.

13-3 续表 Continued

项目	Item	#应交所得税 Income Tax Payable (10000 yuan)	#应交增值税 Value Added Tax Payable	流动比率(倍) Current Ratio (times)	速动比率(倍) Quick Ratio (times)	资产负债率(%) Assets-Liabilities Ratio (%)	资本金利润率(%) Capital-Profit Ratio (%)
合　计	**Total**	**611045**	**1180315**	**1.12**	**0.96**	**67.4**	**23.6**
按企业登记注册类型分	**By Registration Type**						
内资企业	Domestically-funded Enterprises	593709	1149702	1.12	0.96	67.4	23.6
国有企业	State-owned Enterprises	13839	43877	1.23	0.76	76.9	12.4
集体企业	Collectively-owned Enterprises	12230	20020	1.07	0.77	73.6	28.0
股份合作企业	Joint-Equity Cooperative Enterprises	3694	11693	1.32	0.94	67.3	11.6
联营企业	Associate Enterprises			***	***	***	***
有限责任公司	Limited Liability Companies	439178	826122	1.08	0.91	79.9	17.2
股份有限公司	Companies Limited by Shares	75462	107134	1.25	1.16	40.1	43.0
私营企业	Private Enterprises	49306	140856	1.34	1.17	67.1	4.1
港、澳、台商投资企业	Hong Kong, Macao and Taiwan-invested Enterprises	6386	14387	1.20	1.01	80.4	8.6
外商投资企业	Foreign-invested Enterprises	10950	16225	1.25	1.06	71.3	31.2
按隶属关系分	**By Affiliation**						
中　央	Central	370965	470216	1.10	0.95	63.7	30.3
地　方	Local	240081	710099	1.16	0.96	76.3	9.7
按国民经济行业分	**Grouped by Sector**						
房屋建筑业	Construction of Buildings	206073	464066	1.12	0.91	72.2	30.6
土木工程建筑业	Civil Engineering Construction	284479	401164	1.10	0.97	62.3	20.7
建筑安装业	Construction Installation	64418	125986	1.21	1.05	67.6	18.6
建筑装饰和其他建筑业	Building Decoration and Other Construction	56075	189098	1.20	1.09	74.9	9.3

13-4 建筑业施工企业竣工率
PROJECT COMPLETION RATE OF CONSTRUCTION ENTERPRISES

单位：% (%)

项　　目	Item	产值竣工率 Completion Rate by Output Value		面积竣工率 Completion Rate by Floor Space	
		2016	2015	2016	2015
合　计	**Total**	**48.9**	**50.8**	**17.5**	**16.5**
按企业登记注册类型分	**By Registration Type**				
内资企业	Domestically-funded Enterprises	48.7	50.8	17.6	16.6
国有企业	State-owned Enterprises	67.6	78.8	15.4	20.7
集体企业	Collectively-owned Enterprises	69.3	62.0	15.0	15.2
股份合作企业	Joint-equity Cooperative Enterprises	55.9	71.6	25.4	31.3
联营企业	Associate Enterprises	***	***		
有限责任公司	Limited Liability Companies	49.5	50.3	17.6	
股份有限公司	Companies Limited by Shares	11.4	18.4	27.5	33.2
私营企业	Private Enterprises	61.1	70.5	19.4	
港、澳、台商投资企业	Hong Kong, Macao and Taiwan-invested Enterprises	87.2	70.5		3.0
外商投资企业	Foreign-invested Enterprises	33.4	32.8	14.7	8.2
按隶属关系分	**By Affiliation Relationship**				
中　央	Central	45.3	41.1	16.7	14.1
地　方	Local	54.0	64.7	19.3	21.9
按国民经济行业分	**By Sector**				
房屋建筑业	Construction of Buildings	61.2	60.9	17.7	16.8
土木工程建筑业	Civil Engineering Construction	27.4	32.7	14.8	11.5
建筑安装业	Construction Installation	49.8	46.6	18.1	13.4
建筑装饰和其他建筑业	Building Completion, Finishing and Other Construction	55.9	64.0	27.0	333.0

注：行业划分执行2011年国民经济行业分类标准(GB/T 4754—2011)。
Note: Sectors in this table are classified in accordance with the Standard for Classification of National Economic Sectors in 2011 (GB/T 4754-2011).

主要统计指标解释

建筑业总产值 是以货币表现的建筑业企业在一定时期内生产的建筑产品和服务的总和。它包括建筑工程产值、设备安装工程产值、其他产值三部分内容。

(1)**建筑工程产值** 指列入建筑工程预(概)算内的各种工程价值。

(2)**安装工程产值** 指为设备安装而发生的安装工程费用，在设备安装产值中，不得包括被安装设备本身价值。

(3)**其他产值** 建筑业总产值中除建筑工程、安装工程以外的产值，包括房屋构筑物修理产值、非标准设备制造产值、总包企业向分包企业收取的管理费，以及不能明确划分的施工活动所完成的产值。

年末从业人员 指年末最后一日24小时在本单位工作并取得劳动报酬或收入的期末实有人员数。该指标为时点指标，不包括最后一日当天及以前与单位解除劳动合同关系的人员，是在岗职工、劳务派遣人员及其他从业人员之和。

房屋施工面积 指报告期内施工的全部房屋建筑面积，包括：本期新开工的房屋面积、上期施工跨入本期继续施工的房屋面积、上期停缓建本期复工的房屋面积、本期开工又停缓建和本期竣工的房屋面积。

房屋竣工面积 指在报告期内房屋建筑按照设计要求已全部完工，达到了住人和使用条件，经验收鉴定合格或达到竣工验收标准，可正式移交使用的各栋房屋建筑面积的总和。

签订合同额 指建筑业企业在报告期直接同建设单位签订的各种国内工程合同的总价款和以前年度同建设单位签订的各种国内工程合同的未完工程跨入本年度继续施工工程合同的总价款余额。

主营业务收入 指企业确认的销售商品、提供劳务等主营业务的收入。

主营业务成本 指企业经营主要业务所发生的成本总额。

主营业务税金及附加 指企业经营主要业务应负担的营业税、消费税、城市维护建设税、教育费附加等。

利润总额 指企业在一定会计期间的经营成果，是生产经营过程中各种收入扣除各种耗费后的盈余，反映企业在报告期内实现的亏盈总额。

Explanatory Notes on Main Statistical Indicators

Gross Output Value of Construction refers to total of construction products and services, expressed in money terms, completed by construction and installation enterprises during a given period of time. It includes: output value of construction works, output value of installation works and other output value.

(1) Output Value of Construction Works means the value of works involved in project budgets.

(2) Output Value of Installation Works means the costs of installation works incurred for equipment installation. Output value of equipment installation does not include the value of installed equipment itself.

(3) Other Output Value means, of the total output value of construction, the output value other than that of construction and installations works. It includes the repair output value of houses and structures, manufacturing output value of non-standard equipment, management charges collected by general contracting enterprises from subcontracting enterprises, as well as the output value of construction activities falling in no specific categories.

Year-end Employed Persons refers to the actual number of employed persons who still work during the 24 hours of the last day at year-end and acquire labor compensation or income. This time-spot index, which does not include persons who terminate their labor contracts at or before the last day of the year, is the sum of fully employed persons, dispatched personnel of labor service and other employed persons.

House Construction Area means the building area of all houses in the reporting period, including: the area of houses newly started in current period, area of houses built in the previous period and continued in current period, area of houses suspended in the previous period and restarted in current period, area of houses started and suspended in current period, and area of houses completed in current period.

Area of Houses Completed means the total area of all houses and buildings entirely completed in line with requirements of design, meeting conditions of living and use, being eligible after acceptance or reaching inspection standards of completed projects and officially delivered and used in the reporting period.

Value of Signed Contracts means total price of all kinds of domestic engineering contracts signed directly between construction and installation enterprises and builders in the reporting period and the balance of total price of domestic engineering contracts signed with builders in previous year and continued the implementation in the current year.

Main Business Income means the income recognized by an enterprise from main business such as sale of commodities and rendering of service.

Main Business Cost means the total cost incurred in an enterprise for the operation of main business.

Main Business Tax and Surtax means the sales tax, excise, urban maintenance and construction tax, educational surcharge, etc. to be paid by an enterprise for the operation of main business.

Total Profits mean the operating result of an enterprise in certain accounting period. It is the surplus of all revenues deducting all costs in its production and operation, reflecting its total profit and loss realized in the reporting period.

14

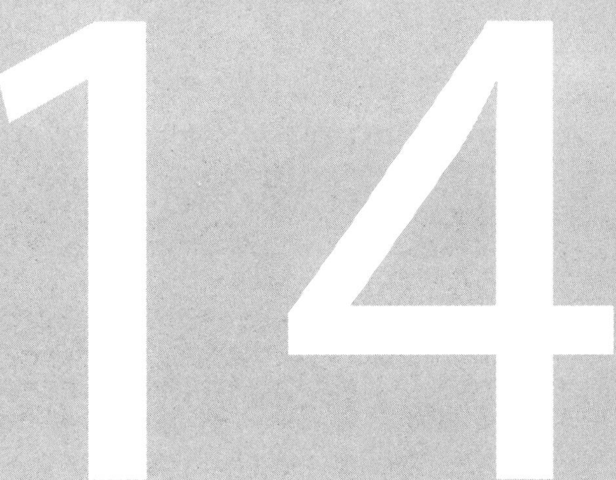

北京统计年鉴2017　BEIJING STATISTICAL YEARBOOK

第三产业
TERTIARY INDUSTRY

简要说明

一、本章资料的主要内容

本章主要内容包括第三产业主要指标、规模以上第三产业主要指标、规模以上第三产业企业财务状况、北京地区服务贸易、文化创意产业、物流业、会展活动和体育及相关产业活动情况等。

二、本章资料的数据来源

本章除北京地区服务贸易情况由北京市商务委员会提供外，其他资料由北京市统计局提供。

三、本章资料的统计范围

本章规模以上第三产业是指除国际组织以外的各行业限额以上的法人单位。具体为：房地产开发业的全部法人单位；金融业为全部金融监管法人单位及年营业收入500万元及以上的非金融监管的金融业法人单位；批发业为年主营业务收入2000万元及以上的企业；零售业为年主营业务收入500万元及以上的企业；住宿业为星级饭店和星级以外年主营业务收入200万元及以上企业；餐饮业为年主营业务收入200万元及以上的企业；居民服务、修理和其他服务业，文化、体育和娱乐业为年营业收入500万元及以上或从业人员期末人数50人及以上的企业；其余行业为年营业收入1000万元及以上或从业人员期末人数50人及以上的企业；执行行政事业、民间非营利组织会计制度收入合计1000万元及以上的法人单位。

文化创意产业资料根据文化创意产业法人单位的统计年报等有关资料测算取得。

物流业资料根据物流业法人单位财务状况统计年报以及其他有关统计资料测算取得。

会展业统计对象涉及会展活动的举办服务单位和接待单位。具体包括限额以上住宿业法人单位、从事各种会展活动的场馆、大型会展活动的举办单位（名单主要由北京市公安局提供）以及为会展活动提供各类专业服务的规模以上单位和旅行社。由于每年的统计对象单位范围不完全相同（有新增或撤销单位），为保持数据的可比性，同时列出统计对象本年和上年数据。

体育及相关产业情况根据体育及相关产业单位的统计年报等有关资料汇总计算，执行2015年国家体育总局、国家统计局颁布的《体育及相关产业分类（试行）》标准。

四、有关统计标准的变化说明

（一）关于行业划分。根据国家统计局规定，自2012年开始执行《国民经济行业分类》GB/T 4754-2011标准。

（二）关于三次产业划分。根据国家统计局《三次产业划分规定》（国统字[2012]108号），该规定对三次产业的范围进行了调整。其中第一产业是指农、林、牧、渔业（不含农、林、牧、渔服务业）；第二产业是指采矿业（不含开采辅助活动），制造业（不含金属制品、机械和设备修理业），电力、热力、燃气及水生产和供应业，建筑业；第三产业是指除第一产业、第二产业以外的其他行业。自2012年开始执行此规定。

Brief Introduction

I. Main Content

This chapter includes: main indicators for tertiary industry, main indicators for tertiary industry above designated size, financial status of tertiary industry above designated size, service trade, cultural and creative industry, logistics industry, exhibition activities, sports and activities in related sectors in Beijing.

II. Date Source

Except for the data on service trade in Beijing, which are acquired from Beijing Municipal Commission of Commerce, other data are provided by Beijing Municipal Bureau of Statistics.

III. Scope of Statistics

In this chapter, the tertiary industry above designated size refers to corporate enterprises above designated size other than international organizations. It includes all corporate enterprises in real estate development sectors, all corporate enterprises under financial regulation and the ones without financial regulation whose annual business income hitting RMB 5 million and more in finance, enterprises with annual main business income of RMB 20 million and more in wholesale trade, enterprises with annual main business income of RMB 5 million and more in retail trade, star-level hotels and non-star-level enterprises with annual main business income of RMB 2 million and more in accommodation, enterprises with annual main business income of RMB 2 million and more in restaurants, enterprises with annual business income of RMB 5 million and above or with period-end employees of 50 and above in resident service, repair, other services, culture, sports and entertainment, enterprises with annual business income of RMB 10 million and above or with period-end employees of 50 and above in other sectors, and corporate enterprises with total income of RMB 10 million and more following accounting system designed for administrative institutions and non-profit private organizations.

Data on cultural and creative industry were calculated based on annual statistical reports and other related materials of corporate enterprises in cultural and creative sector.

Data on logistics industry were calculated based on annual statistical report on financial status and other related materials of impersonal entity in logistics industry.

Statistical scope of MICE industry covers service companies and reception companies holding the exhibitions, in details, including: star-level hotels and those hotels with annual main business income of RMB 2 million and more; venues for exhibitions; sponsors of large exhibitions (with the list provided by Beijing Municipal Bureau of Public Security) together with organizations providing various professional services to exhibitions. Statistics for MICE in 2013 are calculated after collecting data from annual statistical report and relevant departments. As the scope of companies under survey is not completely the same (there are companies newly added and phasing out), data in both the current year and previous year are collected from the surveyed companies to keep the data comparable.

Data on sports and related industry were calculated according to the data in annual statistical reports and other related materials. And the standards in the *Classification of Sports and Related Industry (Temporary)* issued by the State Sport General Administration of China for Sports and National Bureau of Statistics in 2015were applicable.

Ⅳ. Changes in Relevant Statistical Standards

(I) Classification of Sectors. According to relevant provisions of National Bureau of Statistics, the *Standard for Classification of National Economic Sectors* (GB/T4754-2011) became effective in 2012.

(II) Classification of Three Industries. According to the Provisions of the National Bureau of Statistics on *Classification of Three Industries* (GTZ [2012] No. 108), the scope of three industries was changed. The primary industry refers to agriculture, forestry, animal production and hunting, fishing (excluding service for agriculture, forestry, animal production and hunting, fishing); the secondary industry refers to mining and quarrying (excluding mining support activities), manufacturing (excluding metal products, machinery and equipment repair), production and distribution of electricity, heating power, gas and water, and construction; the tertiary industry refers to sectors other than the primary and secondary industries. the Provisions of the National Bureau of Statistics on *Classification of Three Industries* (GTZ [2012] No. 108) came into effect in 2012.

14-1 第三产业主要指标及占全市比重(2000-2016年)

项 目	Item		2000	2001	2002	2003
增加值	(亿元) Value Added	(100 million yuan)	2092.9	2541.6	3054.2	3522.1
占全市比重	(%) Percentage of the Total	(%)	65.1	67.4	69.5	69.0
劳动生产率	(元/人) Overall Labor Productivity	(yuan/person)	62841.6	74751.5	85062.2	89043.9
相当于全市比例	(%) Percentage of the Total	(%)	121.1	123.8	126.6	120.6
从业人员年末人数	(万人) Year-end Employed Persons	(10000 persons)	338.2	341.8	376.3	414.8
占全市比重	(%) Percentage of the Total	(%)	54.6	54.4	55.4	59.0
固定资产投资	(亿元) Investment in Fixed Assets	(100 million yuan)	510.3	1367.9	1621.8	1875.4
占全市比重	(%) Percentage of the Total	(%)	39.3	89.3	89.4	86.9
实际利用外资金额	(亿美元) Actual Use of Foreign Capital	(USD 100 million)	22.2	12.8	12.5	14.0
占全市比重	(%) Percentage of the Total	(%)	90.5	72.4	69.8	65.3
能源消费总量	(万吨标准煤) Energy Consumption	(10000 tons of SCE)	1080.9	1196.2	1334.5	1391.0
占全市比重	(%) Percentage of the Total	(%)	26.1	28.3	30.1	29.9

注：1.2016年，地区生产总值实施研发支出核算方法改革，并对历史数据进行了修订；
2.三次产业划分执行国家统计局《三次产业划分规定》(国统字[2012]108号)。

MAIN INDICATORS OF THE TERTIARY INDUSTRY AND THEIR PERCENTAGES OF BEIJING'S TOTAL (2000-2016)

2004	2005	2006	2007	2008	2009	2010	2011	2012	2013	2014	2015	2016
4211.9	5008.9	6007.7	7438.4	8638.8	9445.4	10930.9	12740.2	14141.7	15777.4	17121.5	18884.7	20594.9
68.3	70.1	72.3	73.9	75.8	76.1	75.7	76.6	77.1	77.6	78.0	79.7	80.2
86432.4	87529.6	98592.1	115529.9	126650.1	130551.6	145358.0	163451.2	173646.1	184305.1	193562.6	206459.0	215371.5
109.2	106.1	106.6	106.8	106.9	104.0	102.2	103.3	103.0	101.9	101.3	102.1	100.9
559.8	584.7	634.0	653.7	710.5	736.5	767.5	791.4	837.4	874.7	894.4	935.0	977.5
65.5	66.6	68.9	69.3	72.4	73.8	74.4	74.0	75.6	76.7	77.3	78.8	80.1
2112.7	2405.6	2993.8	3465.8	3434.4	4389.5	4922.3	5101.3	5597.5	6101.7	6681.6	7202.8	7639.0
83.6	85.1	88.8	87.4	89.2	90.3	89.6	86.3	86.6	86.8	88.4	90.1	90.3
19.2	23.0	34.5	40.8	44.4	52.0	56.3	62.4	69.1	70.1	79.3	123.2	123.2
62.4	65.2	75.9	80.6	72.9	84.9	88.5	88.5	85.9	82.2	87.7	94.8	94.6
1638.0	1771.7	1962.8	2198.4	2394.3	2527.3	2654.4	2818.9	2967.0	3109.1	3236.5	3312.6	3414.4
31.9	35.1	36.4	38.2	41.4	42.1	41.7	44.1	45.2	46.2	47.4	48.3	49.0

Note: a) In 2016, the reform of R&D expenditure calculation method was implemented on GDP, and historical data were revised in this table;
b) Three industries classifications are subject to Regulations on Three Industries Classification from State Statistics Bureau(G.T.Z. [2012] No. 108).

14−2 北京地区服务贸易情况(2016)
STATISTICS FOR SERVICE TRADE IN BEIJING (2016)

单位：亿美元 (USD 100000000)

项 目	Item	进出口总额 Total export-import volume	出口额 Export volume	进口额 Import volume	差额 Balance
合 计	**Total**	**1508.60**	**532.13**	**976.47**	**-444.34**
旅 行	Tourism	762.64	176.88	585.77	-408.89
运输服务	Transportation	157.81	50.33	107.48	-57.15
专业和管理咨询服务	Professional and management consulting services	113.28	84.10	29.18	54.92
电信、计算机和信息服务	Telecommunications, computer and information services	119.96	63.24	56.72	6.52
建筑服务	Construction services	85.07	48.71	36.36	12.35
技术服务	Technical services	34.93	20.27	14.66	5.61
知识产权使用费	Charge for use of intellectual properties	33.55	1.72	31.83	-30.11
保险服务	Insurance services	98.06	25.05	73.00	-47.95
金融服务	Financial services	19.96	15.57	4.39	11.18
文化和娱乐服务	Cultural and recreational services	11.69	2.17	9.51	-7.34
其他服务	Other services	59.83	36.02	23.81	12.21

资料来源：北京市商务委员会。
Source: Beijing Municipal Commission of Commerce .

14−3 规模以上第三产业主要指标(2004−2016年)
MAIN INDICATORS FOR TERTIARY INDUSTRY ENTERPRISES ABOVE DESIGNATED SIZE (2004-2016)

项 目	Item	2004	2005	2006	2007	2008	2009
单位数 (个)	Number of Enterprises (unit)	25725	23661	24921	25651	34820	36177
从业人员平均人数 (万人)	Average Number of Employed Persons (10000 persons)	301.4	323.3	340.4	373.5	443.6	472.1
资产总计 (亿元)	Total Assets (100 million yuan)	184985.5	274180.3	336485.9	422458.7	579095.5	712313.4
收入合计 (亿元)	Income (100 million yuan)	21467.2	24444.6	29468.7	38361.8	47524.3	55390.3
应交税金合计 (亿元)	Total Tax Payable (100 million yuan)	908.1	1004.0	1376.0	2360.9	1855.2	2560.8
企业利润总额 (亿元)	Total Profits (100 million yuan)	1544.8	2696.1	2967.2	4511.2	4577.6	10540.8

注：应交税金合计主要包括应交增值税、应交所得税、营业税金及附加和管理费用中的税金等。
Note: Total tax payable mainly includes VAT payable, income tax payable, business tax and surtax, and tax in management expenses, etc.

14−3 续表 Continued

项 目	Item	2010	2011	2012	2013	2014	2015	2016
单位数 (个)	Number of Enterp (unit)	36064	36102	36616	36504	36361	32698	33308
从业人员平均人数 (万人)	Average Number of Employed Persons (10000 persons)	487.9	509.9	545	565.2	586.6	616.9	635.5
资产总计 (亿元)	Total Assets (100 million yuan)	798485.4	909953.5	1022849.7	1093973	1242344.8	1397969.4	1583118.8
收入合计 (亿元)	Total Income (100 million yuan)	69106.8	79246.0	92138.2	103398.8	110308.2	110154.4	116751.1
应交税金合计 (亿元)	Total Tax Payable (100 million yuan)	3122.4	4018.9	4652.8	5415.4	5998.0	6725.2	5928.1
企业利润总额 (亿元)	Total Profits (100 million yuan)	10236.3	11413.1	14248.4	18410.6	20601.7	24752.9	23973.9

14-4 规模以上第三产业单位主要经济指标(2016年)
MAIN INDICATORS FOR TERTIARY INDUSTRY ENTERPRISES ABOVE DESIGNATED SIZE (2016)

项目	Item	单位数(个) Enter-prises (unit)	从业人员平均人数(万人) Average Number of Employed Persons (10000 persons)	资产总计(亿元) Total Assets (100 million yuan)	收入合计(亿元) Total Incomes (100 million yuan)	应交税金合计(亿元) Total Tax (100 million yuan)	利润总额(亿元) Total Profits (100 million yuan)
合计	**Total**	**33308**	**635.5**	**1583118.8**	**116751.1**	**5928.1**	**23973.9**
按隶属关系分	**By Affiliation**						
中央	Central	3948	129.8	1252965.1	46986.6	2885.1	17221.6
地方	Local	29360	505.7	330153.7	69764.5	3043.0	6752.3
按行业分	**By Sector**						
批发和零售业	Wholesale and Retail Trade	6010	70.4	39732.7	46427.6	784.0	1080.1
交通运输、仓储和邮政业	Transport, Storage and Post	988	58.7	16392.0	4680.2	153.8	414.6
住宿和餐饮业	Accommodation and Restaurants	2281	34.5	1773.9	918.3	51.6	31.4
信息传输、软件和信息技术服务业	Information Transmission,Software and Information Technology Services	3004	76.3	34768.7	7873.3	390.0	1841.0
金融业	Financial Intermediation	1910	50.0	1276438.7	22661.5	2753.2	14488.6
房地产业	Real Estate	4250	46.7	62910.1	6007.5	871.0	974.2
租赁和商务服务业	Leasing and Business Services	5361	98.1	108858.8	9017.2	549.4	4524.2
科学研究和技术服务业	Scientific Research and Technical Services	3367	60.5	21845.1	8195.9	238.5	457.1
水利、环境和公共设施管理业	Management of Water Conservancy, Environment and Public Facilities	553	10.1	2174.7	648.4	23.7	41.5
居民服务、修理和其他服务业	Resident Services, Repair and Other Services	429	9.4	191.9	178.4	8.7	2.1
教育	Education	1500	40.3	4781.3	1942.2	21.4	18.0
卫生和社会工作	Health Care and Social Works	725	26.0	1686.1	1845.9	3.1	-6.0
文化、体育和娱乐业	Culture, Sports and Entertainment	1258	15.8	5079.7	1658.8	75.1	107.2
公共管理、社会保障和社会组织	Pulic Administration,Social Security and Social Organizations	1672	38.8	6485.0	4695.9	4.6	
按登记注册类型分	**By Registration Type**						
内资	Domestic Investment Economy	30381	537.9	1521456.0	95539.0	5024.7	21406.6
国有	State-owned Units	5855	157.6	338951.0	17900.5	422.3	3746.2
集体	Collective-owned Units	447	5.3	1652.8	305.7	13.0	16.9
股份合作	Share Holding	247	2.5	694.3	109.1	5.4	2.2
联营	Joint Ownership Units	25	0.2	80.8	15.0	1.3	3.0
有限责任公司	Limited-Liability Corporations	11736	191.1	260890.2	48052.4	1873.6	9381.8
股份有限公司	Share Holding Corporations Ltd.	1111	64.4	902339.4	18680.0	2373.6	7905.2
私营	Private Units	10532	109.9	15750.5	9865.3	329.3	342.3
其他	Others	428	6.9	1097.0	611.0	6.2	9.0
港澳台商投资	Hong Kong, Macao and Taiwan-invested Enterprises	1263	48.3	21363.3	8524.7	365.9	681.0
外商投资	Foreign Funded Units	1664	49.3	40299.5	12687.4	537.4	1886.4

注：1. 行业划分执行2011年国民经济行业分类标准(GB/T 4754—2011)。
2. 应交税金合计主要包括应交增值税、应交所得税、营业税金及附加和管理费用中的税金等。

Note: a) Sectors in this table are classified in accordance with the Standard for Classification of National Economic Sectors 2011 (GB/T 4754-2011).
b) Total Tax mainly includes payable VAT,payable income tax, business tax and surtax, and tax in management expenses, etc.

14-5 规模以上第三产业企业财务状况(按登记注册类型分)(2016年)

单位：万元

项目	Item	企业单位个数(个) Number of Enterprises (unit)	资产负债 资产总计 Total Assets	流动资产合计 Total Current Assets	#应收账款 Accounts Receivable
合计	**Total**	**28415**	**13545130552**	**1447420143**	**134765439**
按隶属关系分	**By Affiliation**				
中央	Central	2522	10317500730	445552821	39918420
地方	Local	25893	3227629822	1001867321	94847019
按登记注册类型分	**By Registration Type**				
内资企业	Domestically-invested Enterprises	25491	12928544050	1231602869	107160407
国有企业	State-owned Enterprises	1433	1113750043	161029276	8869281
集体企业	Collectively-owned Enterprises	377	15274517	9070825	501727
股份合作企业	Joint-equity Cooperative Enterprises	243	6924334	4732545	285195
联营企业	Associated Enterprises	21	795757	191329	4112
有限责任公司	Limited-Liability Companies	11731	2608885869	744849537	61970387
股份有限公司	Companies Limited by Shares	1111	9023393953	195723376	16630035
私营企业	Private Enterprises	10496	157326146	114405705	18861236
其他企业	Others	79	2193431	1600276	38435
港澳台商投资企业	Hong Kong, Macao and Taiwan-invested Enterprises	1263	213632729	91085253	8589073
外商投资企业	Foreign-invested Enterprises	1661	402953774	124732021	19015960

注：1. 行业划分执行2011年国民经济行业分类标准(GB/T 4754—2011)。
2. 应交税金合计主要包括应交增值税、应交所得税、营业税金及附加和管理费用中的税金。
3. 执行《2006年会计准则》的银行、证券、保险业企业，其“主营营业税金及附加”用“营业税金及附加”代替，“营业成本”和“主营业务成本”用“营业支出—营业税金及附加”代替。

14-5 续表

单位：万元

项目	Item	损益及分配 营业收入 Revenue from Main Businesses	#主营业务收入 Main Business Income	营业成本 Business Cost	#主营业务成本 Main Business Cost
合计	**Total**	**1053323781**	**1036402261**	**766337234**	**758411377**
按隶属关系分	**By Affiliation**				
中央	Central	408204795	400657216	267438685	262563561
地方	Local	645118986	635745045	498898549	495847816
按登记注册类型分	**By Registration Type**				
内资企业	Domestically-invested Enterprises	841228997	828504387	606964468	600500032
国有企业	State-owned Enterprises	71140978	68756488	61812371	61211178
集体企业	Collectively-owned Enterprises	2279871	2180068	1602794	1569277
股份合作企业	Joint-equity Cooperative Enterprises	1064850	1042160	701482	697072
联营企业	Associated Enterprises	138621	136796	87988	87554
有限责任公司	Limited-Liability Companies	480507321	472307307	359862609	354671026
股份有限公司	Companies Limited by Shares	186799727	185483982	106320038	105894241
私营企业	Private Enterprises	98508179	97818719	76146306	75943903
其他企业	Others	789450	778868	430880	425780
港澳台商投资企业	Hong Kong, Macao and Taiwan-invested Enterprises	85247230	84204590	62322141	61957618
外商投资企业	Foreign-invested Enterprises	126847553	123693284	97050625	95953726

FINANCIAL STATUS OF TERTIARY INDUSTRY ENTERPRISES ABOVE DESIGNATED SIZE(BY REGISTRATION TYPE) (2016)

(10000 yuan)

Assets and Liabilites						
固定资产合计 Total Fixed Assets	固定资产原价 Total Original Value of Fixed Assets	负债合计 Total Liabilities	#流动负债合计 Total Current Liabilities	#应付账款 Accounts Payable	所有者权益合计 Total Owner's Equity	#实收资本 Paid-up Capital
199780248	**289254804**	**10214575822**	**1122835475**	**151087683**	**3330554730**	**1415370732**
86826723	128005529	7833867490	391454527	52948357	2483633240	969771196
112953525	161249275	2380708332	731380948	98139327	846921490	445599535
162568380	221923278	9862391786	963925829	115922270	3066152264	1305701756
43131676	58627751	643126959	128685460	9355709	470623084	261759350
2445851	3308058	10923893	8018275	386488	4350624	1028221
867127	1071938	4954692	3922409	238269	1969642	453751
44706	91479	164779	150676	5109	630978	595157
69731250	95628847	1316666858	564785176	75816284	1292219012	634267527
39559292	52512641	7771466306	158878005	14724566	1251927647	373930690
6520955	10276167	114258856	98704170	15234426	43067291	32923254
267522	406398	829443	781659	161419	1363987	743807
28800004	49817167	123805494	65612410	15148244	89827235	59868254
8411864	17514359	228378542	93297237	20017170	174575232	49800722

Note:a)Sectors in this table are classified in accordance with the Standard for Classification of National Economic Sectors in 2011(GB/T4754-2011).
b) Total taxes payable mainly include VAT payable, income tax payable, business tax and surtax, and tax in management expenses, etc.
c) For banks, security and insurance enterprises implementing 2006 Standard of Accounting System, the indicator of "Main Business Tax and Surtax" is replaced with "Business Tax and Surtax" and indicators of "Business Cost" and "Main Business Cost" are replaced with "Business Cost-Busniess Tax and Surtax".

14-5 continued

(10000 yuan)

Profits and Losses							
销售费用 Sales Expenses	管理费用 Manage-ment Expenses	财务费用 Financial Expenses	利润总额 Total Profits	应交税金合计 Total Tax Payable	#营业税金及附加 Business Tax and Surtax	#主营业务税金及附加 Business Tax and Surtax	#应交所得税 Income Tax Payable
49158027	**58263029**	**16987260**	**239739209**	**58761723**	**10129446**	**9895144**	**31025937**
5353896	11906210	5506554	172216190	28422073	2629291	2513756	19813498
43804131	46356819	11480706	67523019	30339651	7500155	7381388	11212440
30318023	41487013	14208500	214065851	49727798	8855393	8639810	27360223
1258195	5384327	1624751	37461885	3735801	798899	728966	1978531
137249	407123	51136	168971	128339	37892	36452	45470
98958	244610	4769	21950	54215	12173	12152	16464
7124	21498	-1746	30298	12865	1504	1097	7064
15731681	20463829	9193006	93817807	18735509	5211795	5097857	7707943
3179274	5113395	2362178	79052404	23735877	2153857	2131663	16811162
9784543	9665128	996562	3422806	3291439	629563	622019	786205
120999	187103	-22156	89731	33754	9711	9605	7385
8013433	7477721	2006656	6809791	3659482	640917	633073	1613365
10826571	9298296	772105	18863567	5374444	633135	622261	2052349

14-6 规模以上第三产业企业财务状况(按行业分)(2016年)

单位：万元

项目	Item	企业单位个数(个) Number of Enterprises (unit)	资产负债 资产总计 Total Assets	流动资产合计 Total Current Assets
合计	**Total**	**28415**	**13545130552**	**1447420143**
批发和零售业	**Wholesale and Retail Trade**	**6010**	**397326956**	**274231081**
批发业	Wholesale	4090	352129965	240406945
零售业	Retail Trade	1920	45196991	33824136
交通运输、仓储和邮政业	**Transport, Storage and Post**	**988**	**163919880**	**33100390**
铁路运输业	Railway Transport	17	70481974	8880338
道路运输业	Road Transport	482	26710007	5885548
水上运输业	Water Transport	5	54881	19203
航空运输业	Air Transport	28	28784075	5000388
管道运输业	Transport Via Pipelines	***	***	***
装卸搬运和运输代理业	Loading, Unloading, Portage and Other Transport Services	319	7391917	4774938
仓储业	Storage	106	21861209	5321382
邮政业	Post	30	5080925	2812925
住宿和餐饮业	**Accommodation and Restaurants**	**2281**	**17738875**	**7365337**
住宿业	Accommodation	964	13750189	4898952
餐饮业	Restaurants	1317	3988686	2466385
信息传输、软件和信息技术服务业	**Information Transmission, Software and Information Technology Services**	**2953**	**344608671**	**119353566**
电信、广播电视和卫星传输服务	Telecommunications, Broadcasting, Television and Satellite Transmission Services	208	215719923	38168282
互联网和相关服务	Internet and Related Services	325	24939572	17414037
软件和信息技术服务业	Software and Information Technology Services	2420	103949176	63771248
金融业	**Finance**	**1890**	**10687398524**	**66321973**
货币金融服务	Monetary Financial Services	512	8736651320	10191188
资本市场服务	Capital Market Services	549	430581359	15753409
保险业	Insurance	400	534431344	1105030
其他金融业	Other Financial Services	429	985734500	39272346

FINANCIAL STATUS OF TERTIARY INDUSTRY ENTERPRISES ABOVE DESIGNATED SIZE(BY SECTOR) (2016)

(10000 yuan)

Assets and Liabilites							
#应收账款 Accounts Receivable	固定资产合计 Total Fixed Assets	固定资产原价 Total Original Value of Fixed Assets	负债合计 Total Liabilities	#流动负债合计 Total Current Liabilities	#应付账款 Accounts Payable	所有者权益合计 Total Owner's Equity	#实收资本 Paid-up Capital
134765439	**199780248**	**289254804**	**10214575822**	**1122835475**	**151087683**	**3330554730**	**1415370732**
47404057	**9686847**	**15997692**	**266300378**	**231325396**	**60677855**	**131026578**	**57703573**
44126778	6597614	10531683	231856382	200518519	53450221	120273584	51476409
3277279	3089233	5466009	34443996	30806877	7227634	10752995	6227164
6255449	**71337271**	**97150392**	**81793803**	**53741566**	**9590143**	**82126077**	**65686693**
2482113	37058717	47315434	22786166	12615419	3913089	47695808	50171118
886012	14989168	19223848	13797845	7329788	2071266	12912162	5852159
1526	33699	73504	23471	16331	327	31410	14788
1030976	15086276	23396735	17433964	7444809	2084411	11350111	3917559
***	***	***	***	***	***	***	***
1218052	465157	861078	3520417	2996983	896367	3871500	1906712
121030	485753	705847	20922799	20432711	36860	938410	384191
509980	405583	870596	2242183	1888568	236771	2838742	1917967
330092	**5671981**	**9911316**	**13503601**	**9942729**	**977626**	**4235273**	**4622440**
181234	5184904	8838975	10287933	6946290	381813	3462256	3891338
148858	487077	1072341	3215668	2996439	595814	773018	731102
24842687	**16309868**	**36096702**	**124252728**	**105976117**	**19326900**	**220355943**	**129637436**
6453686	9044264	22590256	62591293	52280355	8210761	153128630	103368505
2140277	2266360	4450759	13247729	12316481	2608391	11691842	3332101
16248724	4999244	9055687	48413706	41379281	8507749	55535471	22936830
3415699	**21390365**	**28375184**	**8667190212**	**52689338**	**1373123**	**2020208312**	**696072456**
1219762	13480061	20521790	7839655798	10485632	196953	896995522	245361469
707848	954889	1423224	178181367	12415391	102602	252399992	61926283
174112	5470992	4240936	359739147	479726	121527	174692196	57161611
1313977	1484423	2189234	289613899	29308589	952041	696120601	331623094

14-6 续表 1

单位：万元

项目	Item	损益及分配 营业收入 Business Income	#主营业务收入 Revenue from Main Business	营业成本 Business Cost
合计	**Total**	**1053323781**	**1036402261**	**766337234**
批发和零售业	**Wholesale and Retail Trade**	**464276021**	**455229643**	**425895402**
批发业	Wholesale	394250577	387199098	365103580
零售业	Retail Trade	70025444	68030545	60791822
交通运输、仓储和邮政业	**Transport, Storage and Post**	**46802417**	**45876500**	**39744708**
铁路运输业	Railway Transport	12654575	12304119	10524752
道路运输业	Road Transport	6461671	6349089	7153447
水上运输业	Water Transport	24347	24347	12413
航空运输业	Air Transport	11530483	11146797	9132091
管道运输业	Transport Via Pipelines	***	***	***
装卸搬运和运输代理业	Loading, Unloading, Portage and Other Transport Services	8008701	7971867	6880443
仓储业	Storage	4084536	4072337	3859774
邮政业	Post	2884123	2860977	1837853
住宿和餐饮业	**Accommodation and Restaurants**	**9183227**	**9070025**	**3263943**
住宿业	Accommodation	3545260	3504008	971417
餐饮业	Restaurants	5637967	5566018	2292526
信息传输、软件和信息技术服务业	**Information Transmission, Software and Information Technology Services**	**77676585**	**76716963**	**47696781**
电信、广播电视和卫星传输服务	Telecommunications, Broadcasting, Television and Satellite Transmission Services	13285970	13089287	9272582
互联网和相关服务	Internet and Related Services	14401034	14324330	7727151
软件和信息技术服务业	Software and Information Technology Services	49989581	49303347	30697048
金融业	**Finance**	**226147377**	**225906494**	**82042861**
货币金融服务	Monetary Financial Services	78035029	77973258	32985335
资本市场服务	Capital Market Services	17066452	17004526	4552575
保险业	Insurance	61599666	61592477	36229702
其他金融业	Other Financial Services	69446231	69336233	8275249

14-6 continued 1

(10000 yuan)

Profits and Losses								
#主营业务成本 Main Business Cost	销售费用 Sales Expenses	管理费用 Management Expenses	财务费用 Financial Expenses	利润总额 Total Profits	应交税金合计 Total Tax Payable	#营业税金及附加 Business Tax and Surtax	#主营业务税金及附加 Business Tax and Surtax	#应交所得税 Income Tax Payable
758411377	**49158027**	**58263029**	**16987260**	**239739209**	**58761723**	**10129446**	**9895144**	**31025937**
420585410	**19628094**	**9495293**	**2732867**	**10800869**	**7840187**	**1022479**	**982319**	**2307529**
360211451	13733948	7231515	2251632	9334734	6078677	788360	759501	1915456
60373959	5894146	2263778	481235	1466135	1761511	234119	222817	392073
39111022	**1628460**	**2539933**	**1468958**	**4146155**	**1537579**	**136777**	**127375**	**968826**
10154426	5161	491507	395339	1229328	588777	38431	33297	251379
7091816	216114	663795	298739	131617	240555	40213	37351	61795
12413	2617	5127	404	7106	1440	34	34	1178
8940103	621345	337402	759769	1068851	298385	28380	28380	273908
***	***	***	***	***	***	***	***	***
6877089	306493	541162	-9468	529012	143120	7939	7660	83022
3856285	64477	99182	7852	98989	-171393	4048	3935	8995
1836336	385289	375671	12727	280383	127683	5360	5254	87441
3216631	**3425986**	**1918760**	**226729**	**314037**	**515717**	**207648**	**203933**	**138516**
963559	1087592	1262047	181521	113140	303152	98085	95527	60395
2253072	2338394	656712	45209	200897	212565	109563	108407	78121
47225992	**9974025**	**13249018**	**461707**	**18409951**	**3890083**	**473600**	**463183**	**1287449**
9163997	1133998	1714017	362981	11161321	545335	51476	45325	211532
7628447	3233042	2250637	-139676	1707736	666254	152085	151890	271435
30433548	5606985	9284363	238402	5540894	2678495	270039	265968	804482
81974896	**807071**	**2473896**	**760329**	**144885612**	**27531845**	**2426868**	**2413495**	**20083605**
32958608	68484	192933	217267	45795131	20552685	1798828	1798695	15035262
4541741	66881	1026994	232325	12410566	2334381	264498	258135	1634882
36228092	101245	232449	-1465	24959025	2532729	214474	214091	1701366
8246455	570461	1021520	312202	61720892	2112051	149068	142575	1712095

14-6 续表 2

单位：万元

项 目	Item	企业单位个数（个）Number of Enterprises (unit)	资产负债 资产总计 Total Assets
房地产业	**Real Estate**	**4233**	**628804799**
租赁和商务服务业	**Renting and Leasing Activities, Business Services**	**5112**	**1080819181**
租赁业	Renting and Leasing	105	9731308
商务服务业	Business Services	5007	1071087873
科学研究和技术服务业	**Scientific Research and Development, Technical Services**	**2803**	**169110421**
研究和试验发展	Research and Experimental Development	237	22056320
专业技术服务业	Professional Technical Services	1324	104487582
科技推广和应用服务业	Technique Generalization and Application Services	1242	42566519
水利、环境和公共设施管理业	**Management of Water Conservancy, Environment and Public Facilities**	**344**	**18884308**
水利管理业	Management of Water Conservancy	11	755777
生态保护和环境治理业	Ecological Protection and Environmental Control	53	3720956
公共设施管理业	Management of Public Facilities	280	14407576
居民服务、修理和其他服务业	**Resident Services, Repair and Other Services**	**388**	**1542668**
居民服务业	Resident Services	103	560452
机动车、电子产品和日用产品修理业	Repair of Motor Vehicles, Electronics and Household Appliances	135	599856
其他服务业	Other Services	150	382361
教 育	**Education**	**193**	**3414733**
卫生和社会工作	**Healthcare and Social Works**	**233**	**2006555**
卫 生	Healthcare	225	1911623
社会工作	Social Works	8	94932
文化、体育和娱乐业	**Culture, Sports and Entertainment**	**987**	**29554982**
新闻和出版业	Journalism and Publishing	411	12555139
广播、电视、电影和影视录音制作业	Radio Broadcasting, Television, Movies, Videos and Sound Recording	239	12235988
文化艺术业	Culture and Arts	146	1203734
体 育	Sports Activities	134	1821149
娱乐业	Entertainment	57	1738972

14-6 Continued 2

(10000 yuan)

Assets and Liabilites								
流动资产合计 Total Current Assets	#应收账款 Accounts Receivable	固定资产合计 Total Fixed Assets	固定资产原价 Total Original Value of Fixed Assets	负债合计 Total Liabilities	#流动负债合计 Total Current Liabilities	#应付账款 Accounts Payable	所有者权益合计 Total Owner's Equity	#实收资本 Paid-up Capital
475084270	**12358750**	**20024274**	**27768005**	**474953899**	**307936665**	**21629929**	**153850900**	**86339285**
342995514	**17803322**	**26508515**	**36300127**	**462533451**	**264574482**	**13252354**	**618285730**	**336331993**
3616635	471654	3273006	4374600	6896930	2955884	376272	2834379	2104600
339378879	17331668	23235510	31925527	455636522	261618597	12876083	615451351	334227393
98661302	**18174344**	**20055934**	**25507252**	**96589960**	**77447985**	**20067518**	**72520461**	**29136621**
15580033	1406381	1864127	2948554	13896613	10534383	3343462	8159708	3618703
55868239	12083787	15877716	18969551	55849163	45032878	12754659	48638418	15165499
27213031	4684175	2314091	3589148	26844185	21880725	3969396	15722335	10352420
7694082	**1764581**	**4946539**	**5685731**	**10952916**	**5088682**	**1429724**	**7931392**	**2742518**
217967	14967	104756	205657	395482	190645	7488	360295	207391
2412064	841956	596616	781836	2059619	1496892	511849	1661337	836794
5064051	907658	4245167	4698238	8497816	3401145	910386	5909760	1698334
1076039	**183237**	**222647**	**409459**	**1265740**	**1073330**	**157533**	**276928**	**330880**
383573	13420	58833	130800	584503	483289	29921	-24051	78219
430599	92191	70313	133466	413360	395798	77002	186496	171078
261868	77626	93502	145193	267877	194244	50611	114484	81584
2404788	**116355**	**393367**	**712945**	**2203607**	**2135010**	**249713**	**1211126**	**434298**
1126000	**151263**	**523519**	**867258**	**1560831**	**1238531**	**258197**	**445724**	**476239**
1050336	150540	506750	825922	1469373	1147567	245743	442250	472499
75665	724	16769	41336	91458	90964	12454	3474	3740
18005802	**1965604**	**2709122**	**4472741**	**11474695**	**9665646**	**2097069**	**18080287**	**5856299**
8218948	640706	1394055	2190396	4292501	3569790	811798	8262638	2674763
6719883	1064591	486314	908302	4157313	3638103	930172	8078676	2351066
780924	155736	195500	291691	606098	546653	116564	597635	295209
936522	74766	440426	815336	1829411	1413214	197516	-8262	368965
1349525	29805	192828	267015	589372	497888	41020	1149600	166296

14-6 续表 3

单位：万元

项 目	Item	损益及分配 营业收入 Business Income	#主营业务收入 Revenue from Business Income
房地产业	**Real Estate**	**59939259**	**58717738**
租赁和商务服务业	**Renting and Leasing Activities, Business Services**	**88330675**	**85079749**
租赁业	Renting and Leasing	1874729	1840046
商务服务业	Business Services	86455946	83239704
科学研究和技术服务业	**Scientific Research and Development, Technical Services**	**60847491**	**60139749**
研究和试验发展	Research and Experimental Development	4132431	3935989
专业技术服务业	Professional Technical Services	41387138	41131838
科技推广和应用服务业	Technique Generalization and Application Services	15327922	15071923
水利、环境和公共设施管理业	**Management of Water Conservancy, Environment and Public Facilities**	**4226201**	**4188962**
水利管理业	Management of Water Conservancy	87544	85534
生态保护和环境治理业	Ecological Protection and Environmental Control	1363355	1357966
公共设施管理业	Management of Public Facilities	2775302	2745462
居民服务、修理和其他服务业	**Resident Services, Repair and Other Services**	**1578968**	**1536362**
居民服务业	Resident Services	418043	410508
机动车、电子产品和日用产品修理业	Repair of Motor Vehicles, Electronics and Household Appliances	694242	667478
其他服务业	Other Services	466683	458376
教 育	**Education**	**1997345**	**1952296**
卫生和社会工作	**Healthcare and Social Works**	**1862705**	**1854611**
卫 生	Healthcare	1843868	1837191
社会工作	Social Works	18838	17421
文化、体育和娱乐业	**Culture, Sports and Entertainment**	**10455511**	**10133169**
新闻和出版业	Journalism and Publishing	4332267	4076206
广播、电视、电影和影视录音制作业	Radio Broadcasting, Television, Movies, Videos and Sound Recording	4364301	4330092
文化艺术业	Culture and Arts	750493	742716
体 育	Sports Activities	729914	706822
娱乐业	Entertainment	278536	277333

14-6 continued 3

(10000 yuan)

Profits and Losses									
营业成本 Business Cost	#主营业务成本 Main Business Cost	销售费用 Sales Expenses	管理费用 Manage-ment Expenses	财务费用 Financial Expenses	利润总额 Total Profits	应交税金合计 Total Taxes Payable	#营业税金及附加 Business Tax and Surtax	#主营业务税金及附加 Main Business Tax and Surtax	#应交所得税 Income Tax Payable
38799190	**38364811**	**2346437**	**5264248**	**3292479**	**9741550**	**8708866**	**4687330**	**4623452**	**2225785**
65784042	**65345042**	**6929298**	**13832577**	**7572597**	**45242085**	**5452582**	**708466**	**628815**	**2950597**
1263401	1260476	59235	222898	79812	259056	118178	7620	7610	63415
64520641	64084566	6870063	13609679	7492784	44983030	5334405	700845	621205	2887182
49317196	**48955553**	**2389707**	**6184272**	**422783**	**4571368**	**2244327**	**303752**	**291704**	**744105**
3108671	3011111	167513	822154	-37883	544657	190425	23052	21635	58074
34773404	34666849	836342	3213229	324069	3451327	1424347	214379	206570	464665
11435121	11277593	1385852	2148889	136598	575384	629555	66322	63498	221366
3194826	**3179643**	**145624**	**446362**	**58856**	**415456**	**227245**	**37723**	**37475**	**66235**
45433	44590	393	30851	6548	10672	3867	432	432	1502
1011775	1011173	41732	100720	17158	203589	92537	4877	4865	26761
2137618	2123880	103499	314791	35150	201195	130841	32414	32179	37973
929072	**915940**	**354290**	**261268**	**4894**	**20649**	**85061**	**18489**	**18189**	**17496**
170157	168740	132732	90001	1179	21328	21884	5246	5170	8811
487750	481173	119550	80786	3128	2282	37572	4639	4458	6403
271165	266027	102008	90481	586	-2961	25606	8604	8562	2282
968436	**953005**	**400194**	**445647**	**-19904**	**180232**	**108436**	**28727**	**28534**	**35427**
1322293	**1319895**	**174682**	**438916**	**25987**	**-60327**	**23723**	**987**	**939**	**19261**
1303985	1301603	174415	427732	25941	-50284	23365	950	902	19240
18308	18292	267	11185	47	-10044	358	38	38	21
7378484	**7263538**	**954161**	**1712841**	**-21023**	**1071571**	**596071**	**76601**	**75731**	**181106**
2530360	2450456	503308	1030608	-37727	711941	325183	40066	39650	57061
3673524	3667383	238122	348306	6639	301050	152978	13108	12911	86253
487560	483664	72697	123703	1269	83405	43588	6680	6654	16805
523156	499248	100666	162385	10725	-59328	52844	12927	12699	11662
163885	162787	39368	47839	-1929	34504	21479	3821	3818	9326

14-7 文化创意产业活动单位基本情况
STATISTICS FOR CULTURAL AND CREATIVE INDUSTRY

单位：亿元 (100 million yuan)

项 目	Item	资产总计 Total Assets		收入合计 Total Income		从业人员平均人数（万人） Average Number of Employed Persons (10000 persons)	
		2016	2015	2016	2015	2016	2015
合 计	**Total**	**37921.3**	**31893.9**	**17885.8**	**15877.8**	**198.1**	**202.3**
文化艺术	Culture and Arts	1344.5	1497.8	502.8	421.8	10.3	12.6
新闻出版	Journalism and Publications	2493.7	2453.3	923.0	1026.4	11.1	15.2
广播、电视、电影	Radios, Televisions amd Movies	3698.2	2934.2	1002.8	917.4	8.1	7.4
软件、网络及计算机服务	Software, Network & Computer Services	16801.8	13719.4	7010.7	6442.2	98.3	101.4
广告会展	Advertisements & Exhibitions	2729.4	2462.2	2548.3	2178.4	17.3	16.8
艺术品交易	Transaction of Artworks	1181.8	978.5	1329.6	1021.8	3.2	2.5
设计服务	Design Services	1562.2	1116.9	757.6	563.6	14.6	16.6
旅游、休闲娱乐	Tourism and Enterainment	1836.1	1947.6	1253.8	1207.0	13.6	13.1
其他辅助服务	Other Auxiliary Services	6273.5	4783.9	2557.2	2099.2	21.6	16.7

14-8 物流业活动情况
STATISTICS FOR LOGISTICS

项 目	Item	2016	2015	2016年为2015年% 2016 as % of 2015
物流业务收入 （亿元）	**Business Income of Logistics Sector (100 million yuan)**	**2517.3**	**2409**	**104.5**
运输收入	Transportation Income	1801.4	1712.9	105.2
保管收入	Storage Income	649.4	633.2	102.6
一体化物流业务收入	Integrated Logistics Income	66.5	63.0	105.6
社会物流总额 （亿元）	**Total Amount of Social Logistics (100 million yuan)**	**63877.6**	**67648.7**	**94.4**
农产品	Agricultural Products	286.5	312.8	91.6
工业品	Industrial Products	14602.6	17829.2	81.9
进口货物	Imported Goods	15207.1	16442.6	92.5
再生资源	Renewable Resources	219.0	131.5	166.6
外省市流入物品	Goods from Other Provinces and Cities	33300.3	32691.8	101.9
单位与居民物品	Entities and Residents' Goods	262.0	240.8	108.8
物流业从业人员平均人数 （万人）	**Employment in Logistics Sector (10000 persons)**	**47.7**	**50.3**	**94.8**
交通运输、邮政、仓储业	Transportation, Post, Storage	33.0	35.7	92.6
采掘业、制造业、批发和零售业	Excavation, Manufacturing, Wholesale and Retail Trade	14.6	14.6	100.1

14-9 会展业活动情况
STATISTICS FOR MICE INDUSTRY IN BEIJING

项目		Item		2016	2015	2016年为2015年% 2016 as % of 2015
人员情况		**Employed Persons**				
从业人员平均人数	(万人)	Year-end Employed Persons	(10000 person)	14.2	14.9	95.5
接待设施情况		**Facilities**				
接待场所会议室个数	(个)	Number of Meeting Rooms	(unit)	5000	4909	101.9
#座位数超过500座的会议室	(个)	Number of Meeting Rooms with More Than 500 Seats	(unit)	184	178	103.4
接待场所会议室使用面积	(万平方米)	Usable Area of Meeting Rooms	(10000 sq.m)	74.0	72.0	102.8
接待场所会议室可容纳人数	(万人)	Capacity of Meeting Rooms	(10000 person)	45.6	44.5	102.4
会议情况		**Meetings**				
接待会议个数	(万个)	Number of Meetings Held in Beijing	(10000 unit)	21.0	20.5	102.6
#国际会议	(万个)	International Meetings	(10000 unit)	0.5	0.5	91.5
接待会议人数	(万人次)	Number of Meeting Participants	(10000 person-times)	1605.7	1480.9	108.4
#国际会议	(万人次)	International Meeting Participants	(10000 person-times)	65.5	59.6	109.9
展览情况		**Exhibitions**				
接待展览个数	(个)	Number of Exhibitions Held in Beijing	(unit)	867	788	110.0
#国际展览	(个)	International Exhibitions	(unit)	159	173	91.9
#展览面积1万(不含)以下的展览个数	(平方米) (个)	Number of Exhibitions with Exhibition Area under 10,000 sq.m (10,000 sq.m excluded)	(unit)	651	609	106.9
展览面积1万平方米及以上的展览个数	(个)	Number of Exhibitions with Exhibition Area of 10,000 sq.m and over	(unit)	216	179	120.7
接待展览累计面积(含室外展览面积)	(万平方米)	Total Exhibition Area (including outdoor exhibition area)	(10000 sq.m)	673.8	601.9	111.9
#国际展览累计面积	(万平方米)	International Exhibition Area	(10000 sq.m)	361.0	325.8	110.8
接待展览观众人数	(万人次)	Number of Exhibition Visitors	(10000 person-times)	924.0	785.2	117.7
#国际展览观众人数	(万人次)	International Exhibition Visitors	(10000 person-times)	167.8	146.6	114.5
收入情况		**Revenues**				
会展收入	(亿元)	Total Revenues from MICE Industry	(100 million yuan)	232.6	219.2	106.1
会议收入	(亿元)	Revenues from Meetings	(100 million yuan)	109.6	100.8	108.8
#国际会议收入	(亿元)	Revenues from International Meetings	(100 million yuan)	7.4	5.7	130.3
展览收入	(亿元)	Revenues from Exhibitions	(100 million yuan)	116.5	107.6	108.3
#国际展览收入	(亿元)	Revenues from International Exhibitions	(100 million yuan)	41.4	37.0	111.9

注：会展业统计范围包括会展场馆、限额以上住宿业法人单位、会展举办单位以及规模以上会议及展览服务业法人单位和旅行社等。由于统计范围内的单位名录每年均有变化，为保证数据的可比性，需要调整上年同期数据以计算可比增速。

Note: Statistical scope in MICE industry includes MICE venue, star-level hotel and main organizer of MICE, etc. As items in the said statistical scope change every year, so in order to ensure figure comparability, figures of the same period in the previous year need to be adjusted to calculate comparable growth rate.

14-10 体育及相关产业情况
STATISTICS FOR SPORTS AND RELEVANT INDUSTRY

项目	Item	收入合计 (亿元) Total Income (100 million yuan)		从业人员平均人数 (万人) Average Number of Employed Persons (10000 persons)	
		2016	2015	2016	2015
合计	**Total**	**1154.6**	**1063.1**	**14.0**	**14.0**
体育管理活动	Sports Management Activities	32.3	27.8	0.2	0.2
体育竞赛表演活动	Sports Contests and Performance Activities	89.2	70.6	1.2	1.2
体育健身休闲活动	Sports, Body Building and Entertainment Activities	33.9	34.7	2.4	2.4
体育场馆服务	Sports Venues Service	37.1	28.7	1.4	1.4
体育中介服务	Sports Agency Service	36.3	26.0	0.3	0.3
体育培训与教育	Sports Training and Education	17.6	19.1	0.7	0.6
体育传媒与信息服务	Sports Media and Information Service	69.6	62.9	0.5	0.5
其他与体育相关服务	Other Service Related to Sports	95.3	93.1	1.3	1.3
体育用品及相关产品制造	Manufacture of Sports Goods and Related Products	68.4	65.9	0.8	0.9
体育用品及相关产品销售、贸易代理与出租	Sales of Sports Goods and Related Products Trade Agency and Rent	668.1	627.2	4.9	5.0
体育场地设施建设	Construction of Sports Venues and Facilities	6.8	7.1	0.1	0.1

主要统计指标解释

物流业务收入 指通过物流业务活动取得的收入。包括企业完成运输、存储、装卸、搬运、包装、流通加工、配送、信息等物流业务取得的收入之和。反映物流相关行业物流活动的总规模。

物流业从业人员 指企业中直接或间接从事物流活动的人数。直接从事物流活动的人员包括在企业中从事运输、配送、装卸搬运、仓储保管等物流活动并取得劳动报酬的从业人员；间接从事物流活动的人员包括在企业中从事物流管理活动并取得劳动报酬的从业人员，包括采购、销售部门的主管人员，但不包括采购、销售部门内部办事人员。

社会物流总额 指第一次进入市内需求领域，产生从供应地向接受地实体流动的物品的价值总额。包括六个方面的内容：进入需求领域的农产品物流总额、工业品物流总额、进口货物物流总额、外省市调入物品物流总额、再生资源物流总额、单位与居民物品物流总额。.

接待会议个数 指报告期内，接待的各种类型会议的个数。包括国际会议和国内会议。

接待国际会议个数 指报告期内，接待的国际会议的个数。国际会议是指在我国境内举办的，与会者来自 3 个或 3 个以上中国大陆以外国家和地区（含港、澳、台地区）的会议、论坛、研讨会、报告会、交流会等。

接待展览个数 指报告期内，接待的各种类型展览的个数。包括国际展览和国内展览。

接待国际展览个数 指报告期内，接待的国际展览的个数。国际展览指中国大陆以外国家和地区（含港、澳、台地区）的参展商参展面积达到该次展出面积 20%以上的展览个数。

服务贸易 服务贸易包括跨境提供、境外消费、商业存在和自然人移动等内容。

Explanatory Notes on Main Statistical Indicators

Business Income of Logistics Sector refers to the income earned from logistics business activities, which is equal to the sum of incomes from such logistics operations completed by enterprises as transportation, storage, loading and unloading, handling, package, circulation and processing, delivery, and information. It reflects the overall scale of logistics activities in logistics related sector.

Employees in Logistics Sector refers to the number of persons directly and indirectly engaged in logistics activities in enterprises. Persons directly engaging in logistics activities are those engaging in logistics activities such as transportation, delivery, loading and unloading, handling, storage and warehouse keeping in enterprises and receiving labor remuneration; persons indirectly engaging in logistics activities are those engaging in management activities in enterprises and receiving labor remuneration, including executives in purchase and sales departments, but excluding clerks in purchase and sales departments.

Total Amount of Social Logistics refers to the total value of goods entering the demand area in the city for the first time and having physical flow from the supply place to the receiving place, consisting of value on six aspects: total logistics amount of agricultural products, total logistics amount of industrial products, total logistics amount of imported goods, total logistics amount of goods transferred from other provinces and cities, total logistics amount of recycled resources, and total logistics amount of corporate and household supplies entering the demand field.

Number of Meeting Held in Beijing refers to the number of various types of conference held in Beijing in the reporting period, including international and domestic conferences.

Number of International Meeting refers to the number of international conferences held in Beijing in the reporting period. International conference means any conference, forum, seminar, report conference, and workshops, etc. held in our country, with participants coming from 3 or more countries and regions (including Hong Kong, Macao and Taiwan) outside Chinese mainland.

Number of Exhibitions Held in Beijing refers to the number of various types of exhibitions held in Beijing in the reporting period, including international and domestic exhibitions.

Number of International Exhibitions Received refers to the number of international exhibitions received in the reporting period. International exhibition means any exhibition with participants from countries and regions (including Hong Kong, Macao and Taiwan) outside Chinese mainland whose exhibition floorage accounts for more than 20% of the exhibition.

Service Trade includes overseas provision, overseas consumption, commercial existence, movement of natural persons, and so on.

北京统计年鉴2017　BEIJING STATISTICAL YEARBOOK

交通运输邮电

TRANSPORT, POST AND TELECOMMUNICATON SERVICES

简要说明

一、本章资料的主要内容

本章资料反映北京市交通运输业和邮政电信业发展的基本状况。

交通运输业资料主要包括：铁路、公路、民航、管道四种运输方式的线路条数、里程、总运量及周转量、主要技术经济指标（不含管道）；机动车拥有情况。

邮政电信业资料主要包括：邮电业务完成情况、邮政电信发展水平等资料。

二、各部分资料的调查范围及数据来源

1．铁路资料：主要是国家铁路运营情况，不含地方铁路、合资铁路和军用铁路及由厂矿企事业单位自建的铁路专用线和专用铁道，资料来源于北京铁路局。

2．公路资料：(1)公路里程为年末通车里程数，不含在建和未正式投入使用的公路里程；(2)公路运输统计范围包括在北京市注册从事公路货运的全部企事业单位和私人(包括个体联户)，资料来源于北京市交通委员会。

3．管道运输资料：包括输送原油、成品油、天然气以及其他气体的管线长度、输送能力及完成的运输量。管道运输统计数据主要来源于中石油北京天然气管道有限公司和中国石油化工股份有限公司北京燕山分公司所属的管道运输企业，由两家集团公司分别负责收集审核本部门统计数据。

4．民航运输资料：不包括在京运输飞行的外省市及外国航空公司。统计范围为各航空公司从事国内运输、港澳台运输、国际运输的定期航班航线条数及里程、运输量等。2009年及以前数据主要来源于中国国际航空公司、新华航空有限责任公司，2010年起为北京地区的民航运输法人单位。

5．邮政电信资料：包括邮政和电信运营企业为社会公众提供的各类邮政和电信服务，不含专用网业务资料。邮电业务量按业务种类分为邮政业务量和电信业务量。数据主要来源于北京市邮政公司、中国联合网络通信有限公司北京市分公司、中国移动通信集团北京有限公司、中国铁通集团有限公司北京分公司、中国电信股份有限公司北京分公司。

6．民用汽车拥有量资料：民用汽车指在公安交通管理部门已注册登记领有民用车辆牌照的全部汽车数量。民用汽车根据汽车结构分为载客汽车、载货汽车及其他汽车；根据汽车所有者不同分为私人汽车、单位汽车。民用汽车数据来自于北京市公安局公安交通管理局。

Brief Introduction

I. Main Content

Figures in this chapter show the basic situation of development of transport, post and telecommunication in Beijing.

Transportation statistics include the number of lines, mileage, total volume of transport, turnover and main technological and economic indicators (excluding pipelines) for four transport modes, i.e. railway, highway, civil aviation, and pipeline,; and number of motor vehicles.

Post and telecommunication statistics include: performance of post and telecom services, development level of post and telecommunication sector, and so on.

II. Scope of Survey and Source of Data

1. Data on railways: including the operation of national railways, excluding local railways, railways built by joint ventures, military railways, and dedicated lines and railways built by factories, mines, enterprises and public institutions. These data are from Beijing Railway Bureau.

2. Data on highways: (1) highway mileage covers highways open to traffic at the year end, excluding those under construction and not put into use; (2) highway transport statistics cover all enterprises and public institutions as well as individuals (including self-employed) registered in Beijing for highway cargo transportation. These data are from Beijing Municipal Commission of Transport.

3. Data on pipeline transport: including the length, capacity and completed traffic of pipelines for transport of crude oil, refined oil, natural gas, and other gases. These data are mainly from Beijing Natural Gas Pipelines Co., Ltd. of Sinopec and CNPC. Statistical data on the pipelines transportation business affiliated to Beijing Yanshan Branch were collected and reviewed by the two corporations mentioned above respectively.

4. Data on civil aviation: excluding non-local and foreign airlines flying and operating in Beijing. Statistics consist of the number, mileage, and traffic volume of regular flight lines for domestic transport, transport from and to Hong Kong, Macao and Taiwan, and international transport. Data for 2009 and earlier are sourced from Air China and Xinhua Airline; from 2010, from corporate entities of civil aviation transport in Beijing area.

5. Data on post and telecommunication: including those on postal and telecom services offered by post and telecom operators, excluding data on services of dedicated networks. Business volume falls into two categories, namely postal service and telecommunication service. Data are mainly sourced from Beijing Post and Telecom Company, Beijing Branch of China Unicom, China Mobile Beijing Company, Beijing Branch of China Tietong, and Beijing Branch of China Telecom.

6. Data on number of civil automobiles: civil automobiles refer to all vehicles registered with traffic administration and granted license plates. In terms of automobile structure, civil automobiles consist of passenger automobiles, cargo automobiles, and so on; in terms of ownership, they include private and company ones. These data are sourced from Beijing Traffic Management Bureau.

15-1 交通运输邮电业基本情况(1978-2016年)
TRANSPORT, POST AND TELECOMMUNICATION (1978-2016)

年 份 Year	铁路里程(公里) Railway Mileage (km)	公路里程(公里) Highway Mileage (km)	客运量(万人) Passenger Traffic (10000 persons)	铁 路 Railway	公 路 Highway	民 航 Civil Aviation	货运量(万吨) Freight Traffic (10000 tons)	铁 路 Railway	公 路 Highway	民 航 Civil Aviation	管 道 Pipeline
1978	699	6562	4431	2264	2120	47	7394	3370	4023	1	
1979	700	7278	4777	2504	2220	53	7764	3485	4277	2	
1980	707	7487	5285	2762	2465	58	7571	3356	4213	2	
1981-1985			**33230**	**17688**	**15058**	**484**	**45456**	**15425**	**29063**	**14**	**954**
1981	858	7566	5877	2982	2824	71	8546	3046	5498	2	
1982	858	7683	6215	3205	2931	79	9097	3065	5812	2	218
1983	860	8058	6662	3546	3038	78	9403	3152	6016	3	232
1984	864	8271	7273	3877	3287	109	9671	3133	6301	3	234
1985	876	8482	7203	4078	2978	147	8739	3029	5436	4	270
1986-1990			**38506**	**21290**	**16160**	**1056**	**121771**	**15518**	**104929**	**41**	**1283**
1986	876	8995	7337	4106	3059	172	22121	3030	18794	6	291
1987	876	9103	7763	4418	3117	228	23068	3125	19734	8	201
1988	876	9124	8491	4782	3460	249	24749	3168	21308	9	264
1989	876	9371	7434	4214	3034	186	25184	3144	21767	8	265
1990	876	9648	7480	3770	3490	220	26648	3051	23326	10	262
1991-1995			**40918**	**20615**	**18010**	**2292**	**147385**	**14923**	**131956**	**79**	**427**
1991	876	10259	7704	4036	3378	289	26804	2983	23739	11	71
1992	875	10827	8158	4196	3593	369	27707	2912	24700	14	80
1993	875	11260	7607	4374	2781	452	29865	3048	26730	17	70
1994	875	11532	8537	3992	4008	537	30825	3006	27700	19	99
1995	875	11811	8913	4017	4250	646	32184	2974	29087	17	106
1996-2000			**62554**	**19683**	**38888**	**3983**	**154376**	**13491**	**140455**	**125**	**304**
1996	922	12084	8801	3650	4395	756	32907	2851	29960	18	78
1997	924	12306	9263	3613	4902	748	32351	2883	29360	20	87
1998	924	12498	11228	3762	6704	762	30127	2563	27490	22	52
1999	997	12825	14866	4201	9878	788	28275	2583	25635	30	27
2000	997	13600	18396	4458	13009	929	30717	2612	28010	35	60
2001-2005			**191964**	**25350**	**157061**	**9553**	**156702**	**11053**	**144049**	**277**	**1323**
2001	987	13891	22469	4750	16630	1090	30607	2505	28007	38	57
2002	987	14359	28384	5032	22103	1249	30961	2348	28375	44	194
2003	964	14453	30520	4352	24940	1228	30925	2265	28361	45	254
2004	964	14630	49750	5437	41463	2850	31700	1959	29256	73	412
2005	966	14696	60841	5779	51925	3137	32509	1976	30050	77	406
2006-2010			**435377**	**37892**	**376377**	**21107**	**121931**	**8820**	**106451**	**508**	**6151**
2006	962	20503	12276	6269	2482	3525	33547	1956	30953	89	549
2007	962	20754	20040	6915	9275	3850	20770	1925	17872	98	875
2008	956	20340	128525	7644	117118	3763	21885	1733	18689	93	1369
2009	956	20755	133872	8161	121373	4339	22017	1635	18753	98	1531
2010	956	21114	140663	8903	126130	5630	23712	1572	20184	130	1827
2011-2015			**507504**	**57086**	**417017**	**33402**	**136546**	**5826**	**117312**	**709**	**12700**
2011	1067	21347	145773	9755	129918	6100	26849	1380	23276	132	2061
2012	1115	21492	149037	10315	132333	6389	28650	1232	24925	134	2359
2013	1116	21673	71056	11588	52481	6988	28294	1078	24651	136	2429
2014	1124	21849	71715	12609	52354	6752	29518	1132	25416	149	2821
2015	1124	21885	69924	12821	49931	7172	23236	1004	19044	158	3030
2016	1103	22026	69292	13380	48040	7872	24099	725	19972	163	3239

注：1. 铁路数据为北京市市辖范围，2005年以前取自北京铁路分局，2005年及以后取自北京铁路局。
2. 从2006年开始，公路里程包括村道数据。
3. 2006-2007年公路客运量为持有道路运输经营许可证的客运车辆发生的旅客运输量；从2008年开始，公路客运量根据交通运输部《公路水路运输量专项调查方案》调整旅客运输量统计口径，调整后包括旅游客运、省际客运企业、郊区客运和市郊公交的运输量。2013年公路客运量、公路旅客周转量按照《交通运输部办公厅关于印发公路水路运输量统计试行方案(2014)的通知》，统计范围调整为省际客运、旅游客运和郊区客运，市郊公交不再纳入客运量统计。
4. 从2007年开始，公路货物运输为营业性运量。
5. 民航统计范围为北京地区的民航运输法人单位，不包括在京运输飞行的外省市及外国航空公司。

Note: a) Railway figures are statistics within Beijing's jurisdiction. Figures for years before 2005 were from Beijing Railway Branch, those in and after 2005 were from Beijing Railway Bureau.
b) From 2006, road mileage includes figures of rural roads.
c) In 2006 and 2007, highway passenger traffic refered to numbers of passengers traveled by vehicles with road transportation permit ; From 2008, highway passenger traffic refers to passengers travelled for tourism, cross-provincial, suburban and peri-urban purposes, in line with the adjustments made in Special Survey Program for Highway and Water Way Transportation Volume by the Ministry of Traffic and Transportation. In 2013, according to the Notice by the General Office of the Ministry of Transport on Printing and Issuing Provisional Plan for Counting Highway and Water Way Transportation Volume,the statistical scope of highway passenger traffic and highway passenger turnover was changed to inter-provincial, tourist and suburban transport, and suburban buses are no longer counted.
d) From 2007, highway freight traffic refers to freight for operational purpose.
e) Civil aviation covers legal entities of civil aviation registered in Beijing, excluding airlines of other provinces and other countries with transport and flight in Beijing.

15-1 续表 1 Continued 1

年份 Year	旅客周转量（万人公里）Total Passenger Turnover (10000 passengers-km)	铁路 Railway	公路 Highway	民航 Civil Aviation	货物周转量（万吨公里）Total Freight Turnover (10000 ton-km)	铁路 Railway	公路 Highway	民航 Civil Aviation	管道 Pipeline
1978			59367				92247		
1979			64033				97616		
1980			73692				93899		
1981–1985			**498768**				**540035**		
1981			81879				93254		
1982	755815	641550	90092	24173	3451037	3329450	106767	13530	1290
1983	853655	723200	103742	26713	3794223	3666600	110118	16099	1406
1984	968481	821431	113871	33179	4309798	4171789	115740	20896	1373
1985	1089919	936300	109184	44435	4719663	4576400	114156	27437	1670
1986–1990	**6333894**	**2608550**	**649210**	**3076133**	**13703344**	**11007906**	**2496086**	**191715**	**7637**
1986	1133620	496288	119065	518267	2569579	2133836	405645	28281	1817
1987	1281763	534720	133735	613308	2792589	2282106	471393	37966	1124
1988	1503508	588947	141625	772936	2887270	2344684	498391	42612	1583
1989	1216981	521263	122435	573283	2765660	2179878	546022	38194	1566
1990	1198022	467332	132350	598339	2688246	2067402	574635	44662	1547
1991–1995	**8690001**	**2645880**	**842807**	**5201314**	**15220745**	**11382191**	**3488944**	**346841**	**2769**
1991	1383465	506431	139041	737993	2799731	2153176	591187	54929	439
1992	1666810	531574	161735	973501	2938746	2230406	642200	65614	527
1993	1656130	551392	127461	977277	3143512	2301941	767790	73216	565
1994	1906718	547488	180030	1179200	3107722	2303265	725740	78142	575
1995	2076879	508995	234540	1333344	3231034	2393403	762027	74940	663
1996–2000	**12752549**	**2649587**	**1744526**	**8358436**	**14987253**	**10458031**	**3918017**	**609517**	**1688**
1996	2219196	459514	250488	1509194	3176234	2311011	784888	79983	352
1997	2272177	477538	261204	1533435	3129097	2263274	769190	96202	431
1998	2419787	505554	304592	1609641	2846652	1952602	783237	110470	343
1999	2701471	579759	400597	1721115	2838857	1929269	754264	155171	153
2000	3139918	627222	527645	1985051	2996414	2001875	826438	167691	410
2001–2005	**27318106**	**3454437**	**5282581**	**18581088**	**18786284**	**12470145**	**4130198**	**1121536**	**1064404**
2001	3462571	677146	529776	2255649	3159848	2167201	826437	165832	378
2002	3961623	642676	603510	2715437	3405498	2213728	835873	195792	160105
2003	3933077	619631	693100	2620346	3620777	2409620	789952	208058	213147
2004	7580057	738956	1582441	5258660	4022791	2571459	822992	270182	358158
2005	8380778	776028	1873754	5730996	4577370	3108137	854944	281672	332617
2006–2010	**53738139**	**4632513**	**10259436**	**38846188**	**22812698**	**12714298**	**4414583**	**1906235**	**3777583**
2006	8254536	890691	791947	6571898	4231243	2625719	885991	335693	383840
2007	9603464	908438	1474249	7220776	4490390	2684862	792883	376074	636572
2008	10419977	902281	2409604	7108091	4542168	2535249	840878	356744	809297
2009	11464758	935596	2677144	7852018	4412317	2293902	878887	355257	884271
2010	13995404	995507	2906492	10093405	5136580	2574567	1015944	482467	1063602
2011–2015	**79736122**	**6279416**	**10129420**	**63327285**	**32326572**	**14512331**	**7498424**	**2647241**	**7668576**
2011	15286501	1086609	3036655	11163237	6169272	3113203	1323259	474856	1257955
2012	15957877	1163833	3047757	11746287	6383052	3076143	1397736	489845	1419328
2013	14987719	1179555	1360831	12447333	6809063	3231824	1561929	491861	1523448
2014	16027249	1356313	1382967	13287969	6728238	2843623	1651938	553661	1679016
2015	17476775	1493106	1301210	14682459	6236947	2247538	1563562	637018	1788829
2016	18893132	1508200	1176740	16208192	6713288	2290438	1613192	671413	2138246

15-1 续表 2 Continued 2

年 份 Year	机动车拥有量(万辆) Possession of Motor Vehicles (10000 units)	#民用汽车拥有量 Possession of Civil Motor Vehicles	#私人 Private	邮电业务总量(万元) Business Volume of Post and Telecommunications Service (10000 yuan)	年末固定电话用户数(万户) Number of Fixed Telephone Subscribers (10000 subscribers)	年末移动电话用户数(万户) Number of Mobile Phone Subscribers (10000 subscribers)	固定电话主线普及率(线/百人) Popularization Rate of Landline Telephones (lines/100 persons)	移动电话普及率(户/百人) Popularization Rate of Mobile Phones (subscribers/100 persons)	互联网宽带接入用户数(万户) Subscribers of Broad Band Internet (10000 subscribers)
1978		6.1		24114	7.3		0.8		
1979		7.0		26724	7.8		0.9		
1980		8.1		30047	8.4		0.9		
1981–1985				**204839**					
1981		8.9		31907	9.2		1.0		
1982		9.3		34777	9.8		1.1		
1983		9.8		38525	10.9		1.2		
1984		12.1		45629	12.1		1.3		
1985		16.0		54002	13.6		1.4		
1986–1990				**434582**					
1986		18.6		62079	16.5		1.6		
1987		19.3	0.7	71152	19.5		1.9		
1988		22.2	1.3	84331	23.8		2.2		
1989		24.8	2.4	98124	27.8		2.6		
1990		27.1	2.8	118896	33.3	0.3	3.1	0.03	
1991–1995				**1664508**					
1991		29.7	3.5	157418	39.5	0.7	3.6	0.1	
1992		34.1	4.9	215769	48.0	1.2	4.4	0.1	
1993		41.6	6.7	311251	66.5	3.2	6.0	0.3	
1994		48.1	8.5	418774	100.4	7.7	8.9	0.7	
1995		58.9	12.8	561296	150.5	16.9	12.0	1.4	
1996–2000				**6756754**					
1996		62.2	17.4	729022	195.7	31.0	15.5	2.5	
1997		78.4	29.8	930137	251.2	62.0	20.3	5.0	
1998		89.8	40.7	1290967	313.3	104.2	25.1	8.4	
1999		95.1	44.7	1659133	376.3	186.2	29.9	14.8	
2000	157.8	104.1	49.4	2147496	451.2	347.2	33.1	25.5	
2001–2005				**15331552**					
2001	169.9	114.5	62.4	2182782	525.7	629.4	38.0	45.4	
2002	189.9	133.9	81.1	2540454	585.5	919.5	41.1	64.6	
2003	212.4	163.1	107.1	3040327	682.7	1109.0	46.9	76.1	
2004	229.6	187.1	129.8	3438376	847.8	1340.9	56.8	89.8	
2005	258.3	214.6	154.0	4129614	943.5	1459.8	61.3	94.9	228.9
2006–2010				**40044606**					
2006	287.6	244.1	181.0	5046014	905.2	1571.1	56.5	98.1	281.2
2007	312.8	277.8	212.1	6726273	914.5	1598.3	54.6	95.4	347.2
2008	350.4	318.1	248.3	8008147	884.9	1616.2	50.0	91.3	382.7
2009	401.9	372.1	300.3	9175072	893.1	1825.4	48.0	98.1	451.7
2010	480.9	452.9	374.4	11089100	885.6	2129.8	45.1	108.6	545.6
				(4284217)					
2011–2015				**34291472**					
2011	498.3	473.2	389.7	4878792	883.9	2575.9	43.8	127.6	523.4
2012	520.0	495.7	407.5	5464681	883.1	3168.0	42.7	153.1	572.0
2013	543.7	518.9	426.5	6524689	867.6	3373.8	41.0	159.5	534.7
2014	559.1	532.4	437.2	7511309	831.1	4076.2	38.6	189.4	552.7
2015	561.9	535.0	440.3	9912001	784.7	4051.6	36.2	186.7	491.7
2016	571.7	548.4	452.8	14685910	694.4	3868.7	32.0	178.0	475.5

注：1．邮电业务总量2000年及以前按1990年不变价格计算，2001–2010年按2000年不变价格计算，2011年开始按2010年不变价格计算。表内2010年邮电业务总量是按2000年价格计算，括号内数据是按2010年价格计算。

2．2006–2010年主线普及率和移动电话普及率根据第六次人口普查数据进行了调整。

Note: a) Business volume of post and telecommunications before 2000 was calculated at 1990's constant prices; that of 2001-2010 was calculated at 2000's constant prices; and from 2011, the volume was calculated at 2010's constant prices. In this table, the volume of post and telecommunication service in 2010 was calculated at 2000's price, and figures in () were calculated at 2010's price.

b) Data of popularization rate of landline telephones and mobile phones for 2006-2010 were adjusted based on the results from the 6th population census .

15-2 社会客货运总量(换算周转量) PASSENGER AND FREIGHT TRAFFIC (CONVERTED TURNOVER)

单位：万吨公里 (10000 tons-km)

项目	Item	2016	2015	2016年为2015年% 2016 as % of 2015	构成(%) Composition(%)	
					2016	2015
运输总量	**Total**	**9768407.0**	**9158904.0**	**106.7**	**100.0**	**100.0**
铁路	Railway	3798637.5	3740643.9	101.6	38.9	40.8
公路	Highway	1730866.0	1693683.0	102.2	17.7	18.5
民航	Civil Aviation	2100658.0	1935748.1	108.5	21.5	21.1
管道	Pipeline	2138245.5	1788829.1	119.5	21.9	19.5

15-3 运输线路 TRANSPORTATION ROUTES

项目	Item	条数(条) Number (line)		长度(公里) Length (km)	
		2016	2015	2016	2015
铁路	Railway	56	56	1103.1	1123.6
公路	Highway	9902	9853	22026	21885.0
民航	Civil Aviation				
#中国国际航空公司	Air China	378	360		
中国新华航空有限责任公司	China Xinhua Airlines	459	396		
管道	Pipeline	23	17	4314.0	4058.9

注：铁路长度为营业里程，管道长度为管输里程。
Note: Railway length refers to operating mileage, and pipeline length refers to transportation mileage.

15−4 铁路、民航主要技术经济指标
MAIN TECHNICAL AND ECONOMIC INDICATORS OF RAILWAY AND CIVIL AVIATION

项　目	Item	2016	2015	2016年为2015年% 2016 as % of 2015
铁　路	**Railway**			
内燃机车每万吨公里耗柴油　(千克)	Diesel Consumption of Diesel Locomotives per 10 000 Ton-km (kg)	38.4	36.4	105.5
电力机车每万吨公里耗电　(千瓦小时)	Electricity Consumption of Electric Locomotives per 10000 Ton-km (kWh)	109.8	106.5	103.1
民　航	**Civil Aviation**			
每吨公里耗航空油　(千克)	Aviation-oil Consumption per Ton-km (kg)	0.23	0.28	82.1

15−5 机动车拥有量
NUMBER OF CIVIL MOTOR VEHICLES

单位：万辆　(10000 units)

项　目	Item	2016	2015	2016年为2015年% 2016 as % of 2015
机动车	**Motor Vehicles**	**571.7**	**561.9**	**101.7**
#民用汽车	Civil Automobiles	548.4	535.0	102.5
#载货汽车	Trucks	33.0	30.6	107.8
载客汽车	Passanger Vehicles	509.4	498.1	102.3
#私人汽车	Private Cars	452.8	440.3	102.8
#轿　车	Sedans	316.2	316.5	99.9

资料来源：北京市公安局公安交通管理局。
Source: Beijing Traffic Management Bureau.

15-6 邮电业务主要指标
MAIN INDICATORS OF POST AND TELECOMMUNICATION SERVICE

项目		Item		2016	2015	2016年为2015年% 2016 as % of 2015
邮电业务总量	**(万元)**	**Business Volume of Post and Telecommunications**	**(10000 yuan)**	**14685909.5**	**9912001.3**	**148.2**
邮政业务量		Post		721894.5	678364.7	106.4
电信业务量		Telecommunications		13964015.0	9233636.6	151.2
邮电业务		**Total Amount of Post and Telecommunication Businesses**				
函 件	(万件)	Letters	(10000 pcs)	39243.7	61139.6	64.2
包 件	(万件)	Parcels	(10000 pcs)	257.1	670.4	38.4
特快专递业务量	(万件)	Express Mail Services	(10000 pcs)	196029.0	141447.3	138.6
汇 票	(万件)	Money Orders	(10000 pcs)	194.3	286.7	67.8
订销报纸(累计)	(万份)	Newspapers Subscribed	(10000 copies)	67818.7	70901.5	95.7
订销杂志(累计)	(万份)	Magazines Subscribed	(10000 copies)	2849.2	3526.7	80.8
邮政储蓄期末余额	(亿元)	Post Savings Deposit Balance	(100 million yuan)	812.9	746.9	108.8
长途电话通话量(固定)	(亿分钟)	Long-distance Calls (Fixed-line Telephon	(100 million minutes)	57.7	44.9	128.5
本地电话通话量(固定)	(亿分钟)	Local Calls (Fixed-line Telephone)	(100 million times)	98.3	117.4	83.7
移动电话通话量	(亿分钟)	Calls of Mobile Phones	(100 million minutes)	1529.3	1558.7	98.1
移动短信业务量	(亿条)	Short Message Services	(100 million messages)	541.7	517.2	104.7
年末移动电话用户	(万户)	Mobile Phone Subscribers	(10000 subscribers)	3868.7	4051.6	95.5
年末固定电话用户	(万户)	Fixed Telephone Subscribers	(10000 subscribers)	694.4	784.7	88.5
#住宅电话用户	(万户)	Household Telephone Subscribers	(10000 subscribers)	318.3	417.6	76.2
长途光缆纤芯长度	(芯公里)	Fiber Core Length of Long-distance Optic Cables	(core-km)	217542.0	198183.0	109.8
长途电话交换机容量	(万路端)	Capacity of Long-distance Telephone Exchanges	(10000 roadheads)	45.8	48.7	94.1
局用交换机容量	(万门)	Capacity of Office Telephone Exchanges	(10000 units)	1228.5	1587.4	77.4
移动电话交换机容量	(万户)	Capacity of Mobile Phone Exchanges	(10000 subscribers)	5230.0	5102.0	102.5
固定电话主线普及率	(线/百人)	Popularization Rate of Fixed-line Telephones	(lines/100 persons)	32.0	36.2	88.3
移动电话普及率	(户/百人)	Popularization Rate of Mobile Phones	(subscribers/100 persons)	178.0	186.7	95.4
固定互联网宽带接入用户数	(万户)	Subscribers of Broad Band Internet	(10000 subscribers)	475.5	491.7	96.7
互联网上网人数	(万人)	Number of Internet Users	(10000 persons)	1690.0	1647.0	102.6

注：1．邮电业务总量为2010年不变价计算。
2．“互联网上网人数”来源于中国互联网络信息中心(CNNIC)发布的《中国互联网络发展状况统计报告》。
3．从2013年开始，特快专递业务量填报范围扩大为取得快递业务经营许可企业及其备案分支机构。

Note: a) Business volume of post and telecommunications is calculated based on constant price in 2010.
b) “Number of Internet Users” was sourced from the Statistical Report on Internet Development in China issued by CNNIC.
c) Since 2013, enterprises permitted to conduct express delivery businesses and their filed branches are required to submit the business volume of Express Mail Services.

主要统计指标解释

货（客）运量 指在一定时期内，各种运输工具实际运送的货物（旅客）数量。是反映运输业为国民经济和人民生活服务的数量指标，也是制定和检查运输生产计划，研究运输发展规模和速度的重要指标。货运按吨计算，客运按人计算。货物不论运输距离长短，货物类别，均按实际重量统计；旅客不论行程远近或票价多少，均按一人一次作为客运量统计。半价票、小孩票也按一人统计。

货物（旅客）周转量 指在一定时期内，由各种运输工具运送的货物（旅客）数量与其相应运输距离的乘积之总和，是反映运输业生产总成果的重要指标，也是编制和检查运输生产计划、计算运输效率、劳动生产率以及核算运输单位的主要基础资料。计算货物周转量通常按发出站与到达站之间的最短距离，也就是计费距离计算。

邮电业务总量 是以货币形式表示的邮政电信企业为社会提供各类邮政通信服务的总数量。计算公式为：

$$\text{邮电业务总量} = \sum\left(\begin{array}{l}\text{各类邮政通信业务量} \times \text{不变} \\ \text{单价}\end{array}\right) + \text{出租代维及其他业务收入}$$

函件 是指邮政部门为用户传递以书面信息为主的邮件，包括信件、印刷品和邮送广告。

包件 指符合包裹准寄范围，通过邮政渠道寄递的物品。包括国内普通包裹、国内快递包裹、国际及港澳台包裹。

长途电话交换机容量 是指用于接入长途电话网的电话交换机的设备额定容量。

局用交换机容量 是指安装在本地电信企业内用于接续本地固定电话的电话交换机容量。包括现用和备用的人工或自动交换机（含远端模块）的全部容量，包括接入网设备容量。

移动电话交换机容量 分为 GSM、CDMA 两种。指移动电话交换机根据一定话务模型和交换机处理能力计算出来的最大同时服务用户的数量。

固定电话主线普及率 是指报告期行政区域常住人口中，平均每百人拥有的固定电话主线数。计算公式为：

$$\text{固定电话主线普及率} = \frac{\text{电话主线数（本地电话用户）}}{\text{行政区域常住人口数}}$$

移动电话普及率 是指报告期行政区域常住人口中，平均每百人拥有的移动电话的用户数。计算公式为：

$$\text{移动电话普及率} = \frac{\text{移动电话用户总数}}{\text{行政区域常住人口数}}$$

固定互联网宽带接入用户数 指报告期末在电信企业登记注册，通过 xDSL、FTTx+LAN 以及其他宽带接入方式和普通专线接入公众互联网的用户。

Explanatory Notes on Main Statistical Indicators

Freight (Passenger) Traffic refers to the volume of freight (passenger) transported with various means during a certain period of time. It is a quantitative measure to show how the transport industry serves the national economy and people's life, and is also an important indicator for preparing and reviewing transport plan and studying the development scale and speed of the transport industry. Freight transport is calculated in tons and passenger traffic is calculated in the number of persons. Regardless of the types or traveling distance of freight, freight transport is calculated in the actual weight of goods: and regardless of the traveling distance or ticket price, passenger traffic is calculated following the principle that one person can be counted only once in one travel. The passenger who travels with a half-price ticket or a child ticket is also calculated as one person.

Freight (Passenger) Turnover refers to the sum of the transported cargo (passengers) multiplied by the transport distance during a certain period of time. This is an important indicator to show the total results of the transport industry, and also serves as main basic data for preparing and reviewing transport plans and measuring transport efficiency, labor productivity and the transport unit. Freight Turnover is usually calculated by the shortest distance between the departure station and the arrival station, namely the charging distance.

Business Volume of Post and Telecommunications refers to the total amount of post and telecommunication services, expressed in monetary terms, provided by the post and telecommunication sectors for the society. The formula is as follows:

Business Volume of Post and Telecommunications= ∑(Transactions of Post and Telecommunication Service x Constant Price) + Income from Leasing, Maintenance and other Services

Correspondences mean mails mainly in the form of written information delivered by postal authorities, including letters, prints and delivered advertisements.

Parcels means articles permitted for mailing, and mailed through postal channels, including domestic express parcels, international parcels, and parcels from and to Hong Kong, Macao and Taiwan.

Capacity of Long-distance Phone Exchanges means the rated capacity of phone exchangers used for connecting to the long-distance phone network.

Capacity of Local Exchanges means the capacity of phone exchangers installed in local telecom businesses and used for linking local fixed telephones. It is the sum of all capacity of existing and backup manual or automatic exchangers (with far-end modules), including the capacity of network access equipment.

Capacity of Mobile Phone Exchanges, divided into GSM and CDMA, means the maximum number of users receiving services simultaneously from mobile phone exchangers, calculated from certain traffic model and exchanger processing capacity.

Popularization Rate of Fixed-line Telephones means the average number of main lines of fixed-line telephones owned per one hundred persons of permanent population in administrative areas in the reporting period. It is calculated with the following formula:

Popularization Rate of Landline= Number of Main Lines of Telephone (Local Phone Users) / Number of Permanent Population in Administrative Areas

Popularization Rate of Mobile Phones means the average number of mobile phones owned per 100 persons among permanent population in administrative areas in the reporting period. It is calculated with the following formula:

Popularization Rate of Mobile Phones = Total Number of Mobile Phone Users / Permanent Population in Administrative Areas

Subscribers of Broadband Internet means subscribers registered at telecom companies to connect with public Internet through xDSL, FTTx+LAN as well as other broadband connections and general special lines at the end of reporting period.

北京统计年鉴2017　BEIJING STATISTICAL YEARBOOK

批发和零售业、住宿和餐饮业

WHOLESALE AND RETAIL TRADE, ACCOMMODATION AND RESTAURANTS

简要说明

一、本章资料的主要内容

本章资料反映北京市商品流通市场发展及批发和零售业、住宿和餐饮业经营情况。主要内容有社会消费品零售总额；批发和零售业商品购进、销售、库存总值、商品分类销售情况及主要商品销售情况；住宿业和餐饮业经营情况；限额以上批发和零售业、住宿业和餐饮业财务状况；连锁企业基本情况；商品交易市场基本情况、成交额；北京消费者信心指数。

二、本章的统计范围

社会消费品零售总额指标于1993年、1997年和2003年做了较大调整。1993年起不再包括对农民的农业生产资料；1997年起不再包括居民购买住房；2003年起不再包括由各种经济类型的制造业法人企业、产业活动单位直接售给城乡居民（包括本企业职工）和社会集团的商品以及农民对非农业居民的零售额。

限额以上批发和零售业、住宿业和餐饮业统计限额标准：2008年以前，批发业为年销售额2000万元及以上；零售业为年销售额500万元及以上；住宿业为星级饭店和星级以外年营业收入500万元及以上；餐饮业为年营业额200万元及以上。2008年调整后，批发业为年主营业务收入2000万元及以上；零售业为年主营收入500万元及以上；住宿业为星级饭店和星级以外年主营业务收入200万元及以上；餐饮业为年主营业务收入200万元及以上。

北京消费者信心指数调查范围覆盖全市16个区。

三、本章的资料来源

本章资料中所有资料均由北京市统计局提供。

四、本章的统计调查方法

限额以上批发和零售业、住宿和餐饮业单位采用全面调查；连锁企业、商品交易市场采取全数调查；限额以下批发和零售业、住宿和餐饮业法人单位及个体户采用抽样调查。

北京消费者信心指数调查采用计算机辅助电话方式调查，调查对象为居住在北京市半年以上18-65周岁的城乡居民。

五、有关统计标准的变化说明

2010年以前企业大中小型划分执行2003年《统计上大中小型企业划分办法（暂行）》标准；自2011年开始，大中小微型企业划分标准执行国家统计局《关于统计上大中小微型企业划分办法》（国统字[2011]75号）。

六、本章中关于历史数据调整的问题

按照国家统计局统一要求和统一方法，本章中1978年至2003年的社会消费品零售总额数据，根据第一次经济普查结果，采用“速度推算法”进行了修正，2004年数据为第一次经济普查数据；2005-2007年数据根据第二次经济普查结果，采用“趋势离差法”进行了修正，2008年数据为第二次经济普查数据；2009-2012年数据根据第三次经济普查结果进行了修正，2013年数据为第三次经济普查数据。

Brief Introduction

I. Main Content

Statistics in this chapter show the development of commodity circulation market and the operations of wholesale and retail trades, accommodation and restaurants. Figures mainly include retail sales of consumer goods, total value of commodity purchase, sales and inventory in wholesale and retail trades, sales of commodities by category, and sales of main commodities; operation situation of accommodation and restaurants; financial status of wholesale, retail, accommodation and restaurants enterprises above designated size; basic situation of chain businesses; basic situation and turnover of commodity transaction markets, and trading volume of main commodities; and settlement of consumer complaints; and consumer confidence index.

II. Scope of Statistics

Major adjustments were made to the indicators of Retail Sales of Consumer Goods for 1993, 1997 and 2003. From 1993, the indicator did not cover agricultural means of production for farmers any longer; from 1997, it did not cover houses bought by residents any longer; from 2003, it did not cover goods sold by corporate manufacturing enterprises and industrial activity entities of various economic types to urban and rural residents (including enterprises' own employees) and social groups as well as retail sales by farmers to non-agricultural residents any longer.

As for standards for wholesale and retail trades, accommodation and restaurants above designated size, before 2008, for wholesale trades, the standard was annual sales of RMB 20 million and above; for retail trades, annual sales of RMB 5 million and above; for accommodation, star-rated hotels and non-star-rated hotels with annual turnover of RMB 5 million and above; for restaurants, annual turnover of RMB 2 million and above. After adjustments were made in 2008, the designated size is, for whole sale trades, annual sales of RMB 20 million and above; for retail trades, annual sales of RMB 5 million and above; for accommodation, star-rated hotels and non-star-rated hotels with annual main business income of RMB 2 million and above; for restaurants, annual main business income of RMB 2 million and above.

Survey of consumer confidence index covers 16 districts in the City.

III. Source of Data

Data in settlement are all sourced from Beijing Municipal Bureau of Statistics.

IV. Survey Methodology

The method of comprehensive survey was used for statistics of wholesale and retail trades, accommodation, and restaurants service enterprises above designated size; complete enumeration was used for chain businesses, and commodity trading markets; sample survey was used for wholesale and retail trades, accommodation, and restaurants corporate enterprises below designated size as well as self-employed businesses.

Statistics on consumer confidence index were obtained through computer-aided phone calls to urban and rural residents at 18-65 who have been living in Beijing for more than half a year.

V. Changes in Relevant Statistical Standards

Before 2010，the classification of small, medium and large-sized enterprises should comply with the standard of *Measures for Statistical Classification of Small, Medium and Large-sized Enterprises (Temporary)* 2003. Since 2011, the classification of micro, small, medium and large-sized enterprises has been in line with standards of Circular by National Bureau of Statistics on Printing and Issuing the *Measures for Statistical Classification of Micro, Small, Medium and Large-sized Enterprises* (G.T.Z. [2011] No. 75).

VI. Adjustment to Historical Data

In accordance with the unified requirements and methods put forward by the National Bureau of Statistics, data for 1978-2003 on retail sales of consumer goods were adjusted with the "speed calculation method" according to the first economic census results in 2004. Data for 2004 are gathered from the first economic census. Data for 2005-2007 were revised with the "trend deviation method" in accordance with the second economic census results in 2008. Data for 2008 are gathered from the second economic census. Data for 2009-2012 were revised with the "trend deviation method" in accordance with the third economic census results in 2013. Data for 2013 were gathered from the third economic census.

16–1 历年社会消费品零售总额(1978–2016年)
TOTAL RETAIL SALES OF CONSUMER GOODS (1978-2016)

单位：亿元 (100 million yuan)

年份 Year	社会消费品零售总额 Total Retail Sales of Consumer Goods	按商品类别分 By Category of Commodity			
		吃类商品 Food	穿类商品 Clothing	用类商品 Daily Supplies	烧类商品 Fuels
1978	44.2	18.0	8.9	16.0	1.3
1979	53.3	20.8	11.3	19.7	1.5
1980	62.8	24.9	13.4	22.9	1.6
1981–1985	**472.7**	**180.9**	**85.1**	**196.2**	**10.5**
1981	70.7	28.0	14.5	26.5	1.7
1982	75.4	29.7	13.7	30.3	1.7
1983	86.4	34.0	15.7	34.8	1.9
1984	105.8	39.6	18.7	45.2	2.3
1985	134.4	49.6	22.5	59.4	2.9
1986–1990	**1239.8**	**494.9**	**166.7**	**551.8**	**26.4**
1986	155.0	60.7	22.8	68.0	3.5
1987	188.9	77.4	27.4	80.2	3.9
1988	256.0	100.6	36.0	114.9	4.5
1989	294.8	119.4	34.9	134.1	6.4
1990	345.1	136.8	45.6	154.6	8.1
1991–1995	**3239.5**	**1261.4**	**481.3**	**1422.2**	**74.6**
1991	408.3	158.2	53.7	187.6	8.8
1992	503.0	193.6	66.9	230.5	12.0
1993	611.2	220.7	96.5	277.6	16.4
1994	766.6	283.2	125.3	338.6	19.5
1995	950.4	405.7	138.9	387.9	17.9
1996–2000	**6811.7**	**2177.0**	**858.9**	**3576.5**	**199.3**
1996	1061.6	427.5	152.5	461.8	19.8
1997	1208.5	447.9	161.6	565.6	33.4
1998	1373.6	399.8	167.2	764.2	42.4
1999	1509.3	430.4	178.8	852.9	47.2
2000	1658.7	471.4	198.8	932.0	56.5
2001–2005	**11671.8**	**3061.2**	**1218.6**	**6722.7**	**669.3**
2001	1831.4	528.7	221.9	1016.9	63.9
2002	2005.2	540.2	219.9	1167.4	77.7
2003	2296.9	596.4	252.3	1356.4	91.8
2004	2626.6	644.9	242.1	1538.3	201.3
2005	2911.7	751.0	282.4	1643.7	234.6
2006–2010	**23503.8**	**5388.2**	**2126.1**	**14130.0**	**1859.5**
2006	3295.3	818.8	314.7	1852.6	309.2
2007	3835.2	940.4	359.3	2205.2	330.3
2008	4645.5	1073.3	411.7	2799.4	361.1
2009	5387.5	1201.0	482.2	3319.6	384.7
2010	6340.3	1354.7	558.2	3953.2	474.2
2011–2015	**44193.8**	**9029.0**	**3785.2**	**28590.4**	**2789.2**
2011	7222.2	1636.6	712.7	4310.0	562.9
2012	8123.5	1759.9	769.3	4999.5	594.8
2013	8872.1	1804.7	777.1	5711.1	579.2
2014	9638.0	1860.5	783.3	6413.5	580.7
2015	10338.0	1967.3	742.8	7156.3	471.6
2016	11005.1	2296.7	781.5	7424.1	502.8

16−2 社会消费品零售总额(2010−2016年) TOTAL RETAIL SALES OF CONSUMER GOODS (2010-2016)

单位：亿元 (100 million yuan)

项　目	Item	2010	2011	2012	2013	2014	2015	2016	2016年为2015年% 2016 as % of 2015
社会消费品零售总额	**Total Retail Sales of Consumer Goods**	**6340.3**	**7222.2**	**8123.5**	**8872.1**	**9638.0**	**10338.0**	**11005.1**	**106.5**
按商品类别分	**By Category of Commodity**								
吃类商品	Food	1354.7	1636.6	1759.9	1804.7	1860.5	1967.3	2296.7	105.4
穿类商品	Clothing	558.2	712.7	769.3	777.1	783.3	742.8	781.5	102.1
用类商品	Daily Supplies	3953.2	4310.0	4999.5	5711.1	6413.5	7156.3	7424.1	107.4
烧类商品	Fuels	474.2	562.9	594.8	579.2	580.7	471.6	502.8	104.4
按销售单位所在地分	**By Location of Seller**								
城　镇	Urban	6238.0	7106.1	7995.1	8721.0	9471.5	10162.8	10776.1	106.4
农　村	Rural	102.3	116.1	128.4	151.1	166.5	175.2	229.0	108.7
按消费品形态分	**By Form of Consumer Goods**								
餐饮收入	Food and Beverage Income	678.5	817.8	880.2	836.1	829.7	846.8	918.2	104.0
商品零售	Retail Sales of Commodities	5661.8	6404.4	7243.3	8036.0	8808.3	9491.2	10086.9	106.7

16−3 按登记注册类型分限额以上批发和零售企业商品零售额(2016年) RETAIL SALES OF GOODS IN WHOLESALE AND RETAIL ENTERPRISES ABOVE DESIGNATED SIZE BY REGISTRATION TYPE (2016)

单位：万元 (10000 yuan)

项　目	Item	合计 Total Sales	批发业 Wholesale	零售业 Retail Trade
总　计	**Total**	**77093821**	**6288282**	**70805539**
内资企业	Domestic Funded Enterprises	61821954	5119786	56702168
#国　有	State-owned Enterprises	1039789	57394	982395
集　体	Collectively-owned Enterprises	336402	4514	331888
股份有限公司	Companies Limited by Shares	8622110	1331975	7290135
港澳台商投资企业	Hong Kong, Macao and Taiwan-invested Enterprises	5424842	480395	4944447
外商投资企业	Foreign-invested Enterprises	9847025	688101	9158924

注：本表统计范围为限额以上批发和零售业法人单位、产业活动单位和个体经营户。
Note: Figures in this table cover legal entities in wholesale and retail trade above designated size, activity entities and individual entities .

16-4 批发和零售业商品购进、销售、库存情况
TOTAL VALUE OF PURCHASES, SALES AND INVENTORY OF COMMODITIES IN WHOLESALE AND RETAIL TRADE

单位：万元 (10000 yuan)

项 目	Item	2016	2015	2016年为2015年% 2016 as % of 2015
商品购进额	**Total Purchases of Commodities**	**563497059**	**566605298**	**99.5**
市内购进	In the City	156498073	156727808	99.9
市外购进	From Outside Beijing	332373868	334274499	99.4
进 口	Imported	74625118	75602991	98.7
商品销售额	**Total Sales of Commodities**	**617373843**	**607250902**	**101.7**
批发额	**Wholesale**	**519166946**	**515667760**	**100.7**
市内批发	In the City	165804162	162725943	101.9
市外批发	To Outside Beijing	333159866	329501316	101.1
出 口	Exported	20202918	23440501	86.2
零售额	**Retail**	**98206897**	**91583142**	**107.2**
期末商品库存额	**Inventory (Year-end)**	**54275844**	**54584652**	**99.4**

注：本表统计范围为批发和零售业法人单位、产业活动单位和个体经营户。
Note: Figures in this table cover legal entities in wholesale and retail trade above designated size, activity entities and individual entities.

16-5 限额以上批发和零售业商品购进、销售、库存情况(2016年)
TOTAL VALUE OF PURCHASES, SALES AND INVENTORY IN WHOLESALE AND RETAIL ENTERPRISES ABOVE DESIGNATED SIZE (2016)

单位：万元 (10000 yuan)

项 目	Item	合计 Total Sales	批发业 Wholesale	零售业 Retail
商品购进额	**Total Purchases of Commodities**	**515137774**	**432664834**	**82472940**
市内购进	In the City	112377396	78189035	34188362
市外购进	From Outside Beijing	321654311	275375981	46278331
进 口	Imported	81106067	79099819	2006248
商品销售额	**Total Sales of Commodities**	**548665725**	**461459997**	**87205728**
批发额	**Wholesale**	**471571904**	**455171715**	**16400189**
市内批发	In the City	130246922	121514435	8732487
市外批发	To Outside Beijing	318423776	311049817	7373959
出 口	Exported	22901207	22607463	293743
零售额	**Retail**	**77093821**	**6288282**	**70805539**
期末商品库存额	**Inventory (Year-end)**	**54826449**	**48395299**	**6431150**

注：本表统计范围为限额以上批发和零售业法人单位、产业活动单位和个体经营户。
Note: Figures in this table cover legal entities in wholesale and retail trade above designated size, activity entities and individual entities.

16-6 限额以上批发和零售业商品销售类值(2016年)
SALES BY CATEGORY FOR WHOLESALE AND RETAIL ENTERPRISES ABOVE DESIGNATED SIZE (2016)

单位：万元 (10000 yuan)

项目	Item	商品销售额 Total Sales	批发额 Wholesale	零售额 Retail
合计	**Total**	**548665725**	**471571904**	**77093821**
粮油、食品类	Cereal, Oil and Food	25307123	19327016	5980108
#粮油类	Cereal and Oil	11774605	10914921	859684
肉禽蛋类	Meat, Poultry and Eggs	2967821	2020717	947104
饮料类	Beverages	4403818	3746385	657434
烟酒类	Tobacco and Liquor	10455495	9032193	1423302
服装鞋帽、针、纺织品类	Clothing, Shoes, Hats and Textiles	10971114	4685626	6285488
服装类	Clothing	7171679	2308103	4863576
鞋帽类	Shoes and Hats	2279680	1208487	1071193
针、纺织品类	Knitwear and Textiles	1512472	1168568	343904
化妆品类	Cosmetics	3037794	1266131	1771663
金银珠宝类	Gold, Silver and Jewelry	12620416	10248569	2371848
日用品类	Articles for Daily Use	9491684	5494781	3996904
#儿童玩具类	Children's Toys	219631	101425	118206
五金、电料类	Hardware and Electrical Materials	1123195	1001254	121941
体育、娱乐用品类	Sports and Recreation Goods	7461091	6388181	1072910
书报、杂志类	Newspapers and Magazines	2051921	1185873	866048
电子出版物及音像制品类	E-Journals and Video Products	488409	218144	270265
家用电器和音像器材类	Household Appliances and Audiovisual Products	20040088	15478976	4561112
中西药品类	Traditional Chinese and Western Medicines	19197380	14979987	4217393
#西药类	Western Medicines	13046493	10051839	2994654
中草药及中成药类	Chinese Herbal Medicines and Chinese Patent Medicines	3494894	2382038	1112856
文化、办公用品类	Cultural and Office Goods	29860209	24409609	5450600
家具类	Furniture	1322308	217564	1104745
通讯器材类	Communication Devices	55452279	45482274	9970005
煤炭及制品类	Coal and Coal Products	26202788	26145542	57247
木材及制品类	Wood and Wooden Products	3268893	3268893	
石油及制品类	Petroleum and Its Products	55733211	50969139	4764072
化工材料及制品类	Raw Chemical Materials	54246159	54246159	
#化肥类	Fertilizer	7447293	7447293	
金属材料类	Metal Materials	67004892	67004892	
建筑及装潢材料类	Building and Decoration Materials	2835531	2554015	281516
机电产品及设备类	Electric-mechanic Products and Equipment	23622057	23120436	501621
#农机类	Agricultural Machinery	232269	232269	
汽车类	Automobiles	78926586	58723358	20203228
种子饲料类	Seed and Feedstuff	1689263	1689263	
棉麻类	Cotton and Hemp	1856189	1856189	
其他类	Others	19995832	18831459	1164372

注：本表统计范围为限额以上批发和零售业法人单位、产业活动单位和个体经营户。

Note: Figures in this table cover legal entities in wholesale and retail trade above designated size, activity entities and individual entities .

16-7 限额以上批发和零售业商品销售情况(2016年) COMMODITY SALES OF WHOLESALE AND RETAIL ENTERPRISES ABOVE DESIGNATED SIZE (2016)

项目		Item		商品销售量 Total Sales	批发量 Wholesale Volume	零售量 Retail Volume
大米(稻米)	(百公斤)	Rice	(100 kg)	18560785	16589083	1971702
白面(小麦面)	(百公斤)	Flour (Wheat Flour)	(100 kg)	3658122	2846456	811667
杂粮	(百公斤)	Coarse Cereals	(100 kg)	71894258	71567934	326324
食用植物油	(百公斤)	Edible Vegetable Oil	(100 kg)	49492665	48181594	1311072
猪肉	(百公斤)	Pork	(100 kg)	3841767	3015210	826557
牛肉	(百公斤)	Beef	(100 kg)	941429	779348	162081
羊肉	(百公斤)	Mutton	(100 kg)	306073	218349	87725
禽肉	(百公斤)	Poultry	(100 kg)	3249175	2954387	294788
鲜蛋	(百公斤)	Fresh Eggs	(100 kg)	1331552	687315	644237
鲜菜	(百公斤)	Fresh Vegetable	(100 kg)	7197040	2937550	4259490
鲜瓜果	(百公斤)	Fresh Melons and Fruits	(100 kg)	5472070	2589230	2882840
水产品	(百公斤)	Aquatic Products	(100 kg)	5194930	4669030	525900
食糖	(百公斤)	Sugar	(100 kg)	47827920	46251110	1576810
卷烟	(万支)	Cigarettes	(10000 units)	9384966	8931790	453176
酒	(百升)	Wine	(100 liter)	69409463	67179909	2229553
#白酒	(百升)	Distillate Spirit	(100 liter)	5757688	4467270	1290418
啤酒	(百升)	Beer	(100 liter)	62861942	62244757	617185
数码照相机	(台)	Digital Cameras	(unit)	12731834	11814177	917657
彩色电视机	(台)	Color TV Sets	(unit)	11734638	7423566	4311072
数码摄像机	(台)	Digital Video Cameras	(unit)	2383106	2363117	19989
电冰箱(家用电冰箱)	(台)	Household Refrigerators	(unit)	4304228	3152774	1151454
洗衣机(家用洗衣机)	(台)	Household Washing Machines	(unit)	6838961	5650531	1188430
家用空调器(房间空调器)	(台)	Household Air Conditioners (Room Air Conditioners)	(unit)	9894652	7722506	2172146
电脑(微型计算机)	(台)	Computers (Micro Computers)	(unit)	27862228	20510222	7352006
移动电话机	(部)	Mobile Phones	(unit)	273786276	214970441	58815835
钢材	(吨)	Steel Products	(ton)	89758364	89758364	
水泥	(吨)	Cement	(ton)	40773355	40690436	82919
汽车	(辆)	Motor Vehicles	(unit)	2829625	1938268	891357
#轿车	(辆)	Sedan Cars	(unit)	2219646	1492937	726709
化学肥料	(吨)	Chemical Fertilizers	(ton)	58667350	58667350	
化学农药	(吨)	Chemical Pesticides	(ton)	431876	431876	
铜	(吨)	Copper	(ton)	8515222	8515222	
铝	(吨)	Aluminium	(ton)	6807962	6807962	

注：本表统计范围为限额以上批发和零售业法人单位、产业活动单位和个体经营户。
Note: Figures in this table cover legal entities in wholesale and retail trade above designated size, activity entities and individual entities .

16-8 限额以上住宿和餐饮业经营情况(2016年)
STATISTICS FOR ACCOMMODATION AND RESTAURANTS ABOVE DESIGNATED SIZE (2016)

项　　目	Item	合　计 Total	住宿业 Accommodation Industry	餐饮业 Catering Industry
客房数　(间)	**Number of Rooms　(room)**	**234171**	**228182**	**5989**
床位数　(个)	**Number of Beds　(unit)**	**385892**	**375311**	**10581**
餐位数　(位)	**Number of Tables　(table)**	**1420529**	**332820**	**1087709**
营业额　(万元)	**Turnover　(10000 yuan)**	**10409925**	**4528374**	**5881550**
客房收入	Income from Rooms	2502933	2463091	39842
餐费收入	Income from Money	6821019	1205905	5615114
商品销售额	Sales of Commodities	128894	42415	86479
其他收入	Other Incomes	957080	816964	140115

注：本表统计范围为限额以上住宿和餐饮业法人单位、产业活动单位和个体经营户。
Note:This table covers legal entities in accommodation and restaurants above designated size, activity entities and individual entities .

16-9 限额以上批发和零售企业财务状况(2016年)

单位：万元

项 目	Item	企业单位个数(个) Number of Enterprises (unit)	资产总计 Total Assets	流动资产合计 Total Current Assets
合　计	**Total**	**6010**	**397326956**	**274231081**
按隶属关系分	**By Affiliation**			
中　央	Central	433	161666892	95772951
地　方	Local	5577	235660064	178458130
按企业登记注册类型分	**By Registration Type**			
内　资	Domestically-invested Enterprises	5510	313271312	209723483
国　有	State-owned Enterprises	222	31417355	22796756
集　体	Collectively-owned Enterprises	56	997080	512517
股份合作	Joint-equity Cooperative Enterprises	43	160261	106363
联　营	Associate Enterprises	***	***	***
有限责任公司	Limited Liability Companies	2191	203497995	137396759
股份有限公司	Companies Limited by Shares	140	44454910	21710958
私　营	Private Enterprises	2854	32734166	27192029
其　他	Other	***	***	***
港澳台商投资	Hong Kong, Macao and Taiwan-invested Enterprises	187	20623808	15373422
外商投资	Foreign-invested Enterprises	313	63431836	49134176
按国民经济行业分	**By Sector**			
批发业	**Wholesale**	**4090**	**352129965**	**240406945**
农、林、牧产品批发	Wholesale of Agriculture, Forestry and Animal Production and Hunting Products	94	19421256	9786831
食品、饮料及烟草制品批发	Wholesale of Foods, Beverage and Tobaccos	368	16059333	12459121
纺织、服装及家庭日用品批发	Wholesale of Textile, Clothes and Household Commodities	363	19623473	14989123
文化、体育用品及器材批发	Wholesale of Cultural and Sports Goods and Equipment	196	9880574	6789955
医药及医疗器材批发	Wholesale of Medicine and Medical Devices	509	15001414	11793620
矿产品、建材及化工产品批发	Wholesale of Mineral Products, Building Materials, and Chemical Products	1282	157389236	98438238
机械设备、五金交电及电子产品批发	Wholesale of Mechanical Equipment, Hardware and Electronic Products	1133	88101379	67190356
贸易经纪与代理	Trade Broker and Agent	65	16250493	13463153
其他批发	Others	80	10402807	5496549
零售业	**Retail**	**1920**	**45196991**	**33824136**
综合零售	Integrated Retail	203	13675253	8538952
食品、饮料及烟草制品专门零售	Special Retails of Foods, Beverage and Tobacoos	89	897420	640777
纺织、服装及日用品专门零售	Special Retail of Textile, Clothing and Domestic Commodities	157	1988817	1553277
文化、体育用品及器材专门零售	Special Retail of Cultural and Sports Goods and Equipment	130	3611619	2816428
医药及医疗器材专门零售	Special Retail of Medicine and Medical Devices	92	3488230	2073923
汽车、摩托车、燃料及零配件专门零售	Special Retail of Automobiles, Motorcycles, Fuels and Their Accessories	788	10216276	8084725
家用电器及电子产品专门零售	Special Retail of Household Electrical Appliances and Electronic Products	256	8579286	7913385
五金、家具及室内装修材料专门零售	Special Retail of Hardware, Furniture and Indoor Decoration Materials	66	745418	557858
货摊、无店铺及其他零售业	Stand Retail, Retail Without Shops and Other Retail	139	1994672	1644811
按规模划分	**By Size**			
#大中型企业	Medium-and Large-sized Enterprises	3114	344548520	230467564

FINANCIAL STATUS OF WHOLESALE AND RETAIL ENTERPRISES ABOVE DESIGNATED SIZE (2016)

(10000 yuan)

资产负债 Assets and Liabilities							
#应收账款 Accounts Receivable	固定资产合计 Total Fixed Assets	固定资产原价 Total Original Value of Fixed Assets	负债合计 Total Liabilities	#流动负债合计 Total Current Liabilities	#应付账款 Accounts Payable	所有者权益合计 Total Owner's Equity	#实收资本 Paid-up Capital
47404057	**9686847**	**15997692**	**266300378**	**231325396**	**60677855**	**131026578**	**57703573**
18250188	2365909	3771496	100802843	84788307	20410425	60864049	21955502
29153870	7320938	12226196	165497535	146537089	40267430	70162529	35748072
40145969	8081901	12726863	213922506	182994642	44706144	99348806	45622735
2937274	840741	1365818	20784207	17895323	2714739	10633148	4327521
97293	94100	150032	747655	538252	189745	249425	77588
13820	41555	47107	137424	136892	22624	22836	32908
***	***	***	***	***	***	***	***
26597428	4875696	7475943	140791075	121965110	32168961	62706920	30906043
2893298	1037320	1864826	25092726	17948221	3041594	19362184	5817581
7605282	1191252	1820993	26361721	24503146	6564855	6372446	4459240
***	***	***	***	***	***	***	***
1704411	689250	1250669	14186540	13249317	5352355	6437268	4263670
5553677	915696	2020160	38191331	35081436	10619356	25240505	7817169
44126778	**6597614**	**10531683**	**231856382**	**200518519**	**53450221**	**120273584**	**51476409**
444485	285489	427529	12513617	10752656	1233732	6907639	2878136
1280024	502982	867819	12021434	11391430	2197847	4037900	2208772
1271256	419240	632364	13056526	12669524	5125196	6566947	3923807
1284811	367052	469016	6602835	5512696	756091	3277739	1455298
4576050	287806	585866	10331951	9548831	4321190	4669463	1897370
18063112	2992046	4542312	99498689	82135451	17692893	57890547	25172562
10932112	1497738	2622956	56199506	51575590	14019169	31901873	11077661
5357675	155296	234783	12951093	12380718	7226418	3299400	1977336
917253	89966	149038	8680730	4551623	877685	1722077	885467
3277279	**3089233**	**5466009**	**34443996**	**30806877**	**7227634**	**10752995**	**6227164**
372363	1474900	2582167	9704189	7774167	2160393	3971063	1904506
49258	157664	266557	446773	430899	152491	450647	155189
346715	123699	249056	1655411	1501867	490521	333406	459383
182752	149088	211037	2675692	2479865	656163	935927	357829
509020	31399	66752	2804377	2723923	480956	683853	203552
453067	905565	1625127	8191914	7912329	717766	2024362	1776033
858604	98204	192556	5562118	4645277	789368	3017167	742528
31884	94676	163928	580232	552712	126083	165187	161271
473616	54038	108829	2823290	2785838	1653894	-828618	466873
39124709	7814047	13389356	227113653	197059673	52688561	117434867	44310571

16-9 续表

单位：万元

项目	Item	损益 营业收入 Business Income	#主营业务收入 Main Business Income	营业成本 Business Cost	#主营业务成本 Main Business Cost
合计	**Total**	**464276021**	**455229643**	**425895402**	**420585410**
按隶属关系分	**By Affiliation**				
中央	Central	149475951	145449764	142662137	139024010
地方	Local	314800070	309779879	283233265	281561399
按企业登记注册类型分	**By Registration Type**				
内资	Domestically-invested Enterprises	342678580	336097443	320989927	316670774
国有	State-owned Enterprises	32595969	32428804	30511871	30464607
集体	Collectively-owned Enterprises	881758	842841	813824	801664
股份合作	Joint-equity Cooperative Enterprises	410161	408058	383556	383469
联营	Associate Enterprises	***	***	***	***
有限责任公司	Limited Liability Companies	230145459	224752934	217177888	213199078
股份有限公司	Companies Limited by Shares	30826929	30236387	28333667	28154824
私营	Private Enterprises	47786597	47396722	43739271	43637280
其他	Other	***	***	***	***
港澳台商投资	Hong Kong, Macao and Taiwan-invested Enterprises	42819823	42466783	38546003	38477458
外商投资	Foreign-invested Enterprises	78777618	76665417	66359471	65437177
按国民经济行业分	**By Sector**				
批发业	**Wholesale**	**394250577**	**387199098**	**365103580**	**360211451**
农、林、牧产品批发	Wholesale of Agriculture, Forestry and Animal Poduction and Hunting Products	10035467	9933867	9561888	9528971
食品、饮料及烟草制品批发	Wholesale of Foods, Beverage and Tobaccos	19960507	18974660	16872782	16064101
纺织、服装及家庭日用品批发	Wholesale of Textile, Clothes and Household Commodities	39025679	38782267	34708767	34613119
文化、体育用品及器材批发	Wholesale of Cultural and Sports Goods and Equipment	13307728	13105450	11994169	11937111
医药及医疗器材批发	Wholesale of Medicine and Medical Devices	20324978	20042495	17569057	17469340
矿产品、建材及化工产品批发	Wholesale of Mineral Products, Building Materials, and Chemical Products	174173161	173528803	169056335	168716013
机械设备、五金交电及电子产品批发	Wholesale of Mechanical Equipment, Hardware and Electronic Products	105700886	101198161	94628371	91180685
贸易经纪与代理	Trade Broker and Agent	7136403	7067270	6585590	6581824
其他批发	Others	4585769	4566125	4126622	4120287
零售业	**Retail**	**70025444**	**68030545**	**60791822**	**60373959**
综合零售	Integrated Retail	15659718	14537408	12646569	12517583
食品、饮料及烟草制品专门零售	Special Retails of Foods, Beverage and Tobacoos	1139500	1118928	747190	739014
纺织、服装及日用品专门零售	Special Retail of Textile, Clothing and Domestic Commodities	3068797	3001067	2012838	2006610
文化、体育用品及器材专门零售	Special Retail of Cultural and Sports Goods and Equipment	2564383	2458671	2072725	2001882
医药及医疗器材专门零售	Special Retail of Medicine and Medical Devices	2425333	2399753	2151800	2150968
汽车、摩托车、燃料及零配件专门零售	Special Retail of Automobiles, Motorcycles, Fuels and Their Accessories	24274726	23848069	22387409	22234378
家用电器及电子产品专门零售	Special Retail of Household Electrical Appliances and Electronic Products	15332885	15212442	13911133	13887715
五金、家具及室内装修材料专门零售	Special Retail of Hardware, Furniture and Indoor Decoration Materials	829861	813332	526940	522144
货摊、无店铺及其他零售业	Stand Retail, Retail Without Shops and Other Retail	4730240	4640876	4335219	4313664
按规模划分	**By Size**				
#大中型企业	Medium-and Large-sized Enterprises	411616561	403121949	375593413	370607964

注：应交税金合计包括应交增值税、应交所得税、营业税金及附加和管理费用中的税金。

16-9 Continued

(10000 yuan)

Profits and Losses				应交税金合计	#营业税金及附加		#应交增值税	#应交所得税
销售费用 Sales Expenses	管理费用 Management Expenses	财务费用 Financial Expenses	利润总额 Total Profits	Total Tax Payable	Business Tax and Surcharges	#主营业务税金及附加 Business Tax and Surtax	Value Added Tax Payable	Income Tax Payable
19628094	**9495293**	**2732867**	**10800869**	**7840187**	**1022479**	**982319**	**4288007**	**2307529**
2411035	1637252	756052	3952102	1960270	311661	297824	850797	734975
17217059	7858040	1976815	6848767	5879917	710818	684495	3437210	1572555
10514111	5377664	2544845	6577347	4709730	737099	701538	2430506	1382962
466268	439636	166112	1267609	718947	302254	299124	194571	201454
29384	29878	13254	7677	21	1451	1185	-4707	1083
9392	14538	2173	1171	3665	344	340	2614	496
***	***	***	***	***	***	***	***	***
6616425	2993084	1633154	4107586	2819757	287543	266654	1469327	964451
1211271	553907	421265	933350	449365	75928	66526	268879	87016
2180505	1345887	308923	259668	716801	69544	67673	498752	128403
***	***	***	***	***	***	***	***	***
2413127	1344146	173159	655011	601029	70915	67397	364456	147119
6700856	2773483	14864	3568511	2529429	214465	213384	1493045	777449
13733948	**7231515**	**2251632**	**9334734**	**6078677**	**788360**	**759501**	**3203687**	**1915456**
128586	226839	138126	358602	106242	11554	6934	59070	29468
2001722	459204	67917	653364	903009	325768	323456	419236	146526
2609253	1304397	43335	699942	646496	53544	52890	450433	124246
468089	301301	60691	556842	290489	22390	22318	136648	125453
1347844	617864	101521	744104	630021	50880	50467	369691	202546
1884702	1249602	1527872	1897452	1112534	129201	114674	501566	424721
5013883	2803390	125295	3863806	2217079	180199	174222	1230320	747221
136566	138660	148427	382523	131002	9394	9335	44760	72346
143304	130258	38448	178101	41806	5430	5205	-8037	42930
5894146	**2263778**	**481235**	**1466135**	**1761511**	**234119**	**222817**	**1084320**	**392073**
1890755	713853	157420	773171	524947	97340	89570	254513	153537
252728	74817	1663	60667	91663	8197	7965	61492	20532
801735	181288	19407	33397	162552	21118	20489	121648	17752
288423	133265	25265	61571	59222	9745	9560	29918	17986
147696	78004	53535	114637	52272	5886	5806	41315	3980
871561	542596	178055	264542	431214	40618	38660	275775	97986
969768	283208	25921	428341	362871	36310	36061	251824	70187
150198	77838	3239	64418	64164	8584	8451	36047	17932
521282	178908	16732	-334609	12607	6321	6256	11788	-7820
18514197	8741799	2135498	10650460	7329946	960472	924623	4144010	2028768

Note: Total tax payable mainly includes VAT payable, income tax payable, business tax and surtax, and tax in management expenses.

16-10 限额以上住宿业企业财务状况(2016年)

单位：万元

项　目	Item	企业单位个数(个) Number of Enterprises (unit)	资产总计 Total Assets	流动资产合计 Total Current Assets
合　计	**Total**	**964**	**13750189**	**4898952**
按隶属关系分	**By Affiliation**			
中　央	Central	158	1926397	538980
地　方	Local	806	11823791	4359972
按登记注册类型分	**By Registration Type**			
内　资	Domestically-invested Enterprises	901	9814832	3627379
国　有	State-owned Enterprises	204	2200658	552704
集　体	Collectively-owned Enterprises	33	220217	60761
股份合作	Joint-equity Cooperative Enterprises	21	99312	45443
联　营	Associate Enterprises	***	***	***
有限责任公司	Limited Liability Companies	362	5682067	1976909
股份有限公司	Companies Limited by Shares	7	336980	151786
私　营	Private Enterprises	271	1271126	836859
港澳台商投资	Hong Kong, Macao and Taiwan-invested Enterprises	36	2396308	734246
外商投资	Foreign-invested Enterprises	27	1539049	537327
按行业类别分	**By Sector Type**			
旅游饭店	Tourism Hotels	568	11222384	3716218
一般旅馆	Common Inns	364	1903155	830065
其他住宿服务	Other Accomodation Services	32	624650	352669

注：应交税金合计包括应交增值税、应交所得税、营业税金及附加和管理费用中的税金。

FINANCIAL STATUS OF ACCOMMODATION ENTERPRISES ABOVE DESIGNATED SIZE (2016)

(10000 yuan)

资产负债 Assets and Liabilities							
#应收账款 Accounts Receivable	固定资产合计 Total Fixed Assets	固定资产原价 Total Original Value of Fixed Assets	负债合计 Total Liabilities	#流动负债合计 Total Current Liabilities	#应付账款 Accounts Payable	所有者权益合计 Total Owner's Equity	#实收资本 Paid-up Capital
181234	**5184904**	**8838975**	**10287933**	**6946290**	**381813**	**3462256**	**3891338**
31464	997855	1832085	1108175	805939	46021	818222	757905
149770	4187049	7006890	9179758	6140351	335792	2644033	3133433
148672	4001152	6183583	7979984	5653128	312992	1834847	2652925
29584	1291118	1837049	1416877	912476	51088	783781	792402
1706	135755	250133	161906	68077	6172	58311	27579
1830	28418	61058	82777	69661	3532	16535	11926
***	***	***	***	***	***	***	***
95507	2261386	3568829	4670215	3438036	178459	1011852	1646844
917	59941	105695	301881	203381	14550	35099	42590
19238	223664	356982	1341672	957399	58966	-70546	129184
23701	803388	1766227	1527750	969066	46716	868559	888720
8861	380363	889165	780199	324096	22105	758849	349694
130806	4784511	8136741	8480542	5749754	291343	2741842	3211740
44742	299294	539255	1207061	999653	67469	696093	603796
5685	101099	162979	600330	196883	23001	24321	75802

Note：Total tax payable mainly includes VAT payable, income tax payable, business tax and surtax, and tax in management expenses.

16-10 续表

单位：万元

项目	Item	损益 营业收入 Business Income	#主营业务收入 Main Business Income	营业成本 Business Cost	#主营业务成本 Main Business Cost
合计	**Total**	**3545260**	**3504008**	**971417**	**963559**
按隶属关系分	**By Affiliation**				
中央	Central	689878	680652	185386	181353
地方	Local	2855383	2823356	786031	782207
按登记注册类型分	**By Registration Type**				
内资	Domestically-invested Enterprises	2580923	2545848	690518	684836
国有	State-owned Enterprises	690213	680651	170723	168856
集体	Collectively-owned Enterprises	91216	89834	13489	13488
股份合作	Joint-equity Cooperative Enterprises	28778	28737	8067	8067
联营	Associate Enterprises	***	***	***	***
有限责任公司	Limited Liability Companies	1328093	1308775	357261	354606
股份有限公司	Companies Limited by Shares	40083	38500	23182	23180
私营	Private Enterprises	398380	395208	116718	115562
港澳台商投资	Hong Kong, Macao and Taiwan-invested Enterprises	651384	647188	221181	219529
外商投资	Foreign-invested Enterprises	312953	310972	59718	59194
按行业类别分	**By Sector Type**				
旅游饭店	Tourism Hotels	2777010	2749240	730743	724325
一般旅馆	Common Inns	654927	641924	212458	211045
其他住宿服务	Other Accomodation Services	113323	112843	28217	28190

16-10 continued

(10000 yuan)

Profits and Losses				应交税金合计				
销售费用 Sales Expenses	管理费用 Manage-ment Expenses	财务费用 Financial Expenses	利润总额 Total Profits	Total Tax Payable	营业税金及附加 Business Tax and Surcharges	#主营业务税金及附加 Main Business Tax and Surtax	#应交增值税 Value Added Tax Payable	#应交所得税 Income Tax Payable
1087592	**1262047**	**181521**	**113140**	**303152**	**98085**	**95527**	**85075**	**60395**
204250	259604	994	27692	57415	17130	17113	14433	13055
883342	1002443	180527	85448	245737	80955	78413	70642	47340
885513	956218	122289	-21142	194261	61910	60765	66637	27054
221110	283164	12222	83324	50223	16392	16291	14741	7745
42663	26355	58	6756	9041	2090	2088	2567	2295
10837	9028	740	-366	2204	735	735	945	205
***	***	***	***	***	***	***	***	***
442822	505484	82401	-80269	99324	32914	31924	29573	15258
4283	10192	5642	-4370	3624	885	885	1651	136
162636	120439	21199	-26517	29643	8751	8699	17130	1397
132886	192765	46220	51649	66090	22907	22117	11731	18487
69193	113064	13012	82633	42802	13268	12645	6707	14854
847203	1046210	141693	102996	247433	79395	77547	65053	49369
209139	179839	17644	18486	47310	14799	14094	17564	9974
31250	35999	22185	-8342	8410	3891	3886	2458	1052

16-11 限额以上餐饮业企业财务状况(2016年)

单位：万元

项目	Item	企业单位个数(个) Number of Enterprises (unit)	资产总计 Total Assets	流动资产合计 Total Current Assets
合计	**Total**	**1317**	**3988686**	**2466385**
按隶属关系分	**By Affiliation**			
中央	Central	10	76120	61391
地方	Local	1307	3912566	2404994
按登记注册类型分	**By Registration Type**			
内资	Domestically-invested Enterprises	1203	2731812	1803273
国有	State-owned Enterprises	26	45717	30645
集体	Collectively-owned Enterprises	15	16989	4301
股份合作	Joint-equity Cooperative Enterprise	21	18259	14730
有限责任公司	Limited Liability Companies	377	1026263	641441
股份有限公司	Companies Limited by Shares	15	503185	358548
私营	Private Enterprises	749	1121400	753608
港澳台商投资	Hong Kong, Macao and Taiwan-invested Enterprises	57	889140	528733
外商投资	Foreign-invested Enterprises	57	367733	134379
按行业类别分	**By Sector Type**			
正餐	Dinner	1120	2902008	1836465
快餐	Fast Food	108	808974	432847
饮料及冷饮	Beverage and Cold Drink	25	168152	105903
其他餐饮业	Others	64	109552	91170

注：应交税金合计包括应交增值税、应交所得税、营业税金及附加和管理费用中的税金。

FINANCIAL STATUS OF RESTAURANTS ENTERPRISES ABOVE DESIGNATED SIZE (2016)

(10000 yuan)

资产负债 Assets and Liabilities							
#应收账款 Accounts Receivable	固定资产合计 Total Fixed Assets	固定资产原价 Total Original Value of Fixed Assets	负债合计 Total Liabilities	#流动负债合计 Total Current Liabilities	#应付账款 Accounts Payable	所有者权益合计 Total Owner's Equity	#实收资本 Paid-up Capital
148858	**487077**	**1072341**	**3215668**	**2996439**	**595814**	**773018**	**731102**
4009	7972	18467	52427	52422	15926	23693	8342
144850	479106	1053875	3163241	2944017	579887	749325	722761
124699	289225	656718	2421717	2292730	469225	310095	465930
2022	7158	19087	31823	26615	4260	13894	7561
102	3901	6986	13354	13185	1041	3635	4616
622	1288	4207	17517	17504	1546	742	1266
60924	126187	278285	907915	844750	172806	118348	201797
4579	48909	100323	350244	349212	98893	152941	49023
56450	101783	247829	1100864	1041165	190679	20536	201667
11411	123164	242548	462656	398392	85919	426484	137747
12748	74689	173076	331295	305316	40670	36439	127426
99870	329443	735056	2560823	2380489	438416	341185	532358
24811	130808	276039	474637	444810	105960	334337	147259
5987	17285	38568	101645	95780	20517	66507	18527
18190	9541	22679	78564	75360	30920	30988	32959

Note：Total tax payable mainly includes VAT payable, income tax payable, business tax and surtax, and tax in management expenses.

16-11 续表

单位：万元

项目	Item	损益 营业收入 Business Income	#主营业务收入 Main Business Income	营业成本 Business Cost	#主营业务成本 Main Business Cost
合计	**Total**	**5637967**	**5566018**	**2292526**	**2253072**
按隶属关系分	**By Affiliation**				
中央	Central	81902	77836	35127	32582
地方	Local	5556065	5488182	2257399	2220490
按登记注册类型分	**By Registration Type**				
内资	Domestically-invested Enterprises	3334649	3280210	1416676	1387762
国有	State-owned Enterprises	58232	51599	28718	26172
集体	Collectively-owned Enterprises	15338	15338	8389	8389
股份合作	Joint-equity Cooperative Enterprise	26901	26806	14087	14087
有限责任公司	Limited Liability Companies	1496188	1475615	597583	590922
股份有限公司	Companies Limited by Shares	136210	129995	41725	31528
私营	Private Enterprises	1601781	1580856	726174	716664
港澳台商投资	Hong Kong, Macao and Taiwan-invested Enterprises	1238974	1237002	390499	389438
外商投资	Foreign-invested Enterprises	1064344	1048806	485351	475872
按行业类别分	**By Sector Type**				
正餐	Dinner	3567379	3519349	1479631	1449702
快餐	Fast Food	1546214	1523849	589622	580151
饮料及冷饮	Beverage and Cold Drink	262711	262031	68375	68375
其他餐饮业	Others	261663	260790	154899	154844

16−11 continued

(10000 yuan)

Profits and Losses				应交税金合计 Total Tax Payable				
销售费用 Sales Expenses	管理费用 Management Expenses	财务费用 Financial Expenses	利润总额 Total Profits		#营业税金及附加 Business Tax and Surtax	#主营业务税金及附加 Main Business Tax and Surcharges	#应交增值税 Value Added Tax Payable	#应交所得税 Income Tax Payable
2338394	**656712**	**45209**	**200897**	**212565**	**109563**	**108407**	**19809**	**78121**
20096	22550	-307	3755	5218	1539	1455	2060	1533
2318298	634163	45516	197142	207347	108024	106952	17749	76588
1318008	441805	38246	73817	106940	68666	67538	-1474	35611
17072	10485	-1	1889	3246	1166	1018	1460	475
4770	1814	53	89	635	381	381	188	60
9017	3216	82	-83	867	579	579	218	61
598006	204192	7810	69070	24463	30606	29909	-31889	24013
65139	21412	14268	-41	8386	2745	2712	2436	2609
624003	200686	16033	2893	69343	33190	32940	26112	8393
625445	96129	4504	93151	59434	21225	21225	9898	27723
394941	118779	2459	33930	46192	19672	19644	11386	14787
1437822	472361	40313	73143	117668	73898	73332	-1908	41548
692951	139350	3272	92192	63657	26406	25828	11439	25140
136323	20411	1074	29665	19145	4698	4692	4316	10060
71298	24590	550	5897	12096	4561	4555	5962	1374

16-12 连锁企业基本情况(2001-2016年) STATISTICS FOR CHAIN ENTERPRISES (2001-2016)

年 份 Year	连锁总店 (个) Number of General Chain Stores (unit)	门店总数 (个) Number of Chain Stores (unit)	从业人员年末人数 (人) Number of Employed Persons Year-end (person)	营业面积 (平方米) Operational Area (sq.m)	商品销售总额 (营业额) (万元) Total Sales of Commodities (Turnover) (10000 yuan)	#零售额 Retail Sales
2001	129	2123	139470	1605808	4831168	2186540
2002	146	3523	109089	2356266	6621975	6487185
2003	153	4519	132030	3405562	8404232	7601221
2004	196	5432	153942	3783507	8603560	8337829
2005	188	5973	166598	4376383	10612658	9507168
2006	205	6730	170007	5546003	11229026	9514297
2007	210	7645	185114	6677266	13890913	11573838
2008	240	8611	223954	6745802	15720473	12954839
2009	240	8928	218024	6995047	17366414	13816796
2010	234	9299	228292	7268786	21329783	16255496
2011	233	9845	280798	7953891	25742536	19507890
2012	220	10014	287975	8339674	26758403	20140433
2013	241	11111	299445	9026207	27834646	21495798
2014	243	11433	279567	9252645	28173728	21100845
2015	238	11942	279596	9238023	30453838	24508274
2016	245	12604	303319	11519137	32375249	27797369

16-13 连锁企业基本情况(按登记注册类型、经营业态分)(2016年)
STATISTICS FOR CHAIN ENTERPRISES (BY REGISTRATION TYPE OF ENTERPRISES AND OPERATION FORMS) (2016)

项目	Item	门店总数(个) Number of Chain Stores (unit)	从业人员年末人数(人) Year-end Employed Persons (person)	营业面积(平方米) Operational Area (sq.m)	商品销售额(营业额)(万元) Total sales of Commodities (10000 yuan)	#零售额 Retail Sales
合计	**Total**	**12604**	**303319**	**11519137**	**32375249**	**27797369**
按登记注册类型分	**By Registration Type**					
内资	Domestically-invested Enterprises	7821	194339	8541002	23225224	18855392
国有	State-owned Enterprises	80	1462	18633	57911	51383
集体	Collectively-owned Enterprises	14	461	54905	52858	50070
股份合作	Joint-equity Cooperative Enterprises	7	123	4990	2952	2952
联营	Associate Enterprises	5	26	928	932	932
有限责任公司	Limited Liability Companies	3852	96444	3672187	9864988	8021808
股份有限公司	Companies Limited by Shares	1872	65244	4133320	11840335	9423902
私营	Private Enterprises	1991	30579	656039	1405249	1304344
其他	Others					
港、澳、台商投资	Hong Kong, Macao and Taiwan-invested Enterprises	2330	45285	911154	1809878	1731538
外商投资	Foreign-invested Enterprises	2453	63695	2066981	7340147	7210438
按经营业态分	**By Operation Form**					
零售业态	**Retail**	**7732**	**173478**	**9533809**	**28965113**	**24507299**
便利店	Convenient Stores	970	6607	142155	416559	411332
折扣店	Discount Stores	8	599	57851	136803	136803
超市	Supermarkets	1543	54395	2563123	5671252	4107517
大型超市	Large Supermarkets	322	39789	2341724	3407466	3290493
仓储会员店	Warehouse Club Stores	7	1966	134877	314905	314905
百货店	Department Stores	89	14689	2323278	3186545	3183758
专业店	Specialty Stores	2192	23493	1057679	6085616	5388766
加油站	Gas Stations	702	6614	340251	5094655	3130437
专卖店	Boutiques	1888	24315	509706	4405449	4297427
家居建材商店	Furniture and Building Material Stores	11	1011	63165	245863	245863
餐饮业态	**Chain Catering Enterprises**	**4734**	**126208**	**1977740**	**3304202**	**3285982**
中式正餐	Chinese Dinner	642	49743	919678	1124380	1119592
中式快餐	Chinese Fast Food	1449	23443	316639	599928	590668
外国风味正餐	Exotic Dinner	777	18182	270695	486282	483700
外国风味快餐	Exotic Fast Food	1111	28469	354846	789734	788143
茶馆	Teahouses	9	40	910	330	330
咖啡店	Cafés	717	5780	112112	289119	289119
其他	Others	29	551	2860	14429	14429
住宿业态	**Chain Accomodation Enterprises**	**138**	**3633**	**7588**	**105934**	**4088**
旅游饭店	Tourism Hotels	59	1743	3018	51927	441
一般旅馆	Common Inns	79	1890	4570	54007	3647

16-14 商品交易市场基本情况(2016年)
STATISTICS FOR COMMODITY TRANSACTION MARKETS (2016)

项 目	Item	市场数量 (个) Number of Markets (unit)	总摊位数 (个) Number of Booths (unit)	成交额 (亿元) Turnover (100 million yuan)
全市合计	**Total**	**781**	**244224**	**4111.8**
按经营方式分	**By Business Practice**			
批发市场	Wholesale Market	118	81372	2714.8
零售市场	Retail Market	663	162852	1397.0
按经营环境分	**By Business Environment**			
露天式	Open-air	131	54649	1879.9
封闭式	Closed	608	173333	2026.9
其 他	Others	42	16242	205.0
按市场地理环境分	**By Market Place**			
二环以内	Inside the Second Ring Road	40	8662	38.0
二环至三环以内	Between the Second and Third Ring Road	89	38593	270.3
三环到四环以内	Between the Third and Fourth Ring Road	136	46121	1288.8
四环至五环以内	Between the Fourth and Fifth Ring Road	90	32110	1568.5
五环至六环以内	Between the Fifth and Sixth Ring Road	205	50599	527.7
六环以外	Outside the Sixth Ring Road	221	68139	418.5
按功能区分	**By Functional Area**			
首都功能核心区	Core Functional Area of the Capital	71	29023	278.7
城市功能拓展区	Urban Function Extension Area	348	116702	2996.1
城市发展新区	New Area of Urban Development	267	70821	740.0
生态涵养发展区	Ecological Conservation Area	95	27678	97.1

16–15 亿元及以上商品交易市场基本情况(2016年)
STATISTICS FOR COMMODITY TRANSACTION MARKETS OVER RMB 100 MILLION (2016)

项　　目	Item	市场数量(个) Number of markets (unit)	总摊位数(个) Number of Booths (unit)	#出租摊位数 Number of Booths on Lease	成交额(亿元) Turnover (100 million yuan)
全市合计	**Total**	**136**	**119956**	**101729**	**3999.6**
按经营方式分	**By Business Practice**				
批发市场	Wholesale Market	56	66682	52647	2699.6
零售市场	Retail Market	80	53274	49082	1300.0
按经营环境分	**By Business Environment**				
露天式	Open-air	21	23503	13710	1857.4
封闭式	Closed	108	86404	78776	1943.9
其　他	Others	7	10049	9243	198.4
按市场地理环境分	**By Market Place**				
二环以内	Inside the Second Ring Road	6	4511	3539	33.0
二环至三环以内	Between the Second and Third Ring Road	13	21535	20574	256.4
三环到四环以内	Between the Third and Fourth Ring Road	34	28940	27178	1267.3
四环至五环以内	Between the Fourth and Fifth Ring Road	18	18643	17181	1556.4
五环至六环以内	Between the Fifth and Sixth Ring Road	33	20356	18249	503.3
六环以外	Outside the Sixth Ring Road	32	25971	15008	383.2
按功能区分	**By Functional Area**				
首都功能核心区	Core Functional Area of the Capital	13	20064	18349	269.4
城市功能拓展区	Urban Function Extension Area	76	65934	61156	2947.4
城市发展新区	New Area of Urban Development	30	22911	14653	700.5
生态涵养发展区	Ecological Conservation Area	17	11047	7571	82.2

16-16 商品交易市场经营情况(2016年)
STATISTICS FOR COMMODITY TRANSACTION MARKETS (2016)

项目	Item	市场数量(个) Number of Markets (unit)	出租摊位数(个) Number of Booths (unit)	营业面积(万平方米) Operating Area (10,000 sq.m)	成交额(亿元) Turnover (100 million yuan)
合计	**Total**	**781**	**198785**	**1269.5**	**4111.8**
综合市场	**Comprehensive Markets**	**371**	**94695**	**511.8**	**2091.2**
生产资料综合市场	Comprehensive Market of Capital Goods	1	260	1.3	0.3
工业消费品综合市场	Comprehensive Market of Industrial Consumer Goods	49	19874	53.2	90.6
农产品综合市场	Comprehensive Market of Agricultural Products	229	50134	320.3	1804.2
其他综合市场	Other Comprehensive Markets	92	24427	137.0	196.1
专业市场	**Specialized Markets**	**410**	**104090**	**757.6**	**2020.6**
生产资料市场	**Market of Capital Goods**	**57**	**9290**	**115.4**	**108.0**
木材市场	Timber Market	1	190	0.9	0.5
建材市场	Building Material Market	47	7981	68.4	52.7
化工材料及制品市场	Chemical Material and Product Market				
金属材料市场	Metal Material Market	7	571	40.6	35.4
机械设备市场	Mechanical Equipment Market	1	262	3.3	8.0
其他生产资料市场	Other Markets of Capital Goods	1	286	2.1	11.3
农产品市场	**Agricultural Product Market**	**74**	**13882**	**114.9**	**385.6**
粮油市场	Foodstuff and Oil Market	4	417	3.4	3.7
肉禽蛋市场	Meat, Poultry and Egg Market	3	785	2.3	2.4
水产品市场	Aquatic Product Market	6	2811	16.7	121.5
蔬菜市场	Vegetable Market	39	4887	56.0	227.9
干鲜果品市场	Dried and Fresh Fruit Market	3	449	23.8	11.8
其他农产品市场	Other Agricultural Product Markets	19	4533	12.7	18.4
食品、饮料及烟酒市场	**Food, Beverage, Tobacco and Wine Market**	**17**	**1994**	**10.8**	**5.7**
食品饮料市场	Food and Beverage Market	3	323	1.1	0.2
茶叶市场	Tea Market	10	1315	8.2	5.4
其他食品饮料及烟酒市场	Other Food, Beverage, Tobacco and Wine Markets	4	356	1.5	0.1
纺织、服装、鞋帽市场	**Textile, Costume, Shoe and Hat Market**	**65**	**31550**	**102.7**	**254.3**
布料及纺织品市场	Cloth and Textile Market	8	2651	12.3	12.8
服装市场	Clothing Market	44	24113	71.6	223.1
鞋帽市场	Shoe and Hat Market	4	1810	9.4	6.6
其他纺织服装鞋帽市场	Other Textile, Costume, Shoe and Cap Markets	9	2976	9.4	11.8
日用品及文化用品市场	**Domestic Commodity and Cultural Article Market**	**12**	**4907**	**12.7**	**48.4**
小商品市场	Small Commodity Market	2	2752	3.3	23.4

16-16 续表 Continued

项目	Item	市场数量(个) Number of Markets (unit)	出租摊位数(个) Number of Booths (unit)	营业面积(万平方米) Operating Area (10000 sq.m)	成交额(亿元) Turnover (100 million yuan)
文具市场	Stationary Market	1	765	2.0	15.1
图书、报刊杂志市场	Book, Newspaper, and Magazine Market	2	250	1.6	8.5
其他日用品及文化用品市场	Other Domestic Commodity and Cultural Article Market	7	1140	5.9	1.5
黄金、珠宝、玉器等首饰市场	**Market of Gold, Jewelry, and Jade**	**16**	**3622**	**16.3**	**18.1**
电器、通讯器材、电子设备市场	**Market of Electrical Appliances, Communication Devices, and Electronic Equipment**	**18**	**4266**	**11.1**	**42.1**
家电市场	Household Appliance Market	2	92	0.7	0.2
通讯器材市场	Communication Device Market	5	719	2.5	1.3
照相、摄像器材市场	Photographic and Camera Shooting Equipment Market	2	313	1.1	3.5
计算机及辅助设备市场	Computer and Supporting Equipment Market	6	2295	4.8	25.4
其他电器、通讯器材、电子设备市场	Other Electrical Appliance, Communication Device and Electronic Equipment	3	847	2.0	11.7
家具、五金及装饰材料市场	**Furniture, Hardware, and Decoration Material Market**	**73**	**17025**	**202.9**	**175.4**
家具市场	Furniture Market	31	7395	118.2	69.0
装饰材料市场	Decoration Materials Market	20	5389	53.1	75.6
灯具市场	Lamp and Lantern Market	5	777	9.7	2.0
五金材料市场	Hardware Market	11	2199	12.6	26.2
其他装修市场	Other Decoration Market	6	1265	9.3	2.7
汽车、摩托车及零配件市场	**Automobile, Autobike, and Part and Fitting Market**	**23**	**5481**	**104.8**	**966.6**
汽车市场	Automobile Market	12	1833	72.6	904.5
机动车零配件市场	Automobile Part and Fitting Market	11	3648	32.1	62.1
花、鸟、鱼、虫市场	**Flower, Bird, Fish and Insect Market**	**21**	**3518**	**14.3**	**4.6**
花卉市场	Flower Market	18	2918	10.5	4.4
观赏鱼市场	Fish Market	1	88	1.8	0.1
其他花鸟鱼虫市场	Other Flower, Bird, Fish and Insect Market	2	512	2.0	0.1
旧货市场	**Secondhand Goods Market**	**14**	**6530**	**14.7**	**5.7**
古玩、古董、字画市场	Curio, Antique, Calligraphy and Painting Market	7	1334	7.8	1.0
邮票、硬币市场	Stamp and Coin Market	2	933	0.8	0.5
其他旧货市场	Other Secondhand Goods Market	5	4263	6.1	4.1
其他专业市场	**Other Specialized Markets**	**20**	**2025**	**37.1**	**6.2**

16-17 北京消费者信心指数(2016年)
BEIJING CONSUMER CONFIDENCE INDEX (2016)

项 目	Item	一季度 First Quarter	二季度 Second Quarter	三季度 Third Quarter	四季度 Fourth Quarter
消费者信心指数	**Consumer Confidence Index**	**104.5**	**104.0**	**105.5**	**106.8**
消费者满意指数	**Consumer Satisfaction Index**	**107.4**	**106.3**	**107.8**	**109.5**
就业状况满意指数	Index of Satisfaction with Employment Status	119.2	120.4	119.3	121.6
家庭收入状况满意指数	Index of Satisfaction with Household Income Status	99.1	97.5	99.6	100.2
耐用消费品购买时机满意指数	Index of Satisfaction with Durable Consumer Goods	103.8	101.0	104.6	106.7
消费者预期指数	**Consumer Expectation Index**	**102.6**	**102.4**	**103.9**	**105.0**
就业状况预期指数	Index of Expectation for Employment Status	102.4	104.8	107.5	109.4
家庭收入状况预期指数	Index of Expectation for Household Income Status	102.7	99.9	100.2	100.6

主要统计指标解释

社会消费品零售总额 指企业（单位、个体户）通过交易直接售给个人、社会集团非生产、非经营用的实物商品金额，以及提供餐饮服务所取得的收入金额。个人包括城乡居民和入境人员，社会集团包括机关、社会团体、部队、学校、企事业单位、居委会或村委会等。

批发和零售业单位 指在流通环节从事商品批发活动和零售活动的单位。

商品购进额 指从本企业（单位）以外的单位和个人购进(包括从国外直接进口)作为转卖或加工后转卖的商品金额（含增值税）。本指标反映批发和零售业从国内外市场上购进商品的总量。

商品销售额 指对本企业以外的单位和个人出售的商品金额（包括售给本单位消费用的商品，含增值税）。本指标反映批发和零售业在国内市场上销售商品以及出口商品的总量。

期末商品库存额 对于批发和零售业法人企业和个体经营户，是指取得所有权的全部商品金额（含增值税）；对于批发和零售业产业活动单位，是指期末实际在库且归属法人具有所有权的全部商品金额（含增值税）。这个指标反映批发和零售业的商品库存情况，以及对市场商品供应的保证程度。

连锁总店（总部） 负责连锁企业资源（商号、商誉、经营模式、服务标准、管理模式等）的开发、配置、控制或使用等功能的企业核心管理机构。连锁经营是指经营同类商品或服务，使用统一商号的若干店铺，在同一总店（总部）的管理下，采取统一采购或特许经营等方式,实现规模效益的组织形式，包括直营连锁、特许连锁和自愿连锁三种形式。直营连锁是指连锁店铺由连锁公司全资或控股开设，在总部的直接控制下，开展统一经营的连锁经营形式；特许连锁是指拥有注册商标、企业标志、专利、专有技术等经营资源的企业（特许人），以合同形式将其拥有的经营资源许可其他经营者（被特许人）使用，被特许人按合同约定在统一的经营模式下开展经营，并向特许人支付特许经营费用的连锁经营形式；自愿连锁是指若干个店铺或企业自愿组合起来，在不改变各自资产所有权关系的情况下，以同一个品牌形象面对消费者，以共同进货为纽带开展的连锁经营形式。

连锁门店 在连锁企业经营管理的基础上，按照总店（总部）的指示和服务规范要求，承担日常销售业务的店铺，称连锁门店，包括直营店（控股店）和加盟店。

（1）直营店（控股店） 是指由连锁企业总部投资开设，按连锁经营管理模式，由总部统一管理的店铺。

（2）加盟店 是指在特许连锁中，被特许人获得特许人授权后，使用其商标、商号、经营模式、专利和专有技术等经营资源建立的店铺，也包括自愿连锁的成员店。

门店总数 指该连锁企业所拥有的全部门店（包括直营店和加盟店）数量。其中，总店（如果总公司有门店的话）作为一个直营店处理。此外，有的地区分出控股店，控股店按直营店统计。

餐饮业企业 指在一定场所，专门从事对食物进行现场烹饪、调制，并出售给顾客主要供现场消费服务活动的企业。如各种饭馆、中西餐厅、酒馆、茶馆和火车餐车、车站食堂、飞机场餐厅等。

住宿业企业 指有偿为顾客提供临时住宿服务活动的单位。如旅游饭店、宾馆、酒店和旅馆、旅店等。

商品交易市场 指经有关部门和组织批准设立，有固定场所、设施，有经营管理部门和监管人员，若干市场经营者入内，常年或实际开业三个月以上，集中、公开、独立地进行生活消费品、生产资料等现货商品交易以及提供相关服务的交易场所，包括各类消费品市场，生产资料市场等。

消费者信心指数 是综合反映并量化消费者对当前经济形势评价和对经济前景、收入水平、收入预期以及消费心理状态的主观感受，是预测经济走势和消费趋向的一个先行指标，是监测经济周期变化不可缺少的依据。消费者信心指数由消费者满意指数和消费者预期指数构成。其中消费者满意指数反映了消费者对当前经济生活的评价；消费者预期指数反映了消费者对未来一段时期经济发展变化的预期。

指数值的含义 指数取值介于 0 和 200 之间，100 为指数强弱临界点。指数超过 100，表明消费者信心处于强信心区，数值由 100 趋近 200，表明消费者信心逐渐增强；反之，指数小于 100 时，表示消费者信心处于弱信心区，数值由 100 趋近 0，表明消费者信心逐渐减弱。

Explanatory Notes on Main Statistical Indicators

Total Retail Sales of Consumer Goods refer to the total prices of physical commodities sold by enterprises (entities or self-employed businesses) through transaction directly to individuals and social groups to be used for non-productive and non-operating purposes, combined with the amount of income from provision of food and beverage services. Individuals include urban and rural residents and persons entering China. Social groups include government agencies, social organizations, armies, schools, enterprises and public institutions, residents' committee or villagers' committee, and so on.

Wholesale and Retail Entities refer to entities engaged in commodity wholesale and retail activities in circulation.

Total Purchases of Commodities refer to the total value (including value added tax) of purchases (including direct imports from foreign countries) of commodities by the enterprises (entities) from other entities or individuals for the purpose of re-selling, either with or without further processing of the commodities purchased. This indicator is used to show the total value of purchases of retail and wholesale commodities from domestic and overseas markets.

Total Sales of Commodities refer to value of commodities sold by the enterprises to other entities and individuals (including the commodities consumed by the enterprises themselves, including value added tax). This indicator is used to show the total value of wholesale and retail commodities sold in domestic markets and exported.

Inventory (year-end) refers to, for wholesale and retail enterprises and self-employed businesses, the value of all commodities with ownership gained (VAT included); for wholesale and retail entities, refer to the value of all commodities with ownership, actually in storage at the end of a period, and owned by the legal person (VAT included). This indicator shows the commodity inventory in wholesale and retail trades, and to what extent the commodities will be supplied to the market.

General Chain Store (Headquarters) means the core management organization in an enterprise, responsible for the development, deployment, control or use of resources (trade name, goodwill, operating model, service standards and management model, etc.) of the chain enterprise. Chain operation means an organization form in which several stores using unified trade name merchandise the same commodities or provide the same services through uniform purchase or franchise operation under the management of the same general store (headquarters) to achieve benefits of scale. Chain operation falls into direct-sale chain, franchised chain and voluntary chain. Direct-sale chain is a form of chain operation that chain stores are wholly funded or controlled by chain companies, carrying out uniform operation under the direct control of headquarters; franchised chain is a form of chain operation that any enterprise (the franchiser) owning operating resources, such as trademarks, logos, patents and proprietary technologies, authorize such operating resources to any other operator (the franchisee) by contract, and the franchisee operates under uniform operating model as stated in the contract, and pays franchise fees to the franchiser; voluntary chain is a form of chain operation that several stores or enterprises combine together voluntarily to face consumers with the same brand image without changing their own asset ownership relations, and link together through joint purchase.

Chain Stores Based on the operation and management of chain enterprises, stores carrying out daily sales business by following the general store's (headquarters) instruction and required service standards are called chained stores. They include direct-sale stores (controlled stores) and franchise stores.

(1) Direct-sale Stores (Controlled Stores) refer to stores opened with funds from the headquarters of chain enterprises, using the chain operation and management model, and under the uniform management of the headquarters.

(2) Franchised Stores refer to, in franchise chains, stores established after the franchisee is authorized by the franchiser to use its trademark, trade name, operating mode, patent and proprietary technologies and other operating resources. Voluntary chain members are also included.

Total Number of Stores refers to the number of all stores owned by the chain enterprises (including direct-sale stores and franchised stores). The general store (if the parent company has stores) is regarded as a direct-sale store. In addition, controlled stores are considered separately in some areas, which are regarded as direct-sale stores.

Restaurants Enterprises refer to enterprises specialized in cooking and seasoning food which is sold to clients for on-site consumption at a specific site, such as various restaurants, Chinese food and Western food restaurants, pubs, teahouses, dining compartments on trains, canteens at railway stations, and restaurants at airports.

Accommodation Enterprises refer to entities providing clients with temporary accommodation services, such as tourist hotels, guesthouses, rest houses and inns.

Commodity Transaction Markets refer to transaction sites approved by competent authorities and organizations, with fixed places and facilities. There are operation management departments and regulating personnel in the markets, where several operators stay over years or open for over three months, conducting transactions of on-hand commodities such as living consumables and capital goods, and offering relevant services in a concentrated, open and independent manner.

Commodity transaction markets include various markets of consumer goods and capital good market, etc.

Consumer Confidence Index is an indicator reflecting and quantifying the consumers' evaluation on current economic situation, and their personal feeling about the economic prospects, income level, income expectation, and psychological state of consumption. It serves as a leading indicator predicting the trend of economy tendency of consumption, and an essential basis for monitoring the changes in economic cycle and other conditions as well as expectation on the economic prospects in the future. Consumer Confidence Index consists of consumer satisfaction index and consumer expectation index, and the latter one reflects consumers' evaluation on current economic life; consumer expectation index reflects consumers' expectation on the development and changes in the economic prospect in the future.

Indexes range from 0 to 200. 100 represents a critical point between strong and weak confidence. An index greater than 100 indicates the consumers' confidence is strong. An index going toward 200 from 100 shows the consumers' confidence is becoming gradually strong; in contrary, an index smaller than 100 means the consumers' confidence is weak. When the indexes go toward 0 from 100, it means the consumers' confidence is weakening gradually.

北京统计年鉴2017　　BEIJING STATISTICAL YEARBOOK

旅游业
TOURISM

简要说明

一、本章资料的主要内容和统计范围

本章内容主要包括来京旅游者人数及其在京花费情况、星级饭店经营及接待住宿者情况、旅行社接待及出境旅游情况、A级及以上重点旅游景区活动情况等。

统计范围包括国际旅游和国内旅游。

二、本章资料的数据来源

本章中的旅游外汇收入、国内旅游者人数、国内旅游收入、在京旅游花费情况资料来源于北京市旅游发展委员会。入境旅游者人数根据北京市统计局的星级饭店、限额以上非星级饭店全面调查、限额以下饭店抽样调查，以及北京市旅游发展委员会的其他住宿设施抽样调查结果汇总得出。星级饭店、旅行社、A级及以上和重点旅游景区有关数据通过全面调查取得，由北京市统计局提供。

Brief Introduction

I. Main Content and Scope of Statistics

This chapter includes statistics for the number and cost of tourists to Beijing, operation and reception of star-rated hotels, reception and outbound tours made through travel agencies, activities at Level A-or-above key scenic spots, and so on.

Statistics include international and domestic tours.

II. Source of Data

Data of foreign exchange income from tourism, number of domestic tourists, domestic tourism income, and cost of tourists in Beijing are sourced from Beijing Municipal Commission of Tourism Development. The number of inbound tourists is summed from the results of comprehensive survey of star-rated hotels and non-star-rated hotels above designated size, sample survey of hotels below designated size conducted by Beijing Municipal Bureau of Statistics, as well as the results of sample survey of other accommodation facilities conducted by Beijing Municipal Commission of Tourism Development. Data concerning star-rated hotels, travel agencies, Level A-or-above key scenic spots were obtained through comprehensive survey, and provided by Beijing Municipal Bureau of Statistics.

17-1 国际、国内旅游情况(1978-2016年)
STATISTICS FOR INTERNATIONAL AND DOMESTIC TOURISM (1978-2016)

年份 Year	来京旅游者人数(万人次) Number of Tourists to Beijing (10000 person-times)	入境旅游者人数 Inbound Tourists	国内旅游者人数 Domestic Tourists	旅游外汇收入总额(万美元) Foreign Exchange Earnings of Tourism (USD 10000)	国内旅游收入(亿元) Revenue from Domestic Tourism (100 million yuan)
1978		18.7		10000	
1979		25.2		9000	
1980		28.6		12000	
1981-1985		**295.4**		**94000**	
1981		39.4		12000	
1982		45.7		13000	
1983		50.9		14000	
1984		65.7		23000	
1985		93.7		32000	
1986-1990		**492.0**		**280901**	
1986		99.0		46000	
1987		108.1		55000	
1988		120.4		67000	
1989		64.5		47195	
1990		100.0		65706	
1991-1995		**919.6**		**735519**	
1991		132.0		85001	
1992		174.8		107286	
1993		202.8		124128	
1994	6913.0	203.0	6710.0	200904	298.0
1995	6527.0	207.0	6320.0	218200	352.6
1996-2000	**45284.7**	**1203.3**	**44081.4**	**1214800**	**2388.4**
1996	7901.9	218.9	7683.0	225200	359.6
1997	8450.8	229.8	8221.0	224800	391.3
1998	8951.5	220.1	8731.4	238400	424.5
1999	9512.4	252.4	9260.0	249600	530.0
2000	10468.1	282.1	10186.0	276800	683.0
2001-2005	**57116.7**	**1459.7**	**55657.0**	**1475000**	**4968.7**
2001	11292.8	285.8	11007.0	295000	887.7
2002	11810.4	310.4	11500.0	311000	930.0
2003	8885.1	185.1	8700.0	190000	706.0
2004	12265.5	315.5	11950.0	317000	1145.0
2005	12862.9	362.9	12500.0	362000	1300.0
2006-2010	**77925.4**	**2107.4**	**75818.0**	**2247000**	**9712.9**
2006	13590.3	390.3	13200.0	402600	1482.7
2007	14715.5	435.5	14280.0	458000	1753.6
2008	14560.0	379.0	14181.0	446000	1907.0
2009	16669.5	412.5	16257.0	436000	2144.5
2010	18390.1	490.1	17900.0	504400	2425.1
2011-2015	**123156.6**	**2318.8**	**120837.7**	**2457238**	**18148.8**
2011	21404.4	520.4	20884.0	541600	2864.3
2012	23134.6	500.9	22633.7	514900	3301.3
2013	25189.0	450.1	24738.8	479468	3666.3
2014	26149.7	427.5	25722.2	460770	3997.0
2015	27279.0	420.0	26859.0	460500	4320.0
2016	28531.5	416.5	28115.0	506900	4683.0

资料来源：旅游外汇收入总额、国内旅游者人数、国内旅游收入来源于北京市旅游发展委员会。

Source: Data of "Foreign Exchange Earnings of Tourism,Number of Domestic Tourists,Revenue from Domestic Tourism"were provided by Beijing Municipal Commission of Tourism Development.

17-2 按客源地分入境旅游者人数(1978-2016年)
NUMBER OF INBOUND TOURISTS BY COUNTRY/REGION (1978-2016)

单位：万人次 (10000 person-times)

年 份 Year	入境旅游者人数 Number of Inbound Tourists	港澳台同胞 Hong Kong, Macao and Taiwan Tourists	#中国香港 Hong Kong, China	外国人 Foreigner	#日 本 Japan	#韩 国 Korea	#美 国 United States	#英 国 United Kingdom	#法 国 France	#德 国 Germany	#俄罗斯 Russia
1978	18.7	3.3		15.4							
1979	25.2	4.1		21.1							
1980	28.6	5.8		21.7	6.0		3.7	1.3	0.9	0.9	
1981-1985	**295.4**	**47.5**		**233.0**	**68.3**		**47.1**	**10.1**	**9.2**	**10.6**	
1981	39.4	6.8		31.3	5.3		3.8	1.1	1.1	1.0	
1982	45.7	8.2		35.9	8.2		6.6	1.3	1.3	1.4	
1983	50.9	8.9		39.7	10.0		9.4	1.5	1.5	1.7	0.1
1984	65.7	10.0		52.1	17.2		12.5	2.3	2.1	2.5	0.1
1985	93.7	13.6		74.0	27.6		14.8	3.9	3.2	4.0	0.2
1986-1990	**492.0**	**117.7**		**357.0**	**110.0**		**63.8**	**18.1**	**15.7**	**22.4**	**3.8**
1986	99.0	15.8		79.0	25.5		14.7	4.1	3.1	4.6	0.3
1987	108.1	21.8		81.7	26.3		16.5	4.5	4.3	5.1	0.3
1988	120.4	28.8		86.5	27.8		16.7	4.2	4.2	5.4	0.7
1989	64.5	16.6		46.0	12.2		7.3	2.4	2.1	3.3	1.0
1990	100.0	34.7	11.4	63.8	18.2		8.6	2.9	2.0	4.0	1.5
1991-1995	**919.6**	**217.9**	**122.7**	**683.4**	**188.0**	**47.2**	**68.9**	**25.2**	**30.1**	**45.9**	**27.4**
1991	132.0	38.2	17.6	91.4	27.6	4.3	9.5	4.3	3.7	6.0	3.5
1992	174.8	51.2	24.6	120.5	37.6	5.6	12.3	4.4	6.6	9.4	5.1
1993	202.8	52.8	29.4	145.0	39.3	7.3	14.3	5.3	6.9	12.0	7.7
1994	203.0	39.4	25.7	160.0	41.1	12.7	15.4	5.4	6.7	9.7	4.9
1995	207.0	36.3	25.4	166.5	42.4	17.3	17.4	5.8	6.2	8.8	6.2
1996-2000	**1203.3**	**206.2**	**128.3**	**984.3**	**229.4**	**92.6**	**118.6**	**43.8**	**37.5**	**53.0**	**28.1**
1996	218.9	38.6	25.5	176.2	43.0	18.0	18.5	7.5	6.6	10.0	6.9
1997	229.8	40.3	26.3	186.9	43.0	19.4	21.7	9.0	6.5	9.1	6.5
1998	220.1	39.1	25.0	178.2	43.5	8.2	23.2	8.8	6.9	11.3	6.2
1999	252.4	44.1	26.5	205.0	45.6	19.2	24.1	8.8	7.9	10.5	4.6
2000	282.1	44.1	25.0	238.0	54.3	27.8	31.1	9.7	9.6	12.1	3.9
2001-2005	**1459.7**	**220.9**	**133.2**	**1238.8**	**233.7**	**182.9**	**173.8**	**57.8**	**51.7**	**56.9**	**33.2**
2001	285.8	45.9	26.9	239.9	50.7	32.7	33.1	11.1	10.2	12.3	4.9
2002	310.4	43.9	25.5	266.5	56.5	38.0	37.4	12.9	11.3	12.2	5.2
2003	185.1	32.4	21.7	152.7	29.2	24.5	19.4	8.1	5.5	6.3	5.2
2004	315.5	47.4	27.7	268.1	52.3	42.4	37.4	11.8	11.1	11.5	8.2
2005	362.9	51.3	31.4	311.6	45.0	45.3	46.5	13.9	13.6	14.6	9.7
2006-2010	**2107.4**	**286.2**	**174.4**	**1821.1**	**248.2**	**207.9**	**291.8**	**82.4**	**72.3**	**85.7**	**85.2**
2006	390.3	52.0	30.3	338.3	50.6	42.4	49.8	14.8	14.2	15.3	15.0
2007	435.5	52.9	31.3	382.6	58.8	44.4	60.3	17.0	16.4	17.5	18.3
2008	379.0	43.3	28.1	335.7	40.0	35.3	53.8	17.5	14.5	16.0	17.9
2009	412.5	69.6	44.4	342.9	46.2	35.2	57.9	16.3	12.9	16.8	15.0
2010	490.1	68.4	40.3	421.6	52.6	50.6	70.0	16.8	14.3	20.1	19.0
2011-2015	**2318.9**	**326.4**	**185.5**	**1992.5**	**170.3**	**215.6**	**369.6**	**88.9**	**72.2**	**113.5**	**81.2**
2011	520.4	73.0	43.4	447.4	51.0	53.4	78.9	18.8	15.0	22.2	20.5
2012	500.9	66.5	37.6	434.4	43.7	44.2	75.1	18.5	15.1	24.5	20.0
2013	450.1	62.5	35.4	387.6	24.9	37.7	74.7	17.5	13.4	23.0	16.7
2014	427.5	62.0	34.2	365.5	24.9	38.7	71.5	16.9	13.4	22.6	13.7
2015	420.0	62.4	34.9	357.6	25.8	41.6	69.4	17.2	15.3	21.2	10.3
2016	416.5	61.8	35.3	354.8	24.8	37.9	70.3	18.3	13.2	20.6	9.5

注：1. 1980-1999年的入境旅游者人数由外国游客、港澳台游客、华侨三部分组成。
2. 1990-1999年香港游客人数为香港、澳门合计。

Note: a) "Number of inbound tourists"in 1980-1999 consisted of foreign visitors,visitors from Hong Kong,Macao and Taiwan,and overseas Chinese.
b) Tourists from Hong Kong in 1990-1999 were the total number of tourists from Hong Kong and Macao.

17-3 来京旅游者人数
NUMBER OF TOURISTS TO BEIJING

单位：万人次 (10000 person-times)

项目	Item	2016	2015	2016年为2015年% 2016 as % of 2015
合计	**Total**	**28531.5**	**27279.0**	**104.6**
国内旅游人数	**Number of Domestic Tourists**	**28115.0**	**26859.0**	**104.7**
外地来京旅游者人数	Number of Tourists to Beijing from Outside Beijing	17122.0	16253.0	105.3
市民在京游人数	Number of Beijing Citizens Touring in Beijing	10993.0	10606.0	103.6
入境旅游者人数	**Number of Inbound Tourists**	**416.5**	**420.0**	**99.2**
港澳台同胞	Hong Kong, Macao and Taiwan Tourists	61.8	62.4	99.0
中国香港	Hong Kong, China	35.3	34.9	101.1
中国澳门	Macao, China	1.6	2.1	76.2
中国台湾	Taiwan, China	24.9	25.4	97.8
外国人	Foreigners	354.8	357.6	99.2
亚洲	Asia	126.4	133.1	95.0
#日本	Japan	24.8	25.8	96.2
韩国	Korea	37.9	41.6	91.1
菲律宾	Philippines	2.1	2.3	91.3
印度尼西亚	Indonesia	4.4	4.9	89.8
马来西亚	Malaysia	8.1	7.8	103.8
新加坡	Singapore	11.9	11.0	108.2
泰国	Thailand	5.4	5.0	108.0
印度	India	7.5	8.0	93.8
蒙古	Mongolia	3.5	4.4	79.5
美洲	America	95.6	91.6	104.3
#美国	United States	70.3	69.4	101.3
加拿大	Canada	15.3	13.0	117.7
欧洲	Europe	105.9	106.9	99.1
#英国	United Kingdom	18.3	17.2	106.4
法国	France	13.2	15.3	86.1
德国	Germany	20.6	21.2	97.0
意大利	Italy	6.5	6.2	104.7
西班牙	Spain	5.4	4.4	122.7
瑞典	Sweden	3.6	3.8	94.7
瑞士	Switzerland	2.8	2.9	96.6
俄罗斯	Russia	9.5	10.3	92.2
大洋洲	Oceania	17.6	16.3	108.0
#澳大利亚	Australia	14.6	13.6	107.4
新西兰	New Zealand	2.5	2.1	119.0
非洲	Africa	8.8	8.9	98.9
其他	Others	0.6	0.7	85.7

资料来源：表中“国内旅游人数”的相关资料来自北京市旅游发展委员会。
Source: Data related to "Number of Domestic Tourists" in this table were provided by Beijing Municipal Commission of Tourism Development.

17-4 在京旅游花费构成情况(2005-2016年)
COMPOSITION OF EXPENDITURES FOR TOURISM IN BEIJING (2005-2016)

单位：% (%)

项目	Item	2005	2006	2007	2008	2009	2010	2011	2012	2013	2014	2015	2016
入境旅游者花费构成	**Compositition of Expenditures for Inbound Tourists**	**100.0**	**100.0**	**100.0**	**100.0**	**100.0**	**100.0**	**100.0**	**100.0**	**100.0**	**100.0**	**100.0**	**100.0**
长途交通费	Long-distance Transportation Expenses	35.3	30.0	29.0	31.1	37.4	28.1	26.4	28.0	26.9	27.0	36.8	38.3
民　航	Air	30.9	29.6	24.4	25.3	27.1	19.8	20.5	22.3	21.2	21.4	30.8	38.0
铁　路	Railway	1.1	0.3	3.0	3.6	5.5	5.3	3.4	3.3	3.7	3.6	3.2	0.2
公　路	Highway	3.3	0.1	1.6	2.2	4.8	3.0	2.5	2.4	2.0	2.0	2.7	0.1
市内交通费	Local Transportation Expenses	1.1	1.7	2.6	2.4	2.7	3.4	3.5	3.5	2.5	2.6	2.4	2.5
住　宿	Accommodation	17.3	32.0	16.9	16.4	14.5	14.4	15.5	16.5	16.9	16.7	12.8	18.3
餐　饮	Restaurants	9.2	11.7	8.7	8.7	7.5	8.7	6.8	7.4	7.3	7.4	6.2	11.4
购　物	Shopping	19.9	15.9	22.5	19.1	20.4	25.1	25.3	23.5	27.6	26.7	19.9	18.5
邮电通讯	Post and Telecommunications	3.4	0.8	2.7	3.8	2.7	3.2	2.0	2.2	1.7	1.7	2.4	0.2
景区游览	Scenic Spot Sightseeing	4.7	2.3	4.2	4.8	3.9	4.7	4.2	5.0	4.2	4.3	3.3	4.2
文化娱乐	Culture and Entertainment	4.6	3.2	5.0	4.5	4.6	5.0	6.0	5.4	3.8	4.0	4.2	4.6
其　他	Others	4.5	2.4	8.4	9.2	6.3	7.4	10.3	8.5	9.1	9.6	12.1	2.0
外地来京游客花费构成	**Compositition of Expenditures for Tourists from Outside Beijing**	**100.0**	**100.0**	**100.0**	**100.0**	**100.0**	**100.0**	**100.0**	**100.0**	**100.0**	**100.0**	**100.0**	**100.0**
长途交通费	Long-distance Transportation Expenses	12.8	15.1	16.3	15.4	12.9	12.8	13.5	15.5	17.0	17.6	17.0	15.8
民　航	Air		8.0	9.2	9.1	6.6	6.0	6.2	7.7	7.5	7.1	7.4	7.5
铁　路	Railway		6.1	6.4	4.5	1.3	5.8	6.9	7.5	9.1	10.2	9.3	8.0
公　路	Highway		1.1	0.7	1.8	5.0	1.0	0.3	0.3	0.4	0.3	0.3	0.3
市内交通费	Local Transportation Expenses	5.7	5.1	5.5	5.6	4.9	5.0	4.5	4.0	3.8	3.8	4.0	3.9
住　宿	Accommodation	17.2	14.9	17.3	15.1	17.7	19.6	20.0	19.8	19.5	20.2	18.7	17.8
餐　饮	Restaurants	19.8	18.7	20.5	23.2	21.8	20.2	20.9	21.4	21.4	22.1	22.1	22.8
购　物	Shopping	24.1	22.2	25.8	32.7	34.5	34.5	34.3	32.1	30.9	28.2	30.2	31.3
邮电通讯	Post and Telecommunications	1.0	1.2	1.8	1.0	0.6	0.5	0.3	0.2	0.2	0.3	0.3	0.2
景区游览	Scenic Spot Sightseeing	9.1	9.5	7.2	4.5	6.1	6.2	5.7	6.1	6.6	6.5	6.2	6.6
文化娱乐	Culture and Entertainment	3.1	2.5	1.9	1.6	1.2	1.0	0.8	0.7	0.5	0.6	0.7	0.9
其　他	Others	7.1	10.8	3.7	0.9	0.3	0.2	0.1	0.1	0.1	0.7	0.8	0.7

资料来源：北京市旅游发展委员会。
Source: Beijing Municipal Commission of Tourism Development.

17−5 旅游服务设施情况(1978−2016年)
TOURISM SERVICE FACILITIES (1978-2016)

年 份 Year	饭店个数(个) Number of Hotels (unit)	五星 5-star	四星 4-star	三星 3-star	二星 2-star	一星 1-star	饭店客房数(万间) Number of Hotel Guest Rooms (10,000 rooms)	旅行社家数(个) Number of Travel Agencies (unit)	#国际社 International Travel Agencies	A级及以上景区个数(个) Number of Scenic Spots at Grade-A and Above (unit)	5A	4A	3A	2A	1A
1978	11						0.39								
1979	13						0.44								
1980	20						0.49								
1981	35						0.69								
1982	39						1.00								
1983	41						1.03								
1984	50						1.30								
1985	63						1.66								
1986	80						2.10								
1987	97						2.40								
1988	96						2.80	30							
1989	101						3.50	77							
1990	122						3.95	77							
1991	213						4.40	69							
1992	226						5.20	69							
1993	226						5.20	55							
1994	175	14	20	32	72	37	5.40	297	113						
1995	197	15	25	43	79	35	5.90	310	125						
1996	204	15	25	46	82	36	6.10	349	128						
1997	248	16	26	60	109	37	6.80	350	130						
1998	258	16	32	65	113	32	7.00	380	135						
1999	268	17	32	71	117	31	7.20	419	144						
2000	409	21	34	132	176	46	8.40	456	150						
2001	506	21	43	154	230	58	9.30	490	160	47		17	4	22	4
2002	572	26	56	175	252	63	10.30	505	161	86		25	9	43	9
2003	614	30	62	195	267	60	10.90	530	165	93		28	9	46	10
2004	613	34	70	207	260	42	9.10	585	170	93		28	9	46	10
2005	652	36	79	224	267	46	10.97	714	196	124		36	26	50	12
2006	700	37	91	228	292	52	11.20	790	212	124		36	26	50	12
2007	806	42	114	257	338	55	13.00	844	239	154	4	41	35	54	20
2008	836	52	127	272	334	51	13.40	860	266	158	4	44	36	54	20
2009	757	54	129	268	269	37	12.95	888	265	179	4	55	53	51	16
2010	729	64	139	262	237	27	13.05	819		201	4	66	72	44	15
2011	598	63	127	207	181	20	11.64	919		211	6	63	80	46	16
2012	612	62	130	207	191	22	11.71	1021		203	8	64	78	40	13
2013	614	62	131	207	193	21	11.64	1147		213	8	67	86	42	10
2014	581	65	133	205	165	13	11.38	1243		221	8	69	89	45	10
2015	528	63	127	193	135	10	10.86	1238		227	8	72	95	44	8
2016	523	61	126	193	135	8	10.75	1162		241	8	74	106	47	6

注：1. 1993年及以前饭店数为涉外饭店口径，1994年以后为星级饭店口径。

2. 1994—1996年国际旅行社为一、二类旅行社合计。从2010年起，旅行社不再按国际旅行社和国内旅行社分组。

资料来源：北京市旅游发展委员会。

Note: a) Number of hotels in 1993 and before was the number of hotels for foreign tourists, and after 1994,the number of star-rated hotels.

b) International travel agencies were the total number of travel agencies of categories I and II after 1994-1996. From 2010, statistics of travel agencies were no more grouped into international and domestic angencies.

Source: Beijing Municipal Commission of Tourism Development.

17-6 星级饭店接待及经营情况(1995-2016年)
RECEPTION AND OPERATION OF STAR-RATED HOTELS (1995-2016)

年份 Year	企业个数(个) Number of Enterprises (unit)	接待住宿人数(万人次) Tourists Received (10000 person-time)	接待住宿人天数(万人天) Persons-Day Received (10000 person-day)	出租率(%) Renting Rate (%)	平均房价(元/间天) Average Prices (yuan/room.day)	营业收入(万元) Business Income (10000 yuan)	利润总额(万元) Total Profits (10000 yuan)	从业人员平均人数(人) Average Number of Employed Persons (person)
1995	191	484.6	1843.4	67.0	491	1136136	188095	98535
1996–2000		**3168.1**	**10110.0**			**5388348**	**286868**	
1996	207	485.3	1691.6	63.0	483	1132827	153145	94352
1997	235	541.8	1801.4	59.0	463	1145884	104918	103255
1998	262	605.0	1867.7	55.0	397	1038991	-24239	104391
1999	263	681.5	1918.6	57.0	352	970907	22383	103827
2000	294	854.5	2830.6	61.0	394	1099739	30661	96115
2001–2005		**5931.5**	**14152.9**			**7243160**	**316031**	
2001	363	1038.5	3191.7	62.0	384	1202746	50466	105792
2002	390	1071.2	2437.6	62.0	392	1307094	27212	107091
2003	441	1007.4	2497.2	52.0	389	1227956	-33471	105994
2004	464	1270.8	2798.9	65.0	409	1654198	117541	107386
2005	594	1543.6	3227.5	62.0	425	1851166	154283	126817
2006–2010		**8761.5**	**17721.0**			**11799293**	**650440**	
2006	597	1578.5	3284.5	61.3	460	2055300	194460	126430
2007	638	1664.2	3403.6	60.2	494	2369964	219891	129523
2008	694	1566.1	3206.6	52.0	605	2504849	232746	130609
2009	815	1827.3	3652.8	49.2	430	2261411	-76121	134159
2010	729	2125.4	4173.5	56.4	450	2607769	79464	130050
2010–2015		**10119.8**	**19429.6**			**13756636**	**518904**	
2011	598	2111.1	4119.6	59.9	482	2853358	162374	128609
2012	612	2101.0	4085.2	60.0	523	3031116	179495	122379
2013	614	1958.8	3769.5	58.4	530	2727974	111669	112512
2014	581	1940.3	3664.6	57.6	513	2568185	12499	99258
2015	528	2008.6	3790.7	60.6	520	2576003	52866	92606
2016	523	2017.1	3704.0	62.6	533	2614497	274585	84868

注：1. 表中企业个数为全市星级宾馆饭店数，其余指标1995—1999年为涉外饭店数据，2000年及以后为星级宾馆饭店数据。
2. 从2011年开始北京市旅游发展委员会每年对全市星级饭店进行重新评定，对未达标饭店取消星级。

Note: a) Number of Enterprises refer to the number of star-rated hotels in Beijing, Other indicators covered hotels for foreign tourists for 1995-1999, and star-rated hotels after 2000.
b) From 2011, Beijing Municipal Tourism Development Commission reevalutaed star-rated hotels across the city , and cancelled the rating of hotels that did not meet the standard.

17-7 星级饭店经营情况
OPERATION OF STAR-RATED HOTELS

项目	Item	企业个数(个) Number of Enterprises (unit)		出租率(%) Renting Rate (%)		平均房价(元/间天) Average Prices (yuan/room.day)	
		2016	2015	2016	2015	2016	2015
合计	**Total**	**523**	**528**	**62.6**	**60.6**	**533**	**520**
四星、五星合计	**Hotels of 4 and 5 Star Grade**	**187**	**190**	**63.8**	**62.5**	**622**	**640**
五星	5-Star	61	63	67.3	64.0	785	821
四星	4-Star	126	127	64.6	61.4	488	491
一星至三星合计	**Hotels of 1 to 3-Star Grade**	**336**	**338**	**56.1**	**57.8**	**344**	**331**
三星	3-Star	193	193	57.5	57.6	378	361
二星	2-Star	135	135	57.3	58.8	264	253
一星	1-Star	8	10	28.2	42.9	263	204

17-7 续表 Continued

项目	Item	营业收入(万元) Business Income (10000 yuan)		利润总额(万元) Total Profits (10000 yuan)		从业人员平均人数(人) Average Number of Employed Persons (person)	
		2016	2015	2016	2015	2016	2015
合计	**Total**	**2462773**	**2576003**	**250519**	**52866**	**83324**	**92606**
四星、五星合计	**Hotels of 4 and 5 Star Grade**	**1899618**	**1986642**	**248099**	**64208**	**58109**	**63294**
五星	5-Star	1103967	1180293	168620	65453	29083	30995
四星	4-Star	795651	806349	79479	-1244	29026	32299
一星至三星合计	**Hotels of 1 to 3-Star Grade**	**563155**	**589361**	**2420**	**-11342**	**25215**	**29312**
三星	3-Star	470259	491043	-1340	-14208	20711	24108
二星	2-Star	92696	98097	3682	2778	4484	5183
一星	1-Star	200	222	78	88	20	21

17-8 星级饭店接待住宿者情况(按住宿者类别分)
TOURSITS RECEIVED BY STAR-RATED HOTELS (BY TYPE OF TOURISTS)

项目	Item	2016 接待量 Tourists Received	2016 构成(%) Composition (%)	2015 接待量 Tourists Received	2015 构成(%) Composition (%)	2016年为2015年% 2016 as % of 2015
接待住宿人数 (万人次)	**Tourists Received (10000 person-times)**	**2017.1**	**100.0**	**2008.6**	**100.0**	**100.4**
国内住宿者	Domestic Tourists	1780.3	88.3	1775.7	88.4	100.3
外国人	Foreigners	204.3	10.1	200.9	10.0	101.7
香港同胞	Compatriots from Hong Kong, China	18.9	0.9	18.5	0.9	102.1
澳门同胞	Compatriots from Macao, China	0.8	0.0	0.9	…	91.2
台湾同胞	Compatriots from Taiwan, China	12.8	0.6	12.6	0.6	102.0
接待住宿人天数 (万人天)	**Persons-day Received (10000 persons-day)**	**3704.0**	**100.0**	**3790.7**	**100.0**	**97.7**
国内住宿者	Domestic Tourists	3218.2	86.9	3298.3	87.0	97.6
外国人	Foreigners	417.8	11.3	425.0	11.2	98.3
香港同胞	Compatriots from Hong Kong, China	38.2	1.0	37.3	1.0	102.4
澳门同胞	Compatriots from Macao, China	1.9	0.1	2.2	0.1	85.6
台湾同胞	Compatriots from Taiwan, China	27.9	0.8	27.8	0.7	100.5

17-9 星级饭店接待住宿者情况(按饭店星级分)
TOURSITS RECEIVED BY STAR-RATED HOTELS (BY STAR RATING)

单位：万人次 (10000 person-times)

项目	Item	2016 接待量 Tourists Received	2016 构成(%) Composition (%)	2015 接待量 Tourists Received	2015 构成(%) Composition (%)	2016年为2015年% 2016 as % of 2015
接待住宿人数	**Tourists Received**	**2017.1**	**100.0**	**2008.6**	**100.0**	**100.4**
五星级	5-Star	639.7	31.7	550.9	27.4	116.1
四星级	4-Star	674.3	33.4	670.4	33.4	100.6
三星级	3-Star	503.8	25.0	556.9	27.7	90.5
二星级	2-Star	197.2	9.8	225.8	11.2	87.3
一星级	1-Star	2.1	0.1	4.6	0.2	45.7
接待入境住宿人数	**Inbound Tourists Received**	**236.8**	**100.0**	**232.9**	**100.0**	**101.7**
五星级	5-Star	135.8	57.4	131.1	56.3	103.6
四星级	4-Star	84.2	35.6	83.2	35.7	101.2
三星级	3-Star	13.4	5.7	14.1	6.0	95.2
二星级	2-Star	3.3	1.4	4.4	1.9	75.9
一星级	1-Star	…	…	…	…	…

17-10 旅行社接待及经营情况(1990-2016年)
RECEPTION AND OPERATION OF TRAVEL AGENCIES (1990-2016)

年 份 Year	企 业 个 数 (个) Number of Enterprises (unit)	外联(组团) 人 数 (万人次) Number of Inbound Tourists (Organized) (10000 person-times)	接 待 人 数 (万人次) Tourists Received (10000 person-times)	国内居民 出境人数 (万人次) Number of Outbound Chinese Tourists (10000 person-times)	营 业 收 入 (万元) Business Income (10000 yuan)	利 润 总 额 (万元) Total Profits (10000 yuan)	从业人员 平均人数 (人) Average Number of Employed Persons (person)
1990		32.5	54.7				
1991-1995		**355.6**	**451.7**				
1991		53.3	69.1				
1992		61.2	100.7				
1993		71.3	103.6				
1994		84.1	91.0	1.0			
1995	100	85.7	87.4	1.2	290987.9	107654.6	
1996-2000		**487.1**	**417.5**	**37.9**	**2187374.9**	**106167.0**	
1996	105	88.0	78.6	2.7	351634.7	13520.8	
1997	110	87.3	76.0	3.8	386254.1	16009.6	
1998	131	85.0	69.0	6.6	387562.7	21319.9	
1999	120	103.1	92.9	11.1	485678.8	26572.0	
2000	127	123.7	101.0	13.7	576244.6	28744.7	6280
2001-2005		**986.2**	**919.6**	**185.4**	**4453919.0**	**51899.5**	
2001	140	143.4	130.1	21.9	700529.0	18682.5	8259
2002	151	179.4	176.3	28.5	823551.0	23362.0	9350
2003	147	80.2	82.4	31.9	553787.0	-11829.0	8382
2004	147	274.8	252.6	51.4	1059989.0	11444.0	7760
2005	147	308.4	278.2	51.7	1316063.0	10240.0	8752
2006-2010		**2036.3**	**1852.4**	**515.9**	**11530195.8**	**82083.6**	
2006	147	343.9	315.7	79.2	1610265.0	7012.0	8659
2007	189	424.1	377.9	100.2	2101874.5	28409.2	11597
2008	245	359.6	310.1	102.0	2166898.1	18121.6	14369
2009	265	370.6	306.6	84.9	2134058.8	5904.6	15262
2010	819	538.1	542.2	149.6	3517099.4	22636.2	21454
2011-2015		**3223.2**	**2408.0**	**1731.1**	**31300961.3**	**131080.7**	
2011	919	593.9	552.3	184.3	4436713.3	20879.2	23871
2012	1021	684.5	519.1	272.5	5415692.9	35274.4	28022
2013	1147	661.3	441.6	331.0	6103603.4	64177.5	31694
2014	1243	628.0	427.0	410.2	6989125.4	27881.7	33591
2015	1238	655.5	468.0	533.1	8355826.3	-17132.1	37780
2016	1162	667.9	466.8	571.3	8788779.0	-29589.9	40812

注：1．本表2009年及以前为国际旅行社口径，从2010年起调整为全部旅行社口径。
2．国内居民出境人数为旅行社组织出境游客的实际人次数，不重复统计。

Note: a) Figures in this table refer to international travel agencies in and before 2009, and all travel agencies after 2010.
b) Number of outbound Chinese visitors is the actual number of tourists going abroad that were organized by travel agencies, which has not been calculated repeatedly.

17-11 旅行社外联(组团)及接待情况
TOURISTS GROUPED (ORGANIZED) AND RECEIVED BY TRAVEL AGENCIES

项　目	Item	2016	2015	2016年为2015年% 2016 as % of 2015
外联(组团)人数　(万人次)	**Tourists Grouped (Organized)　(10000 person-times)**	**667.9**	**655.5**	**101.9**
国内旅游者	Domestic Tourists	537.3	515.0	104.3
港澳同胞	Compatriots from Hong Kong and Macao, China	5.9	6.3	93.7
台湾同胞	Compatriots from Taiwan, China	4.0	5.1	78.4
外国人	Foreigners	120.7	129.1	93.5
接待人数　(万人次)	**Tourists Received　(10000 person-times)**	**466.8**	**468.0**	**99.7**
国内旅游者	Domestic Tourists	335.6	344.0	97.6
港澳同胞	Compatriots from Hong Kong and Macao, China	7.9	8.7	90.8
台湾同胞	Compatriots from Taiwan, China	3.4	3.8	89.5
外国人	Foreigners	119.8	111.5	107.4
外联(组团)人天数(万人天)	**Persons-day of Tourists Grouped (Organized) (10000 persons-day)**	**2812.7**	**2687.7**	**104.7**
国内旅游者	Domestic Tourists	2170.9	2009.2	108.0
港澳同胞	Compatriots from Hong Kong and Macao, China	24.5	27.2	90.1
台湾同胞	Compatriots from Taiwan, China	22.0	26.5	83.0
外国人	Foreigners	595.3	624.8	95.3
接待人天数　(万人天)	**Persons-day of Tourists Received　(10000 persons-day)**	**1960.2**	**1935.8**	**101.3**
国内旅游者	Domestic Tourists	1406.4	1371.7	102.5
港澳同胞	Compatriots from Hong Kong and Macao, China	40.5	43.1	94.0
台湾同胞	Compatriots from Taiwan, China	17.8	21.4	83.2
外国人	Foreigners	495.5	499.7	99.2

17-12 旅行社组织国内居民出境旅游情况 OUTBOUND CHINESE TOURISTS ORGANIZED BY TRAVEL AGENCIES

单位：万人次 (10000 person-times)

项　　目	Item	2016	2015	2016年为2015年% 2016 as % of 2015
旅行社个数(个)	**Number of Travel Agencies (unit)**	**407**	**400**	**101.8**
国内居民出境人数	**Number of Outbound Chinese Tourists**	**571.3**	**533.1**	**107.2**
前往国别及地区	**Countries and Regions of Destination**			
#中国香港	Hong Kong, China	18.5	21.5	85.8
中国澳门	Macao, China	13.2	15.1	87.3
中国台湾	Taiwan, China	14.6	30.1	48.5
泰　国	Thailand	104.6	93.4	112.0
新加坡	Singapore	17.1	14.7	116.3
马来西亚	Malaysia	11.9	10.7	111.1
菲律宾	Philippines	4.6	2.5	183.2
韩　国	Korea	93.5	68.0	137.6
日　本	Japan	97.7	89.7	108.9
澳大利亚	Australia	13.4	12.7	105.8
新西兰	New Zealand	8.4	7.9	106.7

注：1. 本表统计范围为有特许经营出境旅游业务权的旅行社。
2. 国内居民出境人数为旅行社组织出境游客的实际人次数，不重复统计。
3. 前往国别及地区统计中，游客一次出境旅游去往多个国家及地区的，分别计入前往国家及地区。

Note: a) Figures in this table cover the travel agencies that are franchised to operate outbound travelling business.
b) Number of outbound Chinese tourists is the actual number of tourists going abroad who were organized by travel agencies,which has not been calculated repeatedly.
c) In the statistics for "countries and regions of destination", if a tourist went to several countries and regions, he/she would be included in each country and region.

17−13 旅行社经营情况
OPERATION OF TRAVEL SERVICES

单位：万元 (10000 yuan)

项 目	Item	2016	2015	2016年为2015年% 2016 as % of 2015
企业个数 (个)	Number of Enterprises (unit)	1162	1238	93.9
营业收入	Business Income	8788779.0	8355826.3	105.2
主营业务成本	Main Business Cost	8205259.9	6969927.9	117.7
营业费用	Business Expenses	320865.0	326021.3	98.4
主营业务税金及附加	Main Business Tax and Surtax	14460.6	29739.4	48.6
主营业务利润	Main Business Profits	548903.0	436187.4	125.8
管理费用	Management Expenses	287706.4	251488.1	114.4
营业利润	Business Profits	-35414.0	-24962.0	-
利润总额	Total Profits	-29589.9	-17132.1	-
从业人员平均人数 (人)	Average Number of Employed Persons (person)	40812	37780	108.0

17−14 A级及以上和重点旅游景区活动情况
STATISTICS FOR KEY SIGHT SPOTS ABOVE GRADE A

项 目	Item	2016	2015	2016年为2015年% 2016 as % of 2015
A级及以上和重点旅游景区数 (个)	Number of Key Sight Spots Above Grade A (unit)	243	248	98.0
收入合计 (万元)	Total Income (10000 yuan)	771493	728568	105.9
门票收入	Ticket Income	475262	462318	102.8
商品销售收入	Commodity Sales	26456	19299	137.1
其他收入	Other Income	269775	246951	109.2
接待人数 (万人次)	Tourists Received (10000 person-times)	30350	29405	103.2
#入境旅游者人数	Inbound Tourists	790	844	93.7

主要统计指标解释

入境旅游者 指来中国（大陆）观光、度假、探亲访友、就医疗养、购物、参加会议或从事经济、文化、体育、宗教活动，且在中国（大陆）的旅游住宿设施内至少停留一夜的外国人、港澳台同胞等游客。入境旅游者不包括以下人员：（1）应邀来华访问的政府部长以上官员及其随行人员；（2）外国驻华使领馆官员、外交人员以及随行的家庭服务人员和受赡养者；（3）常住中国（大陆）一年以上的外国专家、留学生、记者、商务机构人员等；（4）乘坐国际航班过境不需要通过护照检查进入中国（大陆）口岸的中转旅客；（5）边境地区往来的边民；（6）回大陆定居的港澳台同胞；（7）已在中国（大陆）定居的外国人和原已出境又返回在中国（大陆）定居的外国侨民；（8）归国的中国（大陆）出国人员。

国内旅游者 指中国（大陆）居民离开惯常居住地在境内其他地方的旅游住宿设施内至少停留一夜，最长不超过12个月的国内游客。

旅游外汇收入 指入境游客在中国（大陆）境内旅行、游览过程中用于交通、参观游览、住宿、餐饮、购物、娱乐等全部花费。

国内旅游收入 指国内游客在国内旅行、游览过程中用于交通、参观游览、住宿、餐饮、购物、娱乐等全部花费。

外联（组团）入境旅游者人数 指报告期内旅行社自组外联的入境旅游者人数，反映旅行社对外招徕的能力。旅行社按以下要求统计外联人数：入境游客不论其停留时间多少、旅游线路长短，只统计一次；旅行社只统计本社自组外联团的实到人数，不包括非本社外联、仅由本社接受委托办理签证的人数。

接待入境旅游者人数 指报告期内本旅行社派地陪接待的入境人数。

出境旅游总人数 指中国（大陆）公民因公或因私出境前往其他国家、中国香港特别行政区、澳门特别行政区和台湾省观光、度假、探亲访友、就医疗养、购物、参加会议或从事经济、文化、体育、宗教活动的人数。统计时，出境游客按每出境一次统计1人次。

Explanatory Notes on Main Statistical Indicators

Inbound Tourists refer to tourists from foreign countries, Hong Kong, Macao and Taiwan to (mainland of) China for sightseeing, holidays, visiting relatives and friends, medical service and rehabilitation, shopping, conferences, or economic, cultural, sports and religious activities, and staying in a tour accommodation facility in (the mainland of) China for at least one night. They do not include: (1) officials above the rank of governmental ministers, and their accompanying persons who visit China upon invitation; (2) officials in foreign embassies and consulates in Beijing, diplomatic personnel, and their accompanying family service personnel and dependents; (3) foreign experts, students, reporters, and personnel in business institutions who have been in (the mainland of) China for more than one year; (4) transit passengers via (the mainland of) China by international flights without passport checking; (5) people living on the frontiers who pass through borders; (6) compatriots from Hong Kong, Macao and Taiwan who settle down in the mainland of China; (7) Foreigners that have settled down in China and foreign nationals that have left the country and then come back to settle down in (the mainland of) China; (8) Chinese (Mainland) people who have gone abroad and returned to China.

Domestic Tourists refer to domestic visitors as residents in (the mainland of) China who leave their regular dwelling places to stay at least one night and at most 12 months in a travel accommodation facility of other domestic places.

Foreign Exchange Earnings of Tourism means the total spending of international tourists on traffic, tour, accommodation, restaurants, shopping, entertainment and so on during their tour and travel in (the mainland of) China.

Revenue from Domestic Tourism means the total spending of domestic tourists on traffic, tour, accommodation, restaurants, shopping and entertainment, and so on during their tour and travel in China.

Number of Inbound Tourists Organized by Travel Agencies means the number of inbound tourists organized by travel agencies in the reporting period. It shows the capacity of travel agencies in attracting inbound tourists; travel agencies shall count the tourists organized as follows: an inbound tourist is regarded as one visit regardless of the duration and distance of the tour; only the actual tourists organized by travel agencies are included. Those organized by other travel agencies or those who have visa submitted by the travel agencies are not included.

Number of Inbound Tourists Received means the number of inbound tourists received by local guides dispatched by travel agencies in the reporting period.

Total Number of Outbound Tourists means the number of citizens from (the mainland of) China who visit other countries, Hong Kong Special Administrative Region of PRC, Macao Special Administrative Region of PRC, and Taiwan for sightseeing, holiday, visiting relatives and friends, medical service and rehabilitation, shopping, conferences, or economic, cultural, sport and religious activities for official or private purpose. One visit is calculated as one person-time.

18

北京统计年鉴2017　BEIJING STATISTICAL YEARBOOK

金融和保险
FINANCE AND INSURANCE

简要说明

一、本章资料的主要内容

本章反映北京地区金融业发展情况。主要包括以下四个部分：

1．金融机构信贷收支情况；

2．证券市场交易情况；

3．保险业务情况；

4．上市公司基本情况。

二、本章资料的数据来源

1．信贷收支数据来源于中国人民银行营业管理部。

2．证券市场交易量数据来源于北京市统计局。

3．银行、保险系统机构及人员数据来源于北京市统计局。

4．保险业务数据来源于中国保险监督管理委员会北京监管局。

5．上市公司数据来源于中国证券监督管理委员会北京证监局。

Brief Introduction

I. Main Content

This chapter reflects the development of the financial industry in Beijing, mainly consisting of four parts:

1. Balance of credit for financial institutions;

2. Transactions in securities market;

3. Insurance business;

4. Basic information of listed companies.

II. Source of Data

1. Figures of balance of credit are gathered from the Banking Management Department of the People's Bank of China.

2. Data of transactions in securities market are gathered from Beijing Municipal Bureau of Statistics.

3. Data of banks, insurance institutions and personnel are gathered from Beijing Municipal Bureau of Statistics.

4. Data of insurance business are gathered from Beijing Bureau of China Insurance Regulatory Commission.

5. Data of basic information of listed companies are gathered from Beijing Securities Regulatory Bureau of China Securities Regulatory Commission.

18-1 北京市金融机构(含外资)存贷款余额(1978-2016年)
DEPOSIT AND LOAN BALANCE OF FINANCIAL INSTITUTIONS (INCLUDING FOREIGN BANKS) (1978-2016)

单位：亿元 (100 million yuan)

年份 Year	金融机构本外币存款 Balance of Savings Deposit in Domestic and Foreign Currencies in Financial Institutions	#人民币存款 RMB Deposits	金融机构本外币存款 Deposits in Domestic and Foreign Currencies in Financial Institutions					
			中资金融机构 Chinese Financial Institutions			外资银行 Foreign-funded Financial Bank		
			存款合计 Total Deposits	人民币存款 RMB Deposits	外汇(亿美元) Foreign Exchange (USD 100 million)	存款合计 Total Deposits	人民币存款 RMB Deposits	外汇(亿美元) Foreign Exchange (USD 100 million)
1978				114.7				
1979				139.1				
1980				168.0				
1981				220.5				
1982				279.2				
1983				321.3				
1984				375.5				
1985				411.0				
1986				508.8				
1987				610.8				
1988				609.9				
1989				717.6				
1990				893.9				
1991				1244.1				
1992				1528.3				
1993				1873.1				
1994				2677.3				
1995				3527.2				
1996				4378.9				
1997				5228.0				
1998				6666.8				
1999				8267.2				
2000	11526.0			9759.8	205.6			…
2001	14109.2		14042.1	12223.4	219.8			7.3
2002	17438.4		17369.9	15392.7	238.9			8.3
2003	20476.0		20398.2	18321.9	250.9			9.4
2004	23781.3	21625.9	23679.3	21625.9	248.1			12.3
2005	28969.9	26785.9	28800.9	26731.3	256.4		54.6	14.2
2006	33793.3	31313.8	33484.1	31179.2	295.2		134.5	22.4
2007	37700.3	35369.7	37087.5	35014.1	283.8		355.6	35.2
2008	43980.7	42107.6	43094.4	41500.0	233.3	886.3	607.5	40.8
2009	56960.1	54275.5	55804.8	53428.8	348.0	1155.3	846.6	45.2
2010	66584.6	64453.9	64897.6	63025.2	282.7	1687.0	1428.7	39.0
2011	75001.9	72655.4	73018.9	70985.1	322.8	1983.1	1670.3	49.6
2012	84837.3	81389.6	82615.9	79620.6	476.5	2221.4	1769.1	72.0
2013	91660.5	87990.6	89187.4	85897.2	539.6	2473.1	2093.4	62.3
2014	100095.5	95370.5	97645.9	93326.0	706.0	2449.6	2044.5	66.2
2015	128573.0	123767.4	126164.8	121878.9	660.0	2461.0	1941.3	80.0
2016	138408.9	132791.9	135510.3	130648.0	700.9	2933.1	2178.5	108.8

资料来源：中国人民银行营业管理部。
Source: Operations Office of People's Bank of China.

18-1 续表 Continued

单位：亿元 (100 million yuan)

年份 Year	金融机构本外币贷款余额 Balance of Loans in Domestic and Foreign Currencies in Financial Institutions	#人民币贷款 RMB Loans	#中长期贷款 Medium-term &Long-term Loans	金融机构本外币贷款 Loans in Domestic and Foreign Currencies in Financial Institutions 中资金融机构 Chinese Financial Institutions 贷款合计 Total Loans	人民币贷款 RMB Loans	外汇(亿美元) Foreign Exchange (USD 100 million)	外资银行 Foreign-funded Financial Bank 贷款合计 Total Loans	人民币贷款 RMB Loans	外汇(亿美元) Foreign Exchange (USD 100 million)
1978					53.9				
1979					74.2				
1980					87.3				
1981					91.3				
1982					109.1				
1983					149.5				
1984					174.3				
1985					249.8				
1986					299.2				
1987					346.1				
1988					415.7				
1989					487.1				
1990					573.1				
1991					735.8				
1992					894.7				
1993					1128.1				
1994					1429.0				
1995					1779.1				
1996					2082.8				
1997					2720.7				
1998					3326.6				
1999					4007.8				
2000	6407.9		3106.7	6306.3	6008.2	27.7			9.0
2001	7612.2		3797.3	7514.9	7202.9	37.4			10.8
2002	9704.3		5026.9	9602.6	9230.8	44.9			12.1
2003	12057.7		6352.0	11884.4	11314.7	68.8			20.9
2004	13577.7		7506.4	13312.3	12600.2	86.0			32.0
2005	15335.5		8632.4	14996.6	13792.2	149.2		42.3	36.8
2006	18131.6	15632.7	11142.8	17631.7	15486.9	274.7		145.8	45.4
2007	19861.5	17812.5	12217.6	19053.9	17360.2	231.9	807.5	452.3	48.6
2008	23010.7	19985.0	14688.9	22160.5	19431.1	399.4	850.2	554.0	43.3
2009	31052.9	25421.8	21163.8	30151.6	24805.1	783.0	901.3	616.7	41.7
2010	36479.6	29563.8	26180.2	35352.0	28748.1	997.2	1127.6	815.6	47.1
2011	39660.5	33367.0	24886.3	38410.3	32434.6	948.4	1250.2	932.5	50.4
2012	43189.5	36441.3	26333.5	41839.8	35441.7	1017.9	1349.7	999.6	55.7
2013	47880.9	40506.7	28171.7	46539.5	39557.5	1145.2	1341.4	949.2	64.3
2014	53650.6	45458.7	30882.3	52254.3	44438.8	1277.3	1396.2	1019.9	61.5
2015	58559.4	50559.5	33671.3	57281.2	49530.8	1193.6	1994.3	1676.9	48.9
2016	63739.4	56618.9	37471.3	62492.2	55553.2	1000.3	2005.9	1725.8	40.4

资料来源：中国人民银行营业管理部。
Source: Operations Office of People's Bank of China.

18-2 北京市金融机构(含外资)本外币信贷收支表(2016年)
BALANCE OF CREIT IN DOMESTIC AND FOREIGN CURRENCIES FOR FINANCIAL INSTITUTIONS (INCLUDE FOREIGN BANKS)(2016)

单位：万元，汇率：6.9370 (10000 yuan ,at an exchange rate of 6.9370)

项　目	Item	余　额 Balance	比年初增减额(+、-) Increase or Decrease than the Beginning of the Year
各项存款	**Total Deposits**	**1384088546**	**98335896**
#人民币存款	RMB Deposits	1327919063	90222390
境内存款	Domestic deposits	1372931527	97953692
住户存款	Resident deposits	295056832	18018229
非金融企业存款	Non-financial corporate deposits	537350081	74069513
广义政府存款	General government deposits	299165929	32806502
#财政性存款	Fiscal deposits	13991728	-559764
非银行业金融机构存款	Deposits of non-banking financial institutions	241358685	-26940551
境外存款	Overseas deposits	11157019	382203
各项贷款	**Total Loans**	**637394336**	**51800312**
#人民币贷款	RMB Loans	566188715	60593536
境内贷款	Domestic Loans	595891668	48821127
住户贷款	Resident loans	141505676	29688415
非金融企业及机关团体贷款	Loans of non-financial companies and organizations	443305096	12480525
非银行业金融机构贷款	Loans of non-banking financial institutions	11080896	6652187
境外贷款	Overseas Loans	41502667	2979186

资料来源：中国人民银行营业管理部。
Source: Operations Office of People's Bank of China.

18-3 北京市中资金融机构本外币信贷收支表(2016年)
BALANCE OF CREDIT IN DOMESTIC AND FOREIGN CURRENCIES FOR DOMESTICALLY-FUNDED FINANCIAL INSTITUTIONS(2016)

单位：万元，汇率：6.9370 (10000 yuan ,at an exchange rate of 6.9370)

项目	Item	余额 Balance	比年初增减额(+、-) Increase or Decrease than Year-beginning
各项存款	**Total Deposits**	**1355103108**	**93455052**
#人民币存款	RMB Deposits	1306479732	87691175
境内存款	Domestic deposits	1345901878	93133189
住户存款	Resident deposits	292756656	17661212
非金融企业存款	Non-financial corporate deposits	514897985	70023455
广义政府存款	General government deposits	299157097	32802377
#财政性存款	Fiscal deposits	13991728	-559764
非银行业金融机构存款	Deposits of non-banking financial institutions	239090140	-27353856
境外存款	Overseas deposits	9201230	321864
各项贷款	**Total Loans**	**624921673**	**52109205**
#人民币贷款	RMB Loans	555531902	60224394
境内贷款	Domestic Loans	584124983	49091934
住户贷款	Resident loans	139655717	29276496
非金融企业及机关团体贷款	Loans of non-financial companies and organizations	433388371	13063251
非银行业金融机构贷款	Loans of non-banking financial institutions	11080896	6752187
境外贷款	Overseas Loans	40796690	3017271

资料来源：中国人民银行营业管理部。
Source: Operations Office of People's Bank of China.

18-4 银行、保险系统机构及人员(2016年)
INSTITUTIONS AND PERSONNEL OF BANKING AND INSURANCE SYSTEMS (2016)

项目	Item	银行系统 Banking System		保险系统 Insurance System	
		机构(个) Institutions (unit)	人员(人) Personnel (person)	机构(个) Institutions (unit)	人员(人) Personnel (person)
全市	**Total**	**4303**	**191529**	**648**	**157817**
首都功能核心区	Core Functional Area of the Capital	765	94961	169	56259
城市功能拓展区	Urban Function Extension Area	2210	76220	221	64208
城市发展新区	New Area of Urban Development	921	14776	176	26739
生态涵养发展区	Ecological Conservation Area	407	5572	82	10611

注：1. 本表口径为在北京地区经营的银行、保险公司的总行(总公司)、分行(分公司)及所属分支机构。
2. 保险系统人员构成中含营销员。

Note: a) Figures in this table cover the headquarters (head offices), branches banks (branch companies) and subsidiaries of banks and insurance companies operating in Beijing.
b) Personnel of insurance system includes marketing personnel.

18-5 上市公司基本情况(1993-2016年)
LISTED COMPANIES (1993-2016)

年 份 Year	年末上市公司(家) Companies Listed by Year-end (unit)	上市公司总股本(万股) Total Equity of Listed Companies (10000 Shares)	股票首发数量(万股) Initial Public Offering Shares (10000 Shares)	首发募集资金(亿元) Funds Raised Through IPO (10000 yuan)	增发募集资金(亿元) Funds Raised Through Right Offerings (10000 yuan)	配股募集资金(亿元) Funds Raised Through Seasoned Equity Offerings (10000 yuan)
1993	3	24592	3924	58.0		28.8
1994	7	124038	20300	11.7		0.5
1995	7	133309				3.8
1996-2000			**439955**	**304.4**	**33.0**	**85.8**
1996	13	198956	29763	12.8		1.9
1997	26	470026	80200	52.2		7.0
1998	33	723561	52750	32.9		20.2
1999	43	1439894	121242	63.0	10.8	10.7
2000	54	2015049	156000	143.5	22.2	46.0
2001-2005			**764200**	**413.8**	**49.2**	**26.3**
2001	63	9764783	345500	191.6		17.0
2002	68	11929954	23800	16.8	14.9	
2003	74	11493598	373600	188.7	2.8	2.2
2004	83	12553074	21300	16.7	28.4	7.1
2005	83	13159721			3.1	
2006-2010			**11456582**	**6506.1**	**1665.5**	**852.8**
2006	92	58156652	2667911	1073.4	79.4	
2007	104	86151941	2428976	2433.3	304.7	12.1
2008	109	90486962	698853	546.9	502.0	63.8
2009	126	97911881	2179290	1154.2	430.7	
2010	165	137726461	3481552	1298.3	348.7	777.0
2011-2015			**1232164**	**1040.8**	**4024.0**	**282.1**
2011	194	143088054	420483	462.0	661.7	175.6
2012	217	146788089	211752	191.4	436.2	69.1
2013	219	151694399			183.9	32.5
2014	235	214359521	67787	74.9	1319.0	4.9
2015	264	225020500	532142	312.5	1423.3	
2016	281	232028500	149046	130.3	1859.3	49.4

注：1. 此表数据统计口径为注册地统计。
2. 1995年、2005年和2013年没有新股发行。
资料来源：中国证券监督管理委员会北京证监局。
Note: a) Statistics in this table are counted in terms of registered area.
b) There were no shares issued in 1995, 2005 and 2013.
Source: Beijing Regulatory Bureau of China Securities Regulatory Commission.

18-6 证券市场交易额情况(1994–2016年)
TRADE VOLUME OF SECURITIES MARKETS (1994-2016)

单位：亿元 (100 million yuan)

年份 Year	证券市场交易额 Trading Volume of Securities Market	#股票交易 Stock Trading	#基金交易 Fund Trading	#债券交易 Bond Trading	年末证券市场资金账户数(万户) Capital Accounts in Securities Market (year-end) (10000 Accounts)
1994	183.3	135.5		47.8	
1995	1619.0	520.5		152.3	
1996	5224.8	2900.6		2324.1	
1997	7934.4	3900.9		3844.8	
1998	10241.5	3426.4	187.0	6435.4	
1999	10694.5	5268.2	341.7	5005.5	88.9
2000	14457.0	9136.5	346.0	4825.9	115.2
2001	12596.5	5339.6	400.6	6729.7	149.0
2002	12565.9	3788.2	485.8	8216.5	155.0
2003	23369.8	5041.4	110.5	18048.4	162.4
2004	18512.9	7247.7	78.9	10928.9	166.2
2005	9322.5	4343.7	91.3	4567.3	169.8
2006	19557.1	14851.5	298.3	2075.2	189.4
2007	97978.7	77487.8	1535.0	2060.1	314.9
2008	62773.6	46231.3	1389.4	4052.5	373.6
2009	92148.0	78339.5	2253.5	1791.3	426.1
2010	87575.4	79843.1	1714.9	3384.3	475.1
2011	79103.1	61743.2	1494.8	15275.3	521.5
2012	85412.9	44993.4	2355.9	37388.6	551.5
2013	145932.7	61596.3	4104.8	69625.4	563.6
2014	232318.6	85714.5	7311.7	110657.5	587.5
2015	597169.7	305252.9	24054.2	182495.0	758.8
2016	421962.9	135890.9	14212.4	240689.6	883.4

注：2016年起“年末证券市场累计资金账户开户数”指标改为“年末证券市场资金账户数”。

Note: The indicator of "Accumulative Capital Accounts Opened in Securities Market (year-end)" has been modified as "Capital Accounts in Securities Market (year-end)" since 2016.

18-7 证券市场交易额情况
TRADE VOLUME OF SECURITIES MARKETS

项 目	Item	2016	2015	2016年为2015年% 2016 as % of 2015
成交额合计 （亿元）	**Total Trade Volume (100 million yuan)**	**421962.9**	**597169.7**	**70.4**
股票交易	Stock Trading	135890.9	305252.9	44.5
债券交易	Bond Trading	240689.6	182495.0	131.9
债券现货	Bonds in Stock	4457.4	3559.6	125.2
债券回购	Bond Repurchasing	235166.1	178394.4	131.8
募集资金交易	Trading of Funds Raised	1489.6	3258.2	45.7
基金交易	Fund Trading	14212.4	24054.2	59.1
其他交易	Other Tradings	29680.4	82109.4	36.1
年末证券市场资金账户数 （万户）	**Capital Accounts in Securities Market (year-end) (10000 Accounts)**	**883.4**	**758.8**	**116.4**

注：2016年起"年末证券市场累计资金账户开户数"指标改为"年末证券市场资金账户数"。

Note: The indicator of "Accumulative Capital Accounts Opened in Securities Market (year-end)" has been modified as "Capital Accounts in Securities Market (year-end)" since 2016.

18-8 保险业务情况(1997-2016年)
INSURANCE BUSINESS (1997-2016)

单位：亿元 (100 million yuan)

年份 Year	原保险保费收入 Premium Income of Original Insurance	人身险 Life Insurance	财产险 Property Insurance	赔付支出 Compensation Expenses	人身险 Life Insurance	财产险 Property Insurance
1997	102.5					
1998	88.6					
1999	91.8			29.9		
2000	93.4			28.4		
2001	141.3			32.0		
2002	234.1			46.9		
2003	282.5			48.0		
2004	279.3			55.3		
2005	498.2			75.4		
2006	411.5	327.2	84.4	84.0	45.1	38.9
2007	498.1	386.3	111.8	135.4	85.7	49.7
2008	585.9	451.8	134.1	188.9	121.0	67.9
2009	697.6	533.2	164.4	196.0	110.6	85.4
2010	966.5	754.2	212.3	199.7	105.9	93.7
2011	820.9	588.4	232.6	232.8	113.8	119.0
2012	923.1	656.1	267.0	286.2	133.9	152.3
2013	994.4	706.4	288.0	318.2	152.9	165.3
2014	1207.2	892.5	314.8	407.2	224.6	182.7
2015	1403.9	1059.2	344.7	506.6	300.0	206.6
2016	1839.0	1469.7	369.2	596.6	367.3	229.3

资料来源：中国保险监督管理委员会北京监管局。
Source: Beijing Regulatory Bureau of China Insurance Regulatory Commission.

18-9 保险业务情况
STATISTICS FOR INSURANCE BUSINESS

单位：亿元 (100 million yuan)

项目	Item	原保险保费收入 Premium Income of Original Insurance		赔付支出 Compensation Expenses	
		2016	2015	2016	2015
合计	**Total**	**1839.0**	**1403.9**	**596.6**	**506.6**
人身险业务小计	**Subtotal of Life Insurance**	**1469.7**	**1059.2**	**367.3**	**300.0**
人寿保险	Life Insurance	1101.6	778.2	280.9	231.7
非分红产品	Non-participating Products	699.8	350.0	33.0	22.6
分红产品	Participating Products	397.7	424.0	246.5	207.8
投资连接产品	Investment-linked Products	0.4	0.5	0.4	0.3
万能产品	Universal Products	3.8	3.7	1.0	1.0
意外伤害保险	Accident Insurance	44.9	37.7	13.7	11.5
健康保险	Health Insurance	323.2	243.3	72.7	56.8
财产险业务小计	**Subtotal of Property Insurance**	**369.2**	**344.7**	**229.3**	**206.6**
#企业财产保险	Enterprise Property Insurance	33.0	34.9	35.8	30.6
家庭财产保险	Household Property Insurance	2.4	1.6	1.3	0.4
机动车辆及第三者责任保险	Motor Vehicle and Third Party Liability Insurance	261.5	243.6	150.9	143.0
货物运输保险	Freight Transport Insurance	8.7	9.9	7.9	5.2
责任保险	Liability Insurance	35.2	24.7	17.4	11.5
工程险	Construction Insurance	7.5	7.8	2.9	3.0

资料来源：中国保险监督管理委员会北京监管局。
Source: Beijing Regulatory Bureau of China Insurance Regulatory Commission.

主要统计指标解释

存款 企业、机关、团体或居民根据可以收回的原则，把货币资金存入银行或其他信用机构保管并取得一定利息的一种信用活动形式。根据存款对象的不同可划分为企业存款、财政存款、机关团体存款、储蓄存款、农业存款等科目。它是银行信贷资金的主要来源。

贷款 银行或其他信用机构根据必须归还的原则，按一定利率，为企业、个人等提供资金的一种信用活动形式。我国银行贷款分为短期贷款、中长期贷款、委托及信托类贷款、其他类贷款等。

原保险保费收入 是指保险企业确认的原保险合同保费收入。是投保人根据保险合同的有关规定，为被保险人取得因约定危险事故发生所造成的经济损失补偿（或给付）权利，付给保险人的代价。包括财产险和人身险收入。

保险赔付支出 公司按保险合同约定支付给被保险人（或受益人）的赔款、保险金、给付等。包括赔款支出、死伤医疗给付、满期给付和年金给付。

股票交易额 指报告期投资者在各类证券交易场所进行股票买卖交易活动的金额。包括A股、B股、股份转让等。不含申购新股及申购中签交易额，也不含配股、分红、送股及转增交易额。

基金交易额 指报告期投资者在各类证券交易场所进行基金买卖交易活动的金额。包括封闭式基金、开放式基金中的ETF、LOF等。填报时，不在交易所挂牌交易的开放式基金的交易额不计在内。

债券交易额 指报告期投资者在各类证券交易场所进行债券买卖交易活动的金额。包括国债、地方政府债、金融债、企业债、公司债、分离债、可转债、私募债、资产支持类债券等。

债券现货交易额 指报告期投资者在各类证券交易场所进行债券买卖交易活动现货成交金额。

Explanatory Notes on Main Statistical Indicators

Deposit is a form of credit activity that enterprises, public institutions, groups or residents save their money, on a reclaimable basis, in banks or other credit institutions and receive certain interest. In terms of depositors, there are enterprise deposit, fiscal deposit, government agency deposit, savings deposit, agricultural deposit and so on, which constitute a main source of bank funds for extending credit..

Loan is a form of credit activity that banks or other credit institutions provide funds which must be repaid for enterprise and individuals at a given interest rate,. In China, bank loans are classified as short-, medium-, and long-term loans, entrusted and trust loans, and others.

Premium Income means the income of insurance premium of original insurance contracts confirmed by insurance companies. It is the price paid by policy holders to the insurer for the right to receive compensation (claim settlement) for any economic loss caused by agreed dangerous accidents pursuant to relevant provisions in the insurance contract. There are property insurance and life insurance incomes.

Insurance Indemnity Payments refer to indemnity, insurance money, and claim settlement, etc. paid by the insurance company to the insurant (or beneficiary) as agreed in the insurance contract, including indemnity payment, claim settlement for medical costs of death and injury, maturity payment and annuity payment.

Stock Market Turnover means the value of shares traded by investors in various securities exchanges, including: A share, B share and share transfer, etc., excluding turnover related to IPO subscription, IPO lot-winning, allotment, dividend, share-granting and capital reserve converted into share capital.

Funds Turnover means the value of funds traded by investors in various securities exchanges during the reporting period, including ETF and LOF, etc. in the closed-end funds and open-end funds. The turnover of open-end funds not listed and traded in exchanges shall not be included in the funds turnover reported.

Bonds Turnover means the value of bonds traded by investors in various securities exchanges during the reporting period, including treasury bonds, local government bonds, financial bonds, enterprise bonds, corporate bonds, convertible bonds, warrants bonds, private placement bonds and asset-backed bonds.

Bonds Spot Turnover means the spot turnover of bonds traded by investors in various securities exchanges during the reporting period.

北京统计年鉴2017　BEIJING STATISTICAL YEARBOOK

教育、文化
EDUCATION AND CULTURE

简要说明

一、教育部分的主要内容和资料来源

教育统计资料包括高等教育（研究生教育、普通本专科教育、成人本专科教育、其他各类高等学历教育）、中等教育(高中阶段、初中阶段)、小学教育、学前教育、特殊教育(盲聋哑和弱智儿童学校等)、工读学校等资料。主要指标包括学校数、在校学生数、招生数、毕业生数、教职工数、专任教师数等内容。

除技工学校数据来源于北京市人力资源和社会保障局外，其他教育统计资料均由北京市教育委员会提供。

二、文化部分的主要内容和资料来源

文化部分主要包括专业艺术剧团、公共图书馆、博物馆、文化馆、档案馆、文化站、广播、电影、电视以及新闻等文化单位的机构、人员和业务活动情况。

文化部分数据中，专业艺术剧团、公共图书馆和群众文化活动的资料主要来自北京市文化局；档案馆资料来自北京市档案局；博物馆资料来自北京市文物局；广播、电影和电视，报纸、期刊、图书出版资料来自北京市新闻出版广电局。

Brief Introduction

I. Main Content and Sources of Data for the Part of Education

Educational statistics include those for higher education (postgraduate education, undergraduate and junior college education, undergraduate and junior college education for adults, and other kinds of higher education for diplomas); secondary education (senior high school, junior high school); primary education; preschool education; special education (schools for the blind, deaf and mute, and mentally handicapped children, etc.); work-study schools for delinquent children. Main indicators include the number of schools, student enrollment, , number of new enrollment, number of teachers and staff, and number of full-time teachers, etc.

Date of Technician Training Schools from Beijing Municipal Bureau of Human Resources and Social Security, the other educational data were provided by Beijing Municipal Commission of Education.

II. Main Content and Sources of Data for the Part of Culture

Cultural statistics include the number, personnel and activities of professional art troupes, public libraries, museums, cultural centers, archives, broadcast, films, television and press, and other cultural organizations.

In Cultural data, figures of art, libraries, and mass culture are from Beijing Municipal Bureau of Culture; data of archives are from Beijing Municipal Bureau of Archives; data of museums are from Beijing Municipal Administration of Cultural Heritage; radio, film and television, newspaper, magazine and book publications data are from Beijing Municipal Administration of Press, Publication, Radio, Film and Television.

19-1 教育基本情况(1978-2016年)
BASIC STATISTICS FOR EDUCATION (1978-2016)

年 份 Year	全市各类学校数(个) Total Number of Various Schools (unit)	#普通高等学校 General Institutions of Higher Education	#普通中等学校 General Middle Schools	#高 中 Senior Middle Schools	#小 学 Primary Schools	全市各类学校在校学生数(人) Enrolled Students in Various Schools (person)	#普通本专科 Regular Undergraduates and College Students	#普通中等学校 General Middle Schools	#高 中 Senior Middle Schools	#小 学 Primary Schools
1978		35			4666		48618		415612	937336
1979		48			4534		55073		299974	968723
1980		50			4485		83032		312188	951763
1981		51			4445		98044		175180	900350
1982		51			4381		93878		92401	854516
1983		54			4269		90894		88657	838078
1984		57			4168		102962		110916	763204
1985		61			4059		122791		119876	733605
1986		66			3995		129647		109862	749101
1987		67			3875		136694		109023	777982
1988		67			3793		145134		108106	850577
1989		67			3703		141625		110745	934696
1990		67			3611		139646		100669	995831
1991	8496	67	1168	282	3482	2142085	136940	565357	93728	1013268
1992	8052	67	1150	279	3306	2194268	139978	617847	82894	1001762
1993	7789	66	1145	280	3190	2266932	158906	679821	78261	1022166
1994	7574	67	1150	280	3035	2348406	175203	758310	86584	1024503
1995	7158	65	1170	286	2867	2380096	182173	834903	102522	1007301
1996	7121	65	1189	296	2780	2388002	189953	881912	118476	999740
1997	6858	65	1181	288	2696	2361438	195842	887644	133461	977323
1998	6456	63	1190	282	2511	2325043	212984	895042	145966	919531
1999	5807	64	1182	275	2352	2297673	234033	931029	161473	836655
2000	5458	59	1159	302	2169	2299433	282585	972930	179002	743109
2001	4873	61	1111	289	1960	2297107	340284	988985	194283	664443
2002	4447	62	998	325	1824	2294947	398573	984117	220667	594241
2003	4158	74	977	329	1652	2299416	458898	968035	250959	546530
2004	3971	77	945	338	1504	2291594	500245	919178	274803	516042
2005	3782	79	917	335	1403	2264004	536724	859132	278358	494482
2006	3751	82	888	335	1310	2910228	554702	799074	259414	473275
2007	3593	83	863	328	1235	3195763	567875	839038	243818	666617
2008	3508	82	838	325	1202	3208704	575639	782866	219163	659500
2009	3425	88	804	305	1160	3214354	577154	740396	203477	647101
2010	3330	89	779	289	1104	3299555	577828	727741	198415	653255
2011	3367	89	769	290	1090	3426025	578633	711130	195072	680457
2012	3314	91	760	289	1081	3568273	581844	732224	193505	718655
2013	3439	89	757	291	1093	3736003	589234	706713	187586	789276
2014	3437	89	766	306	1040	3774868	594614	651443	177554	821152
2015	3454	90	768	306	996	3734245	593448	587112	169412	850321
2016	3524	91	767	305	984	3733544	588389	552468	163130	868417

注：1．从2007年开始，普通中学、小学、工读学校、特殊教育、学前教育在校学生数包括外省市户口借读学生。
2．1991—2005年，普通中等学校包括普通中专、技工学校、职业中学、普通中学和工读学校。2006年及以后普通中等学校为中等教育口径，包括普通中专、成人中专、技工学校、职业高中和普通中学。

Note: a) From 2007, enrolled students in general high schools, primary schools, work-study schools for delinquent children, special education schools, and pre-school education included those from outside Beijing and studying in Beijing on temporary basis.
b) In 1991-2005, general middle schools included technical secondary schools, technician training schools, vocational schools, general high schools, and work-study schools. In and after 2006, middle schools included technical secondary schools, technical secondary schools for adults, technician training schools, vocational senior high schools and general high schools.

19-1 续表 1 Continued 1

年份 Year	全市各类学校招生数（人）New Enrollment in Various Schools (person)	#普通本专科 Regular Undergraduates and College Students	#普通中等学校 General Middle Schools	#高中 Senior Middle Schools	#小学 Primary Schools	全市各类学校毕业生数（人）Number of Graduates in Various Schools (person)	#普通本专科 Regular Undergraduates and College Students
1978		17445		161288	199076		10881
1979		15848		160340	154809		8585
1980		17972		131961	138751		8233
1981		17921		54296	121744		2289
1982		21936		35212	104357		25753
1983		27988		40282	96028		31009
1984		31805		47068	103482		20110
1985		40670		35265	135048		21442
1986		35390		27863	160513		26953
1987		41163		41186	156954		34894
1988		42187		35429	184516		33066
1989		33557		33254	184609		35863
1990		36275		30596	161742		36171
1991	571685	37700	205107	28589	148300	487740	37702
1992	622142	41517	232765	25790	157145	520787	37075
1993	651729	52205	242274	26275	175853	526982	32888
1994	704933	51884	287642	34704	186315	528199	34855
1995	691972	52868	308786	40803	168903	554690	45094
1996	628772	55269	289612	42603	156898	575969	46471
1997	581091	56884	289719	49566	124231	584120	49973
1998	581786	62264	308157	52956	100415	600662	49322
1999	603332	78354	320731	56998	94358	603027	49936
2000	635328	99397	324862	65890	92002	604900	51556
2001	641432	116344	313257	69195	91230	617889	55831
2002	671956	128320	326835	84679	86406	624329	67621
2003	662877	143483	302071	94894	82631	610826	83816
2004	635842	147298	271396	93519	73577	614137	99637
2005	630515	156124	259133	88605	71020	622974	117367
2006	851808	154969	234524	76375	73138	787596	132488
2007	927144	156222	252709	71590	109203	851126	138834
2008	938891	157238	236714	68397	110440	832585	149459
2009	962648	158992	240937	65983	102414	865025	152336
2010	1002141	155228	238954	65649	113728	834340	150156
2011	1050131	157543	243754	64146	132719	838521	151277
2012	1108574	162042	254790	63381	141738	881804	152980
2013	1182301	163081	239010	59983	165807	923050	148689
2014	1113688	160056	202434	55184	153249	937209	147023
2015	1091756	152741	186517	56743	145876	961180	152118
2016	1115515	154715	180881	53544	145274	924267	153005

19-1 续表 2 Continued 2

年 份 Year	#普通中等学校 General Middle Schools	#高 中 Senior Middle Schools	#小 学 Primary Schools	专任教师数(人) Full-time Teachers (person)	平均每一专任教师负担学生数(人) Average Number of Students Instructed by a Full-time Teacher(person) 普通中学 General Middle Schools	小 学 Primary Schools
1978		174899	151950		19.9	20.7
1979		239813	114047		16.1	21.3
1980		145501	144025		14.8	21.7
1981		170992	162306		13.4	19.7
1982		111153	135562		12.3	19.5
1983			95919		11.5	19.6
1984		24498	169251		13.2	18.2
1985		24720	156035		13.9	17.4
1986		36942	138350		14.1	17.3
1987		43589	121599		12.8	16.8
1988		36127	105948		11.4	17.6
1989		29267	97208		11.0	19.1
1990		40369	102782		10.1	18.6
1991		34428	132544	168485	10.5	18.0
1992		32471	156306	169249	11.3	17.4
1993		27428	157838	170361	12.1	17.4
1994		24112	184566	175025	13.1	16.9
1995		23353	183894	176591	13.6	16.5
1996		25170	162030	178006	13.7	16.1
1997		33010	146023	179080	13.2	15.7
1998		39683	156194	178210	12.8	14.9
1999		40660	175656	175496	13.2	13.7
2000		47569	185059	167040	14.1	12.8
2001		51263	167076	168080	14.3	12.1
2002		51180	156683	166490	14.2	11.2
2003		56601	123580	166510	13.7	11.0
2004		66556	100139	172055	12.9	10.6
2005		73260	93486	174589	11.8	10.3
2006	290047	78037	90799	191365	10.8	9.8
2007	272651	78408	112332	195568	11.5	13.8
2008	262871	78468	112268	199114	10.9	13.5
2009	253067	70132	110730	203825	10.0	13.0
2010	233837	62305	102971	206602	10.2	13.2
2011	223955	58275	101678	199789	9.8	13.4
2012	224938	55657	109492	204812	9.7	13.7
2013	240225	58072	111839	216463	9.5	14.4
2014	229640	57773	112819	225165	9.0	14.4
2015	205795	57738	103893	226043	8.4	14.3
2016	182511	52841	111481	231251	7.9	14.0

19-2 幼儿园基本情况(1978-2016年)
BASIC STATISTICS FOR KINDERGARTENS (1978-2016)

单位：人 (person)

年份 Year	园数(所) Number of Kindergartens (unit)	班数(个) Number of Classes (unit)	离园人数 Children Leaving	入园人数 Children Entering	在园人数 Children Enrollment	教职工数 Teachers and Staff	#专任教师 Full-time Teachers
1978	5074				235923	39982	8369
1979	4623				237037	40424	8777
1980	3991				219407	38475	7765
1981	3888				233089	38832	8814
1982	3849				254458	42663	9271
1983	1999				306975	48666	8234
1984	3682				295427	47721	9499
1985	2955				316024	47033	10523
1986	3503				342824	52654	12690
1987	3732				364011	54211	14449
1988	3563				354367	52105	14705
1989	3509				344394	50280	17208
1990	3798				372555	49587	17972
1991	3761		133788	172884	402699	49472	18788
1992	3510		158740	181299	404779	48007	18513
1993	3369		165963	170580	372368	44741	18114
1994	3301		113652	167267	352979	42118	17413
1995	3024		103355	148272	315277	38549	16084
1996	3056		135376	112449	271752	33586	14792
1997	2892		110345	95140	253478	32811	14596
1998	2662		99279	93819	245046	30362	13841
1999	2180		91996	89463	237055	29367	13216
2000	2047		85301	91724	229012	27257	12595
2001	1719	8259	85842	87892	217521	26106	12479
2002	1540	8494	79447	91092	213794	25402	12127
2003	1430	7733	76879	86465	199390	26324	13056
2004	1422	8087	71677	86672	205532	28326	14208
2005	1358	8148	71926	83485	202301	28026	14813
2006	1361	8051	70400	68299	197546	28958	15632
2007	1306	8132	70681	83969	214423	30465	17013
2008	1266	8382	72119	85938	226681	32535	18176
2009	1253	9036	65684	89761	247778	34973	17952
2010	1245	9883	68135	105048	276994	37227	21677
2011	1305	11213	76790	115539	311417	44458	24170
2012	1266	11882	79131	115248	331524	48080	26330
2013	1384	12580	88322	128106	348681	53049	28806
2014	1426	13245	96478	133977	364954	57950	31692
2015	1487	14098	101928	149042	394121	61903	34040
2016	1570	14913	99626	152769	416982	65806	36071

19-3 各类学校基本情况
BASIC STATISTICS FOR VARIOUS SCHOOLS

单位：人 (person)

项目	Item	校数(所) Number of Schools (unit)		教职工数 Teachers and Staff		#专任教师 Full-time Teachers	
		2016	2015	2016	2015	2016	2015
合计	**Total**	**3524**	**3454**	**372328**	**366571**	**231251**	**226043**
高等教育	**Higher Education**	**175**	**175**	**146082**	**146318**	**69374**	**68506**
研究生培养机构(不计校数)	Institutions Providing Postgraduate Programs (Number of Schools Not Counted)	(139)	(138)			(57161)	(54481)
高等学校	Institutions of Higer Education	(58)	(58)			(46975)	(44391)
科研机构	Research Institutes	(81)	(80)			(10186)	(10090)
普通高等学校	General Institutions of Higher Education	91	90	138544	138396	66149	65230
成人高等学校	Adult Institutions of Higher Education	19	19	3211	3332	1510	1542
民办的其他高等教育机构	Privately-funded Institutions of Higher Education	65	66	4327	4590	1715	1734
中等教育	**Secondary Education**	**767**	**768**	**99117**	**98479**	**72784**	**72265**
高中阶段教育	Senior Secondary Education	426	428	99117	98479	51093	50794
普通高中	General Middle Schools	305	306	85352	83970	42858	41920
中等职业教育	Secondary Vocational Schools	121	122	13765	14509	8235	8874
普通中专	General Technical Secondary Schools	31	31	3401	3514	1940	1963
成人中专	Technical Secondary Schools for Adults	11	11	596	618	328	340
职业高中	Vocational Senior High Schools	50	51	6455	7098	4413	4745
技工学校	Technician Training Schools	29	29	3313	3279	1554	1826
初中阶段教育	Junior Secondary Education	341	340			21691	21471
小学教育	**Primary Schools**	**984**	**996**	**59716**	**58308**	**51787**	**50053**
工读学校	**Work-Study Schools for Delinquent Children**	**6**	**6**	**273**	**287**	**199**	**200**
特殊教育	**Special Education**	**22**	**22**	**1334**	**1276**	**1036**	**979**
学前教育	**Pre-school Education**	**1570**	**1487**	**65806**	**61903**	**36071**	**34040**

注：1. 普通高中的教职工数中包含普通初中的教职工数。
2. 表中带()数据不计入“校数”的合计数据中。

Note: a) Number of "Teachers and Staff" in general senior high schools includes those in general junior high schools.
b) In this table data with () were not be calculated in the total number of schools.

19-3 续表 Continued

单位：人 (person)

项目	Item	毕业生数 Graduates 2016	2015	招生数 New Enrollment 2016	2015	在校学生数 Total Enrollment 2016	2015
合计	**Total**	**924267**	**961180**	**1115515**	**1091756**	**3733544**	**3734245**
高等教育	**Higher Education**	**528800**	**547403**	**635415**	**609060**	**1888112**	**1894894**
研究生	Postgraduates	82625	79699	97449	95087	291778	283831
高等学校	Institutions of Higher Education	77465	74840	91426	89545	273066	265888
科研机构	Scientific Research Institutions	5160	4859	6023	5542	18712	17943
普通本专科	General Undergraduates and College Students	153005	152118	154715	152741	588389	593448
中央部委属高校	Under Central Ministries and Commissions	74110	73588	79733	78780	313313	310399
市属高校	Under Municipal Government	78895	78530	74982	79093	275076	283049
公办高校	Public Colleges and Universities	58662	58189	58006	61410	211743	215939
民办高校	Privately-funded Colleges and Universities	20233	20341	16976	17683	63333	67110
成人本专科	Adult Undergraduates and College Students	82494	95277	61052	74980	171790	204311
成人高等学校	Adult Institutions of Higher Education	7795	7999	5192	7287	14379	18413
普通高等学校	General Institutions of Higher Education	74699	87278	55860	67693	157411	185898
在职人员攻读硕士学位	Employees Enrolled in Graduate Programes Leading to Master Degrees			17523	14794	78117	83022
网络本专科生	Students Enrolled in Internet-based Courses	210676	220309	304676	271458	758038	730282
中等教育	**Secondary Education**	**182511**	**205795**	**180881**	**186517**	**552468**	**587112**
高中阶段教育	Senior Secondary	96068	113022	89027	97365	284195	303746
普通高中	General Middle Schools	52841	57738	53544	56743	163130	169412
#北京市户籍	Registered Residents of Beijing	47423	52337	49069	52387	151163	154455
中等职业教育	Secondary Vocational Schools	43227	55284	35483	40622	121065	134334
普通中专	General Technical Secondary Schools	13618	14644	11486	12129	43895	47465
成人中专	Technical Secondary Schools for Adults	9687	10042	8550	9948	27042	30412
职业高中	Vocational High Schools	6532	16715	3373	5031	14843	18400
技工学校	Technical Schools	13390	13883	12074	13514	35285	38057
初中阶段教育	Junior Secondary Education	86443	92773	91854	89152	268273	283366
#北京市户籍	Registered Residents of Beijing	65713	70924	60356	55754	182957	188608
小学教育	**Primary Education**	**111481**	**103893**	**145274**	**145876**	**868417**	**850321**
#北京市户籍	Registered Residents of Beijing	59987	55878	99411	99685	536327	496523
工读学校	**Work-study School for Delinquent Children**	**261**	**375**	**260**	**331**	**638**	**661**
特殊教育	**Special Education Schools**	**1588**	**1786**	**916**	**930**	**6927**	**7136**
学前教育	**Preschool Education**	**99626**	**101928**	**152769**	**149042**	**416982**	**394121**

19−4 全市高等教育学生情况(2016年) STATISTICS FOR STUDENTS IN INSTITUTIONS OF HIGHER EDUCATION (2016)

单位：人 (person)

项　　目	Item	毕(结)业生人数 Number of Graduates	招生数 New Enrollment	在校学生数 Total Enrollment
普通本科、专科生	General Undergraduates and Junior College Students	153005	154715	588389
专　科	Enrolled in Specialized Courses Education	35320	26960	87434
本　科	Enrolled in Full Undergraduate Courses	117685	127755	500955
成人本科、专科生	Adult Undergraduates and Junior College Students	82494	61052	171790
专　科	Enrolled in Specialized Courses Education	34674	24021	61601
本　科	Enrolled in Full Undergraduate Courses	47820	37031	110189
网络本科、专科生	Students Enrolled in Internet-based Courses	210676	304676	758038
专　科	Enrolled in Specialized Courses	124409	181148	422638
本　科	Enrolled in Full Undergraduate Courses	86267	123528	335400
研究生	Postgraduates	82625	97449	291778
硕　士	Master Degree	68382	77985	208280
博　士	Doctor Degree	14243	19464	83498
在职人员攻读硕士学位	Employees Enrolled in Graduate Programes Leading to Master Degrees		17523	78117
自考助学班	Classes for Self-Learning Programs	273		555
普通预科生	College Preparatory Courses			
研究生课程进修班	Postgraduate Courses for Advanced Study	8342		10122
进修及培训	In-Service Training Courses	894827		769826
留学生	Overseas Students	24039	27562	40486

19—5 普通高等学校本专科基本情况(2016年)
BASIC STATISTICS FOR GENERAL INSTITUTIONS OF HIGHER EDUCATION (2016)

单位：人 (person)

项目	Item	校数(所) Number of Schools (unit)	毕业生数 Graduates	招生数 New Enrollment	在校学生数 Total Enrollment	教职工数 Teachers and Staff	#专任教师 Full-time Teachers
合计	**Total**	**91**	**153005**	**154715**	**588389**	**138544**	**66149**
#女性	Females		80285	78489	302036	70231	30566
综合大学	Comprehensive Universities	5	19995	19299	73274	23226	10508
理工院校	Science and Engineering	31	62432	62993	242265	53140	26722
农业院校	Agriculture	3	6062	6154	22756	4770	2530
林业院校	Forestry	1	3211	3306	13271	1875	1193
医药院校	Medicine	4	3324	4489	16050	17928	3642
师范院校	Teacher Training	2	4914	5540	21828	5626	3554
语文院校	Literature	9	11481	11333	42285	7108	4083
财经院校	Finance and Economics	16	22161	20149	77973	10825	6458
政法院校	Politics and Law	8	10455	12033	41113	6601	3031
体育院校	Physical Culture	3	2885	3134	12097	1671	1057
艺术院校	Art	8	3319	3519	14207	3801	2153
民族院校	Minorities Colleges	1	2766	2766	11270	1973	1218

19-6 全市分学科研究生情况(2016年)
BASIC STATISTICS FOR POSTGRADUATES BY SUBJECT OF STUDY (2016)

单位：人 (person)

项目	Item	毕业生 Graduates 合计 Total	硕士 Master Degree	博士 Doctor Degree	招生数 New Enrollment 合计 Total	硕士 Master Degree	博士 Doctor Degree	在校学生数 Student Enrollment 合计 Total	硕士 Master Degree	博士 Doctor Degree
合计	**Total**	**82625**	**68382**	**14243**	**97449**	**77985**	**19464**	**291778**	**208280**	**83498**
#女性	Females	41383	35821	5562	50043	42016	8027	141130	108766	32364
学术型学位	**Academic Degree**	**51677**	**38218**	**13459**	**60193**	**41569**	**18624**	**197616**	**116887**	**80729**
哲学	Philosophy	589	407	182	693	448	245	2455	1348	1107
经济学	Economics	6132	5454	678	6807	5878	929	17517	13359	4158
法学	Law	7471	6559	912	8203	6994	1209	23764	18449	5315
教育学	Education	3228	2917	311	3823	3409	414	10734	8879	1855
文学	Literature	4860	4279	581	5405	4672	733	15089	11944	3145
历史学	History	615	502	113	786	572	214	2577	1583	994
理学	Science	7348	4103	3245	10140	5683	4457	33562	15592	17970
工学	Engineering	30273	25357	4916	35850	28641	7209	112795	79878	32917
农学	Agriculture	2643	2109	534	3210	2453	757	8818	5878	2940
医学	Medicine	4660	3048	1612	5920	4139	1781	17078	11535	5543
军事学	Military	20	11	9	11	8	3	67	39	28
管理学	Management	11835	10979	856	13253	12085	1168	37396	31149	6247
艺术学	Art	2951	2657	294	3348	3003	345	9926	8647	1279

19-7 高等教育外国留学生情况(2016年)
STATISTICS FOR FOREIGN STUDENTS STUDYING IN BEIJING FOR HIGHER EDUCATION (2016)

单位：人 (person)

项目	Item	毕(结)业生数 Graduates	授予学位人数 Number of Students Conferred with Degree	招生数 New Enrollment	在校学生数 Total Enrollment
合计	**Total**	**24039**	**5163**	**27562**	**40486**
#女性	Females	11971	2188	13594	18241
按学历划分	**By Educational Background**				
专科	Enrolled in Specialized Courses	72		191	239
本科	Enrolled in Full Undergraduate Courses	4216	3047	5120	15417
硕士	Master Degree	2111	1837	3502	7036
博士	Doctor Degree	324	279	1055	3647
培训	Training	17316		17694	14147
按地区划分	**By Region**				
亚洲	Asia	12756	3437	14790	25926
非洲	Africa	1212	587	2070	3757
欧洲	Europe	6233	615	6777	6774
北美洲	North America	2737	330	2815	2594
南美洲	South America	572	148	589	850
大洋洲	Oceania	529	46	521	585
按经费来源	**By Source of Funds**				
国际组织资助	From International Organizations	19	5	171	430
中国政府资助	From Chinese Government	3685	1450	6216	11207
本国政府资助	From the Government of the Students' Home Country	150	136	278	780
学校间交换	Interscholastic Exchange	3399	85	3690	3361
自费	Self Funding	16786	3487	17207	24708

19–8 普通中专分科情况(2016年)
BASIC STATISTICS FOR SPECIALIZED SECONDARY SCHOOLS BY MAJOR (2016)

单位：人 (person)

项 目	Item	毕业生数 Graduates	招生数 New Enrollment	在校学生数 Total Enrollment
合 计	**Total**	**13618**	**11486**	**43895**
#女 生	Females	6229	5397	20243
按类别分	**By Category**			
农林牧渔类	Agriculture, Forestry, Animal Production and Hunting, Fishing	205	57	415
资源环境类	Resources and Environment	68		201
能源与新能源类	Energy and New Energy	115	13	247
土木水利类	Construction and Water Conservancy	792	271	1728
加工制造类	Processing and Manufacturing	1336	295	2432
石油化工类	Petroleum and Chemicals			
轻纺食品类	Light Industry, Textile and Foods	99	24	166
交通运输类	Transportation	2558	1589	8665
信息技术类	IT	977	461	2160
医药卫生类	Medicine and Health	2927	1543	7769
休闲保健类	Recreation and Healthcare			
财经商贸类	Finance, Business and Trade	1433	1319	4503
旅游服务类	Tourism Services	159	123	656
文化艺术类	Culture and Arts	1692	1280	6778
体育与健身	Sports and Fitness	518	381	1275
教育类	Education	342	1107	1747
司法服务类	Judicial Services	143	307	738
公共管理与服务类	Public Management and Services	192	129	757
其 他	Others	62	2587	3658

19-9 职业高中分科情况(2016年)
BASIC STATISTICS FOR VOCATIONAL SCHOOLS BY MAJOR (2016)

单位：人 (person)

项　　目	Item	毕业生数 Graduates	招生数 New Enrollment	在校学生数 Total Enrollment
合　　计	**Total**	**6532**	**3373**	**14843**
#女　生	Females	3166	1604	7482
按类别分	**By Category**			
农林牧渔类	Agriculture, Forestry, Animal Production and Hunting, Fishing	136	30	249
资源环境类	Resources and Environment			
能源与新能源类	Energy and New Energy			
土木水利类	Construction and Water Conservancy	36	16	92
加工制造类	Processing and Manufacturing	231	47	400
石油化工类	Petroleum and Chemicals			
轻纺食品类	Light Industry, Textile and Foods	41	19	87
交通运输类	Transportation	863	540	2252
信息技术类	IT	893	501	1923
医药卫生类	Medicine and Health	145	86	319
休闲保健类	Recreation and Healthcare	97	36	164
财经商贸类	Finance, Business and Trade	985	372	2022
旅游服务类	Tourism Services	706	374	1635
文化艺术类	Culture and Arts	1176	424	2454
体育与健身	Sports and Fitness	18	20	49
教育类	Education	1032	724	2738
司法服务类	Judicial Services	18	42	81
公共管理与服务类	Public Management and Services	155	58	253
其　他	Others		84	125

19—10 校外教育情况(2016年)
STATISTICS FOR AFTER-SCHOOL EDUCATION (2016)

单位：人 (person)

项目	Item	单位数(个) Number of Organizations(unit)	活动小组数(个) Activity Groups(unit)	参加小组学生数 Participating Students	教职工人数 Teachers and Staff	#专职辅导员 Full-time Coaches	兼职辅导员 Part-time Coaches
合计	**Total**	**716**	**9854**	**582510**	**4965**	**1825**	**3275**
少年宫	Children's Palaces	22	5653	125607	1439	745	880
少年科技馆	Children's Scientific Museums	8	699	48354	265	194	128
少年之家	Children's Homes	33	1583	347364	540	344	502
少年活动站	Children's Clubs	653	1919	61185	2721	542	1765

19—11 幼儿园基本情况(2016年)
STATISTICS FOR KINDERGARTENS (2016)

单位：人 (person)

项目	Item	总计 Total	#女 Females	城区 In City	镇区 In Counties and Towns	乡村 In Villages
园数(所)	Number of Kindergartens (unit)	1570		1149	192	229
班数(个)	Number of Classes (unit)	14913		12188	1579	1146
在园幼儿数	Children Enrollment	416982	200725	343683	44773	28526
教职工数	Teachers and Staff	65806	60194	56050	6203	3553
#园长	Headmasters	2296	2187	1807	260	229
专任教师	Full-time Teachers	36071	35246	30211	3702	2158
保健医	Health Workers	2725	2699	2365	245	115

19-12　高等教育自学考试情况
STATISTICS FOR HIGHER EDUCATION SELF-STUDY EXAMINATION

项　目	Item	2016	2015
报考人次　(人次)	Number of Registered Person-times　(person-time)	136639	144357
报考科次　(科次)	Number of Registered Subject-times　(person-time)	446936	475744
发出专科毕业证书　(个)	Number of Junior College Diplomas Issued　(unit)	3034	3103
发出本科毕业证书　(个)	Number of General College Diplomas Issued　(unit)	3738	4362
开考专业　(个)	Number of Majors Examined　(unit)	90	99

19-13　特殊教育情况(2016年)
STATISTICS FOR SPECIAL EDUCATION (2016)

单位：人　(person)

项　目	Item	毕业生 Graduates	招生数 New Enrollment	在校学生数 Total Enrollment
合　计	**Total**	**1588**	**916**	**6927**
#女　性	Females	564	313	2463
特殊教育学校	Special Education Schools	409	325	2643
小学附设特教班	Special Classes Attached to Primary Schools		9	131
小学随班就读	Studying in Primary Schools	473	176	2381
普通(职业)初中随班就读	Studying in General Junior Secondary (Vocational) Classes	706	406	1772

19-14 职业技术培训机构基本情况(2016年)
BASIC STATISTICS FOR VOCATIONAL AND TECHNICAL TRAINING INSTITUTIONS(2016)

项 目	Item	学校数(所) Schools (unit)	教学班(点、个) Teaching Classes (site,unit)	结业生数(人次) Students Completing Courses (person-time)	#女 性 Females
合 计	**Total**	**3579**	**46538**	**2873164**	**1426470**
#少数民族	National Miniorities			14671	8072
按培训机构分	**By Training Institution**				
职工技术培训学校(机构)	**Technical Training Schools (Institutions) for Employees**	**28**	**466**	**29890**	**12041**
教育部门和集体办	Run by Education Authorities and Collectively-run	3	132	4986	2472
其他部门办	Run by Other Authorities	8	142	7465	3026
民 办	Privately-funded	17	192	17439	6543
农村成人文化技术培训学校(机构)	**Cultural and Technical Training Schools (Institutions) for Rural Adults**	**2202**	**10800**	**920952**	**511466**
#教育部门和集体办	Run by Education Authorities and Collectively-run	2197	10779	918073	510035
县 办	Run by Counties	2	59	2057	1025
乡 办	Run by Townships	169	6019	554870	312277
村 办	Run by Villages	2026	4701	361146	196733
其他培训机构(含社会培训机构)	**Other Training Institutions (Including Social Training Institutions)**	**1349**	**35272**	**1922322**	**902963**
教育部门和集体办	Run by Education Authorities and Collectively-run	65		75980	32741
其他部门办	Run by Other Authorities	150		665074	273520
民 办	Privately-funded	1134	35272	1181268	596702
按培训时间分	**By Training Duration**				
一个月以内	within 1 month			1307442	666656
一个月至三个月以内	1-3 months			439866	226827
三个月至半年以内	3-6 months			601827	273739
半年至一年以内	6 months to 1 year			356148	164538
一年及以上	over 1 year			167881	94710
按培训形式分	**Group by Form of Training**				
#资格证书培训	Qualification Certificate Training			249521	117750
岗位证书培训	Job Post Certificate Training			250987	111579

19-14 续表 Continued

单位：人 (person)

项目	Item	注册学生数 Student Enrollment 合计 Total	#女性 Females	教职工数 Teachers and Staff 合计 Total	#专任教师 Full-time Teachers	聘请校外教师 External Teachers Retained
合计	**Total**	**2784059**	**1330975**	**54884**	**19831**	**16997**
#少数民族	National Miniorities	13751	7750	116	56	43
按培训机构分	**By Training Institution**					
职工技术培训学校(机构)	**Technical Training Schools (Institutions) for Employees**	**23549**	**10638**	**382**	**284**	**129**
教育部门和集体办	Run by Education Authorities and Collectively-run	3936	2866	103	86	99
其他部门办	Run by Other Authorities	2606	1232	152	94	27
民办	Privately-funded	17007	6540	127	104	3
农村成人文化技术培训学校(机构)	**Cultural and Technical Training Schools (Institutions) for Rural Adults**	**733350**	**405619**	**1405**	**775**	**2871**
#教育部门和集体办	Run by Education Authorities and Collectively-run	730471	404188	1405	775	2871
县办	Run by Counties	1327	599	51	16	26
乡办	Run by Townships	472758	255927	724	461	1681
村办	Run by Villages	256386	147662	630	298	1164
其他培训机构(含社会培训机构)	**Other Training Institutions (Including Social Training Institutions)**	**2027160**	**914718**	**53097**	**18772**	**13997**
教育部门和集体办	Run by Education Authorities and Collectively-run	80453	70571	2647	1127	958
其他部门办	Run by Other Authorities	687395	210141	17350	6542	5134
民办	Privately-funded	1259312	634006	33100	11103	7905
按培训时间分	**By Training Duration**					
一个月以内	within 1 month	1116342	527682			
一个月至三个月以内	1-3 months	392232	197097			
三个月至半年以内	3-6 months	636998	287551			
半年至一年以内	6 months to 1 year	409109	205068			
一年及以上	over 1 year	229378	113577			
按培训形式分	**Group by Form of Training**					
#资格证书培训	Qualification Certificate Training	238888	112952			
岗位证书培训	Job Post Certificate Training	206531	87500			

19–15 民办教育基本情况(2016年)
STATSTICS FOR PRIVATELY-FUNDED EDUCATION (2016)

单位：人 (person)

项目	Item	校数(所) Number of Schools (unit)	毕业生数 Graduates	招生数 New Enrollment	在校学生数 Total Enrollment	教职工数 Teachers and Staff	#专任教师 Full-time Teachers	聘请校外教师数 External Teachers Retained
合计	**Total**	**893**	**77613**	**91262**	**307785**	**53268**	**27802**	**3872**
民办高等教育	**Privately-funded Higher Education**	**81**	**20233**	**16976**	**63333**	**10356**	**4817**	**3418**
普通高校	General Institutions of Higher Education	16	20233	16976	63333	6029	3102	1909
民办高等教育机构	Other Privately-funded Higher Education Institutions	65				4327	1715	1509
民办中等教育	**Privately-funded Secondary Education**	**116**	**13710**	**10817**	**33723**	**12263**	**7376**	**354**
高中阶段教育	Senior High School Education	91	6248	3061	10341	12263	7376	354
民办普通高中	Privately-funded Senior High Schools	69	5393	2173	8122	11308	6897	102
民办中等职业教育	Privately-funded Secondary Vocational Education	22	855	888	2219	955	479	252
初中阶段教育	Junior High School Education	25	7462	7756	23382			
民办小学	**Privately-funded Primary Schools**	**61**	**10889**	**6866**	**59788**	**2510**	**1928**	**2**
民办幼儿园	**Privately-funded Kindergartens**	**635**	**32781**	**56603**	**150941**	**28139**	**13681**	**98**

注：普通中学教职工数、专任教师及聘请校外教师数为初中高中合计数。

Note: Number of teachers,staff,full-time teachers,substitutive and part-time teachers in regular secondary schools includes those in junior and senior middle schools.

19–16 高校办学条件(2016年)
SCHOOL CONDITIONS OF HIGHER EDUCATION INSTITUTIONS (2016)

项目	Item	合计 Total	中央 Central	市属市管 Municipal
普通高校	**General Institutions of Higher Education**			
校舍建筑面积 (平方米)	Building Area (sq.m)	38604181	26811148	11793033
占地面积 (平方米)	Floor Space (sq.m)	46221347	30249315	15972033
图书 (万册)	Books (10000 volumes)	11165	7073	4092
电子图书藏量 (册)	E-books Collections (volumes)	148423574	100639228	47784346
拥有教学用计算机 (台)	Computers for Teaching (unit)	434753	230039	204714
成人高校	**Institutions of Higher Education for Adults**			
校舍建筑面积 (平方米)	Building Area (sq.m)	934755	338433	596322
占地面积 (平方米)	Floor Space (sq.m)	1408417	444870	963547
图书 (万册)	Books (10000 volumes)	226	51	176
电子图书藏量 (册)	E-books Collections (volumes)	47784346	3766278	44018068
拥有教学用计算机 (台)	Computers for Teaching (unit)	10736	1203	9533

19-17 基础教育办学条件(2016年)
SCHOOL CONDITIONS OF BASIC EDUCATION (2016)

单位：平方米 (sq.m)

项目	Item	普通中学 General Middle Schools	小学 Primary Schools
学校占地面积	Floor Space	24126796	14142792
校舍建筑面积	Building Area	13770982	7010201
#当年新增	Newly Added in the Year	459070	170223
#危房面积	Area of Dangerous Buildings		
教学及辅助用房	Teaching and Auxiliary Houses	5060882	3205482
普通教室	Classrooms	2923757	2504770
实验室	Laboratories	871163	199258
图书室	Libraries	375944	173299
微机室	Computer Rooms	216690	142884
语音室	Language Labs	34224	13610
体育馆	Gymnasiums	639104	171661
行政办公用房	Administrative Houses	1502985	814619
生活用房	Houses for Life (Residencial Houses)	3858581	1197768
其他用房	Houses for Other Purposes	3348534	1792332
计算机 (台)	Computers (unit)	293454	243148
图书藏量 (册)	Books Collections (volume)	29309302	27612508
电子图书藏量 (册)	E-book Collections (volumes)	4833438	3526710

19-18 非本市户籍、外国籍学生情况(2016年)
STATISTICS FOR STUDENTS FROM OTHER PROVINCES, MUNICIPALITIES AND AUTONOMOUS REGIONS ALONG WITH OTHER COUNTRIES (2016)

单位：人 (person)

项目	Item	非本市户籍学生数 Students from Other Provinces, Municipalities and Autonomous Regions	#民办学校 Privately-funded Schools	外国籍学生数 Overseas Students	#民办学校 Privately-funded Education
合计	**Total**	**569820**	**120054**	**5680**	**2318**
普通中学	General Middle Schools	97283	13265	1707	366
初中	Junior Secondary Schools	85316	12624	730	179
高中	Senior Secondary Schools	11967	641	977	187
中等职业教育	Vocational Secondary Schools	32508	1398	116	
小学	Primary Schools	332090	47927	2070	599
特殊教育	Special Education Schools	554	2	4	
幼儿园	Kindergartens	107385	57462	1783	1353

19-19 图书馆、文化馆、档案馆情况(1978-2016年) LIBRARIES, CULTURAL CENTERS AND ARCHIVES (1978-2016)

年份 Year	公共图书馆 Public Libraries				群众艺术馆、文化馆 Mass Art Centers, Cultural Centers		档案馆 Archiving Institutions			
	个数 (个) Number (unit)	总藏数 (万册、万件) Total Collections (10000 volumes)	建筑面积 (万平方米) Building Area (10000 sq.m)	书刊文献外借人次 (万人次) Person-times Borrowing Books, Magazines, and Documents (10000 person-times)	个数 (个) Number (unit)	组织文艺活动 (次) Art Activities Organized (times)	个数 (个) Number (unit)	建筑面积 (平方米) Building Area (sq.m)	利用档案资料人次 (万人次) Persons of Using Files (10000 person-times)	案卷 (万卷件) Records (10000 rolls)
1978	18	1423		168.5	19	516				
1979	21	1502		173.7	19	1033				
1980	20	1606	1.8	210.4	19	778				
1981	21	1614	1.9	211.0	19	1131				
1982	21	1676	2.0	228.4	20	1334				
1983	21	1733	1.9	243.0	20	1015				
1984	22	1824	2.3	223.7	22	489				
1985	22	1860	3.0	219.9	23	469				
1986	23	1874	6.0	219.9	23	883				
1987	23	1959	20.6	169.8	23	1067	20	10695	1.30	86.13
1988	23	2050	23.4	300.4	23	647	20	21472	1.46	115.98
1989	23	2128	24.5		23	1411	20	31280	1.48	156.28
1990	23	2205	25.0		23	1429	20	23618	2.51	167.37
1991	23	2281	25.3		23	1128	20	33491	3.24	177.45
1992	23	2397	25.4	147.0	23	978	20	35950	2.64	181.31
1993	23	2461	25.5	212.0	23	764	20	37650	1.73	192.39
1994	23	2548	23.8	383.8	23	1034	20	42641	1.50	192.35
1995	23	2629	24.1	139.3	23	1127	20	65489	1.42	204.06
1996	22	2652	25.3	145.6	23	2277	20	62994	3.03	223.70
1997	23	2789	25.7	188.0	23	1875	20	64147	2.69	227.42
1998	24	2848	25.6	189.0	23	2554	20	67759	2.71	240.78
1999	24	2934	26.4	607.0	23	1490	20	72597	2.52	259.50
2000	26	3020	27.0	283.0	23	1809	20	72596	3.01	278.29
2001	26	3133	31.4	287.7	23	1822	20	72730	4.17	297.02
2002	26	3248	30.7	337.5	20	1817	20	72946	4.53	328.42
2003	26	3355	30.9	334.8	20	2023	20	81519	6.27	358.95
2004	26	3451	30.9	405.0	22	1826	20	83162	7.03	379.13
2005	26	3626	31.7	480.0	22	3697	20	84656	6.97	404.69
2006	25	3776	31.0	515.0	21	2200	20	93773	10.59	436.70
2007	25	3940	31.5	479.0	21	4752	20	93463	9.51	461.67
2008	25	4100	33.4	450.0	20	3007	20	97605	9.00	495.70
2009	25	4368	41.9	471.0	20	3470	20	97605	9.88	523.84
2010	25	4613	42.4	441.0	20	3564	18	97611	13.45	557.99
2011	25	5049	42.1	333.0	20	3401	18	97976	12.30	582.92
2012	25	5556	47.6	317.0	20	3848	18	98879	12.37	602.54
2013	25	5316	48.4	325.0	20	4769	18	101896	23.85	636.10
2014	25	5601	52.7	407.0	20	2158	18	98220	22.18	697.90
2015	25	5943	52.4	438.0	20	2587	18	96256	14.90	733.23
2016	25	6229	55.3	549.0	21	3417	18	119930	21.95	764.67

注：1978-1981年，群众艺术馆、文化馆数据不包括群众艺术馆。

资料来源：北京市文化局、国家图书馆、北京市档案局。

Note: In 1978-1981, the data of mass art centers and cultural centers didn't include those of mass art centers.

Source: Beijing Municipal Bureau of Culture, National Library of China, and Beijing Municipal Bureau of Archives.

19－20 博物馆情况(1982－2016年)
STATISTICS FOR MUSEUMS (1982-2016)

年 份 Year	北京地区博物馆数 (个) Number of Museums in Beijing (unit)	文 物 藏品数 (万件) Cultural Relic Collections (10000 units)	博物馆及其他文物保护机构(文物局系统内) Museums and Other Cultural Relic Protection and Administration Organizations (under the jurisdiction of Beijing Municipal Administration of Cultural Heritage) 个 数 (个) Number (unit)	#博物馆 Museums	文物藏品数 (万件) Cultural Relic Collections (10000 units)	#一级品 (件) Grade-I Collections (unit)	参观人次 (万人次) Visitors (10000 person-times)
1982			28		8.4	294	9.7
1983			29		4.0		58.0
1984							
1985			32		9.0		20.0
1986			39	7	21.0		905.0
1987							
1988			42	11	21.0		1098.0
1989			46	12	14.0		992.0
1990							
1991			46	12	11.7	2901	6629.1
1992							
1993			50	16	17.4	479	2423.4
1994			51	17	16.7	447	955.0
1995			51	17	16.7	447	2100.3
1996			51	17	18.0	443	2009.3
1997			54	24	18.2	443	935.8
1998			56	26	18.3	387	697.8
1999			54	26	18.5	374	5641.8
2000			53	25	18.2	367	702.7
2001			58	26	17.3	366	99.1
2002			48	27	20.1	716	170.8
2003			55	27	112.4	716	119.2
2004			66	31	370.4	656	599.9
2005			73	34	115.1	620	1370.9
2006			70	33	115.5	643	1416.7
2007			69	34	113.5	439	1493.0
2008	148	331	71	37	116.0	678	1368.4
2009	151	331	76	40	117.0	722	1647.9
2010	156	332	79	41	117.0	725	1712.1
2011	162	430	78	41	117.0	852	1373.4
2012	165	430	78	41	117.0	903	1887.9
2013	167	430	78	41	117.0	903	1760.0
2014	171	430	78	41	128.0	891	1848.0
2015	173	430	77	40	126.0	931	2069.1
2016	178	430	79	43	128.0	960	1994.3

资料来源：北京市文物局。
Source: Beijing Municipal Administration of Cultural Heritage.

19-21 博物馆及其他文物保护管理机构情况(2016年) STATISTICS FOR MUSEUMS AND OTHER CULTURAL RELIC PROTECTION AND ADMINISTRATION ORGANIZATIONS (2016)

项目	Item	合计 Total	市属 Under the Jurisdiction of the City	区属 Under the Jurisdiction of a District
全市按行业管理登记的博物馆	**Museums Registered by Industry Administration**			
博物馆数 (个)	Museums (unit)	**178**	**43**	**44**
#免费开放的博物馆数 (个)	Museums Open for Free (unit)	80	24	24
文物藏品数 (万件)	Cultural Relic Collections (10000 units)	430		
参观人次 (万人次)	Visitors (10000 person-times)	3550		
文物古迹个数 (处)	Cultural Relics and Historical Sites (unit)	3840		
文物拍卖机构数 (个)	Organizations of Cultural Relic Aucti (unit)	176		
举办文物艺术品拍卖场次 (场)	Cultural Relic Auctions (time)	437		
文物拍卖标的数 (件、套)	Auction Targets (unit)	140890		
文物拍卖标的成交金额 (万元)	Turnover of Cultural Relic Auctions (10000 yuan)	2041495		
文物局系统内博物馆及文物保护管理机构 (个)	**Museums and Cultural Relic Protection and Administration Organizations under the Municipal Administration of Cultural Heritage (unit)**	**79**	**29**	**50**
#博物馆 (个)	Museums (unit)	43	18	25
博物馆按类别分	Grouped by Category			
综合性 (个)	Comprehensive (unit)	12	2	10
历史性 (个)	Historical (unit)	18	8	10
艺术性 (个)	Art (unit)	6	5	1
自然科技类 (个)	Natural Science (unit)	2	1	1
其他类 (个)	Others (unit)	5	2	3
从业人员 (人)	Employment (person)	3992	1135	2857
文物藏品数 (万件)	Cultural Relic Collections (10000 units)	128	122	6
#一级品 (件)	Grade-I Collections (unit)	960	670	290
参观人次 (万人次)	Visitors (10000 person-times)	1994	458	1536
本年收入 (万元)	Revenues in the Year (10000 yuan)	247293	130088	117205
#财政收入 (万元)	Fiscal Revenue (10000 yuan)	158326	87551	70775
门票收入 (万元)	Ticket Revenue (10000 yuan)	42037	905	41132
本年支出 (万元)	Expenditures in the Year (10000 yuan)	229207	86903	142304

注：全市博物馆数为北京地区按行业管理登记的博物馆数。
资料来源：北京市文物局。
Note: Number of museums in the city means the number of museums registered by industrial administration in Beijing.
Source: Beijing Municipal Administration of Cultural Heritage.

19—22 公共图书馆(2016年)
PUBLIC LIBRARIES (2016)

项目	Item	合计 Total	中央属 Under Central Jurisdiction	市属 Under the Jurisdiction of the City	区县属 Under the Jurisdiction of a District/ County
个数 (个)	Number (unit)	25	1	1	23
从业人员 (人)	Employed Persons (person)	2782	1533	351	898
总藏数 (万册、万件)	Total Collections (10000 volumes)	6229	3635	808	1786
#图书 (万册、万件)	Books (10000 volumes)	3656	1332	664	1660
建筑面积 (万平方米)	Building Area (10000 sq.m)	55.3	27.8	9.4	18.1
阅览座席 (个)	Seating Capacity of Reading Rooms (unit)	22619	5303	2995	14321
总流通人次 (万人次)	Total Number of Visitors (10000 person-times)	1800	398	525	877
#书刊文献外借人次 (万人次)	Person-times Borrowing Books, Magazines and Documents (10000 person-times)	549	38	54	457
#书刊文献外借册次 (万册次)	Volume-times of Borrowed Books, Magazines and Documents (10000 volunme-times)	1081	56	235	790

资料来源：北京市文化局、国家图书馆。
Source: Beijing Municipal Bureau of Culture, and National Library of China.

19—23 群众艺术馆、文化馆和文化站情况(2016年)
STATISTICS FOR MASS ART CENTERS, CULTURAL CENTERS AND CULTURAL STATIONS(2016)

项目	Item	合计 Total	群众艺术馆 Mass Art Centers	文化馆 Cultural Centers	文化站 Cultural Stations
个数 (个)	Number (unit)	352	1	20	331
从业人员 (人)	Employed Persons (person)	2748	56	849	1843
举办展览个数 (个)	Exhibitions Held (unit)	2017	3	191	1823
组织文艺活动 (次)	Art Activities Organized (times)	30725	20	3397	27308

资料来源：北京市文化局。
Source: Beijing Municipal Bureau of Culture.

19-24 档案事业基本情况(2016年)
STATISTICS FOR ARCHIVING INSTITUTIONS (2016)

项目		Item		合计 Total	市属 Under the Jurisdiction of the City	区属 Under the Jurisdiction of a District/County
档案馆个数	**(个)**	**Number of Archives**	**(unit)**	**18**	**2**	**16**
建筑面积	**(平方米)**	**Building Areas**	**(sq.m)**	**119930**	**30962**	**88968**
馆藏档案情况		**Files Colllected in Archives**				
全宗	(个)	Full Archives	(unit)	3420	934	2486
案卷	(万卷件)	Records	(10000 rolls)	764.67	311.20	453.48
建国前档案	(万卷件)	Files Prior to the Foundation of PRC	(10000 rolls)	100.55	98.84	1.71
建国后档案	(万卷件)	Files After the Foundation of PRC	(10000 rolls)	664.12	212.35	451.77
录音、录像、影片档案	(盘)	Tape, Video, and Film Files	(piece)	44049	35235	8814
照片档案	(张)	Photo Files	(disc)	729950	356953	372997
缩微胶片		Microfiches				
平片、开窗卡	(张)	Flat and Window-open Microfiches	(disc)	289067	289067	
卷片	(万幅)	Rolled Microfiches	(10000 rolls)	5460	5410	50
档案利用情况		**File Utilization**				
本年利用档案人次	(人次)	Person-times Using Files in the Year	(person-times)	219165	11384	207781
本年利用档案	(万卷件次)	Files Used in the Year	(10000 roll.times)	30.61	6.33	24.28
本年利用资料册次	(册次)	Data Books Used in the Year	(volume-times)	893	145	748
本年利用资料人次	(人次)	Person-times Using Data in the Year	(person-times)	290	62	228
本年编研档案、资料	(万字)	Files and Data Edited and Studied in the Year	(10000 Chinese characters)	813	104	709
档案馆网站来访IP次数	**(万次)**	**IPs Visiting Archive Websites**	**(10000 times)**	**133**	**33**	**100**

资料来源：北京市档案局。
Source: Beijing Municipal Bureau of Archives.

19-25 电影、电视、广播电台情况(1978-2016年)

年 份 Year	电 影 Films			电 视 TVs		
	放映场次 (万场次) Show Times (10000 Times)	观众人次 (万人次) Audience (10000 Person-times)	票房收入 (亿元) Ticket Revenue (100 million yuan)	电视节目套数 (套) Number of TV Programs (unit)	平均每日电视节目播出时间 (小时) Daily Show Hours of TV Programs (hour)	电视综合覆盖率 (%) Comprehensive Coverage Rate of TVs (%)
1978	31.9	29924.1				
1979	35.5	34626.0				
1980	33.1	31189.5		1	4.25	
1981	31.9	30067.0		1	5.46	100.00
1982	32.8	28743.5		1	6.85	91.00
1983	30.1	27345.5		1	7.07	90.00
1984	27.8	23966.7		1	7.15	98.00
1985	23.0	18875.0		1	7.54	98.00
1986	20.6	15904.4		2	19.07	98.00
1987	19.0	13517.7		2	13.64	98.00
1988	19.2	13269.4		2	19.39	98.00
1989	21.5	14492.6		4	25.43	98.00
1990	20.7	12771.2		4	29.43	98.00
1991	21.3	12558.3		4	27.79	98.00
1992	22.1	11587.4		6	45.02	98.00
1993	11.9	5369.8		7	58.18	98.00
1994	10.6	2166.5	0.51	9	77.79	98.30
1995	9.2	1598.6	0.93	12	98.36	98.30
1996	11.5	1644.1	1.07	12	101.01	98.81
1997	12.6	1742.3	1.17	12	111.00	99.12
1998	12.3	1443.5	1.28	12	110.68	99.60
1999	11.7	964.7		12	118.36	99.80
2000	12.2	873.2		12	122.45	99.80
2001	12.6	804.7	0.92	16	200.15	99.91
2002	12.3	827.4	1.09	18	329.40	99.82
2003	11.8	683.0	1.35	19	259.32	99.90
2004	18.1	814.4	1.86	24	244.17	99.50
2005	22.6	873.8	2.29	25	329.81	99.99
2006	28.0	1221.0	3.02	25	294.23	99.99
2007	38.0	1711.0	3.70	25	309.12	99.99
2008	46.8	1767.3	5.37	24	309.06	99.99
2009	62.4	2451.5	8.19	26	319.13	99.99
2010	74.3	2923.3	11.81	26	319.24	99.99
2011	97.4	3235.9	13.52	25	334.22	100.00
2012	120.0	3954.6	16.23	26	343.68	100.00
2013	137.8	4288.5	18.60	26	347.89	100.00
2014	162.8	5281.3	22.90	26	344.02	100.00
2015	198.1	7212.7	31.56	26	351.08	100.00
2016	228.5	6926.7	30.33	26	360.27	100.00

资料来源：北京市新闻出版广电局。

STATISTICS FOR FILMS, TELEVISIONS, AND BROADCASTING STATIONS (1978-2016)

电视 TVs				广播电台 Broadcasting Stations			
农村电视综合覆盖率 (%) Comprehensive Coverage Rate of TVs in Rural Area (%)	无线电视综合覆盖率 (%) Comprehensive Coverage Rate of Wireless TVs (%)	有线电视注册用户数 (万户) Subscnbers of Cable Televisions (10000 households)	有线广播电视入户率 (%) Access Rate of Cable Televisions (%)	广播节目套数 (套) Number of Radio Programs (unit)	平均每日广播节目播出时间 (小时) Daily Show Hours of Radio Programs (hour)	广播综合覆盖率 (%) Comprehensive Coverage Rate of Broadcast (%)	广告收入 (万元) Advertising Income (10000 yuan)
				4	56.08		
				4	57.22	100.00	139
				4	59.37	98.00	166
				5	61.97	98.00	117
				5	73.67	98.00	668
				5	65.87	98.00	645
				5	66.17	98.00	555
				6	68.75	98.00	771
				6	76.33	98.00	964
				7	78.67	98.00	1668
				7	77.87	98.00	2885
				7	77.87	98.00	5115
				10	94.75	98.00	9680
				12	134.75	98.00	15225
		52.71		12	134.85	98.00	26480
		82.21		13	148.25	91.00	45398
		182.97		13	150.25	96.97	93428
		202.75		15	156.05	98.44	100546
		230.97		16	174.67	99.98	106773
		165.78	43.24	16	178.20	99.96	115072
		175.71	45.80	16	188.90	97.70	149661
		205.95	51.76	16	192.43	99.91	136451
		231.24	57.05	16	197.43	99.88	154317
		243.00	58.39	16	197.86	99.91	157210
	97.57	265.50	62.09	16	229.55	100.00	212091
	99.99	282.00	64.12	17	281.88	100.00	236334
99.97	94.90	319.58	70.75	17	282.88	100.00	240146
99.97	93.13	345.06	74.43	17	288.92	99.98	317437
99.97	93.19	383.13	81.00	17	297.40	99.98	385231
99.97	94.38	413.50	85.90	18	316.58	99.99	453932
99.97	98.72	448.12	91.68	18	324.82	99.99	613672
100.00	99.74	475.92	95.90	18	329.56	100.00	796113
100.00	99.75	495.70	99.13	25	471.69	100.00	1081857
100.00	99.75	524.59	103.00	25	473.62	100.00	1689443
100.00	99.75	551.57	106.85	25	472.61	100.00	1753933
100.00	99.75	569.13	108.88	25	470.42	100.00	2153546
100.00	99.75	580.42	109.66	26	493.55	100.00	2549300

Source: Beijing Municipal Administration of Press, Publication, Radio, Film and Television.

19−26 电影、电视剧制作情况
STATISTICS FOR PRODUCTION OF FILMS AND TV PLAYS

项目		Item		2016 全国 National Total	2016 北京 Beijing	2016 占全国比重(%) As % of National Total	2015 全国 National Total	2015 北京 Beijing	2015 占全国比重(%) As % of National Total
生产故事片	(部)	Feature Films	(Piece)	944	314	33.3	888	291	32.8
制作电视剧	(部)	TV Plays	(Piece)	334	64	19.2	394	75	19.0
	(集)		(Episode)	14932	2673	17.9	16540	2878	17.4
电视剧出口量部	(部)	TV Plays Exported	(Piece)	419	34	8.1	381	53	13.9
	(集)		(Episode)	25455	1325	5.2	15902	2116	13.3
电视剧出口额	(万元)	Value of TV Plays Exported	(10000 yuan)	29732	2370.32	8.0	37705	6211	16.5

资料来源：北京市新闻出版广电局。
Source: Beijing Municipal Administration of Press, Publication, Radio, Film and Television.

19−27 电影放映单位情况(2016年)
STATISTICS FOR MOVIE PROJECTION ORGANIZATIONS (2016)

项目	Item	放映单位数(个) Number of Projection Organizations (unit)	总银幕数(块) Total Screens (Piece)	#3D银幕数 3D Screens	#IMAX巨幕数 IMAX Large Screens	放映场次(万场次) Show Times (10000 Times)	观影人次(万人次) Audience (10000 Person-times)	票房收入(亿元) Ticket Revenues (100 million yuan)
合计	**Total**	**207**	**1273**	**873**	**14**	**228.50**	**6926.73**	**30.33**
院线影院	Cinema Chains	207	1273	873	14	228.35	6873.43	30.28
二级市场	Secondary Market					0.15	53.30	0.05

资料来源：北京市新闻出版广电局。
Source: Beijing Municipal Administration of Press, Publication, Radio, Film and Television.

19–28 电视台情况
STATISTICS FOR TELEVISION STATIONS

项　　目	Item	2016		2015	
		中　央 Central	地　方 Local	中　央 Central	地　方 Local
基本情况	**Basic Statistics**				
电视台　(座)	Television Stations　(unit)	1	1	1	1
公共节目套数　(套)	Number of Public Programs　(unit)	29	26	43	26
全年公共节目播出时间　(小时)	Annual Broadcast Time of Public Programs　(hour)	241175.7	131859.2	359898.6	128143.5
播放节目情况	**Shows of TV Programs**				
新闻咨询类节目　(小时)	News and Consulting Programs　(hour)	71546	22056	75766	22792
专题服务类节目　(小时)	Special Service Programs　(hour)	77337	51290	90699	49656
综艺益智类节目　(小时)	Entertainment and Education Programs　(hour)	38019	10392	41613	10007
影视剧类节目　(小时)	Movie and TV Play Programs　(hour)	50091	28780	73926	26981
广告类节目　(小时)	Commercial Programs　(hour)	4183	8579	5666	9270
其他类节目　(小时)	Other Programs　(hour)		10761	72228	9437

注：电视台数不包括区电视台。
资料来源：北京市新闻出版广电局。
Note: Number of television stations excludes TV stations of districts.
Source: Beijing Municipal Administration of Press, Publication, Radio, Film and Television.

19-29 广播电台情况
STATISTICS FOR BROADCASTING STATIONS

项目	Item	2016 中央 Central	2016 地方 Local	2015 中央 Central	2015 地方 Local
基本情况	**Basic Statistics**				
电台数 (座)	Number of Broadcasting Stations (unit)	2	1	2	1
公共节目套数 (套)	Number of Public Programs (unit)	23	26	23	25
全年公共节目播出时间 (小时)	Annual Broadcast Time of Public Programs (hour)	270579	180641	262963	171702
播放节目情况	**Shows of Radio Programs**				
新闻咨询类节目 (小时)	News and Consulting Programs (hour)	71479	18733	68043	19811
专题服务类节目 (小时)	Special Service Programs (hour)	103436	39641	99244	39010
综艺类节目 (小时)	Entertainment and Education Programs (hour)	66363	93714	65204	82092
广播剧类节目 (小时)	Radio Plays (hour)	1463	8792	8170	11519
广告类节目 (小时)	Commercial Programs (hour)	10250	12623	12851	12308
其他类节目 (小时)	Other Programs (hour)	17589	7138	9451	6963

注：1. 广播电台数不包括区县电台。
2. 公共节目套数中含县级广播电视台的广播节目套数。
资料来源：北京市新闻出版广电局。
Note: a) Number of broadcasting stations excluded those of districts and counties.
b) Public programs included broadcast programs of radio stations at county levels.
Source: Beijing Municipal Administration of Press, Publication, Radio, Film and Television.

19-30 广播电视综合覆盖率(2016年)
COMPREHENSIVE COVERAGE RATE OF BROADCASTS AND TELEVISIONS (2016)

项目	Item	2016
广播综合覆盖率 (%)	Comprehensive Coverage Rate of Broadcasts (%)	100.0
农村广播综合覆盖率 (%)	Comprehensive Coverage Rate of Broadcasts in Rural Areas (%)	100.0
无线广播综合覆盖率 (%)	Comprehensive Coverage Rate of Radios (%)	100.0
电视综合覆盖率 (%)	Comprehensive Coverage Rate of Televisions (%)	100.0
农村电视综合覆盖率 (%)	Comprehensive Coverage Rate of Televisions in Rural Areas (%)	100.0
无线电视综合覆盖率 (%)	Comprehensive Coverage Rate of Wireless Televisions (%)	99.75
有线电视入户率 (%)	Access Rate of Wire Broadcasting and Cable TVs (%)	109.66
有线电视注册用户数 (万户)	Registered Subscribers of Cable TVs (10000 households)	580.42
#高清交互数字电视用户数 (万户)	Subscribers of High-definition Interactive Digital Televisions (10000 households)	483.04
付费电视用户数 (万户)	Subscribers of Pay TVs (10000 households)	76.40
农村有线广播电视用户数 (万户)	Subscribers of Wire Broadcasting and Cable TVs in Rural Areas (10000 households)	85.02

资料来源：北京市新闻出版广电局。
Source: Beijing Municipal Administration of Press, Publication, Radio, Film and Television.

19-31 报纸、期刊、图书出版情况(1978-2015年)
NEWSPAPER, JOURNAL AND BOOK PUBLICATIONS (1978-2015)

年份 Year	报纸出版 Newspaper Publications				期刊出版 Journal Publications				图书出版 Books Publications		
	种数(种) Types (kind)	平均期印数(万份) Average Printed Copies Per Issue (10000 copies)	总印数(亿份) Total Printed Copies (100 million copies)	总印张(亿印张) Total Sheets Printed (100 million pieces)	种数(种) Types (kind)	平均期印数(万册) Average Printed Copies Per Issue (10000 copies)	总印数(亿册) Total Printed Copies (100 million copies)	总印张(亿印张) Total Sheets Printed (100 million pieces)	种数(种) Types (kind)	总印数(亿册、亿张) Total Sheets Printed (100 million copies)	总印张(亿印张) Total Sheets Printed (100 million pieces)
1978	11		68.50		468		4.50		5253	5.12	
1979	16		81.60		697		5.92		6723	5.91	
1980	41		84.50		839		5.80		9534	6.28	
1981	55		83.10		886		6.69		11139	7.84	
1982	57		78.30		882		6.67		13862	8.71	
1983	61		79.90		940		6.84		14384	8.49	
1984	73		83.00		987		7.89		15636	8.43	
1985	99		86.00		1098		8.21		17178	9.01	
1986	126		82.00		1206		7.95		19362	5.82	
1987	129		86.00		1409		8.24		21843	6.94	
1988	151		87.00		1514		8.23		23689	7.28	
1989	161		66.00		1580		6.24		25980	6.31	
1990	148		68.00		1415		5.90		27345	6.17	
1991	157		76.70		1499		6.83		29609	7.05	
1992	164	3886	81.38	88.39	1594	6043	7.79	22.30	31320	7.83	58.67
1993	170	3965	81.70	87.71	1597	6037	7.80	22.36	34393	8.60	70.96
1994	233	3759	69.98	92.59	1854	5328	6.29	19.11	38498	8.28	71.71
1995	240	3823	72.92	108.32	1884	5018	6.38	19.62	38819	8.33	70.15
1996	242		70.52		2129		6.13		41572	9.45	
1997	242	3624	71.80	122.17	2162	5396	6.61	22.87	45775	9.93	78.62
1998	247	3561	71.70	130.01	2274	5797	7.28	26.54	50155	10.95	86.05
1999	247	3520	71.65	144.65	2273	6116	8.04	35.18	54783	11.34	93.38
2000	240	3343	68.67	149.58	2352	5909	7.91	32.96	57821	9.63	92.98
2001	243	3339	69.35	153.22	2374	5761	8.09	32.61	63928	10.27	105.06
2002	247	3364	71.02	169.87	2377	5708	8.23	34.34	73836	12.16	127.48
2003	250	3393	72.45	190.35	2382	5702	8.18	34.25	85244	13.82	140.77
2004	253	3405	70.40	206.53	2791	5233	7.97	35.53	98312	15.22	157.17
2005	255	3169	66.16	227.22	2809	4957	7.72	40.80	108152	17.07	180.51
2006	256	3651	74.01	240.39	2809	5077	8.29	47.39	113232	17.19	186.10
2007	256	3454	73.09	218.55	2809	5340	9.17	54.21	125412	18.68	195.30
2008	259	3328	73.21	241.27	2898	5392	9.36	55.39	136284	20.78	220.00
2009	260	3232	71.63	232.50	3030	5373	9.70	59.35	144211	21.04	220.21
2010	262	3406	77.54	275.62	3063	5519	10.03	69.61	155209	21.45	251.18
2011	254	3453	83.07	293.72	3044	5991	10.19	76.74	167942	22.60	243.05
2012	257	3725	89.49	300.17	3064	5940	10.31	76.68	179634	22.54	250.70
2013	254	3737	91.72	298.20	3053	6094	10.36	78.02	192137	24.01	269.54
2014	256	3550	89.90	289.30	3123	5867	9.95	74.04	194259	23.56	258.65
2015	253	3389	87.35	267.51	3168	5539	9.32	67.96	205992	24.45	270.97

注：1991年及以前，报纸、期刊、图书为出版数；1992年及以后均为总印数。

资料来源：北京市新闻出版广电局。

Note: Figures on newspaper, journals and books in and before 1991 were figures of publications; after 1992, they were total sheet printed.

Source: Beijing Municipal Administration of Press, Publication, Radio, Film and Television.

19－32 报纸出版情况 NEWSPAPER PUBLICATION

项目	Item	种数(种) Types of Publications (kind)		平均期印数(万份) Average Printed Copies Per Issue (10000 copies)		总印数 (亿份) Total Printed Copies (100 million copies)		总印张 (亿印张) Total Sheets Printed (100 million pieces)	
		2015	2014	2015	2014	2015	2014	2015	2014
合　计	**Total**	**253**	**256**	**3389**	**3550**	**87.4**	**89.9**	**267.5**	**289.3**
综合报	Comprehensive	31	30	1262	1337	43.5	45.8	157.0	169.5
专业报	Professional	222	226	2127	2213	43.8	44.1	110.5	119.8

资料来源：北京市新闻出版广电局。
Source: Beijing Municipal Administration of Press, Publication, Radio, Film and Television.

19－33 期刊出版情况 JOURNAL PUBLICATION

项目	Item	种数 (种) Types of Publications (kind)		平均期印数 (万册) Average Printed Copies Per Issue (10000 copies)		总印数 (亿册) Total Printed Copies (100 million copies)		总印张 (亿印张) Total Sheets Printed (100 million pieces)	
		2015	2014	2015	2014	2015	2014	2015	2014
合　计	**Total**	**3168**	**3123**	**5539**	**5867**	**9.32**	**9.95**	**67.96**	**74.04**
综　合	Comprehensive	69	68	106	123	0.26	0.30	1.74	2.09
哲学、社会科学	Philosophy and Social Sciences	950	939	3581	3705	6.14	6.33	33.50	34.57
自然科学技术	Natural Sciences and Technology	1615	1595	1040	1151	1.40	1.58	18.13	18.10
文化、教育	Culture and Education	381	373	642	705	1.15	1.34	12.19	16.57
文学、艺术	Literature and Art	153	148	170	183	0.37	0.40	2.40	2.71

资料来源：北京市新闻出版广电局。
Source: Beijing Municipal Administration of Press, Publication, Radio, Film and Television.

19—34 图书出版情况
BOOK PUBLICATION

项 目	Item	出版图书种数合计(种) Types of Publications (kind)		#新 书 New Publications		总印数(万册、万张) Total Printed Copies (10000 volumes, 10000 pieces)		总印张(万印张) Total Sheets Printed (10000 print sheets)	
		2015	2014	2015	2014	2015	2014	2015	2014
合 计	**Total**	**205992**	**194259**	**115397**	**113605**	**244489**	**235632**	**2709742**	**2586544**
书籍合计	**Books**	**205772**	**194189**	**115286**	**113565**	**242841**	**233165**	**2702355**	**2575153**
马列主义、毛泽东思想	Maxism, Leninism, Mao Zedong Thought	492	516	365	321	1326	1737	22699	29666
哲 学	Philosophy	5486	4820	3648	3197	3912	3288	55989	48599
社会科学总论	General Social Sciences	3616	3477	2105	2175	2141	1743	34180	29952
政治、法律	Politics and Law	14601	13470	10320	9914	15996	14877	188399	169374
军 事	Military Science	1083	975	845	810	588	448	8823	7099
经 济	Economics	23139	22224	14208	13741	11693	10886	198285	187999
文化、科学、教育、体育	Culture,Science,Education and Sports	42918	37775	19325	19067	133140	129651	1090815	1049900
语言、文字	Languages	12176	11891	5290	5644	13009	11875	224582	211571
文 学	Literature	16517	15731	12208	11844	16539	14619	197774	180654
艺 术	Art	8826	8858	5836	6250	5286	5433	52929	50653
历史、地理	History and Geography	9464	8637	6936	6194	8267	8097	105156	93850
自然科学总论	General Natural Sciences	349	342	234	220	229	175	3255	2442
数学科学、化学	Mathematics and Chemistry	5573	5232	1949	1925	2653	2620	45270	46562
天文学、物理科学	Astronomy and Physics	1749	1561	1204	1091	631	588	8193	6593
生物科学	Biology	1931	1580	1018	858	1017	799	14492	11131
医药、卫生	Medicine and Healthcare	13124	11484	7819	6532	7863	6590	144661	124175
农业科学	Agricultural Sciences	3571	3327	2007	2037	1214	1298	14482	14327
工业技术	Industrial Technologies	33877	35286	15715	17649	13214	14231	235054	252816
交通运输	Transportation	3818	4014	1849	1893	2323	2567	31537	35004
航空、航天	Aeronautics and Aerospace	390	319	258	240	107	85	1533	1339
环境科学	Environmental Sciences	1540	1443	994	1032	453	497	5965	6051
综合性图书	General Books	1532	1227	1153	931	1239	1060	18283	15394
图片及小件印品合计	**Pictures and Small Printed Publications**	**220**	**70**	**111**	**40**	**1649**	**2467**	**7388**	**11392**

资料来源：北京市新闻出版广电局。
Source: Beijing Municipal Administration of Press, Publication, Radio, Film and Television.

19-35 录音制品出版情况
PUBLICATION OF AUDIO PRODUCTS

项目 Item	录音带 Audio-tapes				激光唱盘 CDs				高密度激光唱盘及其他 DVDs-A and Others			
	种数(种) Types (kind)		数量(万盒) Number (10000 cassettes)		种数(种) Types (kind)		数量(万张) Number (10000 pieces)		种数(种) Types (kind)		数量(万张) Number (10000 pieces)	
	2015	2014	2015	2014	2015	2014	2015	2014	2015	2014	2015	2014
合计 Total	**907**	**1095**	**10360.7**	**12366.6**	**1632**	**1654**	**3605.6**	**2657.8**	**1068**	**1069**	**1422.1**	**830.4**
#市属 Municipal	25	78	2.3	6.2	107	192	100.6	157.3	5	31	1.4	89.1

资料来源：北京市新闻出版广电局。
Source: Beijing Municipal Administration of Press, Publication, Radio, Film and Television.

19-36 录像制品出版情况
PUBLICATION OF VIDEO PRODUCTS

项目 Item	录像带 Videotapes				激光视盘 VCDs				高密度激光视盘 DVD-Vs			
	种数(种) Types (kind)		数量(万盒) Number (10000 cassettes)		种数(种) Kind (kind)		数量(万张) Number (10000 pieces)		种数(种) Types (kind)		数量(万张) Number (10000 pieces)	
	2015	2014	2015	2014	2015	2014	2015	2014	2015	2014	2015	2014
合计 Total	**64**	**93**	**18.0**	**18.5**	**578**	**523**	**1082.1**	**1456.7**	**1912**	**1799**	**2915.8**	**2669.8**
#市属 Municipal									53	54	25.2	287.0

资料来源：北京市新闻出版广电局。
Source: Beijing Municipal Administration of Press, Publication, Radio, Film and Television.

19—37 电子出版物出版情况(2015年)
PUBLICATION OF E-PUBLICATIONS (2015)

项 目	Item	只读光盘 CD-ROMs		交互式光盘及其他 CD-Is and Others		高密度只读光盘 DVD-ROMs	
		种数(种) Types (kind)	数量(万盒) Number (10000 cassettes)	种数(种) Types (kind)	数量(万张) Number (10000 pieces)	种数(种) Types (kind)	数量(万张) Number (10000 pieces)
合 计	**Total**	**3516**	**12015.97**	**860**	**986.46**	**2304**	**1816.96**
#市 属	Municipal	12	16.51	14	1	28	11.82

资料来源：北京市新闻出版广电局。
Source: Beijing Municipal Administration of Press, Publication, Radio, Film and Television.

19—38 引进版权量情况
NUMBER OF IMPORTED COPYRIGHTS

项 目		Item		2015	2014
引进版权量	**(件)**	**Number of Imported Copyrights**	**(set)**	**8578**	**8647**
软件和电子出版物	(件)	Softwares and E-Publications	(set)	139	92
图 书	(件)	Books	(set)	8439	8555

资料来源：北京市新闻出版广电局。
Source: Beijing Municipal Administration of Press, Publication, Radio, Film and Television.

主要统计指标解释

教　育

研究生培养机构　指经国家批准按国家计划招收和培养硕士、博士和其他研究生的高等学校和科学研究机构。

普通高等学校　指按国家规定的设置标准和审批程序批准举办的，通过国家统一招生考试，招收高中毕业生为主要培养对象，实施高等教育的全日制大学、独立设置的学院和高等专科学校、短期职业大学。

成人高等学校　指按国家规定的设置标准和审批程序批准举办的，通过全国成人高等教育统一招生考试，招收具有高中毕业或同等学历的人员为主要培养对象，利用函授、业余、脱产等多种形式对其实施高等学历教育的学校。包括：职工高等学校、农民高等学校、管理干部学院、教育学院、独立函授学院、广播电视大学和其他机构。

高等教育机构　指经省、自治区、直辖市教育行政部门审批并颁发办学许可证，不具有颁发学历文凭资格的实施高等教育的单位。

民办学校　指经有关主管部门批准，公民个人、社会团体及其他社会组织等利用非国家财政性教育经费，面向社会举办的学校及其他教育机构。

学历文凭考试机构　经教育行政部门专门批准，进行全日制高等教育的民办其他高等教育机构。

专科教育　应当使学生掌握本专业必备的基础理论、专门应用技术知识，具有从事本专业实际工作的基本技能和技术应用能力。全日制专科教育的基本修业年限为二至三年。

本科教育　应当使学生比较系统地掌握本学科、专业必需的基础理论、基本知识，掌握本专业必要的基本技能、方法和相关知识，具有从事本专业实际工作和研究工作的初步能力。全日制本科教育的基本修业年限为四至五年。

硕士研究生教育　应当使学生掌握本学科坚实的基础理论、系统的专业知识，掌握相应的技能、方法和相关知识，具有从事本专业实际工作和科学研究工作的能力。硕士研究生教育的基本修业年限为二至三年。

博士研究生教育　应当使学生掌握本学科坚实宽广的基础理论、系统深入的专业知识、相应的技能和方法，具有独立从事本学科创造性科学研究工作和实际工作的能力。博士研究生教育的基本修业年限为三至四年。

网络学生　指经教育部批准的现代远程教育试点学校设立的网络教育学院，基于互联网上实施高等学历教育所招收的普通和成人本科、专科学生。

在职人员攻读博士、硕士学位学生　指经国务院学位委员会批准的，为提高在职人员业务水平，通过攻读博士、硕士学位入学全国联考所招收的学生。培养的学生只有学位没有学历。

证书教育　指由各类高等教育机构举办的，招收具有高中毕业文化程度，从事专业技术工作或专业性较强的管理工作人员，经过学校学习及考试合格，取得达到岗位要求的专业知识水平证明的非学历教育。证书教育形式包括单科班和专业证书班。

单科班　指学生在学校只学一个科目中的一门或几门课程，考试合格可获得单科结业证书。

专业证书班　学生在学校学习 8 至 10 门课程，考试合格可获得岗位要求的大专层次专业知识水平的证书。

岗位培训　指由各类高等教育机构举办的，以提高本职工作能力为目的的非学历教育和培训活动。接受培训的各类人员按要求经考核合格，颁发岗位合格证书和上岗任职聘任书。岗位培训形式包括资格性培训和适应性培训。

资格性培训　指学生按照岗位规范要求取得上岗(在岗)、转岗、晋升等资格的培训。

适应性培训　指学生根据本岗位工作的发展需要而进行各种适应性的培训。

进修及培训　指对具有大学专科以上学历和中级以上职称的专业人员和管理人员进行扩展知识，提高技能的非学历教育。

外国留学生　指接受来中国学习的外籍学生。

毕业生数　指上学年度内，具有学籍的学生学完教学计划规定的全部课程，考试及格，取得毕业证书，实际毕业的学生数。不包括结业生和肄业生数。

招生数　指新学年开始时，按照国家计划实际招收入学的新生数。不包括留级生和复读学生数。

在校学生数　指学年初开学以后，具有学籍的注册学生数。

结业生数　指具有学籍的学生学习期满，有一门以上主要课程(包括毕业论文或毕业设计)不及格或其他方面不合格，未予毕业而发给结业证书的学生数。不包括短训班和单科结业学生。

教职工数　指在学校(机构)工作并由学校(机构)支付工资的教职工人数。教职工数包括校本部教职工、科研机构人员、校办企业职工、其他附设机构人员。

专任教师　指主要从事教育工作的人员。包括临时（一年以内）调去帮助做其他工作的教学人员。不包括调离教学岗位，担任行政领导工作或其他工作的原教学人员；不包括兼任教师和代课教师。

特殊教育学校 指招收盲聋哑青少年进行初中等教育的学校。

校舍建筑面积 指产权归学校所有，已经使用的各种用房的建筑面积。不包括尚未竣工的在建工程和借用、租用的房舍或临时搭用的棚舍。

危房面积 指年久失修、结构构件受到严重损坏，有倒塌危险，经房管部门鉴定属于危房的面积。

学校占地面积 指学校校园内的土地面积，不包括校园外学校拥有的农场、林场及校办工厂等的土地面积。

文 化

公共图书馆藏书 指各级文化部门举办的面向社会服务的独立的图书馆（不包括文化馆的图书室，也不包括文化系统以外的图书馆）藏书数量。

广播综合覆盖率 根据国家广电总局制定的《广播电视人口覆盖率统计技术标准和方法》进行统计调查的，在对象区内能接收到广播节目的覆盖人口数占本行政区域内人口总数的比率。

农村广播综合覆盖率 根据国家广电总局制定的《广播电视人口覆盖率统计技术标准和方法》进行统计调查的，在对象区内能接收到广播节目的农村人口数占本行政区域内农村人口总数的比率。农村是指经国家批准设立的乡镇人民政府的乡和农村建制镇所辖区，不包括县政府驻地镇。

无线广播综合覆盖率 根据国家广电总局制定的《广播电视人口覆盖率统计技术标准和方法》进行统计调查的，在对象区内能接收到用中、短波、调频等无线传输技术发射转播的广播节目的人口数占本行政区域内人口总数的比率。包括中央、省、地市、县四级无线广播综合覆盖人口。

电视综合覆盖率 根据国家广电总局制定的《广播电视人口覆盖率统计技术标准和方法》进行统计调查的，在对象区内能接收到电视节目的人口数占本行政区域内人口总数的比率，包括中央、省、地市、县电视节目综合覆盖人口。

农村电视综合覆盖率 根据国家广电总局制定的《广播电视人口覆盖率统计技术标准和方法》进行统计调查的，在对象区内能接收到电视节目的农村人口数占本行政区域内农村人口总数的比率，包括中央、省、地市、县电视节目综合覆盖农村人口。农村是指经国家批准设立的乡镇人民政府的乡和农村建制镇所辖区，不包括县政府驻地镇。

无线电视综合覆盖率 根据国家广电总局制定的《广播电视人口覆盖率统计技术标准和方法》进行统计调查的，在对象区内能接收到用中、短波、调频等无线传输技术发射转播的电视节目的人口数占本行政区域内人口总数的比率。包括中央、省、地市、县四级无线电视综合覆盖人口。

有线电视入户率 指通过广播电视有线传输网收看电视节目的家庭用户数（包括接收模拟信号和接收数字信号的有线电视用户数，不包括宾馆、单位、写字楼等集体用户）与本行政区域内总户数的比率。

数字电视用户数 指通过广播电视有线传输网收看数字信号电视节目的家庭用户数。

付费电视用户数 指通过广播电视有线传输网收看数字信号的电视节目，并交纳收看费的有线电视家庭用户数。

Explanatory Notes on Main Statistical Indicators

Education

Institutions Providing Postgraduate Programs refer to colleges and universities, research institutions recruiting and educating postgraduates of master's degree, doctor's degree and other degree upon approval by the government and under the State Plan.

Regular Institutions of Higher Education refer to educational establishments set up according to the government evaluation and approval procedures, recruiting graduates from senior secondary schools as the main target by National Matriculation Test. They include full-time universities, independent colleges and higher professional schools, short-term vocational colleges.

Adult Institutions of Higher Education refer to educational establishments, set up in line with relevant rules approved by the government, recruiting personnel with senior high school or equivalent educational diploma through national college entrance test for adults, and providing higher education courses in many forms of correspondence, spare-time, or full-time teaching for adults. Institutions of higher learning for adults include schools of higher education for staff and workers, schools of higher education for farmers, colleges for management cadres, pedagogical colleges, independent correspondence colleges, Radio and TV universities and other educational establishments.

Higher Education Institutions refer to institutions offering higher education upon examination and approval by administrative departments in charge of education in provinces, autonomous regions and municipalities, with an education license, which are not eligible for conferring diploma.

Civilian-run Schools refer to schools and other educational institutions run by individuals, social groups and other social organizations upon approval by relevant competent authorities, by using educational funds not from state revenues.

Diploma Test Institutions refer to other civilian-run higher education institutions offering full-time higher education upon special approval by educational administration.

Secondary Technical Education shall enable students to understand necessary basic theories and special knowledge on applied technologies of a specialty, have basic skills and technical application ability for practice of the specialty. Full-time secondary technically education offers a basic study term of 2-3 years.

Undergraduate Education shall enable students to understand necessary basic theories and knowledge of a subject or specialty, have necessary basic skills, methodology and relevant knowledge of the specialty, and have preliminary skills for practical work and research of the specialty. Full-time undergraduate education offers a basic study term of 4-5 years.

Master's-degree Postgraduate Education shall enable students to understand solid basic theories, systematic professional knowledge of a subject, have relevant skills, methodology and relevant knowledge of the specialty, and have preliminary skills for practical work and research of the specialty. Master's-degree postgraduate education offers a basic study term of 2-3 years.

Doctor's-degree Postgraduate Education shall enable students to understand solid and extensive basic theories, systematic and in-depth professional knowledge, relevant skills and methodology of a subject, have relevant skills, methodology and relevant knowledge of the specialty, and have preliminary skills for independent creative research and practical work of the specialty. Doctor's-degree postgraduate education offers a basic study term of 3-4 years.

Online Students refer to students for Internet-based general higher courses, undergraduate courses for adults, and secondary technical courses recruited in online education colleges opened in schools as modern remote education pilots approved by the Ministry of Education.

Employees Enrolled in Graduate Programs refer to students recruited through national joint test for studies of Doctor's and Master's degrees approved by the Academic Degree Commission of the State Council, in order to improve the practical skills of on-the-job personnel. Graduated students will be conferred academic degree only, without academic credentials.

Certificate Education refers to education not for academic credentials, run by various higher education institutions that recruit management personnel who are graduated from senior high schools and engaged in professional technical work or strongly professional management work, and receive a certificate for professional knowledge level meeting the requirements of their job position after studying in the school and pass the test. It consists of single-subject program and professional certificate program.

Single-subject Program means that students study only one or more courses of one subject, and will be awarded a certificate of completion of single subject.

Professional Certificate Program means that students study 8-10 courses in the school, and will be awarded a certificate for professional knowledge at junior college level required for their job.

Occupational Training refers to educational and

training activities not for academic credentials, aiming to improve the competence, run by various higher education institutions. Various trainees will be awarded Occupational Incumbency Certification and Engagement Certification. The occupational training is in the form of qualification training and adaptability training.

Qualification Training means any training for students to become qualified for being employed (reemployed) on a job, transfer of job, and promotion as required by job criterion.

Adaptability Training means that students receive training for adaptability in line with needs of their own job.

Advanced Studies and Trainings means education not for academic credentials, offered for professional and managers with educational background of college and above, and technical title above middle rank, to expand their knowledge and improve their skill.

Foreign Students Studying in China refers to foreign students who study in China.

Number of Graduated Students means the number of enrolled students who are actually graduated after passing all exams and receiving a diploma upon completing all courses stated in the teaching plan within the last academic year. This does not include the number of students completing all courses with any one course not passed, and students not completing all courses or discontinuing their schooling.

Number of New Students refers to the number of students actually recruited at the beginning of an academic year in line with State plan, excluding the number of students failing to go up to the next grade and those resuming their interrupted studies.

Number of Enrolled Students means the number of students enrolled at the beginning of a new academic year.

Number of Students Completing Courses means the number of enrolled students completing their schooling with one and more courses not passed (including the graduation paper or graduation design) or other aspects not passed, who are not granted for graduation and awarded a certificate of completion, excluding the number of students completing short-term training courses and single-subject programs.

Faculty Number means the number of faculty working in and paid by schools (institutions). It includes the number of teachers and workers in the principal campus, in research institutions, school-run enterprises and other subsidiaries.

Full-time Teachers refer to personnel mainly engaged in teaching, including persons temporarily (within one year) transferred to other jobs, excluding persons transferred from teaching to administrative leadership or other jobs; excluding part-time teachers and teachers taking over a class for absent teachers.

Schools for Special Education mean schools recruiting blind, deaf and mute teenagers for primary and secondary education.

Floor Space of Schoolhouse refers to the building area of various houses of which the property right is owned by the school and which have been used, excluding houses not completed and under construction, borrowed and rented, or temporarily built sheds and houses.

Area of Dilapidated Houses refers to the area of those houses that have not been repaired for many years, have seriously damaged components, are at the risk of collapse, and are identified by the house administration authority as dilapidated houses.

Area of Land Occupied by School means the area of land within campus, excluding the area of land for farms and forest land outside schools and school-run factories.

Culture

Collection of Books in Public Libraries means the number of books collected in independent libraries open to the public and run by all-level cultural bodies (excluding book rooms in culture centers, and books collected in libraries not included in the cultural system).

Comprehensive Coverage Rate of Broadcast means the share of population who can receive broadcasting programs in the target area, calculated in line with *Statistical Standard and Method on Television and Radio Coverage of Population* established by the State Administration of Broadcasting, Film and Television, of the total population in the administrative area.

Comprehensive Coverage Rate of Broadcast in Rural Area means the share of rural population who can receive broadcasting programs in the target area, calculated in line with *Statistical Standard and Method on Television and Radio Coverage of Population* established by the National Administration of Broadcasting, Film and Television, of the total rural population in the administrative area. Rural area means villages of towns with people's governments approved by the State and areas under the jurisdiction of rural towns with organizational system, excluding towns where people's governments of counties are located.

Comprehensive Coverage Rate of Radio means the share of population who can receive broadcasting programs transmitted with short-wave, medium-wave, FM and other radio transmission technologies in the target area, calculated in line with *Statistical Standard and Method on Television and Radio Coverage of Population* established by the National Administration of Broadcasting, Film and Television, of the total population in the administrative area, including the population covered by broadcasting programs from central, provincial, prefectural cities and county radio stations.

Comprehensive Coverage Rate of TV means the share of population who can receive TV programs in the target area, calculated in line with *Statistical Standard and Method on Television and Radio Coverage of Population* established by the National Administration of Broadcasting, Film and Television, of the total population in the administrative area, including the population covered by TV programs from central, provincial, prefectural cities and county TV stations.

Comprehensive Coverage Rate of TV in Rural Area means the share of rural population who can receive TV programs in the target area, calculated in line with *Statistical Standard and Method on Television and Radio Coverage of*

Population established by the National Administration of Broadcasting, Film and Television, of the total rural population in the administrative area, including the population covered by TV programs from central, provincial, prefectural cities and county TV stations. Rural area means villages of towns with people's governments approved by the State and areas under the jurisdiction of rural towns with organizational system, excluding towns where people's governments of counties are located.

Comprehensive Coverage Rate of Wireless TV means the share of population who can receive TV programs transmitted with short-wave, medium-wave, FM and other radio transmission technologies in the target area, calculated in line with *Statistical Standard and Method on Television and Radio Coverage of Population* established by the National Administration of Broadcasting, Film and Television, of the total population in the administrative area, including the population covered by radio television programs from central, provincial, prefectural cities and county TV stations.

Access Rate of CATV refers to the percentage of households which can watch television programs by cable broadcasting and television transmission network (including cable TV households receiving analog signals and digital signals, excluding collective subscribers such as hotels, companies and entities, office buildings), to the total households in the administrative area).

Number of Digital Broadcast/TV Subscribers means the number of households watching digital-signal TV programs through the TV and radio cable transmission network.

Number of Pay TV Subscribers means the number of cable TV households watching digital-signal TV programs through the TV and radio cable transmission network and paying fees for watching.

北京统计年鉴2017 BEIJING STATISTICAL YEARBOOK

科 技
SCIENCE AND TECHNOLOGY

简要说明

一、本章资料的主要内容

本章主要包括：研究与试验发展（R&D）人员情况，研究与试验发展（R&D）经费情况，研究与试验发展（R&D）项目（课题）情况，研究机构情况，规模以上工业企业 R&D 活动基本情况，限额以上信息传输、软件和信息技术服务业企业研究与试验发展(R&D)活动基本情况，规模以上高技术制造业主要科技指标，高等学校科技活动情况、研究与开发机构研发活动、专利申请及授权情况等。

二、本章资料的统计范围

国民经济中研究与试验发展（R&D）活动相对密集行业的法人单位，主要数据包括：农、林、牧、渔业，采矿业，制造业，电力、热力、燃气及水的生产和供应业，建筑业，交通运输、仓储和邮政业，信息传输、软件和信息技术服务业，金融业，租赁和商务服务业，科学研究和技术服务业，水利、环境和公共设施管理业，教育，卫生和社会工作，文化、体育和娱乐业，公共管理、社会保障和社会组织等。

三、本章资料的数据来源

本章由北京市统计局、北京市科学技术委员会、北京市教育委员会、北京市经济和信息化委员会、北京市人力资源和社会保障局、北京市知识产权局、北京市科学技术协会、北京技术市场管理办公室等部门提供。

四、有关统计标准的变化说明

（一）关于行业划分。根据国家统计局规定，自 2012 年开始执行《国民经济行业分类》（GB/T 4754-2011）标准。

（二）关于三次产业划分。根据国家统计局《三次产业划分规定》（国统字[2012]108 号），该规定对三次产业的范围进行了调整。其中第一产业是指农、林、牧、渔业（不含农、林、牧、渔服务业）；第二产业是指采矿业（不含开采辅助活动），制造业（不含金属制品、机械和设备修理业），电力、热力、燃气及水生产和供应业，建筑业；第三产业是指除第一产业、第二产业以外的其他行业。自 2012 年开始执行此规定。

（三）关于高技术制造业。根据国家统计局《关于印发高技术产业（制造业）分类（2013）的通知》（国统字〔2013〕55 号），本分类在《高技术产业统计分类目录》（国统字〔2002〕33 号）的基础上修订完成，采用了原分类的基本结构框架。自 2013 年开始执行此标准。

Brief Introduction

I. Main Content

Data in this chapter reflect the situation of scientific and technological activities and patents, R&D personnel, R&D funds, R&D projects (tasks), research institutions, basic information on R&D of industrial enterprises above the designated size, basic information on R&D of information transmission, software and information technology service enterprises, scientific and technological activities of colleges and universities, R&D of research institutions and personnel, patent application and licensing, etc.

II. Scope of Statistics

Included in this chapter are the corporate entities in sectors with relatively intensive R&D activities in national economy, such as agriculture, forestry, animal production and hunting, fishing, mining, manufacturing, generation and distribution of electricity, heating, gas and water, construction, transport, storage and post, scientific research and development, technology services, information transmission, software and information technology services, finance, renting and leasing activities and business services, management of water conservancy, environment and public facilities, education, healthcare and social works, culture, sports and entertainment, public administration, social security and social organizations, etc.

III. Source of Data

Data in this chapter are from Beijing Municipal Bureau of Statistics, Beijing Municipal Science & Technology Commission, Beijing Municipal Commission of Education, Beijing Municipal Commission of Economy and Information Technology, Beijing Municipal Bureau of Human Resources and Social Security, Beijing Intellectual Property Bureau, Beijing Municipal Association of Science and Technology, and Beijing Technical Market Management Office, etc.

IV. Changes in Relevant Statistical Standards

(I) Classification of Sectors. According to relevant provisions of National Bureau of Statistics, the Standard for *Classification of National Economic Sectors* (GB/T4754-2011) became effective in 2012.

(II) Classification of Primary, Secondary, and Tertiary Industries. According to the *Provision of Classification of Three Industries* (G.T.Z. [2012] No. 108) issued by National Bureau of Statistics, the scope of three industries has changed. The primary industry includes agriculture, forestry, animal production and hunting, fishing (excluding agricultural, forestry, animal production and hunting, fishing services); the secondary industry includes mining (excluding mining support activities), manufacturing (excluding metal products, machinery and equipment repairing), production and distribution of electricity, heating, natural gas and water and construction industry; the tertiary industry means industries other than the primary and secondary industries. The *Provisions of Classification of Three Industries* (G.T.Z. [2012] No. 108) came into effect in 2012.

(III) High-tech Manufacturing. According to the *Circular of National Bureau of Statistics on Printing and Issuing the Classification of High-tech Industry (Manufacturing) 2013* (G.T.Z. [2013] No. 55). This Classification is revised on the basis of *Classified Catalog of High-tech Industry Statistics* (G.T.Z. [2002] No. 33), following the structure of the original classification. The standard has been put in place since 2013.

20-1 科技活动及专利情况(1985-2016年)
SCIENCE AND TECHNOLOGY ACTIVITIES AND PATENTS (1985-2016)

年 份 Year	科技活动人员 (人) Personnel Engaged in Science and Technology Activities (person)	研究与试验发展(R&D)人员折合全时当量 (人年) Full-time Equivalent of R&D Professionals (person-year)	研究与试验发展(R&D)经费内部支出 (万元) Internal R&D Expenditures (10000 yuan)	研究与试验发展(R&D)经费内部支出相当于地区生产总值比例(%) Internal R&D Expenditures as Percentage of GDP (%)
1985				
1986-1990				
1986				
1987				
1988				
1989				
1990				
1991-1995				
1991	228167			
1992	247525			
1993	252811			
1994	240386			
1995	252232			
1996-2000			**4307457**	
1996	265552	84793	418614	2.32
1997	273161	84913	532257	2.54
1998	237127	86602	861138	3.58
1999	229584	85740	938437	3.46
2000	261113	98723	1557011	4.85
2001-2005			**13434129**	
2001	240609	95255	1711696	4.54
2002	257326	114919	2195402	4.99
2003	270921	110358	2562518	5.02
2004	301202	152132	3169064	5.14
2005	383153	177765	3795450	5.31
2006-2010			**30706037**	
2006	382756	168875	4329878	5.21
2007	450331	204668	5270591	5.23
2008	450147	200080	6200983	5.44
2009	529985	191779	6686351	5.38
2010	529811	193718	8218234	5.69
2011-2015			**58378733**	
2011	605980	217255	9366440	5.63
2012	651003	235493	10633640	5.79
2013	681346	242175	11850469	5.83
2014	726792	245384	12687953	5.78
2015	747461	245728	13840231	5.84
2016	810195	253337	14845762	5.78

资料来源：北京市统计局、北京市科学技术委员会、北京市教育委员会、北京市经济和信息化委员会、北京市知识产权局。
Source: Beijing Municipal Bureau of Statistics, Beijing Municipal Science & Technology Commission, Beijing Municipal Commission of Education, Beijing Municipal Commission of Economy and Information Technology, Beijing Intellectual Property Office.

20-1 续表 Continued

年 份 Year	专 利 申请量 (件) Patent Applications (unit)	发 明 Inventions	实用新型 Utility Models	外观设计 Industrial Designs	专 利 授权量 (件) Patents Granted (unit)	发 明 Inventions	实用新型 Utility Models	外观设计 Industrial Designs
1985	1540	754	720	66				
1986-1990	**15087**	**3332**	**11003**	**752**	**6700**	**737**	**5614**	**349**
1986	1692	535	1091	66	491	43	408	40
1987	2425	523	1796	106	776	102	630	44
1988	3342	702	2494	146	1376	169	1147	60
1989	3344	742	2408	194	1789	207	1497	85
1990	4284	830	3214	240	2268	216	1932	120
1991-1995	**31126**	**6604**	**21787**	**2736**	**19379**	**1801**	**15835**	**1743**
1991	4624	1023	3324	277	2369	263	1917	189
1992	6316	1340	4493	483	3265	312	2724	229
1993	6972	1483	4931	558	5806	530	4780	496
1994	6852	1506	4666	680	3914	368	3245	301
1995	6362	1252	4372	738	4025	328	3169	528
1996-2000	**37296**	**10344**	**20395**	**6557**	**22156**	**2483**	**14836**	**4837**
1996	6595	1441	4255	899	3295	246	2563	486
1997	6313	1678	3667	968	3327	281	2340	706
1998	6321	1754	3444	1123	3800	309	2522	969
1999	7723	2062	4045	1616	5829	573	3948	1308
2000	10344	3409	4984	1951	5905	1074	3463	1368
2001-2005	**83993**	**39312**	**30960**	**13721**	**39944**	**10960**	**20019**	**8965**
2001	12174	4984	5114	2076	6246	946	3600	1700
2002	13842	5785	5920	2137	6345	1061	3721	1563
2003	17003	7833	6665	2505	8248	2261	4244	1743
2004	18402	8608	6321	3473	9005	3216	3956	1833
2005	22572	12102	6940	3530	10100	3476	4498	2126
2006-2010	**209275**	**124175**	**62237**	**22863**	**100371**	**35532**	**48350**	**16489**
2006	26555	14226	8200	4129	11238	3864	5490	1884
2007	31680	18763	8819	4098	14954	4824	7364	2766
2008	43508	28394	11157	3957	17747	6478	8776	2493
2009	50236	29326	15424	5486	22921	9157	10141	3623
2010	57296	33466	18637	5193	33511	11209	16579	5723
2011-2015	**588019**	**332390**	**208281**	**47348**	**322762**	**115260**	**170445**	**37057**
2011	77955	45057	26615	6283	40888	15880	19628	5380
2012	92305	52720	32609	6976	50511	20140	24672	5699
2013	123336	67554	47586	8196	62671	20695	36301	5675
2014	138111	78129	48228	11754	74661	23237	44071	7353
2015	156312	88930	53243	14139	94031	35308	45773	12950
2016	189129	104643	64496	19990	100578	40602	44710	15266

20-2 研究与试验发展(R&D)活动人员情况

项　目	Item	研究与试验发展(R&D)人员(人) R&D Personnel (person)		#本科及以上学历 Bachelor Degree or above	
		2016	2015	2016	2015
合　计	**Total**	**373406**	**350721**	**313037**	**246741**
按执行部门分	**By Executive Department**				
企　业	Enterprises	169480	146896	133066	66173
工业企业	Industrial Enterprises	70658	72802	50713	28613
非工业企业	Non-industrial Enterprises	98822	74094	82353	37560
科研机构	Scientific Research Institutions	113675	111272	101492	99291
高等学校	Institutions of Higher Education	77397	80744	71493	75311
事业单位	Public Institutions	12854	11809	6986	5966
按隶属关系分	**By Affiliation**				
中　央	Central	213211	208503	188441	172781
地　方	Local	160195	142218	124596	73960
按行业门类分	**By Sector**				
#制造业	Manufacturing	66228	69756	48360	27412
信息传输、软件和信息技术服务业	Information Transmission, Software and Information Technology Services	51758	34590	43809	10994
科学研究和技术服务业	Scientific Research and Development, Technical Services	155650	142575	138721	127945
教　育	Education	77397	80744	71493	75311

资料来源：北京市统计局、北京市科学技术委员会、北京市教育委员会、北京市经济和信息化委员会。

RESEARCH AND EXPERIMENTAL DEVELOPMENT PERSONNEL

研究与试验发展(R&D)人员折合全时当量(人年) Full-time Equivalent of R&D Professionals (person-year)		基础研究 Basic Research		应用研究 Applied Research		试验发展 Experimental Development	
2016	2015	2016	2015	2016	2015	2016	2015
253337	**245728**	**46337**	**41324**	**63694**	**61644**	**143306**	**142763**
114590	106625	1006	535	7541	4614	106045	101478
51143	50773	47	17	978	878	50119	49879
63447	55852	960	519	6563	3737	55925	51599
99099	97988	30397	26121	34534	34857	34168	37010
32327	34460	13258	13690	18231	19989	839	781
7320	6655	1676	977	3389	2184	2255	3495
149024	151047	41415	36405	51036	50183	56573	64460
104312	94681	4924	4919	12657	11461	86732	78303
48222	48385	15	6	840	865	47368	47514
36494	26322	323	25	1627	1231	34544	25066
123502	122751	32153	27055	39687	37802	51663	57894
32327	34460	13258	13690	18231	19989	839	781

Source: Beijing Municipal Bureau of Statistics, Beijing Municipal Science & Technology Commission, Beijing Municipal Commission of Education, Beijing Municipal Commission of Economy and Information Technology.

20-3 研究与试验发展(R&D)经费情况

单位：万元

项目	Item	研究与试验发展(R&D)经费内部支出 Internal R&D Expenditures		按活动类型分 Group by Type of Activity			
				基础研究 Basic Research		应用研究 Applied Research	
		2016	2015	2016	2015	2016	2015
合计	**Total**	**14845762**	**13840231**	**2111730**	**1909930**	**3480597**	**3182637**
按执行部门分	**By Executive Department**						
企业	Enterprises	5604315	4964801	26912	26790	372424	249601
工业企业	Industrial Enterprises	2548433	2440875	372	1170	32097	30272
非工业企业	Non-industrial Enterprises	3055881	2523927	26540	25620	340328	219329
科研机构	Scientific Research Institutions	7301166	7027642	1366529	1232527	2164983	1940278
高等学校	Institutions of Higher Education	1604357	1626476	645067	622028	850159	932921
事业单位	Public Institutions	335925	221312	73223	28585	93031	59837
按隶属关系分	**By Affiliation**						
中央	Central	10014677	9888233	1972424	1806243	3048573	2835007
地方	Local	4831086	3951998	139305	103687	432025	347630
按行业门类分	**By Sector**						
#制造业	Manufacturing	2471279	2365034	313	76	30391	29065
信息传输、软件和信息技术服务业	Information Transmission, Software and Information Technology Services	1742949	1181114	7103	545	105493	90853
科学研究和技术服务业	Scientific Research and Development, Technical Services	8596262	8260041	1451934	1279558	2423960	2092820
教育	Education	1604357	1626476	645067	622028	850159	932921

资料来源：北京市统计局、北京市科学技术委员会、北京市教育委员会、北京市经济和信息化委员会。

RESEARCH AND EXPERIMENTAL DEVELOPMENT FUNDS

(10000 yuan)

试验发展 Experimental Development		按支出用途分 Group by Purpose of Payment							
		日常性支出 Routine Expenses		#人员劳务费 Labor Cost		资产性支出 Expenditures for Assets		#仪器和设备 Instruments and Equipment	
2016	2015	2016	2015	2016	2015	2016	2015	2016	2015
9253435	**8747665**	**12810394**	**11677460**	**4414919**	**3889660**	**2035369**	**2162771**	**1567068**	**1639922**
5204979	4688410	5291977	4514413	2645152	2320791	312338	450389	307610	420826
2515965	2409432	2407294	2212021	1030765	969877	141140	228853	138671	226534
2689014	2278978	2884683	2302392	1614387	1350914	171198	221535	168938	194292
3769654	3854837	5871000	5597785	1434615	1277295	1430166	1429857	999017	972218
109130	71528	1374138	1380680	251358	216615	230219	245796	211543	221517
169672	132890	273278	184583	83795	74959	62647	36729	48899	25360
4993680	5246984	8340084	8109519	2138058	1983695	1674592	1778715	1216729	1279604
4259756	3500681	4470309	3567941	2276861	1905965	360777	384056	350340	360318
2440575	2335892	2331869	2139398	1001092	940664	139410	225636	137115	223427
1630353	1089716	1622023	1129526	1017864	827693	120925	51589	119975	50086
4720368	4887663	7060449	6668450	2005350	1739215	1535813	1591591	1090029	1098061
109130	71528	1374138	1380680	251358	216615	230219	245796	211543	221517

Source: Beijing Municipal Bureau of Statistics, Beijing Municipal Science & Technology Commission, Beijing Municipal Commission of Education, Beijing Municipal Commission of Economy and Information Technology.

20-3 续表 Continued

单位：万元 (10000 yuan)

项目	Item	按资金来源分 Group by Fund Source							
		政府资金 Governmental Funds		企业资金 Enterprise Funds		国外资金 Foreign Funds		其他资金 Others	
		2016	2015	2016	2015	2016	2015	2016	2015
合　计	**Total**	**8026073**	**7916391**	**5636747**	**4722359**	**322625**	**403247**	**860317**	**798234**
按执行部门分	**By Executive Department**								
企　业	Enterprises	335159	412517	4916212	4117110	270519	356319	82425	78855
工业企业	Industrial Enterprises	195161	244291	2274450	2097799	14571	41929	64252	56856
非工业企业	Non-industrial Enterprises	139998	168227	2641762	2019312	255949	314390	18173	21999
科研机构	Scientific Research Institutions	6313337	6196676	238991	150103	16890	20088	731948	660775
高等学校	Institutions of Higher Education	1079835	1132410	473306	448191	34170	25868	17045	20007
事业单位	Public Institutions	297742	174788	8239	6955	1046	972	28899	38597
按隶属关系分	**By Affiliation**								
中　央	Central	7475813	7330742	1692533	1766315	51403	49041	794928	742136
地　方	Local	550260	585649	3944214	2956044	271222	354207	65389	56098
按行业门类分	**By Sector**								
#制造业	Manufacturing	192277	237717	2200180	2028532	14571	41929	64252	56856
信息传输、软件和信息技术服务业	Information Transmission, Software and Information Technology Services	19550	27242	1508374	914137	206013	232148	9011	7588
科学研究和技术服务业	Scientific Research and Development, Technical Services	6705343	6484699	1059429	961873	65107	101687	766383	711781
教　育	Education	1079835	1132410	473306	448191	34170	25868	17045	20007

20-4 单位内部办研发机构情况 STATISTICS FOR IN-HOUSE RESEARCH AND DEVELOPMENT INSTITUTIONS

项 目	Item	机构数 (个) Number of Institutions (unit)		机构研究与试验发展(R&D)人员 (人) R&D Personnel (Person)		机构研究与试验发展(R&D)经费支出 (万元) R&D Expenditures (10000 yuan)	
		2016	2015	2016	2015	2016	2015
合 计	**Total**	**2368**	**2658**	**170957**	**191232**	**9530969**	**10317729**
按机构所属学科分	**By Subject of Institution**						
自然科学	Natural Science	148	156	26147	29114	1186259	1299660
农业科学	Agricultural Science	87	93	6056	6361	316056	274982
医药科学	Medical Science	134	128	11820	12911	362314	427325
工程与技术科学	Engineering and Techical Science	1646	1942	113701	131710	7443413	8105250
人文与社会科学	Humanities and Social Science	353	339	13233	11136	222928	210512
按机构组成类型分	**By Institution Composition**						
政府部门办	Run by Government Agency	533	528	118401	116031	7389105	7106379
与国内高校合办	Jointly Run with Domestic Colleges and Universities	52	43	943	804	43955	41670
与国内独立研究机构合办	Jointly Run with Domestic Independent Research Institutions	9	9	168	144	240	824
与境外机构合办	Jointly Run with Overseas Institutions	5	5	57	65	967	531
与境内注册外商独资企业合办	Jointly Run with Solely Foreign-invseted Enterprises Registered in China						
与境内注册其他企业合办	Jointly Run with Other Enterprises Registered in China	71	68	1601	1314	51206	45113
单位自办	Self Run	1693	2001	49724	72784	2044716	3122802
其 他	Others	5	4	63	90	779	411

资料来源：北京市统计局、北京市科学技术委员会、北京市教育委员会、北京市经济和信息化委员会。

Source: Beijing Municipal Bureau of Statistics, Beijing Municipal Science & Technology Commission, Beijing Municipal Commission of Education, Beijing Municipal Commission of Economy and Information Technology.

20-5 研究与试验发展(R&D)项目(课题)情况
RESEARCH AND EXPERIMENTAL DEVELOPMENT PROJECTS (TASKS)

项目	Item	项目(课题)数 (项) Number of Projects (Tasks) (unit)		项目(课题)人员折合全时当量 (人年) Full-time Equivalent of Project (Task) Personnel (person-year)		项目(课题)经费内部支出 (万元) Internal Project (Task) Expenditures (10000 yuan)	
		2016	2015	2016	2015	2016	2015
合计	**Total**	**135387**	**136969**	**226138**	**223637**	**11487262**	**10497955**
按项目(课题)来源分	**By Source**						
国家科技项目	National Science and Technology Projects	55604	57827	89855	97296	5355036	5272977
地方科技项目	Local Science and Technology Projects	15281	13978	11990	11491	314063	223341
企业委托科技项目	Science and Technology Projects Entrusted by Enterprises	32188	32496	16998	20877	787005	872256
自选科技项目	Self-chosen Science and Technology Projects	26256	26534	87268	71166	3928956	2872489
来自国外的科技项目	Science and Technology Projects from Foreign Countries	1849	2127	7870	9925	503453	492927
其它科技项目	Other Science and Technology Projects	4209	4006	12159	12881	598750	763965
按项目(课题)合作形式分	**By Form of Cooperation**						
与境外机构合作	Cooperating with Overseas Institutions	1535	1745	5518	6324	330787	297178
与国内高校合作	Cooperating with Domestic Colleges and Universities	6900	7253	8306	10387	414912	431168
与国内独立研究机构合作	Cooperating with Domestic Independent Research Institutions	8139	8853	15457	18319	971663	1045808
与境内注册外商独资企业合作	Cooperating with solely Foreign-invested Enterprises Registered in China	216	207	170	160	6621	7669
与境内注册其他企业合作	Cooperating with Other Enterprises Registered in China	7158	7371	9514	11164	531608	597067
独立完成	Independent	108718	108368	178025	170151	8692991	7831323
其他	Others	2721	3171	9148	7133	538681	287743
按项目(课题)活动类型分	**By Type of Project (Task) Activity**						
基础研究	Basic Research	50429	47864	40899	39086	1390635	1322954
应用研究	Applied Research	66262	68234	58036	58459	2388676	2295658
试验发展	Experimental Development	18696	20871	127204	126092	7707951	6879344
按项目(课题)社会经济目标分	**By Social and Economic Objective**						
#环境保护及污染防治	Environmental Protection and Pollution Prevention and Control	7792	6983	8109	7137	316242	263796
促进能源的生产、分配和合理利用	Promotion of Production, Allocation and Reasonable Utilization of Energy	8097	10686	7742	13600	393799	613675
促进卫生事业的发展	Promotion of Public Health	10607	9992	15520	17279	251869	298404
促进教育事业的发展	Promotion of Education	12700	11488	2934	3008	66602	57053
基础设施以及城市和农村规划	Infrastructure,Urban and Rural Planning	6138	7053	2965	9344	82116	299837

资料来源：北京市统计局、北京市科学技术委员会、北京市教育委员会、北京市经济和信息化委员会。
Source: Beijing Municipal Bureau of Statistics, Beijing Municipal Science & Technology Commission, Beijing Municipal Commission of Education, Beijing Municipal Commission of Economy and Information Technology.

20-5 续表 Continued

项　目	Item	项目(课题)数 (项) Number of Projects (Tasks) (unit)		项目(课题)人员折合全时当量 (人年) Full-time Equivalent of Project (Task) Personnel (person-year)		项目(课题)经费内部支出 (万元) Internal Project (Task) Expenditures (10000 yuan)	
		2016	2015	2016	2015	2016	2015
社会发展和社会服务	Social Development and Social Service	16414	16078	11000	10656	302583	274831
地球和大气层的探索和利用	Exploration and Exploitation of Earth and Aerosphere	3011	3325	4182	4812	159488	167354
民用空间的探测及开发	Exploration and Exploitation of Civil Space	1719	1018	4226	3293	510456	239263
促进农林牧渔业发展	Promotion of Agriculture, Forestry, Animal Production and Hunting, Fishing	6954	8190	5946	7151	208959	240186
促进工商业发展	Promotion of Industry and Commerce	26246	22877	105886	82554	5014957	3555276
非定向研究	Non-oriented Research	27926	30365	20100	24204	840585	864724
按项目(课题)服务的国民经济行业分	**By Sector of National Economy Served**						
农、林、牧、渔业	Agriculture, Forestry, Animal Production and Hunting, Fishing	7958	8799	5196	6491	213395	224657
采矿业	Mining and Quarrying	2374	3187	2586	4727	93865	231829
制造业	Manufacturing	23368	25352	64532	73081	3594887	3740985
电力、热力、燃气及水生产和供应业	Production and Distribution of Electricity, Heating Power, Gas, Water	2210	2577	1860	3083	54294	124741
建筑业	Construction	2452	2972	5087	6547	246199	195989
批发和零售业	Wholesale and Retail Trade	154	185	41	53	2040	3894
交通运输、仓储和邮政业	Transport, Storage and Post	2381	2491	2266	2565	36081	77773
住宿和餐饮业	Accommodation and Restaurants	200	279	74	117	3547	6298
信息传输、软件和信息技术服务业	Information Transmission,Software and Information Technology Services	5328	5309	36364	26159	1906295	1143231
金融业	Finance	1272	1201	345	300	7486	4844
房地产业	Real Estate	132	133	34	35	589	532
租赁和商务服务业	Renting and Leasing Activities and Business Services	2594	2746	1299	1960	55501	75368
科学研究和技术服务业	Scientific Research and Development, Technical Services	48344	46885	82028	72035	4768552	4123470
水利、环境和公共设施管理业	Management of Water Conservancy, Environment and Public Falicities	4035	3566	4438	4283	167115	155874
居民服务、修理和其他服务业	Resident Services, Repair and Other Services	921	1065	308	339	11835	15809
教　育	Education	11198	10664	2717	2965	79079	71080
卫生和社会工作	Healthcare and Social Works	9303	8360	12018	13139	155394	204276
文化、体育和娱乐业	Culture, Sports and Entertainment	4976	5314	2521	3521	30751	35203
公共管理、社会保障和社会组织	Public Management, Social Security and Social Organizations	6044	5744	2393	2196	59843	61385
国际组织	International Organizations	143	140	32	42	514	719

20-6 规模以上工业企业研究与试验发展(R&D)活动基本情况(2016年)

项　目	Item	企业数(个) Number of Enterprises (unit)	#有研究与试验发展(R&D)活动的企业数 Enterprises with R&D Activities	研究与试验发展(R&D)人员(人) R&D Personnel (person)	研究与试验发展(R&D)人员折合全时当量(人年) Full-time Equivalent of R&D Personnel (person-year)	研究与试验发展(R&D)经费内部支出(万元) Internal R&D Expenditures (10000 yuan)
合　计	**Total**	**3340**	**1155**	**70658**	**51143**	**2548433**
按企业规模分	**By Size of Enterprise**					
#大中型企业	Medium and Large-sized	676	357	51045	36894	2039078
按隶属关系分	**By Affiliation**					
中　央	Central	221	138	13708	10490	528172
地　方	Local	3119	1017	56950	40653	2020262
按登记注册类型分	**By Registration Type**					
内资企业	Domestically-invested Enterprises	2594	948	55771	40056	1688614
#国有企业	State-owned Enterprises	65	22	3079	2194	85718
港澳台商投资企业	Hong Kong, Macao and Taiwan-invested Enterprises	181	60	4961	3442	343823
外商投资企业	Foreign-invested Enterprises	565	147	9926	7646	515996
按重点产业分	**By Key Sector**					
#高技术制造业	High-tech Manufacturing	795	476	29802	23138	1299264
#现代制造业	Modern Manufacturing	1412	670	45161	34167	1944304

BASIC INFORMATION ON RESEARCH AND EXPERIMENTAL DEVELOPMENT ACTIVITIES OF INDUSTRIAL ENTERPRISES ABOVE DESIGNATED SIZE (2016)

政府资金 Governmental Funds	企业资金 Enterprise Funds	国外资金 Foreign Funds	其他资金 Others	专利申请数(件) Patent Applications (unit)	#发明专利 Inventions	新产品产值(万元) Output Value of New Products (10000 yuan)	新产品销售收入(万元) Sales Income of New Products (10000 yuan)	#出口 Exports
195161	**2274450**	**14571**	**64252**	**20065**	**9392**	**41002789**	**40858562**	**2772815**
179361	1791435	11841	56442	15085	7487	34434273	34172167	2384234
58347	418628	303	50894	3925	2111	4683475	4946224	96802
136814	1855822	14268	13358	16140	7281	36319314	35912337	2676014
132492	1490707	2564	62851	14633	6877	23027196	22984464	1327551
7359	76466		1893	848	420	1266934	1297715	2343
1948	338705	1769	1401	3400	2013	9021504	8872246	569284
60721	445039	10237		2032	502	8954089	9001852	875980
171646	1066144	3072	58401	6775	4114	17755406	17684341	1832618
132646	1735569	14529	61560	12871	6260	32540501	31846709	2105657

20-7 规模以上工业企业研究与试验发展(R&D)活动基本情况(按行业分)(2016年)

项目	Item	企业数(个) Number of Enterprises (unit)	#有研究与试验发展(R&D)活动的企业数 Enterprises with R&D Activities	研究与试验发展(R&D)人员(人) R&D Personnel (person)
合计	**Total**	**3340**	**1155**	**70658**
采矿业	**Mining and Quarrying**	**19**	**8**	**2911**
煤炭开采和洗选业	Mining and Washing of Coal	1	1	1656
石油和天然气开采业	Extraction of Petroleum and Natural Gas	2	1	219
黑色金属矿采选业	Mining and Processing of Ferrous Metal Ores	7	1	315
有色金属矿采选业	Mining and Processing of Non-Ferrous Metal Ores			
非金属矿采选业	Mining and Processing of Nonmetal Ores	2		
开采辅助活动	Mining Support Service Activities	6	5	721
其他采矿业	Mining of Other Ores	1		
制造业	**Manufacturing**	**3204**	**1137**	**66228**
农副食品加工业	Processing of Food from Agriculture Products	133	31	896
食品制造业	Manufacture of Foods	124	20	988
酒、饮料和精制茶制造业	Manufacture of Wine, Beverage and Refined Tea	42	5	996
烟草制品业	Manufacture of Cigarettes and Tobacco	1	1	20
纺织业	Manufacture of Textile	19	5	121
纺织服装、服饰业	Manufacture of Textile Wearing Apparel and Ornament	117	7	243
皮革、毛皮、羽毛及其制品和制鞋业	Manufacture of Leather, Fur, Feather and Its Products, and Footwear	8		
木材加工和木、竹、藤、棕、草制品业	Processing of Timbers, Manufacture of Wood, Bamboo, Rattan, Palm, and Straw Products	12	1	243
家具制造业	Manufacture of Furniture	60	5	398
造纸和纸制品业	Manufacture of Paper and Paper Products	41	3	130
印刷和记录媒介复制业	Printing, Reproduction of Recording Media	99	15	663
文教、工美、体育和娱乐用品制造业	Manufacture of Articles for Culture,Education, Artwork, Sport and Entertainment Activities	30	4	64
石油加工、炼焦和核燃料加工业	Processing of Petroleum, Coking, Processing of Nuclear Fuel	16	1	18
化学原料和化学制品制造业	Manufacture of Raw Chemical Materials and Chemical Products	184	71	1811
医药制造业	Manufacture of Medicines	209	124	7063
化学纤维制造业	Manufacture of Chemical Fibers	3	3	153
橡胶和塑料制品业	Manufacture of Rubber and Plastics Products	108	16	402
非金属矿物制品业	Manufacture of Non-Metallic Mineral Products	219	54	2204
黑色金属冶炼和压延加工业	Smelting and Pressing of Ferrous Metals	20	4	247
有色金属冶炼和压延加工业	Smelting and Pressing of Non-Ferrous Metals	35	15	831
金属制品业	Manufacture of Fabricated Metal Products	182	36	1216
通用设备制造业	Manufacture of General-Purpose Machinery	213	87	4989
专用设备制造业	Manufacture of Special-Purpose Machinery	287	168	6740
汽车制造业	Manufacture of Motor Vehicles	240	54	8779
铁路、船舶、航空航天和其他运输设备制造业	Manufacture of Railway Locomotives, Building of Ships and Boats, Manufacture of Air and Spacecrafts and Other Transportation Equipment	78	44	5466
电气机械和器材制造业	Manufacture of Electrical Machinery and Equipment	233	92	4661
计算机、通信和其他电子设备制造业	Manufacture of Computers, Communication Equipment and Other Electronic Equipment	284	154	12692
仪器仪表制造业	Manufacture of Measuring Instruments and Meters	158	102	3688
其他制造业	Other Manufacturing	24	10	361
废弃资源综合利用业	Recycling and Disposal of Waste	9	1	12
金属制品、机械和设备修理业	Repair of Fabricated Metal Products, Machinery and Equipment	16	4	133
电力、热力、燃气及水的生产和供应业	**Production and Distribution of Electricity, Heating Power, Gas and Water**	**117**	**10**	**1519**
电力、热力生产和供应业	Production and Distribution of Electricity and Heating Power	74	6	657
燃气生产和供应业	Production and Distribution of Gas	20	1	484
水的生产和供应业	Production and Distribution of Water	23	3	378

BASIC INFORMATION ON RESEARCH AND EXPERIMENTAL DEVELOPMENT ACTIVITIES OF INDUSTRIAL ENTERPRISES ABOVE ESIGNATED SIZE (BY SECTOR) (2016)

研究与试验发展(R&D)人员折合全时当量(人年) Full-time Equivalent of R&D Personnel (person-year)	研究与试验发展(R&D)经费内部支出(万元) Internal R&D Expenditures (10000 yuan)	政府资金 Governmental Funds	企业资金 Enterprise Funds	国外资金 Foreign Funds	其他资金 Others	专利申请数(件) Applications Patents (unit)	#发明专利 Inventions	新产品产值(万元) Output Value of New Products (10000 yuan)	新产品销售收入(万元) Sales Income of New Products (10000 yuan)	#出口 Exports
51143	**2548433**	**195161**	**2274450**	**14571**	**64252**	**20065**	**9392**	**41002789**	**40858562**	**2772815**
1819	**58122**	**1456**	**56667**			**307**	**182**		**5050**	
745	7539		7539			34	3			
212	16513	261	16252			6	5			
306	10621	728	9893			157	122			
556	23450	467	22983			110	52		5050	
48222	**2471279**	**192277**	**2200180**	**14571**	**64251**	**18293**	**8494**	**40991628**	**40842350**	**2772815**
671	23904	742	23107		55	157	86	326234	327791	6872
699	29478	987	28492			67	52	224258	212774	14071
600	13624	101	13523			94	5	273881	275200	3302
19	970		970					929	687	
71	2184		2184			47	17	30215	37574	2451
68	7242	209	7034			23	4	198625	191387	
87	2569		2569							
139	4891		4891			272	3	118418	93521	12
34	1910		1910			12	7	60267	64230	12704
335	8910	59	8817		33	66	7	194330	198590	144
35	618		618			42	12	29481	40822	137
2	725	2	723			10	8	270610	430692	
1373	48087	2107	45839		140	322	246	560711	682601	55530
5468	206074	7961	195069	496	2548	369	262	1925823	1738715	20735
88	1051		1051			8	7	4255	3982	
339	6486		6486			48	6	108644	116601	2730
1370	59647	1822	57824			940	307	1670964	1860177	27289
134	3097	252	2845			54	22	82519	80813	1539
567	25533	702	24188		644	223	121	464947	442998	82197
860	29083	1767	27193		124	379	131	601890	640855	61629
3607	125614	3224	122252	55	83	1671	754	2023103	1939860	446866
4701	199260	11122	187121	42	974	2159	1004	2324728	2225348	338569
5934	394425	2537	388677	1810	1401	3294	1012	9467665	8999643	103931
4373	213884	28646	134716	303	50219	797	446	1626283	1690225	4668
3649	227886	1956	216074	9591	265	1951	741	3783315	3794161	89883
9986	718263	120066	595955	1	2241	4447	2867	13083283	13171348	1443715
2759	99990	6409	86950	2273	4358	743	336	1411882	1394480	53683
226	12987	1603	11144		240	73	25	89218	94513	
4	82	3	79			4	2	27130	33289	158
22	2808		1882		926	20	4	8021	59476	
1102	**19032**	**1428**	**17604**			**1465**	**716**	**11161**	**11161**	
592	3779	1068	2710			1378	683			
182	8990	127	8864			44	11			
329	6263	233	6030			43	22	11161	11161	

20-8 规模以上高技术制造业主要科技指标

项　目	Item	R&D人员折合全时当量（人年） Full-time Equivalent of R&D Personnel (person-year)	
		2016	2015
高技术制造业	**High-tech Manufacturing**	**23138**	**22344**
医药制造业	Manufacture of Medicines	5468	4220
#化学药品制造	Manufacture of Chemical Medicine	1981	1850
生物药品制造	Manufacture of Biological Medicine and Biochemical Chemical Products	1873	1625
航空、航天器及设备制造业	Manufacture of Aircrafts and Spacecrafts	3156	3258
#航空航天器修理	Repair of Air and Spacecrafts	4	146
电子及通信设备制造业	Manufacture of Electronic Equipment and Communication Equipment	9037	8591
#通信设备制造	Manufacture of Communication Equipment	4587	4382
电子器件制造	Manufacture of Electronic Appliances	1663	1480
电子元件制造	Manufacture of Electronic Components	536	478
其他电子设备制造	Manufacture of Other Electronic Equipment	1453	1408
计算机及办公设备制造业	Manufacture of Computers and Office Equipments	1117	1687
#计算机整机制造	Manufacture of Entired Computer	616	1048
医疗仪器设备及仪器仪表制造业	Manufacture of Medical Equipments and Meters	4250	4383
医疗仪器设备及器械制造	Manufacture of Medical Equipment and Appliances	1491	1581
仪器仪表制造	Manufacture of Measuring Instrument and Meter	2759	2802

注：本表高技术行业中不包括信息化学品制造业。

MAJOR SCIENCE AND TECHNOLOGY INDICATORS OF HIGH-TECH MANUFACTURING ABOVE DESIGNATER SIZE

R&D经费支出 (亿元) R&D Expenditures (100 million yuan)		新产品销售收入 (亿元) Sales Income of New Products (100 million yuan)		专利申请数 (件) Patent Applications (unit)		#发明专利 Inventions	
2016	2015	2016	2015	2016	2015	2016	2015
129.9	**120.2**	**1768.4**	**1597.8**	**6775**	**7837**	**4114**	**5305**
20.6	18.4	173.9	153.5	369	414	262	288
8.6	8.4	48.2	50.1	136	146	102	116
8.0	7.9	63.5	49.7	157	162	107	113
17.1	15.0	56.9	37.9	527	368	320	251
0.1	0.6			16	9	1	7
53.8	50.9	1041.1	925.9	2744	2549	1677	1711
21.1	17.0	685.8	612.5	1040	978	717	824
18.0	21.8	200.3	171.2	924	825	495	415
2.2	1.9	33.2	25.4	123	81	56	42
8.5	7.1	65.2	59.3	485	473	318	311
20.1	18.3	307.2	303.0	1766	3038	1224	2336
18.1	15.9	238.3	222.3	1468	2741	1102	2206
17.9	17.4	182.6	171.3	1307	1388	576	642
7.9	8.0	43.2	40.3	564	730	240	342
10.0	9.4	139.4	131.1	743	658	336	300

Note: Photographic equipment manufacturing is not included in the high-tech sector stated in this table.

20-9 限额以上信息传输、软件和信息技术服务业企业研究与试验发展(R&D)活动基本情况(2016年)

项目	Item	企业数(个) Number of Enterprises (unit)	#有研究与试验发展(R&D)活动的企业数 Enterprises with R&D Activities	研究与试验发展(R&D)人员(人) R&D Personnel (person)	研究与试验发展(R&D)人员折合全时当量(人年) Full-time Equivalent of R&D Personnel (person-year)
合计	**Total**	**1302**	**257**	**51758**	**36494**
按隶属关系分	**By Affiliation**				
中央	Central	82	29	3494	2162
地方	Local	1220	228	48264	34332
按登记注册类型分	**By Registration Type**				
内资企业	Domestically-invested Enterprises	1039	218	27447	18713
#国有企业	State-owned Enterprises	8	4	499	402
港澳台商投资企业	Hong Kong, Macao and Taiwan-invested Enterprises	114	19	8984	4569
外商投资企业	Foreign-invested Enterprises	149	20	15327	13212
按行业分	**By Sector**				
电信、广播电视和卫星传输服务	Telecommunications, Broadcasting, Television and Satellite Transmission services	66	13	8068	6540
互联网和相关服务	Internet and Related Services	150	20	12844	7186
软件和信息技术服务业	Software and Information Technology Services	1086	224	30846	22767

BASIC INFORMATION ON R&D ACTIVITIES OF INFORMATION TRANSMISSIOM, SOFTWARE AND INFORMATION TECHNICIAL SERVICE ENTERPRISES ABOVE DESIGNATED SIZE (2016)

研究与试验发展(R&D)经费内部支出(万元) Internal R&D Expenditures (10000 yuan)	政府资金 Govern-mental Funds	企业资金 Enterprise Funds	国外资金 Foreign Funds	其他资金 Others	专利申请数(件) Patent Applications (unit)	#发明专利 Inventions
1742949	**19550**	**1508374**	**206013**	**9011**	**21455**	**16641**
72755	4227	67098		1431	1921	1763
1670193	15323	1441276	206013	7581	19534	14878
764936	19361	737817		7758	16553	13473
12354	815	9865		1674	896	887
325544	77	322092	2123	1253	1768	1116
652468	112	448465	203891		3134	2052
436258	288	379720	55190	1060	666	637
518512		518436		76	5392	4453
788179	19262	610218	150823	7876	15397	11551

20-10 研究与开发机构研发活动情况(2007-2016年)

项　目		Item		2007
研究与开发机构基本情况		**Basic Information on R&D Institutions**		
机构数	(个)	Number	(unit)	265
中　央	(个)	Central	(unit)	221
地　方	(个)	Local	(unit)	44
研究与试验发展(R&D)投入情况		**R&D Input**		
R&D人员	(万人)	R&D Personnel	(10000 persons)	4.6
按隶属关系分		By Affiliation		
中　央	(万人)	Central	(10000 persons)	4.4
地　方	(万人)	Local	(10000 persons)	0.2
R&D人员折合全时当量	(万人年)	Full-time Equivalent of R&D Personnel	(10000 persons-year)	3.8
基础研究	(万人年)	Basic Research	(10000 persons-year)	1.2
应用研究	(万人年)	Applied Research	(10000 persons-year)	1.6
试验发展	(万人年)	Experimental Development	(10000 persons-year)	1.0
R&D经费内部支出	(亿元)	Internal R&D Expenditures	(100 million yuan)	103.1
按隶属关系分		By Affiliation		
中　央	(亿元)	Central	(100 million yuan)	99.0
地　方	(亿元)	Local	(100 million yuan)	4.1
按活动类型分		By Type of Activity		
基础研究	(亿元)	Basic Research	(100 million yuan)	26.4
应用研究	(亿元)	Applied Research	(100 million yuan)	45.2
试验发展	(亿元)	Experimental Development	(100 million yuan)	31.5
按资金来源分		By Source of Funds		
政府资金	(亿元)	Governmental Funds	(100 million yuan)	88.6
企业资金	(亿元)	Enterprise Funds	(100 million yuan)	3.2
境外资金	(亿元)	Foreign Funds	(100 million yuan)	1.3
其他资金	(亿元)	Others	(100 million yuan)	10.0
研究与试验发展(R&D)项目(课题)情况		**R&D Projects (Tasks)**		
R&D项目(课题)数	(项)	Number of R&D Projects (Tasks)	(unit)	15079
R&D项目(课题)人员折合全时当量	(万人年)	Full-time Equivalent of R&D Personnel	(10000 persons-year)	2.2
R&D项目(课题)经费内部支出	(亿元)	Internal R&D Expenditures	(100 million yuan)	57.1
科技产出及成果情况		**Science & Technology Output and Achievement**		
发表科技论文	(篇)	Published Articles on Science and Technolog	(unit)	37232
#国外发表	(篇)	Published Abroad	(unit)	9005
出版科技著作	(种)	Published Writings on Science and Technolog	(Sort)	1489
专利申请数	(件)	Number of Patents Applications	(unit)	1993
#发明专利	(件)	Invention Patents	(unit)	1784
专利授权数	(件)	Number of Patents Granted	(unit)	985
#发明专利	(件)	Invention Patents	(unit)	752

注：研究与开发机构范围是北京市政府部门属的科学研究与技术开发机构、科技情报与文献机构。
资料来源：北京市科学技术委员会。

STATISTICS FOR R&D ACTIVITIES IN RESEARCH AND DEVELOPMENT INSTITUTIONS (2007-2016)

2008	2009	2010	2011	2012	2013	2014	2015	2016
266	275	281	280	288	287	299	296	303
225	228	231	231	238	237	248	245	254
41	47	50	49	50	50	51	51	49
4.8	5.2	5.7	5.9	6.3	6.6	6.6	6.8	6.9
4.5	4.9	5.4	5.6	5.9	6.2	6.2	6.3	6.4
0.3	0.3	0.3	0.3	0.4	0.4	0.4	0.5	0.5
3.9	4.2	4.6	4.7	5.3	5.5	5.5	5.6	5.6
1.3	1.4	1.5	1.6	1.8	1.9	2.0	2.1	2.5
1.6	1.7	2.0	2.1	2.2	2.3	2.3	2.2	2.2
1.0	1.1	1.1	1.0	1.3	1.3	1.2	1.3	0.9
123.8	150.3	187.0	195.1	222.0	246.8	271.2	295.6	301.5
117.4	143.9	178.9	185.1	211.5	236.3	253.6	277.0	280.4
6.4	6.4	8.1	10.0	10.5	10.5	17.6	18.6	21.1
28.3	39.2	49.9	58.5	65.1	73.6	86.5	96.8	109.1
49.0	61.5	78.0	84.0	92.0	102.2	108.9	120.5	131.3
46.5	49.6	59.1	52.6	64.9	71.0	75.8	78.3	61.1
106.6	126.3	164.4	168.0	192.6	220.0	244.6	266.3	262.1
4.0	4.4	3.6	6.6	6.5	8.2	8.2	12.1	16.1
1.8	2.0	1.5	2.5	1.5	1.9	1.8	2.0	1.7
11.4	17.6	17.5	18.0	21.4	16.7	16.6	15.2	21.6
16383	17816	19545	20333	22842	23949	25550	26762	26998
2.3	3.8	4.1	4.3	4.9	5.0	5.0	5.0	4.7
70.9	87.1	107.2	115.0	142.7	156.8	161.0	173.5	162.0
37149	39380	39384	41442	44218	45509	48040	48734	49517
9184	12011	11696	13361	14003	17216	17905	18915	19800
1636	1873	1601	1828	1670	1921	2058	2261	2453
2488	3182	3879	4880	5456	6192	6004	6464	6657
2119	2772	3450	4373	4798	5144	5115	5164	5543
1146	1574	1879	2260	3251	3646	3932	4702	5522
922	1299	1455	1756	2635	2763	3001	3529	4184

Note: R&D institutions cover scientific research and technological development institutions, scientific and technological information institutions subordinate to government authorities of Beijing.

Source: Beijing Municipal Science & Technology Commission.

20-11 高等学校研发活动情况
STATISTICS FOR R&D ACTIVITIES IN COLLEGES & UNIVERSITIES

项目		Item		2016	2015
高等学校基本情况		**Basic Information of Colleges & Universities**			
学校数	(个)	Number of Colleges and Universities	(unit)	118	115
#理工农医	(个)	Colleges & Universities of Science, Engineeri Agriculture, Medical Science	(unit)	74	72
#人文社科	(个)	Colleges & Universities of Arts and Social Sciences	(unit)	91	90
研究与试验发展(R&D)机构数	(个)	Number of R&D Institutions	(unit)	905	863
研究与试验发展(R&D)投入情况		**R&D Input**			
R&D人员	(万人)	R&D Personnel	(10000 person)	7.74	8.07
R&D人员折合全时当量	(万人年)	Full-time Equivalent of R&D Personnel	(10000 persons-year)	3.23	3.45
基础研究	(万人年)	Basic Research	(10000 persons-year)	1.33	1.37
应用研究	(万人年)	Applied Research	(10000 persons-year)	1.82	2.00
试验发展	(万人年)	Experimental Development	(10000 persons-year)	0.08	0.08
R&D经费内部支出	(亿元)	Internal R&D Expenditures	(100 million yuan)	160.44	162.65
按活动类型分		By Type of Activity			
基础研究	(亿元)	Basic Research	(100 million yuan)	64.51	62.20
应用研究	(亿元)	Applied Research	(100 million yuan)	85.02	93.29
试验发展	(亿元)	Experimental Development	(100 million yuan)	10.91	7.15
按资金来源分		By Source of Funds			
#政府资金	(亿元)	Governmental Funds	(100 million yuan)	107.98	113.24
企业资金	(亿元)	Enterprise Funds	(100 million yuan)	47.33	44.82
研究与试验发展(R&D)项目(课题)情况		**R&D Projects (Tasks)**			
R&D项目(课题)数	(项)	Number of R&D Projects (Tasks)	(unit)	91089	92243
R&D项目(课题)人员折合全时当量	(万人年)	Full-time Equivalent of R&D Personnel	(10000 persons-year)	3.23	3.44
R&D项目(课题)经费内部支出	(亿元)	Internal R&D Expenditures	(100 million yuan)	121.93	125.17
科技产出及成果情况		**Science & Technology Output and Achievement**			
发表科技论文	(篇)	Published Articles on Science and Technology	(unit)	118193	118985
#国外发表	(篇)	Published Abroad	(unit)		
出版科技著作	(种)	Published Writings on Science and Technolog	(Sort)	5354	5225
专利申请数	(件)	Number of Patent Applications	(unit)	14960	13363
#发明专利	(件)	Invention Patents	(unit)	12308	10795
专利授权数	(件)	Number of Patents Granted	(unit)	10656	9212
#发明专利	(件)	Invention Patents	(unit)	8038	7161

资料来源：北京市教育委员会。
Source: Beijing Municipal Commission of Education.

20–12 科学技术协会及所属学会工作情况(2016年)
STATISTICS FOR SCIENCE AND TECHNOLOGY ASSOCIATION AND SUBORDINATE INSTITUTES (2016)

项 目		Item		合 计 Total	市科协 Municipal Science and Technology Association	市级学会 Institutes at Municipal Level
基本情况		**Basic Information**				
机构数	(个)	Number of Institutions	(unit)	183	1	182
机构从业人员	(人)	Number of Employed Persons in the Institutions	(person)	1391	392	999
学术交流活动		**Academic Exchange Activities**				
国内学术会议	(次)	Domestic Academic Meetings	(time)	1176	1	1175
参加人数	(人次)	Number of Participants	(person-time)	632386	120	632266
交流论文	(篇)	Number of Papers Exchagned	(unit)	17395	6	17389
境内国际学术会议	(次)	Domestically-held International Academic Meetings	(time)	71		71
参加人数	(人次)	Number of Participants	(person-time)	17907		17907
交流论文	(篇)	Number of Papers Exchagned	(unit)	2142		2142
港澳台地区学术会议	(次)	Academic Meetings Held in Kong Kong, Macao and Taiwan	(time)	4		4
参加人数	(人次)	Number of Participants	(person-time)	682		682
交流论文	(篇)	Number of Papers Exchagned	(unit)	72		72
科技期刊		**Science and Technology Journals**				
主办科技期刊种数	(种)	Types of Science and Technology Journals Sponsored	(sort)	39	7	32
科技期刊总印数	(万册)	Number of Total Printings of Science and Technology Journals	10000 copies)	130.16	19.45	110.71
科技期刊发表论文数	(篇)	Papers Published on Science and Technology Journals	(unit)	22278	69	22209
科普活动		**Activities to Popularize Scientific Knowledge**				
举办科普宣讲活动	(次)	Scientific Knowledge Lectures	(time)	4351	584	3767
播放科技广播、影视节目	(分钟)	Playing Radio, Films and TV Programs on Science and Technology	(minute)	3249		3249
举办实用技术培训	(次)	Holding Practical Technology Trainings	(time)	790	520	270
推广新技术、新品种	(项)	Promoting New Technologies and New Varieties	(unit)	225	45	180
参加活动科技人员总数	(人次)	Participating in Science and Technology Personnel	(person-time)	51914	13440	38474
参加活动的学会、协会、研究会	(个次)	Participating in Socieities, Associations and Research Institutes	(unit-time)	3196	90	3106
科技传播		**Science and Technology Dissemination**				
主办科技报纸种数	(种)	Types of Science and Technology Newspaper Sponsored	(sort)			
制作科普挂图种数	(种)	Types of Scientific Knowlede Flip Charts Produced	(sort)	175	23	152
制作科技广播、影视节目套数	(套)	Science and Technology Raido, Films and TV Programs Produced	(unit)	16		16
制作科技光盘种数	(种)	Types of Science and Technology CDs Produced	(sort)	28	4	24
制作科普动漫作品套数	(套)	Scientific Knowledge Animation Works Produced	(unit)	16	1	15
主办科技网站	(个)	Science and Technology Websites Sponsored	(unit)	55	5	50
科技开放与交流		**Science and Technology Opening-up and Exchange**				
加入国际民间科技组织	(个)	International Cilvilian Science and Technology Organizations Joined	(unit)	18		18
参加国外科技活动人数	(人次)	Number of Persons Participating in Foreign Science and Technology Activities	(person-time)	563	183	380
参加港澳台地区科技活动人数	(人次)	Number of Persons Participating in Science and Technology Activities in Hong Kong, Macao and Taiwan	(person-time)	167	23	144
接待国外专家学者	(人次)	Foreign Experts and Scholars Received	(person-time)	992	315	677
接待港澳台地区专家学者	(人次)	Experts and Scholars from Kong Kong, Macao and Taiwan Received	(person-time)	407	80	327
科技服务		**Science and Technology Service**				
提供决策咨询报告	(篇)	Providing Policy-making Consulting Reports	(unit)	111	14	97
举办决策咨询活动	(次)	Holding Policy-making Consulting Activities	(time)	179	21	158

注：本表统计范围是北京市科学技术协会所属学会、研究会。
资料来源：北京市科学技术协会。
Note: Figures in this table cover societies and research institutes affiliated with Beijing Association for Science & Technology.
Source: Beijing Association for Science & Technology.

20-13 公有经济企事业单位专业技术人员(2016年)
NUMBER OF PORFESSIONAL TECHNICAL PERSONNEL IN PUBLIC ENTERPRISES AND INSTITUTIONS (2016)

单位：人 (person)

项目	Item	合计 Total	#高级 Senior	#中级 Intermediate	#初级 Junior
合计	**Total**	**533737**	**74574**	**172101**	**191008**
#工程技术人员	Engineering Technicians	127370	13860	28835	39858
农业技术人员	Agricultural Technicians	4400	524	1238	1964
科学研究人员	Science Research Personnel	8408	2223	3236	1178
卫生技术人员	Medical Technicians	98450	12969	34024	48163
教学人员	Teaching Personnel	175668	36849	75940	59403
经济人员	Economic Personnel	65070	3561	14034	17151
会计人员	Accountants	27550	1586	6536	12644
统计人员	Statisticians	3024	93	695	1275

注：公有经济是指北京市属国有和集体企事业单位，不包含在京中央属企事业单位。

资料来源：北京市人力资源和社会保障局。

Note: Public sector means state-owned and collectively-owned enterprises and institutions in Beijing, excluding central enterprises and institutions located in Beijing.

Source: Beijing Municipal Bureau of Human Resources and Social Security.

20−14 技术合同成交情况(1990−2016年) STATISTICS FOR CONCLUSION OF TECHNOLOGICAL CONTRACTS (1990-2016)

年 份 Year	合同数 (项) Number of Contracts (unit)	技术合同成交总额 (亿元) Total Volume of Transaction of Technological Contracts Concluded (100 million yuan)	#技术交易额 Total Volume of Transaction of Technology	#流向外省市技术合同额 Amount of Transaction Flowing to Other Provinces and Municipalities	实现合同总金额 (亿元) Total Volume of Transaction Achieved in Contracts (100 million yuan)	#技术交易实现金额 Amount of Technological Transactions Achieved
1990	18588	20.3	10.5		15.4	8.4
1991−1995	**93970**	**167.7**	**120.0**		**115.4**	**83.8**
1991	18547	22.4	13.1		15.3	9.1
1992	23395	31.3	22.2		20.0	14.4
1993	20461	35.6	25.6		24.9	17.6
1994	15220	37.2	26.9		26.9	20.4
1995	16347	41.2	32.2		28.4	22.3
1996−2000	**91421**	**414.2**	**375.9**		**206.7**	**188.1**
1996	14850	45.8	39.2		29.6	25.4
1997	13866	54.3	48.1		31.1	27.8
1998	20724	81.6	73.9		42.1	37.6
1999	20711	92.2	88.5		43.6	41.0
2000	21270	140.3	126.3	65.5	60.3	56.3
2001−2005	**156114**	**1443.8**	**1217.2**	**688.9**	**669.5**	**628.1**
2001	23921	191.0	164.8	85.4	97.6	93.0
2002	27037	221.1	181.0	100.4	101.9	97.2
2003	32173	265.5	226.8	132.4	119.9	113.9
2004	35478	331.8	294.3	165.8	148.7	143.4
2005	37505	434.4	350.4	204.9	201.4	180.6
2006−2010	**256074**	**5422.8**	**3984.7**	**2372.7**	**2226.7**	**2006.7**
2006	51575	697.3	572.6	325.3	349.5	319.7
2007	50972	882.6	660.3	407.4	418.1	353.5
2008	52742	1027.2	778.1	487.0	406.2	375.0
2009	49938	1236.2	906.9	498.2	516.8	452.9
2010	50847	1579.5	1066.7	654.8	536.0	505.6
2011−2015	**315814**	**13788.6**	**10868.6**	**7237.5**	**3942.1**	**3811.6**
2011	53552	1890.3	1268.3	635.9	580.4	563.3
2012	59969	2458.5	2048.6	1385.0	739.8	707.0
2013	62743	2851.2	2252.4	1615.9	684.0	659.3
2014	67278	3136.0	2531.5	1722.0	708.2	675.1
2015	72272	3452.6	2767.8	1878.7	1229.7	1206.9
2016	74965	3940.8	2919.3	1997.2	749.2	717.0

资料来源：北京技术市场管理办公室。
Source: Beijing Technical Market Management Office.

20-15 技术合同成交情况
CONCLUSION OF TECHNICAL CONTRACTS

项目	Item	合同数(项) Number of Contracts (unit)		成交额(万元) Volume of Transaction (10000 yuan)	
		2016	2015	2016	2015
合计	**Total**	**74965**	**72272**	**39407994.2**	**34525661.6**
按合同类别分类	**By Type of Contract**				
技术开发合同	Technological Development	26314	27886	6871123.0	6479482.5
技术转让合同	Technology Transfer	1460	1338	845345.3	607524.9
技术咨询合同	Technical Consultation	4559	4907	1462764.7	536515.7
技术服务合同	Technical Service	42632	38141	30228761.3	26902138.4
按合同卖方类别分类	**By Type of Seller**				
机关法人	Government Organisations		22		2606.3
事业法人	Public Institutions	12242	13918	1461049.5	1503626.3
社团法人	Mass Organisations	12	14	955.4	572.5
企业法人	Enterprises	62646	57727	37125314.9	30713014.6
自然人	Natural Persons	27	27	3125.5	8240.1
其他组织	Other Organizations	38	564	817548.9	2297601.7
按合同买方类别分类	**By Type of Buyer**				
机关法人	Government Organisations	5857	5570	4845268.3	4953626.5
事业法人	Public Institutions	17937	15274	4241244.0	2097516.8
社团法人	Mass Organisations	566	473	17409.5	20373.1
企业法人	Enterprises	49049	49678	29707251.1	26613959.4
自然人	Natural Persons	594	336	27365.2	42918.8
其他组织	Other Organizations	962	941	569456.0	797267.0
按服务社会经济目标分类	**By Social and Economic Service Objectives**				
环境保护、生态建设及污染防治	Environmental Protection, Ecological Development and Pollution Control	2959	2857	5517919.4	4743858.5
能源生产、分配和合理利用	Energy Production, Allocation and Reasonable Utilization	4112	4463	2156718.5	3605908.6
卫生事业发展	Health Services	1958	2236	1065402.2	786368.9
教育事业发展	Education Development	4436	2388	282410.4	216182.7
基础设施以及城市和农村规划	Infrastructure and Rural and Urban Planning	3485	4018	8196269.6	6249296.6
社会发展和社会服务	Social Development and Social Services	33304	32962	14020732.4	11121994.1
地球和大气层的探索与利用	Exploration and Utilization Of The Earth and Atmosphere	85	71	10526.9	34369.0
民用空间探测及开发	Private Space Exploration and Development	381	481	359702.6	97514.8
农林牧渔业发展	Development in Agriculture, Forestry, Animal Production and Hunting, Fishing	1762	1778	180761.9	104089.0
工商业发展	Industrial and Commercial Development	2879	3326	776830.8	841931.8
非定向研究	Non-Directional Research	5119	2880	2457262.3	2157559.0
其他民用目标	Other Civilian Target	9615	9624	3415950.6	3494623.2
国防	National Defense	4870	5188	967506.5	1071965.3
按技术流向分类	**By Spread Area of Technology**				
流向本市	To Beijing	34759	33514	11313055.1	6250403.1
天津流入	From Tianjin	2407	2043	858563.1	974300.0
河北流入	From Hebei	370	384	65072.7	21100.0
流向外省市	To Other Provinces and Municipalities	38928	37447	19971841.0	18786775.4
流向天津	To Tianjin	1486	1407	560382.5	576200.0
流向河北	To Hebei	2362	2291	986598.2	539200.0
技术出口	Exports	1278	1311	8123098.0	9488483.1

资料来源：北京技术市场管理办公室。
Source: Beijing Technical Market Management Office.

20–16 科技成果及获奖情况(2001–2016年)
STATISTICS FOR SCIENTIFIC AND TECHNOLOGICAL ACHIEVEMENTS AND AWARDS (2001-2016)

单位：项 (unit)

年 份 Year	科技成果登记数 Registered Number of Scientific and Technological Achievements	#国家技术发明奖 National Awards of Technical Invention	#国家科学技术进步奖 National Awards of Scientific and Technological Advancement
2001–2005	**3063**	**25**	**233**
2001	326	1	38
2002	275	5	48
2003	468	5	52
2004	976	6	43
2005	1018	8	52
2006–2010	**5081**	**56**	**257**
2006	1002	12	64
2007	1010	9	44
2008	1016	13	42
2009	1023	11	54
2010	1030	11	53
2011–2015	**5205**	**78**	**238**
2011	1035	5	56
2012	1040	22	53
2013	1043	19	38
2014	1042	15	49
2015	1045	17	42
2016	728	10	47

资料来源：北京市科学技术委员会。
Source: Beijing Municipal Science & Technology Commission.

20-17 专利申请及授权情况
APPLICATIONS AND GRANTING OF PATENTS

单位：件 (unit)

项目	Item	申请量 Patent Applications 2016	申请量 Patent Applications 2015	授权量 Patents Granted 2016	授权量 Patents Granted 2015
合计	**Total**	**189129**	**156312**	**100578**	**94031**
按种类分	**By Type**				
发明	Inventions	104643	88930	40602	35308
实用新型	Utility Models	64496	53243	44710	45773
外观设计	Industrial Designs	19990	14139	15266	12950
按对象分	**By Applicant**				
工矿企业	Industrial and Mining Enterprises	131375	107921	72236	66007
大专院校	Universities & Colleges	17805	14887	9026	8700
科研单位	Scientific Research Institutes	17707	14779	9067	8692
机关团体	Government Organizations	2939	2296	1410	1309
个人	Individuals	19303	16429	8839	9323

资料来源：北京市知识产权局。
Source: Beijing Intellectual Property Office.

20-18 有效发明专利情况
STATISTICS FOR VALID INVENTION PATENTS

单位：件 (unit)

项目	Item	2016	2015
合计	**Total**	**166722**	**133040**
按对象分	**By Applicant**		
工矿企业	Industrial and Mininig Enterprises	98720	74594
大专院校	Universities & Colleges	29461	25698
科研单位	Scientific Research Institutes	29785	24907
机关团体	Government Organizations	1890	1476
个人	Individuals	6866	6365

资料来源：北京市知识产权局。
Source: Beijing Intellectual Property Office.

主要统计指标解释

科技活动人员　指报告年度调查单位直接从事科技活动、以及从事科技活动管理和为科技活动提供直接服务的人员。直接从事科技活动人员包括：在单位办的研究室、实验室、技术开发中心及中试车间（基地）等机构中从事科技活动的人员；虽不在上述机构工作，但编入科技活动项目（课题）组的人员等。从事科技活动管理和为科技活动提供直接服务的人员包括：与科技活动相关的行政管理人员，以及直接为科技活动提供资料文献、材料供应、设备维护等服务的人员。

研究与试验发展（R&D）　指在科学技术领域，为增加知识总量、以及运用这些知识去创造新的应用而进行的系统的创造性的活动，包括基础研究、应用研究、试验发展三类活动。

研究与试验发展（R&D）人员　指单位内部从事基础研究、应用研究和试验发展三类活动的人员。包括直接参加上述三类项目活动的人员以及这三类项目的管理人员和直接服务人员。为研发活动提供直接服务的人员包括直接为研发活动提供资料文献、材料供应、设备维护等服务的人员。

研究与试验发展（R&D）人员折合全时当量　是国际上通用的、用于比较科技人力投入的指标。指 R&D 全时人员（全年从事 R&D 活动累积工作时间占全部工作时间的 90% 及以上人员）工作量与非全时人员按实际工作时间折算的工作量之和。

研究与试验发展（R&D）内部支出　指调查单位在报告年度用于内部开展 R&D 活动（基础研究、应用研究和试验发展）的实际支出。包括用于 R&D 项目（课题）活动的直接支出，以及间接用于 R&D 活动的管理费、服务费、与 R&D 有关的基本建设支出以及外协加工费等，不包括生产性活动支出、归还贷款支出以及与外单位合作或委托外单位进行 R&D 活动而转拨给对方的经费支出。

专业技术人员　指从事专业技术工作的人员以及从事专业技术管理工作且已在 1983 年以前评定了专业技术职称或在 1984 年以后聘任了专业技术职务的人员。从事专业技术工作的人员具体指工程技术人员，农业技术人员，科学研究人员（含自然科学研究及实验技术人员），卫生技术人员，教学人员（含高等院校、中等专业学校、技工学校、中学、小学），民用航空飞行技术人员，船舶技术人员，经济专业人员，会计人员，统计人员，翻译人员，图书资料、档案、文博人员，新闻、出版人员，律师、公证人员，广播电视播音人员，工艺美术人员，体育人员，艺术人员及企业政治思想工作人员。从事专业技术管理工作的人员是指企业、事业单位领导；企业、事业单位下设的职能机构、企业的生产车间的辅助车间（或附属辅助生产单位）中从事生产、技术、经济管理和政治工作的人员；按照公务员管理或参照公务员管理的人员不统计为专业技术人员。

专利　是专利权的简称，是对发明人的发明创造经审查合格后，由专利局依据专利法授予发明人和设计人对该项发明创造享有的专有权。包括发明、实用新型和外观设计。

发明专利　指专利法及其实施细则所称的发明，指对产品、方法或者改进所提出的新的技术方案。

实用新型专利　指专利法及其实施细则所称的实用新型，指对产品的形状、构造或者其结合所提出的适于实用的新的技术方案。

外观设计专利　指专利法及其实施细则所称的外观设计，指对产品的形状、图案、色彩或者其结合所做出的富有美感并适于工业上应用的新设计。

Explanatory Notes on Main Statistical Indicators

Personnel Engaged in Science and Technology Activities refer to persons directly engaged in science and technology activities as well as persons engaged in science and technology management and persons offering direct services to science and technology activities in the surveyed entities in the reporting year. Persons directly engaged in science and technology activities include: persons engaged in science and technology activities in such institutions as research labs of entities, laboratories, technical development centers and middle-stage test workshops (bases); persons not working in the above-mentioned institutions but included in the science and technology activity project (task) team, etc. Persons engaged in science and technology management and persons offering direct services for science and technology activities include administrative staff related to science and technology activities, as well as persons directly providing information and literature, supply of materials, equipment maintenance and other services.

R&D refers to systematic and creative activities in the field of science and technology to increase the total knowledge, and apply such knowledge to create new applications, including three kinds of activities, i.e. basic research, applied research, and experimental development.

R&D Personnel refer to persons in the surveyed entities who are engaged in three kinds of activities, i.e. basic research, applied research and experimental development. They include those who participate in the above-mentioned three kinds of activities directly, research management personnel and persons directly serving these activities. Persons providing direct services include those who provide information and literature, supply of materials, equipment maintenance and other services.

Full-Time Equivalent of R&D Personnel is an indicator globally used to compare input of scientific talents. It refers to the sum of workload of full-time R&D personnel (the personnel whose accumulative annual working time involved in R&D activities takes 90% and above of the whole working time) plus the workload of non-full time personnel that is equivalent of the actual working time.

Internal R&D Expenditure means the actual disbursement of investigated entities on internal R&D activities (basic research, applied research, and experimental development) in the reporting year, including direct spending on R&D project (task) activities, and management expenses and service fees indirectly spent on R&D activities, R&D related basic construction expense and external assisting processing charges, etc., excluding production-based activity expense, loan repayment expense and fund transferred to external institution cooperated or entrusted to conduct R&D activities.

Professional Technical Personnel refer to persons engaged in professional technological work and professional technological management whose professional technological titles were assessed and granted before 1983 or who have been retained at professional technological positions after 1984. Persons engaged in professional technological work refer to engineering technicians, agricultural technicians, research personnel (including natural science research and experiment technicians), medical technicians, teaching staff (including those in colleges and universities, technical secondary schools, vocational schools, high schools, and elementary schools), civil aviation flight technicians, watercraft technicians, economics professionals, accountants, statisticians, translators and interpreters, librarians, archivists, cultural expo personnel, journalists, publishers , lawyers, notaries, TV and radio broadcasters, industrial arts staff, sportspersons, artists, as well as personnel responsible for political ideology work in enterprises.. The professional technological management refer to leaders of enterprises and public institutions; persons engaged in management of production, technology and economy as well as political work in functional organs under enterprises and public institutions, auxiliary workplaces (or affiliated auxiliary production entities) of production workplaces of enterprises; persons managed as civil servants or with reference to civil servants are not counted as professional technicians.

Patent is the abbreviation of patent right, referring to the exclusive right granted by patent authorities upon examination and approval of inventions and creations to the inventors and designers with regard to the invention, including inventions, utility models and industrial designs.

Invention means the invention mentioned in the Patent Law and its detailed rules for implementation, i.e. the new technological solutions presented for the product, methodology, or improvement.

Utility Model means the utility model mentioned in the Patent Law and its detailed rules for implementation, i.e. the new practical technological solutions presented for the product shape, structure, color or combination.

Industrial Design means the industrial design mentioned in the Patent Law and its detailed rules for implementation, i.e. new designs of product shape, pattern, color or combination which are aesthetic and suitable for industrial applications.

21

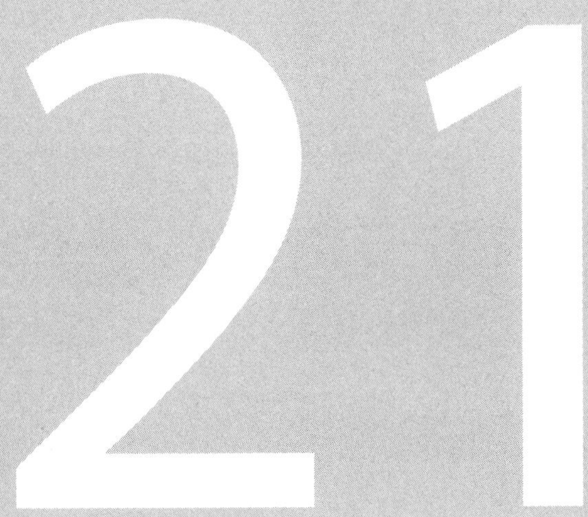

卫生、体育
HEALTH CARE AND SPORTS

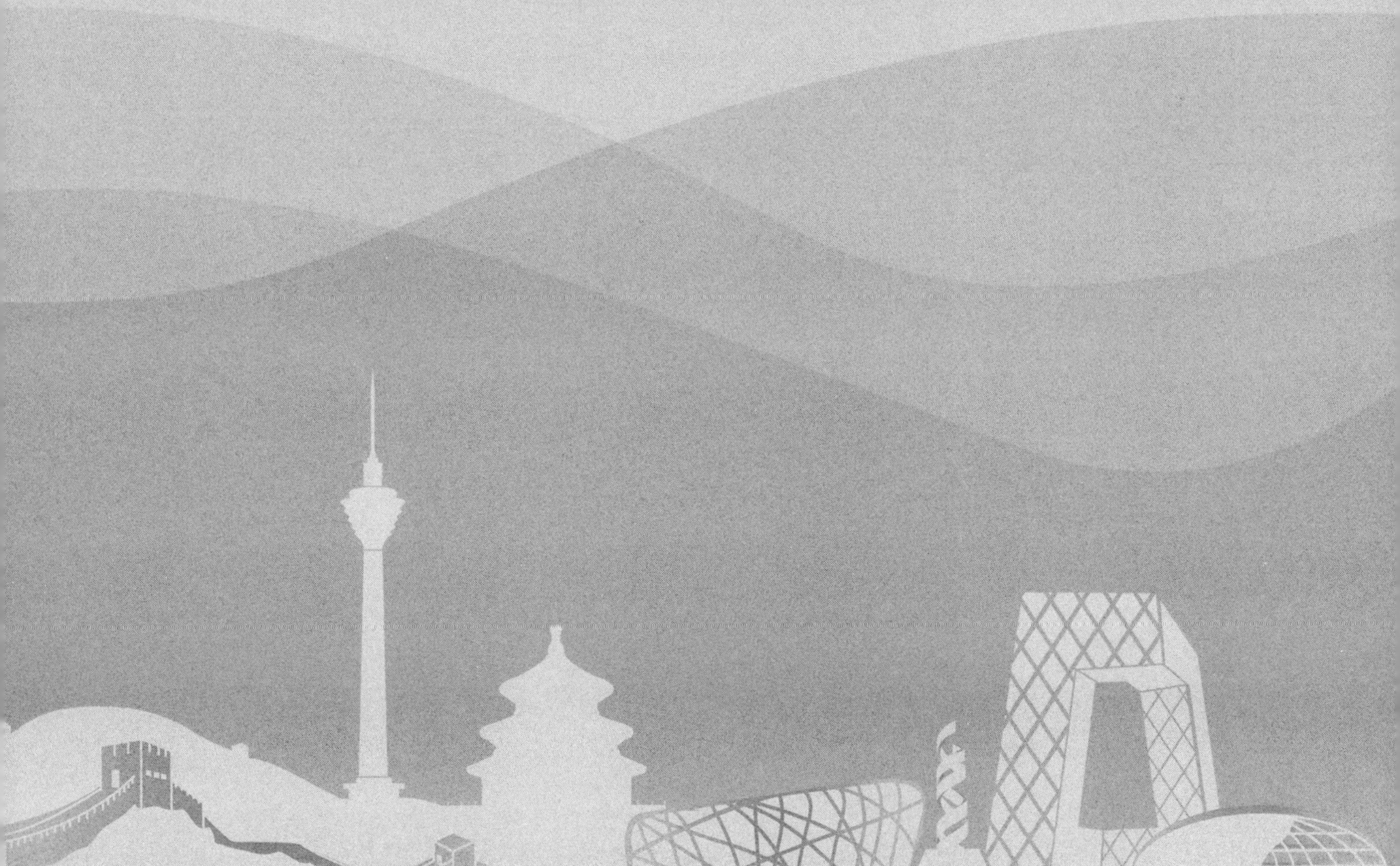

简要说明

一、本章资料的主要内容

本章主要反映卫生、体育的发展情况。

卫生部分主要内容包括卫生总费用、卫生机构、卫生技术人员、床位数，医院诊疗人次及入院人数，主要疾病死亡原因及构成，全市主要健康指标等情况。体育部分主要包括体育场地情况、运动员和裁判员情况、运动员获奖情况、体育彩票情况等。

二、本章资料的数据来源

卫生部分的资料由北京市卫生和计划生育委员会提供，体育部分的资料由北京市体育局提供。

Brief Introduction

I. Main Content

This chapter mainly reflects the development of health and sports.

Health statistics include the total health expenditures, the number of health institutions, health technicians, ward beds, patients treated and hospitalized persons, major causes of death and composition, main health indicators of Beijing, and so on. Sports statistics include the situation of sports venues, athletes and referees, awards received by athletes, and sports lottery tickets, etc.

II. Source of Data

Health data are from Beijing Municipal Commission of Health and Family Planning. Sports data are from Beijing Municipal Bureau of Sports.

21-1 卫生事业基本情况(1978-2016年)

年份 Year	卫生机构(个) Healthcare Institutions (unit)	#医院 Hospitals	#疾病预防控制中心(防疫站) Centers for Disease Control and Prevention	#妇幼保健院(所、站) Maternity and Child Care Centers (Stations)	#社区卫生服务中心(站) Community Health Services Centers (Stations)
1978	3263		22	15	
1979	3614		22	17	
1980	3818		22	19	
1981	4135		22	19	
1982	4389		22	18	
1983	4312		22	19	
1984	4173		22	18	
1985	4248		22	18	
1986	4483		22	20	
1987	4744		22	19	
1988	4342		22	17	
1989	4398		22	17	
1990	4953		22	17	
1991	4970	337	22	17	
1992	4868	345	22	16	
1993	4962	364	32	16	
1994	4958	387	33	16	
1995	4955	387	33	15	
1996	6470	405	33	13	
1997	6577	435	33	13	
1998	5723	449	32	11	
1999	5990	460	32	8	
2000	6176	458	30	8	
2001	5969	458	30	9	
2002	4998	461	24	19	35
2003	5075	459	29	19	36
2004	4835	503	29	19	43
2005	4818	519	28	18	93
2006	4878	541	28	18	90
2007	6189	535	31	18	1126
2008	6523	537	31	19	1282
2009	6603	522	31	19	1395
2010	6539	550	31	19	1587
2011	9699	569	32	19	1744
2012	9974	608	32	19	1897
2013	10141	647	32	19	1926
2014	10265	672	32	19	1958
2015	10425	701	30	19	1979
2016	10637	713	29	20	1997

注：1. 2010年及以前，本表中所有数据都不包含村卫生室及驻京部队医院情况。2011年开始，包含村卫生室情况。 2012年开始，除床位数外均包含驻京部队医院数据(下表同)。
2. 2010年开始，原卫生院数据并入到社区卫生服务中心(站)等其他卫生机构。

BASIC STATISTICS ON HEALTH CARE (1978-2016)

卫生机构人员(人) Employed Persons in Healthcare Institutions (person)	#卫生技术人员 Medical Technical Personnel	#执业(助理)医师 Certified (Assistant) Physicians	#注册护士 Registered Nurses
90174	65943	28435	16085
97942	72131	31842	17398
102601	74753	34365	17492
110774	81183	37886	20025
114420	83843	39385	20389
119222	86593	41216	21181
124664	89362	42112	22286
127771	90831	42216	23782
132865	94433	43403	25383
142556	101829	46007	27786
145362	105237	48216	30250
150062	108108	49361	32056
156304	111614	50934	34565
161103	114342	52309	35714
164213	115825	53254	36768
165170	116173	53906	36687
164867	116818	53865	36608
164436	115967	54114	36719
164981	116849	54091	37712
167090	119256	54909	38630
162609	115976	51902	38883
161823	116597	52646	39625
160258	115510	51570	39900
158185	115935	52100	40537
144021	109564	47236	38879
148406	112212	47887	39912
153154	116610	48988	41547
157133	119874	50617	42897
166278	126904	52795	45647
182475	139275	54989	50890
193799	149916	58773	55349
208156	160435	62348	61604
219762	171093	65954	67308
235708	181938	69749	72812
276654	219714	82192	95202
294012	229720	85819	100652
304990	242923	89590	106167
321151	256531	96445	114294
330777	264850	100878	117760

Note: a) In and before 2010, figures in this table did not include village health clinics and hospitals of troops stationed in Beijing. From 2011, figures included village health clinics. From 2012,figures in this table include troops stationed in Beijing with the bed number excluded. stationed in Beijing (the same to the follow tables).

b) From 2010, data on health centers were incorporated into other health institutions such as community health service centers (stations).

21-1 续表 Continued

年 份 Year	实有床位数(张) Beds (unit)	#医院 Hospitals	每千户籍人口执业(助理)医师数(人) Certified Physicians (assistant) per 1,000 households (person)	每千户籍人口注册护士数(人) Registered nurses per 1,000 households (person)	每千户籍人口医院床位数(张) Number of hospital beds per 1,000 households (unit)	每千常住人口执业(助理)医师数(人) Certified Physicians (assistant) per 1,000 permanent residents (person)	每千常住人口注册护士数(人) Registered nurses per 1,000 permanent residents (person)	每千常住人口医院床位数(张) Number of hospital beds per 1,000 permanent residents (unit)
1978	29767		3.35	1.89	3.11			
1979	30231		3.66	1.87	3.08			
1980	32453		3.88	1.97	3.22			
1981	33666		4.20	2.20	3.30			
1982	34574		4.30	2.23	3.40			
1983	35987		4.40	2.26	3.50			
1984	38580		4.40	2.33	3.70			
1985	41603		4.44	2.48	3.99			
1986	43956		4.47	3.72	4.21			
1987	47538		4.66	2.81	4.49			
1988	53078		4.82	3.02	4.87			
1989	55623		4.83	3.14	5.08			
1990	59036		4.93	3.35	5.37			
1991	61744	54888	5.03	3.44	5.65			
1992	63230	55858	5.10	3.52	5.73			
1993	65621	58605	5.13	3.49	5.93			
1994	67112	60661	5.07	3.45	6.07			
1995	66925	60337	5.06	3.43	6.00			
1996	66760	60997	5.02	3.50	6.02			
1997	67946	61865	5.06	3.56	6.06			
1998	69095	63144	4.76	3.56	6.13			
1999	69465	63660	4.79	3.60	6.15			
2000	71245	65138	4.66	3.60	6.25			
2001	73053	66537	4.64	3.61	6.31			
2002	75188	67750	4.18	3.44	6.46			
2003	74298	66990	4.21	3.51	5.89			
2004	77359	69850	4.25	3.60	6.54			
2005	79067	72329	4.32	3.66	6.65			
2006	81440	74762	4.41	3.84	6.77	4.44	3.84	6.77
2007	83736	76915	4.53	4.19	6.34	3.37	3.12	4.71
2008	86196	79089	4.78	4.50	6.43	3.47	3.27	4.67
2009	90100	82471	5.00	4.94	6.62	3.55	3.51	4.70
2010	92871	85935	5.24	5.35	6.83	3.36	3.43	4.38
2011	94735	87596	5.46	5.70	6.85	3.46	3.61	4.34
2012	100167	92610	6.33	7.34	7.14	3.97	4.60	4.48
2013	104034	96558	6.52	7.65	8.76	4.06	4.76	4.57
2014	109789	102851	6.72	7.96	7.71	4.16	4.93	4.78
2015	111555	104644	7.17	8.50	7.76	4.44	5.27	4.82
2016	116963	110021	7.40	8.64	8.58	4.64	5.42	5.06

21-2 卫生总费用(2000-2015年) TOTAL HEALTH EXPENDITURES (2000-2015)

年份 Year	卫生总费用(亿元) Total Health Expenditures (100 million yuan)	政府卫生支出 Health Expenditures by Governments		社会卫生支出 Social Health Expenditures		个人现金卫生支出 Health Expenditures in Cash by Individuals		相当于地区生产总值比例(%) Total Health Expenditure as % of GDP Total (%)
		绝对数(亿元) Absolute Number (100 million yuan)	占卫生总费用比重(%) As % of Total (%)	绝对数(亿元) Absolute Number (100 million yuan)	占卫生总费用比重(%) As % of Total (%)	绝对数(亿元) Absolute Number (100 million yuan)	占卫生总费用比重(%) As % of Total (%)	
2000	166.72	34.70	20.81	61.78	37.05	70.25	42.13	5.19
2001	201.12	45.28	22.52	73.18	36.39	82.65	41.10	5.33
2002	262.36	48.51	18.49	99.61	37.97	114.23	43.54	5.97
2003	314.16	65.80	20.94	132.04	42.03	116.33	37.03	6.16
2004	357.19	69.35	19.41	150.72	42.20	137.12	38.39	5.79
2005	432.80	85.73	19.81	187.84	43.40	159.22	36.79	6.06
2006	497.41	115.89	23.30	208.00	41.82	173.52	34.88	5.98
2007	523.20	142.03	27.15	212.00	40.52	169.17	32.33	5.19
2008	668.52	180.01	26.93	271.26	40.58	217.25	32.50	5.87
2009	689.60	201.14	29.17	296.25	42.96	192.21	27.87	5.55
2010	814.74	226.84	27.84	385.10	47.27	202.80	24.89	5.64
2011	977.26	275.48	28.19	453.16	46.37	248.62	25.44	5.88
2012	1190.01	320.40	26.92	600.96	50.50	268.65	22.58	6.49
2013	1349.62	356.42	26.41	717.75	53.18	275.45	20.41	6.64
2014	1594.64	394.38	24.73	890.57	55.85	309.69	19.42	7.27
2015	1834.75	445.81	24.30	1069.88	58.31	319.07	17.39	7.75

21−3 卫生机构基本情况
BASIC STATISTICS FOR HEALTH CARE INSTITUTIONS

项　目	Item	2016	2015	构　成 (%) Composition (%)	
				2016	2015
卫生机构　（个）	**Health Care Institutions (unit)**	**10637**	**10425**	**100.0**	**100.0**
#医　院	Hospitals	713	701	6.7	6.7
社区卫生服务中心(站)	Health Service Centers (Stations) for Community	1997	1979	18.8	19.0
门诊部	Outpatient Departments	1141	1070	10.7	10.3
妇幼保健院(所、站)	Maternity and Child Care Hospitals	20	19	0.2	0.2
疾病预防控制中心(防疫站)	Disease Prevention and Control Center (Epidemic Prevention Station)	29	30	0.3	0.3
专科疾病防治院(所、站)	Specific Disease Prevention and Cure Centers	25	25	0.2	0.2
诊所、卫生所、医务室、护理站	Clinics, Health Centers, Infirmaries, Nursing Stations	3757	3630	35.3	34.8
床　位　（张）	**Beds (unit)**	**116963**	**111555**	**100.0**	**100.0**
#医　院	Hospitals	110021	104644	94.1	93.8
社区卫生服务中心(站)	Health Service Centers (Stations) for Community	4417	4412	3.8	4.0
妇幼保健院(所、站)	Maternity and Child Care Hospitals	1971	1935	1.7	1.7
专科疾病防治院(所、站)	Specific Disease Prevention and Cure Centers	554	534	0.5	0.5
卫生技术人员　（人）	**Medical Technical Personnel (person)**	**264850**	**256531**	**100.0**	**100.0**
#医　院	Hospitals	199719	194203	75.4	75.7
社区卫生服务中心(站)	Health Service Centers (Stations) for Community	27343	26193	10.3	10.2
妇幼保健院(所、站)	Maternity and Child Care Hospitals	5482	5135	2.1	2.0
专科疾病防治院(所、站)	Specific Disease Prevention and Cure Centers	632	550	0.2	0.2
#执业(助理)医师	Certified Doctors	100878	96445	38.1	37.6
注册护士	Registered Nurses	117760	114294	44.5	44.6

注：本表数据除床位数外均包含驻京部队医院数据。

Note: Figures in this table include troops stationed in Beijing with the bed number excluded.

21-4 全市医院基本情况(2016年)
BASIC STATISTICS ON HOSPITALS (2016)

项 目	Item	医院数 (个) Hospitals (unit)	床位数 (张) Beds (unit)	职工人数 (人) Employed Persons (person)	#卫生技术人员 Medical Technical Personnel	#执业医师 Certified Doctors	#中医 Doctors of Traditional Chinese Medicine
合 计	**Total**	**713**	**110021**	**244807**	**199719**	**69351**	**10519**
按隶属关系分	**By Affiliation**						
#市 级	Municipal	29	22473	48040	38944	12769	892
区	Districts and Counties	98	30773	56093	45946	16227	3448
按专业分	**By Specialty**						
综合医院	General Hospitals	318	62157	156602	132676	46294	2285
中医医院	Hospital Specialized in Traditional Chinese Medicine	164	14112	27820	22061	8939	6243
中西医结合医院	Hospitals Combining Western Medicine with Traditional Chinese Medicine	38	8482	11490	9297	3336	1345
民族医院	Nationality Hospitals	3	198	400	282	80	48
口腔医院	Stomatology Hospitals	21	477	4590	3638	1428	5
眼科医院	Ophthalmology Hospitals	11	436	874	488	171	11
肿瘤医院	Tumor Hospitals	8	3432	5927	4355	1326	44
心血管病医院	Hospitals for Cardiovascular Diseases	2	1298	3244	2761	687	5
胸科医院	Thorax Hospitals	1	533	838	650	167	2
妇(产)科医院	Hospitals for Gynecology and Obstetrics	16	1276	4061	2757	773	29
儿童医院	Children's Hospitals	12	2081	5469	4260	1339	81
精神病医院	Psychiatric Hospital	22	7450	5885	4250	952	50
传染病医院	Infectious Disease Hospitals	4	1426	4932	4180	1371	50
骨科医院	Hospitals of Orthopedics	8	1098	1384	965	324	71
整形外科医院	Orthopaedics Hospitals	1	328	788	572	194	1
其他专科医院	Other Specialized Hospitals	37	2500	5743	3843	1117	101
护理院	Nursing Hospitals	8	150	96	46	17	4

注：本表数据除床位数外均包括驻京部队数据。

Note: Figures in this table include troops stationed in Beijing with the bed number excluded.

21-4 续表 Continued

单位：人 (person)

项 目	Item	#执业助理医师 Certified Assistant Doctors	#中医 Doctors of Traditional Chinese Medicine	#注册护士 Registered Nurses	#药师(士) Pharmacists (Assistant Pharmacists)	#技师(士) Technicians (Assistant Technicians)	#检验师(士) Laboratorians (Assistant Laboratorians)
合 计	**Total**	**1701**	**358**	**98227**	**8963**	**8357**	**5241**
按隶属关系分	**By Affiliation**						
#市 级	Municipal	136	3	18922	1840	2051	1236
区	Districts and Counties	479	61	20884	2645	2188	1519
按专业分	**By Specialty**						
综合医院	General Hospitals	791	96	67851	4958	5130	3199
中医医院	Hospital Specialized in Traditional Chinese Medicine	362	182	8289	2086	1092	707
中西医结合医院	Hospitals Combining Western Medicine with Traditional Chinese Medicine	147	46	4106	550	381	262
民族医院	Nationality Hospitals	4	2	127	26	16	8
口腔医院	Stomatology Hospitals	37		1597	38	91	24
眼科医院	Ophthalmology Hospitals	10	1	230	24	23	16
肿瘤医院	Tumor Hospitals	10		2197	179	250	108
心血管病医院	Hospitals for Cardiovascular Diseases	1		1532	61	76	48
胸科医院	Thorax Hospitals			380	30	53	24
妇(产)科医院	Hospitals for Gynecology and Obstetrics	21	1	1495	101	184	123
儿童医院	Children's Hospitals	19	4	1948	229	289	215
精神病医院	Psychiatric Hospitals	64	1	2298	213	149	116
传染病医院	Infectious Disease Hospitals	3		2347	133	181	132
骨科医院	Hospitals of Orthopedics	26	14	446	47	56	30
整形外科医院	Orthopaedics Hospitals			270	13	19	10
其他专科医院	Other Specialized Hospitals	165	6	1872	146	248	140
护理院	Nursing Hospitals	1		23	2	3	2

21-5 医院工作情况(2016年)
WORKS OF HOSPITALS (2016)

项目	Item	诊疗人次数(千人次) Patients Treated (1000 person times)	#门诊 Out-patients	健康检查人数(千人次) Health Check (1000 person times)	平均开放病床数(张) Beds in Use (unit)	入院人数(千人次) In-patients (1000 person times)	出院人数(千人次) Discharged Patients (1000 person times)
合计	**Total**	**172674.1**	**144544.2**	**3427.7**	**105984**	**2975.4**	**3555.4**
综合医院	General Hospitals	112848.7	87939.1	2489.1	60813	1980.7	2524.0
中医医院	Hospital Specialized in Traditional Chinese Medicine	32431.6	31411.1	377.3	13354	279.2	280.3
中西医结合医院	Hospitals Combining Western Medicine with Traditional Chinese Medicine	7516.6	7031.9	372.8	8170	129.6	128.3
民族医院	Nationality Hospitals	137.6	137.6	4.0	174	2.7	2.7
口腔医院	Stomatology Hospitals	2728.0	2624.6	1.2	378	9.3	9.3
眼科医院	Ophthalmology Hospitals	281.8	280.3	30.8	397	11.0	11.0
肿瘤医院	Tumor Hospitals	1492.0	1467.6	88.9	2910	140.9	140.4
心血管病医院	Hospitals for Cardiovascular Diseases	738.1	709.2	3.5	1298	65.2	65.1
胸科医院	Thorax Hospitals	279.5	273.4		533	11.6	11.6
妇(产)科医院	Hospitals for Gynecology and Obstetrics	1876.8	1831.5	2.8	1065	54.0	53.9
儿童医院	Children's Hospitals	6723.7	6150.5	14.3	1911	119.5	116.6
精神病医院	Psychiatric Hospitals	1316.3	1299.7	5.0	7322	21.2	21.0
传染病医院	Infectious Disease Hospitals	2134.4	1316.4		1402	50.7	92.2
骨科医院	Hospitals of Orthopedics	443.9	431.8	19.5	1090	20.5	20.2
整形外科医院	Orthopaedics Hospitals	155.9	149.8	0.3	328	12.5	12.5
其他专科医院	Other Specialized Hospitals	909.2	834.6	16.0	2319	38.7	38.4
护理院	Nursing Centers	1.5	1.5	0.4	120	…	…

21-5 续表 Continued

项目	Item	病死率 (%) Case Fatality Rate (%)	病床周转次数 (次) Turnover Beds (time)	病床使用率 (%) Utilization Rate of Beds (%)	出院者平均住院日 (日) Average Hospitalization Period (day)
合计	**Total**	**1.1**	**28.0**	**82.0**	**9.7**
综合医院	General Hospitals	1.2	32.5	83.2	9.2
中医医院	Hospital Specialized in Traditional Chinese Medicine	1.3	21.0	74.1	12.5
中西医结合医院	Hospitals Combining Western Medicine with Traditional Chinese Medicine	2.3	15.7	74.9	17.0
民族医院	Nationality Hospitals	0.9	15.4	70.4	17.1
口腔医院	Stomatology Hospitals	…	24.6	55.4	8.2
眼科医院	Ophthalmology Hospitals		27.6	68.9	8.3
肿瘤医院	Tumor Hospitals	0.3	48.3	90.6	7.3
心血管病医院	Hospitals for Cardiovascular Diseases	0.2	50.2	98.4	7.2
胸科医院	Thorax Hospitals	1.1	21.7	95.2	16.1
妇(产)科医院	Hospitals for Gynecology and Obstetrics	…	50.6	66.0	4.7
儿童医院	Children's Hospitals	0.1	61.0	107.8	6.1
精神病医院	Psychiatric Hospital	0.7	2.9	98.5	118.5
传染病医院	Infectious Disease Hospitals	1.8	36.0	108.1	10.9
骨科医院	Hospitals of Orthopedics	0.2	18.5	75.7	14.8
整形外科医院	Orthopaedics Hospitals		38.2	66.9	6.4
其他专科医院	Other Specialized Hospitals	1.6	16.6	58.1	11.8
护理院	Nursing Centers		0.1	10.2	3.0

21-6 全市居民前十位死因顺位、死亡率及构成(2016年)
DEATH RATE AND COMPOSITION OF 10 MAJOR DISEASES (2016)

顺 位 No.	死因名称	Cause of Death	死亡率(1/10万) Death Rate (1/100 thousands)	构 成(%) Composition (%)
	全 市	**Total**		
1	恶性肿瘤	Malignant Tumour	177.32	26.80
2	心脏病	Heart Disease	170.44	25.76
3	脑血管病	Cerebrovasular Disease	130.60	19.74
4	呼吸系统疾病	Disease of the Respiratory System	65.07	9.83
5	损伤和中毒	Trauma and Toxicosis	25.06	3.79
6	内分泌、营养、代谢及免疫疾病	Endocrine, Nutrition, Metabolite and Immunity Disease	21.18	3.20
7	消化系统疾病	Disease of the Gigestive System	16.56	2.50
8	神经系统疾病	Neurological Disease	8.47	1.28
9	泌尿生殖系统疾病	Disease of the Genitourinary System	5.30	0.80
10	传染病	Infectious Disease	4.42	0.67
	男 性	**Male**		
1	恶性肿瘤	Malignant Tumour	211.74	28.41
2	心脏病	Heart Disease	179.37	24.07
3	脑血管病	Cerebrovasular Disease	147.40	19.78
4	呼吸系统疾病	Disease of the Respiratory System	75.32	10.11
5	损伤和中毒	Trauma and Toxicosis	30.08	4.04
6	内分泌、营养、代谢及免疫疾病	Endocrine, Nutrition, Metabolite and Immunity Disease	21.32	2.86
7	消化系统疾病	Disease of the Gigestive System	18.87	2.53
8	神经系统疾病	Neurological Disease	9.46	1.27
9	传染病	Infectious Disease	5.80	0.78
10	泌尿生殖系统疾病	Disease of the Genitourinary System	5.39	0.72
	女 性	**Female**		
1	心脏病	Heart Disease	161.45	27.94
2	恶性肿瘤	Malignant Tumour	142.82	24.71
3	脑血管病	Cerebrovasular Disease	113.70	19.67
4	呼吸系统疾病	Disease of the Respiratory System	54.82	9.49
5	内分泌、营养、代谢及免疫疾病	Endocrine, Nutrition, Metabolite and Immunity Disease	21.05	3.64
6	损伤和中毒	Trauma and Toxicosis	20.00	3.46
7	消化系统疾病	Disease of the Gigestive System	14.25	2.47
8	神经系统疾病	Neurological Disease	7.48	1.29
9	泌尿生殖系统疾病	Disease of the Genitourinary System	5.20	0.90
10	肌肉骨骼和结缔组织疾病	Diseases of Musculoskeletal and Connective Tissue	3.62	0.63

21-7 全市主要健康指标情况(1978-2016年)
MAJOR HEALTH INDICATIONS OF BEIJING (1978-2016)

年份 Year	婴儿死亡率(‰) Infant Mortality (‰)	新生儿死亡率(‰) Newborn Baby Mortality (‰)	孕产妇死亡率(1/10万) Pregnant & Lying-in Women Mortality (1/100000)	甲乙类传染病发病率(1/10万) Incidence Rate of Catogory A and B Epidemics (1/100000)
1978	17.11	12.21	31.00	
1979	16.97	10.08	34.70	1584.25
1980	14.79	10.24	26.30	2165.23
1981	13.84	9.22	48.50	2225.71
1982	12.97	8.02	24.50	2193.16
1983	13.79	8.78	28.10	1904.55
1984	10.98	7.78	16.80	1666.68
1985	13.94	10.41	22.90	1335.23
1986	16.05	12.13	30.50	1120.19
1987	15.56	11.08	26.60	826.51
1988	14.98	10.48	24.80	640.98
1989	14.96	10.53	34.50	547.61
1990	11.66	8.49	25.00	509.55
1991	12.46	8.56	24.00	448.23
1992	12.12	8.93	30.10	385.98
1993	10.38	7.21	16.50	356.66
1994	10.93	7.29	18.94	374.31
1995	11.45	7.52	22.27	309.99
1996	10.05	6.97	15.32	340.24
1997	9.45	6.36	23.69	294.41
1998	7.58	5.53	10.46	306.37
1999	7.95	5.94	17.53	308.10
2000	5.36	3.70	9.70	301.19
2001	6.01	4.05	11.71	276.85
2002	5.56	3.70	15.12	282.95
2003	5.89	3.83	15.60	228.00
2004	4.61	3.49	15.19	408.03
2005	4.35	3.29	15.91	445.91
2006	4.66	3.42	7.87	448.70
2007	3.89	2.65	16.74	421.02
2008	3.70	2.45	18.52	312.99
2009	3.49	2.47	14.55	339.89
2010	3.29	2.06	12.14	268.99
2011	2.84	1.88	9.09	226.76
2012	2.87	1.91	6.05	174.45
2013	2.33	1.52	9.45	155.87
2014	2.33	1.46	7.19	165.49
2015	2.42	1.52	8.69	150.86
2016	2.21	1.48	10.83	138.00

21－8 主要年份体育场地情况
SITUATION OF THE GYMNASIUMS AND STADIUMS IN MAIN YEARS

单位：个 (unit)

年 份 Year	合 计 Total	#体育场 Stadiums	#体育馆 Gymnasiums	#游泳场馆 Natatoriums	#室 内 Indoor	#各种训练房 Exercise Rooms
1950	19	1				2
1955	61	1		2	2	10
1960	124	2		4	3	19
1970	188	2	2	8	3	24
1975	234	3	2	11	4	28
1980	293	3	2	12	4	32
1985	405	4	2	20	8	54
1990	780	12	12	49	26	153
1995	1381	18	18	88	56	291
2000	2815	35	24	214	161	863
2001	3500	42	27	283	216	1101
2002	4176	57	33	334	263	1358
2003	6100	93	36	443	371	1729
2004	6104	93	36	443	371	1729
2005	6112	93	36	446	374	1731
2006	6122	93	36	446	374	1734
2007	6146	94	37	446	374	1736
2008	6149	94	37	446	374	1739
2009	6149	94	37	446	374	1739
2010	6151	94	37	446	374	1741
2011	6151	94	37	446	374	1741
2012	6156	94	37	447	375	1742
2013	20075	131	70	590	548	2836
2014	20075	131	70	590	548	2836
2015	20075	131	70	590	548	2836
2016	20075	131	70	590	548	2836

注：本表2013年以后数据口径为第六次全国体育场地普查数据资料，此次普查时点为2013年12月31日。

Note: The data in the table after 2013 werr collected according to the sixth national census on gymnasiums and stadiums. The date of this census is December 31st, 2013.

21–9 运动员、裁判员情况
ATHLETES AND REFEREES

单位：人 (person)

项目	Item	2016	#女性 Females	2015	#女性 Females
分等级运动员发展人数	**Number of Graded Athletes**	**1621**	**587**	**1449**	**588**
国际级运动健将	World-class Athletes	6	4	15	9
国家级运动健将	National Grade Athletes	136	79	118	62
一级	First Grade Athletes	566	227	374	155
二级	Second Grade Athletes	913	277	942	362
分等级裁判员发展人数	**Number of Graded Referees**	**1188**	**260**	**1790**	**438**
国家级	National Grade Referees				
一级	First Grade Referees	197	81	320	91
二级	Second Grade Referees	991	179	1470	347

21–10 运动员获奖牌情况(2016年)
STATISTICS FOR MEDALS WON (2016)

单位：块 (piece)

项目	Item	金牌 Gold	银牌 Silver	铜牌 Copper
合计	**Total**	**50**	**32**	**46**
国际比赛	International Competitions	14	3	4
国内比赛	Domestic Competitions	36	29	42

21–11 体育彩票
SPORTS LOTTERY

项目	Item	2016	2015
电脑体育彩票销售点数 (个)	Number of Computer Sports Lottery Tickets Sold (unit)	2750	2680
体育彩票发行额 (万元)	Circulation of Sports Lottery (10000 yuan)	603753	502981
体育彩票公益金提取额 (万元)	Public Welfare Funds Drawn from Sports Lottery (10000 yuan)	158962	133204

主要统计指标解释

卫　生

卫生机构　指从卫生行政部门取得《医疗机构执业许可证》，或从民政、工商行政、机构编制管理部门取得法人单位登记证书，为社会提供医疗保健、疾病控制、卫生监督服务或从事医学科研和医学在职培训等工作的单位。

卫生技术人员　指由卫生机构支付工资的全部固定职工和合同制职工中现任职务为卫生技术工作的专业人员，不包括从事管理工作的人员。

执业医师和注册护士　指领取医师执业证书和注册护士证书的人员，不包括从事管理工作的医师和护士。

死亡率（死因死亡率）　是指某种原因（如疾病）所致的死亡人数占户籍人口比重。

婴儿死亡率　指某地区一年内每 1000 名活产婴儿与未满 1 岁的婴儿死亡人数之比。婴儿死亡率可以衡量一个国家或地区经济文化、居民健康状况和卫生保健事业发展情况，同时也是人口平均期望寿命研究的重要内容。

新生儿死亡率　指年内新生儿死亡数与活产数之比，一般以千分率表示。新生儿死亡指出生至 28 天以内（即 0-27 天）死亡人数。

孕产妇死亡率　指某年某地每十万活产中的孕产妇死亡比例。同婴儿死亡率一样，孕产妇死亡率是评价某一地区社会发展状况的重要指标，它的高低与社会经济状况、孕产妇社会环境及卫生保健服务有直接的联系。

体　育

体育场地　指专门用于体育训练、比赛和健身活动的，有一定投资的公益性或经营性体育建筑设施，包括必要的附属功能用房。

等级运动员人数　指经考核正式批准授予等级运动员称号的人数。运动员等级分为国际级运动健将、国家级运动健将、一级运动员、二级运动员、三级运动员、少年级运动员。

等级裁判员人数　指经考核正式批准授予等级裁判员称号的人数。裁判员等级分为国际级裁判、国家级裁判、一级裁判、二级裁判、三级裁判。

运动员获奖牌情况　指当年北京市运动员在世界比赛、亚洲比赛、全国比赛中获得金、银、铜牌的数量。

Explanatory Notes on Main Statistical Indicators

Health

Healthcare Institutions refer to institutions granted with *License for Medical Institution* by the health administration authority, or granted with certificate of corporate unit by the civil affair, administration for industry and commerce, management authority of institutional organization, and providing medical service and healthcare, disease control, health supervision service or carrying out medical research and education, and so on.

Medical Technical Personnel refer to all fixed employees and of contract-based employees, professional personnel in health technology, who receive pays from health institutions, excluding personnel engaged in management.

Certified Doctors and Registered Nurses refer to personnel who have received a physician practicing certificate and certified nurse certificate, excluding physicians and nurses engaged in management.

Mortality (Cause-specific Death Rate) means the proportion of persons dead due to certain cause (such as disease) in the permanent population.

Infant Mortality means the rate of dead infants under 1 year old to 1,000 live infants in an area in a year. Infant death rate measures the development of economy, culture, citizen health and health care in a country or region. It is also an important component of study on average life expectancy of population.

Neonatal mortality rate refers to the rate of dead newborn babies to live births in a year, generally expressed in permillage. Death toll of newborns refers to the number of newborns that died within 28 days after birth (i.e. 0-27 days).

Pregnant and Lying-in Women Mortality refers to the rate of dead pregnant and lying-in women to 100,000 live pregnant and lying-in women in an area in a year. This is an important indicator to evaluate the social development status in an area. The figure of this indicator is directly related to the social and economic status, social environment and health care service for pregnant and lying-in women.

Sports

Sports Venues refer to sports building facilities for public welfare or operating purpose, specially used for sports training, games and fitness activities, and with certain investment.

Number of Graded Athletes means the number of athletes formally granted with the title of graded athlete upon examination. Grades of athletes include international master sportsman, national maser sportsman, grade-I athlete, grade-II athlete, grade-III athlete and juvenile athlete.

Number of Graded Referees means the number of referees formally granted with the title of graded referees upon examination. Grades of referees include international referee, national referee, grade-I referee, grade-II referee and grade-III referee.

Medals Won by Athletes mean the number of gold, silver and copper medals won by athletes of Beijing in world games, Asian games and national games.

北京统计年鉴2017 BEIJING STATISTICAL YEARBOOK

社会福利、社区、政法及其他
SOCIAL WELFARE, COMMUNITY, LAW AND OTHERS

简要说明

一、本章资料的主要内容

本章资料主要包括社会活动参与、公检法司、民政事业、劳动保障、残疾人事业、妇女及儿童发展规划监测情况等内容。

二、本章资料的数据来源

1.社会活动参与的内容主要包括历届北京市人大代表和政协委员人数及议案情况、妇联组织和工会组织情况等。资料分别由北京市人民代表大会常务委员会、中国人民政治协商会议北京市委员会、北京市妇女联合会和北京市总工会提供。

2.公检法司的资料主要包括公安机关的刑事案件立案情况和治安案件查处情况，交通、火灾事故情况，检察机关的办案情况，人民法院审理案件和收结案情况，以及司法局提供的律师、公证、调解工作等情况。资料分别由北京市公安局、北京市高级人民法院、北京市人民检察院和北京市司法局提供。

3.民政事业和劳动保障统计资料主要包括社会福利企事业机构、人员、优抚和社会救济情况、婚姻登记情况。资料分别由北京市民政局、北京市人力资源和社会保障局提供。

4.残疾人资料主要包括残疾人康复、教育、就业、扶贫和残联组织建设等情况。资料由北京市残疾人联合会提供。

5.妇女与儿童发展规划监测资料主要包括妇女参与决策和管理、就业、教育、健康、法律保护等情况；儿童的健康、教育、法律保护社会生活环境等情况。资料由北京市统计局依据部门统计报表资料整理提供。

6.安全生产情况由北京市行政工商管理局、北京市食品药品监督管理局、北京市公安局公安交通管理局、北京市安全生产监督管理局提供。

Brief Introduction

I. Main Content

This chapter consists of statistics for social activity participation, public security institutions, procuratorates, courts, judicial authorities, civil affairs, labor security, undertakings for disabled people, women and children development planning and monitoring.

II. Data Sources

1. Statistics for social activity participation consist of the numbers of deputies and proposals at people's congress and political consulting conferences of Beijing in previous years, women's federation and organizations, and labor unions. Data were provided respectively by the Standing Committee of Beijing Municipal People's Congress, Beijing Committee of CPPCC, Beijing Women's Federation, and Beijing Federation of Labor Unions.

2. Statistics for public security institutions, procuratorates, courts, and judicial authorities cover criminal cases put on the record of public security organs as well as public security investigation and punishments, traffic accidents and fires, case settlements in procuratorates, cases accepted and settled by people's courts, information on lawyers, notary, mediation provided by juridical bureaus. Data were provided by Beijing Municipal Bureau of Public Security, People's High Court of Beijing, People's Procuratorate of Beijing, and Beijing Municipal Bureau of Justice.

3. Statistics for civil affairs and labor security mainly consist of social welfare institutions, personnel, social relief, special care, and marriage registration. Data were provided by Beijing Municipal Bureau of Civil Affairs, and Beijing Municipal Bureau of Human Resources and Social Security.

4. Statistics for disabled persons mainly include information on rehabilitation, education, employment and poverty reduction, and building of federations for disabled persons, etc. Data were provided by Beijing Disabled Persons' Federation.

5. Supervision data on women and children development are composed of women's participation in decision making and management, employment, education, health, legal protection, and so on; children's health, education, legal protection, social living environment, etc. Data were provided respectively by Beijing Municipal Bureau of Statistics in accordance with statistic reporting system of different departments.

6. Safe production data were provided by Beijing Administration for Industry and Commerce, Beijing Municipal Food and Drug Administration, Beijing Municipal Bureau of Traffic Management, Beijing Administration of Work Safety.

22-1 北京市历年社会保障相关待遇标准(1994-2016年)
HISTORICAL LEVEL ON SOCIAL WELFARE IN BEIJING (1994-2016)

单位：元/月 (yuan/month)

年 份 Year	标 准 Standard	职 工 最低工资 Minimum Wages of Employed Persons	失业保险金 最低标准 Minimum Unemployment Insurance	城市居民最低生活保障标准 Minimum Subsistence for Allowance Urban Residents	企业退休人员基本养老金最低标准 Minimum of Basic Pensions for Retired Persons	企业退职人员基本养老金最低标准 Minimum of Basic Pensions for Resigned Persons	企业退养人员基本养老金最低标准 Minimum of Basic Pensions for Early-retired Persons
1994		210					
1995		240	174				
1996		270	189	170	263	202	170
1997		290	203	190	293	232	200
1998		310	217	200	336	265	233
1999年第一次	First-time in 1999	320	224	210			
1999年第二次	Second-time in 1999	400	291	273	396	335	288
2000		412	300	280	421	360	308
2001		435	305	285	441	380	317
2002		465	326	290	466	405	367
2003		465	326	290	466	405	367
2004年第一次	First-time in 2004	495					
2004年第二次	Second-time in 2004	545	347	290	510	443	402
2005		580	382	300	563	488	443
2006		640	392	310	620	537	487
2007		730	422	330	675	592	527
2008		800	502	390	775	682	607
2009		800	562	410	900	800	700
2010		960	632	430	1000	900	800
2011		1160	782	500	1100	1000	900
2012		1260	842	520	1210	1100	1000
2013		1400	892	580	1330	1210	1100
2014		1560	1012	650	1463	1331	1210
2015		1720	1122	710	1609	1464	1331
2016		1890	1212	800	1714	1559	1418

资料来源：城市居民最低生活保障标准由北京市民政局提供，本表其他资料由北京市人力资源和社会保障局提供。

Source: Data on minimum subsistence allowance for urban residents was provided by Beijing Municipal Bureau of Civil Affairs,others were provided by Beijing Municipal Bureau of Human Resources and Social Security.

22-2 北京市历年参加社会保障情况(1995-2016年)

单位：万人

年 份 Year	参加职工基本养老保险人数 Employed Persons Participating in Basic Pension Insurance	参加职工基本医疗保险人数 Staff and Workers Participating in Basic Medical Care Insurance	参加失业保险人数 Employed Persons Participating in Unemployment Insurance	参加工伤保险人数 Employed Persons Participating in Work-related Injury Insurance	参加生育保险人数 Employed Persons Participating in Maternity Insurance
1995	261.1		219.8		
1996	252.0		214.5		
1997	264.3		214.0		
1998	359.2		222.9		
1999	379.0		289.0		
2000	391.6		287.8	212.0	
2001	425.9	210.2	287.2	212.7	
2002	436.2	353.8	299.5	221.0	
2003	448.5	436.1	306.6	242.9	
2004	460.0	484.0	308.0	259.0	
2005	520.0	574.8	394.6	328.9	226.1
2006	604.1	679.5	482.2	465.3	263.3
2007	671.7	783.0	535.3	609.2	290.6
2008	758.1	871.0	614.3	666.5	324.1
2009	827.7	938.4	675.7	747.1	346.8
2010	982.5	1063.7	774.2	823.8	372.2
2011	1091.9	1188.0	881.0	862.4	395.3
2012	1206.4	1279.7	1006.7	897.2	844.7
2013	1311.3	1354.8	1025.1	920.3	883.2
2014	1392.6	1431.3	1057.1	961.0	915.6
2015	1424.2	1475.7	1082.3	1020.1	941.6
2016	1459.1	1517.6	1117.5	1060.2	981.0

注：1. 2001年开始设置基本医疗保险指标，以前年份称为大病统筹，2000年参加大病统筹人数为232.6万人。
2. 2005年7月1日《北京市企业职工生育保险规定》开始实施。全市农村社会养老保险1992年试点，1996年全市正式实施。
3. 从2006年起，农村最低生活保障人数不含农村五保供养人员。
4. 农村居民参加城乡居民养老保险人数在2007年及以前为参加农村社会养老保险人数口径；2008年为参加新型农村社会养老保险人数；2009年及以后为参加城乡居民养老保险人数中农村参保人数。

资料来源：城市居民最低生活保障人数和农村最低生活保障人数来源于北京市民政局，其他资料来源于北京市人力资源和社会保障局。

SOCIAL SECURITY PARTICIPATION IN BEIJING (1995-2016)

参加城乡居民养老保障人数 Residents Participating in Basic Pension Insurance	参加城镇居民基本医疗保险人数 Residents Participating in Basic Urban Medical Insurance	参加新型农村合作医疗人数 Residents Participating in New-type Rural Cooperative Medicare	城市居民最低生活保障人数 Persons Receiving Subsistence Allowances in Urban Areas	农村最低生活保障人数 Persons Receiving Subsistence Allowances in Rural Areas
			0.9	
			0.9	
			2.8	
			4.3	1.2
			6.7	1.6
			7.8	1.8
			12.0	5.4
			16.1	6.7
		234.0	16.1	7.5
		250.4	15.5	7.8
		261.0	15.2	7.1
		268.5	14.8	7.8
		272.5	14.5	7.9
		274.9	14.7	8.0
	143.7	278.5	13.7	7.7
	159.8	276.8	11.7	7.0
	151.9	267.5	11.0	6.3
	160.1	254.4	10.4	6.0
	173.0	242.6	8.9	5.1
	181.0	223.9	8.5	4.9
215.7	191.2	211.9	8.2	4.7

Note: a)The basic medicare indicator was set from 2001.Before that it was called general healthcare program for major diseases which covered 2.326 million people in 2000.

b) Regulations of Beijing on Maternity Insurance for Enterprise Employed Persons became effective from July 1st, 2005. Pilots were made for social pension program in rural area of Beijing in 1992. The program was formally effective in 1996 across the city.

c) Rural persons receiving minimum subsistence allowance excluded rural persons enjoying five guarantees from 2006.

d) In and before 2007, the number of rural people participating in urban and rural pension insurance covered the people participating in rural social pension insurance; in 2008, this figure covered the people participating in new-type rural social pension insurance; since 2009, this figure covered the rural people of those participating in the urban and rural pension insurance.

Source: Figures on persons receiving subsistence allowances in urban and rural areas are from Beijing Municipal Bureau of Civil Affairs;other data are from Beijing Municipal Bureau of Human Resources and Social Security.

22-3 城镇职工参加社会保险情况(2016年)
PARTICIPATION OF EMPLOYED PERSONS FOR SOCIAL SECURITY INSURANCE PROGRAMS IN THE URBAN AREA (2016)

项目	Item	职工基本养老保险 Basic Pension Insurance		职工基本医疗保险 Basic Medical Insurance	
		单位个数(个) Number of Entities (unit)	人数(人) Number of Persons (person)	单位个数(个) Number of Entities (unit)	人数(人) Number of Persons (person)
合计	**Total**	**472331**	**14590760**	**447963**	**15176243**
按登记注册类型分	**By Registration Type**				
国有	State-owned	6726	1995450	5402	1899884
集体	Collectively-owned	6363	250412	5000	238658
其他	Others	459242	12344898	437561	13037701
按隶属关系划分	**By Affiliation**				
中央单位	Central	7259	1879043	6491	1815176
地方单位	Local	465072	12711717	441472	13361067

资料来源：北京市人力资源和社会保障局。
Source: Beijing Municipal Bureau of Human Resources and Social Security.

22-3 续表 Continued

项目	Item	失业保险 Unemployment Insurance		工伤保险 Industrial Injury Insurance		生育保险 Maternity Insurance	
		单位个数(个) Number of Entities (unit)	人数(人) Number of Persons (person)	单位个数(个) Number of Entities (unit)	人数(人) Number of Persons (person)	单位个数(个) Number of Entities (unit)	人数(人) Number of Persons (person)
合计	**Total**	**471058**	**11175010**	**484739**	**10601808**	**468362**	**9809944**
按登记注册类型分	**By Registration Type**						
国有	State-owned	6051	977688	6230	1011309	6089	936152
集体	Collectively-owned	5789	126713	5989	130083	5757	115171
其他	Others	459218	10070609	472520	9460416	456516	8758621
按隶属关系划分	**By Affiliation**						
中央单位	Central	6948	1455740	7287	1437619	6961	1192569
地方单位	Local	464110	9719270	477452	9164189	461401	8617375

资料来源：北京市人力资源和社会保障局。
Source: Beijing Municipal Bureau of Human Resources and Social Security.

22-4 城乡居民参加社会保险情况(2010-2016年)
PARTICIPATION OF RURAL AND URBAN RESIDENTS FOR SOCIAL SECURITY INSURANCE PROGRAMS (2010-2016)

单位：万人 (10000 persons)

年 份 Year	城乡居民基本养老保障人数 Basic Pension Insurance	城镇居民基本医疗保险人数 Basic Medical Care Insurance			
		合 计 Total	学生儿童 Students and Children	无保障老人 Unguaranteed Aged Persons	无业居民 Unemployed Residents
2010		143.7	121.3	17.7	4.7
2011		159.8	135.5	19.1	5.3
2012		151.9	128.6	18.5	4.8
2013		160.1	137.5	18.8	3.7
2014		173.0	149.8	19.7	3.6
2015		181.0	157.7	19.8	3.4
2016	215.7	191.2	168.0	19.9	3.3

资料来源：北京市人力资源和社会保障局。
Source: Beijing Municipal Bureau of Human Resources and Social Security.

22-5 优抚及主要救助对象情况
STATISTICS FOR PERSONS RECEIVING SPECIAL CARE AND RELIEF

单位：人 (person)

项 目	Item	人 数 Number of Persons 2016	2015	2016年为2015年% 2016 as % of 2015
抚恤、补助优抚对象总人数	**Total Number of Persons Receiving Pensions, Subsidies, and Special Care Treatment**	**45044**	**44391**	**101.5**
定期抚恤人数	Number of Persons Receiving Regular Pensions	1512	1572	96.2
定期补助人数	Number of Persons Receiving Regular Subsidies	31669	31107	101.8
伤残人数	Total Number of Disabled Persons	11863	11712	101.3
医疗救助人次数	**Total Number of Persons Receiving Medical Assistance**	**94607**	**97698**	**96.8**
社会救助对象总人数	**Total Number of Persons Receiving Social Relief**	**133135**	**138161**	**96.4**
城市居民最低生活保障人数	Number of Persons Receiving Subsistence Allowances in Urban Areas	81882	84860	96.5
农村居民最低生活保障人数	Number of Persons Receiving Subsistence Allowances in Rural Areas	46779	48850	95.8
农村五保供养人数	Rural Residents Enjoying Five Guarantees	4474	4451	100.5
农村集中五保供养人数	Collective Rural Residents Enjoying Five Guarantees	1711	1837	93.1
农村分散五保供养人数	Scattered Rural Residents Enjoying Five Guarantees	2763	2614	105.7

注：“农村居民最低生活保障人数”不含“农村五保供养人数”。
资料来源：北京市民政局。
Note: Number of persons receiving subsistence allowances in rural areas excludes "Rural Residents Enjoying the Five Guarantees".
Source: Beijing Municipal Bureau of Civil Affairs.

22-6 社会福利事业、社区情况情况
STATISTICS FOR SOCIAL WELFARE AND COMMUNITY

项目		Item		2016	2015	2016年为2015年% 2016 as % of 2015
社区服务机构数	(个)	Number of Service Facilities in Urban Communities	(unit)	11913	11528	103.3
#社区服务中心	(个)	Community Service Centers	(unit)	198	199	99.5
社区服务志愿者组织数	(个)	Number of Community Service Volunteer Organizations	(unit)	15158	11801	128.4
城市便民利民服务网点数	(个)	Number of Urban Convenient Service Outlets	(unit)	2244	5247	42.8
社会福利企业单位数	(个)	Number of Social Welfare Enterprises	(unit)	496	528	93.9
社会福利企业年末职工人数	(人)	Year-end Employed Persons in Social Welfare Enterprises	(person)	22992	23936	96.1
#残疾职工	(人)	Disabled Employed Persons	(person)	9080	9649	94.1

资料来源：北京市民政局。
Source: Beijing Municipal Buresu of Civil Affairs.

22-7 收养性单位情况(2016年)
STATISTICS ON ADOPTING INSTITUTIONS (2016)

项目		Item		合计	#光荣院 Homes for Disabled Veterans	#社会福利院 Social Welfare Institutions	#儿童福利院 Children's Welfare Institutions	#福利类精神病院和医院 Welfare Mental Hospitals and Hospitals	#城市养老服务机构 Urban Elderly Care Agencies	#农村养老服务机构 Rural Elderly Care Agencies
单位数	(个)	Institutions	(unit)	641	10	8	10	1	184	267
职工人数	(人)	Employed Persons	(person)	15746	176	1029	479	173	6047	5348
床位数	(张)	Beds	(unit)	143470	660	3168	1460	52	36305	53120
年末在院人数	(人)	Persons Received	(person)	81172	127	2801	1190	30	15371	17421
#自费	(人)	Self-supported	(person)	31429	24	1907	118	4	14216	15160

资料来源：北京市民政局。
Source: Beijing Municipal Buresu of Civil Affairs.

22–8 离婚、青少年刑事案犯情况
STATISTICS FOR DIVORCE AND JUVENILE CRIMINAL CASES

项　　目		Item		2016	2015
婚姻家庭纠纷案件数(结案)	(件)	Marriage and Family Disputes (Closed)	(case)	31699	33694
#离婚案件数	(件)	Divorce Cases	(case)	18847	21799
#调离案件数	(件)	Cases of Divorce Reconciled	(case)	5443	6113
#判离案件数	(件)	Cases of Divorce Judged	(case)	2780	3082
建立少年法庭个数	(个)	Juvenile Courts Established	(unit)		20
青少年罪犯人数	(人)	Teenager Offenders	(person)	4135	5215
14周岁以上不满16周岁罪犯人数	(人)	Teenager Offenders 14-16	(person)	32	29
16周岁以上不满18周岁罪犯人数	(人)	Teenager Offenders 16-18	(person)	383	444
18周岁以上不满25周岁罪犯人数	(人)	Teenager Offenders 18-25	(person)	3720	4742
青少年刑事案犯占全部		Teenager Criminal Offenders as %			
刑事案犯的比重	(%)	of Total Criminal Offenders	(%)	19.4	22.1

资料来源：北京市高级人民法院。
Source: The People's High Court of Beijing.

22-9 婚姻登记(1981-2016年)
BASIC STATISTICS FOR MARRIAGE AND DIVORCE REGISTRATIONS (1981-2016)

年 份 Year	结 婚 对 数 (对) Registered Marriages (couple)	#涉外及华侨、港澳台居民登记结婚对数 Registered Marriages Involving Foreigners and Citizens of Hong Kong, Macao and Taiwan	初 婚 总人数 (人) First Marriages (person)	离 婚 对 数 (对) Registered Divorces (couple)	#民政部门登 记 离婚对数 Divorces Registered in the Civil Affair Department (couple)
1981	200352		389936	5170	1780
1982	141253		261851	5359	1581
1983	117976		227676	5322	1465
1984	113362		217649	5654	1387
1985	134462		258255	5874	1746
1986	143105		274634	7541	2474
1987	149952		267424	8916	3218
1988	113333		212544	10664	4198
1989	103829		188287	12515	5174
1990	92988		169510	14748	5791
1991	91979		165752	15287	6483
1992	89095		158241	15567	6477
1993	89938		160127	17829	7589
1994	90379		160793	19928	8327
1995	85511		148722	20160	8096
1996	86803		146666	20716	8225
1997	84208		144040	22257	8628
1998	85534		146750	23708	9381
1999	83312		141740	23922	8502
2000	80212		136500	26616	6384
2001	79385	873	133259	27683	5425
2002	76136	606	126371	27691	5810
2003	93526	761	158729	30637	10142
2004	126436	974	214443	32657	21013
2005	96956	937	158736	34244	23991
2006	171286	1172	294223	35505	24954
2007	117926	991	193387	36622	26432
2008	147516	1165	246309	37619	27277
2009	181771	1176	305803	41299	29998
2010	138104	1085	222269	43970	32595
2011	173238	1260	288406	43521	32999
2012	174114	1242	287436	48575	38243
2013	163676	1070	251636	64610	54536
2014	170027	1149	253774	65623	56192
2015	166018	1018	229546	82195	73000
2016	166207	1012	200750	105806	97583

注：离婚对数包括在民政部门登记的对数和经法院调离和判离的对数。
资料来源：北京市民政局、北京市高级人民法院。
Note: Registered divorces include those registered in the civil affair department and those mediated and judged in courts.
Source: Beijing Municipal Bureau of Civil Affairs, and The People's High Court of Beijing.

22-10 婚姻登记情况
BASIC STATISTICS ON MARRIAGE AND DIVORCE REGISTRATIONS

项目		Item		2016	2015	2016年为2015年% 2016 as % of 2015
登记结婚对数	**(对)**	**Registered Marriages**	**(couple)**	**166207**	**166018**	**100.1**
按婚前状况分		**By Pre-marriage Status**				
初婚人数	(人)	First Marriages	(person)	200750	229546	87.5
再婚人数	(人)	Remarriages	(person)	131664	102490	128.5
#女　性	(人)	Females	(person)	64185	49274	130.3
按居住地分		**By Place of Residence**				
内地居民登记结婚对数	(对)	Registered Marriages in Mainland	(couple)	165195	165000	100.1
涉外及华侨、港澳台居民登记结婚对数	(对)	Registered Marriages with involving Foreigner and the Citizens of Hong Kong, Macao and Taiwan	(couple)	1012	1018	99.4
内地居民	(人)	Mainland Residents	(person)	919	933	98.5
#女　性	(人)	Females	(person)	645	664	97.1
香港居民	(人)	Hong Kong Residents	(person)	57	68	83.8
澳门居民	(人)	Macao Residents	(person)	6	5	120.0
台湾居民	(人)	Taiwan Residents	(person)	125	143	87.4
华　侨	(人)	Overseas Chinese	(person)	18	18	100.0
外国人	(人)	Foreigners	(person)	899	869	103.5
离婚登记对数	**(对)**	**Registered Divorces**	**(couple)**	**97583**	**73000**	**133.7**
内地居民登记离婚对数	(对)	Mainland Residents	(couple)	97327	72746	133.8
涉外及华侨、港澳台居民登记离婚对数	(对)	Overseas Chinese,Hong Kong,Macao, Taiwan Residents	(couple)	256	254	100.8

注：离婚对数不含法院判离数。
资料来源：北京市民政局。
Note: Number of registered divorces excludes the divorces ruled by courts.
Source: Beijing Municipal Bureau of Civil Affairs.

22-11 残疾人事业基本情况
BASIC INFORMATION OF UNDERTAKINGS FOR DISABLED PERSONS

项目		Item		2016	2015
康复		**Rehabilitation**			
0-6岁残疾儿童享受康复政策人数	(人)	Number of Disabled Children of 0 to 6 Years Old Enjoying Rehabilitation Policies	(person)	1065	977
7-15岁残疾儿童少年享受康复政策人数	(人)	Number of Disabled Children and Teenagers of 7 to15 Years Old Enjoying Rehabilitation Policies	(person)	1478	960
残疾人接受辅助器具服务人数	(人)	Number of Disabled Persons With Assistive Devices	(person)	9512	8596
精神残疾人接受免费服药人数	(人)	Number of Mentally Disabled Persons Receiving Free Drug Treatment	(person)	18438	12047
贫困白内障患者接受减免费复明手术人数	(人)	Number of Poor Cataract Patients Receiving Free Cataract Surgery or That of Preferential Price	(person)	3377	2947
盲人接受定向行走训练人数	(人)	Number of Blind Persons Receiving Mobility and Orientation Training	(person)	988	1422
肢残人在社区接受康复训练人数	(人)	Number of The Physical Disabled Receiving Rehabilitation Training In Communities	(person)	6469	7677
智障人在社区接受康复训练人数	(人)	Number of Retarded Persons Receiving Rehabilitation Training In Communities	(person)	6958	6476
精神残疾人在社区接受康复训练人数	(人)	Number of Mentally Disabled Persons Receiving Rehabilitation Training In Communities	(person)	3897	3485
家庭康复培训残疾人亲友、家属总人数	(人)	Total Number of Family Members and Friends of Disabled Persons Receiving Family Rehabilitation Training	(person)	48063	44169
教育		**Education**			
未入学适龄残疾儿童少年	(人)	School-age Disabled Children Without Schooling	(person)	43	31
培训		**Training**			
职业教育与培训机构数(残联认定)	(个)	Number of Vocational Education and Training Institutions (recognized by China Disabled Persons' Federation)	(unit)	53	62
职业技能培训人数	(人次)	Number of Persons Receiving Vocational Skill Training	(person-time)	11499	12374
就业		**Employment**			
城镇残疾人就业状况		Employment of Urban Disabled Persons			
当年安排就业人数	(人)	Persons Employed by Arrangement in the Year	(person)	4817	3541
#按比例就业人数	(人)	Employed by Quota Scheme	(person)	1067	1388
集中就业人数	(人)	Disabled Persons Employed in Concentrated Way	(person)	134	228
个体就业人数	(人)	Self-employed	(person)	128	1336
残疾人就业服务机构数	(个)	Employment Placement Service Facilities for Disabled Jobseekers	(unit)	17	17
盲人按摩		Massage by Persons with Visual Disability			
保健按摩机构	(家)	Healthcare Massage Institutions	(unit)	473	458
医疗按摩机构	(家)	Medical Massage Institutions	(unit)	4	4
保健按摩员培训人次	(人次)	Massage Therapists Training	(person-time)	333	389
医疗按摩员培训人次	(人次)	Keep-fit Massager Training	(person-time)	125	124
扶贫		**Poverty Alleviation**			
享受城镇廉租住房的残疾人户数	(户)	Number of Households with Disabled Persons Enjoying Low-cost Urban House Leasing	(household)	2449	1654
扶持农村残疾人数	(人)	Number of Disabled Persons Supported in Rural Areas	(person)	1389	2398
社会保障		**Social Security**			
城镇		Urban Areas			
已纳入最低生活保障范围人数	(人)	Covered by the Basic Living System	(person)	18053	19082
享受失业且无稳定收入生活补助重残人数	(人)	Number of Severely Disabled Persons Enjoying Allowance For Unemployment and Unsteady Income	(person)	14796	14428
享受失业且无稳定收入生活补助非重残人数	(人)	Number of Non-Severely Disabled Persons Enjoying Allowance For Unemployment and Unsteady Income	(person)	8709	7882
参加城乡居民养老保险残疾人数	(人)	Number of Disabled Persons Insured by Urban Resident Pension Insurance	(person)	22117	26551
参加城镇居民医疗保险残疾人数	(人)	Number of Disabled Persons Insured by Urban Resident Medical Insurance	(person)	37660	43226
其他救助救济人数	(人)	Number of Other Persons Assisted and Supported	(person)	52250	10204
农村		Rural Areas			
已纳入最低生活保障范围人数	(人)	Covered by The Basic Living System	(person)	16681	17665
享受失业且无稳定收入生活补助重残人数	(人)	Number of Severely Disabled Persons Enjoying Allowance For Unemployment and Unsteady Income	(person)	23590	24746
享受失业且无稳定收入生活补助非重残人数	(人)	Number of Non-severely Disabled Persons Enjoying Allowance For Unemployment and Unsteady Income	(person)	25502	29827
参加城乡居民养老保险残疾人数	(人)	Number of Disabled Persons Insured by Urban Resident Pension Insurance	(person)	63219	66398
参加新型农村合作医疗保险残疾人数	(人)	Number of Disabled Persons Insured by New Rural Cooperative Medical Service	(person)	155469	141912
其他救助救济人数	(人)	Number of Other Persons Assisted and Supported	(person)	55416	15914
残联组织建设		**Organization Building of Disabled Persons' Federation**			
残疾人工作者数	(人)	Workers for Disabled Persons	(person)	1274	1255

资料来源：北京市残疾人联合会。
Source: Beijing Disabled Persons' Federation.

22-12 残疾人就业、维权援助情况
STATISTICS FOR EMPLOYMENT AND AID FOR RIGHT PROTECTION OF DISABLED PERSONS

项目	Item	2016	2015
残疾人职业培训人数 (人)	Number of Disabled Persons Trained for Employment (person)	11499	13817
#女性 (人)	Females (person)	2680	6460
新安置残疾人员就业人数 (人)	New Employment of Disabled Persons (person)	4817	4622
#女性 (人)	Females (peoson)	2206	2106
维权信访咨询件数 (件)	Right Protection Letters, Visits and Consulting (case)	21552	22055
维权法律服务件数 (件)	Right Protection Legal Aid (case)	2296	2568

资料来源：北京市残疾人联合会。
Source: Beijing Disabled Persons Federation.

22-13 律师工作
STATISTICS FOR LAWYERS

项目	Item	2016	2015	2016年为2015年% 2016 as % of 2015
律师事务所 (个)	Law Firms (unit)	2249	2100	107.1
执业律师 (人)	Number of Practicing Lawyers (person)	26953	25542	105.5
专职律师 (人)	Full-time Lawyers (person)	25595	24163	105.9
兼职律师 (人)	Part-time Lawyers (person)	973	943	103.2
公司律师 (人)	Company Lawyers (person)	286	325	88.0
公职律师 (人)	Government Lawyers (person)	99	111	89.2
担任法律顾问 (家)	Legal Counsel (unit)	30358	25366	119.7
民事诉讼代理 (件)	Civil Case Litigation Agencies (case)	93990	94480	99.5
行政诉讼代理 (件)	Administrative Case Litigation Agencies (case)	6852	6614	103.6
刑事诉讼辩护及代理 (件)	Criminal Case Litigation Agencies (case)	26162	26976	97.0
非诉讼法律事务 (件)	Off-court Cases (case)	90046	89638	100.5

资料来源：北京市司法局。
Source: Beijing Municipal Bureau of Justice.

22-14 调解工作
MEDIATION

项目	Item	2016	2015	2016年为2015年% 2016 as % of 2015
人民调解委员会个数 (个)	People's Mediation Committees (unit)	7531	7850	95.9
调解员人数 (万人)	Mediators (10000 persons)	7.81	7.68	101.7
调解各类纠纷件数 (万件)	Disputes Mediated (10000 cases)	28.96	18.56	156.0
#调解各类纠纷成功件数 (万件)	Succeed Disputes Mediated (10000 cases)	28.25	17.80	158.7
防止民间纠纷激化件数 (件)	Civil Disputes Prevented from Intensification (case)	443	1251	35.4
防止民间纠纷激化人数 (人次)	Persons Involved in Civil Disputes Prevented from Intensification (person)	4635	9970	46.5

资料来源：北京市司法局。
Source: Beijing Municipal Bureau of Justice.

22-15 公证工作
NOTARIZATIONS

项目	Item	2016	2015	2016年为2015年% 2016 as % of 2015
公证机构个数 (个)	Notary Offices (unit)	25	25	100.0
执业公证员人数 (人)	Certified Notaries (person)	369	310	119.0
总办证数 (件)	Certificates Issued (case)	1268346	1077217	117.7
国内公证业务 (件)	Domestic Notarial Services (case)	761567	570486	133.5
涉外公证业务 (件)	Foreign-Relatesd Notarial Documments (case)	500913	500956	100.0
涉港澳公证业务 (件)	Hongkong,Macao affairs (case)	2996	2810	106.6
涉台公证业务 (件)	Naiwan Notarial Services (case)	2870	2965	96.8

资料来源：北京市司法局。
Source: Beijing Municipal Bureau of Justice.

22-16 法律援助工作情况
STATISTICS FOR LEGAL AID

项目		Item		2016	2015	2016年为2015年% 2016 as % of 2015
法律援助机构个数	(个)	Number of Legal Aid Agencies	(unit)	32	29	110.3
法律援助机构人员数	(人)	Number of Legal Aid Persons	(person)	155	215	72.1
承办民事法律援助案件数	(件)	Civil Cases Aided	(case)	23430	18229	128.5
承办刑事法律援助案件数	(件)	Criminal Cases Aided	(case)	4443	3256	136.5
承办行政法律援助案件数	(件)	Administrative Cases Aided	(case)	112	47	238.3
法律援助机构接待咨询人次	(万人次)	Consultations by Legal Aid Agencies	(10000 person-times)	23.8	16.8	141.7
得到法律援助机构援助的		Females Receiving Aids from				
妇女人数	(人次)	Legal Aid Agencies	(person-times)	8559	6247	137.0
得到法律援助机构援助的		Children Receiving Aids from				
儿童人数	(人次)	Legal Aid Agencies	(person-times)	1431	1505	95.1

资料来源：北京市司法局。
Source: Beijing Municiapl Bureau of Justice.

22-17 司法鉴定工作情况
STATISTICS FOR JUDICIAL APPRAISAL

项目		Item		2016	2015
司法鉴定机构个数	(个)	Judicial Appraisal Organizations	(unit)	109	109
司法鉴定人员数	(人)	Judicial Appraisal Personnel	(person)	1780	1691
司法鉴定业务量	(件)	Judicial Appraisal Cases Proceeded	(case)	75764	78686

注：本表中司法鉴定机构数为“北京市司法局审核登记的全部司法鉴定机构”个数。
资料来源：北京市司法局。
Note: In the table, the number of judicial appraisal organizations is the number of "all judicial appraisal organizations approved by and registered with Beijing Municipal Bureau of Justice".
Source: Beijing Municipal Bureau of Justice.

22-18 公安、法院、检察院收案、结案情况(2005-2016年)

CASES ACCEPTED AND SETTLED BY PUBLIC SECURITY DEPARTMENTS, COURTS AND PROCURATORATES (2005-2016)

项 目		Item		2005	2006	2007	2008	2009
公安部门侦破刑事案件		**Criminal Cases Detected by Public Security Departments**						
立 案	(起)	Cases Put on File	(case)	107988	120554	127446	90045	98750
破 案	(起)	Cases Settled	(case)	59035	66399	74232	63294	71950
法院刑事案件收、结案情况		**Criminal Cases Accepted and Settled in Courts**						
收 案	(件)	Cases Accepted	(case)	17488	17725	19592	20024	18819
结 案	(件)	Cases Settled	(case)	17624	17701	19536	20004	18773
法院婚姻家庭、继承纠纷案件收、结案情况		**Marriage and Inheritance Dispute Cases Accepted and Settled in Courts**						
收 案	(件)	Cases Accepted	(case)	26739	27860	28089	30402	33056
结 案	(件)	Cases Settled	(case)	27002	27845	27916	29499	32902
法院合同纠纷案件收、结案情况		**Contract Dispute Cases Accepted and Settled in Courts**						
收 案	(件)	Cases Accepted	(case)	133534	141485	135099	144948	153766
结 案	(件)	Cases Settled	(case)	135612	141439	134829	140512	152128
法院权属、侵权纠纷及其他民事案件收、结案情况		**Ownership, Infringement Dispute and Other Civil Cases Accepted and Settled in Courts**						
收 案	(件)	Cases Accepted	(case)	42690	44890	46892	53864	58057
结 案	(件)	Cases Settled	(case)	43166	45005	46372	51668	57135
检察机关查办反贪污贿赂案件		**Anti-Corruption and Bribery Cases Handled by Procuratorates**						
受 案	(件)	Cases Accepted	(case)	1202	1330	1276	1060	1113
立 案		Cases Put on File						
件 数	(件)	Number of Cases	(case)	292	321	322	282	319
人 数	(人)	Number of Persons Involved	(person)	356	363	372	333	369
挽回经济损失	(万元)	Economic Losses Redeemed	(10000 yuan)	30701	29545	14703	21148	62542
检察机关办理渎职侵权案件		**Misconduct and Infringement Cases Handled by Procuratorates**						
受 案	(件)	Cases Accepted	(case)	218	162	205	150	206
立 案		Cases Put on File						
件 数	(件)	Number of Cases	(case)	37	30	34	29	48
人 数	(人)	Number of Persons Involved	(person)	38	31	36	31	53
挽回经济损失	(万元)	Economic Losses Redeemed	(10000 yuan)	1320	458	71	3019	25

资料来源：北京市公安局、北京市人民检察院、北京市高级人民法院。

Source: Beijing Municipal Bureau of Public Security, the People's Procuratorate of Beijing, and the People's High Court of Beijing.

22-18 续表 Continued

项目		Item		2010	2011	2012	2013	2014	2015	2016
公安部门侦破刑事案件		**Criminal Cases Detected by Public Security Departments**								
立案	(起)	Cases Put on File	(case)	104327	142835	145724	140498	153334	174374	150312
破案	(起)	Cases Settled	(case)	80401	89156	101776	112594	122383	115807	65376
法院刑事案件收、结案情况		**Criminal Cases Accepted and Settled in Courts**								
收案	(件)	Cases Accepted	(case)	19824	19574	22168	19109	20556	19980	16737
结案	(件)	Cases Settled	(case)	19870	19423	22084	19012	20357	19667	16905
法院婚姻家庭、继承纠纷案件收、结案情况		**Marriage and Inheritance Dispute Cases Accepted and Settled in Courts**								
收案	(件)	Cases Accepted	(case)	36799	35251	35418	37347	39390	43869	43141
结案	(件)	Cases Settled	(case)	37160	35149	35201	35296	38565	40436	43606
法院合同纠纷案件收、结案情况		**Contract Dispute Cases Accepted and Settled in Courts**								
收案	(件)	Cases Accepted	(case)	148655	144433	145017	149237	162893	237850	253456
结案	(件)	Cases Settled	(case)	153130	144766	143153	141642	155472	207012	255852
法院权属、侵权纠纷及其他民事案件收、结案情况		**Ownership, Infringement Dispute and Other Civil Cases Accepted and Settled in Courts**								
收案	(件)	Cases Accepted	(case)	64379	65972	62736	64747	69541	85554	100574
结案	(件)	Cases Settled	(case)	65763	66405	62235	61688	67444	76644	100399
检察机关查办贪污贿赂案件		**Anti-Corruption and Bribery Cases Handled by Procuratorates**								
受案	(件)	Cases Accepted	(case)	1138	988	1070	871	1087	880	855
立案		Cases Put on File								
件数	(件)	Number of Cases	(case)	356	343	379	299	382	312	383
人数	(人)	Number of Persons Involved	(person)	418	425	459	357	429	339	439
挽回经济损失	(万元)	Economic Losses Redeemed	(10000 yuan)	14634	36469	29955	16171	9050	30435	37956
检察机关办理渎职侵权案件		**Misconduct and Infringement Cases Handled by Procuratorates**								
受案	(件)	Cases Accepted	(case)	213	193	351	443	291	104	113
立案		Cases Put on File								
件数	(件)	Number of Cases	(case)	57	55	77	74	75	46	57
人数	(人)	Number of Persons Involved	(person)	60	66	94	81	78	49	60
挽回经济损失	(万元)	Economic Losses Redeemed	(10000 yuan)	16	58	735	962	210	919	9512

22-19 法院行政案件收、结案情况(2016年) STATISTICS FOR ADMINISTRATIVE CASES ACCEPTED AND SETTLED BY COURT (2016)

单位：件 (case)

项目	Item	收案 Cases Accepted	结案 Cases Settled	#判决 Judgment	#裁定 Mediation
合计	**Total**	**19641**	**18871**	**9435**	**9429**
公安	Public Security	752	678	260	589
资源	Resources	271	234	137	134
城建	City Construction	1655	1401	583	1074
工商	Industry and Commerce	367	277	162	196
专利	Patents	1054	641	613	202
劳动和社会保障	Labor and Social Security	236	201	113	121
教育	Education	37	44	22	22
其他	Others	15269	15395	7545	7091

资料来源：北京市高级人民法院。
Source: The People's High Court of Beijing.

22-20 法院刑事案件收、结案情况(2016年) STATISTICS FOR CRIMINAL CASES ACCEPTED AND SETTLED BY COURT (2016)

项目	Item	收案(件) Cases Accepted (case)	结案(件) Cases Settled (case)	判决发生法律效力 Judgment with Legal Forces	
				件数(件) Number of Cases (case)	人数(人) Number of Persons(person)
合计	**Total**	**16737**	**16905**	**17817**	**21287**
#危害公共安全罪	Offences against Public Security	3079	3073	3208	3283
破坏社会主义市场经济秩序罪	Offences against the Socialist Market Economy Order	1399	1377	1480	1905
侵犯公民人身权利、民主权利罪	Offences against Civil Personal Rights and Democratic Rights	3457	3508	3451	4054
侵犯财产罪	Offences against Property	5361	5387	5619	6767
妨害社会管理秩序罪	Offences against Social Administration	3087	3137	3674	4813
危害国防利益罪	Offences against National Defense Interest	16	18	22	28
贪污贿赂罪	Crimes of Corruption and Bribery	296	364	327	393
渎职罪	Crimes of Misconduct in Office	17	14	13	13

资料来源：北京市高级人民法院。
Source: The People's High Court of Beijing.

22-21 法院婚姻家庭、继承纠纷案件收、结案情况(2016年)
STATISTICS FOR MARRIAGE AND FAMILY AND INHERITANCE DISPUTE CASES ACCEPTED AND SETTLED BY COURT (2016)

单位：件 (case)

项　　目	Item	收　案 Cases Accepted	结　案 Cases Settled	#判　决 Judgment	#调　解 Mediation
合　计	Total	43141	43606	11151	19055
婚姻家庭纠纷	Marriage and Family Disputes				
离　婚	Divorces	18310	18847	6418	5588
解除非法同居关系	Relieving the Relation of Illicit Cohabitation	309	317	84	113
抚养、扶养关系纠纷	Child-support Disputes	1290	1285	262	698
抚育费纠纷	Child-support Payment Disputes	1053	1080	443	360
赡养纠纷	Support Disputes	1044	1040	454	242
分家析产	Family Property Division	6043	6146	613	3891
其　他	Others	2964	2984	887	850
继承纠纷	Inheritance Disputes				
法定继承	Legal Inheritance	8388	8261	985	5622
遗嘱继承	Testamentary Inheritance	1096	1067	395	414
继承权确认纠纷	Inheritance Right Dispute				
其　他	Others	2644	2579	610	1277

资料来源：北京市高级人民法院。
Source: The People's High Court of Beijing.

22-22 法院合同纠纷案件收、结案情况(2016年)
STATISTICS FOR CONTRACT CASES ACCEPTED AND SETTLED BY COURT (2016)

单位：件 (case)

项　　目	Item	收　案 Cases Accepted	结　案 Cases Settled	#判　决 Judgment	#调　解 Mediation
合　计	Total	253456	255852	96138	36846
#买卖合同纠纷	Trade Contracts	31618	31944	11616	5309
房地产开发经营合同纠纷	Real Estate Development & Operation Contracts	7810	7801	4029	1207
供用电、水、气、热力合同纠纷	Electricity, Water, Gas, Heating Supply contracts	21355	21560	2135	3763
借款合同纠纷	Loan Contracts	60650	60615	30287	6646
租赁合同纠纷	Lease Contracts	13254	13606	5641	2137
建设工程合同纠纷	Construction Contracts	4443	4638	1891	934
承揽合同纠纷	Contracts for Hire of Work	2882	3039	1216	640
运输合同纠纷	Transportation Contracts	760	808	424	121
经营合同纠纷	Management Contracts	1633	1771	759	259
农村承包合同纠纷	Rural Contracts	43	48	26	5
劳动争议	Labor Disputes	20675	21588	11415	4389

资料来源：北京市高级人民法院。
Source: The People's High Court of Beijing.

22-23 法院权属、侵权纠纷及其他民事案件收、结案情况(2016年)
STATISTICS FOR OWNERSHIP, TORTIOUS DISPUTES AND OTHER CIVIL CASES ACCEPTED AND SETTLED BY COURT (2016)

单位：件 (case)

项目	Item	收案 Cases Accepted	结案 Cases Settled	#判决 Judgment	#调解 Mediation
合计	**Total**	**100574**	**100399**	**33426**	**29170**
所有权及与所有权相关权利纠纷	Ownership and Related Rights	37863	37535	7003	20206
票据、证券权益纠纷	Bill and Securities Rights	338	270	141	2
股东权纠纷	Shareholder's Rights	1654	1622	738	121
不正当竞争纠纷	Unfair Competition	494	637	237	80
人身权纠纷	Personal Rights	13523	13370	5869	2500
特殊侵权纠纷	Special Infringements	19489	20373	10958	4691
适用特别程序案件	Special-poceeding Cases	8251	8367	3980	
其他	Others	18962	18225	4473	1570

资料来源：北京市高级人民法院。
Source: The People's High Court of Beijing.

22-24 检察机关办理各类案件情况(2016年)
STATISTICS FOR CASES HANDLED BY PROCURATORIAL ORGANS (2016)

项目	Item	受案(受理) Cases Accepted		审结案合计 Cases Settled	
		件 Case	人 Person	件 Case	人 Person
审查逮捕	**Arrests to Be Examined and Approved**	**14307**	**18006**	**14265**	**17897**
批准逮捕	Approved			10274	12456
不批准逮捕	Disapproved			3991	5447
审查起诉	**Prosecution to Be Reviewed and Made**	**18786**	**23107**	**18361**	**22107**
起诉	Prosecuted			16642	19909
不起诉	Non-prosecution			1561	2112
附条件不起诉	Conditional Non-prosecution			58	86
举报案件	**Reported Cases**	**2156**		**2006**	
控告案件	**Complaints**	**3844**		**3691**	
申诉案件	**Appeal Cases**	**6633**		**6667**	
民事检察案件	**Civil Cases**	**1424**		**1451**	
行政检察案件	**Administrative Cases**	**403**		**419**	

资料来源：北京市人民检察院。
Source: The People's Procuratorate of Beijing.

22-25 查办贪污贿赂、渎职侵权案件情况(2016年) STATISTICS FOR CORRUPTION, BRIBERY, MALPRACTICE AND INFRINGEMENT CASES (2016)

项目		Item		查办贪污贿赂案件 Corruption and Bribery Cases	贪污案 Corruption Cases	贿赂案 Bribery Cases	挪用公款案 Misappropriation of Public Funds	其他 Others	渎职侵权案件 Malpractice and Infringement Cases
受案	(件)	**Cases Accepted**	(case)	**855**	**341**	**463**	**33**	**18**	**113**
立案		**Cases Registered**							
件数	(件)	Number of Cases	(case)	383	136	222	21	4	57
人数	(人)	Persons involved	(person)	439	170	242	22	5	60
大案	(件)	**Major Cases**	(case)	**371**	**134**	**218**	**19**		**34**
按查办贪污贿赂案件类型分		**By Type of Corruption and Bribery Case**							
5万至10万元(不含)	(件)	50000-100000 Yuan	(case)	34	12	22			
10万至50万元(不含)	(件)	100000-500000 Yuan	(case)	138	56	79	3		
50万至100万元(不含)	(件)	500000-1000000 Yuan	(case)	64	14	44	6		
100万至1000万元(不含)	(件)	1000000-10000000 Yuan	(case)	122	41	71	10		
1000万元及以上	(件)	Above 10000000 Yuan	(case)	13	11	2			
按查办渎职侵权案件类型分		**By Type of Malpractice and Infringement Case**							
重大	(件)	Serious Cases	(case)						13
特大	(件)	Extraordinary Serious Cases	(case)						21
要案	(人)	**Important Cases**	(person)	**94**	**23**	**65**	**4**	**2**	**10**
县处级	(人)	County Level	(person)	70	19	45	4	2	9
地厅级	(人)	Departmental Level	(person)	24	4	20			1
省部级以上	(人)	Above Provincial Level	(person)						
侦结		**Cases Closed**							
件数	(件)	Number of Cases	(case)	382	130	224	24	4	54
人数	(人)	Number of Persons	(person)	431	157	241	28	5	58
#移送起诉		Handed over to Law Suit							
件数	(件)	Number of Cases	(case)	365	125	215	21	4	49
人数	(人)	Number of Persons	(person)	411	151	230	25	5	52
#移送不起诉		Handed over yet Immunity from Suit							
件数	(件)	Number of Cases	(case)	6	2	1	3		2
人数	(人)	Number of Persons	(person)	7	3	1	3		2
挽回经济损失	(万元)	**Economic Losses Redeemed**	**(10000 yuan)**	**37956**	**20652**	**15167**	**2137**		**9512**

资料来源：北京市人民检察院。
Source: The People's Procuratorate of Beijing.

22-26 刑事案件情况
STATISTICS FOR CRIMINAL CASES

单位：起 (case)

项目	Item	2016	2015	2016年为2015年% 2016 as % of 2015
刑事案件	**Criminal Cases**			
立案	Cases Registered	150312	174374	86.2
破案	Cases Settled	65376	115807	56.5

资料来源：北京市公安局。
Source: Beijing Municipal Bureau of Public Security.

22-27 消防建设情况(1996-2016年)
STATISTICS FOR FIRECONTROL (1996-2016)

年份 Year	公安消防队数(支) Number of Fire Brigades of Public Security (unit)	公安消防车辆(辆) Number of Fire-fighting Vehicles of Public Security (unit)	企业专职消防队队数(支) Number of Full-time Fire Brigades in Enterprises (unit)	企业专职消防队人数(人) Persons of Full-time Fire-fighters in Enterprises (person)
1996	36	180	101	1865
1997	38	190	104	1885
1998	41	210	108	1993
1999	44	236	120	2447
2000	47	259	120	2447
2001	50	266	120	2447
2002	52	296	112	2228
2003	56	303	112	2147
2004	57	381	120	2477
2005	57	342	120	2477
2006	64	357	109	2269
2007	69	401	109	2269
2008	77	558	109	2269
2009	86	572	109	2269
2010	91	664	109	2269
2011	98	604	87	1766
2012	107	670	76	1405
2013	122	735	76	1405
2014	125	799	76	1405
2015	134	858	78	1410
2016	143	916	65	1307

资料来源：北京市公安局消防局。
Source: Fire Department of Beijing Municipal Bureau of Public Security.

22-28 火灾及损失
FIRE ACCIDENTS AND LOSSES

项目	Item	数量 Number 2016	数量 Number 2015	直接经济损失(万元) Direct Economic Losses (10000 yuan) 2016	直接经济损失(万元) Direct Economic Losses (10000 yuan) 2015
火灾起数 (起)	**Fire Accidents (case)**	**4296**	**3769**	**5957.4**	**6104.0**
特别重大火灾	Extraordinarily Serious				
重大火灾	Serious				
较大火灾	Big Fire	3	2	42.1	62.6
一般火灾	Relatively Big Fire	4293	3767	5915.3	6041.3
起火原因	**Cause of Fire**				
电 气	Electricity and Gas	1246	1244	2979.3	2982.5
生产作业	Violation of Operation	109	113	256.6	260.0
生活用火不慎	Carelessness in Fire Use	506	511	327.3	289.1
吸 烟	Smoking	89	103	74.4	69.7
玩 火	Fire Playing	61	59	34.6	435.7
自 燃	Spontaneous Combustion	133	93	168.9	78.3
雷 击	Thunderstroke	2	4	0.6	
静 电	Static	3	5	0.2	10.6
放 火	Incendiarism	98	78	250.2	294.8
其 他	Others	2049	1559	1865.3	1683.4
受伤人数 (人)	**Number of Injuries (person)**	**21**	**23**		
死亡人数 (人)	**Number of Deaths (person)**	**56**	**48**		

资料来源：北京市公安局消防局。
Source: Fire Department of Beijing Municipal Bureau of Public Security.

22-29 安全生产情况
STATISTICS FOR SAFE PRODUCTION

项目	Item	2016	2015
亿元地区生产总值安全生产事故死亡率 (人/亿元)	Death Rate of Work Accidents Per 100 million yuan GDP (person/100 million yuan)	0.024	0.045
工矿商贸企业从业人员10万人生产安全事故死亡率 (人/10万人)	Death Rate of Work Accidents in the Mining, Commercial and Trade Industries Per 100,000 Persons (1/100000)	1.03	0.43
煤矿百万吨死亡率 (人/百万吨)	The Death Rate of Coal Mines Per Million Tons (Person/million tons)	0.63	0.22
道路交通万车死亡率 (人/万车)	Road Traffic Death Rate Per 10000 Vehicles (person/10000 vehicles)	2.38	1.64
65大类食品检验合格率 (%)	Up-to -standard Rate in Inspection on 65 Categories of Food (%)	97.92	97.60
#重点食品安全监测抽检合格率 (%)	Up-to-standard Rate of Key Foods Security Monitor Spot Checks (%)	98.50	98.42
药品抽验合格率 (%)	Up-to-standard Rate of Drug Spot Checks (%)	99.85	99.71

数据来源：北京市食品药品监督管理局、北京市公安局公安交通管理局、北京市安全生产监督管理局。
Source:Beijing Municipal Food and Drug Administration,Beijing Municipal Bureau of Traffic Management,Beijing Administration of Work Safety.

22-30 交通事故及损失
STATISTICS FOR TRAFFIC ACCIDENTS AND LOSSES

项目		Item		2016	2015	2016年为2015年% 2016 as % of 2015
交通事故		**Traffic Accidents**				
交通事故发生数	(起)	Number of Traffic Accidents	(case)	3160	2639	119.7
受伤人数	(人)	Number of Injuries	(person)	2781	2619	106.2
死亡人数	(人)	Number of Deaths	(person)	1359	921	147.6
机动车事故		**Motor Vehicle Accidents**				
机动车事故发生数	(起)	Number of Motor Vehicle Accidents	(case)	2676	2187	122.4
受伤人数	(人)	Number of Injuries	(person)	2381	2222	107.2
死亡人数	(人)	Number of Deaths	(person)	1207	792	152.4
直接经济损失	(万元)	**Direct Economic Losses**	**(10000 yuan)**	**2817.3**	**2089.6**	**134.8**
每万辆机动车死亡人数	(人)	**Persons Died Per 10,000 Motor Vehicles**	**(person)**	**2.38**	**1.64**	**145.1**

资料来源：北京市公安局公安交通管理局。
Source: Beijing Municipal Bureau of Traffic Management.

22-31 地震应急避难场所情况
EMERGENT EARTHQUAKE REFUGES

项目		Item		2016	2015
地震应急避难场所累计个数	(个)	Total Number of Emergent Earthquake Refuges	(unit)	120	106
地震应急避难场所累计面积	(万平方米)	Total Area of Emergent Earthquake Refuges	(10000 sq.m)	1831	2809

资料来源：北京市地震局。
Source: Beijing Municipal Bureau of Earthquake.

22-32 妇联组织状况
STATISTICS FOR WOMEN'S FEDERATIONS AND ORGANIZATIONS

单位：个，人 (unit,person)

项目	Item	2016	2015	2016年为2015年% 2016 as % of 2015
妇联组织状况	**Status of Women's Federations and Organizations**			
区妇联数	Number of Women's Federations in Districts	16	16	100.0
乡、镇妇联组织数	Number of Women's Federations in Townships	182	182	100.0
街道妇联组织数	Number of Women's Federations in Subdistricts	147	147	100.0
妇联干部状况	**Status of Cadres in Women's Federation**			
区妇联干部数	Cadres in Women's Federations in Districts	303	295	102.7
乡、镇、街道妇联干部数	Cadres in Women's Federations in Townships, Towns and Subdistricts	327	333	98.2
妇联基层妇代会组织个数	**Number of Grass-root Women Congresses of Women's Federations**			
城市	Urban	2918	2903	100.5
农村	Rural	3844	3936	97.7
各类妇女联谊组织数	**Women's Sodalities**	**31**	**31**	**100.0**

资料来源：北京市妇女联合会。
Source: Beijing Women's Federation.

22-33 工会组织建设情况(2016年)
STATISTICS FOR LABOR UNIONS (2016)

项目	Item	基层工会组织(个) Grassroot Labor Unions (unit)	职工人数(人) Number of Employed Persons (person)	会员人数(人) Number of Members (person)
合计	**Total**	**34352**	**4802485**	**4335030**
按单位类别划分	**By Registration Type**			
国有企业	State-owned Enterprises	1391	598342	576227
集体企业	Collectively-owned Enterprises	1751	153537	142775
股份合作企业	Joint-equity Cooperative Enterprises	525	75801	69192
联营企业	Associated Enterprises	38	2863	2801
国有独资公司	Solely State-owned Enterprises	435	168579	158175
其他有限责任公司	Other Limited-Liability Companies	11048	1119929	945699
国有控股公司	State-holding Companies	420	353996	336429
其他股份有限公司	Other Holding Companies	1026	195065	170887
私营企业	Private Enterprises	7113	549766	460614
其他内资企业	Other Domestically-invested Enterprises	65	5098	3622
港澳台商投资企业	Hong Kong, Macao and Taiwan-invested Enterprises	364	74554	66479
外商投资企业	Foreign-invested Enterprises	918	285716	253101
事业单位	Public Institutions	4269	600804	560193
机关	Governmental Agencies and Organizations	1582	260011	253477
其他	Others	3407	358424	335359
按系统分	**By System**			
工业国防工会	Labor Unions for Industry and National Defence	727	323571	308534
工业	Industry	711	312317	297491
国防	National Defence	16	11254	11043
建筑工会	Construction	1640	790270	606576
本市	Local	499	271191	258478
市外	Non-local	1141	519079	348098
服务业工会	Services	723	253918	235827
交通运输工会	Transportation	193	324887	315987
机关事业部	Governmental Institutions	307	108054	106609
教育工会	Education	47	90790	83741
金融工会	Finance	62	111309	107158
市直机关工会	Institutions under Direct Municipal Leadership	433	48134	46015
区工会	Labor Unions in Districts and Counties	30051	2667268	2460706
经济技术开发区	Economic-Technological Development Area	169	84284	63877

资料来源：北京市总工会。
Source: Beijing Federation of Labor Unions.

22-34 北京市妇女发展规划监测统计资料
SUPERVISORY STATISTICS ON WOMEN DEVELOPMENT PROGRAMS OF BEIJING

项目	Item	2016	2015
城镇单位就业人员数（万人）	Employed Persons in Urban Entites (10000 persons)	791.5	777.3
#女性	Females	323.5	314.8
城镇登记失业人员总数（万人）	Urban Registered Unemployment (10000 persons)	24.8	24.0
#女性	Females	10.0	9.6
城镇登记失业人员就业人数（万人）	Employed Persons from Urban Registered Unemployment (10000 persons)	15.9	15.3
#女性	Females	6.5	6.1
参加基本养老保险人数（万人）	Number of Participants in Basic Pension Insurance (10000 persons)	1459.1	1424.2
#女性	Females	660.6	647.1
参加基本医疗保险人数（万人）	Number of Participants in Basic Medical Insurance (10000 persons)	1517.6	1475.7
#女性	Females	697.7	680.7
参加失业保险人数（万人）	Number of Participants in Unemployment Insurance (10000 persons)	1117.5	1082.3
#女性	Females	490.3	474.5
参加工伤保险人数（万人）	Number of Participants in Work Injury Insurance (10000 persons)	1060.2	1020.1
#女性	Females	452.5	435.7
城乡居民养老保险参保人数（万人）	Number of Urban and Rural Residents Participating in Basic Pension Insurance for Urban and Rural Residents (10000 persons)	215.7	187.6
#女性	Females	104.9	97.3
市人大女代表领衔提出的议案数（件）	Number of Proposals Put Forward by Women Deputies of Beijing Municipal People's Congress(BMPC) (case)	66	84
市政协女委员提出的提案数（件）	Number of Proposals Put Forward by Women Deputies of Beijing Committee of Chinese People's Political Consultative Conference (case)	507	429
普通高校在校学生人数（万人）	Enrollment in Institutions of Higher Education (10000 persons)	58.8	59.3
#女性	Females	30.2	30.6
在读研究生人数（万人）	Number of Enrolled Postgraduates (10000 persons)	29.2	28.4
#女性	Females	14.1	13.5
成人本专科在校生人数（万人）	Enrollment of Technical Higher and Secondary Education for Adults (10000 persons)	17.2	20.4
#女性	Females	9.6	11.2
妇科病普查率（%）	Rate of Gynaopathy General Surveys (%)	63.9	54.2
高危孕产妇住院分娩率（%）	Birth-giving Rate of High-risk Lying-in Women in Hospitals (%)	100.0	100.0
抓获刑事作案成员中女性比例（%）	Share of Females in Criminal Suspects Captured (%)	16.7	20.1
得到法律援助机构援助的妇女人数（人）	Number of Women Receiving Aids from Law Aid Institutions (person)	8559	6247

22-35 北京市儿童发展规划监测统计资料
SUPERVISORY STATISTICS FOR CHILDREN DEVELOPMENT IN BEIJING

项 目	Item	2016	2015
婚前医学检查率 (%)	Rate of Premarital Medical Checks (%)	10.4	9.4
新生儿遗传代谢性疾病筛查率 (%)	Screening Rate of Genic Metabolic Diseases for Newborn (%)	98.4	100.0
出生缺陷监测率 (%)	Monitoring Rate of Birth Deficiencies (%)	100.0	100.0
新生儿听力筛查率 (%)	Screening Rate of Hearing for Newborns (%)	96.63	96.92
出生缺陷发生率 (‰)	Rate of Birth Deficiencies (‰)	13.52	16.37
7岁以下儿童保健管理率 (%)	Rate of Health Management for Children Under 7 Years Old (%)	98.63	98.02
0-6个月婴儿纯母乳喂养率 (%)	Rate of Exclusive Breast Breeding for Infants of 0-6 Months (%)	73.52	70.33
婴儿死亡率 (‰)	Mortality Rate of Infants (‰)	2.21	2.42
5岁以下儿童死亡率 (‰)	Mortality Rate of Children below 5 Years Old (‰)	2.67	3.02
儿童肥胖率(0-6岁) (%)	Rate of Obesity for Children of 0-6 Years Old (%)	3.84	3.95
儿童龋齿率(0-6岁) (%)	Rate of Decayed Teeth for Children of 0-6 Years Old (%)	19.06	17.30
卡介苗疫苗接种率 (%)	Rate of Inoculation of BCG Vaccines (%)	99.85	99.94
脊髓灰质炎疫苗接种率 (%)	Rate of Inoculation of Poliomyelities Polio Vaccines (%)	99.82	99.73
百白破疫苗接种率 (%)	Rate of Inoculation of Pertussis, Diphtheria and Tetanus Vaccines (%)	99.79	99.94
含麻疹成分疫苗接种率 (%)	Rate of Inoculation of Vaccines with Measle Ingredients (%)	99.91	99.88
孕产妇系统管理率 (%)	Rate of Systematic Management for Pregnant and Lying-in (%)	97.49	97.27
孕产妇健康教育普及率 (%)	Popularization Rate of Health Education for Pregnant and Lying-in Women (%)	99.97	99.98
孕产妇住院分娩率 (%)	Birth-giving Rate of Pregnant and Lying-in Women in Hospital (%)	100.0	100.0
孕产妇死亡率 (1/10万)	Mortality Rate of Pregnant and Lying-in Women (1/100000)	10.83	8.69

22-36 北京市历届人代会代表人数性别构成及议案、建议数
NUMBER AND SEX COMPOSITION OF DEPUTIES、NUMBERS OF PROPOSALS AND SUGGESTIONS AT PREVIOUS SESSIONS OF PEOPLE'S CONGRESS OF BEIJING

单位：人、%、件 (person,%,case)

项目 Item		代表人数 Number of Deputies			性别比例 Sex Percentage		议案立案数 Number of Proposals on Record	建议数 Suggestions
		合计 Total	女性 Females	男性 Males	女性 Females	男性 Males		
第一届	1st	564	106	458	18.8	81.2		
第二届	2nd	619	142	477	22.9	77.1		
第三届	3rd	618	162	456	26.2	73.8		
第四届	4th	745	202	543	27.1	72.9		
第五届	5th	751	203	548	27.0	73.0		
第七届	7th	1195	325	870	27.1	72.9		
第八届	8th	973	252	721	25.9	74.1	55	6644
第九届	9th	880	217	663	24.7	75.3	86	7921
第十届	10th	885	224	661	25.3	74.7	156	7281
第十一届	11th	763	197	566	25.8	74.2	166	9717
第十二届	12th	762	235	527	30.8	69.2	276	9859
第十三届	13th	779	237	542	30.4	69.6	153	7576
第十四届	14th	771	257	514	33.3	66.7	179	4718

注：1. 北京市人大常委会是经北京市七届三次人民代表大会选举成立的，故一至七届人代会无议案及建议数。
2. 代表人数为届首选举数，议案及建议数均是本届五年会上及平时议案及建议的合计数。
3. 第十四届议案立案及建议数截止到2016年12月底。

资料来源：北京市人民代表大会常务委员会。

Note: a) Standing Committee of Beijing People's Congress was established upon election at the 3rd Session of Beijing 7th People's Congress. As a result, there were no proposals and suggestions at the 1st-7th People's Congresses.

b) Deputies were those first elected for that term. Proposals and suggestions at other terms of Congress included those at the meeting of the term and/or at ordinary times.

c) Data of proposals and suggestions of 14th Congress was counted by the end of december of 2016.

Source: Standing Committee of Beijing Municipal People's Congress (BMPC).

22-37 北京市历届政协会委员人数及提案立案数
NUMBER OF MEMBERS AND PROPOSALS AT HISTORICAL BEIJING CPPCC

单位：人、件 (person,case)

届别 Term	起止年月 Beginning-ending Month	委员人数 Number of Members			提案立案数 Number of Proposals on Record
		合计 Total	女性 Females	男性 Males	
第一届 1st	1955.04-1959.09	270	40	230	37
第二届 2nd	1959.09-1962.12	463	84	379	13
第三届 3rd	1962.12-1965.09	519	92	427	884
第四届 4th	1965.09-1977.11	529	88	441	23
第五届 5th	1977.11-1983.03	779	161	618	1610
第六届 6th	1983.03-1988.01	766	168	598	3122
第七届 7th	1988.01-1993.01	703	179	524	4276
第八届 8th	1993.01-1998.01	740	185	555	4975
第九届 9th	1998.01-2003.01	782	203	579	6240
第十届 10th	2003.01-2008.01	824	226	598	6871
第十一届 11th	2008.01-2013.01	737	233	504	5354
第十二届 12th	2013.01-2017.08	758	237	521	5410

资料来源：中国人民政治协商会议北京市委员会。
Source: The Chinese People's Political Consultative Conference Beijing Committe.

主要统计指标解释

优抚对象 依照法律和政策的规定，享受国家、社会和群众抚恤优待的人员，包括中国人民解放军（包括中国人民武装警察部队）现役军人、革命伤残人员、复员退伍军人、革命烈士家属、因公牺牲军人家属、病故军人家属、现役军人家属。

社会救助对象总人数 指在报告期末生活在当地规定的最低生活保障线以下的家庭人员及国家规定由民政部门救济的特殊人员和60年代精简退职老职工救济人员等。

城市居民最低生活保障人数 指报告期末家庭平均收入在当地规定的最低生活保障线以下的城镇居民数。包括“三无”对象、失业人员和在职、下岗、退休人员等。

农村居民最低生活保障人数 指报告期末在建立农村最低生活保障制度的地区，得到当地政府或集体给予最低生活保障的农业人口家庭人数。

参加基本养老保险人数 指报告期末按照国家法律、法规和有关政策规定参加基本养老保险并在社保经办机构已建立缴费记录档案的职工人数，包括中断缴费但未终止养老保险关系的职工人数和参加基本养老保险的离休、退休和退职人员的人数。不包括只登记未建立缴费记录档案的人数。

参加基本医疗保险人数 指报告期末按国家有关规定参加基本医疗保险的人数。包括参加保险的职工人数和退休人员数。

参加失业保险人数 指报告期末按照国家法律、法规和有关政策规定参加了失业保险的城镇企业事业单位的职工及地方政府规定参加失业保险的其他人员的人数。参加失业保险人数为参加失业保险的职工人数。

参加工伤保险人数 指报告期末参加工伤保险的职工人数。

参加生育保险人数 指报告期末参加生育保险的职工人数。

农村居民参加城乡居民养老保险人数 指截止报告期末参加城乡居民养老保险的农村居民人数。

参加农村新型合作医疗人数 指截止报告期末乡镇已参加农村新型合作医疗的总人数。农村新型合作医疗制度是由政府组织、引导、支持，农民自愿参加，集体、个人和政府多方筹资，以大病统筹为主的农民医疗互助共济制度。

社区服务机构数 指报告期末社区服务站、社区服务中心、其它社区服务设施的总和。

律师 指受聘参加律师事务所工作，提任法律顾问、刑（民）事代理人、刑事辩护人，办理非诉讼事件、解答法律询问，代写法律事务文书等主要从事律师业务的专职法律工作者和兼职律师。

公证人员 指在国家公证机关依法办理公证事务的司法人员。包括公证员、助理公证员和在公证处工作的其他人员。

办理公证文书 指公证处在一定时期内办结的公证文书件数。公证文书系按司法部规定或批准的格式制作。

调解人员 指人民调解委员会担负调解民间一般民事纠纷和轻微违法行为所引起的纠纷的工作人员。包括调解委员会的委员和调解小组调解员。

调解民间纠纷 指调解委员会依照法律规定，根据自愿原则，用说服教育的方法调解民间发生的有关民事权利和义务的争执，促成当事双方达到协议和谅解，解决纠纷。包括婚姻家庭纠纷，财产权益纠纷等。不包括法院受理调解的民事案件数。

地震应急避难场所 指适用于地震等自然灾害，也适用于其他事件应急状态下，供居民紧急疏散的公园、公共绿地、城市广场、体育场、学校运动场等场地数量。

Explanatory Notes on Main Statistical Indicators

Persons Receiving Special Care refer to persons receiving special treatment from the country, society and the public in accordance with provisions in laws and policies, including active servicemen of PLA (including the People's Armed Policy Army), persons wounded and disabled due to revolution, veterans, military dependents of revolutionary martyrs, military dependents of servicemen who sacrificed on duty, military dependents of servicemen who died of illness, military dependents of active servicemen.

Total Number of Persons Receiving Social Relief refer to the number of family members living under the minimum living standard provided by local governments, special persons receiving relief by civil affair authorities in line with national regulations, as well as employed persons retired because of streamlining in the 1960s, at the end of the reporting period.

Number of Persons Receiving Subsistence Allowances in Urban Areas refers to the number of urban residents whose average family income is below locally provided minimum living standard, including elderly persons, minors, psychotic patients and disables who have no statutory guardian, no fixed pocketbook, no labor ability, unemployed persons, on-the-job persons, laid-off persons, and retired persons, etc.

Number of Persons Receiving Subsistence Allowances in Rural Areas refers to the number of persons in agricultural families covered by subsistence allowances of local government or collective entities in an area where rural minimum living standard guarantee system is established, at the end of reporting period.

Number of People Participating in Basic Pension Insurance refers to the number of employed persons participating in basic pension insurance and keeping insurance premium payment records with social security organizations in accordance with provisions in national laws, rules and relevant policies at the end of reporting period, including the number of employed persons suspending the payment of insurance premium without terminating the pension insurance relation as well as retired employed persons participating in basic endowment insurance, excluding the number of persons only registered but having no insurance premium payment records.

Number of People Participating in Basic Medical Insurance refers to the number of persons participating in medical insurance programs at the end of the reporting period in accordance with relevant national regulations, including the number of employed persons and retired persons participating in the insurance.

Number of People Participating in Unemployment Insurance refers to the number of employed persons in urban enterprises and public institutions participating in unemployment insurance programs at the end of the reporting period in accordance with provisions in national laws, rules and relevant policies, as well as other persons specified by local governments to participate in unemployment insurance. The number of persons participating in unemployment insurance program is the number of employees who participate in unemployment insurance.

Number of People Participating in Work-related Injury Insurance refers to the number of persons participating in work injury insurance programs at the end of the reporting period.

Number of People Participating in Maternity Insurance refers to the number of persons participating in maternity insurance programs at the end of the reporting period.

Number of People Participating in Rural Basic Pension Insurance refers to the number of rural residents who had participated in urban and rural pension insurance programs by the end of the reporting period.

Number of People Participating in New-type Rural Cooperative Medicare refers to the total number of persons who had participated in the rural new-type cooperative medical service by the end of reporting period. The rural new-type cooperative medical service system is a mutual aid medical system for farmers, focusing on general health care programs for major diseases, organized, guided and supported by government, with farmers' voluntary participation.

Number of Service Facilities in Urban Communities refers to the total number of community service stations, service centers, and other service facilities, by the end of reporting period.

Lawyer refers to a full-time legal worker and part-time lawyer joining a law firm, serving as a legal consultant, criminal (civil) proxy, criminal counsel, handling non-lawsuit events, answering legal questions, writing legal documents for others, and other lawyer business.

Notary refers to any judicial person handling notarization matters in national notarization agencies according to laws, including notaries, assistant notaries, and other personnel working in notarization offices.

Notarization Documents Executed refers to the number of notarization documents executed at notarization offices within a given period of time. Notarization documents are prepared in the format specified or approved by the Ministry of Justice.

Mediator refer to working personnel responsible for mediating general civil disputes as well as disputes caused by slightly illegal acts in any people's mediation committee, including members of people's mediation committees and mediators of mediation teams.

Mediation of Civil Disputes refers to the mediation of disputes against civil rights and obligations by mediation committees on voluntary basis and in accordance with provisions in laws in order to urge both parties to reach an agreement and understanding to resolve the dispute, including marriage and family disputes, property rights and interest disputes, etc., excluding the number of civil cases accepted by courts.

Emergent Earthquake Refuges refer to the number of parks, public green land, city squares, gyms, school playgrounds for residents' emergent evacuation in the event of natural disasters such as earthquake, and under the condition of other emergent events.

23

北京统计年鉴2017　BEIJING STATISTICAL YEARBOOK

开发区
DEVELOPMENT ZONES

简 要 说 明

一、本章资料的主要内容

本章资料主要反映北京市开发区的基本情况，招商、入资，企业生产经营、财务、研发活动和人力资源情况，重点介绍了北京经济技术开发区、中关村国家自主创新示范区及北京天竺综合保税区的主要情况。其中，中关村国家自主创新示范区亦庄园在中关村国家自主创新示范区与北京经济技术开发区中为重叠部分。

二、本章资料的数据来源

本章中关村国家自主创新示范区的统计资料由北京市统计局提供；其他各开发区中涉及招商、土地、投资的统计资料由各开发区管委会提供，财务资料由北京市统计局提供；北京经济技术开发区的统计资料由北京经济技术开发区统计局、调查队提供；北京天竺综合保税区中涉及招商、土地、投资等方面的统计资料由北京天竺综合保税区管委会提供，财务资料由北京市统计局提供。

三、本章的有关变化说明

根据 2012 年《国务院关于同意调整中关村国家自主创新示范区空间规模和布局的批复》，自 2013 年起，中关村国家自主创新示范区的统计范围在原有的海淀园、丰台园、昌平园、电子城科技园、亦庄园、德胜园、雍和园、石景山园、通州园和大兴生物医药产业基地的基础上，增加了平谷园、门头沟园、顺义园、房山园、密云园、怀柔园和延庆园七个园区。同时，“电子城科技园”更名为“朝阳园”；“德胜园”更名为“西城园”；“雍和园”更名为“东城园”。

Brief Introduction

I. Main Content

Data in this chapter mainly shows the basic condition of development zones in Beijing, business invitation, investment, production and operation of enterprises, financial status, scientific and technological activities, and human resources. This chapter mainly focuses on the situation of Beijing Economic-Technological Development Area, Zhongguancun National Innovation Demonstration Zone and Beijing Tianzhu Bonded Zone. Data of Zhongguancun Yizhuang Sub-park is counted in both Zhongguancun National Innovation Demonstration Zone and Beijing Economic-Technological Development Area.

II. Source of Data

Data of Zhongguancun National Innovation Demonstration Zone in this chapter are sourced from Beijing Municipal Bureau of Statistics; statistics for other development zones in terms of business innovation, land and investment are gathered and provided by Beijing Municipal Commission of Economy and Information Technology and financial data are provided by Beijing Municipal Bureau of Statistics; data for Beijing Economic- Technological Development Area are from the Statistics Bureau and Survey Team of Beijing Economic-Technological Development Area; data for business invitation and land in Beijing Tianzhu Bonded Zone are provided by the Administrative Committee of the Bonded Zone, while other data are from Beijing Municipal Bureau of Statistics.

III. Notes on Changes in This Chapter

According to the *Official Reply of the State Council on Approving the Adjustment of Spatial Scale and Layout of Zhongguancun National Innovation Demonstration Area* issued in 2012, the statistic scope of Zhongguancun Area has been enlarged to include Pinggu Sub-park, Mentougou Sub-park, Shunyi Sub-park, Fangshan Sub-park, Miyun Sub-park, Huairou Sub-park and Yanqing Sub-park to supplement Haidian Sub-park, Fengtai Sub-park, Changping Sub-park, Electronic Park, Yizhuang Sub-park, Deshengyuan Sub-park, Yonghe Sub-park, Shijingshan Sub-park, Tongzhou Sub-park and Daxing Ecological Sub-park Pharmaceutical Base. At the same time, Electronic Park is changed into Chaoyang Sub-park, Deshengyuan Sub-park into Xicheng Sub-park and Yonghe Sub-park into Dongcheng Sub-park.

23-1 开发区基本情况(2016年)
STATISTICS ON DEVELOPMENT ZONES (2016)

项目	Item	国家级 National	市级 Municipal
开发区个数 (个)	Number of Development Zones (unit)	3	16
区规划总面积 (公顷)	Total Planned Area of Development Zones (hectare)	45395.9	9252.6
累计已开发土地面积 (公顷)	Accumulated Area of Developed Land (hectare)	31549.3	6644.2
累计已供应土地面积 (公顷)	Accumulated Area of Supplied Land (hectare)	29020.8	5271.0
累计已建成城镇建设用地面积 (公顷)	Accumulated Area of Land for Urban Development (hectare)	26087.8	5198.0
累计招商项目企业个数 (个)	Accumulated Number of Enterprises of Business Inviting Programs (unit)	59429	20647
累计招商项目总投资 (亿元)	Accumulative Total Investment of Business Inviting (100 million yuan)	20612.2	3526.6
累计招商项目注册资本 (亿元)	Accumulative Registered Capital of Business Inviting Programs (100 million yuan)	19373.8	2586.5
#三资企业 (亿元)	Three Kinds of Foreign-funded Enterprises (100 million yuan)	2557.4	346.8
累计招商项目合同外资金额 (亿美元)	Accumulative Contracted Foreign Capital of Business Inviting Programs (USD 100 million)	315.5	55.2
累计招商项目外商实际投资 (亿美元)	Accumulated Actual Foreign Investment of Business Inviting Programs (USD 100 million)	250.0	62.5
固定资产投资 (亿元)	Investment in Fixed Assets (100 million yuan)	1010.0	111.2
总收入 (亿元)	Total Revenue (100 million yuan)	49765.3	5022.1
工业总产值(当年价格) (亿元)	Gross Output Value Of Industry (at current prices) (100 million yuan)	10185.8	1345.5
工业销售产值(当年价格) (亿元)	Sales Value of Industry (at current prices) (100 million yuan)	9956.0	1325.3
利润总额 (亿元)	Total Profits (100 million yuan)	3775.5	298.8
应缴税金 (亿元)	Total Taxes Payable (100 million yuan)	2331.4	205.2

注：1. 本表所指开发区包括北京市级及国家级开发区情况。
2. 表内"累计"指自开始至年末的累计数。
3. 本表"总收入"、"工业总产值(当年价格)"、"工业销售产值"(当年价格)、"利润总额"和"应缴税金"数据的统计范围为注册在开发区内的规模(限额)以上法人单位。

Note: a) Development zones in this table include those at Beijing municipal level and national level.
b) Accumulative data in this table refer to the accumulation from the beginning to the end of this year.
c) The statistical scope of total revenue, gross output value of industry (at current prices), sales value of industry (at current prices), total profits and total taxes payable in this table cover legal entities above designated size that are registered in the development zones.

23-2 开发区土地开发情况(2016年)
LAND EXPLOITATION OF DEVELOPMENT ZONES(2016)

单位：公顷 (hectare)

名　　称	Item	规划总面积 Total Planned Area	累计已开发土地面积 Accumulated Area of Developed Land	累计已供应土地面积 Accumulated Area of Supplied Land	累计已建成城镇建设用地 Accumulated Area of Land for Urban Development
国家级开发区	**State-level Development Zone**	**45395.9**	**31549.3**	**29020.8**	**26087.8**
北京经济技术开发区	Beijing Economic-Technological Development Area	4680.0	3700.0	3948.8	3700.0
中关村国家自主创新示范区	Zhongguancun National Independent Demonstration Zone	42799.5	30177.8	24756.0	24816.6
中关村示范区海淀园	Zhongguancun Haidian Sub-park	17430.6	13930.3	13673.2	13506.3
中关村示范区丰台园	Zhongguancun Fengtai Sub-park	1763.0	367.5	237.4	191.6
中关村示范区昌平园	Zhongguancun Changping Sub-park	5140.0	2890.7	2306.3	2766.3
中关村示范区朝阳园	Zhongguancun Chaoyang Sub-park	2610.0	1471.9	1447.1	1047.6
中关村示范区亦庄园	Zhongguancun Yizhuang Sub-park	2678.0	2678.0		2678.0
中关村示范区西城园	Zhongguancun Xicheng Sub-park	1000.0	1000.0	1000.0	
中关村示范区东城园	Zhongguancun Dongcheng Sub-park	603.0	288.8		288.8
中关村示范区石景山园	Zhongguancun Shijingshan Sub-park	1334.0	133.4	71.9	133.4
中关村示范区通州园	Zhongguancun Tongzhou Sub-park	3434.6	2553.3	2088.9	1718.2
中关村示范区大兴园	Zhongguancun Daxing Sub-park	1124.7	710.2	559.0	299.5
中关村示范区平谷园	Zhongguancun PingGu Sub-park	508.0	227.7	103.4	85.2
中关村示范区门头沟园	Zhongguancun MenTouGou Sub-park	189.0	120.0	120.0	
中关村示范区房山园	Zhongguancun FangShan Sub-park	1573.0	1231.3	1060.6	678.9
中关村示范区顺义园	Zhongguancun ShunYi Sub-park	1208.5	912.4	567.5	410.7
中关村示范区密云园	Zhongguancun MiYun Sub-park	1000.8	699.3	607.0	462.4
中关村示范区怀柔园	Zhongguancun HuaiRou Sub-park	711.0	693.1	664.3	359.2
中关村示范区延庆园	Zhongguancun YanQing Sub-park	491.2	270.0	249.6	190.6
北京天竺综合保税区	Beijing Tianzhu Bonded Area	594.4	349.5	316.0	249.2
市级开发区	**Municipal-level Development Zone**	**9252.6**	**6644.2**	**5271.0**	**5198.0**
北京石龙经济开发区	Shilong Economic Development Zone	189.0	120.0	120.0	
北京良乡经济开发区	Liangxiang Economic Development Zone	240.9	136.1	132.7	110.7
北京大兴经济开发区	Daxing Economic Development Zone	414.8	294.3	282.4	278.5
北京通州经济开发区	Tongzhou Economic Development Zone	1947.6	770.7	750.5	637.3
北京雁栖经济开发区	Yanqi Economic Development Zone	1096.0	1096.0	722.2	637.6
北京兴谷经济开发区	Xinggu Economic Development Zone	503.2	571.7	421.6	596.0
北京密云经济开发区	Miyun Economic Development Zone	1249.5	1249.5	1000.4	910.0
北京林河经济开发区	Linhe Economic Development Zone	416.0	385.0	260.0	349.0
北京天竺空港经济开发区	Tianzhu Economic Development Zone	660.0	660.0	449.2	432.2
北京八达岭经济开发区	Badaling Economic Development Zone	480.8	318.6	209.6	295.1
北京永乐经济开发区	Yongle Economic Development Zone	459.8	219.3	137.1	137.1
北京延庆经济开发区	Yanqing Economic Development Zone	418.6	173.2	143.0	221.0
北京昌平小汤山工业园区	Changping Xiaotangshan Industrial Park	257.3	14.3	23.5	45.3
北京采育经济开发区	Caiyu Economic Development Zone	355.0	327.1	319.7	314.0
北京房山工业园区	Fangshan Industrial Park	218.5	159.5	150.7	122.8
北京马坊工业园区	Mafang Bonded Area Industrial Park	345.6	149.0	148.4	111.5

注：1. 本表所指开发区包括北京市级及国家级开发区情况。
2. 中关村国家自主创新示范区亦庄园数据在中关村国家自主创新示范区与北京经济技术开发区中为重叠部分。
3. 自2013年起，平谷园、门头沟园、房山园、顺义园、密云园、怀柔园和延庆园七个园区纳入中关村国家自主创新示范区统计范围，后表同(详见简要说明)。
4. 除中关村国家自主创新示范区海淀园外，中关村国家自主创新示范区各园"规划总面积"指标均填报批复土地面积，范围较2012年有所变化。
5. 表内"累计"指自开始至年末的累计数。

Note: a) Development zones in this table include those at Beijing municipal level and national level.
b) Data on Yizhuang Sub-park of Zhongguancun Demonstration Zone are overlapped in Zhongguancun National Innovation Demonstration Zone and Beijing Economic and Technological Development Area.
c) Since 2013, the Pinggu Sub-park, Mentougou Sub-park, Fangshan Sub-park, Shunyi Sub-park, Huairou Sub-park and Yanqing Sub-park are incorporated into the statistical scope of Zhongguancun National Independent Innovation Demonstration Zone (the same in the following tables). (For details, please refer to the Brief Introduction to this chapter.)
d) Apart from Haidian Sub-park, the total planned area of all sub-parks of Zhongguancun National Independent Innovation Demonstration Zone refers to the approved area of land. The statistical scope is slightly different from that of 2012.
e) "Accumulated" in this table refers to the accumlation from the beginning to the end of the year.

23-3 开发区招商、入资情况(2016年)

名　称	Item	招商项目企业个数(个) Number of Enterprises Involved in Business Inviting Programs (unit)
国家级开发区	**State-level Development Zone**	**59429**
北京经济技术开发区	Beijing Economic-Technological Development Area	12722
中关村国家自主创新示范区	Zhongguancun National Independent Innovation Demonstration Zone	47264
中关村示范区海淀园	Zhongguancun Haidian Sub-park	23963
中关村示范区丰台园	Zhongguancun Fengtai Sub-park	10181
中关村示范区昌平园	Zhongguancun Changping Sub-park	3778
中关村示范区朝阳园	Zhongguancun Chaoyang Sub-park	1635
中关村示范区亦庄园	Zhongguancun Yizhuang Sub-park	852
中关村示范区西城园	Zhongguancun Xicheng Sub-park	649
中关村示范区东城园	Zhongguancun Dongcheng Sub-park	2207
中关村示范区石景山园	Zhongguancun Shijingshan Sub-park	2656
中关村示范区通州园	Zhongguancun Tongzhou Sub-park	296
中关村示范区大兴园	Zhongguancun Daxing Sub-park	101
中关村示范区平谷园	Zhongguancun PingGu Sub-park	147
中关村示范区门头沟园	Zhongguancun MenTouGou Sub-park	118
中关村示范区房山园	Zhongguancun FangShan Sub-park	150
中关村示范区顺义园	Zhongguancun ShunYi Sub-park	283
中关村示范区密云园	Zhongguancun MiYun Sub-park	136
中关村示范区怀柔园	Zhongguancun HuaiRou Sub-park	54
中关村示范区延庆园	Zhongguancun YanQing Sub-park	58
北京天竺综合保税区	Beijing Tianzhu Bonded Area	295
市级开发区	**Municipal-level Development Zone**	**20647**
北京石龙经济开发区	Shilong Economic Development Zone	11065
北京良乡经济开发区	Liangxiang Economic Development Zone	84
北京大兴经济开发区	Daxing Economic Development Zone	2849
北京通州经济开发区	Tongzhou Economic Development Zone	87
北京雁栖经济开发区	Yanqi Economic Development Zone	1720
北京兴谷经济开发区	Xinggu Economic Development Zone	207
北京密云经济开发区	Miyun Economic Development Zone	260
北京林河经济开发区	Linhe Economic Development Zone	316
北京天竺空港经济开发区	Tianzhu Economic Development Zone	961
北京八达岭经济开发区	Badaling Economic Development Zone	1608
北京永乐经济开发区	Yongle Economic Development Zone	26
北京延庆经济开发区	Yanqing Economic Development Zone	1242
北京昌平小汤山工业园区	Changping Xiaotangshan Industrial Park	78
大兴采育经济开发区	Caiyu Economic Development Zone	54
北京房山工业园区	Fangshan Industrial Park	26
北京马坊工业园区	Mafang Industrial Park	64

注：中关村国家自主创新示范区亦庄园数据在中关村国家自主创新示范区与北京经济技术开发区中为重叠部分。

STATISTICS FOR BUSINESS INVITATION AND INVESTMENT IN DEVELOPMENT ZONES (2016)

自开始至报告期累计 Accumulative Number from Beginning				
项目总投资(万元) Total Investment (10000 yuan)	注册资本(万元) Registered Capital (10000 yuan)	#三资企业 Foreign-funded Enterprises	合同外资金额(万美元) Contracted Foreign Capital (USD 10000)	外商实际投资(万美元) Actual Foreign Investment (USD 10000)
206121862	**193738392**	**25574349**	**3154503**	**2500266**
50330270	42046517	8376568	927701	733557
169368988	159821679	21117550	2445823	1977264
68101834	67565490	10432231	1461440	986423
21944409	21944409	227253	26905	33239
25601069	25415898	1247443	86573	86573
10666826	10666826	1500567	125578	125578
17213168	9480050	4549670	365887	357421
9426511	9426511	1345977	202637	202637
2255929	2255929	101275	3293	3142
3256892	3264034	203505	31308	34210
2022938	1277495	347442	19848	19848
264984	246500	16000	5200	4750
349604	349604	11800	2168	2168
1135329	1135329	10372	1019	319
107255	1127291	280108	75	1451
5370136	4948601	800251	109770	111510
758500	556481	41020	3759	7609
816005	98938			
77600	62294	2636	363	386
3635772	1350246	629901	146866	146866
35265809	**25864630**	**3467679**	**552366**	**624958**
5163430	5163430	41465	8028	6454
304676	142579	13663	1532	1532
478512	1708942	151535	10675	9491
2981539	851549	272846	46220	41208
3403598	958253	460489	240471	252780
899986	324498	234743	57008	58506
3137471	582010	131210	24807	56459
924762	610864	94631	12622	7889
5940018	4202013	1951652	142353	181154
681764	841915	20061	70	70
193769	47139	1000		1487
9925464	9601021		5857	6494
52800	34731	6242	989	655
690041	436242	9808	1735	780
232722	104187			
255258	255258	78334		

Note: Data on Yizhuang Sub-park of Zhongguancun Demonstration Zone are overlapped in Zhongguancun National Innovation Demonstration Zone and Beijing Economic and Technological Development Area.

23-4 开发区投资、生产情况(2016年)
INVESTMENT AND PRODUCTION OF DEVELOPMENT ZONES (2016)

名称	Item	自年初累计 Accumulative Number from Year-beginning		
		固定资产投资(万元) Investment in Fixed Assets (10000 yuan)	总收入(万元) Total Revenue (10000 yuan)	利润总额(万元) Total Profits (10000 yuan)
国家级开发区	**State-level Development Zone**	**10100405**	**497652684**	**37755260**
北京经济技术开发区	Beijing Economic-Technological Development Area	3910369	80131999	4018242
中关村国家自主创新示范区	Zhongguancun National Independent Innovation Demonstration Zone	7410788	460476182	37325320
中关村示范区海淀园	Zhongguancun Haidian Sub-park	1358662	183553601	14078899
中关村示范区丰台园	Zhongguancun Fengtai Sub-park	1280000	44032802	3456339
中关村示范区昌平园	Zhongguancun Changping Sub-park	224624	36691286	2031068
中关村示范区朝阳园	Zhongguancun Chaoyang Sub-park	330000	46035935	4419209
中关村示范区亦庄园	Zhongguancun Yizhuang Sub-park	1356102	44369315	3714492
中关村示范区西城园	Zhongguancun Xicheng Sub-park	73036	26869228	2616377
中关村示范区东城园	Zhongguancun Dongcheng Sub-park	1102794	19104337	1810722
中关村示范区石景山园	Zhongguancun Shijingshan Sub-park	98271	18814871	3083000
中关村示范区通州园	Zhongguancun Tongzhou Sub-park	568643	6276446	633305
中关村示范区大兴园	Zhongguancun Daxing Sub-park	208931	5628465	407756
中关村示范区平谷园	Zhongguancun PingGu Sub-park	51792	1222230	77321
中关村示范区门头沟园	Zhongguancun MenTouGou Sub-park	91912	1745658	-2112
中关村示范区房山园	Zhongguancun FangShan Sub-park	392543	3021033	193081
中关村示范区顺义园	Zhongguancun ShunYi Sub-park	139469	14845663	299427
中关村示范区密云园	Zhongguancun MiYun Sub-park	27404	2133504	123854
中关村示范区怀柔园	Zhongguancun HuaiRou Sub-park	92426	5228006	348644
中关村示范区延庆园	Zhongguancun YanQing Sub-park	14179	903804	33939
北京天竺综合保税区	Beijing Tianzhu Bonded Area	135350	1413818	126190
市级开发区	**Municipal-level Development Zone**	**1111821**	**50221415**	**2988338**
北京石龙经济开发区	Shilong Economic Development Zone	91912	7249209	-547474
北京良乡经济开发区	Liangxiang Economic Development Zone	6381	1782283	42693
北京大兴经济开发区	Daxing Economic Development Zone	10392	2489200	59835
北京通州经济开发区	Tongzhou Economic Development Zone	107130	1710741	444419
北京雁栖经济开发区	Yanqi Economic Development Zone	92426	3996512	430412
北京兴谷经济开发区	Xinggu Economic Development Zone	102363	2100095	65996
北京密云经济开发区	Miyun Economic Development Zone	159136	3582381	186285
北京林河经济开发区	Linhe Economic Development Zone	74532	1914358	85097
北京天竺空港经济开发区	Tianzhu Economic Development Zone	305521	19948331	1828509
北京八达岭经济开发区	Badaling Economic Development Zone	17910	1240347	230731
北京永乐经济开发区	Yongle Economic Development Zone	21652	63306	5995
北京延庆经济开发区	Yanqing Economic Development Zone	54954	1498546	32510
北京昌平小汤山工业园区	Changping Xiaotangshan Industrial Park		22273	106
大兴采育经济开发区	Caiyu Economic Development Zone	15259	2070405	103960
北京房山工业园区	Fangshan Industrial Park	20432	428839	19535
北京马坊工业园区	Mafang Industrial Park	31821	124590	-271

注：1.中关村国家自主创新示范区亦庄园数据在中关村国家自主创新示范区与北京经济技术开发区中为重叠部分。

2.北京经济技术开发区、市级各开发区"总收入"、"利润总额"指标的统计范围为规模(限额)以上法人单位。

Note: a) Data on Yizhuang Sub-park of Zhongguancun Demonstration Zone are overlapped in Zhongguancun National Innovation Demonstration Zone and Beijing Economic and Technological Development Area.

b) The statistical scope of total revenue and total profits for Beijing Economic-Technological Development Area and other municipal-level development zones covers legal entities above designated size.

23-5 北京经济技术开发区主要经济指标
MAIN ECONOMIC INDICATORS FOR BEIJING ECONOMIC-TECHNOLOGICAL DEVELOPMENT AREA

项目		Item		2016	2015	2016年为2015年% 2016 as % of 2015
规划面积	(公顷)	Area Planned	(hectare)	4680.0	4680.0	100.0
开发区生产总值	(亿元)	Gross Output Value	(100 million yuan)	1172.6	1081.4	108.4
工业总产值		Gross Output Value of Industry				
(当年价格)	(亿元)	(at current prices)	(100 million yuan)	2842.5	2555.5	111.2
#高新技术企业	(亿元)	High and New Technology Enterprises	(100 million yuan)	2581.7	2333.2	110.6
销售(营业)收入	(亿元)	Sales(Business)Revenue	(100 million yuan)	8044.2	6670.7	120.6
利润总额	(亿元)	Total Profits	(100 million yuan)	399.7	384.6	103.9
进出口总值	(亿美元)	Total Value of Imports and Exports	(USD 100 million)	157.2	146.6	107.2
出　口	(亿美元)	Exports	(USD 100 million)	49.5	52.6	94.2
进　口	(亿美元)	Imports	(USD 100 million)	107.7	94.0	114.6
公共财政预算收入	(亿元)	Local Public Finance Budget Revenue	(100 million yuan)	169.3	134.9	125.5
公共财政预算支出	(亿元)	Local Public Finance Budget Expenditure	(100 million yuan)	163.2	145.4	112.3
实际利用外资	(亿美元)	Actual Use of Foreign Capital	(USD 100 million)	3.1	3.0	101.8
固定资产投资	(亿元)	Investment in Fixed Assets	(100 million yuan)	386.7	397.6	97.2
从业人员期末人数	(人)	Number of Employed Persons	(person)	345490	314059	110.0
从业人员工资总额	(万元)	Total Wages of Employed Persons	(10000 yuan)	3382429	3140220	107.7

注：工业总产值(当年价格)、销售(营业)收入和利润总额指标的统计范围是规模(限额)以上法人单位。

资料来源：北京经济技术开发区统计局、调查队。

Note: The statistical scope of gross output value of industry (at current prices), sales (business) revenue and total profits covers legal entities above designated size.

Source: Statistics Bureau and Survey Team of Beijing Economic-Technological Development Area.

23-6 中关村国家自主创新示范区企业经营及科技活动情况(2008-2016年)
OPERATING ACTIVITIES AND SCIENCE ACTIVITIES OF ENTERPRISES IN ZHONGGUANCUN NATIONAL INNOVATION DEMONSTRATION ZONE (2008-2016)

项目	Item	2008	2009	2010	2011	2012	2013	2014	2015	2016
总收入 (亿元)	**Total Revenue (100 million yuan)**	**10222.4**	**13004.6**	**15940.2**	**19646.0**	**25025.0**	**30497.4**	**36057.6**	**40811.9**	**46047.6**
技术收入 (亿元)	Technological Revenue (100 million yuan)	1693.4	2093.6	2478.3	2845.9	3403.1	4032.4	4837.7	6623.6	7580.4
产品销售收入 (亿元)	Products Sales Revenue (100 million yuan)	5229.2	5923.6	6889.6	7809.4	8741.2	10788.4	12474.2	13300.0	14752.5
#新产品销售收入 (亿元)	Sales Revenue of New Products (100 million yuan)	3327.0	3203.7	3949.2	3405.1	3352.1	4070.4	4614.8	4397.5	4565.6
商品销售收入 (亿元)	Commodity Sales Revenue (100 million yuan)	2398.9	3689.4	5032.2	7161.9	10077.4	11339.6	12832.6	13339.5	14522.4
其他收入 (亿元)	Other Revenues (100 million yuan)	900.9	1298.0	1540.1	1828.9	2803.4	4337.0	5913.1	7548.9	9192.3
出口总额 (亿美元)	Total Exports (USD 100 million)	207.4	208.2	227.4	237.3	261.7	336.2	337.3	299.4	257.9
实缴税费总额 (亿元)	Total Tax Paid (100 million yuan)	504.0	658.7	767.2	925.8	1445.8	1506.6	1857.6	2038.1	2314.1
利润总额 (亿元)	Total Profits (100 million yuan)	726.3	1122.4	1298.9	1533.9	1788.6	2264.8	3031.5	3404.5	3732.5
获奖成果情况	**Statistics on Prize-winning Achievements**									
获奖成果个数 (个)	Number of Prize-winning Achievements (unit)	1448	1909	1811	2329	2509	2852	2636	3577	3911
#国家级 (个)	National (unit)	282	276	256	323	377	450	364	358	496
省部级 (个)	Provincial (unit)	641	1044	1015	1351	1318	1652	1522	2219	2302
专利情况	**Statistics on Patents**									
专利申请数 (件)	Number of Patents Applied (unit)	17219	17226	18515	24894	34192	44275	55009	68944	74923
拥有有效发明专利数(件)	Number of Patents in Force (unit)	9836	11611	13988	15232	23198	35000	44870	63171	82890
专利授权数 (件)	Number of Patents Licensed (unit)	9050	10512	13151	12951	17969	22308	25065	32327	37629

23-7 中关村国家自主创新示范区企业经营活动情况
OPERATING ACTIVITIES OF ENTERPRISES IN ZHONGGUANCUN NATIONAL INNOVATION DEMONSTRATION ZONE

单位：亿元 (100 million yuan)

项目	Item	2016	2015
工业总产值(当年价格)	Gross Output Value of Industry (at current prices)	9937.7	9561.7
工业销售产值(当年价格)	Sales Value of Industry (at current prices)	9714.9	8972.4
#出口交货值	Delivery Value of Exports	719.7	720.1
总收入	Total Revenue	46047.6	40811.9
技术收入	Technological Revenue	7580.4	6623.6
产品销售收入	Products Sales Revenue	14752.5	13300.0
#新产品销售收入	Sales Revenue of New Products	4565.6	4397.5
商品销售收入	Commodity Sales Revenue	14522.4	13339.5
其他收入	Other Revenues	9192.3	7548.9
利润总额	Total Profits	3732.5	3404.5
实缴税费总额	Total Tax Paid	2314.1	2038.1
#增值税	Value Added Tax	1100.5	904.5
营业税	Business Tax	109.7	166.4
所得税	Corporate Income Tax	645.8	534.3
本年实缴关税	Duties Paid in the Year	204.7	196.4
减免税总额	Reduced and Exempted Tax	389.2	359.8
#增值税	Value Added Tax	163.1	159.8
营业税	Business Tax	1.4	4.2
所得税	Corporate Income Tax	219.5	188.0
应交增值税	Value Added Tax Payable	941.3	764.6
出口总额 (亿美元)	Foreign Exchange Created by Export (USD100 million)	257.9	299.4

23-8 中关村国家自主创新示范区企业研发活动情况
SCIENTIFIC ACTIVITIES OF ENTERPRISES IN ZHONGGUANCUN NATIONAL INNOVATION DEMONSTRATION ZONE

项目	Item	2016	2015
研发活动情况	**Statistics on Scientific and Technological Activities**		
研发人员合计 (人)	Total Number of Personnel Engaged in Scientific and Technological Activities (person)	657015	604816
#全职人员	Full-time Personnel	619077	557124
企业内部的日常研发经费支出 (亿元)	Total Expenditures on Research Activities Inside Enterprises (100 million yuan)	1728.7	1522.6
#人员人工费(包括各种补贴)	Labor Cost (Including Various Subsidies)	1003.4	836.1
原材料费	Cost of Raw Materials	265.1	261.0
委托外单位开展研发的经费支出 (亿元)	Expenditures on Scientific and Technological Activities Institutions Conducted by External Institutes Entrusted (100 million yuan)	142.2	149.5
对境外支出	Overseas Spending	8.7	7.4
企业科技活动产出情况	**Scientific and Technological Output**		
获奖成果情况	**Statistics on Prize-winning Achievements**		
获奖成果个数 (个)	Number of Prize-winning Achievements (unit)	3911	3577
#国家级 (个)	National (unit)	496	358
省部级 (个)	Provincial (unit)	2302	2219
地市级 (个)	Prefecture and City-level (unit)	1113	1000
专利情况	**Statistics on Patents**		
当年专利申请受理数 (件)	Number of Patents Applied (case)	74923	68944
#发明专利 (件)	Invention Patents (case)	49525	45939
期末拥有有效发明专利数 (件)	Number of Patents in Force (case)	82890	63171
当年专利授权数 (件)	Number of Patent Licensed (case)	37629	32327
论文、著作情况	**Statistics on Papers and Writings**		
发表科技论文 (篇)	Number of Published Scientific Papers (unit)	20697	16693
技术改造和技术获取情况	**Technical Rennovation and Acquisition**		
技术改造经费支出 (亿元)	Expenditures on Technical Rennovation (100 million yuan)	30.3	24.1
引进境外技术经费支出 (亿元)	Expenditures on Introduction of Foreign Technologies (100 million yuan)	13.0	20.7
引进境外技术的消化吸收经费支出 (亿元)	Expenditures on Absorption of Imported Technologies (100 million yuan)	7.5	7.6
购买境内技术经费支出 (亿元)	Expenditures on Purchasing Domestic Technologies (100 million yuan)	10.1	13.3

23-9 中关村国家自主创新示范区企业人力资源情况
HUMAN RESOURCES OF ENTERPRISES IN ZHONGGUANCUN NATIONAL INNOVATION DEMONSTRATION ZONE

单位：人 (person)

项　目	Item	2016	2015
企业人力资源情况	**Statistics on Human Resource**		
从业人员年末人数	**Number of Employeed Persons at the Year End**	**2482615**	**2316372**
#留学归国人员	Returned Students Studying Abroad	30197	27435
#在岗长期职工	On-the-post Long-term Employed Persons	2275145	2125468
按文化程度分	**By Educational Background**		
博士及以上	Doctor Degree and Above	25498	23492
#留学归国人员	Returned Students Studying Abroad	2799	2782
硕　士	Masters	263469	238324
#留学归国人员	Returned Students Studying Abroad	21346	18864
大　本	Undergraduates	1030955	944733
大　专	Junior College	526412	499736
按技术职称分	**By Technical Post**		
高　级	Senior	153537	140654
中　级	Middle	264359	249076
初　级	Junior	271713	262349
按年龄分	**By Age**		
#29岁及以下	Age 29 and Below	1070536	1024651
30-39岁	30-39	897809	814472
40-49岁	40-49	347527	320017
从业人员平均人数	**Average Number of Empolyed Persons**	**2455429**	**2298503**
在岗职工参加社会保险人数	**Number of Employees Covered by the Social Insurance**	**2207884**	**1996831**

23-10 中关村国家自主创新示范区企业财务状况
FINANCIAL STATUS OF ENTERPRISES IN ZHONGGUANCUN NATIONAL INNOVATION DEMONSTRATION ZONE

单位：亿元 (100 million yuan)

项　目	Item	2016	2015
资产总计	Total Assets	97824.6	79917.4
流动资产合计	Total Current Assets	52197.9	57221.4
固定资产合计	Total Fixed Assets	7891.6	7745.4
固定资产原价	Original Value of Fixed Assets	12597.4	11861.8
累计折旧	Accumulative Depreciation	4890.6	4350.3
负债合计	Total Liabilities	55956.7	43795.3
所有者权益合计	Total Owner's Equity	41867.9	36122.1
实收资本	Paid-up Capital	24245.0	16264.7
主营业务收入	Operating Income	43636.3	38991.2
主营业务成本	Main Business Cost	35391.8	31627.8
主营业务税金及附加	Main Business Tax and Surtax	278.1	338.7
利润总额	Total Profits	3732.5	3404.5

主要统计指标解释

已开发土地面积 指在规划范围内达到“七通一平”标准的，具备进行房屋建筑物施工或出让条件的土地面积。

已供应土地面积 指开发区内通过各种方式获得土地使用权的土地面积，包括出让、划拨、租赁等。

已建成城镇建设用地面积 截至报告期，已经建设并通过竣工验收的国有建设用地。包括已建成的住宅用地、工矿仓储用地、多功能用地、交通运输用地、商服用地、公共管理与公共服务用地，以及其他城镇建设用地等。海关特殊监管区域的已建成城镇建设用地包括现状围网范围内已建成的城镇建设用地，及开发区四至范围与围网范围间的海关专属办公用地。

累计招商项目企业个数 指自开始至报告期末累计招商入区，并经工商管理机关注册取得法人营业执照的企业个数。

累计招商项目总投资 指自开始至报告期末累计批准的合同（章程）规定的投资总额。

累计招商项目注册资本 指自开始至报告期末累计为设立经营企业在工商行政管理机关注册的资本总额。

累计招商项目合同外资金额 指自开始至报告期末累计批准的合同（章程）中，外商和港、澳、台商的出资额。

累计招商项目外商实际投资 指自开始至报告期末累计按合同规定的外方和港、澳、台方以现金、实物、工业产权及专有技术的计价实缴资本投资额。

总收入 指企业全年的生产产品销售收入、技术性收入和与本企业产品相关的商品的销售收入、其它收入等各种收入的总和，总收入等于主营业务收入加上其他业务收入。总收入应按不含增值税的价格计算，不包括补贴收入、营业外收入、投资收益。

出口总额 指出售给外贸部门或直接出售给外商的产品、商品、技术或服务的总金额。包括来料加工装配出口，境外技术合同实现金额及在国内以外汇计价的商品出售和技术服务的总额等。以千美元计价。

留学归国人员 指出国学习，取得学位的归国人员。

Explanatory Notes on Main Statistical Indicators

Area of Developed Land refers to the area of land that meets the standard of "seven connections and one leveling" and is qualified for construction or sale.

Area of Supplied Land refers to the area of land whose right of use is acquired in the development zones by various means including sale, transfer, and lease.

Area of Land for Urban Development refers to state-owned construction land that has already gone through construction and acceptance check by the end of the reporting period. It includes land for complete residential buildings, land for industrial, mining and storage use, multi-functional land, land for transportation, land for commercial services, land for public administration and services and other lands for urban development. Land for urban development under special administration of customs includes urban development land completed inside the current seine and land for office buildings of customs inside the development zones and between the seines.

Accumulated Number of Enterprises Involved in Business Inviting Programs refers to the total number of enterprises invited to development zones and awarded with business licenses for legal persons from the administration for industry and commerce from the beginning to the end of the reporting period.

Accumulative Investment of Business Inviting Programs refers to the total investment of contracts (articles of incorporation) approved from the beginning to the end of the reporting period.

Accumulative Registered Capital of Business Inviting Programs refers to the total capital registered with the administration for industry and commerce for the purpose of establishment of operating enterprises from the beginning to the end of the reporting period.

Accumulative Contracted Foreign Capital of Business Inviting Programs refers to the cumulative capital contribution of investors from foreign countries, Hong Kong, Macao and Taiwan as approved in contracts (articles of incorporation) from the beginning to the end of the reporting period.

Accumulative Actual Foreign Investment of Business Inviting Programs refers to the cumulative amount of paid-up capital investment from foreign countries, Hong Kong, Macao and Taiwan made in cash, in physical material, industrial property right and proprietary technology, as stated in contracts, from the beginning to the end of the reporting period.

Total Revenue refers to the sum of income earned by enterprises from sales of their own products, technological income, and income from selling commodities related to their own products, and other income. Total revenue is the sum of main business income and other business income. Total revenue shall be calculated at VAT-excluded prices, and exclude subsidies, non-operating income and return on investment across the year.

Total Exports refers to the total amount of products or commodities sold to foreign trade organizations or directly sold to foreign traders. It includes the value of export of investor's raw materials processed, the value of technical contracts completed at home and abroad, and the total value of domestic commodity sales and technical services measured in foreign currency.

Returned Students Studying Abroad refer to persons who have come home after studying abroad and been conferred with academic degrees.